TOP

ARGENTINA
CHILE
SPAIN
MEXICO

2013/14

TEAM:

Director: Carlos González
Editor in Chief: Javier Luengo
Tasting Team: Carlos González, Javier Luengo and Pablo Vecilla
Texts: Javier Luengo, Carlos González and José Peñín
Database Manager: Erika Laymuns
Advertising: Mª Carmen Hernández
Cover design, layout and desktop publishing: Raúl Salgado and Luis Salgado
Supervising Editor: José Peñín

Published by: PI&ERRE
Santa Leonor, 65. Edificio A - Bajo A
28037 - MADRID
Tel.: 914 119 464 - Fax: 915 159 499
comunicacion@guiapenin.com
www.guiapenin.com

Translation: John Mullen Connelly

ISBN: 978-84-95203-94-6
Copyright library: M-9358-2013
Printed by: Gamacolor

DISTRIBUTED BY: GRUPO COMERCIAL ANAYA
Juan Ignacio Luca de Tena, 15
Tel: 913 938 800
28027 MADRID

DISTRIBUTED BY: ACC PUBLISHING GROUP
Antique Collector's Club Ltd.
Sandy Jane, Old Martlesham
Woodbridge, Suffolk
IP12 45D, United Kingdom

A CONSOLIDATION TRIP

You have before you the 2nd edition of The Guide to the Best Wines of Argentina, Chile, Spain and Mexico. This is a unique Guide for the sector and, for the first time, it will be available in the main countries where the wines described and scored here are consumed.

In order to achieve more than 3,700 wines which appear here, we tasted approximately 11,000 wines over a period of one year. This tasting was always carried out in the source countries. This made it possible for us to understand each and every one of the terroirs which characterize the main producer zones.

In this second edition, we wish to share the experience of being witnesses to the extensive diversity of wines in the world with you. In this regard, the Hispano American wines are highly important. From the exoticism of the Mexican wines to the traditions of La Rioja, to the high altitude wines of Salta and the ocean wines of Chile, all the styles all the styles are included and demonstrate that they have nuances with sufficient quality to make it worthwhile to purchase and drink them.

Breaking down by countries, we have found that wine production in Mexico is going through a boom in the new production regions, there are more and more projects which are progressively scoring higher. From a total of 320 wines tasted, mainly in the State of Lower California, approximately 113 are scored in this Guide. We hope that such a high percentage of wines, ≥90, from Mexico serve to position them as they deserve within the global wine growing sector. We have already done so.

Argentina continues to make progress thanks to its recognized and recognizable style of wines based on malbec, its main strength and weakness. As much as 25% of the wines tasted are single varietal from this variety, and in 63% it appears as the base variety. The latter wines, the blends, are those which have the high scores: Catena Zapata Estiba Reservada 2006, Finca el Origen 2011, Norton Privada 2010, etc.. this is logical as these wines have the freshness and elegance provided by the variety mixture. The future of Argentinean wine involves adapting to the new world production tendencies which give importance to balsamic, herbal and fresh fruit nuances rather than potency, structure and tannin.

Chile is giving a new image to the world. While it maintains its international image of wine with the carmenére grape, it is on target with its explorations of other oenological riches provided by the more "oceanic" valleys, where the wines made from pinot noir and sauvignon blanc from Limarí, Leyda and Casablanca are outstanding. More than 300 wines tasted, 75% of which (the highest percentage in the Guide) score more than 90 points. The red wines of Las Niñas de Apalta 2012, Almaviva 2009, Montes Purple 2010, Carmín de Peumo 2008 and Outer Limits Pinot Noir should be highlighted.

Finally, Spain continues to show it has a wide variety of wines produced from over 200 domestic and international varieties. A priori this question might confuse a consumer at the beginning, and this is the opportunity the wineries have in order to open up international markets which are somewhat overstocked with French varieties. The deficit in the Spanish wine sector arises from the commercialization as the winery owner must understand that the promotion, the marketing and the image of the country is as important as the quality of the wine. The highest scoring Spanish wines are sherry wines, whose singularity makes them unique in the world. Again the most outstanding are those of the Equipo Navazos. In the area of red wines, those made from tempranillo and garnacha are dominant (Artadi and L'Ermita), these two varieties amount to more than 20% of the wines which appear within the Spain brand. However, we must not forget the cavas, Spanish champagne sparkling wines, which are on a level with the best French champagnes thanks to the Gramona winery.

Carlos González Sáez
Director Guía Peñín

the wines of the anticyclone

We are pleased with the congratulations we have received from wine enthusiasts and from the owners of Latin American wineries regarding the precision and depth of content of the first edition of the Guía Peñín of the Best Wines of Argentina, Chile, Mexico and Spain 2012. It was not expected that we could x-ray the varied geographical areas of Latin America from "such a distance". The substantial volume of the Spanish "green guide" meant that it was necessary to inform on the wine growing environment of Latin America with the same criteria. On my travels and those of the tasting team, we have stressed the geo-climatic differences in the zones rather than specifying the business or oenological values of the brands or their producers. This is the old model of the European tasters who were sensitive to the "terroir" and the peculiarities of each territory.

This experience led me to an even more lengthy conclusion: the wines of Mexico, Argentina, Chile and ours have something in common: they are the sun wines, the so called "Mediterranean type" as, during the vegetative epoch of the plant and at harvest time, not a drop of water falls and the sun solemnly reigns due to the summer anticyclone, which forces artificial hydration. These characteristics may be extended to the rest of the wines of the Anglo-American New World.

LIGHT AND DARKNESS

The advantages of these wines lies in the fact that, due to their greater alcohol content, they are warm in the palate, with mature tannins which in some cases are sweet, full bodied, oily and rounded for the palate. These features are easier for new consumers to assimilate, as opposed to the dry tannins and acid sensation of the "Atlantic" wines. Increased maturity which is currently in vogue in all the vineyards in the world, including France is intended to cater for new consumers who drink more as opposed to the traditional wine drinkers (generally from European wine growing countries) who are progressively drinking less wine. Never in the history of wine has the standard consumer had so many possibilities of making a successful purchase. Today it is difficult to find a bad wine unless the winery owner makes it on purpose.

The other side of the coin is the uniformity of the wines, this is called "photocopy wine", with only slight differences between each other. It is almost impossible to differentiate a malbec from a tempranillo, merlot from a cabernet or a mencía from Spanish Bierzo from a monastrell from Jumilla. For those who are knowledgeable or for those, like me, who embrace the philosophy of sensorial diversity, this model may be boring. Why? Because it is due to the total phenol maturing at the time the aromatic or identifying maturing of the variety declines. In order t achieve sensorial diversity, it would be necessary to harvest earlier, assuming the risk of perceiving sensations of immaturity. Total maturity scarcely leaves any traces which might enable the detection the geographical or varietal origin.

OBJECTIVE: DIVERSITY

The advantages of these wines lies in the fact that, due to their greater alcohol content, they are warm in the palate, with mature tannins which in some cases are sweet, full bodied, oily and rounded for the palate. These features are easier for new consumers to assimilate, as opposed to the dry tannins and acid sensation of the "Atlantic" wines. Increased maturity which is currently in vogue in all the vineyards in the world, including France is intended to cater for new consumers who drink more as opposed to the traditional wine drinkers (generally from European wine growing countries) who are progressively drinking less wine. Never in the history of wine has the standard consumer had so many possibilities of making a successful purchase. Today it is difficult to find a bad wine unless the winery owner makes it on purpose.

In order to achieve different wines in warm countries with a multiplicity of styles can only be attained using long cycle Mediterranean varieties as opposed to the generalized Bordeaux varieties. Mexico has the fresher thermal alternative of the ocean, which is not sufficient to reduce the maturing of the grapes in an arid climate such as Lower California, with a lower thermal range than the Chilean vineyards. This results in wines with sweeter tannins, hints of high candied maturing (some near to the flavour of raisins). Some have been daring enough to use varieties such as tempranillo, merlot and pinot noir which are more advisable for fresher climates.

With regard to Argentina, I am very interested in the new biodynamic and organic approaches in Mendoza, with initiatives concerning diversity with less incidence of the single malbec variety, avoiding the frenzy of the eighties in Spain with tempranillo planted in almost all the zones. The fact is that the best results are produced by a combination of several vines. As opposed to the varietal peculiarity of the torrontés of Salta, malbec endeavours to be different when, in fact, its nocturnal acidity is overshadowed by its excessive day-time maturity owing to the effect of the ultraviolet rays. Only if the vineyard falls within the shade of a nearby mountain can it generate greater varietal expression. If we go to Neuquén or Río Negro in Patagonia, the colder latitude can provide more than sufficient acidity, but the strong insolation and the Patagonian winds are not the elements to preserve or better define the varietal aromas. It is important that merlot can be used to successfully produce wine in this latitude although it does have the inconvenience of "total maturing". The new initiatives in the Province of Córdoba are also defined as "high level" wines of Mendoza and San Juan. As regards the Province of Buenos Aires, I was curious about the possibilities of its new wines with sufficient rainfall but which is irregular in the vegetative season and a thermal latitude similar to the coast of Morocco. The latitude is temperate and, therefore, it is necessary to work patiently in order to achieve a quality wine while the yield of each vine.

Chile is possibly the country with all the climates: from desert to polar. However, the differences become radical as we move south where there is no Atlantic moderation as in Europe. On approaching the Pacific or going farther south, the aromatic maturing of the grape becomes more difficult. This is why most Chilean wines are produced in the Mediterranean-continental climate of the Central Valley and the foothills of the Andes, subject to the thermal range. It is only possible to find better terroirs with more diverse soils (including slate in the pre-mountain range) with a climate similar to Ribera del Duero in the area of Maule, within the pre mountain range towards the sea, but before reaching the coast, and in the Valley of Malleco (the most southern in Chile).

With regard to Spain, the anticyclone of the Azores is the reason why the "sun wine" model is the leading model in Europe. This is not a privilege as our history of great wines only includes the fortified wines (Sherry, Montilla, Malaga, Fondillón de Alicante or the old mellow wines of Medina del Campo and Catalonia). At the present time, the craze for vineyards with varieties of French origin during the eighties is being replaced by our historical native vines, which are mainly late cycle (monastrell, garnacha, bobal, cariñena, graciano, etc.) as is normal in warm continental climates, while other less well known varieties are being recuperated. In Spain we have the enormous advantages of a greater varietal range, a plurality of orientations, altitudes and types of soils, only the northwest (Galicia, Asturias, and León) is less affected by the aforementioned anticyclone, while the climate is more moderate, more in the style of Bordeaux. Vines such as mencía, prieto picudo, godello, caíño, brancellao, sousón, dona blanca, bastardo, etc. are more expressive and diverse.

José Peñín

SUMMARY

Fariña

III GENERACIÓN
1942-2012
70
1942-2012
ANIVERSARIO

III GENERACIÓN
1942-2012
70
1942-2012
ANIVERSARIO
Fariña

WINEinMODERATION.eu
Art de Vivre

SUMMARY

SUMMARY

ACKNOWLEDGEMENTS

To all the Regulatory Boards and Wineries which have efficiently collaborated with us so that we might simple their wines. Moreover, we wish to express our special thanks to: (Chile) ProChile, Iberico Restaurant in Santiago de Chile; (Argentina) The Vines of Mendoza, Winifera, Wines of Argentina; (Mexico) the Secretariat of Tourism of Lower California, the Secretariat of Farming, the Association of Wine Growers, the Vine Product System, the Representative Office of the State of Baja California in Spain and the Universidad Autónoma of Lower California.

HOW TO USE THIS GUIDE

All the countries appear in alphabetical order and the list of wineries and wines tasted from each country are included under each geographical zone.

The following sections are specified in each chapter by country:

- A practical record with the main relevant data required to understand each producer country at a glance: population, surface area, varieties, grape harvest dates, climatology, commercialization, average annual production, number of wineries and altitudes of the vineyards.
- An introduction to each country: overview.
- An illustrative map of the country and its wine growing areas.
- The keys to the year: commentary on the current situation, the keys to the year as regards the qualities of the wines in the light of the results of the tasting and the foreseeable future.
- General characteristics of the wines by type (white and red) classified by the more relevant grape varieties
- Description of the wine growing categories and zones in each country according to their legal classifications.
- Exportation data of the domestic wines of each country.
- Records of production zones: each country has several explanatory records of the current production zones. These records are previous to the exhibition of the wines which have achieved the minimum 90 points required to appear in the Guide. In the four countries there are cases of certain production zones which have no wines mentioned as these have not achieved the minimum points required. In these cases, it was decided to maintain these records in the Guía Peñín in order to provide the reader with more complete information on each country.
- List of wineries and tasting of wines.

WINERIES

The wineries are listed in alphabetical order within the wine growing areas where they are located. Each winery is specified by its name, address, telephone number, email address and website. This information is supplied by the producers each year. All the basic information (addresses, telephone numbers and brands) is almost 100% updated in this edition.

If the same firm produces wine under different protected Denominations of Origin or from different wine growing areas, the data available on these will appear for all of them and the entries, zones or regions where they work will be included in the index of wineries. The more frequent cases involve firms which simultaneously produce Spanish sparkling wine and still wines although this only occurs in Spain.

In order to create the structure of this guide, we intend that the consumer locate wines mainly by zones and once they are located, he tries to contact the wineries which own the brands in order to make a purchase or search for information.

WINES

The wines and their tasting take up most of the text. They always appear after the information on the producer winery in accordance with the following specifications:

- Spanish wines are the most numerous considering the wine producing tradition of the country and the number of brands which far outnumber those of Chile, Argentina and Mexico. In Spain there are more than 2,300 wineries, while there are far fewer in the other countries included in this guide.

- Each wine appears with its brand, ageing and harvest (when these details are included by the producer on the label). In addition, the type of wine, the protected Denomination of Origin (in the case of Spain) or the geographical region it comes from.
- All the wines which appear in this Guide are located within specific production areas clearly defined by their legal denomination in the case of Spain (Protected Denomination of Origin, Single Estate Wines, Regional Wines, etc.) or by their production regions. In many cases, the difficulty involved in locating each wine in a specific production zone and sub-zone – fundamentally in Chile and Argentina – made it necessary to include a section on the production sub-zones of these countries in order to be as precise as possible as regards location. As the reader will acknowledge, in Chile and Argentina there are wineries whose wines may be located in different sub-zones.
- Considering that the number of pages should be kept at such a level so that the Guide can be handled with ease, it only includes wines with a tasting grade equal to or above 90 points.
- The remarks on the tasting give emphasis to the main characteristics of the wines with criteria and a uniform vocabulary common to all the countries.

INDEXES

At the end of the Guide there are alphabetical indices of wine brands and wineries, in order to facilitate the search for specific wines and wineries.

The objective of the guide is to inform efficiently and rapidly on the characteristics of the wines which can be found on the market in the last quarter of 2013 and in 2014. The opinions given are the full responsibility of the Guía Peñín through its tasting team and must only be evaluated insofar as the reader trusts the diagnosis of the team. Moreover, the grading must be interpreted with a maximum margin of flexibility equivalent to a deviation of 6%.

The tasting has been simplified in order to highlight the most significant aspects which are easily detectable by any consumer, except as regards those wines with a strong sensorial character. Descriptions which are too meticulous or technical have been avoided as we consider that these are too confusing for the average consumer.

TYPE OF GRADING

Due to the fact that it is used more commonly at international level, we have chosen the American grading system, where 0 is equivalent to 50. This grading expresses the different qualities of the wines in general, taking into account concepts listed in each band of 10 points, except in the 90 to 100 band, which we have divided into two parts in order to ensure more rigor and responsibility as regards the higher grades. It should be pointed out that these evaluations are not equivalent to the more traditional 10 point scale used by other guides.

In view of this, the reader must use this page in order to understand the general description regarding the specific grading and then examine the particular description of the wine according to the following scale:

95-100 EXCEPTIONAL WINE
This stands out among those of its type, year and the characterization of the zone. It leaves an extraordinary impression on all the senses. It is complex, full of olfactory and taste properties due to the value of the soil, variety, production and ageing; it is elegant and out of the ordinary; that is to say, it goes beyond the commercial standards and, in some cases, it is strange for the public in general.
90-94 EXCELLENT WINE
Wine with the same values as in the previous section but with less impact and clarity of nuances.

TABLE OF EQUIVALENCES

Sometimes the wineries complain of the difficulty involved in understanding the equivalencies of the numerical grading systems which appear in the media and those in the wine guides. The Guía Peñín adopted the American grading system for the simple reason that, in 1992, in the world wine market relevance was given to the system of icons (wineglasses, stars, bunches of grapes, etc.) and the grading from 0 to 20, both of which were implemented in Europe.

The culmination was the rapid dissemination of the Wine Advocate grading led by Robert Parker in the world market. Our intention was to project Spanish wines to the world as the first independent catalogue of brands with evaluations of quality and price in order to adapt to the model which is progressively more extended throughout the world, a catalogue which we now extend to Argentinean, Chilean and Mexican wines.

HOW ARE WINES CLASSIFIED AND GRADED?

The wine team of the Guía is reluctant to use numerical grading. However, the pure and simple description of the tasting, with no nuances regarding points, does not sufficiently explain the differences between brands to the consumer, who is faced with the dilemma of which wine to choose from two or several similar descriptions.

Jancis Robinson, Bettane et Desseauve, Vinum, elmundovino.com, Revista Vinho, Wine "Esencia do Vinho"	0-20	0	2	4	6	8	10	12	14	16	18	20
Wine Enthusiast, Wine Spectator, Wine Advocate (Robert Parker), Vino y Gastronomía, Wine Cellar (Stephen Tanzer's), Guía Peñín	50-100	50	55	60	65	70	75	80	85	90	95	100

HOW IS THE TASTING DONE?

Unlike the comparative and competitive tastings, the team of the Guía carries out the tasting with the labels on view and each wine must be evaluated depending on its country of origin, production area and varieties used, data which, to a certain extent, will establish the standard of the wines to be graded.

The experience of the tasting team enables them to go beyond the influence of the labels, therefore, their knowledge of the progress of the winery makes it possible for them to make a fairer evaluation as it is rare that there are extensive differences in quality which are not related to the natural factors of the harvest.

It is evident that, unless the tasting of the same wines is carried out by several groups or commissions of tasters in several series, the results obtained in a single blind tasting session for a guide with the validity of one year will never be fair unless they are compared with tastings carried out with the labels on view and the members know the general working lines of the winery, depending on the country, varieties, climate, etc.

This is how the tasting is carried out:

- A general impression is obtained not only from the results of the tasting carried out in different places, situations and at different times, but the line, style and segmentation of the quality of the winery is also taken into account.

It is strange that two bottles of the same brand, type and ageing method obtain a difference greater than three points even though they are from different harvests. However, it is more probable that higher grading is given due to profound changes in the style of production and in the raw materials obtained by the winery.

- The general knowledge of the team as regards the style (generally one of continuity) of each winery reduces the errors of blind tasting, where the defects arising in a determined bottle (not evaluable) can sometimes be confused with the deficiencies in the production and ageing (evaluable) of the wine.
- Furthermore, we are aware that the differences of year are progressively lower than the changes in style due to the introduction of new technical systems in the vineyards and wineries. In addition, these styles tend to become standardized in order to cater for the demands of international taste, fostered by the large corporations.

TASTING OF EARLY BOTTLED WINES

It is possible that relatively lower scores are given to high quality wines bottled within periods of less than three months. Clearly, after six months, this wine would deserve a higher grading due to its improvement, as regards aroma and taste, and as there is no possibility of rectification, it would be necessary to wait for the edition of the following year.

Even knowing the negative factors involved in wine testing in the period mentioned (hermetic fruitiness, unassembled oak and wine, sometimes drying tannins) and apart from this, grading above what is perceived by the senses is risky. Therefore, the tasting team recommends that the wineries which are not sure of the total taste and olfactory development of the wine refrain from sending samples in these circumstances as this may involve a risk for them and for the team which might be discredited due to mistakenly grading a brand. In these cases, it would be advisable to send the previous harvest with the characteristics fully established even if this is out of stock in the winery as it may continue to be on the market, which is the most essential factor for publication in the Guide.

HOW IS TASTING INTERPRETED?

Each description of a wine provides two concepts:

OBJECTIVE:
These are the "evaluable" descriptions which are not conditioned by the status of the taster and his customs and which can be checked by any amateur. These are the most reliable factors.

> **Colour:** intensity and transparency, for example, whether the wine is intense, open, pale, cloudy, crystalline, etc.
> **Aroma:** the intensity, defects, excess aroma of an element in the wine (e.g. wood and variety, fruity or not, aged, etc.).
> **Taste:** : the intensity and structure; whether it is thick, has body, rounded, the essential flavours (sourness, bitterness –tannins – sweet, sour, salty) and all those regarding aroma.

SUBJECTIVE:
These are the "non-evaluable" personal type descriptions referring to comparisons with other products which the tasting team knows by experience, and their value is to serve as orientation for the reader. Examples: colour "golden, cherry, old gold, auburn, straw yellow, etc."; aroma and taste "roasted, candied, cherry, wooden, etc..."

For another taster, for example, roasted could be equivalent to a toasted nuance and "wooden" might be described as dusty or old wood.

It is becoming more and more common that wine comes onto the market after three or four months in barrels, especially in Spain so that the wine is more formed and polished.

In this regard, we only inform that the wine has been aged in barrels, with no mention of the number of months. If the label mentions "oak", we include this in the identification of the wine.

Furthermore, abbreviations are used to identify the different types of wine described. These must be interpreted as follows:

B **White**
BC **Aged white**
BFB **White fermented in wood**
RD **rosé**
T **red**
TC **aged red**
TR **red vintage wine**
TGR **grand reserve wine**
FI **very dry pale**
MZ **manzanilla (very pale dry)**
OL **oloroso**
OLV **oloroso viejo**
AM **amontillado**
PX **pedro ximénez**
PC **palo cortado (between oloroso and amontillado)**
CR **cream**
PCR **pale cream**
GE **fortified**
ESP **sparkling wine**
BR **brut**
BN **brut nature**
SC **dry**
SS **semi-dry**
S/C **no harvest**

THE UNPUBLISHED WINES

It may be that the reader might note the absence of a brand which he considers to be relevant. There may be two reasons for this:
1.- The wine is out of stock in the winery (an absurd reason as the wine may be on the market), or that the producer believes that, as these are lower quality brands, they will receive a lower grading. In the latter case, we deduce that these are wines at a lower level than those tasted and classified for these firms. As the brands received enable us to know the style of the winery, we do not pursue the missing labels.
2.- The wine has not achieved the 90 points required to be considered as "The Best Wines of ...". As regards this point, all the wines which do not achieve this grade will not appear in this Guide.

NOTIONS FOR BECOMING A GOOD TASTER

1.- THE GRAPE HARVEST

This consists of gathering the fruit to be transported to the winery, where the wine will be produced. In the northern hemisphere, the time of the harvest depends on the latitude and the altitude, from July (the earliest), until October and even November. In the southern hemisphere, from February to May. There are two fundamental factors concerning the harvest: the grape is healthy (that is to say, free from disease and bruising) and that the maturity of the grape is right.

How is the date of the grape harvest decided?

This aspect is fundamental for the quality of the wine. Thus, as opposed to the balance between sugar and sourness which was traditionally sought, the so called "polyphenolic maturity" is becoming more and more relevant. This is based on an analysis of the level of tannins and anthocyanes in the fruit. Tasting the grape is fundamental in order to detect this "maturity" and, in particular, tasting the woody part: the seeds. If these are fully mature, there will be no risk of the transfer of herbaceous and vegetable signs during the long periods of maceration employed today for high quality wines.

The big debate at global level is the problem of wines in warm climates, where, due to the heat, the amount of sugar in the grape is greater despite the fact that the phenolic maturing (that of the peel and the seeds) is not speeded up. In order to mature the peel, it is necessary that the must achieve excessive maturing, in excess of 14 degrees, thus, it ends up losing a large amount of identifying aroma and taste. Unfortunately, this theoretical balance does not entail the aromatic maturity of the grape (the maximum or fruit expression of the variety). This contradiction is due to the fact that, in the final maturing phase of the grape, the leaf area undergoes

Water undernourishment from the roots which maintain transpiration. This is a result of the mistaken custom not to irrigate in this key period in order to prevent the grape from "thickening". Due to this lack of irrigation, the plant has recourse to the water of the grape bunches and partially dehydrates these "by boiling them". This is when the first symptoms of aromas and candied tastes common to all the grapes from warm terrain appear.

Does a mechanical grape harvest have the same quality as a manual one?

The debate among the supporters of each system ha not yet ended. The mechanical grape harvest, which meant a revolution as regards reduction of costs, made it possible to harvest the grapes at night and do the job more efficiently, but it shakes the vines (and this may be aggressive for the plant) and the harvest is normally more messy (there are more vegetable remains among the bunches). Of course, it also requires that the vineyard be prepared for the machine with the correct separations between the

rows of vines. On the positive side, besides the savings in salaries, there is a greater standardization of the grapes which fall into the basket once moved by the shakers and, owing to the greater facility to detach the grapes on maturing, the ideal time for the harvest is known.

In any case, the grand wines of the world continue to use manual harvesting, which is more than just picking as it involves expert grape gatherers, the selection of bunches in the vineyard, several pickings are required in each plot in order to harvest the grapes at their precise maturity point, etc.

What is a late grape harvest?

This is a harvest which is carried out later than normal in order to pick the bunches which have been left to mature longer than is usual on the vine and which, normally, owing to their higher concentration of sugar, are used to produce sweet or raisin wine. In some cases, if the variety and the climate permit (the combination of mist in the early morning and sun later in the day), "noble rot" occurs when the fungus known as botrytis cinerea attacks the fruit making it gain sourness and sugar and lose its volume of water, but this also especially enriches its slightly "mushroom" fungus aroma, very recognizable and especially valued in the best fortified wines such as sauternes, tokays and trockenbeerenausleses.

NEW CONCEPTS OF WINE GROWING

Work in the vineyard has changed radically in recent times. Theories from California and Australia have led to a revolution which has led to the obtaining of relatively high productions. However, the European producers also endeavour to obtain the maximum profit from their vines. There are a number of old and new concepts related to new wine growing.

Among the main promoters of wine growing techniques in the New World is the University of Davis (California), one of the most outstanding research universities in this area, together with the New Zealand expert, Richard Smart, who revolutionized wine growing with his work "Sunlight into Wine" and whose theories have taken root in the vineyards of half the world (in Europe including Spain) due to his success as a travelling consultant.

~ **The clones.** Clone selection, that is to say, the selection of a determined botanical species of the same variety is the most appropriate for the ecosystem of the zone, and has become a recent factor to take into account. Only among the international and some indigenous varieties with some prestige can clones be chosen whose vines have characteristics which are slightly different from each other. A cabernet sauvignon clone from California will be more adapted to most of the Spanish climates than a Bordeaux clone which is intended for fresher climates.

~ **Canopy management.** This can be explained as "management of the vegetable canopy" and is the term used to describe the set of techniques which are employed in the vineyard. This concept is not exclusive to the New World and has been widely studied in Europe although it was especially applied in the new producer companies as it functions especially well in the cases of vigorous vineyards. Basically it is focused on the microclimate of the plant and the search for good exposure of the leaves and bunches to the sun. This is an important quality factor which helps to improve the yields and makes it possible to obtain better grapes and combat diseases such as mildew and botryotinia. In order to obtain the desired exposure, work is carried out with vine canes (the most famous are the lyre system and those systems named in honour of their inventors, Scott-Henry and Smart-Dyson) and all the pruning work, summer pruning and thinning of leaves is intended to allow a greater exposure to the sun. Of course, all these modern vine canes are intended to enable mechanical grape harvesting.

~ **Hydric stress.** This is one of the favourite terms of the new wine growers. It describes the "psychological state" of a plant which suffers a lack of water. This fact which occurs naturally during the maturing phase in the vineyards in warm and Mediterranean climates is considered to be a quality factor especially with regard to red wines (greater concentration of fruit, control of yields) and this type of pressure is currently placed on the plant in a controlled form depending on the intentions of the wine grower. The present irrigation systems, associated to modern vine canes employ sophisticated computer controlled techniques in order to apply determined amounts of water to the plant alternating the two sides of the plant. Underground irrigation reduces the effect of untimely evaporation due to the aforementioned computerized controls of the level of humidity required for the plant in order to prevent over-ripening or candying of the grape while maintaining the levels of the richness of the identifying nuances although the sugar level might rise. It is possible to achieve aromatic freshness features of the grape even though the level of 14 degrees of alcohol is exceeded.

~ **Old vines.** Vines constitute one of the most sought after quality factors by European wine growers, taking into account their wealth in this area. The old vines have lower productions (yield is progressively reduced in the older vines), but the amount of grapes is much more stable and consistent considering the greater quantity of wood or woody material which they contain. The greater amount of roots (root mass) and, therefore, the greater power to retain nutritional substances which, acting as reserves, preserve the plant against the imbalances of the water provisions. The roots which go deeper reach constant humidity quotas and, consequently, a greater power to self-regulate water.

The old vines are less vigorous, which involves (as regards the theory of canopy management) improved exposure of leaves and bunches.

~ **Root mass.** Another aspect which the wine growers take more and more into account are the roots of the vines. A large part of current work is oriented to stimulating their growth towards the lower layers of the subsoil so that they provide the wine with a greater amount of mineral hints and, consequently, a more definitive character of the vine with the water nutrition of the subsoil. It is necessary to start from the basis that some subsoil is of interest to the vine. The water stress also helps in this regard since, if the upper layers of the terrain are deprived of water, the plant will be forced to seek this deeper down in the subsoil. The greater the mass of the roots in search of deeper humidity, the plant will ensure more constant humidity.

2.- THE PRODUCTION OF WINE

Wine making is another crucial component for obtaining quality wines. Basically, the production process involves the following steps. These are explained globally here without going into too much detail:

~ **Grape harvest.** Spain is possibly the one country in the world where the dates of the grape harvests are so varied. The first harvests begin in the first fortnight of July in the coastal areas of the Canary Islands with the white grape varieties and the last harvests take place at the beginning of November in certain places in the north of Granada.

The most careful harvesting is made with a selection of the bunches which are more damaged or are excessively mature on the vine.

~ **Transport to the winery.** This must be carried out with the minimum aggression possible so that the grape does not deteriorate due to excessive pressure and in order to avoid premature fermentation. The best method is to use boxes with a capacity not exceeding 15 kilos.

~ **Unloading.** This is carried out in the "reception skip", a type of inverted pyramid which, like a funnel, will place t the grapes on a "worm drive", where they pass to the grape crusher. In the skip, the fruit is analysed in order to determine its state of health and its sugar and acid content.

As regards quality wines, the complete bunches may go directly to the steel or wooden containers with or without stripping the stem if this is sufficiently wooden and not herbaceous.

~ **Crushing.** The crusher presses the grape but only enough to prevent the seeds or stems – the structural support of the bunch– breaking and contaminating the must. The resulting paste is transferred to the presses avoiding contact with the air in order to prevent fermentation starting.

WHITE WINES

~ **Crushing.** The winepresses crush the grapes at different pressures producing must of several qualities:

The first must press, run juice or free run juice are the finest, most aromatic, softest and fruitiest –, therefore, they are of superior quality–, obtained statically (by gravity) due to the pressure of the grape bunches.

First, second and third or pressed must are the result of growing pressure on the grapes in this order (the greater the pressure the lower the quality). Each will be separated and will result in different types of wines.

Orujo: this is the excess paste which remains in the press. This may be distilled in order to produce orujo liquor or be transformed into feed or fertiliser.

~ **Clarifying.** This is how the must is separated into the herbaceous and the aggressive parts of the grape. The must is left to repose for some hours so that the solids suspended in the must are deposited by decantation at the bottom of the deposit and the fermentation can be carried out with a clean, fruity must.

~ **Fermentation.** This is the process in which the sugars contained in the must are transformed into alcohol. This alcoholic fermentation is possible due to the action of the yeast –micro- fungus which are in the soils of the vineyards or are added by selection and, on being bereft of air, they metabolize the sugars into alcohol and carbonic gas.
During this process, the temperature must be controlled as an excessively high temperature may give rise to a stoppage in fermentation as the yeast may die, as well as the control of density in order to determine the amount of sugar which remains in the must. This latter factor will determine the type of wine obtained. Distinctions can be made among the following:

Dry white wine: the residual sugar content does not exceed five grams per litre.
Semi-dry wine: : the residual sugar content is 15-30 grams/litre.
Sweet wine: more than 50 grams/litre of residual sugar.

In order to obtain the last two types of wines, it is necessary to stop the fermentation by chemical means (the addition of sulphur dioxide) or by physical means (cooling which blocks the action of the yeast or overheating which kills off the yeast) at the time when the sugar content is right for the type of wine it is intended to obtain. Later, deep micro-filtering takes place before bottling in order to clean out the yeast from sweet wine as this continues to "ingest" the residual sugar of the wine and transform this into more alcohol.

"Virgin" fermentation. This is the most normal and is solely used with must; that is to say there is no contact with the skins.

~ **Cold maceration.** This is a way to increase the aromatic potential of the wine. Before the fermentation, the bunches of grapes are left to repose in the press (after light pressure so that the must is ejected from the grape) for 6 to 12 hours, extracting the most abundant aromatic molecules from the skins. The must is macerated with the grape skins at low temperature (maximum 10º), which prevents the fermentation which is not required at this time. This method is fashionable at he present time and provides the wine with more body, enriches the sensations in the mouth, increases its aromatic potency and provides part of the colour which is achieved in the fermentation, reducing the time of maceration after fermentation.

~ **Racking.** This consists of passing the wine from one container to another, regardless of whether this is steel, cement or wood in order to leave the solid remains in the previous container. In the case of white wine, the wine is subjected to racking two or three times, between November and January as, at these times, the low temperatures prevent contamination by microorganisms. Then, a selection is made of qualities and the corresponding mixtures in order to achieve the desired result.

~ **Clarifying.** This involves using a clarifying substance which, in the form of a veil, drags the final remains of the wine in suspension and which have not been eliminated by the racking to the bottom.

BASIC PRODUCTION OF WHITE WINES

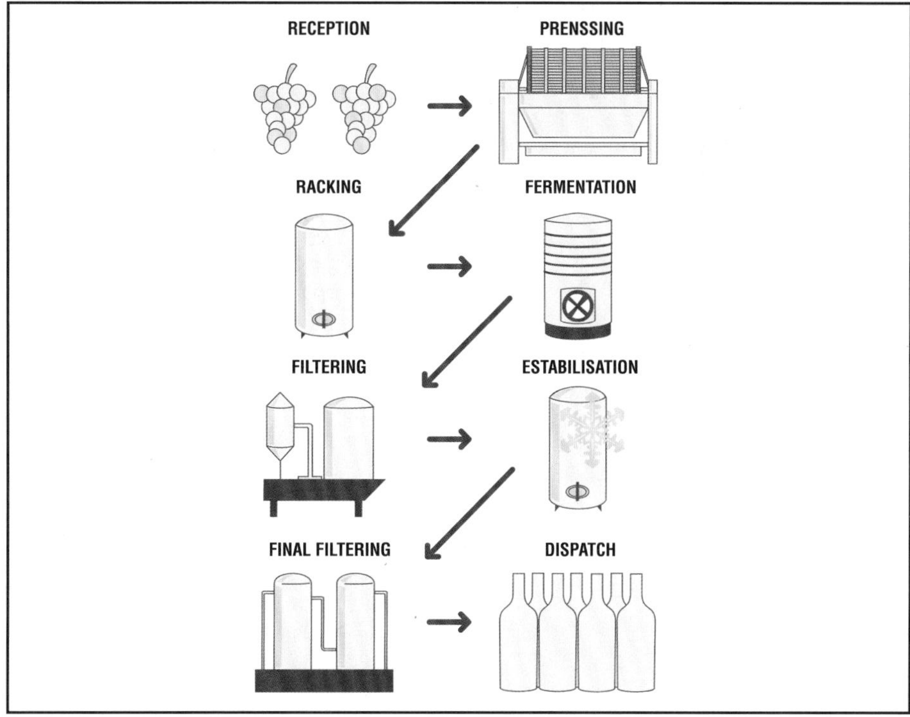

~ **Filtering.** The objective is the same as clarifying, but the means employed differ as, in this case, the wine is passed through a porous device or a membrane in order to retain the suspended matter.

~ **Bottled.** The wine from barrels or containers is standardized in another supply deposit in the bottling plant and is finally bottled there to be put on the market.

ROSÉ

Production is similar to white wine except that red grapes are used, or a mixture of white and red.

~ **Maceration.** Before fermentation, the must is subjected to a short period of cold maceration so that it does not ferment, together with the skins (only a few hours of maceration) so that the colour and certain aromatic substances can be extracted from the skins.

~ **Settling and fermentation.** The solid matter in the must is separated in order to carry out the fermentation without skins (as if it were a white wine) with the consequent transformation of sugar into alcohol due to the action of the yeast.

RED WINES

These are produced from the must of red grapes fermented together with the solid parts of the grapes (skins and seeds).

~ **Destemming** Unlike white wines, the paste resulting from the crushing must go through a "destemming" process, which consists of separating the grape stem so that, during the maceration required in order to take on the

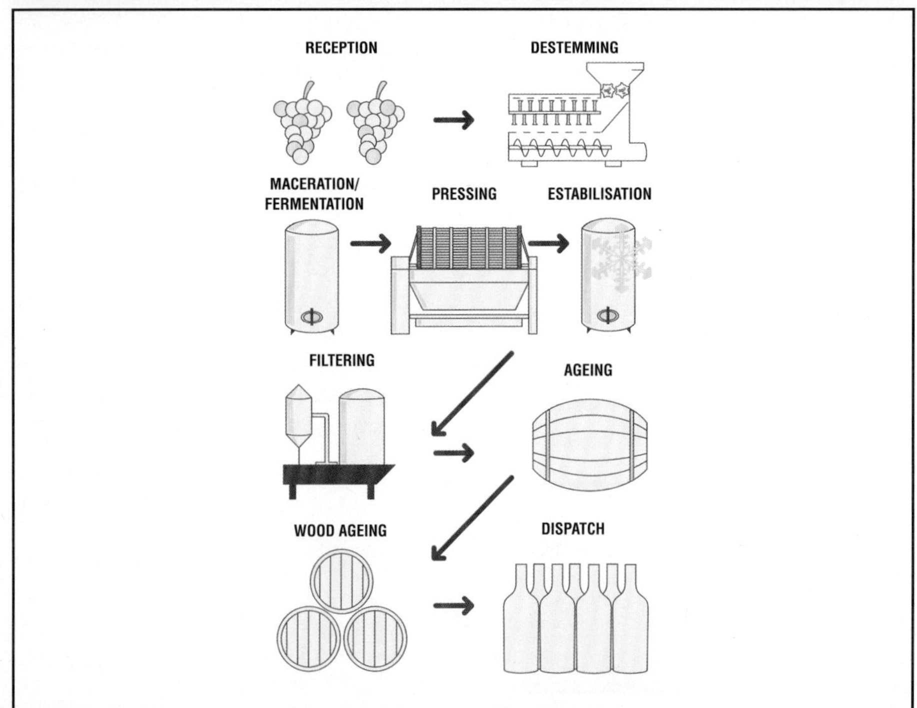

colour, herbaceous and bitter tastes are not transferred from this wooden part of the bunch. Some producers in certain harvests, generally very mature grapes, usually include the very wooden non-herbaceous stem together with the grape. This is a very old formula (until the XIX century, all wines were made this way) but it requires a lot of responsibility. The result is a more voluminous wine, with the aromatic potency distributed between the values of the must itself and the complexity of the vegetable material of the wooden part of the bunch, which is capped with greater volume in the mouth but without the aggressiveness of immature tannins.

~ **Alcoholic fermentation.** This is also called "tumultuous" due to the exceptional activity of the yeasts at this stage. The sugars are split into alcohol while the colouring material in the skins is dissolved in the must.

~ **Remontage.** During the alcoholic fermentation carbonic gas is generated. This pushes the skins upwards and these form a natural barrier called the "cap". Remontage consists of wetting this layer with must in order to activate the extraction of colour. The skins must also be stirred periodically; this is called "pigeage". There are several formulas at this stage depending on the objective set: rack and return, Ganymede or several techniques using nitrogen, etc..

~ **Devatting.** Once the colour is obtained, the principal aromatic components are extracted from the skin and there is a sufficient tannic "framework" provided by this solid part together with the seeds, the liquid is transferred to other containers and separated from the solid material mentioned which goes to the presses.

~ **Malolactic fermentation.** With red wine a second fermentation occurs called malolactic fermentation, through which a strong vegetable acid, malic acid, is turned into a smoother creamier acid, lactic acid, which provides the wine with fineness and smoothness.

What is press wine? This is obtained from pressing the remaining solids from the first fermentation. It is very rich in colour and tannins, but it must not be mixed with the rest unless it is of high quality and comes from mature grapes.
Once the fermentations are over, the wine is subjected to racking and processing in order to clarify and stabilize it so that the limpidity of the bottled product is conserved. Finally, the wines are selected by quality and bottled in the case of new wine or put into barrels to be aged in wood.

SPARKLING WINES

These are wines which contain carbonic gas from the addition of sucrose and yeasts which provoke a second fermentation, either in the bottle (Spanish sparkling wine, champagne) or in the container ("granvás" which is fermentation in large deposits with no disgorgement and elimination of lees in the container).

The traditional method for the production of sparkling wines.

In the past this was called the "champenoise method" or champagne method due to its French origin. This involves those sparkling wines which are fermented for the second time in bottles and are those of the highest quality on the market. In this case, production takes place as follows:

~ **Base wine.** This is a pale, clean, fruity wine which does not exceed 11 degrees of alcohol content and is produced in steel or cement tanks.

~ **Second fermentation.** AIn the tanks there is a mixture of sugar and yeast (tirage liqueur) before bottling. This mixture is bottled with a metallic shutter. With the added sugar, the yeasts go through a second fermentation in the bottle.

~ **Ageing.** The bottles age in caves, which are usually underground bays with uniform temperature and humidity conditions for a period of nine months. They are piled up horizontally, (which is called "stacking") so that, once the second fermentation ends, the dead yeasts are located along the bottle in a horizontal position.

~ **Stirring.** In order to extract the dead yeasts and other remains from the second fermentation once the ageing terminates, the bottles are taken to remuage, where they will be spun and little by little tilted until the yeasts concentrate in the necks of the bottles upside down.

At the present time, this process can be carried out with computer controlled machines, which are called gyropalettes.

~ **Disgorging.** The neck of the bottle is frozen and the shutter opened so that all the yeasts exit the bottle in a small block of ice. Subsequently, the bottles are filled with the tirage liqueur (wine of the same type or aged wine which contains different doses of sugar). It is then sealed, labelled and is ready for sale.

The production of sparkling wine with large containers

~ **Base wine.** This is a pale, clean, fruity wine which does not exceed 11 degrees of alcohol content, produced in steel or cement tanks.

~ **Second fermentation.** A mixture of sugar and yeasts (tirage liqueur) is added to the base wine in the tanks. On being fed with the added sugar, the yeasts make it possible to have a second fermentation in a larger contained, for a period of 20 days, thus, carbonic gas will be generated which is the characteristic of sparkling wines, which is the result of the splitting of the sugar through the action of the yeasts.

The Transfer Method

Today this is less relevant and is hardly used. The second fermentation takes place in the bottle, but is subsequently transferred to another bottle or a container. The difference is that no ageing takes place in the bottle with the yeasts as the wine is stacked only for two months.

~ Types of sparkling wines in relation to the level of sweetness:

The type will depend on the amount of sugar used in the tirage liqueur or in the ageing period. A distinction can be made between the following:

Brut nature: dry, with no added sugar or up to 6 grams/litre of residual sugar.**Brut:** contiene hasta 15 gr./l.
Brut: This contains up to 15 grams/litre of sugar.
Dry: between 17 and 35 grams/litre.
Semi-dry: More than 50 grams/litre.
Sweet: minimum oak ageing of 30 months.

BASIC PRODUCTION OF SPARKLING WINES

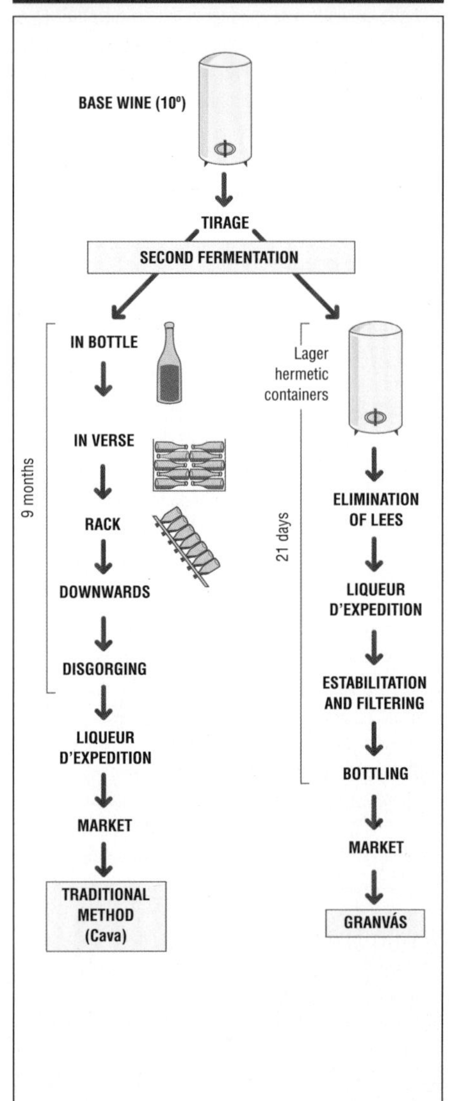

3.- NEW WINES, AGED WINES AND AGEING

New wine is the earliest of the young wines, it can be consumed recently produced when it still conserves the features of the grape intact. The French were the pioneers with their beaujolais, which became a genuine commercial success and its coming onto the market is awaited with much excitement.

It is full of floral and fruity aromas, which transforms its newness into a marvellous quality. A new wine best shows the strain of the vines and the taste of the grapes.

However, newness is not only appreciated in white and rosé wines. The red wines are also successful in this fresher and more fruity style, with their natural taste freed from the standardizing action of the wood.

For the wineries, the production and bottling of a new quality wine is more profitable as prolonged storage is not necessary, it requires less investment as regards stocks and prevents the reduction of wine through evaporation which always occurs when ageing is carried out in barrels.
Young wine must not be consumed beyond three or four years from the date of the harvest which appears on the label as the fruit and freshness qualities are the first which are lost.

The production of this wine requires fermentation, clarification and stabilization, and is subjected to centrifuging, filtering and cold processing, unlike what occurs with new wine, where these processes take place more slowly. The fact that these wines have a shorter life span is due to the fact that there are lower levels of tannins because the production processes are very rapid and there are only a few days for the maceration of the skins.

What is carbonic maceration?
This is a very normal production for "new" and young wines and consists of working with complete bunches (with the stems still attached), which are placed in a sealed tank which contains carbon dioxide. It may also happen that, due to the weight of the harvest, the grapes which are in the lower areas break and begin to ferment, issuing carbonic gas. The most important factor is that the fermentation commences inside the grape so that the specific character of each vine is respected. These wines are normally very fruity and aromatic although there is no substantial extraction of tannins, therefore, they are not recommendable for extended conservation. It is better to consume them in one year.

AGEING

During ageing, which includes ageing in barrels and in bottles, the wines can improve their qualities, acquiring characteristics which are derived especially from the contribution of the wood.

What must wines subjected to ageing be like? Normally, these are robust, sharp, aggressive to the taste and with an intense lively colour; aspects which, little by little, will be polished and refined throughout the ageing.

THE BARREL

This is the oak container which will hold the wine during its ageing. The type most used is made of oak wood with a capacity of 225 litres, called Bordeaux type barrels.

WHICH ASPECTS OF THE BARREL INFLUENCE THE AGEING OF THE WINE?

The origin of the wood. The most normal is American oak, generally sawn, due to its cheaper price, however, French oak from the woods of Allier, Limousin and Nevers is being used more and more, and, recently, oak from East European countries.

The way in which the "staves" (each one of the boards which make up the barrel) are cut. American oak is the "sawn" type, and is cut transversally, while in the French or European oak, the cut is of the "cleaved" type, lengthwise.

The age of the barrels. New barrels or those scarcely used transfer their characteristics to the wine more quickly than older barrels as the older ones have lost their characteristic contribution with use and the wine has to stay for a longer period of time in these.

The period of time the wine must remain in the barrel. The longer the ageing period, the more the characteristics of the wood will be transferred to the wine together with increased oxidization, with the consequent loss of fruit.

HOW IS THE WINE TAKEN TO THE BARREL?

Before receiving the wine, the interior of the barrel is burned with sulphur in order to sanitize it and to eliminate the oxygen and all the microbial remains.

The wine is poured in slowly through a pipe which goes down to the bottom in order to prevent the formation of foam which might displace the sulphur dioxide formed by the combustion of sulphur.

The barrel is closed with a cork stopper covered with burlap or silicone so that it is as hermetic as possible.

CONDITIONS REQUIRED FOR ADEQUATE AGEING.

Low temperature (13-15°C) and with no substantial oscillations between winter and summer, with approximately 75% humidity.

What are transfers? At the end of approximately six months in the barrel, the wine is transferred to another barrel, taking care that it is not mixed with the deposits or impurities accumulated at the bottom at this time. Generally, this operation is repeated with the same periodicity until the wine acquires its ideal point according to the criteria of the producer and maintaining the minimum conditions regulated by the pertinent organisms.

When the permanence in barrels ends, qualities are unified, mixing complementary wines from the same harvest. Once the ideal wine is achieved, bottling takes place.

THE BOTTLE

After its passage through the barrel, the wine requires some time in the bottle so that the fruit and wood features join together and harmonize. In the bottle and due to the absence of oxygen, the molecules of the wine have a different conduct and develop a bouquet while smoothing the roughness until the wine attains its maximum expression.

It is important that the bottle be perfectly clean before being filled with wine and that the corks have a minimum length of 44 millimetres and have no smells or porosities.

~ **Placing the bottles.** They are placed horizontally forming "stacks" so as to ensure that the wine and cork are in contact, thus keeping it wet and hermetic.

~ **Where are the bottles kept?** In "cellars", places which are totally isolated and are generally underground. They are not subjected to air currents or temperature changes, and the relative humidity is greater than 70%. In modern wineries, they are stored in large cages made of wood or metal in the same environmental conditions as those underground using artificial air conditioning.

~ **Does evolution in the bottle vary?** EYes, it is not the same for all wines. It will depend on the amount, quality and balance of the phenolic composites they contain, especially the tannins and total acidity.

AGEING IN OAK

WHY IS WOOD FUNDAMENTAL FOR WINE?

The use of wood for wine in the form of casks no larger than 600 litres began in the XVII century, coinciding with the development of sea trade and the consequent transport of wine in large containers which slowly transferred part of their nature. However, due to their large size and the disproportion between the volume and the surface contact of the wine and the wood this transfer was slow and slight.

However, this was the origin of the "oloroso", the first wine from Jerez, which enchanted English people. Its name refers to the contribution of the excellent aromas which the oak containers supplied to the wine as a result of the aromatic potential of the wood.

What happened with Port wine was similar, and this was achieving immortality in the casks of Vilanova de Gaia, which contributed toasted features and aromas of exotic woods. The first oak from Limoges Bordeaux provided an unmistakable vanilla bouquet.

Thus, it was discovered that the wood enlivened the wine as well as giving it certain maturity and solemnity. This fact was more clearly verified with the manufacture of smaller barrels, where the proportion of oak to wine is greater.

~ **The first wines aged in wood.** The taste of oak transferred by the casks from Jerez was mainly due to the southern heat and to the sea sway which produced strong oxidization. Influenced by the barrels from Jerez, Bordeaux began to manufacture its own barrels, where red wine with high amounts of tannin and acidity was stored and was able to withstand the action of the wood. The intention was to achieve the same aromatic intensity as the barrels from Jerez, but in a wetter, fresher environment.

Some years after the legendary classification of 1855, created in Bordeaux involving wines which gave off hints of cedar and resins from the pre-phyloxera oak barrels, the grands crus of the Gironde adopted the manufacture of the 225 litre Bordeaux barrel, which were initially stored in the caves of the traders of the port of Bordeaux.

Meanwhile, Rioja began to use, not the concept of château Bordeaux, but that of the urban storage-trader, which would later be called "producer-bottler" of wines acquired from the harvesters or wine growers. They imported the ageing tools and the new 225 litre barrels which at first were called "Bordeauxe barrels".

~ **Present day barrels.** Today, the ageing bays of each winery are mainly filled with new barrels, carefully selected from the best suppliers of barrels, which provide the guarantee that American, French or Russian oak is used. These barrels supply essential tannins and aromatic principles to the wine.

~ **Present day barrels.** Today, the ageing bays of each winery are mainly filled with new barrels, carefully selected from the best suppliers of barrels, which provide the guarantee that American, French or Russian oak is used. These barrels supply essential tannins and aromatic principles to the wine.

What lies behind the characteristic taste of oak?

Innumerable reactions and exchanges are produced between the wine and the barrel and these affect the evolution of the wine. They include the fusion of the bitter tannins of the oak with the fruity and sometimes sweet tannins of the grape skins or the fine hints of vanilla from the wood, wrapped in the fruity aroma of the variety.

~ **The taste of the past.** Until the beginning of the eighties in the last century, the "wooden" and "carpentry" tastes were normal in some older Rioja wines, but this was due more to the weak constitution of the wine rather than its long storage in the barrel. Generally, these were red wines which were very open in colour and usually matured prematurely, with evolved tastes lacking nuances together with excess oxidization. The reason was the excessive ventilation of the wine in the transfers rather than the entry of oxygen through the pores and staves of the wood.

~ **Present day taste.** Today the ageing times in the barrels have been shortened and the wine is bottled with fewer transfers. The profound tastes of the lees, the fruity nuances of the grape and the complex features of the mature skins are much more evident, providing a pleasant fresh, fruity sensation. Thus, the nuances acquired by the oak join the primary tastes of the fruit and the characteristic hints of the grape varieties.

Which wines age better?

~ **Red wines.** These will be wines with a strong tannic constitution, pigmentation, level of alcohol and acidity which, consumed in the same epoch as an aged wine (three or four years after the harvest) offer certain aggressiveness to the palate and aromas which are not very evident. They may have vegetable hints from the skins (red) and a touch of resin and pitch typical of new oak. Generally, the wineries usually commercialize these from three to five years after the date of the harvest.

~ **White wines.** Normally, although they have few tannins, unless maceration is carried out with the skins, in theory their lifespan is more ephemeral. In fact, the juvenile, aromatic and penetrating features tend to disappear after two years. However, it is possible to taste white wines aged over 20 years which have maintained their liveliness thanks to good acidity and a low pH.

Nevertheless, a slow fermenting white wine, aged in oak and bottled late on will have its lifespan prolonged to that of a red wine. This is possible due to the transfer of tannins from the oak, which offset the lack of tannins in white grapes (it should not be forgotten that the tannins are in the grape skins and, normally, although things are beginning to change, it is not usual to macerate the must with the skins).

Today, as opposed to the classic aged white wines with a long period of storage in wood and produced like red wines, it is now normal that those fermented in barrels with their lees and subjected to correctly understood ageing where the molecules of the lees prevent the features of the oak from becoming overwhelming, as happens with white wines aged in wood.

4.- HOW TO DESIGN A GRAND WINE

Below is a vade mecum which explains the factors required to achieve a high quality wine in order of importance. The work practice described corresponds to a philosophy shared by the majority of the grand labels which set out the quality guidelines in the world of wine.

PRACTICE IN THE VINEYARD

A) Cultivation and harvesting. It is fundamental that the following practices take place so that the grape can achieve its maximum expression:

A1.- Ecological treatment of the vineyard (organic fertilizers, green pruning in order to reduce the yield).

A2.- Dosage of water in order to achieve a certain hydric stress, which produces smaller grapes, therefore, there is a higher proportion of skin to must.

A3.- Control of the leaves (the number of leaves which must achieve a balanced photosynthesis function) and training of the vine shoots which enables a greater number of bunches, which are smaller and with the grapes looser, which mature uniformly.

A4.- The determination of the time of the harvest, depending on the phenol maturing (that is to say, the grape skins are mature and the seeds are dry) and reducing the amount of sugar as far as possible through of the variety the intelligent dosage of water to the plant so that the maturing of the skin coincides with a lower alcohol level, which preserves the fresh aromas of the variety and prevents the grape from candying by insolation.

A5.- Selection of bunches in the vineyard.

A6.- Control of the maturing of the skins.

B) Soil. This is the cause of the mineral nuances in the aroma and taste of the wine. It must be:

B1.- Rich in minerals and poor in organic material.

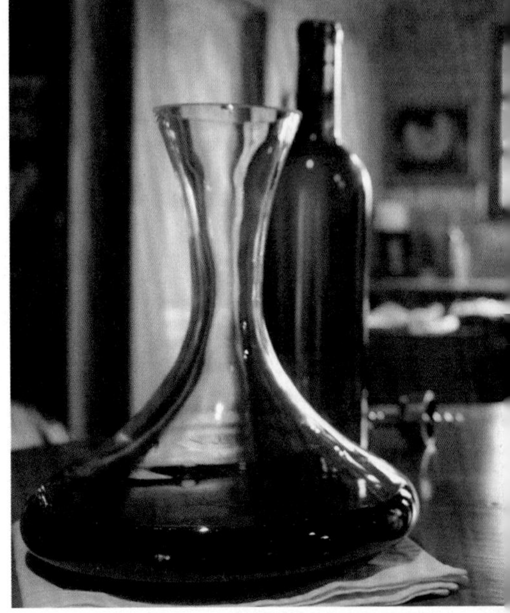

B2.- Have a layer which allows good drainage (sand, stone, pebbles, slate on a clay-limestone substratum, etc.).

B3.- Water in deep layers so that the root mass (the root network) crosses the layers of the terrain and benefits from its contributions.

C) Microclimate. The location of the vineyard is important, depending on whether the plot is oriented north or south, is flat or on a slope.

C1.- The best vineyards. These come from the more ventilated hills at higher altitudes. This situation allows the acidity to be more than sufficient and that, owing to direct insolation, a considerable level of alcohol is obtained.

D) Varieties. These determine the style of the wine. The ideal ones are noble. Old vines (40-80 years old, which are those which have a greater amount of roots, some of which are very deep down). Choose the later varieties in warm climates (garnacha red, petit verdot, cabernet sauvignon, garnacha white, viognier, graciano, verdejo, cariñena, etc.). For climates with wider thermal conditions, (cooler nights and daytme insolation), choose varieties such as malbec, tempranillo, prieto picudo, etc.) and for temperate climates , choose early vines such as cabernet franc, pinot noir, albariño, godello, etc.)

PRACTICE IN THE WINERY

~ **Selection of bunches in the winery** (some boutique wineries even select only the healthiest and most mature parts of the bunches).

~ **Small steel or wooden fermentation** containers with a maximum capacity of 15,000 litres.

~ **Avoid mechanically pumping the grapes.** It is better to use gravity by locating the grape reception area in the higher part of the winery.

~ **Pellicular maceration.** (skins with must). This contributes more fruity features. It is a process used to extract the aromatic features of the grape before fermentation in a purer fashion and at low temperature. Thus, the slight deterioration of the fruity potential produced by the rise in temperature during fermentation is prevented.

~ **Alcoholic fermentation.** Fermentation with complete, millimetric control of the temperature of the must makes it possible to balance the features of the grape with those derived from the fermentation and enables the full maintenance of the features of the fruit during the extraction of the substances contained in the skins and the must.

~ **Remontage** (wetting the solid mass of grapes which float in the container) or "pigeage" (mechanical breaking of the mass or cap so that the wine penetrates through the gaps) achieve a better dissolution of the colour and the tannins.

~ **Malolactic and ageing fermentations.** To a large extent, these determine the personalities of the new quality wines. In the bacterial transformation of the malic acidity into lactic acidity, agents are involved which enrich the tastes (lees), but these are easily corrupted.

How is this done? Generally, it must be carried out in new barrels. The fine lees and the vegetable molecules of the wine which in turn fuse with the aromatic molecules of the oak provide a complexity and "volume" which is oily to the touch and has a persistent taste. If bad smells arise, it is necessary stir these periodically with a wooden shaft (batonnage) in order to improve the transfer of their peculiar features and prevent their reduction and the bad smell, very similar to that of stagnant water.

~ **Selection of barrels.** The key to the fineness of the aroma and taste. Oak has gone from being a container and has become the main ingredient of quality wine. What factors must be taken into account?

The barrels must be new in order to take advantage of the aromatic substances of the oak.

The proportions of different types of wood (American, French or Russian oak), its drying and the periods of use for each wine.

Small wooden containers with no top cover in order to carry out the grape crushing which extracts the most delicate colouring and tastes from the grapes.

Choose the suppliers well. The barrel is still the work of craftsmen and the manual skills and the choice of woods of the cooper make him a genuine cabinetmaker.

~ **Clarifying by decanting without a filter.** The objective is to conserve the pigments and composites which enrich the aromas and tastes of the wine.

In the past. The transparency of red wine was achieved by natural means with prolonged repose in barrels and transfers.

At the present time. Red wines are in the barrel just for the period of time for the wood to transfer the aromatic and tannic composites of the ageing and this is not sufficient for all the sediment to disappear (pigments and bitartrate crystals). That is why many labels warn the consumer of this.

SOME KEYS TO PRODUCTION

Micro-oxygenation

This is also called "microbullage", a French term which refers to the injection of oxygen into the wine conserved in containers with little airing (steel vats) or in barrels for short periods of ageing in order to prevent corrupt aromas ("reduction stinks", similar to the smell of stagnant water) which arise in the post-fermentation processes or due to the lack of airing.

This is carried out as regards young wines, whose bottling is brought forward to the point where it has not obtained the required dose of oxygen, and for wines aged in barrels, substituting the effect of the transfers and long storage of the wine in wood. Thus, there is no need to lengthen the periods for ageing which would give more aroma and taste of oak, which would affect the features of the fruit. Nevertheless, this rapid micro-oxygenation does not achieve the attributes of the oxygenation through the pores of the barrel, as in ageing in oak.

The fine lees

These are the sediments which remain at the bottom of the containers after the fermentation of the wine: dead yeast, non-soluble acids and vegetable remains and waste of the grape. When this wine is transferred immediately after the alcoholic fermentation, the "thick" lees remain in the container, while the fine ones accompany the wine.

These composites dissolved in the liquid enrich the aromas of the wine, and, for this to succeed properly, the fine lees must be sufficiently oxygenated not only through the pores of the wood, but also due to bâtonnage, a French term which means stirring the liquid with a shaft inserted through the mouth of the barrel.

This practice also makes it possible for the lees to remain in suspension and achieves supplementary oxygenation as, otherwise, the lees in repose would facilitate their reduction or putrefaction due to the absence of oxygen, with the resulting hydrogen sulphide (rotten eggs) or mercaptan (stagnant water).

THE FERMENTATION CONTAINERS

Stainless steel

This began to be implemented in Spain at the end of the seventies.

Advantages: strong asepsis and, above all, thermal control of the alcoholic fermentation owing to its sophisticated refrigeration systems.

Inconveniences: its hermetic nature prevents airing and may give rise to the reduction of some vegetable composites; the clarifications are very difficult and in vats with more than 15,000 litres, there are thermal currents as a result of the interaction of the external temperature with the totally controlled internal temperature, as well as strange electrostatic influences caused by the steel.

Wood

This has been the material most traditionally used in the production of quality wines.

Advantages: It allows the wine to "breathe" better through its pores ("natural micro-oxygenation"), the wines stabilize more easily after fermentation and are more rounded.

Inconveniencies: Its high cost, purchase and maintenance, it requires exhaustive cleansing and continual attention (repairs, etc.), as well as qualified staff.

Cement

This was the material used in the older wineries until stainless steel appeared.

Advantages: it was recently discovered that more uniform temperatures are achieved in its interior, therefore, a greater expression of the wine in the difficult storage and ageing phases.

Inconveniencies: care must be taken to prevent alterations to the wine due to the excess temperatures although it is compatible with control systems; it also requires absolute cleanliness to achieve a perfect state; it is not associated with quality wines (although the mythical Petrus continues to use it to ferment its wines).

Currently, some wineries are installing small capacity internal wall cement containers but with no coating although the texture is easily cleaned. The features of the wines as regards special nuances are near to those aged in oak but the hints of wood are not detected.

How is "vin de garage" produced? Basically, the production of "vins de garage" refers to the production of small amounts which allow for improved quality control, a selection of the "terroir", a selection of bunches from the vine and on the table to finish up, in some cases, in very expensive wines, selected "grape by grape", so that each grape is almost identical and with an almost uniform level of maturity.

5.- WINE TASTING STEP BY STEP

This is the sequence which every non-professional must interpret, the recipe for discovering a complex world of sensations, aromas and tastes. The following is the liturgy in slow motion of what every wine lover must follow.

THE COLOUR OF THE WINE

There are a number of nuances in the wine which can only be appreciated through a visual comparison and which provide valuable information on its characteristics.

There is a basic principle as regards the colour of wine. With ageing, white wines darken; red wines become lighter.

The more acidic wines give off more glimmer regardless of whether they are white or red

WHITE WINES:

The darkening of the white wines (tendency to amber colours with red nuances) in the bottle this is due to oxidation by air, by heat and by light. The colouring transfer from the wood as from four months of ageing provides a more yellow colouring.

The greenish tinges reveal that there is greater acidity, apart from the characteristics of the variety, there may be more or less intense yellow tinges.

Chardonnay always has a light yellow background. However, a sauvignon blanc in similar circumstances has paler nuances.

A pale white wine, which is very shiny with rapid foam will be a young wine, from cold areas rich in acids and, if not, it will have been produced, at least, in accordance with the modern rules of oenology with an early harvest with a lack of sugar and rich in acids.

A white wine poured into a glass which seems denser will be from a warm climate. The high level of alcohol is usually parallel to the amount of natural glycerine which "thickens" the wine.

VISUAL INTERPRETATIONS OF THE COLOURS IN WINES

Interpretation of the colours in wines in a glass inclined at 45°, together with the most common wine tasting terms used in this guide:

Rim or border with a slightly violet hue.

Cherry, medium-intensity and quite lively

WHITE WINES

YOUNG WHITE WINE
Palate straw yellow. There are also green nuances, proof of its youth.

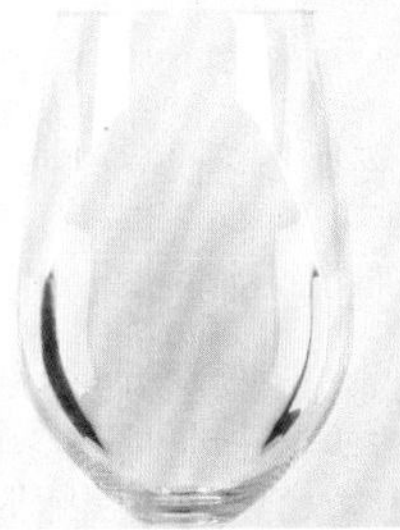

MATURE WHITE WINE, AGED FOR 20 YEARS IN BOTTLE
Golden yellow with hints of amber. (Due to oxidation the yellow becomes more intense and turns to shades of red).

ROSE WINES

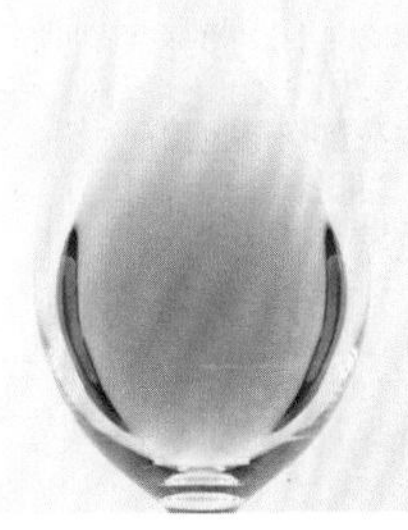

THE LATEST VINTAGE
Brilliant blush with strawberry-raspberry hue. The blue tones that, combined with the reddish tones give a raspberry hue, are associated with youth.

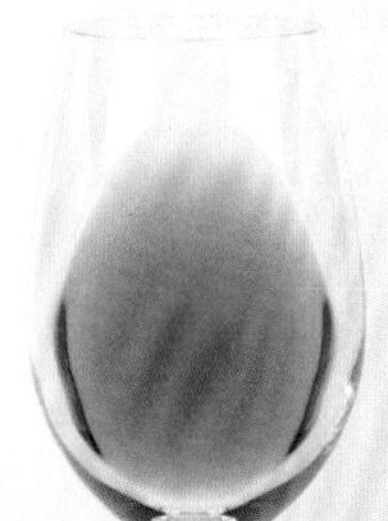

20 YEARS OF AGEING IN BOTTLE
Blush salmon colour with coppery hints. (In roses, over time the colour changes to orangey hues, losing the lively blue tone that gives it the raspberry colour.

RED WINES

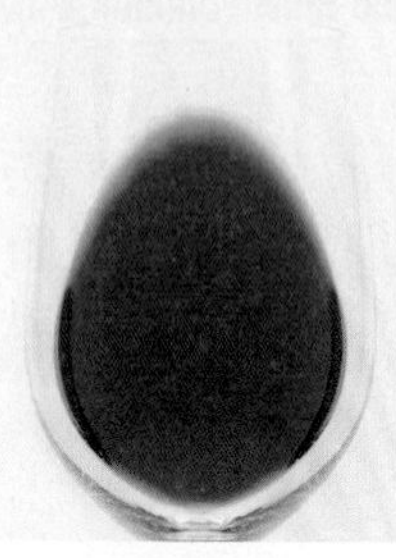

LATEST VINTAGE
medium-intensity cherry red with a violet rim (characteristic of its youth).

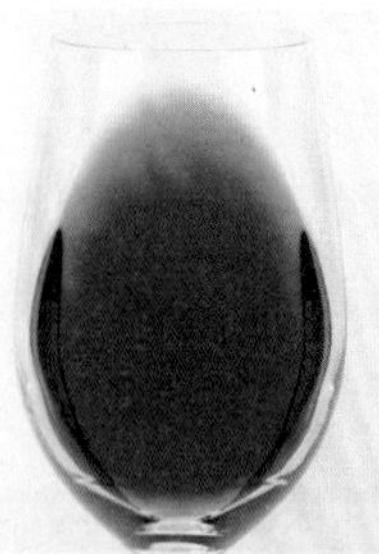

AGED FOR 20 YEARS IN BOTTLE
Ruby red with an orangey hue and a rim between ochre and brick. (This red wine is on the decline, the very brick coloured ochre is a sign of excessive oxidation).

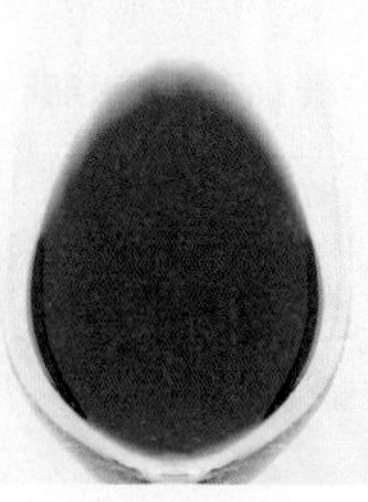

TEMPRANILLO, CABERNET SAUVIGNON
the differences between these two varieties are quite clear: while the colour of the Tempranillo(first glass) is dark cherry with more orangey rim, the colour of the Cabernet is more intense with a more violet rim, due to greater pigmentation from the skins as the grapes are smaller than the Tempranillos.

RED WINES

The time required for the extraction of colouring material during the maceration of the skins with the must depends on the level of insolation which the grape has undergone during its vegetative period.

In its first period, the wine has a solid, intense colour. With the passage of the years, this will open up due to the fact that the molecules of the colour tend to fuse with each other and become thicker (passing from the soluble to the colloidal stage and from this to insoluble, with precipitation to the bottom of the barrel or bottle; these are the inoffensive sediments which many confuse with the term "chemical").

A red wine with bright tinges and vermillion-rose coloured edges will come from northern areas and will have a high acidity level.

A red wine with violet nuances and with brown tones means that it is from warm climates.

In short, the colour of the wine depends on the type of grape, the maceration of the skins, the maturity of the grapes, the duration of the ageing in wood and the age in the bottle.

The influence of the production

FIRST PRACTICAL CASE: WHITE WINES

We can take two white wines as examples: one is produced with current technology and the other with the more elementary classical procedure applied to table or common wines. Later we will examine the white wines produced with the progressively more normal pellicular maceration.

a) Technological wine. This will be a pale wine, the fruit of controlled production and an early harvest. The must is filtered before fermentation so that the herbaceous parts will not excessively transfer colours and tastes to the wine; subsequently, the fermentation is controlled without going beyond 18 degrees and, finally, it is clarified. This wine has substantial transparency and a high level of acidity which is seen in its slightly greenish shine.

b) Common wine. This has straw-yellow tones which result from more elementary wine making and from a less rigorous racking than in the first. Perhaps there was not a precise con-

trol of the fermentation temperature and a greater incidence of oxidization is noted.

c) Wine with pellicular maceration. These are white wines which have macerated with the skins (peel or skin of the grape) in its pre-fermentation phase (must) in order to achieve a greater structure, taste-olfactory complexity and density. They have a certain amber shine produced by yellow pigments (flavones) in the skins.

SECOND PRACTICAL CASE: RED WINES

The following is an example of the influence of the production of two wines of the same year.

a) Wine with less colour. This has quite an open hue which presupposes early devatting (separation of the must transformed into wine with skins).

More white grapes could have been used in order to smooth it and supply a more extensive spectrum of consumers.

It could also have remained longer in the barrel than the second and this would have precipitated its colouring material to a greater extent. However, this would be doubtful if the taste differences of the wood between one and the other are not apparent.

b) Wine with more colour. This is more intense either because the maceration was longer or simply due to the greater insolation of the grapes in the area.
Its level of anthocyanins (the red colour) and tannins (yellow) are substantially greater, which shows that a wine with these characteristics ages better. However, in its first commercialization phase, it may have to tackle customers not used to its slightly rough taste.

THIRD CASE: ROSÉ WINE

It is said that the most perfect rosé is the one which has a pale rose colour. If the year has been very sunny, the hue will be more reddish as the skins of the red grapes have more colouring material and it is difficult to separate the skins quickly in order to prevent the intensity of the colour. If the year has been rainy or cold, the colouring will not be so intense, with a tendency to onion skin hues.

The typical rosé wine oscillates between an onion skin and a rose colour. If the wine is produced with absolute asepsis, sheltered from the air, with fermentation control and with moderate acidity, a very bright rose coloured hue will appear together with possible slight gleams of mauve.

In time the mauve gleams disappear and the yellow and ochre hues increase.

The influence of age

~ Red wines

A red wine of the latest harvest.

This has the vermillion hints of young wine, the fruit of the large amount of blue pigments which appear at this stage. Moreover, the hint appears as lively and luminous and with strong violet nuances, features which also reveal the short life of this wine (see glass page 40).

A red wine aged for 20 years in a bottle (see glass page 40). As it is declining, it has more open hues, it has lost most of its anthocyanins and the brick red hues with the gleam of mahogany have appeared with a predominant yellow colour, which is the result of greater ageing.

~ Rosé wine

A rosé wine of the latest harvest (see glass page 39). This has a raspberry pink colour as a result of the slight reddish pigmentation with the bluish nuance which determines the raspberry hue.

A twenty year old bottled rosé wine loses the lively bluish pink nuances (raspberry) and takes on a more yellowish-copper hue due to oxidization (see glass page 39).

~ White wines

This occurs inversely. If the young wine (see glass page 39) is characterized by a pale, sharp, shiny hue, the oldest wines (see glass page 39) have a more golden tonality.

This nuance is possibly due to he fact that the must has obtained yellow pigments from the skins, and the flavones which, due to the oxidization, modify the colour throughout time.

The influence of ageing in barrels

~ White wines

The longer the wine is stored in the barrel, the more intense is its colour.

A wine aged in wood begins to **show a golden sheen** as from five months and this will intensify as the ageing is prolonged in time. However, if the wine has fermented in the barrel with its lees, owing to the fermenting reaction of these solid composites with the molecules of the wood, the influence of the oak will be less and the colour will be paler in the case of white wines which have only been aged in oak.

Another illustrative example involves the **vintage wines of Western Andalusia** where the colour is not only established by the wood, but by the defensive action of the yeast in the vinos finos and in the oxidation process in the case of amontillados and olorosos.

Finos (in the County of Huelva "pálidos"). These involve a degradation from the colourless tone of the edge to a pale yellow. This yellowness due to the two epochs of the year when the flor yeast disappears entails a greater contribution of oxygen.

Manzanilla. The flor yeast is more permanent owing to the greater humidity in the wineries of Sanlúcar de Barrameda, therefore, its evolution towards oxidation is slower. So, the wine maintains the paleness and the green highlights are more pronounced.

Amontillado. This is oxidative as it does not maintain its flor yeast in all its purity and usually remains longer in the barrel than the aforementioned wines. So, it takes on a very defined amber colour.

Oloroso. The hues are highly toasted; there is orange and ochre on a background with yellow highlights. There is greater oxidation over time and with higher temperatures in the ageing bays and concentration due to the evaporation of water and alcohol.

~ Red wines
As from 10 months in the barrel, a slight orange hint appears when the intensity of the colour is diminishing due to the precipitation of the colouring molecules owing to the micro-oxygenation through the pores of the wood.

THE AROMA OF THE WINE

Although the nose is the organ which we probably use less, its importance is vital. In fact, many of the pleasures of the mouth would be imperceptible without the sense of smell. For the wine taster, it is an essential tool and should be considered justly, as is beautifully defined by Max Leglise, as "the garden of the senses".

Smell is a complex and mysterious sense, which also has its weaknesses.

Did you know that?
A person does not smell his usual cologne he uses although the other persons do, or that a house has an aroma which everyone except those who live there smell. The nose is inconsistent as regards normal smells; the sense of smell tires.

It is important that a wine enthusiast who attempts to smell for the first time should record the nuances perceived in his mind. Do not insist on smelling as this increases insensibility.

The importance of smell. Of the three gastronomic senses, smell is the most selective. If we smell a rosé wine and we see it, we will be convinced that it is a rosé wine. If our eyes are bound, it would not be so clear; even less so, if we drink it.

On smelling a wine during a tasting, we will have decided approximately 80% of its evaluation. However, if we have not seen the wine, this will fall to 60%. A large part of what we are going to evaluate is based on the "tip off" which seeing the glass has transferred to the other two senses.

The influence of production

The aromas acquired throughout the production process are called "secondary". These may be positive or negative.

~ Positive aromas. These are the aromas of yeast, the lactic nuances which produce a smooth sweet sensation, or the ethereal hints which bring nuances of the fine herbs of the lees.

~ Negative aromas.
Hydrogen sulphide, mercaptan, geraniol. They may appear in young wines and indicate that the wine is not yet terminated or is undergoing microbiological degradation of the sulphurous anhydride due to a lack of airing or late transfer. If it is uncorked some years later, the smell of mercaptans may be notable, like the smell of petroleum and stagnant water. Geraniol has nothing to do with aroma of geranium or the smell of the leaf of the geranium. This is a rustic vegetable feature which is more noticeable when a heat wave affects the vine. As a defensive action, the leaves stop the vegetative process, delaying phenolic maturing (that of the skins and the seeds) but not the alcoholic maturing due to the dehydration of the bunch.

The sulphur smell is due to the insertion of a small dose of sulphur during bottling in order to prevent premature oxidation. Currently this is hardly ever used.

Banana. Although this is not unpleasant, it appears in wines bottled too early. This forms during wine making at low temperatures with certain selected yeasts. The aroma is less perceptible when bottling is carried out late.

Rustic and aroma of orujo (liquor distilled from grape remains). This is typical of wines produced with a lack of hygiene before the arrival of stainless steel containers and the control of temperature during fermentation. Filtering or clarifying the must did not take place and the herbaceous parts transferred unwanted tastes to the wine although these were not unpleasant. Furthermore, neither the alcoholic level nor the acidity were controlled, thus the white wines lacked the freshness which is welcomed today.

"Enclosed". This is noticeable on uncorking a bottle of rosé or young red wine bottled too early and stored in the bottle for a long time although it dissipates a little with airing. Bottling too early will never help the wine to acquire the aromas to reduce ageing; in time it will even lose the primary aromas. Therefore, young wines and rosé wines must be consumed as soon as possible.

"Brett". When the animal smell mixed with a hint of stable is intense, it is probable that this is a case of brettanomyces owing to a yeast which has reduced in the bottles with wines which have their pH altered, generally to a high level.

The influence of ageing

These are the aromas which the wine acquires during its storage in wooden barrels, casks or vats and those produced in the bottle. "Knowing how to age consists of conserving the virtues of youth for a long time", said Peynaud. And this is the case, ageing without losing the aromas which the fruit evokes.

~ **Ageing in wood.** Ageing in wood (generally in oak due to its lower porosity) produces an expansion of the fruity and mineral aromas in the wine owing to the slight airing through the pores of the container. The features are sharper and fused with those transferred from the barrel regardless of whether this is new or semi-new, with creamy toasted hints. When the ageing in wood is prolonged beyond two years, it is probable that the oxygen which has entered during this period begins to take effect. The identifying features are a limited oxidation of the alcohol with slight aldehyde nuances (acetone, resin or nail lacquer), while the wine acquires hints of dried fruits, woodwork, vanilla. If the barrels are old and have been stored in underground bays with little ventilation, a mushroom, rancid vanilla, wax nuance may be noted more clearly than in old brandies.

~ **Ageing in the bottle.** Generally, rather than ageing if compared with the transformations in the barrel, this is a "finishing" of the wine. In the first six months in the glass bottle, a fusion of all the aromatic composites of the wine and the oak takes place. The bottle tempers the aromas, the acidic and tannic sensation is moderated and, after two years, another change appears due to the absence of oxygen. This is called "reduction" and evokes tobacco, leather, honey, incense, spices, etc. These features are more appreciable if the ageing process in wood is over a long period, with greater oxygenation of the wine potentiated by the transfers, this difference is more difficult to appreciate.

Principal ageing aromas

~ **Animal type aroma.** This is typical of old wines which have been bottled for a long time and have been suffocated or reduced substantially in the container. These are noted in wines with little pigmentation and tannins.

New leather, Moroccan leather, wet dog hair.

~ **Balsamic type aroma.** Aroma with the evocation of resin produced by ageing in oak at medium and high conservation temperatures (Eastern Spain, Greek and Tunisian wines and some wines from Australia, California and South Africa). These "pharmacy" aromas are also due to the use of pine and chestnut wood. The caramelizing of the wine which is evaporated between the staves also contributes to its formation. Some smells evoke eucalyptus and bay leaves may be due to phenolic immaturity (seeds and skins of the grapes) which also enrich its fruity nuances. These must not be confused with subtle aromas of the grand wines of the Rhone which may be evoked by the eucalyptus.

Pitch, cedar wood, incense, eucalyptus, bay, dried leaves.

~ **Wooden aroma.** These are produced by recent often excessive ageing in wood, generally in 225 litre barrels.
New oak or woodcraft oak, very dry old wood, cigarette box, green or chip wood.

~ **Roasted or toasted aroma.** Acquired over long ageing in wood toasted and new or from very mature grape skins.
Black pepper, toasted caramel, toasted almond, aroma of coffee, aroma of roasted coffee, cocoa, chocolate, toasted bread, smoked, vanilla, tobacco.

6.- THE FOLLOWING MUST BE TAKEN INTO ACCOUNT

WHAT MUST BE AVOIDED

~ **On purchasing wines,** acquire economical aged red wines over 10 years old as they are declining.

~ **On serving the wine:** uncork by the edge of the bottle and uncork Spanish sparkling wine in a vertical position.

~ **As regards the conservation of wine:** keep the bottles in the kitchen or in a pantry with the aromas of salted food.

~ **Consumption:** a bottle must not be consumed after being transported. A minimum of 24 hours must elapse.

GOOD MANNERS WHEN HAVING GUESTS AT HOME

- **The red wines must be on the table** previously uncorked, and the white wines and rosé wines in the ice bucket with water and ice.

- **The host must know the wine** preferences of the guests.

- **The host must previously taste** the wine he is going to serve in order to verify its state.

- **The host** should give a surprise with a new brand.

- **The host must begin the series** of red wines with the youngest and lightest in order to end with the oldest or most expressive.

ADVICE FOR REQUESTING WINE IN A RESTAURANT

- **Do not order the oldest wines** even if these are economical unless the establishment has a good system for their conservation.

- **Ask for the bottle on the table.** Cold wines must be in the ice bucket beside the table.

- **Do not trust a restaurant** which only has very well known brands.

- **Do not trust the establishment** which piles up bottles in the room.

- **In summer,** do not be ashamed to ask for red wine to be cooled (it is usually served at 23 degrees) in an ice bucket with water and ice for nine minutes (this is the time required to lower it to 18 degrees to serve it).

- **Trust the restaurant** which has an air conditioned wine cabinet.

- **Do not trust the restaurant** which insists on offering a determined wine and does not take the menu requested into account.

- **Do not trust the "dram"** or the free glass of home made fruit or blueberry liquor. It is preferable to pay for a well known brand and return the drink if it is not of the required quality.

- **Be alert to the "house wine"** with no label. If the house wine has the label of the restaurant, it is essential to find out the supplier winery.

- **Do not order a generic wine.** Look at the menu and trust the unknown brands of less reputed areas. This shows that the wine steward or the person in charge of the restaurant recognizes their quality and can provide more creditable information.

EMERGENCY HANDBOOK

Frequently asked questions

~ **Can red wine be drunk with fish?** If the fish are oily, there are no problems, nor is it a mistake to drink red wine with fish such as turbot, cod and other more delicate fish, if these are accompanied by varied garnishing or strong sauces on condition that the red wine is light, with slight body and young, that is to say up to three years old.

~ **Does wine improve over time?** Wine changes or worsens. A wine changes because it gains some attributes (it becomes smoother, more spicy aromas appear), others are lost or reduced, such as the features of the grape and some sensorial components of the terrain (soil and climate).

~ **Does wine become worse when it travels?** Today wines are sufficiently stabilized in order to withstand any type of attack. They are only blocked as regards smell and taste (short aroma with no expression) during the days following the journey. Fifteen days later they recover.

~ **Does white wine become worse over the years?** Some wines aged intensively in wood are better after five years as the wood softens and the carpentry aromas of the oak combined with a slight evocation of the grape become more honeyed and spiced. A white wine fermented in wood, an albariño, rueda or chardonnay are better in the second year.

~ **Are rosé wines only for beginners?** Definitely not. The fact is that the measure of red and white wines (type of ageing, variety of grape and terrain) are not applicable to these wines. The interest in them only lies in their freshness, fruitiness and, especially, their newness. Naturally, these factors are attractive for any consumer, regardless of whether he is an expert or not.

~ **Why do finos and manzanillas last for so little time if they have a high level of alcohol?** All dry or sweet Sherry wines are produced as mellowed wines (they are oxidized by the air and the temperature) except for the finos and manzanillas which are produced with an absence of oxygen under the veil or white cream which covers the surface of the wine inside the barrel (cask) and protects them from the air. From the time the wine exits the cask for bottling and is unprotected by the "yeast layer", it will tend to become rancid. That is why these wines are much paler and fresher even though they have the same ageing as an amontillado or an oloroso.

~ **Is the must of red wines red?** The colour is the same as the white grapes. The pigmentation is only in the skins of the grapes. The only exception is the must of the garnacha tintorera grape, which is very low quality.

~ **Why are red grapes generally used in champagne and the colour is that of white wine?** Because they extract the must very quickly with very wide, shallow presses so that there is no time for the pigmentation of the skins to stain the must. Even so, the colour of these sparkling wines sometimes has reddish glints.

~ **Does a white wine last less than a red wine?** This depends on the state of the cork. If the white wine is aged in oak, its lifespan may be the same as a red wine. However, fruity white wines have been tasted from harvests as old as 15 or more years and these conserved the more important components such as balance, acidity and a variety of features, together with reduced hints although they did lose their fruity nature.

~ **Do old vines give better wines?** On condition that they are healthy, the old vines have a self-regulating system and the reservation of nutrients due to a greater mass of roots with lower production, consequently, they have a higher quality.

A GOOD ENTHUSIAST MUST NOT FORGET THE FOLLOWING:

- **Be curious about less well known wines.**
- **Wine is not only for eating,** but is to be enjoyed at any time in moderation.
- **The sense of smell is the most important.** The mouth only perceives sour, bitter, sweet and salty tastes. The specific tastes of things are processed via aftertaste (the internal via from the mouth to smell), however, we only perceive these in the palate.
- **Do not overwhelm the inexperienced person with a doctoral thesis on wine.** The more efforts made to impress the inexperienced person, the more difficult it becomes for him to understand this culture.
- **Acidity offsets the sugar and the alcohol.** A wine with a level of 12 degrees of alcohol, but with very low acidity, will seem to us to be more alcoholic than a wine with an alcohol level of 14 degrees with higher acidity. A sweet wine will not seem to be less if tartaric acid is added (from the grapes), citric acid (from oranges, lemons and grapefruit) or malic acid (from apples).
- **Be tolerant and modest.** These are the virtues of those who best know wines.
- **Do not attempt to guess the label in a blind tasting** if you do not want to appear to be ridiculous. It is better to say, this red wine reminds me of wine X. If you are not right, nothing happens. If you are lucky enough to be right, glory.
- **With time,** red wine becomes clearer, white wine becomes darker and rosé wine becomes spoiled.
- **As regards red wines,** the violet edge of the glass means that it is young; the orange edge means maturity; and the ochre edge means it is declining. As regards white wines, the straw yellow edge means that it is young; golden yellow that it is mature and red that it is in decline.

SEA CURRENTS

The sea currents are interrelated creating a circular system influenced by the rotation of the earth, the winds which strike the surfaces of the oceans and the density and temperature of the water in each area of the planet. This is a complex, closed circuit which will affect the climates in a large part of the world, benefiting or burying the wine growing possibilities of the countries. The currents with greater influence on vineyards are four, unless these are explained, there would only be a single interdependent system of sea currents.

THE TEMPERATURE OF THE CURRENTS AS A DETERMINING FACTOR

WARM CURRENTS: These are the thermal sea ways which penetrate colder areas moderating the climate and enabling vine growing. The particularity of these warm currents lies in in achieving rainfall of no less than 600 millimetres per year, temperatures not above 30 degrees centigrade in summer and humidity levels no less than 70 per cent. At latitudes nearer to the equator, this phenomenon generates a more tropical, wetter climate, which is less adapted to generating quality wines.

COLD CURRENTS: Warm coasts bathed by cold currents are generally arid as the low temperatures of their waters do not enable evaporation and, therefore, the formation of clouds, which directly leads to the absence of rain, and means that it is necessary to artificially irrigate the vines. The beneficial influence on the vines is seen in the moderation of the daytime and night-time temperatures and levels of sea humidity of the air which does not fall below 60 per cent even though this does not penetrate more than 50 kilometres inland.

PRINCIPAL OCEANIC INFLUENCES

The Gulf Stream, a warm stream from the Gulf of Mexico is responsible for the temperatures in a large part of Western Europe not being excessively cold. The influence of the Gulf Stream is such that Iceland has relatively moderate temperatures in spite of its latitude, while Greenland, which is not influenced by the Gulf Stream despite lying only 400 kilometres to the west, has a polar arctic climate which makes life practically impossible on a large part of its surface. This means that, in the latitude of Iceland, Norway and even Sweden, the normal climate would be that of Greenland in the same way that on this same latitude in the southern hemisphere this last mentioned phenomenon also occurs. Therefore, continental Europe has an abnormally benign climate which enables vines to be cultivated even in the south of England, Sweden and Denmark. What types of wines are produced in these territories? Oceanic types with moderate rainfall, temperate days and nights such as those in Galicia, Leon, Rioja, Bordeaux, the areas of the Loire, Northern Italy and even beyond Burgundy.

East Australian Current: this affects the east of Australia and the totality of the South and North Islands of New Zealand. Due to the subtropical latitude of the North Island of this country and the eastern coast of Australia, this is not an important factor for quality wines. However, in the South Island of New Zealand it is possible to have quality harvests due to its colder latitude, therefore, it has a climate which is more propitious for quality wines, similar to a certain extent to the European Atlantic zone so that wines from early vines such as sauvignon blanc and pinot noir have specific aromatic features due to the benign climate.

The Benguela Current: this lies on the west coast of the south of Africa. It is a cold sea current from the Antarctic which bathes the South African coast, moderating an extremely warm and arid area, enabling a quality cultivation of vines, such as the wine growing area of Stellenboch. The wines are expressive and not over ripe. The cabernet sauvignon, syrah and merlot red wines are outstanding. This miracle of nature evokes astounding images of groups of penguins swimming near the arid African coast.

The North Pacific Current: this is responsible for the climatic peculiarities of California. This current of cold water from Alaska, bathes the western coast of a large part of North America generating two currents, one which goes north and the other south known as the California current. We have all seen the city of San Francisco concealed behind a thick fog. However, San Francisco is a city with a Mediterranean type climate due to the high temperatures which come from the interior contrasting with the notable freshness which comes from the sea. In this area there are several factors which influence the climatic tendency. California has an immense mountain barrier, Sierra Nevada, which acts as insulation from the heat from the desert of Nevada. The miracle which occurs in this area is that, within its Mediterranean influence, there is a current of icy water coming from Alaska which hits the Bay of San Francisco head on. The cold temperature of the water and the environmental heat generate a dense fog, which mitigates the dense Mediterranean heat and generates humidity which is excellent for the vineyards of the area as it provides them with the best of the Mediterranean climate and optimum humidity and freshness for the development of the grapes.

The Humboldt Current: this is responsible for the excellence of Chilean wines. This Antarctic current transforms an area, which should be subtropical owing to its location, into an unusually arid and temperate area. Excellent sauvignon blanc, chardonnay and pinot noir are produced near the coast. (see page 116)

The Canary Island Trade Winds: although these do not constitute a sea current properly speaking, the fact that the trade winds blow from the northeast to the southwest in the northern hemisphere and are cold makes it possible for the summer temperatures of the Canary Islands to be moderate and, therefore, vines can be cultivated. In the Saharan latitude of the archipelago, this would be practically impossible owing to the high temperatures. The wines are stylistically proximate to the wines of Galicia and Western France.

CURRENT MAP

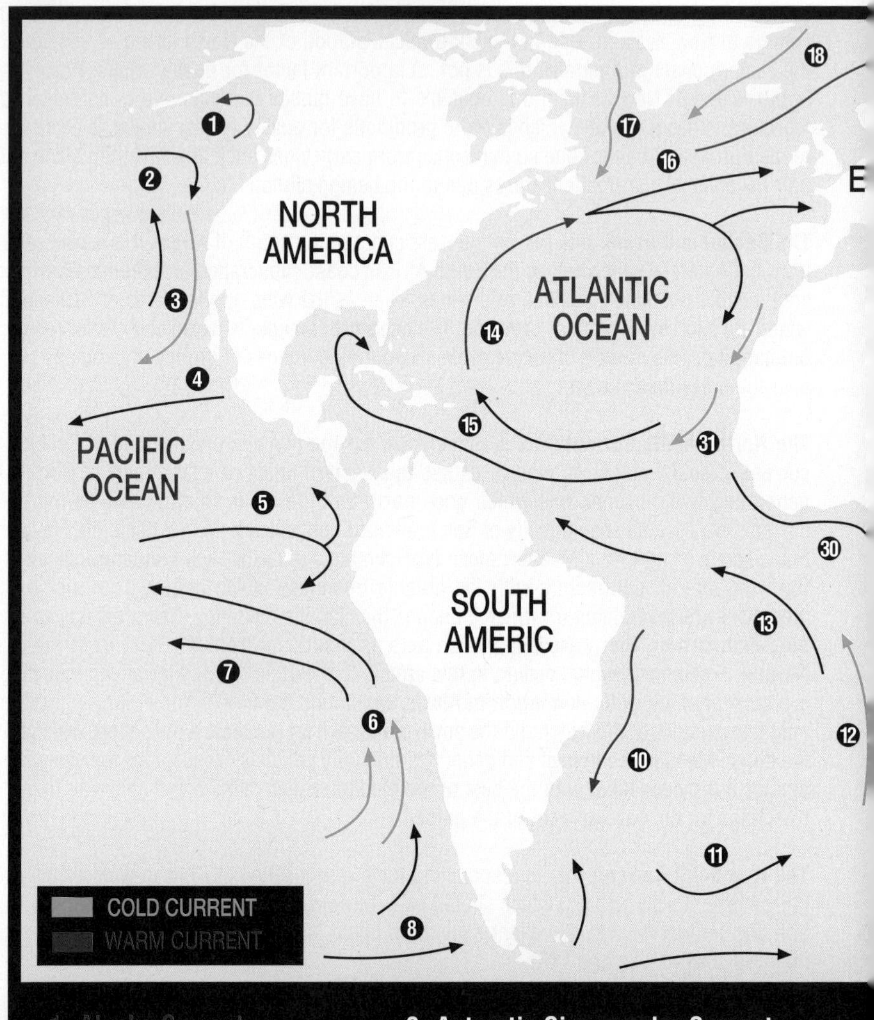

1. Alaska Current
2. North Pacific Current
3. California Current
4. Pacific Equatorial Current
5. Equatorial Counter Current
6. Peruvian Humboldt Current
7. Equatorial Pacific Current
8. Cape Horn Current
9. Antarctic Circumpolar Current (West Wind
10. Brazil Current
11. South Atlantic Current
12. Benguela Current
13. Equatorial Atlantic Current
14. Gulf Stream
15. North Atlantic Equatorial Current
16. North Atlantic Current

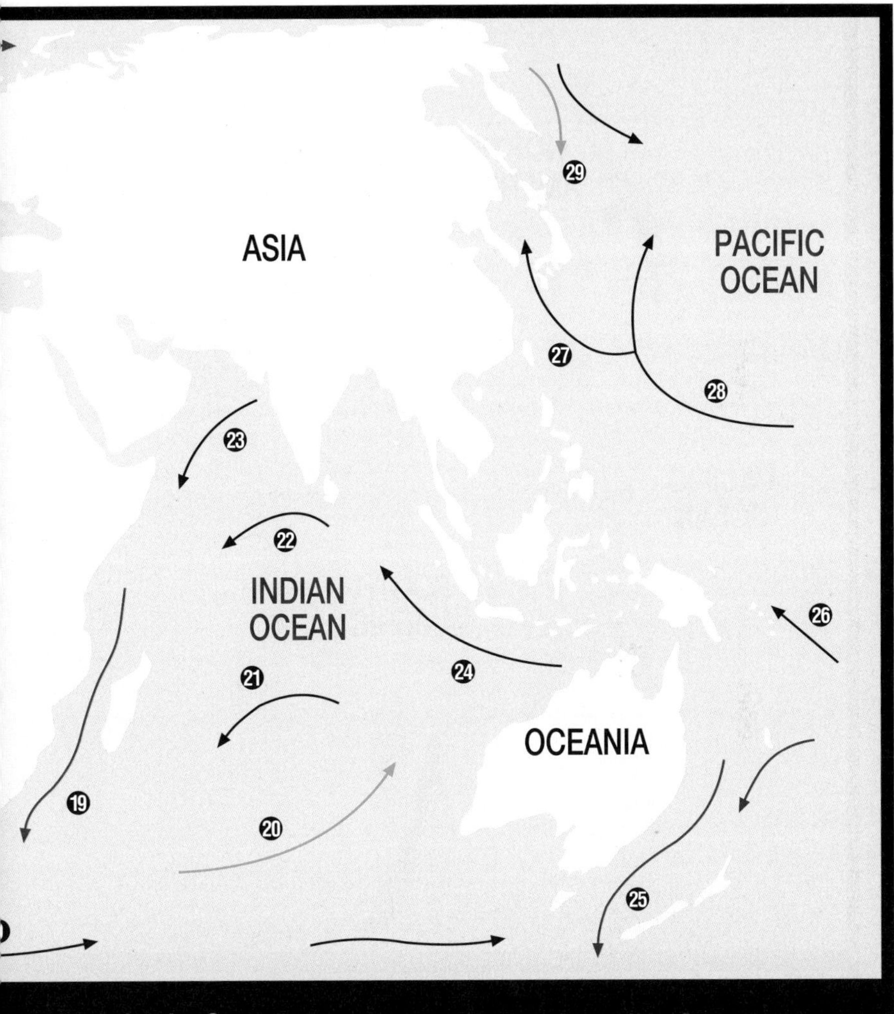

17. Labrador Current
18. Greenland Current
19. Agulhas Current
20. North Australian Current
21. South Equatorial Current
22. North Equatorial Current
23. Monsoon Current
24. Bay of Bengal Current
25. East Australian Current
26. South Pacific Equatorial Current
27. Kuro Shivo
28. North Pacific Equatorial Current
29. Oya Shivo
30. Guinea Current
31. Canary Current

WEATHER MAP OF THE MAIN WINE AREAS

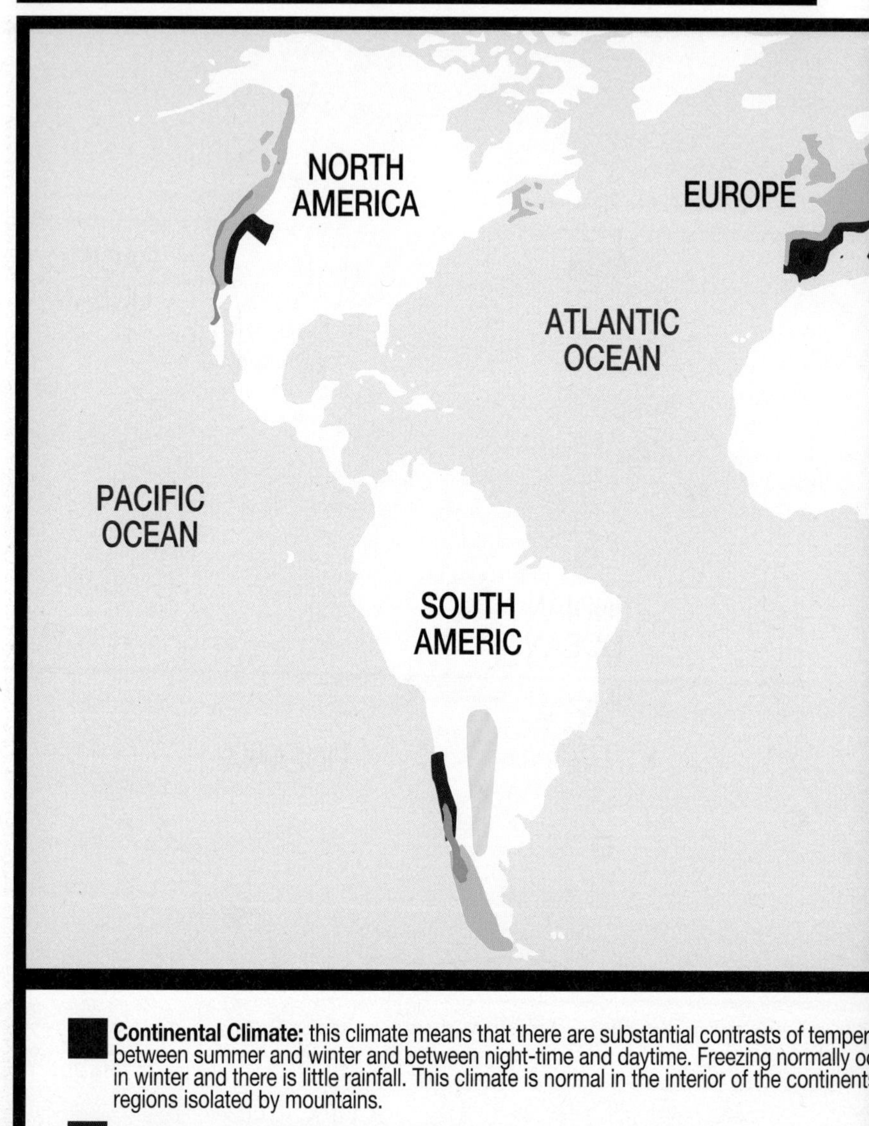

Continental Climate: this climate means that there are substantial contrasts of tempera between summer and winter and between night-time and daytime. Freezing normally oc in winter and there is little rainfall. This climate is normal in the interior of the continents regions isolated by mountains.

Mediterranean climate: this is typical of the countries near to the Mediterranean Sea also affects zones with dry hot summers and more temperate winters.

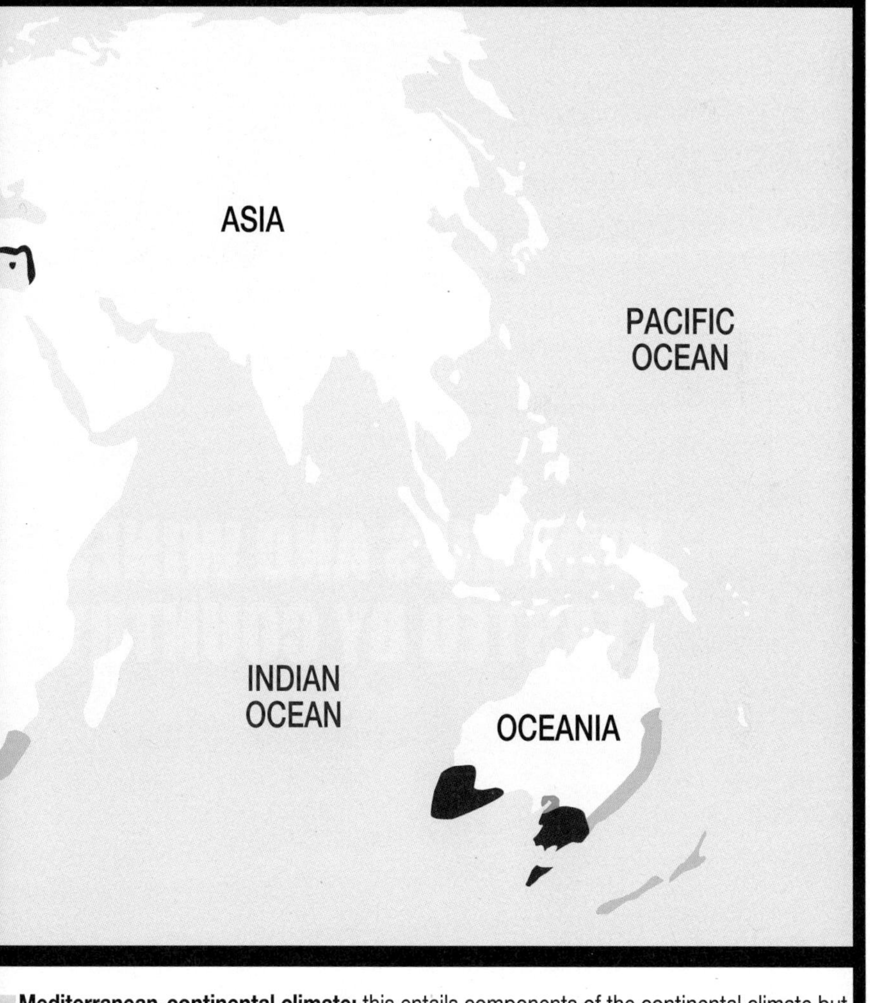

Mediterranean-continental climate: this entails components of the continental climate but with more drastic variations between night and day. This affects the interior of Spain, the north of Italy, the interior of Central Argentina and the interior valley of Santiago de Chile.

Oceanic: due to its proximity to the ocean, this is a climate with heavy rainfall, but with milder temperatures throughout the year.

Mediterranean Oceanic: In overseas regions with a Mediterranean climate, the coast of California, the coast of central Chile, Adelaide in Australia and Cape Town.

WINERIES AND WINES TASTED BY COUNTRY

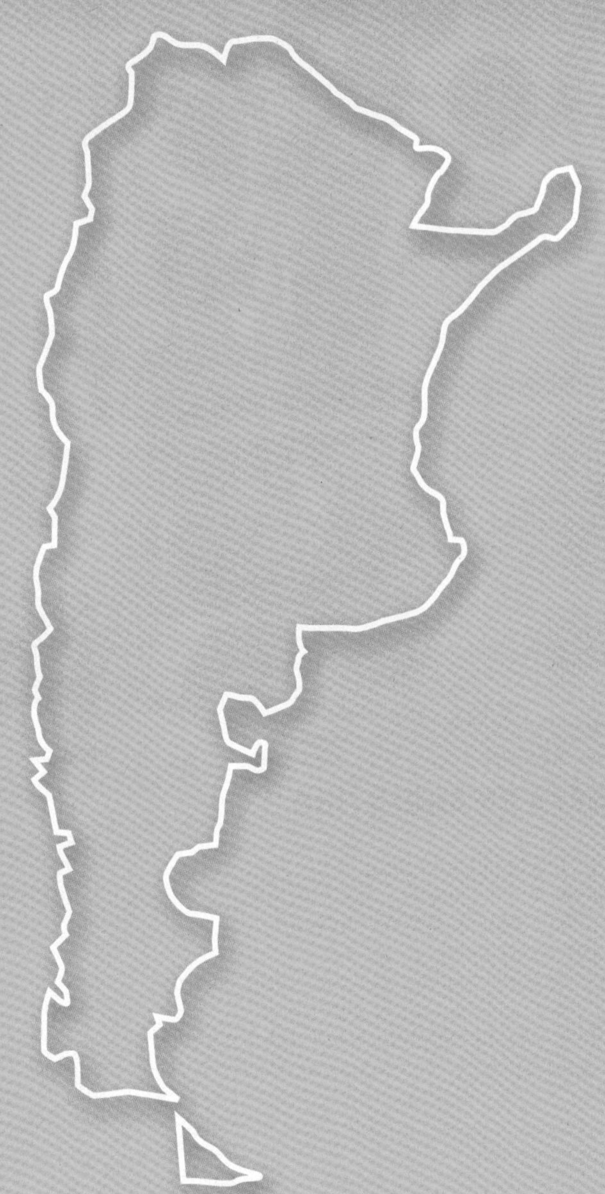

PEÑÍN GUIDE

TOP WINES FROM

ARGENTINA

DATA ON ARGENTINA :

POPULATION: 40.518.951 habitantes
SURFACE AREA: 2.780.400 km^2
SURFACE AREA OF VINEYARDS: 221.000 has.
PREDOMINANT VARIETIES:
RED GRAPES: *malbec, bonarda, cabernet sauvignon, syrah, merlot, tempranillo, sangiovesse, pinot negro, bequignol and barbera.*
WHITE GRAPES: *pedro ximénez, torrontés riojano, chardonnay, chenin, torrontés sanjuanino, sauvignon, semillón, torrontés mendocino, riesling and viognier.*
Harvest Dates:
White grapes: February for the warm zones and March for the fresh zones.
Red grapes: From March to May.
CLIMATE: warm (subtropical, tropical and tropical-highland), temperate, arid and cold (arid windy, snowy and southern wet). The dimensions of the country and its mountain system lead to notable differences in each type of climate. There are many hours of sunshine with a scarcity of rainfall, fundamentally in the more northern part. Argentinean vineyards have irrigation systems.
ANNUAL PRODUCTION 2012: 11,7 million hectoliters
WINERIES: 240
ALTITUDES: The range of altitudes go from 300 in the regions located more to the south to 3,000 m. of the vineyards of Salta, located in the most northern part.

INTRODUCTION

Argentina is the country with the largest surface area of vineyards on al of South America. It is one of the wine growing powers in the planet and the country where the highest vineyard and the most southerly vineyards in the world are located. The particularity of this immense territory lies not only in the diversity of climates and soils of its surface area, but also in the benefits which are contributed by the Andes mountain range, the authentic alma mater of its wines. The country is currently exporting substantial amounts of wine, an increase arising from the drop in internal consumption, where the consumers have changed from the cheaper wine in bulk to bottled wines, which has obliged the wineries to open up markets abroad. This development of exports is led by the province of Mendoza through a variety with a French origin which, over time, has fused with the Argentinean soil contributing new nuances and creating a new dimension of the variety, malbec. From its Bordeaux origin within an oceanic climate to an altitude no greater than 100 metres, it has adapted to a totally opposed cosmos, with a dry, continental climate, which gives it another feature, which is purely "Argentinean". These red wines are easily interpreted by the United States and Canadian consumers who are the main consumers of Argentinean wine abroad. The nomadic character of the Argentineans has served to open up markets in many places which are happy to accept these wines as it considers them to be part of their culture and there is also emotional link these have for those away from their homeland.

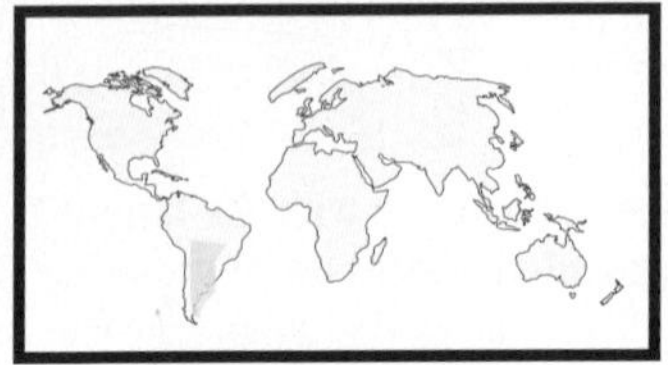

WINE GROWING ZONES MAP

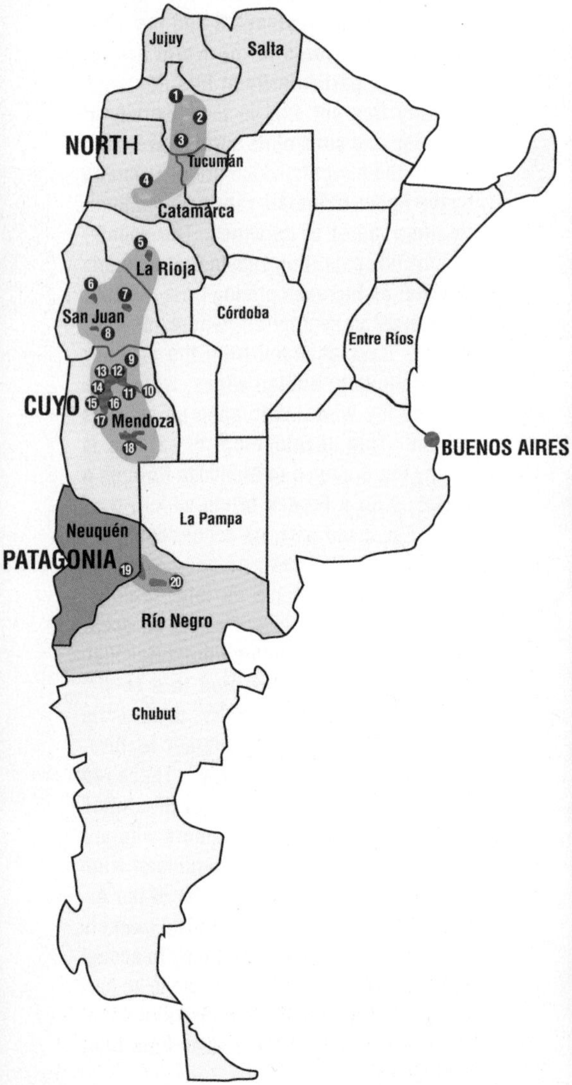

NORTH
Jujuy
Salta
Tucumán
Catamarca
La Rioja
San Juan
Córdoba
Entre Ríos
CUYO
Mendoza
BUENOS AIRES
La Pampa
Neuquén
PATAGONIA
Río Negro
Chubut

NORTH

1. Molinos (Salta)
2. El Arenal (Salta)
3. Cafayate (Salta)
4. Valle de Fiambalá (Catamarca)

CUYO

5. Famatina Valley (La Rioja)
6. Zonda Valley (San Juan)
7. Tulum Valley (San Juan)
8. Pedernal Valley (San Juan)
9. North (Mendoza)
10. East (Mendoza: La Paz, Santa Rosa, Rivadavia, San Martín, Junín)
11. Center (Mendoza: Rusell, Cruz de Piedra, Barrancas, Medrano)
12. Luján/Maipú (Mendoza: Carrodilla, Mayor Drummond, Lunlunta)
13. West Luján (Mendoza: Las Compuertas, Vistalba)
14. South Mendoza River (Mendoza: Perdriel, Agrelo, Ugarteche, Anchoris)
15. West Uco Valley (Mendoza: San José, El Peral, Villa Bastías, Tupungato, Gualtallary, los Árboles, Vista Flores)
16. Uco Valley Center (Mendoza: La Arboleda, El Zampal, Campo Vidal, Cordón de Plata, Agua Amarga, Villa Seca, Los Sauces)
17. San Carlos (Mendoza: Altamira, La Consulta, San Carlos, Eugenio Bustos, El Cepillo)
18. San Rafael (Mendoza)

PATAGONIA

19. San Patricio del Chañar (Neuquén)
20. Alto Valle del Río Negro (Río Negro)

THE KEYS TO THE YEAR

Argentina the differentiation between wines and zones is more related to its altitudes, its proximity or distance from the Andes, rather than to simple climactic differences. The main Argentinean production is concentrated in the zones near to the Andes, from the north in Salta, passing through La Rioja, San Rafael, Mendoza and Río Negro. Going from north to south in the Andes mountain range, the optimum altitudes of the vines descend. Thus, in Salta, a tropical zone, the altitudes are the highest in the world (as high as 3,000 metres), in Mendoza they range from 1,500 to 700 metres, and in the southern zone, Neuqúen and Río Negro, scarcely reach 500 metres.
A good example of this differentiation of wines by altitude is malbec. This is how the different types can be appreciated, a malbec with more jammy and fruity sensations in the lower zones as opposed to others with notable balsamic and fresher features located at altitudes proximate to 1,000 metres. The perseverance of the Argentinean wine producers and the support of its institutions has made it possible that today this variety of French origin is linked more to Argentina than to France. There are substantial reasons for this, time has enabled the Argentinean producers to demonstrate that malbec is also a native variety as the greatest expression has been extracted from the variety in Argentina, with 100% malbec wines, which was not attempted in France. However, there is still a rough patch to be overcome which is the excessive use of barrels and the high maturing levels, which impairs the varietal features in most of the wines tasted. It should be pointed out that there is a growing tendency in the progressively more restrained use of barrels and a more precise adjustment of the harvesting times. Therefore, this type of wine is little by little becoming a more clean tasting wine. Nevertheless, malbec is not the only grape in Argentina, although they are still scarce, there is now much work being done in Luján de Cuyo, with cabernet franc another grape of French origin which is becoming more important in Argentinean vineyards and wineries such as Luigi Bosca and Lamadrid Estate Wines, among others. This is demonstrating its excellent acclimatization to the local soil and climate.

© Catena Zapata

Furthermore, cabernet sauvignon, the third variety which is most extended in Argentina, behind malbec and bonarda, has not yet demonstrated its full Argentinean singularity. This noble type of grape produces wines with good structure and fruitiness, wines capable of reaching scores of approximately 90 points in the Guía Peñín, but at global level, they do not achieve more ambitious scores.

While in Europe (France, Spain and Italy) the producer regions are more well known (Rioja, Bordeaux and Piedmont) than the varieties (tempranillo, cabernet sauvignon and nebbiolo), the regions of the new world offer the consumer single variety wines which are easy to identify and which can be produced in any zone of the country with little differentiation.

© Catena Zapata

This commercial advantage becomes an obstacle for the identification of its wines as, in the case of Argentina, there are very few producers who seek to differentiate a malbec or a cabernet de Rio Negro as opposed to one from Valle de Uco or from Lujan de Cuyo. At the present time, it has been observed that only the leading producers want this identification, therefore, it is only a question of time before the other wineries assimilate this.
Curiously more and more Argentinean winery owners seek the top quality of the winery in blends, through the mixing of varieties which contributes to the whole like an architectonical construction. Wineries such as Catena Zapata, Finca el Origen and Norton are good examples of these lines of wines.

In addition, the development of the white wines of the Andes is not so notable as that of the red wines. It has two star varieties: chardonnay, the white variety most adopted in the world, and torrontés, a grape variety which, if wished, could be the standard bearer Argentinean white wines although as a single variety it is quit bitter and perfumed. Until now the best examples of this variety have been found in Salta.
At legal level, this year we have been able to find labelling which includes the new legislation approved in March 2011 by the Argentinean Instituto Nacional de Vitivinicultura (National Wine Making Institute) (Resolution C.11/2011), which modifies the rules of use of the Reserve and Grand Reserve categories as regards a number of varieties: Chardonnay, Chenin, torrontés, verdello, sauvignon, semillón, sauvignonasse, riesling, viognier, moscato bianco, pinot blanco, prosecco, petit manseng, gewrztraminer, pinot gris and canari. Therefore, as from now the times regulated for each category will be as follows:
Reserves: minimum ageing of 12 months for red wines and six months for white and rosé wines.
Grand Reserves: minimum ageing of 24 months for red wines and one year for white and rosé wines.

HISTORY

After five centuries, the wine industry in Argentina has developed at a dizzying pace. Argentinean wine growing began in the era of the colonization. In South America, the Spanish and Portuguese colonists were the first precursors of the cultivation of vines. The excellent climatic conditions and the particular characteristics of the terrain made it possible to develop wine growing in the country, especially in the XIX century thanks to the substantial Italian emigration which brought the oenological experience and knowledge already developed in Europe.
The first Argentinean vineyards were implemented in the provinces of La Rioja, Mendoza and San Juan, which today are the main engines behind the balance of export trade and are responsible for 93% of the Argentinean vine-

yards. At the beginning of the XVII century, the country had a substantial production of wine, but it was two years later when, owing to the railway, immigration and the start of the first school of agriculture, there was a complete change in the wine growing industry and the bases were laid for the future development of the industry.

In the XX century, the Republic of Argentina expanded its vineyards and expanded in the market for quality wines. To date, a large part of the crop was intended for the consumption of raisins and the production of lower quality wines, which were easily assimilated by the Argentinean consumer whose basic nourishment is meat. It was the powerful domestic market which boosted the sustained growth of the Argentinean wineries to such an extent that there was little interest in exportation due to the substantial domestic demand, curiously this demand was almost totally for bulk wine. This boom period reached its full splendour in the seventies in the last century, when the vineyards occupied 350,000 hectares in 1977 as compared with 228,000 today. This increase suddenly stopped in the nineties with the famous institutional crisis in Argentina. The substantial drop in domestic consumption obliged the Argentinean wineries to open up markets abroad in order to survive, and this gave rise to a spectacular increase in bottled wine. This upward trend continues today.

WINE GROWING ZONES

The geographic classification system of Argentinean wines has three categories, Statement of Origin, Geographical Statement and Controlled Denomination of Origin. The first of these, Statement of Origin, is the most generic of the three and identifies the origin of a minor product in the country. This category is only used for table wines or regional wines. The Geographical Statement locates the place of production of the wine more precisely as it identifies a product originating in a region, locality or geographical area of production on condition that it is not greater than the surface area of the province or acknowledged inter-provincial zone as stated by the Instituto Nacional de Viticultura Argentino (Argentinean National Wine Growing Institute), an organism depending on the Ministry of Agriculture, Cattle Breeding and Fishing. The Geographical Statement is reserved for those wines with a quality which is basically attributable to their geographical origin. In order to obtain the Geographical Statement, the wineries must prove the peculiar characteristics of the terrain which differentiate its wines from the rest of the zones.
Currently there are more than 70 Geographical Statements in Argentina and the most important are Mendoza, San Juan and La Rioja, representing more than 90% of Argentinean vineyards.

GROWING AREAS

CUYO:
Mendoza:
Oasis North (North of Mendoza river): Maipú, Luján de Cuyo and Rivadavia
Oasis South: San Rafael and General Alvear
Oasis Center: Valle de Uco (Tunuyan, Tupungato, San Carlos)
San Juan

NEW CUYO:
La Rioja

NORTH:
Salta, Jujuy, Tucumán and Catamarca

PATAGONIA:
Neuquén, Río Negro and Chubut

THE REST OF ARGENTINA:
Córdoba, Entre Ríos and Buenos Aires

© Catena Zapata

Finally, there is the Controlled Denomination of Origin, which is the most specific of all. As in the Geographical Statement, the Controlled Denomination of Origin must be located within a region, locality or area of production, except that their quality must originate in a geographical environment where the natural and human factors are outstanding. There are only two, Luján de Cuyo and San Rafael, both Denominations of Origin are in the province of Mendoza. It should be stressed that these Denominations of Origin must not be compared with the European style of Denomination of Origin as their objective is not to seek regulations for production and work in the vineyards, but simply to classify the origin of the wine.

Argentina can be divided into three large wine producing regions: Centre-West (Cuyo), North –West and South (Patagonia).

GENERAL CHARACTERISTICS OF THE WINES

TYPOLOGIES OF RED WINES

WINES WITH MALBEC. These are the most identifiable wines of Argentina. The grape is of French origin and is the most extended in Argentinean vineyards. It occupies more than 28,000 hectares, but those which are cultivated in Mendoza are the most popular and there are clear differences between the wines of one region or another due to the geo-climatic differences (the cold nights in Cafayate are beneficial for aromatic depth). The quality of malbec, which is more intense on the slopes at higher altitudes and is deliberately cultivated in the areas of Luján de Cuyo (at altitude and with stony soil) and San Rafael. The young wines tend to be fruity, with an intense violet colour but with the passage of time they become more balanced, with sweet tannins and with plum, spicy aromas (tobacco, truffles, leather). These wines mature better in bottles than cabernet sauvignon and have a better colour and lighter tannins.

WINES WITH CABERNET SAUVIGNON. These are very uniform wines in Argentina because wines which reach adequate maturity are not achieved in all the climates. These form the raw material in most Argentinean wineries. Until recently, these were wines with herbaceous aromas and with hints of green peppers, however, more elegant wines have been achieved (bouquet of spiced black fruit and potent, balanced tannins).

WINES WITH TEMPRANILLO This is one of the grapes recently recovered despite the fact that it was highly extended in Argentinean vineyards, however, this was used in order to make simpler wines. Its origin is Spanish and has shown its tannic power to age.

WINES WITH BONARD, This is called Piedmontese Bonard in Argentina, however, the experts compare this with French corbeau. The wines from this Piedmontese strain are mature while those from are more fruity, delicious and with good acidity. This grape must not be confused with barbera bonarda considering the confusion of strains in the Argentinean vineyards.

WINES WITH MERLOT. One of the grapes recently accepted as a quality variety in the Argentinean production, which has demonstrated its strong potential in Alto Valle (Río Negro), Luján de Cuyo, Maipú and Cruz de Piedra (Mendoza), Valle del Pedernal (San Juan) and even in Patagonia, where these wines have demonstrated their pas concentrated wines with more delicious and balanced tastes. Frequently merlot is blended with cabernet sauvignon.

WINES WITH SYRAH. The wines in the warmer zones provide more Mediterranean wines with bright colours and a very expressive fruity bouquet (full bodied, spicy and cherry aromas). In colder climates longer lasting wines are obtained which are more suited to age in oak. Valle de San Juan is especially adapted to this grape.

WINES WITH PINOT NOIR. A large part of these wines are blended for sparkling wines. This is a very old variety in Argentina which is better expressed in the fresher zones such as the Valle del Uco in Mendoza or in the Valle del Río Neuquén in Patagonia. The wines with low production are scarce, but the Argentinean type normally has hints of raisins, liquorice and more mature red fruits, much more smoked and complex as they evolve in the bottle, but always lighter and soother as corresponds to this grape.

TYPOLOGIES OF WHITE WINES

WINES WITH CHARDONNAY. The white grape wines best known in the world are making immense progress from a more glyceride and heavy style to a more acidic and elegant concept. Their main strongholds are Tupungato and San Rafael in Mendoza and in the Alto Valle of the River Negro.

WINES WITH SEMILLÓN. One of the wines most used for the blends of white wines of Mendoza in the Valle de Uco and the upper regions of the river. This Bordeaux strain has shown that its risk of oxidation may be compensated in cold climates with subsequent ageing in wood. Their greenish colour expresses more honeyed, herbal and citric aromas with a very good balance if its optimum maturity can be achieved and its yield is controlled.

WINES WITH TORRONTÉS. This is the most native grape in the country although it origina-

© Catena Zapata

ted in Spain, where almost none remain, this is why it is known in Argentina as La Rioja torrontés. It is aromatic and has fresh acidity. The wines with torrontés have a grand personality if they are not produced in bulk or as a blend for sparkling wines. Their original aromas evoke orange, rose petals, camomile and muscatel, with excellent acidity. The best wines are usually found in Mendoza (Tupungato, San Rafael and Maipú) and in the Alto Valle del Rio Negro.

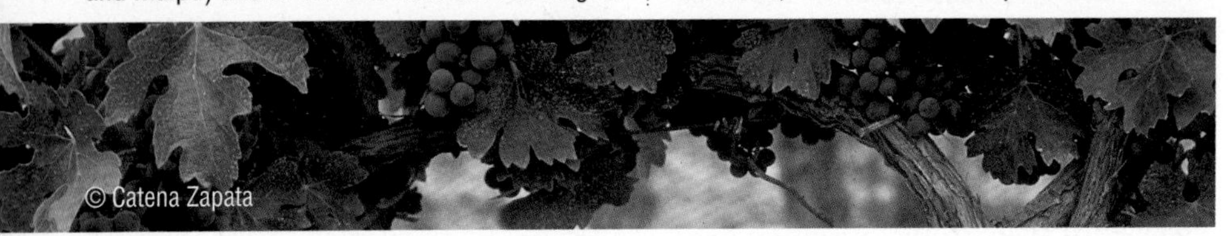
© Catena Zapata

WINES WITH SAUVIGNON BLANC. There are excellent perspective's for the wines with this aromatic strain, especially since the wines of the higher zones have turned to more fruity, balsamic and fresh wines (in the proinces of Luján de Cuyo, Junin and Maipú).

WINES WITH VIOGNIER. One of the most promising Argentinean white grapes entre. It can produce very floral, spicy wines with a high level of alcohol, good raw material for ageing

EXPORTATION

The boom in exports of the countries of the New World took place between 1996 and 2001. The growth was so substantial that producer countries such as Chile, the United States and Argentina accumulated increases of 96%, 69.1% and 86.2%, respectively.

Although the increase in exports are no longer so striking, countries such as Argentina continue to maintain an upward trend in their export balances. Thus, the sales of Argentinean wine abroad were positive as regards both volume and value, according to the figures provided by the National Wine Growing Institute (Instituto Nacional de Vitivinicultura). In total, 3.6 million hectolitres of wine were exported (17% more than in 2011) for a value amounting to $920,000,000 (10% more than the previous year). Among the main importers of Argentinian wine are the United States, Russia, Canada, Brazil, Paraguay, the United Kingdom, the Netherlands, Switzerland and Japan, among others.

Although more Argentinean wine is exported to the world, almost 70% of the production remains in Argentina due to an average per capita consumption of 36 litres, as compared to 17 litres consumed per capita annually in Spain (data of International Wine & Spirit Research 2011).By types of wine, the varietal (wine which contains more than 85% of a single variety) continues to be the wine most exported by the Argentinean Republic, with a balance in 2012 of 2.3 million hectolitres, 12% more than last year, for a total value of $780,000,000 (10% more). However, the wines with no varietal mention varied more significantly, attaining a volume of exports amounting to 1.2 million hectolitres, which supposed an increase of 29% in volume and 10% in value ($113,000,000). Finally, sparkling wines increased 2% with its 41,000 hectolitres exported, achieving invoicing amounting to $22,800,000.

According to the data published by the International Organization of Vine and Wine (OIV) in its Note on the World Situation published in March 2013, in 2012 South America (taking into account the figures of Argentina and Chile) stood in 4th place as exporter at world level, with a total of 11.2 million hectolitres of wine.

It is important to point out that last year Argentina dropped to 6th place in wine production in the world, partly due to an important reduction of its surface area of vineyards, which fell by 24% as compared to the previous year.

DESCRIPTION

Catamarca has a border with La Rioja, another of the provinces which form part of west wine growing region of Argentina, which also has a border with the Andes mountain range.

NUMBER OF HECTARES:2.583 **ALTITUDES:** 1.500 m.

PREDOMINANT VARIETIES:
White gr*apes: torrontés.*
Red grapes: *cabernet sauvignon, malbec, syrah and bonarda.*

CLIMATOLOGY AND SOILS

Warm climate almost desert and with sandy-loam soils.

PRODUCER ZONES

Most of the vineyards as concentrated in the Department of Tinogasta, basically white varieties although Santa María and Belén are also outstanding.

None of the wines tasted achieve the minimum required scoring

DESCRIPTION

The province of Córdoba is geographically speaking the heart of the country. It has a border in the north with the province of Catamarca and Santiago del Estero, to the east with Santa Fe, to the south with La Pampa and Buenos Aires and to the west with San Luis and La Rioja. In Córdoba there are mountain ranges, valleys and plains although the predominant zones in the region are the plains. The wines from this zone have a low alcoholic level, most of them do not exceed 13 degrees due in part to the thermal moderation and the coincidence of the rainfall with the vegetative process of the grape in summer.

NUMBER OF HECTARES:313 **ALTITUDES:** 400 m. – 900 m.

PREDOMINANT VARIETIES:

White grapes: *moscatel de Alejandría, sauvignon blanc and chardonnay.*
Red grapes: *malbec, pinot noir, cabernet sauvignon, sangiovese and merlot.*

CLIMATOLOGY AND SOILS

Córdoba must be considered to be a zone with a purely Mediterranean character, regulated by a temperate climate with very defined meteorological seasons. Generally, the winters in the province of Córdoba are not very cold, except in the zones at a higher altitude, and the summers are wet, with warm days and fresh nights. The rainfall is summer seasonal with approximately 800 millimetres annually, and the average temperatures range between 10 °C and 30 °C.

PRODUCER ZONES

Most of the vineyards are concentrated in Caroya, Athos Pampa, Nono and Berna although these are small disperse vineyards.

None of the wines tasted achieve the minimum required scoring

DESCRICIÓN

Jujuy lies to the north of Salta, it has three hectares and qualities similar to Salta: high altitudes and very notable thermal integrals. This is one of the smallest and poorest provinces in Argentina. It has a northern border with Bolivia and in the west with Chile. Its vineyards are in the Departments of Tilcara and Tumbaya.

None of the wines tasted achieve the minimum required scoring

DESCRIPTION

This is the third province as regards vineyard surface area in Argentina, as well as being the oldest wine producer in the country. It is located to the north of the province of Mendoza, and, as happens in Mendoza, it has a western border with the Andes mountain range, benefiting from the freshness of its air which mitigates the characteristic heat of this zone.

NUMBER OF HECTARES:8.518 **ALTITUDES:** 600m. - 1.350 m.

PREDOMINANT VARIETIES:

White grapes: *torrontés riojano, moscatel de Alejandría and chardonnay.*

Red grapes: *bonarda, malbec, syrah and cabernet sauvignon.*

CLIMATOLOGY AND SOILS

Its climate is warm and it has very scarce rainfall, 130 millimetres per year, which means more mature wines. The burning sun of La Rioja requires a wine growing structure which protects the grapes from the extenuating heat, therefore, it is not uncommon to find vineyards with abundant leaves. The soils are loam (clay, silt and earth) and its thermal integrals are high as occurs in San Juan.

PRODUCER ZONES

The zones with more concentration of vineyards in the province are Chilecito and Nonogasta, while the more famous are the Valle de Famatina, where the vines are protected by two mountain ranges: Sierra de Famatina and Sierra de Velasco.

BELASCO DE BAQUEDANO

Cobos, 8260 Alto Agrelo
5509 Luján De Cuyo
☎: +54 926 130 23491
administracion@grupolanavarra.com
www.belascodebaquedano.com

ROSA DE ARGENTINA TORRONTÉS 2012 B
torrontés La Rioja

90 Colour: bright straw. Nose: complex, characterful, fresh fruit, citrus fruit. Palate: flavourful, sweetness, long.

MELODÍA WINES S.A.

Manuel A. Sáez 831
5519 Guaymallén
☎: +54 261 445 8571
jorge@jorgebenites.com.ar
www.jorgebenites.com.ar

MELODÍA TORRONTÉS 2012 B
100% torrontés La Rioja

90 Colour: bright straw. Nose: neat, fresh, varietal, powerfull. Palate: flavourful, fruity, fresh, good acidity.

VALLE DE LA PUERTA

Ruta Nacional 74, Km. 1185
5374 Vichigasta
☎: +54 382 549 0085 - Fax: +54 382 549 0085
www.valledelapuerta.com

LA PUERTA ALTA BONARDA 2010 T
bonarda La Rioja

90 Color cherry, garnet rim. Aroma ripe fruit, spicy, creamy oak, toasty, complex. Taste powerful, flavourful, toasty, round tannins.

LA PUERTA BLEND 2009 TGR
bonarda, malbec, syrah La Rioja

90 Colour: cherry, garnet rim. Nose: spicy, creamy oak, toasty, characterful. Palate: powerful, flavourful, toasty, round tannins.

LA PUERTA BONARDA 2009 TGR
bonarda La Rioja

92 Colour: cherry, garnet rim. Nose: creamy oak, toasty, characterful, ripe fruit. Palate: powerful, flavourful, toasty, round tannins.

DESCRIPTION

This is the heart of the vineyards of Argentina and boosts Argentinean wines in the world. It has 65% of the vineyards in the country and more than 80% of the Argentinean wine production. It is protected by the imposing Andes mountain range, below the imperishable dominance of the Aconcagua, the highest peak in America standing at 6,959 metres.

NUMBER OF HECTARES:160.704 **ALTITUDES:** 450 m. – 1700 m.

PREDOMINANT VARIETIES:

White grapes: *chardonnay, sauvignon blanc, torrontés and viognier.*
Red grapes: *malbec, merlot and cabernet sauvignon.*

CLIMATOLOGY AND SOILS

Although there are important differences as regards climate and soil depending on the location of the vineyard, generally speaking, the climate of Mendoza is semi-arid continental, with very high temperatures in summer and very low temperatures in winter. Low rainfall is approximately 230 millimetres per year as most of the rainfall comes from the far off Atlantic after crossing most of the country, this obliges the wine growers to use irrigation in most of the vineyards. The great wall of the Andes decisively influences the climate of Mendoza, where it acs as an immense barrier which prevents the passage of humid air from the Pacific.

The success of Mendoza lies fundamentally in the conditioning effect of the Andes and in the wide variety of soils, which confer personality and weight to its most important departments such as Luján de Cuyo, the first zone to obtain the status of denomination of origin in 1987-, Maipú and Valle de Uco.

PRODUCER ZONES

In the north (bordering with San Juan) Mendoza has vineyards at a low altitude (600 – 700 metres) with sandy soils where fundamentally white wines are produced based on chardonnay, chenin blanc, sauvignon blanc and red wine fro cabernet sauvignon, merlot, pinot noir and syrah.

To the south (with borders with La Pampa and Neuquén) the region has altitudes which go from 450 to 800 metres above sea level. This is the predominant zone of the chenin blanc variety and it also concentrates one of the major productions in the region (almost 17% of the vineyards of Mendoza belong to the Department of San Rafael).

The east has some of the most emblematic vineyards in the country. This has borders with San Luis and La Pampa. The zone is composed of the Departments of Junín, San Martín, Rivadavia, Santa Rosa and La Paz. Its thermal nature is very wide due to its desert characteristics. Very near to these vineyards is the high zone of the River Mendoza also known as the first zone of

Argentinean wines where two of the major Mendoza wine growing areas are located: Luján de Cuyo and Maipú. The altitude goes from 650 to 1,060 metres above sea level, and the predominant variety in the area is malbec. This strip is the authentic wine growing engine in the country, and the circle is closed with another exceptional area, the Valle de Uco (15,000 hectares), the highest area in the province which reaches heights of 1,700 metres above sea level. This valley has a privileged geographical position as it lies at the foot of mountains with notable slopes and scarcely fertile soils, with pebbles, thick sand and silt, ingredients which, mixed with the altitude benefit the development of red grape varieties such as malbec, tempranillo, barbera, merlot, cabernet sauvignon, sangiovese and bonarda. In the Valle de Uco the winters are very cold and the summers hot with temperate daytime temperatures. The notable differences between day and night, with up to 15ºC difference, benefits the production of grapes for the production of wines with long-term ageing owing to their excellent acidity. The white wines from the semillón variety, especially in the regions of Tupungato, give the consumer excellent fruitiness and freshness.

CLIMATOLOGY AND SOILS

Although there are substantial differences as regards climate and soils depending on the location of the vineyards, generally speaking, the climate of Mendoza is semi-arid and of a continental nature, with very high temperatures in summer and very low temperatures in winter. Low rainfall scarcely reaches 230 millimetres per year as this comes from the distant Atlantic Ocean, which dissipates, and this forces the wine growers to use irrigation in most of the vineyards. The great wall of the Andes decisively influences the climate of Mendoza, acting as an immense barrier which prevents the passage of wet air from the Pacific Ocean.

PRODUCER ZONES

Within the province of Mendoza, there are several Departments which are outstanding as regards their concentration of vineyards and due to their relevance in the production of quality wines. The most important are the following:

1- Luján de Cuyo 13,468 hectares
2- Maipú 13,900 hectares
3- San Martín 32,574 hectares
4- San Rafael 15,516 hectares
5- Tupungato 8,111 hectares
6- Valle de Uco 15,000 hectares
7- Mendoza 62,135 hectares

ALGODON WINE ESTATE

Ruta Nacional 144, km. 674 Cuadro Benegas
5600 San Rafael
☎: +54 260 442 9020
vandreoni@algodonwineestates.com
www.algodonwines.com

ALGODON WINE ESTATES 2009 T
70% malbec, 30% bonarda — San Rafael

91 Colour: cherry, garnet rim. Nose: powerfull, ripe fruit, red berry notes. Palate: flavourful, powerful, complex, concentrated.

ALGODON WINE ESTATES 2011 B
100% chardonnay — San Rafael

90 Colour: bright straw. Nose: medium intensity, balanced, sweet spices, ripe fruit. Palate: toasty, smoky aftertaste.

ALGODON WINE ESTATES BONARDA 2010 T
100% bonarda — San Rafael

91 Colour: cherry, garnet rim. Nose: ripe fruit, fruit expression, sweet spices, creamy oak. Palate: flavourful, fruity, fleshy.

ALGODON WINE ESTATES MALBEC 2010 T
100% malbec — San Rafael

90 Colour: cherry, garnet rim. Nose: expressive, ripe fruit, creamy oak. Palate: flavourful, fruity, fine bitter notes.

ALPAMANTA

Cobo s/n, Ugarteche
5500 Luján de Cuyo
☎: +54 261 152 034 786
info@alpamanta.com
www.alpamanta.com

ALPAMANTA ESTATE CHARDONNAY 2012 B
chardonnay — Luján de Cuyo

90 Colour: bright straw. Nose: ripe fruit, citrus fruit, dried herbs, sweet spices. Palate: flavourful, fruity, fresh, good acidity, round.

ALPAMANTA ESTATE MALBEC 2010 T
100% malbec — Luján de Cuyo

90 Colour: cherry, garnet rim. Nose: ripe fruit, fruit expression, spicy, cocoa bean. Palate: fine bitter notes, good acidity, balanced.

ALPAMANTA ESTATE MERLOT 2010 T
merlot — Luján de Cuyo

90 Color bright cherry. Aroma ripe fruit, sweet spices, creamy oak, expressive. Taste flavourful, fruity, toasty, round tannins.

ALTA VISTA

Alzaga 3972
5505 Chacras De Coria
☎: +54 261 496 4684 - Fax: +54 261 496 4683
philippe.rolet@altavistawines.com
www.altavistawines.com

ALTA VISTA EXTRA BRUT
chardonnay, pinot noir — Luján de Cuyo

90 Colour: bright straw. Nose: expressive, fresh fruit, floral, fine lees, citrus fruit. Palate: flavourful, fruity, good acidity, round tannins.

ALTA VISTA TERROIR SELECTION 2008 T
100% malbec — Mendoza

92 Colour: deep cherry, garnet rim. Nose: spicy, scrubland, ripe fruit, cocoa bean. Palate: full, good structure, long.

ALTOS LAS HORMIGAS

Tierra del Fuego, 69
5500 Mendoza
☎: +54 261 424 3727
info@altoslashormigas.com
www.altoslashormigas.com

ALTOS LAS HORMIGAS 2009 TR
100% malbec — Valle de Uco

91 Colour: bright cherry. Nose: sweet spices, creamy oak, ripe fruit. Palate: flavourful, fruity, toasty, round tannins.

ALTOS LAS HORMIGAS SINGLE VINEYARD 2007 T
100% malbec — Valle de Uco

91 Colour: cherry, garnet rim. Nose: spicy, creamy oak, toasty, complex, overripe fruit, earthy notes. Palate: powerful, flavourful, toasty, round tannins.

ALTOS LAS HORMIGAS TERROIR 2010 T
100% malbec — Valle de Uco

90 Colour: cherry, garnet rim. Nose: toasty, overripe fruit, powerfull. Palate: fine bitter notes, mineral.

COLONIA DE LAS LIEBRES BONARDA 2012
100% bonarda Luján de Cuyo

90 Colour: cherry, purple rim. Nose: expressive, fresh fruit, red berry notes, violet drops. Palate: flavourful, fruity, good acidity, round tannins, easy to drink.

COLONIA DE LAS LIEBRES RESERVA 2009
100% bonarda Luján de Cuyo

91 Colour: deep cherry, garnet rim. Nose: spicy, ripe fruit, dry stone, expressive. Palate: flavourful, long, fruity aftestaste, round tannins.

BELASCO DE BAQUEDANO

Cobos, 8260 Alto Agrelo
5509 Luján De Cuyo
☎: +54 926 130 234 91
administracion@grupolanavarra.com
www.belascodebaquedano.com

ARGUENTOTA 2009 T
100% malbec Luján de Cuyo/Agrelo

92 Colour: cherry, garnet rim. Nose: ripe fruit, spicy, creamy oak, toasty, balsamic herbs. Palate: powerful, flavourful, toasty, round tannins.

LLAMA 2012 T ROBLE
100% malbec Luján de Cuyo/Agrelo

91 Colour: cherry, garnet rim. Nose: spicy, creamy oak, toasty. Palate: powerful, flavourful, toasty, round tannins.

SWINTO 2010 T
100% malbec Luján de Cuyo/Agrelo

91 Colour: deep cherry. Nose: spicy, overripe fruit, aromatic coffee, roasted coffee. Palate: powerful, sweetness, spicy.

BODEGA ALEANNA

Cobos S/N
5509 Agrelo
☎: +54 261 413 1100
jcrotta@catenazapata.com
www.enemigowines.com

EL ENEMIGO BONARDA 2010 T
90% bonarda, 10% cabernet franc Mendoza

91 Colour: very deep cherry. Nose: expressive, balanced, spicy, scrubland. Palate: flavourful, good acidity, fine bitter notes.

EL ENEMIGO CHARDONNAY 2010 B
100% chardonnay Mendoza

94 Colour: bright yellow. Nose: powerfull, ripe fruit, sweet spices, creamy oak. Palate: rich, smoky aftertaste, flavourful, fresh, good acidity.

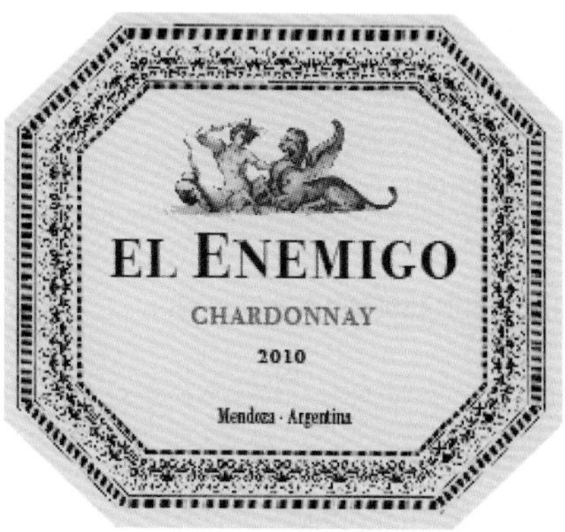

GRAN ENEMIGO 2009 T
Mendoza

91 Colour: cherry, garnet rim. Nose: ripe fruit, cocoa bean, sweet spices. Palate: good structure, flavourful, round tannins, great length, slightly tart.

EL ENEMIGO MALBEC 2010 T
89% malbec, cabernet franc, 4% petit verdot Mendoza

93 Colour: cherry, garnet rim. Nose: medium intensity, ripe fruit, sweet spices. Palate: flavourful, good acidity, fine tannins.

BODEGA ATAMISQUE

Ruta Provincial, 86 Km. 30 San José
5561 Tupungato
☎: +54 261 425 2415
info@atamisque.com
www.atamisque.com

ATAMISQUE ASSEMBLAGE 2008 T
Valle de Uco

91 Colour: deep cherry, garnet rim. Nose: ripe fruit, sweet spices, powerfull, cocoa bean. Palate: good acidity, fine bitter notes, round tannins.

ATAMISQUE ASSEMBLAGE 2012 TR
cabernet franc — Valle de Uco

90 Colour: bright cherry, garnet rim. Nose: balanced, medium intensity, mineral, ripe fruit. Palate: flavourful, spicy, good acidity.

ATAMISQUE CHARDONNAY 2011 B
chardonnay — Tupungato

92 Colour: bright straw. Nose: fresh, fresh fruit, white flowers, varietal. Palate: flavourful, fruity, good acidity, balanced.

ATAMISQUE MALBEC 2009 TR
100% malbec — Valle de Uco

92 Colour: cherry, garnet rim. Nose: ripe fruit, spicy, creamy oak, toasty, complex, varietal. Palate: powerful, flavourful, toasty, round tannins.

CATALPA CHARDONNAY 2010 B
chardonnay — Tupungato

91 Colour: bright straw. Nose: ripe fruit, citrus fruit, sweet spices. Palate: flavourful, fine bitter notes, good acidity.

CATALPA MALBEC 2010 T
100% malbec — Valle de Uco

90 Colour: deep cherry, cherry, purple rim. Nose: sweet spices, cocoa bean, ripe fruit. Palate: flavourful, fruity, round tannins.

SERBAL MALBEC 2011 T
100% malbec — Mendoza

91 Colour: bright cherry, garnet rim. Nose: balanced, ripe fruit, spicy. Palate: flavourful, good structure, good acidity.

BODEGA CAELUM

Ruta 7, Km. 1060, Agrelo
5507 Luján de Cuyo
☎: +54 926 169 928 90
info@bodegacaelum.com.ar
www.bodegacaelum.com.ar

CAELUM CABERNET SAUVIGNON 2010 TR
100% cabernet sauvignon — Mendoza

93 Colour: cherry, garnet rim. Nose: spicy, ripe fruit, balsamic herbs, varietal. Palate: full, long, fleshy, round tannins.

CAELUM CHARDONNAY 2010 B RESERVA
100% chardonnay — Mendoza

91 Colour: bright yellow. Nose: powerfull, ripe fruit, sweet spices, creamy oak, fragrant herbs. Palate: rich, smoky aftertaste, flavourful, good acidity.

CAELUM CLÁSICO CABERNET SAUVIGNON 2010 T
100% cabernet sauvignon — Mendoza

90 Colour: bright cherry. Nose: ripe fruit, balsamic herbs, spicy, varietal. Palate: spicy, ripe fruit, round tannins.

CAELUM CLÁSICO CHARDONNAY 2012 B
100% chardonnay — Mendoza

91 Colour: bright yellow. Nose: powerfull, ripe fruit, sweet spices, fragrant herbs. Palate: rich, smoky aftertaste, flavourful, fresh, good acidity.

CAELUM CLÁSICO TORRONTÉS 2012 B
100% torrontés — Mendoza

90 Colour: bright straw. Nose: fresh, fresh fruit, white flowers. Palate: flavourful, fruity, good acidity, balanced.

CAELUM MALBEC 2010 T
100% malbec — Luján de Cuyo

92 Colour: bright cherry. Nose: floral, red berry notes, ripe fruit, dried herbs. Palate: good acidity, easy to drink, fine bitter notes, spicy.

CAELUM MALBEC 2010 TR
100% malbec — Mendoza

92 Colour: cherry, garnet rim. Nose: sweet spices, toasty, creamy oak. Palate: good structure, fleshy, harsh oak tannins.

BODEGA DIAMANDES

Clodomiro Silva, s/n Vista Flores
5565 Tunuyán
☎: +54 261 476 5400
diamandes@diamandes.com
www.diamandes.com

DIAMANDES 2008 TGR
100% malbec Valle de Uco

93 Colour: cherry, garnet rim. Nose: spicy, creamy oak, toasty, characterful, expressive. Palate: powerful, flavourful, toasty, round tannins.

DIAMANDES DE UCO 2010 T
100% malbec Valle de Uco

91 Colour: cherry, garnet rim. Nose: ripe fruit, sweet spices, toasty, aromatic coffee. Palate: fine bitter notes, good acidity, spicy, ripe fruit.

DIAMANDES DE UCO CHARDONNAY 2012 B
chardonnay Valle de Uco

92 Colour: bright straw, greenish rim. Nose: elegant, expressive, fresh fruit, floral. Palate: long, mineral, fruity, good acidity.

DIAMANDES DE UCO VIOGNIER 2012 B
viognier Valle de Uco

92 Colour: bright straw. Nose: expressive, dry stone, white flowers. Palate: flavourful, good acidity, fine bitter notes, elegant.

PERLITA 2011 T
Valle de Uco

92 Colour: cherry, garnet rim. Nose: spicy, creamy oak, toasty, characterful, fruit expression. Palate: powerful, flavourful, toasty, round tannins.

BODEGA ERAL BRAVO

Emilio Civit, 567
5500
☎: +54 261 429 6864 - Fax: +54 261 429 6864
info@eralbravo.com
www.eralbravo.com

ERAL BRAVO "YBS" 2009 T
60% malbec, 30% cabernet sauvignon, 10% syrah Luján de Cuyo/Agrelo

92 Colour: cherry, garnet rim. Nose: balanced, ripe fruit, spicy, balsamic herbs. Palate: full, long, round tannins.

ERAL BRAVO CABERNET SAUVIGNON 2008 T
Luján de Cuyo/Agrelo

90 Colour: cherry, garnet rim. Nose: ripe fruit, spicy, creamy oak, balsamic herbs. Palate: powerful, flavourful, toasty, round tannins.

ERAL BRAVO MALBEC 2009 T
100% malbec Luján de Cuyo/Agrelo

90 Colour: cherry, garnet rim. Nose: tobacco, spicy, dried herbs. Palate: flavourful, good structure, round tannins.

BODEGA ESCORIHUELA GASCÓN

Belgrano, 1188
5501 Godoy Cruz
☎: +54 261 424 2282 - Fax: +54 261 424 2282
cpesce@escorihuela.com.ar
www.escorihuelagascon.com.ar

1884 LIMITED PRODUCTION MALBEC 2009 T
100% malbec Mendoza

90 Colour: bright cherry. Nose: ripe fruit, sweet spices, creamy oak. Palate: flavourful, fruity, toasty, round tannins.

1884 RESERVADO MALBEC 2012 T

Mendoza

90 Colour: cherry, garnet rim. Nose: expressive, ripe fruit, scrubland. Palate: flavourful, powerful, fine bitter notes.

MIGUEL ESCORIHUELA GASCON 2008 T

85% malbec, 10% cabernet sauvignon, 5% syrah — Mendoza

92 Colour: cherry, garnet rim. Nose: spicy, creamy oak, toasty, characterful. Palate: powerful, flavourful, toasty, round tannins.

Cosecha: 2da. semana de abril de 2008
Variedad: 85% Malbec, 10% Cabernet Sauvignon, 5% Syrah.
Crianza: 12 meses en barricas, 90% en roble francés y 10% en roble americano. 100% barricas de 1er uso.
Notas de degustación: De color rojo violáceo intenso, sus aromas recuerdan a frutos rojos y negros, como frambuesas, grosellas silvestres y cassis combinados con notas de vainilla, chocolate y café aportados durante su crianza en roble. En boca es de buena estructura, concentración y de elegante final.
Botellas: 19.872

Lic. Gustavo Marín
ENÓLOGO

DON MALBEC 2007 T

100% malbec — Mendoza

92 Colour: cherry, garnet rim. Nose: ripe fruit, spicy, creamy oak, toasty, complex, characterful, earthy notes, mineral. Palate: powerful, flavourful, toasty, round tannins, long.

ESCORIHUELA GASCÓN PEQUEÑAS PRODUCCIONES CHARDONNAY 2011 B

chardonnay — Mendoza

92 Color bright yellow. Aroma powerfull, ripe fruit, sweet spices, creamy oak, fragrant herbs. Taste rich, smoky aftertaste, flavourful, fresh, good acidity.

PEQUEÑAS PRODUCCIONES CABERNET 2009 T
Mendoza

92 Colour: very deep cherry. Nose: fruit expression, aromatic coffee, sweet spices. Palate: flavourful, spicy, ripe fruit.

THE PRESIDENT'S BLEND 2008 T
85% malbec, 10% cabernet sauvignon, 5% syrah — Mendoza

93 Colour: cherry, garnet rim. Nose: spicy, creamy oak, toasty, characterful, fruit expression. Palate: powerful, flavourful, toasty, round tannins.

BODEGA FAMILIA ZUCCARDI

Ruta Provincial 33, Km. 7,5
5531 Maipú
☎: +54 261 441 100 10
info@familiazuccardi.com
www.zuccardiwines.com

ALAMBRADO CABERNET SAUVIGNON 2011 T
100% cabernet sauvignon — Maipú

90 Colour: cherry, garnet rim. Nose: ripe fruit, spicy, medium intensity. Palate: flavourful, fruity, good structure.

ALAMBRADO CHARDONNAY 2011 B
100% chardonnay — Mendoza

90 Colour: bright straw, greenish rim. Nose: medium intensity, white flowers, creamy oak. Palate: good acidity, fine bitter notes.

ALAMBRADO MALBEC 2011 T
100% malbec — Mendoza

92 Colour: bright cherry, garnet rim. Nose: red berry notes, ripe fruit, floral. Palate: flavourful, fruity, fine tannins, long.

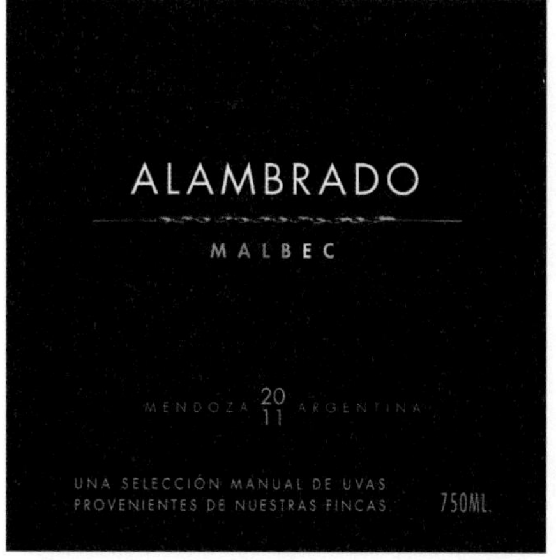

ALAMBRADO SAUVIGNON BLANC 2012 B
sauvignon blanc — Valle de Uco

90 Colour: bright straw. Nose: grassy, fresh fruit, varietal. Palate: fresh, easy to drink, good acidity.

ZUCCARDI ALUVIONAL EL PERAL 2011 T
merlot — Tupungato

92 Colour: bright cherry. Nose: sweet spices, creamy oak, expressive, overripe fruit. Palate: flavourful, fruity, toasty, round tannins.

EMMA ZUCCARDI BONARDA 2011 T
bonarda — Maipú

94 Colour: bright cherry. Nose: sweet spices, creamy oak, expressive, floral, balsamic herbs, mineral. Palate: flavourful, fruity, toasty, round tannins.

ZUCCARDI CHARDONNAY 2011 B
chardonnay — Maipú

91 Colour: bright yellow. Nose: varietal, balanced, expressive, white flowers. Palate: full, fruity, long, good acidity, fine bitter notes, spicy.

ZUCCARDI Q MALBEC 2010 T
100% malbec — Maipú

91 Colour: deep cherry, garnet rim. Nose: expressive, red berry notes, ripe fruit, sweet spices. Palate: good structure, full, round tannins.

ZUCCARDI Q TEMPRANILLO 2010 T
tempranillo — Maipú

90 Colour: bright cherry, garnet rim. Nose: red berry notes, ripe fruit, sweet spices, medium intensity. Palate: good acidity, fine bitter notes.

ZUCCARDI TITO 2010 T
90% malbec, 8% cabernet sauvignon, 2% caladoc — Valle de Uco

93 Colour: cherry, garnet rim. Nose: spicy, complex, candied fruit, dark chocolate. Palate: powerful, flavourful, toasty, round tannins.

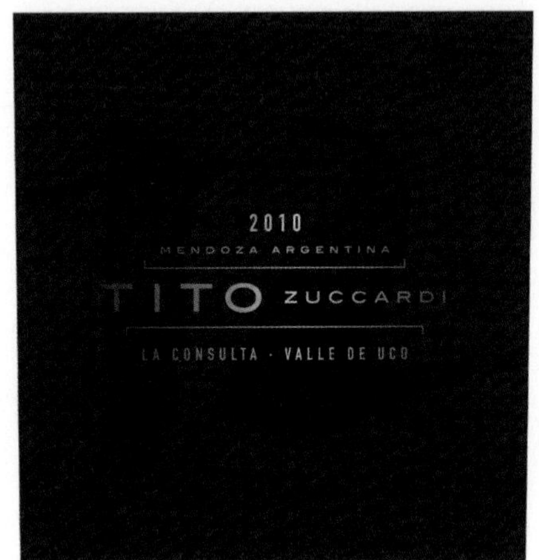

ZUCCARDI ZETA 2009 T
66% malbec, 20% cabernet sauvignon, 14% tempranillo Maipú

92 Colour: bright cherry. Nose: elegant, balanced, ripe fruit, spicy, creamy oak, cocoa bean. Palate: balanced, good acidity, full, fine bitter notes, round tannins.

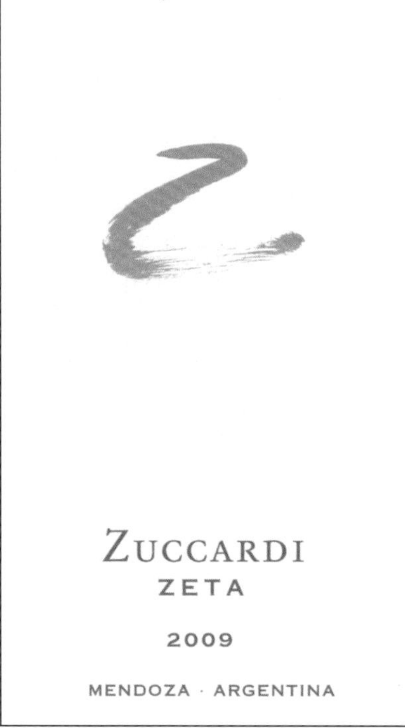

BODEGA FURLOTTI

Pueyrredón 2222
5505 Chacras de Coria, Luján de Cuyo
☎: +54 261 496 0713 - Fax: +54 261 496 6192
info@adalgisawexperience.com.ar
www.bodegafurlotti.com

FINCA ADALGISA 2008 T
100% malbec Luján de Cuyo

90 Colour: cherry, garnet rim. Nose: spicy, old leather, balsamic herbs. Palate: flavourful, good acidity, fine bitter notes.

BODEGA LUIGI BOSCA FAMILIA ARIZU

San Martín 2044
5507 Luján de Cuyo
☎: +54 261 498 1974
turismo@luigibosca.com.ar
www.luigibosca.com.ar

FINCA LA LINDA VIOGNIER 2012 B
100% viognier Maipú

90 Colour: bright straw, greenish rim. Nose: floral, ripe fruit. Palate: flavourful, ripe fruit, long, balanced.

FINCA LOS NOBLES CABERNET BOUCHET 2008 T
cabernet sauvignon, bouchet Luján de Cuyo

90 Colour: very deep cherry. Nose: powerfull, warm, overripe fruit, toasty, spicy. Palate: powerful, concentrated, round.

GALA 1 LUIGI BOSCA 2010 T
85% malbec, 10% petit verdot, 5% tannat Luján de Cuyo

92 Colour: black cherry. Nose: powerfull, characterful, toasty, dark chocolate, aromatic coffee. Palate: powerful, concentrated, fine bitter notes.

GALA 4 LUIGI BOSCA 2010 T
95% cabernet franc, 5% malbec — Luján de Cuyo

92 Colour: cherry, garnet rim. Nose: ripe fruit, spicy, creamy oak, toasty, fruit expression, characterful. Palate: powerful, flavourful, toasty, round tannins.

LUIGI BOSCA DE SANGRE 2010 T
70% cabernet sauvignon, 15% merlot, 15% syrah — Luján de Cuyo

92 Colour: bright cherry. Nose: sweet spices, creamy oak, expressive, complex, characterful, earthy notes. Palate: flavourful, fruity, toasty, round tannins.

LUIGI BOSCA MALBEC D.O.C. 2010 T
100% malbec — Luján de Cuyo

91 Colour: cherry, garnet rim. Nose: spicy, creamy oak, toasty, ripe fruit, earthy notes. Palate: powerful, flavourful, toasty, round tannins.

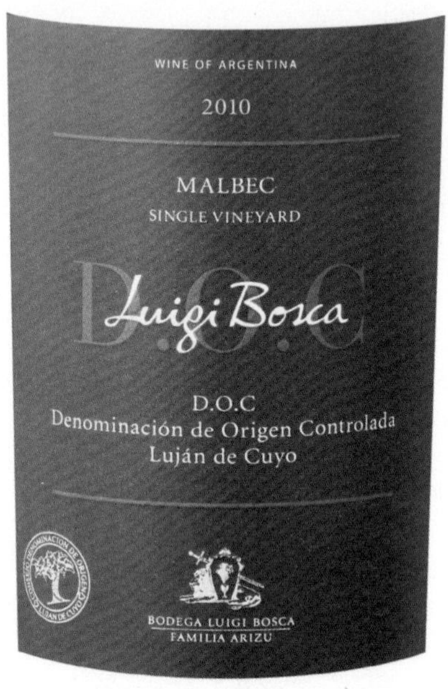

BODEGA MARGOT

Italia 6016
5505 Chacras de Coria
☎: +54 261 496 1877
romina@bodegamargot.com.ar

CELEDONIO 2011 T
100% malbec — Tupungato

91 Colour: cherry, garnet rim. Nose: ripe fruit, spicy, creamy oak, roasted coffee. Palate: powerful, flavourful, toasty, round tannins.

MAULA & MISERY MOUSE 2011 T
100% malbec — Tupungato

90 Colour: cherry, garnet rim. Nose: balanced, scrubland, spicy, ripe fruit. Palate: flavourful, good acidity, fine bitter notes.

BODEGA MI TERRUÑO

Avda. Colón, 241 - Of. 6
5500 Mendoza
☎: +54 261 429 9962 - Fax: +54 261 429 9962
ventas@bodegamiterruno.com.ar
www.bodegamiterruno.com.ar

MI TERRUÑO CABERNET SAUVIGNON 2010 TR
100% cabernet sauvignon — Maipú

91 Colour: cherry, garnet rim. Nose: spicy, scrubland, ripe fruit. Palate: flavourful, good structure, good acidity.

MI TERRUÑO CHARDONNAY 2011 B RESERVA
100% chardonnay — Valle de Uco

90 Colour: bright straw. Nose: fresh, fresh fruit, white flowers. Palate: flavourful, fruity, good acidity, balanced.

MI TERRUÑO EXPRESIÓN MALBEC 2011 T
100% malbec — Maipú

90 Colour: bright cherry. Nose: ripe fruit, sweet spices, creamy oak, varietal. Palate: flavourful, fruity, toasty, round tannins.

MI TERRUÑO EXPRESIÓN CABERNET SAUVIGNON 2011 T
100% cabernet sauvignon — Maipú

91 Colour: bright cherry. Nose: ripe fruit, fruit expression. Palate: flavourful, fruity, toasty, round tannins.

MI TERRUÑO LIMITED RESERVE 2009 T
55% malbec, 45% cabernet sauvignon — Luján de Cuyo

91 Colour: cherry, garnet rim. Nose: ripe fruit, fruit expression, toasty, aromatic coffee. Palate: flavourful, powerful, fine bitter notes, good acidity.

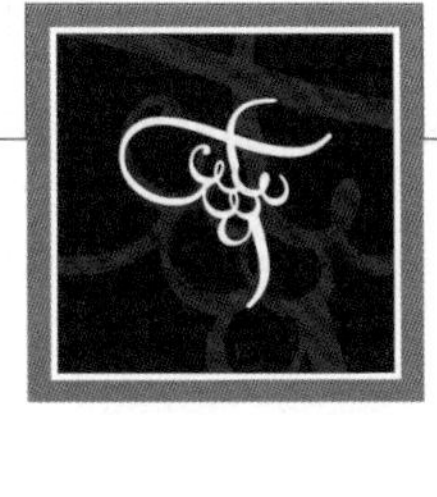

MI TERRUÑO MALBEC 2010 TR
100% malbec — Luján de Cuyo

90 Colour: cherry, garnet rim. Nose: spicy, creamy oak, toasty, complex, scrubland. Palate: powerful, flavourful, toasty, round tannins.

MI TERRUÑO MAYACABA 2007 T
100% malbec — Mendoza

90 Colour: cherry, garnet rim. Nose: spicy, creamy oak, toasty, complex, earthy notes, fruit expression. Palate: powerful, flavourful, toasty, round tannins.

BODEGA PALO ALTO

Videla Aranda 502, Cruz de Piedra
5515 Maipú
☎: +54 261 524 9469 - Fax: +54 261 524 9469
jdelbono@bodegapaloalto.com.ar
www.bodegapaloalto.com.ar

AMADORES CABERNET SAUVIGNON T
cabernet sauvignon — Tupungato

90 Colour: cherry, garnet rim. Nose: ripe fruit, toasty, aromatic coffee. Palate: flavourful, fine bitter notes, good acidity.

BENITO A. RED BLEND 2010 TGR
Tupungato

92 Colour: bright cherry. Nose: fruit expression, scrubland, spicy. Palate: flavourful, fleshy, spicy.

BENITO A. RED BLEND PINOT NOIR 2010 T
Tupungato

93 Colour: deep cherry. Nose: spicy, balsamic herbs, scrubland, ripe fruit. Palate: long, easy to drink, fine bitter notes.

BODEGA PIEDRA NEGRA

Ruta 94 Km. 21, Vista Flores
5565 Tunuyán
☎: +54 261 441 1134
rmalla@bodegalurton.com
www.francoislurton.com

GRAN LURTON CORTE FRIULANO 2012 B
friulano — Valle de Uco

91 Colour: bright straw, greenish rim. Nose: balanced, creamy oak, sweet spices, floral. Palate: flavourful, fine bitter notes.

PIEDRA NEGRA 2009 T
100% malbec — Valle de Uco

91 Colour: cherry, garnet rim. Nose: powerfull, ripe fruit, spicy, red berry notes. Palate: flavourful, fruity, fine bitter notes, good acidity.

BODEGA ROLLAND

Campo Clos de los Siete Clodomiro Silva s/n
5565 Vista las Flores Tunuyan
☎: +33 557 515 243 - Fax: +33 557 515 293
www.rollandcollection.com

MARIFLOR 2010 T
merlot — Valle de Uco

92 Colour: bright cherry. Nose: ripe fruit, sweet spices, creamy oak, powerfull. Palate: flavourful, fruity, toasty, round tannins.

MARIFLOR MALBEC 2010 T
malbec — Valle de Uco

91 Colour: cherry, garnet rim. Nose: spicy, creamy oak, toasty, balsamic herbs, scrubland, characterful. Palate: powerful, flavourful, toasty, round tannins.

MARIFLOR SAUVIGNON BLANC 2012 B
sauvignon blanc — Valle de Uco

91 Colour: bright straw. Nose: fresh, fresh fruit, white flowers, scrubland, sweet spices. Palate: flavourful, fruity, good acidity, balanced.

MIRAFLOR PINOT NOIR 2011 T
pinot noir — Valle de Uco

90 Colour: deep cherry. Nose: aromatic coffee, mineral, floral, balsamic herbs. Palate: flavourful, fruity, fine bitter notes.

VAL DE FLORES 2006 T
malbec — Valle de Uco

93 Color cherry, garnet rim. Aroma ripe fruit, spicy, creamy oak, toasty, complex. Taste powerful, flavourful, toasty, round tannins.

BODEGA TEHO

Viamonte 4620
5505 Chacras de Coria
☎: +54 261 562 8900
asejanovich@tintonegro.com

TEHO MALBEC 2010 T
97% malbec, 2% cabernet franc, 1% petit verdot — Mendoza

93 Colour: bright cherry. Nose: sweet spices, creamy oak, expressive, fruit expression, candied fruit, mineral, earthy notes. Palate: flavourful, fruity, toasty, round tannins.

ZAHA CABERNET FRANC 2011 T
cabernet franc — Neuquén

92 Color bright cherry. Aroma ripe fruit, sweet spices, creamy oak, expressive. Taste flavourful, fruity, toasty, round tannins.

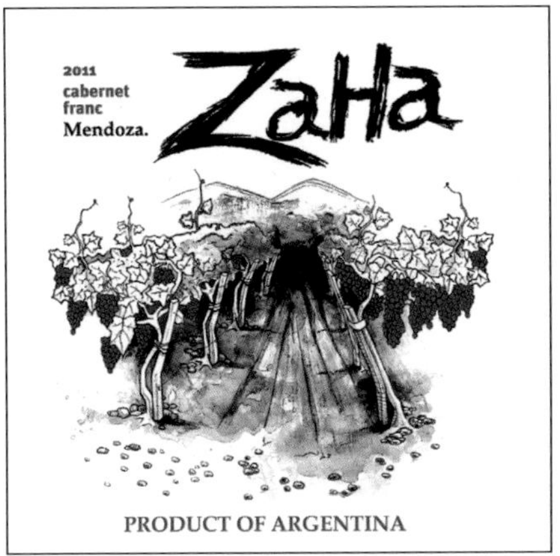

TINTO NEGRO FINCA LA ESCUELA 2010 T
100% malbec — Mendoza

92 Colour: cherry, garnet rim. Nose: ripe fruit, spicy, creamy oak, toasty, expressive, varietal. Palate: powerful, flavourful, toasty, round tannins.

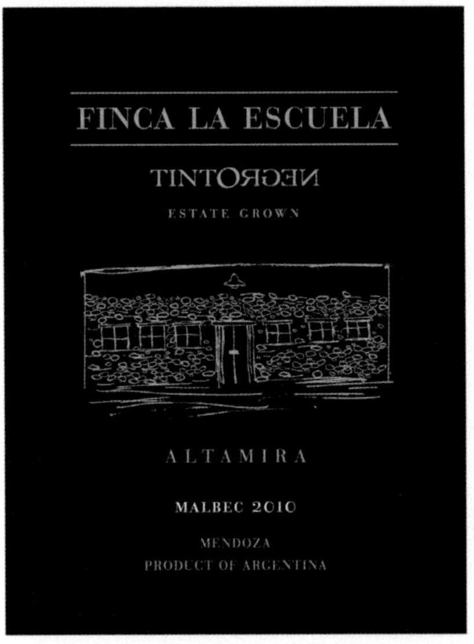

BODEGA VIÑA 1924 DE ANGELES

Roque Sáenz Peña, s/n, Vistalba
5509 Luján de Cuyo
☎: +54 926 151 556 16
info@malbecdeangeles.com
www.malbecdeangeles.com

VIÑA 1924 DE ANGELES, GRAN MALBEC 2009
100% malbec — Vistalba

91 Colour: cherry, garnet rim. Nose: ripe fruit, spicy, creamy oak, toasty. Palate: powerful, flavourful, toasty, fruity aftestaste.

VIÑA 1924 DE ANGELES, MALBEC 2010
100% malbec Vistalba

92 Colour: bright cherry. Nose: ripe fruit, mineral, spicy, balanced, expressive. Palate: flavourful, round tannins, long, balanced, elegant.

BODEGA Y VIÑEDOS O FOURNIER

Calle Los Indios, s/n
5567 La Consulta San Carlos
☎: +54 262 245 1579 - Fax: +54 262 245 1588
info@ofournier.com
www.ofournier.com

ESTIBA ALFA CRUX BLEND 2005 T
Valle de Uco

90 Colour: black cherry. Nose: fruit preserve, toasty, dark chocolate, sweet spices. Palate: powerful, concentrated, fine bitter notes.

ESTIBA ALFA CRUX MALBEC 2008 T
100% malbec Valle de Uco

92 Colour: cherry, garnet rim. Nose: mineral, earthy notes, ripe fruit, creamy oak. Palate: flavourful, concentrated, complex, fleshy.

ESTIBA BETA CRUX BLEND 2008 T
Valle de Uco

91 Colour: bright cherry. Nose: ripe fruit, sweet spices, creamy oak, balanced. Palate: flavourful, fruity, toasty, round tannins.

ESTIBA BETA CRUX SAUVIGNON BLANC 2012 B
sauvignon blanc Valle de Uco

92 Colour: bright straw. Nose: fresh, fresh fruit, white flowers, expressive, sweet spices. Palate: flavourful, fruity, good acidity, balanced.

ESTIBA O. FOURNIER RED BLEND 2006 T
syrah, cabernet sauvignon Valle de Uco

93 Colour: cherry, garnet rim. Nose: ripe fruit, spicy, creamy oak, toasty, earthy notes. Palate: powerful, flavourful, toasty, round tannins.

URBAN UCO BLEND 2012 T
Mendoza

91 Color bright cherry. Aroma ripe fruit, sweet spices, creamy oak, expressive. Taste flavourful, fruity, toasty, round tannins.

URBAN UCO TEMPRANILLO 2012 T
tempranillo Mendoza

90 Colour: bright cherry. Nose: ripe fruit, sweet spices, balsamic herbs. Palate: flavourful, fruity, toasty, round tannins.

BODEGAS ARGENCERES

Av. 25 de Mayo nº 43
5400 San Rafael
☎: +54 260 444 6244
info@bodegasargenceres.com
www.bodegasargenceres.com

LÁGRIMA MALBEC 2010 TR
100% malbec Mendoza

90 Colour: deep cherry, garnet rim. Nose: powerfull, ripe fruit, candied fruit, sweet spices, creamy oak. Palate: flavourful, fleshy.

BODEGAS CARO

Presidente Alvear, 151
5501 Godoy Cruz
☎: +54 261 424 6477 - Fax: +54 261 424 6459
adm@bodegascaro.com.ar
www.lafite.com

ARUMA 2011 T
100% malbec Valle de Uco

91 Colour: cherry, garnet rim. Nose: ripe fruit, spicy, complex, varietal. Palate: round tannins, full, flavourful, fruity, good acidity.

CARO 2010 T
malbec, cabernet sauvignon Valle de Uco

92 Colour: cherry, garnet rim. Nose: balsamic herbs, spicy, tobacco. Palate: flavourful, balanced, fine bitter notes, round tannins.

BODEGAS DEUMAYÉN

Avda. España 1340 Piso 8º - Of. 11/12
5500 Mendoza
☎: +54 261 438 1679 - Fax: +54 261 423 8184
vtosoni@speedy.com.ar
www.bodegasdeumayen.com.ar

TREZ 2008 T
100% malbec Mendoza

90 Colour: bright cherry, garnet rim. Nose: scrubland, spicy, ripe fruit. Palate: balanced, round tannins, fine bitter notes.

CASARENA BODEGA Y VIÑEDOS

Brandsen 505, Perdriel
5500 Lujan De Cuyo
☎: +54 261 423 1573 - Fax: +54 261 423 1573
martin@casarena.com
www.casarena.com

CASARENA 505 ESENCIA 2012 T
50% malbec, 30% cabernet sauvignon, 20% merlot Luján de Cuyo

91 Color cherry, garnet rim. Aroma ripe fruit, spicy, creamy oak, toasty, complex. Taste powerful, flavourful, toasty, round tannins.

CASARENA 505 MALBEC 2012 T
100% malbec — Luján de Cuyo

90 Colour: deep cherry. Nose: red berry notes, grassy, spicy. Palate: flavourful, fruity, fresh.

CASARENA MALBEC LAUREN'S SINGLE VINEYARD AGRELO 2010 T
100% malbec — Luján de Cuyo

93 Colour: very deep cherry. Nose: powerfull, ripe fruit, toasty, spicy, dark chocolate. Palate: flavourful, good acidity, ripe fruit.

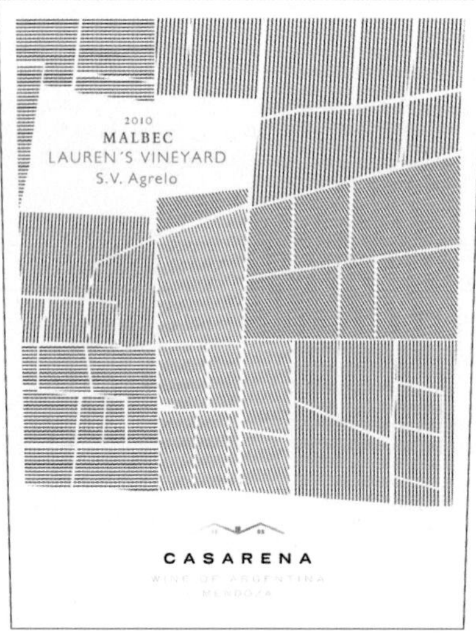

CASARENA RAMANEGRA RESERVA MALBEC 2011 T
100% malbec — Luján de Cuyo

91 Colour: bright cherry. Nose: sweet spices, creamy oak. Palate: flavourful, fruity, toasty, round tannins.

CASARENA RAMANEGRA RESERVA REDBLEND SINERGY 2011 T
70% malbec, 20% cabernet sauvignon, 7% cabernet franc, 3% petit verdot — Luján de Cuyo

91 Colour: cherry, garnet rim. Nose: ripe fruit, spicy, toasty, roasted coffee. Palate: powerful, flavourful, toasty, round tannins.

CATENA ZAPATA

J. Cobos s/n, Agrelo
5509 Luján de Cuyo
☎: +54 261 413 1100 - Fax: +54 261 413 1133
mlabat@catenazapata.com
www.catenazapata.com

ANGELICA ZAPATA 2008 T
cabernet franc — Valle de Uco

92 Colour: very deep cherry. Nose: expressive, fruit expression, red berry notes, spicy, earthy notes. Palate: good acidity, round, long.

CATENA 2012 B
100% chardonnay — Valle de Uco

90 Colour: bright yellow. Nose: powerfull, ripe fruit, sweet spices. Palate: rich, smoky aftertaste, flavourful, fresh, good acidity.

CATENA ALTA CABERNET SAUVIGNON 2010 T
cabernet sauvignon — Mendoza

91 Colour: cherry, garnet rim. Nose: creamy oak, sweet spices, ripe fruit. Palate: flavourful, round tannins, long.

CATENA ALTA CHARDONNAY 2011 B
100% chardonnay — Mendoza

92 Color bright yellow. Aroma powerfull, ripe fruit, sweet spices, creamy oak, fragrant herbs. Taste rich, smoky aftertaste, flavourful, fresh, good acidity.

CATENA ALTA MALBEC 2010 T
100% malbec — Mendoza

92 Colour: bright cherry, garnet rim. Nose: sweet spices, ripe fruit, balsamic herbs. Palate: complex, fruity, flavourful, long, good acidity, round tannins.

CATENA CABERNET SAUVIGNON 2011 T
100% cabernet sauvignon — Mendoza

91 Colour: cherry, garnet rim. Nose: spicy, scrubland, ripe fruit. Palate: flavourful, ripe fruit, good structure.

CATENA MALBEC 2009 T
100% malbec — Mendoza

92 Colour: cherry, garnet rim. Nose: ripe fruit, elegant, spicy, balsamic herbs. Palate: flavourful, good acidity, fine bitter notes, fruity.

CATENA ZAPATA ESTIBA RESERVADA 2006 T
cabernet sauvignon, merlot Mendoza

95 Colour: very deep cherry. Nose: elegant, expressive, fruit expression, ripe fruit, creamy oak. Palate: flavourful, spicy, ripe fruit, long, elegant.

NICOLÁS CATENA ZAPATA 2009 T
Mendoza

93 Colour: cherry, garnet rim. Nose: spicy, creamy oak, toasty, characterful, earthy notes. Palate: powerful, flavourful, toasty, round tannins, elegant.

DOMINIO DEL PLATA WINERY

Cochabamba, 7801 Agrelo
5507 Luján de Cuyo
☎: +54 261 498 9200 - Fax: +54 261 498 9212
info@dominiodelplata.com.ar
www.dominiodelplata.com.ar

BENMARCO CABERNET SAUVIGNON 2011 T
90% cabernet sauvignon, 5% merlot, 5% cabernet franc
Luján de Cuyo/Agrelo

91 Colour: cherry, garnet rim. Nose: balanced, ripe fruit, balsamic herbs, spicy. Palate: full, flavourful, good acidity.

BENMARCO EXPRESIVO 2011 T
50% malbec, 20% cabernet sauvignon, 10% tannat, 10% syrah, 5% petit verdot, 5% bonarda Luján de Cuyo

94 Colour: cherry, garnet rim. Nose: balanced, complex, ripe fruit, red berry notes, sweet spices, cocoa bean, dried herbs. Palate: fine bitter notes, round, long.

CRIOS RED BLEND 2012 T
40% malbec, 40% bonarda, 15% tannat, 5% syrah Luján de Cuyo/Agrelo

90 Colour: bright cherry, garnet rim. Nose: scrubland, red berry notes, ripe fruit, cocoa bean. Palate: fruity, fruity aftestaste, great length.

SUSANA BALBO MALBEC 2011 T
90% malbec, 10% cabernet sauvignon Mendoza

91 Colour: bright cherry, garnet rim. Nose: spicy, balsamic herbs. Palate: balanced, fine bitter notes, fine tannins.

DURIGUTTI WINES

Roque Saenz Peña, 8450 Las Compuertas
5549 Luján de Cuyo
☎: +54 261 562 9134
cinnella@lamadridwines.com
www.durigutti.com

AGUIJÓN DE ABEJA MALBEC 2011 T
100% malbec Luján de Cuyo

90 Colour: bright cherry. Nose: expressive, spicy. Palate: flavourful, fruity, toasty, round tannins.

DURIGUTTI BONARDA 2010 T
100% bonarda Luján de Cuyo

90 Colour: bright cherry. Nose: ripe fruit, sweet spices, fruit expression. Palate: flavourful, fruity, toasty, round tannins.

DURIGUTTI BONARDA 2010 TR
bonarda Luján de Cuyo

90 Colour: cherry, garnet rim. Nose: ripe fruit, aromatic coffee, toasty. Palate: powerful, fine bitter notes, good acidity.

DURIGUTTI CABERNET FRANC 2010 TR
cabernet franc Luján de Cuyo

91 Colour: cherry, garnet rim. Nose: ripe fruit, spicy, creamy oak, toasty, earthy notes, complex, wet leather. Palate: powerful, flavourful, toasty, round tannins.

DURIGUTTI CABERNET SAUVIGNON 2010 TR
cabernet sauvignon Luján de Cuyo

90 Colour: cherry, garnet rim. Nose: ripe fruit, spicy, creamy oak, toasty, roasted coffee. Palate: powerful, toasty, round tannins.

DURIGUTTI FAMILIA 2007 T
malbec, syrah, cabernet franc, bonarda, cabernet sauvignon
Luján de Cuyo

90 Colour: very deep cherry. Nose: powerfull, roasted coffee, dark chocolate, aromatic coffee. Palate: fine bitter notes, good acidity, round tannins, harsh oak tannins.

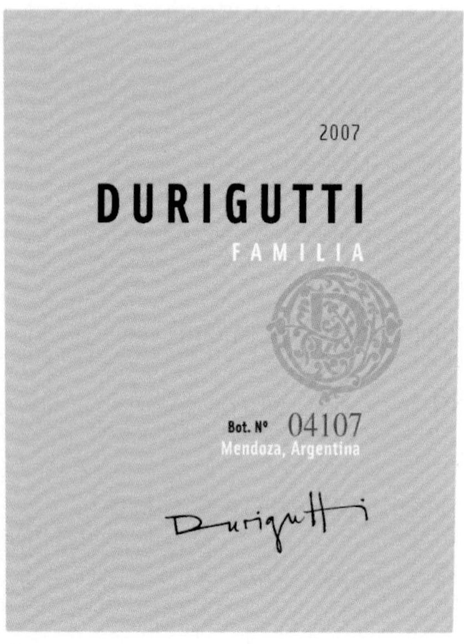

DURIGUTTI MALBEC 2012 T
100% malbec
Luján de Cuyo

91 Colour: bright cherry. Nose: sweet spices, creamy oak, ripe fruit, scrubland. Palate: flavourful, fruity, toasty, round tannins.

HD MALBEC 2008 TGR
100% malbec
Luján de Cuyo

90 Colour: very deep cherry. Nose: roasted coffee, aromatic coffee, overripe fruit. Palate: powerful, long, warm.

HD MALBEC 2010 T
Luján de Cuyo

91 Colour: bright cherry. Nose: sweet spices, creamy oak, ripe fruit, earthy notes. Palate: flavourful, fruity, toasty.

HD MALBEC 2010 TR
100% malbec
Luján de Cuyo

90 Colour: cherry, garnet rim. Nose: ripe fruit, spicy, toasty, characterful, roasted coffee. Palate: powerful, flavourful, toasty, round tannins.

FAMILIA OTERO RAMOS TIERRA DEL ANDE S.A.

Araoz, 2750 (Ruta 60) Mayor Drummond
5507 Luján de Cuyo
☎: +54 261 496 1680 - Fax: +54 261 496 1680
info@oteroramos.com.ar
www.oteroramos.com.ar

GRITOS CLÁSICO CABERNET SAUVIGNON 2011 T
cabernet sauvignon Luján de Cuyo

91 Colour: deep cherry. Nose: earthy notes, fruit expression, ripe fruit. Palate: flavourful, fine bitter notes, good acidity, round tannins.

GRITOS CLÁSICO MALBEC 2008 T
100% malbec Luján de Cuyo

90 Colour: very deep cherry. Nose: toasty, new oak, ripe fruit, mineral. Palate: powerful, fleshy, complex.

FINCA DECERO

Bajo las Cumbres, 9003 Agrelo
5509 Luján de Cuyo
☎: +54 261 524 4747
decero@decero.com
www.decero.com

DECERO AMANO, REMOLINOS VINEYARD 2010 T
64% malbec, 30% cabernet sauvignon, 4% petit verdot, tannat
Luján de Cuyo/Agrelo

91 Colour: deep cherry. Nose: powerfull, roasted coffee, new oak, ripe fruit. Palate: powerful, concentrated, sweetness.

DECERO CABERNET SAUVIGNON, REMOLINOS VINEYARD 2010 T
cabernet sauvignon Luján de Cuyo/Agrelo

91 Colour: cherry, garnet rim. Nose: spicy, creamy oak, toasty, characterful. Palate: powerful, flavourful, toasty, round tannins.

DECERO MALBEC, REMOLINOS VINEYARD 2011 T
100% malbec Luján de Cuyo/Agrelo

90 Colour: deep cherry. Nose: expressive, varietal, ripe fruit, spicy. Palate: spicy, ripe fruit.

DECERO MINI EDICIONES PETIT VERDOT, REMOLINOS VINEYARD 2010 T
100% petit verdot Luján de Cuyo/Agrelo

90 Colour: very deep cherry. Nose: powerfull, spicy, toasty, overripe fruit. Palate: flavourful, fine bitter notes, good acidity.

DECERO SYRAH, REMOLINOS VINEYARD 2011 T
syrah Luján de Cuyo/Agrelo

93 Colour: cherry, garnet rim. Nose: spicy, creamy oak, toasty, characterful, fruit expression, earthy notes. Palate: powerful, flavourful, toasty, round tannins.

FINCA EL ORIGEN

F. Gambarte 220 Barrio Arizu
5501 Godoy Cruz
☎: +54 261 424 5414
info@fincaelorigen.com
www.fincaelorigen.com

FINCA EL ORIGEN CABERNET SAUVIGNON 2010 TGR
85% cabernet sauvignon, 8% petit verdot, 7% malbec Valle de Uco

90 Colour: cherry, garnet rim. Nose: creamy oak, ripe fruit. Palate: flavourful, spicy, long, round tannins.

FINCA EL ORIGEN CABERNET SAUVIGNON 2012 T
100% cabernet sauvignon Valle de Uco

91 Colour: cherry, garnet rim. Nose: spicy, scrubland, medium intensity. Palate: flavourful, fruity, round tannins, good acidity.

FINCA EL ORIGEN CABERNET SAUVIGNON 2012 TR
85% cabernet sauvignon, 8% bonarda, 7% malbec Valle de Uco

90 Colour: bright cherry, garnet rim. Nose: neat, balanced, ripe fruit, creamy oak. Palate: good structure, fleshy, full.

FINCA EL ORIGEN MALBEC 2011 TGR
85% malbec, 7% petit verdot, 6% cabernet sauvignon, 2% cabernet franc Valle de Uco

94 Colour: cherry, garnet rim. Nose: ripe fruit, spicy, creamy oak, complex, dry stone. Palate: powerful, flavourful, round tannins.

FINCA EL ORIGEN MALBEC 2012 T
100% malbec Valle de Uco

90 Colour: cherry, garnet rim. Nose: scrubland, red berry notes, ripe fruit, spicy. Palate: flavourful, good acidity.

FINCA EL ORIGEN MALBEC 2012 TR
85% malbec, 7% bonarda, 6% cabernet sauvignon, 2% syrah Valle de Uco

91 Colour: cherry, garnet rim. Nose: powerfull, spicy, ripe fruit. Palate: balanced, fine bitter notes, good acidity.

FINCA EL ORIGEN MALBEC ROSÉ 2012 RD
100% malbec Valle de Uco

90 Colour: onion pink. Nose: elegant, candied fruit, dried flowers, fragrant herbs, red berry notes. Palate: light-bodied, flavourful, good acidity, long, spicy.

FINCA EL ORIGEN PHI 2009 T
79% malbec, 11% cabernet franc, 7% cabernet sauvignon, 3% petit verdot Valle de Uco

93 Colour: bright cherry. Nose: expressive, complex, spicy, sweet spices, ripe fruit, dried herbs. Palate: balanced, fine bitter notes, good acidity.

FINCA EL ORIGEN SYRAH 2012 T
100% syrah Valle de Uco

90 Colour: bright cherry. Nose: sweet spices, expressive, red berry notes, ripe fruit. Palate: flavourful, fruity, round tannins.

FINCA LA ANITA

Calle Cobos s/n - Agrelo
Luján de Cuyo
☎: +54 261 951 065 01
admin@fincalaanita.com
www.fincalaanita.com

FINCA LA ANITA GRAN MALBEC 2011 T
Luján de Cuyo

91 Colour: deep cherry, garnet rim. Nose: red berry notes, ripe fruit, varietal, spicy. Palate: good acidity, ripe fruit, long, round tannins.

FINCA LA ANITA CORTE G 2011 T
50% malbec, 30% cabernet sauvignon, 15% syrah, 5% petit verdot Luján de Cuyo

90 Colour: bright cherry. Nose: red berry notes, ripe fruit, spicy, dried herbs. Palate: flavourful, round tannins, fruity.

FINCA LA ANITA CORTE UNIVERSITARIO 2011 T
Luján de Cuyo

90 Colour: cherry, purple rim. Nose: balanced, fruit expression, violets. Palate: fruity, flavourful, good acidity, fine bitter notes.

VARÚA 2011 T
merlot Luján de Cuyo

93 Colour: cherry, garnet rim. Nose: sweet spices, red berry notes, ripe fruit, balanced. Palate: good structure, flavourful, good acidity, balanced, fine bitter notes.

FINCA LA CELIA

Circunvalación Celia Bustos de Quiroga 374
5569 San Carlos
☎: +54 262 245 1010 - Fax: +54 262 245 1010
info@fincalacelia.com.ar
www.fincalacelia.com.ar

LA CELIA 2011 T
malbec Valle de Uco

91 Colour: very deep cherry, garnet rim. Nose: balanced, powerfull, ripe fruit, scrubland, spicy. Palate: balanced, long, spicy, fine tannins.

FINCA LA CHAMIZA

Ruta 60 y Canal Pescara, Russell
5517 Maipú
☎: +54 261 413 7182 - Fax: +54 261 413 7116
team@lachamiza.com
www.lachamiza.com

LA CHAMIZA LEGEND OF POLO 2011 T
100% malbec Luján de Cuyo

92 Colour: cherry, garnet rim. Nose: sweet spices, ripe fruit, toasty, creamy oak, fruit expression. Palate: fine bitter notes, good acidity, round tannins.

LA CHAMIZA MARTÍN ALSINA 2009 T
100% malbec Luján de Cuyo

93 Colour: cherry, garnet rim. Nose: spicy, creamy oak, toasty, complex, fruit expression. Palate: powerful, flavourful, round tannins.

LA CHAMIZA POLO PROFESIONAL CABERNET SAUVIGNON 2012 TR
100% cabernet sauvignon Tupungato

91 Colour: cherry, garnet rim. Nose: spicy, creamy oak, toasty, characterful, red berry notes. Palate: powerful, flavourful, toasty, round tannins.

LA CHAMIZA POLO PROFESIONAL MALBEC 2012 T
100% malbec Maipú

92 Colour: bright cherry. Nose: sweet spices, creamy oak, red berry notes. Palate: flavourful, fruity, toasty, round tannins.

FINCA LA ESCARCHA (ENTRELINEAS)

Calle 6 y Calle 8
5561 La Arboleda -Tupungato
☎: +54 261 429 1362
sreta@hotmail.com

LA ESCARCHA SYRAH 2010 T
syrah Tupungato

91 Colour: cherry, garnet rim. Nose: creamy oak, toasty, complex, balsamic herbs. Palate: powerful, flavourful, toasty, round tannins.

FINCA LA LUZ

Cale Armani s/n Villa Seca
5560 Tunuyán
☎: +54 926 168 369 79
marolla.agustin@gmail.com
www.fincalaluz.com.ar

CALLEJÓN DEL CRIMEN 2010 T
100% malbec Valle de Uco

91 Colour: very deep cherry. Nose: ripe fruit, grassy, balsamic herbs, spicy. Palate: fine bitter notes, spicy, good acidity, round tannins.

Callejón del
Crimen
GRAN RESERVA
2010
MALBEC
PRODUCT OF ARGENTINA

FINCA SOPHENIA

Ruta Provincial 89, Km. 12.5
5561 Tupungato
☎: +54 114 781 9840
consultas@sophenia.com.ar
www.sophenia.com.ar

FINCA SOPHENIA MALBEC 2011 TR
100% malbec Tupungato

91 Colour: cherry, garnet rim. Nose: balanced, medium intensity, red berry notes. Palate: good acidity, balanced, fine bitter notes.

FINCA SOPHENIA VIOGNIER 2012 B RESERVA
viognier Tupungato

90 Colour: bright yellow. Nose: floral, sweet spices, ripe fruit. Palate: flavourful, spicy, good acidity.

SOPHENIA SYNTHESIS MALBEC 2010 T
100% malbec Tupungato

92 Colour: very deep cherry, garnet rim. Nose: creamy oak, cocoa bean, balsamic herbs, ripe fruit. Palate: good structure, flavourful, round tannins.

SOPHENIA SYNTHESIS THE BLEND 2009 T
malbec, cabernet sauvignon, merlot Tupungato

92 Colour: cherry, garnet rim. Nose: expressive, creamy oak, ripe fruit, sweet spices. Palate: flavourful, fruity, round tannins.

GAUCHEZCO VIÑEDOS Y BODEGA

Carril Barrancas s/n
5517 Barrancas, Maipú
☎: +54 926 153 327 44
info@gauchezco.com
www.gauchezco.com

GAUCHEZCO ORO MALBEC 2009 T
100% malbec Mendoza

90 Colour: bright cherry, garnet rim. Nose: powerfull, cocoa bean, creamy oak, ripe fruit, candied fruit. Palate: long, round tannins.

GIMENEZ RIILI

Sargento Cabral 450
5506 Luján de Cuyo
☎: +54 261 498 7863
info@gimenezriili.com
www.gimenezriili.com.ar

GIMINEZ RIILI 2011 TR
cabernet sauvignon Valle de Uco

91 Colour: cherry, garnet rim. Nose: spicy, creamy oak, toasty, characterful. Palate: powerful, toasty, round tannins, fresh.

GIMINEZ RIILI LIMITED EDITION 2008 T
100% malbec Valle de Uco

93 Colour: cherry, garnet rim. Nose: spicy, creamy oak, toasty, complex, earthy notes. Palate: powerful, flavourful, toasty, round tannins, fine bitter notes.

GIMINEZ RIILI LIMITED EDITION 2011 TGR
syrah Valle de Uco

90 Colour: black cherry. Nose: ripe fruit, roasted coffee, new oak, dark chocolate. Palate: powerful, fine bitter notes, good acidity, mineral.

GOUGUENHEIM

Laprida, 3278
1642 San Isidro
☎: +54 114 708 0044 - Fax: +54 114 708 0055
patricio@gouguenheimwinery.com.ar
www.gouguenheimwinery.com.ar

ESTACIONES DEL VALLE - INVIERNO 2011 T
100% cabernet sauvignon Valle de Uco

90 Colour: cherry, garnet rim. Nose: ripe fruit, balanced, spicy, balsamic herbs. Palate: good structure, flavourful, good finish.

ESTACIONES DEL VALLE - PRIMAVERA 2011 T
100% syrah Valle de Uco

90 Colour: bright cherry, garnet rim. Nose: red berry notes, ripe fruit, floral. Palate: fruity, flavourful, good acidity.

FLORES DEL VALLE - BLEND 2008 T
50% malbec, 32% cabernet sauvignon, 10% cabernet franc, 8% merlot — Valle de Uco

91 Colour: cherry, garnet rim. Nose: red berry notes, ripe fruit, balanced, expressive, sweet spices. Palate: balanced, flavourful, fruity aftestaste.

GOUGUENHEIM MALBEC RESERVA 2010 TR
100% malbec — Valle de Uco

91 Colour: cherry, garnet rim. Nose: red berry notes, ripe fruit, spicy. Palate: fruity, flavourful, good acidity, balanced.

GOUGUENHEIM MERLOT RESERVA 2009 TR
100% merlot — Valle de Uco

90 Colour: cherry, garnet rim. Nose: toasty, creamy oak, ripe fruit. Palate: balanced, round tannins, good acidity.

MOMENTOS DEL VALLE BONARDA-SYRAH 2011 T
50% bonarda, 50% syrah — Valle de Uco

90 Colour: cherry, garnet rim. Nose: medium intensity, ripe fruit, spicy. Palate: fruity, easy to drink, good acidity.

HUARPE WINES

Ruta Provincial 15, km. 32
5500 Agrelo
☎: +54 261 479 0222
info@huarpewines.com
www.huarpewines.com

GUAYQUIL 2007 T
45% malbec, 30% cabernet sauvignon, 15% petit verdot, 5% bonarda, 5% tannat — Luján de Cuyo

91 Colour: cherry, garnet rim. Nose: balanced, expressive, ripe fruit, spicy, scrubland. Palate: good acidity, fine bitter notes.

HUARPE AGRELO 2010 T
80% malbec, 20% cabernet sauvignon — Luján de Cuyo

93 Colour: cherry, garnet rim. Nose: spicy, creamy oak, toasty, complex, characterful. Palate: powerful, flavourful, toasty, round tannins.

TAYMENTE 2012 B
100% torrontés — Luján de Cuyo

90 Colour: bright straw. Nose: white flowers, fresh fruit. Palate: flavourful, fruity, fresh.

TAYMENTE BONARDA 2011 T
100% bonarda — Luján de Cuyo

90 Colour: cherry, garnet rim. Nose: characterful, ripe fruit, toasty, spicy. Palate: flavourful, fine bitter notes, good acidity.

TAYMENTE MALBEC 2011 T
100% malbec — Luján de Cuyo

91 Colour: bright cherry. Nose: ripe fruit, sweet spices, creamy oak, varietal. Palate: flavourful, fruity, toasty, round tannins.

KAIKEN

Roque Saenz Peña 5516 (ingreso por el Callejón de la Virgen), Vistalba
5507 Luján de Cuyo
☎: +54 261 524 3060 - Fax: +54 261 524 3060
labrahan@kaikenwines.com
www.kaikenwines.com

KAIKEN MAI 2008 T
100% malbec — Luján de Cuyo/Agrelo

90 Colour: very deep cherry, garnet rim. Nose: warm, powerfull, ripe fruit, candied fruit, creamy oak. Palate: good structure, concentrated.

KAIKEN TERROIR SERIES 2011 B
torrontés — Luján de Cuyo/Agrelo

91 Colour: bright straw, greenish rim. Nose: expressive, jasmine, fresh. Palate: flavourful, balanced, good acidity.

KAIKEN ULTRA CHARDONNAY 2011 B
chardonnay — Luján de Cuyo/Agrelo

92 Colour: bright straw. Nose: fresh, white flowers, expressive. Palate: flavourful, fruity, good acidity, balanced.

KAIKEN ULTRA MALBEC 2011 T
100% malbec — Luján de Cuyo/Agrelo

90 Colour: deep cherry, garnet rim. Nose: ripe fruit, sweet spices, varietal, wild herbs. Palate: flavourful, fruity.

LA GIOSTRA DEL VINO

Viamonte, 4038 Chacras de Coria
5505 Luján de Cuyo
☎: +54 926 133 783 68
giuseppe_franceschini@yahoo.it
www.lagiostradelvino.com

BACÁN 2010 TR
100% malbec — Luján de Cuyo

93 Colour: very deep cherry. Nose: expressive, scrubland, fruit expression, spicy. Palate: good structure, round tannins.

BACÁN 2011 B RESERVA
sauvignon blanc — Tupungato

93 Colour: bright straw. Nose: fresh, fresh fruit, white flowers, expressive, new oak, spicy. Palate: flavourful, fruity, good acidity, balanced.

BACÁN 2012 B RESERVA
sauvignon blanc — Tupungato

93 Colour: cherry, purple rim. Nose: expressive, fresh fruit, red berry notes, floral, creamy oak. Palate: flavourful, fruity, good acidity, round tannins.

BACÁN CLÁSICO 2010 T
100% malbec — Luján de Cuyo

91 Colour: cherry, garnet rim. Nose: red berry notes, ripe fruit, spicy, floral. Palate: good acidity, fresh, fruity, flavourful, fine tannins.

BACÁN CLÁSICO 2011 T
100% malbec — Luján de Cuyo

90 Colour: cherry, garnet rim. Nose: ripe fruit, medium intensity. Palate: fruity, flavourful, long, fine tannins.

BACÁN TORRONTÉS DULCE 2011 B
torrontés — Tupungato

90 Colour: bright straw. Nose: ripe fruit, white flowers, candied fruit. Palate: flavourful, fruity, fresh, sweet.

BACÁN VIOGNIER 2011 B
viognier — Tupungato

90 Colour: bright straw. Nose: fresh, fresh fruit, white flowers. Palate: flavourful, fruity, balanced.

LA TRES 14

latres14@gmail.com
www.latres14.com

IMPERFECTO 2011 T
Luján de Cuyo

93 Colour: cherry, garnet rim. Nose: spicy, creamy oak, toasty, complex, red berry notes, fruit expression. Palate: powerful, toasty, round tannins, mineral, long.

LAMADRID ESTATE WINES

Roque Saenz Peña 8450, Las Compuertas
5549 Luján de Cuyo
☎: +54 261 562 9134
cinnella@lamadridwines.com
www.lamadridwines.com

LAMADRID 2008 TGR
100% malbec — Luján de Cuyo/Agrelo

90 Colour: black cherry. Nose: overripe fruit, roasted coffee, aromatic coffee, toasty. Palate: fine bitter notes, good acidity, spicy.

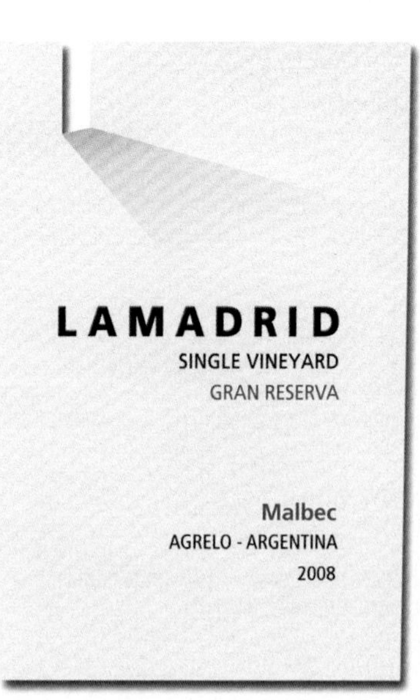

LAMADRID
SINGLE VINEYARD
GRAN RESERVA
Malbec
AGRELO - ARGENTINA
2008

LAMADRID BONARDA 2010 TR
Luján de Cuyo/Agrelo

90 Colour: bright cherry. Nose: sweet spices, creamy oak. Palate: flavourful, fruity, toasty, round tannins.

LAMADRID CABERNET FRANC 2010 TR
cabernet franc Luján de Cuyo/Agrelo

92 Colour: cherry, garnet rim. Nose: ripe fruit, creamy oak, toasty, characterful, varietal. Palate: powerful, flavourful, toasty, round tannins.

LAMADRID CABERNET SAUVIGNON 2010 TR
cabernet sauvignon Luján de Cuyo/Agrelo

91 Colour: cherry, garnet rim. Nose: spicy, creamy oak, toasty, varietal. Palate: powerful, flavourful, toasty, round tannins.

LAMADRID MALBEC 2010 TR
Luján de Cuyo/Agrelo

91 Colour: cherry, garnet rim. Nose: ripe fruit, spicy, creamy oak, toasty. Palate: powerful, flavourful, toasty, round tannins.

MATILDE LAMADRID 2007 T
100% malbec Luján de Cuyo/Agrelo

91 Colour: cherry, garnet rim. Nose: spicy, ripe fruit, fruit expression, balsamic herbs, scrubland. Palate: spicy, ripe fruit, fine bitter notes.

LAS NENCIAS

9 de Julio 309 PB 2
5500 Mendoza
☎: +52 614 240 790 - Fax: +54 261 424 0595
maria@lasnencias.com
www.lasnencias.com.ar

LAS NENCIAS BLEND 2011 TR
56% malbec, 14% bonarda, 20% cabernet sauvignon, 6% cabernet franc, 4% syrah Valle de Uco

94 Colour: bright cherry. Nose: sweet spices, ripe fruit, creamy oak, varietal, fruit expression. Palate: flavourful, fruity, toasty, round tannins.

LAS NENCIAS FAMILY SELECTION 2010 T
100% malbec Valle de Uco

92 Colour: bright cherry. Nose: ripe fruit, sweet spices, creamy oak, expressive, toasty, mineral. Palate: flavourful, fruity, round tannins, great length, mineral.

LAS NENCIAS MALBEC 2010 TR
100% malbec Valle de Uco

91 Colour: cherry, garnet rim. Nose: ripe fruit, fruit expression, cocoa bean, creamy oak. Palate: flavourful, varietal, toasty, great length.

LAS NENCIAS SINGLE VINEYARD 2010 T
100% malbec Valle de Uco

90 Colour: bright cherry. Nose: sweet spices, creamy oak, ripe fruit. Palate: flavourful, fruity, toasty, round tannins.

LUCA VINEYARD AND WINERY

Calle Cobos s/n Agrelo
5509 Luján de Cuyo
☎: +54 261 413 100 - Fax: +54 261 413 1133
info@lucawines.com
www.lucawines.com

LUCA BESO DE DANTE 2010 T
60% malbec, 40% cabernet sauvignon Luján de Cuyo/Agrelo

91 Colour: cherry, garnet rim. Nose: ripe fruit, spicy, characterful, roasted coffee. Palate: powerful, flavourful, toasty, round tannins.

LUCA CHARDONNAY 2012 B
100% chardonnay Tupungato

93 Colour: bright straw. Nose: ripe fruit, citrus fruit, spicy, cocoa bean. Palate: spicy, long, good acidity.

LUCA LABORDE DOUBLE SELECT SYRAH 2011 T
syrah Valle de Uco

91 Colour: cherry, garnet rim. Nose: ripe fruit, spicy, characterful, earthy notes. Palate: powerful, flavourful, toasty, round tannins.

LUCA MALBEC 2011 T
100% malbec Valle de Uco

93 Colour: deep cherry. Nose: sweet spices, ripe fruit, spicy, toasty. Palate: fine bitter notes, spicy, toasty, round tannins.

LUCA PINOT NOIR 2011 T
100% pinot noir Valle de Uco

92 Colour: bright cherry. Nose: ripe fruit, sweet spices, creamy oak, fruit expression, red berry notes. Palate: flavourful, fruity, toasty, round tannins.

NICO BY LUCA 2009 T
100% malbec Valle de Uco

92 Colour: cherry, garnet rim. Nose: ripe fruit, spicy, toasty, complex, new oak, dark chocolate, aromatic coffee. Palate: powerful, flavourful, toasty, round tannins.

MARCELO PELLERITI WINES

9 de Julio 1221 2do piso
5500 Mendoza
☎: +54 261 429 2337
info@marcelopelleriti.com
www.marcelopelleriti.com

MARCELO PELLERITI RESERVE 2008 TR
100% malbec Valle de Uco

90 Colour: cherry, garnet rim. Nose: spicy, creamy oak, toasty, characterful. Palate: powerful, flavourful, toasty, round tannins.

MATIAS RICCITELLI WINES

Callejon Nicolas De La Reta s/n Las Compuertas
5549 Lujan De Cuyo
☎: +54 92 615 465 443
info@matiasriccitelli.com
www.matiasriccitelli.com

REPUBLICCA DEL MALBEC 2011 T
100% malbec Luján de Cuyo

92 Colour: black cherry. Nose: powerfull, overripe fruit, creamy oak, spicy, toasty. Palate: powerful, fine bitter notes, good acidity, round.

THE APPLE DOESN'T FALL FAR
FROM THE TREE 2011 T
100% malbec Luján de Cuyo

92 Colour: cherry, garnet rim. Nose: ripe fruit, spicy, creamy oak, toasty, complex, mineral. Palate: powerful, flavourful, toasty, fine tannins.

VINEYARD SELECTION 2011 T
100% malbec Luján de Cuyo

93 Colour: bright cherry. Nose: sweet spices, creamy oak, expressive, earthy notes, dry stone, overripe fruit. Palate: flavourful, fruity, toasty, round tannins.

MELODÍA WINES S.A.

Manuel A. Sáez 831
5519 Guaymallén
☎: +54 261 445 8571
jorge@jorgebenites.com.ar
www.jorgebenites.com.ar

MELODÍA 2007 T
malbec, cabernet sauvignon, merlot, bonarda, syrah Luján de Cuyo/Agrelo

90 Colour: cherry, garnet rim. Nose: powerfull, ripe fruit, balsamic herbs. Palate: flavourful, fruity, good acidity, fine tannins.

MELODÍA BONARDA 2009 T
100% bonarda Luján de Cuyo

90 Colour: cherry, garnet rim. Nose: powerfull, scrubland, ripe fruit. Palate: full, spicy, good acidity, round tannins.

MELODÍA MALBEC 2007 T
100% malbec Luján de Cuyo/Agrelo

90 Colour: cherry, garnet rim. Nose: medium intensity, scrubland, ripe fruit, old leather. Palate: balanced, easy to drink, good acidity.

MENDEL WINES

Terrada 1863
5507 Luján de Cuyo
☎: +54 261 524 1621 - Fax: +54 261 524 1622
tasting@mendel.com.ar
www.mendel.com.ar

MENDEL CABERNET SAUVIGNON 2011 T
Luján de Cuyo

90 Colour: cherry, garnet rim. Nose: spicy, creamy oak, toasty, complex, overripe fruit. Palate: powerful, flavourful, toasty, round tannins.

MENDEL UNUS 2010 T
70% malbec, 30% cabernet sauvignon Mendoza

91 Colour: cherry, garnet rim. Nose: ripe fruit, spicy, toasty, complex, expressive, varietal, aromatic coffee. Palate: powerful, flavourful, toasty, round tannins.

MONTE QUIETO

Cobos 12290, Agrelo
5509 Luján de Cuyo
☎: +54 261 562 8282 - Fax: +54 261 524 1596
nuestro@montequieto.com
www.montequieto.com

QUIETO 2008 TR
cabernet franc, malbec, cabernet sauvignon Luján de Cuyo

90 Colour: cherry, garnet rim. Nose: ripe fruit, spicy, creamy oak, roasted coffee. Palate: powerful, flavourful, toasty, round tannins.

QUIETO MALBEC 2010 T
Luján de Cuyo

91 Colour: bright cherry. Nose: sweet spices, creamy oak, varietal. Palate: flavourful, fruity, toasty, round tannins.

MOOR BARRIO WINES

Estrada 1848
5521 Villa Nueva, Guaymallén
☎: +54 926 154 667 02
info@moorbarrio.com
www.moorbarrio.com

INITIUM 2011 T ROBLE
100% malbec Luján de Cuyo

92 Colour: very deep cherry. Nose: powerfull, varietal, characterful, ripe fruit, sweet spices. Palate: flavourful, fine bitter notes, good acidity, round.

NORTON

Ruta Provincial 15 Km. 23,5 Perdriel
550 Luján de Cuyo
☎: +54 261 490 9700 - Fax: +54 261 490 9799
ebarzola@norton.com.ar
www.norton.com.ar

NORTON PRIVADA 2010 T
40% malbec, 30% merlot, 30% cabernet sauvignon Luján de Cuyo

94 Colour: cherry, garnet rim. Nose: spicy, creamy oak, toasty, complex, earthy notes, fruit expression. Palate: powerful, flavourful, toasty, round tannins.

NORTON RESERVA CABERNET SAUVIGNON 2010 T
100% cabernet sauvignon Luján de Cuyo

91 Colour: bright cherry. Nose: sweet spices, creamy oak, expressive, fruit expression, varietal. Palate: flavourful, fruity, round tannins.

NORTON RESERVA MALBEC 2010 T
100% malbec Luján de Cuyo

90 Colour: bright cherry. Nose: sweet spices, creamy oak, ripe fruit. Palate: flavourful, fruity, toasty, round tannins.

NORTON WINEMAKER'S RESERVA CABERNET SAUVIGNON 2010 T
100% cabernet sauvignon Luján de Cuyo

92 Colour: cherry, garnet rim. Nose: spicy, creamy oak, toasty, complex, dry nuts, ripe fruit. Palate: powerful, flavourful, round tannins.

NORTON WINEMAKER'S RESERVA MALBEC 2010 T
100% malbec Luján de Cuyo

90 Colour: bright cherry. Nose: sweet spices, creamy oak, expressive, ripe fruit. Palate: flavourful, fruity, toasty, round tannins.

NOVUS ORDO VINEYARDS & WINERY

Ruta 89
Tupungato
www.novusordovineyards.com

NOVUS ORDO 2010 TGR
100% malbec Valle de Uco

90 Colour: very deep cherry. Nose: ripe fruit, balsamic herbs, spicy, toasty. Palate: powerful, fine bitter notes, good acidity.

NOVUS ORDO 2010 TR
Valle de Uco

92 Colour: cherry, garnet rim. Nose: spicy, creamy oak, toasty, characterful. Palate: powerful, flavourful, toasty, round tannins.

NOVUS ORDO CHADONNAY 2011 B
chardonnay Valle de Uco

90 Colour: bright straw. Nose: fresh, fresh fruit, white flowers, expressive. Palate: flavourful, fruity, good acidity, balanced, sweet.

PRIMITIVO 2010 T
97% malbec, 3% cabernet franc Valle de Uco

93 Colour: cherry, garnet rim. Nose: spicy, creamy oak, toasty, characterful, balsamic herbs. Palate: powerful, flavourful, toasty, round tannins.

OJO DE VINO S.A.

Bajo Las Cumbres, s/n Agrelo
5509 Luján de Cuyo, Agrelo
☎: +54 261 479 0145
patricio.eppinger@ojodevino.com
www.ojodevino.ch

DIETER MEIER PURO CORTE 2011 T
malbec, cabernet sauvignon, cabernet franc Luján de Cuyo/Agrelo

90 Colour: cherry, garnet rim. Nose: spicy, creamy oak, toasty, characterful, ripe fruit. Palate: powerful, flavourful, toasty, round tannins.

OJO DE AGUA MALBEC 2012 T
100% malbec Luján de Cuyo/Agrelo

91 Colour: bright cherry. Nose: sweet spices, creamy oak, ripe fruit. Palate: flavourful, fruity, toasty, round tannins.

PURO CORTE D'ORO 2011 T
malbec, cabernet sauvignon, petit verdot Luján de Cuyo/Agrelo

91 Colour: deep cherry. Nose: ripe fruit, red berry notes, spicy, dark chocolate. Palate: fine bitter notes, good acidity, spicy, round tannins.

RIGLOS

Ruta Provincial 89, km. 13 Gualtallary
Tupungato
☎: +54 262 248 9696
jr@bodegariglos.com.ar
www.bodegariglos.com

RIGLOS GRAN CABERNET FRANC 2010 T
cabernet franc Tupungato

92 Colour: deep cherry. Nose: ripe fruit, mineral, balsamic herbs, sweet spices, new oak. Palate: fine bitter notes, good acidity, long.

RIGLOS GRAN CORTE 2010 T
malbec, cabernet sauvignon Tupungato

90 Colour: cherry, garnet rim. Nose: ripe fruit, spicy, creamy oak, toasty, characterful, powerfull. Palate: powerful, flavourful, toasty, round tannins.

RIGLOS GRAN MALBEC 2010 T
100% malbec Tupungato

91 Colour: cherry, garnet rim. Nose: spicy, creamy oak, characterful, overripe fruit. Palate: powerful, flavourful, toasty, round tannins.

RUCA MALEN

Ruta Nacional nº 7, km. 1059, Agrelo
Luján de Cuyo
☎: +54 261 562 8357
www.bodegarucamalen.com

RUCA MALEN 2010 T
malbec Luján de Cuyo

91 Colour: very deep cherry, purple rim. Nose: balanced, ripe fruit, creamy oak, cocoa bean, dried herbs. Palate: flavourful, round tannins, long.

RUTINI WINES

Avda. Rivadavia, 413 Piso 8
☎: +54 261 497 2013
Buenos Aires
promocion@bodegalarural.com.ar
www.bodegalarural.com.ar

ANTOLOGÍA XXVII 2009 T
90% malbec, 5% petit verdot, 5% cabernet franc Mendoza

90 Colour: very deep cherry, garnet rim. Nose: expressive, balanced, fine reductive notes, spicy, dried herbs. Palate: good structure, round tannins, balanced.

RUTINI 2011 T
cabernet sauvignon, malbec Mendoza

91 Colour: deep cherry, garnet rim. Nose: balsamic herbs, ripe fruit, spicy. Palate: flavourful, good acidity, round tannins.

TRUMPETER 2011 B
torrontés Mendoza

90 Colour: bright straw, greenish rim. Nose: faded flowers, ripe fruit, powerfull. Palate: fruity, easy to drink, good finish, balanced.

SERRERA WINES

Echeverria 1654 PB Of. 4
5501 Godoy Cruz
☎: +54 261 517 0353
info@serrera.com.ar
www.serrera.com.ar

SERRERA GRAN GUARDA 2006 T
100% malbec Luján de Cuyo

93 Colour: cherry, garnet rim. Nose: ripe fruit, spicy, creamy oak, toasty, elegant. Palate: powerful, flavourful, toasty, elegant, round tannins.

SERRERA GRAN GUARDA 2008 T
100% malbec Luján de Cuyo

94 Colour: cherry, garnet rim. Nose: ripe fruit, creamy oak, toasty, complex, fruit expression, mineral. Palate: powerful, flavourful, toasty, round tannins.

TERRAZAS DE LOS ANDES/CHEVAL DES ANDES/BODEGAS CHANDON

Thames y Cochabamba, Perdriel
Luján de Cuyo
☎: +54 261 488 0058 - Fax: +54 261 488 0614
info@terrazasdelosandes.com
www.terrazasdelosandes.com

BARON B 2010 BN
Mendoza

90 Colour: bright straw. Nose: fine lees, candied fruit, citrus fruit, ripe fruit, spicy. Palate: good acidity, fine bead, elegant.

CHEVAL DE LOS ANDES 2008 T
Luján de Cuyo

92 Colour: bright cherry. Nose: sweet spices, expressive, ripe fruit, toasty, spicy, aromatic coffee, earthy notes. Palate: flavourful, fruity, toasty, round tannins.

TERRAZAS DE LOS ANDES AFINCADO CABERNET SAUVIGNON 2009 T
cabernet sauvignon — Mendoza

91 Colour: very deep cherry. Nose: characterful, complex, ripe fruit, toasty, dark chocolate. Palate: powerful, concentrated, warm, good acidity.

TERRAZAS DE LOS ANDES AFINCADO MALBEC 2009 T
100% malbec — Mendoza

90 Colour: dark-red cherry. Nose: overripe fruit, fruit preserve, creamy oak, new oak. Palate: warm, round, confected.

TERRAZAS DE LOS ANDES CABERNET SAUVIGNON 2010 TR
cabernet sauvignon — Luján de Cuyo

90 Colour: cherry, garnet rim. Nose: creamy oak, toasty, complex, overripe fruit. Palate: powerful, flavourful, toasty, round tannins.

THE VINES OF MENDOZA

Belgrano 1194
5500 Mendoza
☎: +54 (0261) 438 1031
monofri@vinesofmendoza.com
www.vinesofmendoza.com

RECUERDO GRAN CORTE 2011 T
65% malbec, 20% cabernet franc, 10% merlot, 5% petit verdot
Valle de Uco

92 Colour: deep cherry. Nose: complex, characterful, ripe fruit, red berry notes, creamy oak, sweet spices, earthy notes. Palate: flavourful, spicy, ripe fruit.

RECUERDO 2011 TR
100% malbec — Valle de Uco

91 Colour: deep cherry. Nose: powerfull, ripe fruit, balsamic herbs, toasty, spicy, varietal. Palate: powerful, fleshy, complex, good acidity.

THE VINES CHARDONNAY 2011 B
chardonnay — Valle de Uco

90 Colour: bright straw. Nose: powerfull, characterful, ripe fruit, creamy oak, new oak. Palate: flavourful, fruity, toasty, fine bitter notes.

RECUERDO 2012 T
100% malbec Valle de Uco

90 Colour: bright cherry. Nose: ripe fruit, sweet spices, creamy oak, varietal, scrubland. Palate: flavourful, fruity, toasty, round tannins.

TRIVENTO BODEGAS Y VIÑEDOS

Canal Pescara, 9347 - Russell
5517 Maipú
☎: +54 261 413 7100 - Fax: +54 261 413 7116
press@trivento.com
www.trivento.com

TRIVENTO AMADO SUR TORRONTÉS 2012 B
80% torrontés, 10% chardonnay, 10% viognier Tupungato

90 Colour: bright straw. Nose: floral, expressive, ripe fruit. Palate: flavourful, fruity, long, good acidity.

TRIVENTO GOLDEN RESERVE CHARDONNAY 2011 B
100% chardonnay Luján de Cuyo

90 Colour: bright yellow. Nose: powerfull, ripe fruit, sweet spices, creamy oak, faded flowers. Palate: rich, smoky aftertaste, flavourful, good acidity.

TRIVENTO GOLDEN RESERVE MALBEC 2010 T
100% malbec Luján de Cuyo

91 Colour: deep cherry, garnet rim. Nose: scrubland, spicy. Palate: balanced, fine bitter notes, round, round tannins.

TRIVENTO GOLDEN RESERVE SYRAH 2010 T
100% syrah Valle de Uco

90 Colour: bright cherry, garnet rim. Nose: red berry notes, ripe fruit, expressive, spicy. Palate: balanced, fine bitter notes, long.

URRACA

Cochabamba, 9384 Agrelo
5509 Luján de Cuyo
☎: +54 261 423 5528 - Fax: +54 261 423 5528
info@urracawines.com
www.urracawines.com.ar

URRACA PRIMERA 2008 TR
40% cabernet sauvignon, 40% merlot, 20% malbec Luján de Cuyo

93 Colour: bright cherry. Nose: creamy oak, neat, overripe fruit, powerfull, new oak. Palate: flavourful, fruity, toasty, round tannins.

VIÑA ALICIA

Terrada s/n (Esq. Anchorena)
5507 Luján De Cuyo
☎: +54 261 524 3673 - Fax: +54 261 524 3673
rodrigoarizu@vinaalicia.com
www.vinaalicia.com

VIÑA ALICIA COLECCIÓN DE FAMILIA CUARZO 2008 T
petit verdot Mendoza

95 Colour: very deep cherry. Nose: expressive, spicy, creamy oak, earthy notes. Palate: flavourful, good acidity, elegant, fine tannins.

VIÑA ALICIA COLECCIÓN DE FAMILIA NEBBIOLO 2008 T
nebbiolo Luján de Cuyo

93 Colour: cherry, garnet rim. Nose: ripe fruit, spicy, creamy oak, toasty, complex, earthy notes. Palate: powerful, flavourful, toasty.

DESCRIPTION

This is one of the zones which have been recently incorporated into the Argentinean oenological panorama. In recent years, its growth has been considerable, and it has become the fastest growing wine centre in the Argentinean Republic. Its fertile land contrasts with the aridity of the northern mountains. In this zone, the Andes mountain range falls to 275 metres.

NUMBER OF HECTARES:1.631 **ALTITUDES:** 250 m. - 460 m.

PREDOMINANT VARIETIES:

White grapes: *sauvignon blanc.*

Red grapes: *merlot, pinot noir and malbec.*

CLIMATOLOGY AND SOILS

The vineyards are in the more eastern parts of the province. In this zone, rainfall is less than 150 millimetres per year. The summers are hot, with temperatures reaching 40º C in daytime and nights are fresh. The winters are cold with absolute minimums of up to -14º C below zero and an average winter temperature of -5º C. The soils are fundamentally clay, loam and sand.

In the farthest western side, the climate is much colder due to the proximity of the Andes, with notable thermal integrals. Curiously, the lower the altitude, the less warm is the climate than in Mendoza due mainly to its proximity to the South Pole. These characteristics mean that the grapes mature slowly, thus, the short-cycle varieties such as merlot, savignon blanc and pinot noir moderate, with excellent results in white wines and sparkling wines

.

PRODUCER ZONES

San Patricio del Chañar and Añelo.

BODEGA DEL FIN DEL MUNDO

Honduras, 5663
1414 Buenos Aires
☎: +54 114 852 6660 - Fax: +54 114 852 6660
info@bdfm.com.ar
www.bodegadelfindelmundo.com

POSTALES DEL FIN DEL MUNDO
CABERNET MALBEC 2012 T
cabernet sauvignon, malbec Neuquén

90 Colour: deep cherry, garnet rim. Nose: balanced, ripe fruit, wild herbs. Palate: flavourful, fruity, balanced.

RESERVA DEL FIN DEL MUNDO
CABERNET SAUVIGNON 2008 T
cabernet sauvignon Neuquén

91 Colour: cherry, garnet rim. Nose: ripe fruit, wild herbs, spicy. Palate: balanced, good acidity, round tannins.

RESERVA DEL FIN DEL MUNDO MALBEC 2009 T
malbec Neuquén

93 Colour: cherry, garnet rim. Nose: ripe fruit, spicy, creamy oak, toasty, complex, dark chocolate, wild herbs. Palate: powerful, flavourful, toasty, round tannins.

MANOS NEGRAS

Viamonte 4620
5505 Chacras de Coria
☎: +54 261 562 8900
asejanovich@manosnegras.com.ar
www.manosnegras.com.ar

MANOS NEGRAS RED SOIL SELECT 2010 T
pinot noir Neuquén

93 Colour: bright cherry. Nose: sweet spices, creamy oak, expressive, fruit expression, red berry notes. Palate: flavourful, fruity, toasty, round tannins.

DESCRIPTION

This is the most southerly production zone in the country and, as such, it has the lowest temperatures as regards latitude considering the low temperatures in Salta due to its altitude. This is a zone subjected to climatic extremes, with very cold winters and the appropriate warmth for proper maturing at the time the grape most needs this.

With a climate which is somewhat less cold than its neighbour Neuquén, but with a higher average altitude, Río Negro concentrates the best vineyards of the torrontés riojano and semillón varieties in its region of the Alto Valle del Río Negro although the varieties of French origin merlot, chardonnay and sauvignon blanc must also be taken into account.

NUMBER OF HECTARES:2.636 **ALTITUDES:** 370 m.

PREDOMINANT VARIETIES:

White grapes: *torrontés riojano, semillón and sauvignon blanc.*
Red grapes: *merlot, pinot noir ad malbec.*

CLIMATOLOGY AND SOILS

The climate is purely continental, with a very low relative humidity due to the influence of the strong winds from Patagonia, which means that some vineyards must be protected with rows of trees. The very low rainfall, approximately 190 millimetres per year and the substantial amount of sunlight make Río Negro a zone to take into account for the production of wine with personality and high quality. The lack of water makes it necessary to use irrigation in the vineyards and, even more, if we take into account the soil which is mainly sandy and leads to the loss of water.

PRODUCER ZONES

Alto Valle del Río Negro.

None of the wines tasted achieve the minimum required scoring

DESCRIPTION

This is a world reference due to the peculiarity of its vineyards. Salta, located within the imposing Calchaquíes valleys, has the highest vineyards in the world, standing at 1,700 metres reaching even 3,000 metres above sea level.

Nº DE HECTÁREAS: 2.296 **ALTITUDES:** 1.700 m. - 3.000 m.

PREDOMINANT VARIETIES:

White grapes: *torrontés riojano and chardonnay.*
Red grapes: *malbec, cabernet sauvignon and tannat.*

CLIMATOLOGY AND SOILS

The emblem of Salta is its white wines made from the torrontés riojano variety, cultivated mainly in loam-sandy soils. In this zone the thermal difference entails a day and night-time contrast of more than 30 degrees so that the grape tends to dehydrate quickly, passing from vegetable to candied tastes, but maintaining a very high acidity, which leaves the mouth with very pleasant sweet and sour sensation. The sun in Salta is sharp and burning due to the greater intensity of the ultraviolet rays and as a result of the high altitude. This influence means that the wineries of Salta seek specific slopes which minimize this effect. Its wines, regardless of whether these are red, malbec or cabernet sauvignon mainly, or white, they easily exceed 16º alcoholic volume.

PRODUCER ZONES

The vineyards of Salta are distributed among the Departments of Cafayate, San Carlos, Cachi, Molinos and La Viña.

ALTA VISTA

Alzaga 3972
5505 Chacras De Coria
☎: +54 261 496 4684 - Fax: +54 261 496 4683
philippe.rolet@altavistawines.com
www.altavistawines.com

ALTA VISTA PREMIUM TORRONTÉS 2012 B
torrontés Salta

91 Colour: bright straw. Nose: fresh, fresh fruit, white flowers, grassy, citrus fruit. Palate: flavourful, fruity, good acidity, balanced.

BODEGA "EL TRANSITO"

Belgrano Nº 102
4427 Cafayate
☎: +38 684 223 85 - Fax: +38 684 223 85
abn@bodegaeltransito.com
www.bodegaeltransito.com

PIETRO MARINI MALBEC 2010 T
100% malbec Salta

90 Colour: cherry, garnet rim. Nose: balsamic herbs, scrubland, ripe fruit. Palate: balanced, round tannins. Personality.

BODEGA ROLLAND

Finca Yacochuya C.C. 1
4427 Cafayate
☎: +33 557 515 243 - Fax: +33 557 515 293
contact@rollandcollection.com
www.rollandcollection.com

SAN PEDRO DE YACOCHUYA 2009 T
85% malbec, 15% cabernet sauvignon — Salta

91 Colour: cherry, garnet rim. Nose: spicy, mineral, overripe fruit. Palate: powerful, flavourful, good acidity.

YACOCHUYA 2006 T
100% malbec — Salta

92 Colour: cherry, garnet rim. Nose: spicy, creamy oak, toasty, fruit liqueur notes, earthy notes. Palate: powerful, flavourful, toasty, round tannins.

BODEGA Y VIÑEDOS O FOURNIER

Calle Los Indios, s/n
5567 La Consulta San Carlos
☎: +54 262 245 1579 - Fax: +54 262 245 1588
info@ofournier.com
www.ofournier.com

URBAN UCO TORRONTÉS 2011 B
Salta

90 Colour: bright straw, greenish rim. Nose: medium intensity, fresh fruit, dried flowers. Palate: flavourful, fruity, easy to drink.

BODEGAS ETCHART

Ruta 40, Km.1047
4427 Cafayate
☎: +54 114 469 8000 - Fax: +54 114 469 8023
info@bodegasetchart.com
www.bodegasetchart.com

ETCHART 2010 TR
malbec — Salta

91 Colour: bright cherry. Nose: ripe fruit, sweet spices, creamy oak, balsamic herbs, mineral. Palate: flavourful, fruity, toasty, round tannins.

DOMINIO DEL PLATA WINERY

Cochabamba, 7801 Agrelo
5507 Luján de Cuyo
☎: +54 261 498 9200 - Fax: +54 261 498 9212
info@dominiodelplata.com.ar
www.dominiodelplata.com.ar

CRIOS TORRONTÉS 2012 B
torrontés — Salta

91 Colour: bright straw. Nose: varietal, elegant, white flowers, jasmine. Palate: fresh, fruity, fine bitter notes, good acidity.

FINCA EL ORIGEN

F. Gambarte 220 Barrio Arizu
5501 Godoy Cruz
☎: +54 261 424 5414
info@fincaelorigen.com
www.fincaelorigen.com

FINCA EL ORIGEN CHARDONNAY 2012 B
100% chardonnay — Salta

91 Colour: bright straw. Nose: fresh, fresh fruit, white flowers, expressive. Palate: flavourful, fruity, good acidity, balanced.

FINCA EL ORIGEN TORRONTÉS 2012 B
torrontés — Salta

90 Colour: bright straw. Nose: fresh, white flowers, varietal. Palate: flavourful, fruity, good acidity, balanced.

FINCA EL ORIGEN VIOGNIER 2012 B
100% viognier — Salta

92 Colour: bright straw. Nose: floral, fresh fruit, medium intensity, expressive. Palate: fruity, balanced, fine bitter notes, good acidity.

GAUCHEZCO VIÑEDOS Y BODEGA

Carril Barrancas s/n
5517 Barrancas, Maipú
☎: +54 926 153 327 44
info@gauchezco.com
www.gauchezco.com

GAUCHEZCO CLÁSICO TORRONTÉS 2011 B
100% torrontés — Salta

91 Colour: bright straw. Nose: white flowers, jasmine, fresh fruit. Palate: flavourful, fruity, fresh.

MICHEL TORINO ESTATE

Arenales 460
1638 Vicente López
☎: +54 115 198 9018 - Fax: +54 115 198 8000
jbrea@micheltorino.com.ar
www.elesteco.com.ar

ALTA VISTA PREMIUM 2011 T
100% malbec Salta

91 Colour: cherry, garnet rim. Nose: medium intensity, varietal, wild herbs. Palate: good acidity, fine bitter notes, balanced.

ALTIMVS 2010 T
54% malbec, 25% cabernet sauvignon, 11% cabernet franc, 10% tannat Salta

92 Colour: cherry, garnet rim. Nose: expressive, red berry notes, ripe fruit, spicy, cocoa bean. Palate: flavourful, ripe fruit, good acidity.

DON DAVID FINCA LA URQUIZA
CABERNET SAUVIGNON 2011 T
100% malbec Salta

91 Colour: deep cherry. Nose: powerfull, ripe fruit, earthy notes, toasty. Palate: powerful, concentrated, fine bitter notes, good acidity.

DON DAVID MALBEC 2011 TR
100% malbec Salta

92 Colour: deep cherry. Nose: expressive, varietal, neat, ripe fruit, toasty, fruit expression. Palate: flavourful, fruity, fine bitter notes, good acidity.

TERRAZAS DE LOS ANDES/CHEVAL DES ANDES/BODEGAS CHANDON

Thames y Cochabamba, Perdriel
Luján de Cuyo
☎: +54 261 488 0058 - Fax: +54 261 488 0614
info@terrazasdelosandes.com
www.terrazasdelosandes.com

TERRAZAS DE LOS ANDES 2012 B
torrontés Salta

90 Colour: bright straw. Nose: fresh, white flowers, honeyed notes. Palate: flavourful, fruity, good acidity, balanced.

DESCRIPTION

San Juan is located to the north of the province of Mendoza and also has a border to the west with the Andes mountain range. It is the province with the second highest production in Argentina, behind Mendoza, with more than 21% of Argentinean vineyards and with an altitude which goes from 600 metres to 1,350 above sea level.

NUMBER OF HECTARES:49.492 **ALTITUDES:** 600 m. – 1.350 m.

PREDOMINANT VARIETIES: San Juan was historically known for the production of rosé and white wines. Currently, the predominant variety in this region is the red variety as a consequence of a process of reconversion of the vineyards which began in the nineties. Little by little the syrah variety began to gain predominance in the zone. The most representative varieties in San Juan are syrah, bonarda, cabernet sauvignon and malbec red grapes and muscat of Alexandria, pedro ximénez and torrontés sanjuanino white grapes.

CLIMATOLOGY AND SOILS

It has a warmer climate than its neighbour to the south, but with a high thermal integral owing to the influence of the Andes. It is an area where there is hardly any rainfall, its average annual rainfall is 10 millimetres as compared with the 200 millimetre average in the province of Mendoza.

ZONAS PRODUCTORAS

Calingasta (1,165 metres above sea level), Ullum and the valley of Tullom are the most outstanding provinces in the zone as regards quality.

FINCA DEL ENLACE S.A.

Dardo Rocha, 986
1640 San Isidro
☎: +54 115 368 7300 - Fax: +54 115 368 7340
www.tracia.com.ar

TRACIA ALADOS 2010 T
100% malbec San Juan

90 Colour: cherry, garnet rim. Nose: ripe fruit, spicy, creamy oak, toasty, mineral. Palate: powerful, flavourful, toasty, round tannins.

TRACIA HONORES 2010 T
100% malbec San Juan

90 Colour: black cherry. Nose: powerfull, ripe fruit, spicy, toasty. Palate: flavourful, good acidity.

FINCA LAS MORAS

Rawson, s/n
5439 San Martín
☎: +54 261 520 7214 - Fax: +54 261 520 7221
pbergada@fincalasmoras.com.ar
www.fincalasmoras.com

LAS MORAS BLACK LABEL BONARDA 2011 T
bonarda Valle de Tulum

90 Colour: very deep cherry, garnet rim. Nose: powerfull, dark chocolate, ripe fruit, violets. Palate: flavourful, fruity, good acidity.

LAS MORAS BLACK LABEL CABERNET CABERNET 2011 T
50% cabernet sauvignon, 50% cabernet franc San Juan

90 Colour: bright cherry. Nose: creamy oak, cocoa bean. Palate: fleshy, flavourful, spicy, round tannins.

LAS MORAS BLACK LABEL MALBEC 2011 T
100% malbec Valle de Tulum

91 Colour: bright cherry, garnet rim. Nose: sweet spices, cocoa bean, ripe fruit, candied fruit. Palate: balanced, fine bitter notes.

LAS MORAS BLACK LABEL SHIRAZ 2011 T
syrah San Juan

90 Colour: cherry, garnet rim. Nose: ripe fruit, creamy oak, cocoa bean, candied fruit. Palate: good structure, flavourful, round tannins.

LAS MORAS CHADONNAY 2012 B
chardonnay San Juan

91 Color bright straw. Aroma fresh, fresh fruit, white flowers, expressive. Taste flavourful, fruity, good acidity, balanced.

LAS MORAS GRAN SHIRAZ 3 VALLES 2009 T
syrah Valle de Tulum

90 Colour: black cherry. Nose: candied fruit, fruit preserve, creamy oak, sweet spices. Palate: good acidity, fine bitter notes, round.

LAS MORAS RESERVE SHIRAZ 2011 T
syrah San Juan

91 Colour: bright cherry. Nose: sweet spices, creamy oak, varietal, red berry notes. Palate: flavourful, fruity, toasty, round tannins.

MARIANNE 2012 T
100% malbec Valle de Tulum

91 Colour: cherry, purple rim. Nose: fresh fruit, red berry notes, floral, cocoa bean, spicy. Palate: flavourful, fruity, good acidity, round tannins.

MORA NEGRA 2010 T
malbec, bonarda San Juan

90 Colour: bright cherry. Nose: ripe fruit, sweet spices, creamy oak, roasted coffee. Palate: flavourful, fruity, toasty, round tannins.

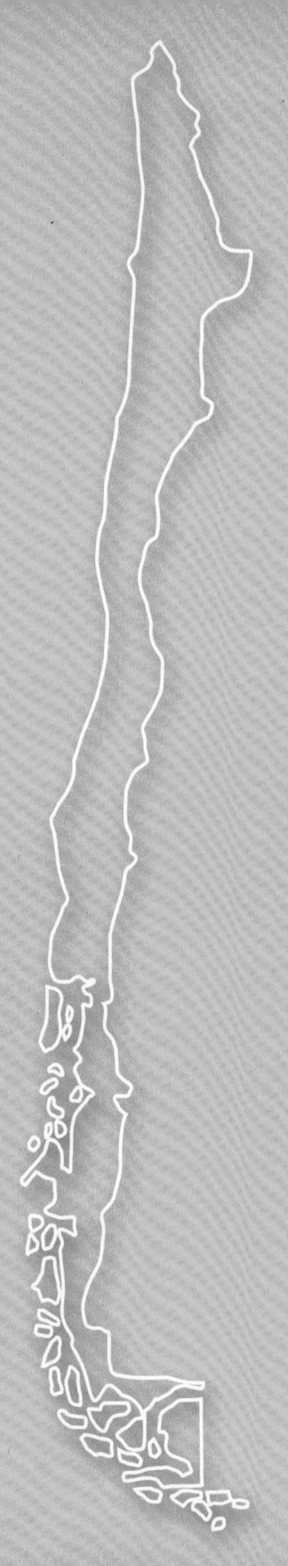

PEÑÍN GUIDE

TOP WINES FROM

CHILE

DATA ON CHILE:

POPULATION: 16.736.740 inhabitants
SURFACE AREA: 756.646 square kilometres.
SURFACE AREA OF VINEYARDS: 205.000 hectares
WINERIES: 339
PREDOMINANT VARIETIES
RED GRAPES: *Cabernet sauvignon*, *merlot*, *carmenère*, *syrah*, *pinot noir*.
WHITE GRAPES: *Sauvignon blanc*, *chardonnay*, *viognier*, *riesling*
HARVESTS: The seasons for harvesting the grapes are the inverse to the northern hemisphere. The vine blooms in December and the harvest begins at the end of February and continues until May. In Chile the harvest depends on the mesoclimate of the cold Antarctic Humboldt and the microclimates of each valley due to the orographic constitution of the valleys which flow towards the sea and the different altitudes of the orography of the Andes.
CLIMATES: Except for the valleys located in the interior and those further north which are the warmest, the climate could be defined as Benign Mediterranean, with average rainfall of approximately between 100 litres in the north and east and 450 to the west. Below Maule, rainfall shoots up to more than 1,000 litres annually.
PRODUCTION 2012: 12,5 million hectolitres
WINERY: 339
ALTITUDE: The differences oscillate between 470 metres in the vineyards near the coast up to the possibility that some of these reach the foothills and the higher properties at 1,500 metres up in the Andes.

INTRODUCTION

Chile forms part of the countries of the New World which, together with Australia as precursors of this movement, have found a niche in the world counterattacking the wines from European countries. This has been achieved with wines made from French grapes and with styles proximate to the fruity, more achievable tastes demanded by the consumer. Thanks to the geographic location of Chile, located between the sea and the Andes mountain range, the vineyards are protected from pathological diseases and mildew is extremely rare. It has the only vineyard in a large estate not devastated by phylloxera , therefore, it is root stock which has not been grafted, which makes its vines the oldest in the world. This fact, together with its sunny, dry weather which ensures excellent maturing of the grape, and it facilitates an ecological footprint. The use of modern technology, the new irrigation systems which offset the lack of rain and a control more adapted to the period of ageing times in the barrel, are part of the reasons for the success of these wines which are sold in more than 90 countries in the five continents. Explorations of new cultivation areas near the ocean breezes in the west or higher up in the Andes to the east are new wine growing trends for the future which distance themselves from the flatter hotter zones of the Central Valley, where most of the Chilean wineries are located. The new tendencies are focussed on a greater diversity of varieties such as pinot noir and syrah together with growing cultivation of carmenère and sauvignon blanc. Cabernet sauvignon and chardonnay are more developed vines in Chile and age and improve thanks to a new awareness of less yield and the new biodynamic criteria which are beginning to flourish among the young oenologists.

WINE GROWING ZONES MAP

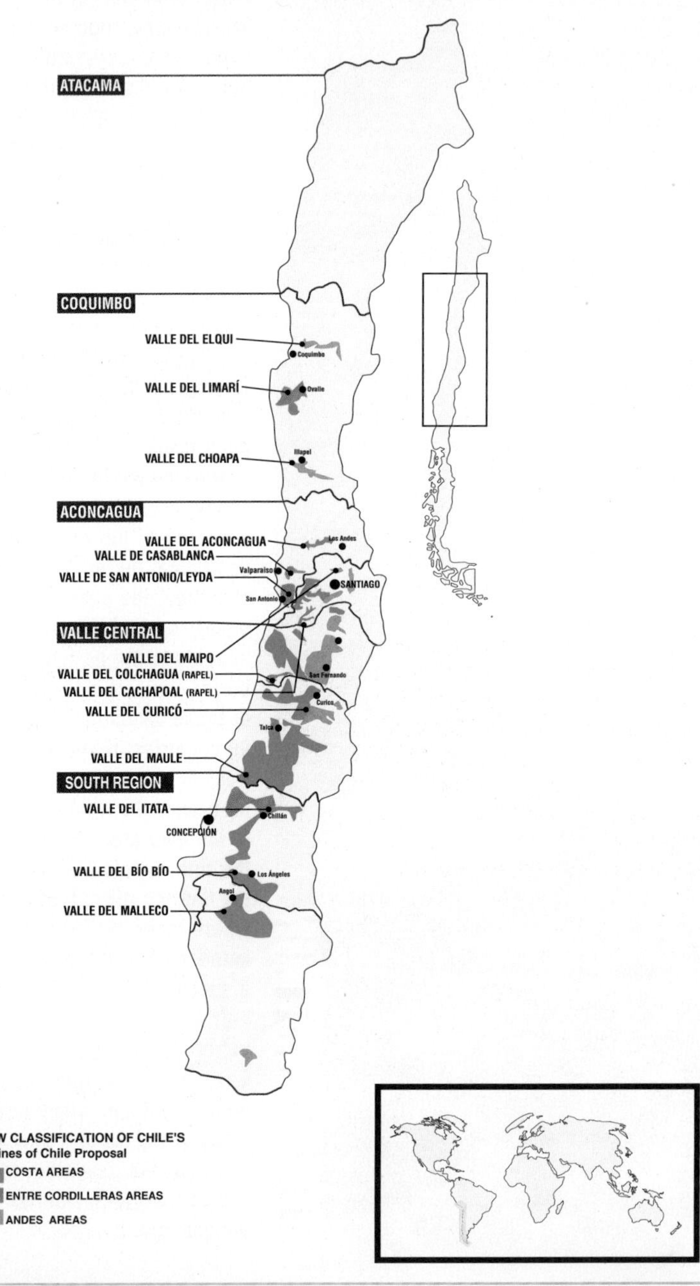
ATACAMA
COQUIMBO
VALLE DEL ELQUI
Coquimbo
VALLE DEL LIMARÍ
Ovalle
VALLE DEL CHOAPA
Illapel
ACONCAGUA
VALLE DEL ACONCAGUA
Los Andes
VALLE DE CASABLANCA
Valparaíso
VALLE DE SAN ANTONIO/LEYDA
San Antonio
SANTIAGO
VALLE CENTRAL
VALLE DEL MAIPO
VALLE DEL COLCHAGUA (RAPEL)
VALLE DEL CACHAPOAL (RAPEL)
San Fernando
VALLE DEL CURICÓ
Curicó
Talca
VALLE DEL MAULE
SOUTH REGION
VALLE DEL ITATA
Chillán
CONCEPCIÓN
VALLE DEL BÍO BÍO
Los Ángeles
Angol
VALLE DEL MALLECO
NEW CLASSIFICATION OF CHILE'S
* Wines of Chile Proposal
COSTA AREAS
ENTRE CORDILLERAS AREAS
ANDES AREAS

THE KEYS TO THE YEAR

Chile continues to be unstoppable on its way to create a definitive, stable oenological identity. Since the boom of Chilean wine, which began in the nineties, with the proliferation of wineries in Chilean valleys, the producers have endeavoured to construct the image of Chilean wine based on work. These endeavours are producing results. The reduction of domestic consumption 13.92 litres per capita per year, according to data of the International Organization of Vine and Wine (OIV) and the globalization of the wine has led to the Chilean producers throwing themselves into exportation as a fundamental part of commercial business. This export vocation is boosting the knowledge of wine in third countries, such as the United Kingdom, the United States, Brazil and Japan, and is attracting the interest of the more curious consumers. It has only 120,000 hectares of vineyards, as compared to the 228,000 Argentinean, the 28,000 Mexican or the astounding 1,077,000 Spanish hectares, but this does not entail a limit to the qualitative expansion of its wines. In countries like Spain the identity of the wines is substantially marked by the production zone, that is to say, soils and climates, together with the varieties as regards their relationship with the environment, in Chile there is a more marked oenological identification due to the sub region where they are located and to the proximity or not of the ocean, than due to the variety origin.

As regards red grapes, *carmenère* demonstrates its full potential in Chilean soil. This variety of French origin has found a place to live comfortably in Chile where it can express unique nuances focussed on very special balsamic features and refreshing acidity. The Chilean *pinot noir* is also outstanding. This is known for its expressivity in Burgundy, and has managed to find good soil for cultivation in Chile, especially in the zones nearer to the sea, such as Casablanca and San Antonio, where the fresh ocean winds help to maintain the hints of flowers and fresh fruit which appear in the wine.

It should be pointed out that the Chilean wine producers achieve an excellent balance with the wood. The wines tasted do not suffer from excessive use of the barrel, in fact, the contrary is true, the wood is present in the wine as a vehicle to boost the fruit nuances of the variety together with the nuances of the toasted barrel. In addition, the fineness of the tannins in many

THE HUMBOLDT CURRENT

Together with the influence of the Andes, this is one of the phenomenon with most repercussions in Chilean vineyards. The current receives its name from Alexander von Humboldt, a XIX century German naturalist and explorer. The origin of this current comes from one which is even bigger, the Antarctic Circumpolar Current, a very cold marine current which flows from west to east around the Antarctic and connects with the Atlantic, Pacific and Indian Oceans. Most of the Circumpolar Current goes round the globe without touching any continent except for a small part which strikes the Chilean coast, creating the Humboldt Current at the point of impact, Chiloé, in a northerly direction, and generating another southerly current, the Cape Horn Current.

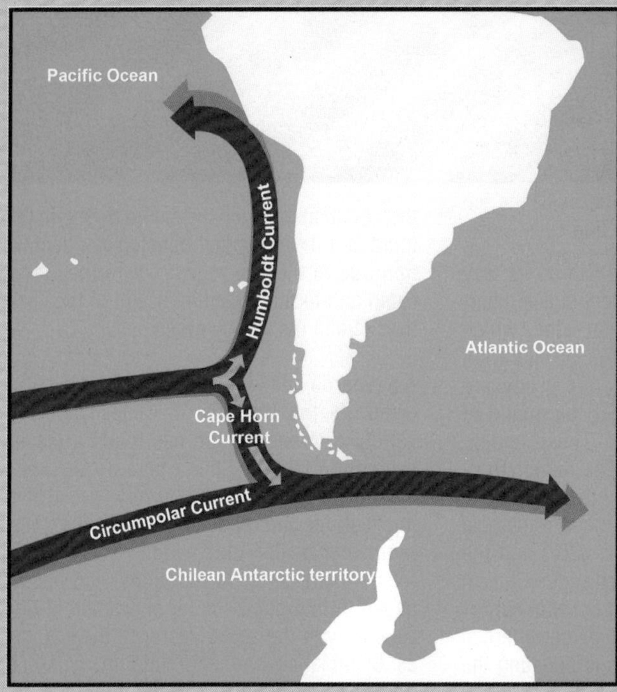

The Humboldt Current produces an ascent of the deep waters of the Antarctic making the climate, which should be subtropical due to its latitude, unusually arid and cold. This phenomenon leads to the appearance of coastal fog and the alteration of the subtropical rainfall system, while it acclimatizes and standardizes the climactic characteristics of many of the Chilean wine producing valleys. Humboldt is also a phenomenon which contributes rich fishing grounds to Chile due to dragging nutrients from the bottom of the ocean to the surface, which boosts marine productivity.

As regards cycles, every 2-7 years, there is a change of current, which entails the passage from the cold waters of the Humboldt Current to much warmer currents. This phenomenon is known as the Corriente del Niño and acts negatively on Chilean vineyards, triggering overriPeñíng of the grapes if measures are not taken quickly enough.

of their wines is outstanding. The wide difference of temperatures between daytime and night-time favours the rounding of very pleasant, fine tannins.

While the acidity is maintained, this makes even those wines which have moderate or high levels of alcohol fresh and easy to consume, with no candied or overripe hints. It is interesting to see the tastes of certain wine producers who offer very sweet tannins, which together with ripe fruit, leave a very pleasant sensation in the mouth.

We also highlight the good examples based on syrah which appear in this new edition of the Peñín Guide, with features marked by substantial fruit expression, somewhat sweetish, and with a structure, which, together with the balance with the barrel and the fine even sweet tannin leave a long, rounded and very pleasant taste for the consumer.

As regards white wines, the *sauvignon blanc* and *chardonnay* show us two very different styles. El de la The freshness and evocations of green herbs in the former. Evocations typical of the pyrazine in the variety. Curiously endeavours are being made to eliminate this in other parts of the world, however, in Chile this contributes substantial singularity in a natural fashion which distinguishes the Chilean origin. The sensorial nuances go from hints of green asparagus to tomato leaf, passing through green grass. Those located in the Valle de Casablanca must be especially taken into account, which also have very marked mineralization. On the other hand, there are wines produced from chardonnay, where the producers seek to boost their more mature features.

HISTORY

Chile as a wine growing country came about mainly because of the arrival of European travellers in search of new opportunities in vineyards

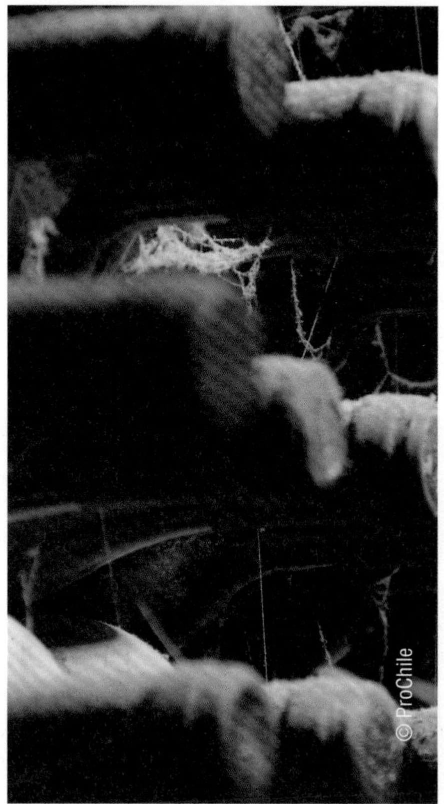
© ProChile

free from phylloxera which devastated France in the XIX century. However, before the French colonization imported new customs, a new architecture and new vines to America, the Spanish missionaries (Fray Francisco de Carabantes, 1548) in the XVI century had already planted the grape of the country which was similar to the mission grape of California. The majority *Alejandria muscatel* grape was replaced by new strains of Bordeaux grapes: *cabernet sauvignon, malbec, carmenère, chardonnay, semillon, riesling*, etc, which became Chilean by adoption, used by the pioneer wineries such as Cousiño Macul, Concha y Toro, Undurraga, Errázuriz, La Rosa, Santa Rita, Carmen and San Pedro as from 1870. To date, these firms continue to be the main actors with their oldest wines and vines. The first wineries which cultivated an average of 17,000 hectares, are concentrated in the perimeter near the in Maipo, Rapel and Aconcagua. Until Chilean wine blossomed, almost all the XX century was marked by the lack of knowledge of the wine growers as regards the imported grapes and their own climate, by an excess production of low quality wine generated by the demand of the war crises in Europe, and the restrictions and redistribution of land imposed by the political regimes of Allende and Pinochet. The exploitation of the vineyards was halved and consumption dropped drastically for some years.

more specific map of sub-regions or delimited soil characteristics given the enormous differences between climates and soils in the same zone. Formulated in 1994, the Law on the Denomination of Origin of Chilean wines gave rise to new modern formulas more adapted to the climatic changes of the valleys by the producers. These claim that there are specifications of the valleys not only north south, but the transversal aspect of the same valley is also taken into account and these entail differences of up to 5°C due to winds, fog and the specifications of each zone.

© ProChile

eighties in the XX century to become a strong quality wine market with the exportation of table wines to the United States. The knowledge of the new oenology and wine growing methods would contribute privileged information, such as the rediscovery of the carmenère grape in 1994, which grew among vines mixed and confused by the Chileans with the clone of merlot.

WINE GROWING ZONES

Chile has based its current promotion of geographical denominations in the valleys from east to west. It is difficult to establish a achieve fresher wines in sunnier climates or more rounded and mature wines in areas with greater ventilation, taking into account the maturing process required by each vine. In Chile the minimum alcohol level is 11.5 degrees.

The differences between valleys is based on two aspects:

1.-The north south latitude: the zones nearer to the equator receive the rays of sunlight with more effect than in the south and the temperatures are higher. This is not so in the south where rainfall is more intense.

2.- From east to west: the vines which are nearer to the sea and those planted at the foot of the Andes will receive the inflow of fresher breezes in the afternoon than those which are located between hills. The Humboldt Current will also serve as a thermometer of the differences between valleys.

WORKING ON NEW ZONING OF CHILEAN WINE

Work is currently being done in order to endeavour to implement a supplementary zoning system which might help the consumer to understand the influences on Chilean wine. This is logical and natural in a country which is seeking to simplify the consumption of wine as far as possible with no distortions, of course, but, in an understandable way, explaining the origin of the wines through the three important influences on its vineyards: the Andes mountain range, the coast and the part in between which is termed the "area between mountain ranges". This supplementary system makes it possible to differentiate each production zone as, in addition to the classical Chilean wine labelling system, there will be a system of symbols (**Costa Area / Entre cordilleras Area / the Andes Area**) included in the final labelling of Chilean wines. The reader can find this zoning project included in the map of Chilean producer zones, page 114.

At Peñín Guide we understand that this new system will speed up the understanding and the positioning of Chilean wine throughout the world. Moreover, at tasting level, there are notable differences between wines from the coast with the influence of the ocean and those located between mountain ranges due to the clash of freshness and maturity. Perhaps we lack more examples of the "Andes" zone, with regard to projects which seek differentiation at the limit of altitude.

Before the proposal of a subdivision, the way to understand the geo climate of Chile was by taking into account the latitude. As we move farther south (the fresher area), the climate

approaches the limits for cultivating vines, therefore, it becomes more interesting for those who are seeking quality red and white wine growing. For this reason, the southern valleys: Maule, Itata and Biobio are valleys with huge potential for the production of fresh, fruity and balsamic wines.

UNDERSTANDING LABELLING

In order to understand the labels of Chilean wines of any origin, it is sufficient to say that these are divided into wines with Denomination of Origin, wines with no Denomination of Origin and Table Wines made from dessert grapes. The wines with Denomination of Origin may include the name of the variety if this is not less than 75%, as well as the year of the harvest if it has a maximum proportion of wine harvested that year.

According to the Chilean Law on Agriculture as regards labelling, five grand, generic regions have been classified: Atacama, Coquimbo, Aconcagua, Valle Central and Región Vitícola del Sur.

The minor zones or sub-regions which appear on the label of the wine will appear on condition that at least 75% of the grape comes from the place stated. The complexity of the geographical classification system of wines in Chile is evident in the complex world of labels. In the event that a wine with denomination of origin is blended and is mostly one variety, it is possible to state up to three regions or up to three sub-regions in decreasing order of importance on condition that the amount of each one involved is not less than 15%. This procedure which is difficult to commercialize was replaced by new marketing tools which highlight a Generic Valley and the variety of grape.

The legislative description of the Chilean wine categories includes five generic regions which take in areas with the names of the valleys and an infinite list of sub-regions classified around small production communes which are added to as new wine growing projects are consolidated.

REGIÓN DE ATACAMA (Arid)
-Valle de Copiapó
-Valle del Huasco

REGIÓN DE COQUIMBO (Warm)
-Valle del Elqui. This includes the areas of Vicuña and Paiguano
-Valle del Limarí. This includes the areas of Ovalle, Monte Patria, Punitaqui and Río Hurtado.
-Valle del Choapa. This includes the areas of Salamanca and Illapel.

REGIÓN DE ACONCAGUA (Maritime warm)
-Valle del Aconcagua. This takes in the provinces of San Felipe de Aconcagua and the Andes. The Andes includes the area of Panquehue.
-Valle de Casablanca. In the commune with the same name.
-Valle de San Antonio. In the province of the same name where the Valle de Leyda is located and which is included in the area of San Juan.

VALLE CENTRAL (Moderate warm)
This extends from the province of Cahacabuco in the Metropolitan Administrative region to the provinces of Cauquenes and Linares. The following sub-regions are classified in this zone:

-Valle del Maipo. This takes in all the provinces of the Metropolitan Region. The same region includes nine sub-zones.
-Valle del Rapel. In the provinces of Cachapoal, Colchagua and Cardenal Caro. This zone includes two of the most commercial brands: Valle de Cachapoal in the regions with the same name (with four more sub-regions) and Valle de Colchagua in the province of Colchagua and Cardenal Caro (with eight sub-zones).
-Valle de Curicó. In the province of Curicó and the commune of Río Claro in the province of Talca in the VII Administrative Region. This zone is divided into: Valle del Teno and Valle del Lontué and the commune of Río Claro.
-Valle del Maule. Comprende la provincia de Talca. En este VallThis includes the province of Talca. Located in this Valley are the zones of Valle del Claro and Valle del Loncomilla and Valle del Tutuvén.

REGIÓN DEL SUR (Fresh warm)
This extends from the province of Nuble in the VIII Administrative Region to where the climate and soil conditions enable vines to develop.
-Valle del Itata. This includes the communes of the province of Ñuble and the commune of Florida in the province of Concepción in the VIII Administrative Region. In turn, it includes four regions.
-Valle del Bío Bío. This takes in the communes of Yumbel, Nacimiento, Mulchén, Negrete and Laja in the provinces of Bío Bío.
-Valle del Malleco. This includes the communes of Angol, Collipulli, Ercilla, Los Sauces, Lumaco, Purén, Renaico, Traiguén and Victoria in the province of Malleco.

GENERAL CHARACTERISTICS OF THE WINES

TYPOLOGIES OF RED WINES

This is the most significant Chilean wine and accounts for 70% of the bottled wines. Most of the bottles blend grapes from Maule and Colchagua. From the common production of red grapes with intense colour, maturity and alcohol level, there has been a change to the generation of single variety red wines. These are better acclimatized, more balanced, with

© ProChile

well integrated wood and a better study of each maturing cycle of the grape. It is possible to distinguish a number of types by variety, as well as the terroir which is most adequate for each one of these.

WINES FROM CABERNET SAUVIGNON GRAPES. This is the most abundant grape (37%) and the almost exclusive formula in almost all the wines, with ageing or as part of a blend. The excellent wines are dark in colour with the character of the variety and only slight hints of preserve with aromas of black fruits, a pleasant menthol feature and dry earth. The freshest cabernets are more southern or planted towards the Andes, while the most full bodied and mature are from the east where the Valle de Colchagua dominates.

WINES WITH CARMENÈRE. This has become positioned as an icon for differentiating between so many Bordeaux grapes although only 9% of wines have this grape. The vineyards with this vine can boast of being old vines. The best wines come from sunny zones with moderate temperatures, such as in the VALLE CENTRAL or beside the coast, such as Peumo, Apalta and Maipú, where better levels of acidity are achieved. These usually taste of mature black fruits, with sweet aromas of toasted spices and smoother tannins than those of cabernet sauvignon.

WINES WITH MERLOT. This s the second most planted grape (9% of the red wines) although at first it was confused with carmenère, which was called Chilean merlot in order to distinguish it. It maintains the original XIX century rootstock. The plantation of new original clones gives better results in fresher and wetter terrain such as San Antonio or Bío Bío. The best versions offer the taste of sweet black fruits and black chocolate.

WINES WITH SYRAH. One of the varieties which has grown most in Chile owing to the advantages of the continental climate of contrasts and the choice of adequate poor granite soil in marginal estates. More robust, spiced syrah can be found, such as the syrah of Colchagua, Aconcagua and Cachapoal, or more elegant and complex with hints of flesh, herbs, pepper and flowers, fruit from fresher latitudes such as in Casablanca and San Antonio.

WINES WITH PINOT NOIR. This is the new promise from Chile once over-riPeñíng and the extra time in barrels can be controlled. The most outstanding examples come from the southeast such as those from Leyda, where the sea breezes refresh the vines.

TYPOLOGIES OF WHITE WINES

A minority of these wines is produced (29%), and most originate in Valparaíso, Colchagua and Maule. The evolution of the quality of the white wines is due to the research done in fresher zones or those near the sea and the new techniques for controlling acidity in the wineries. Grapes such as viognier, semillón, riesling, gewürztraminer and chenin blanc have joined the range of chardonnay and sauvignon blanc, all of which are predominantly fruity and have variety with hardly any time spent in the barrel.

WINES WITH CHARDONNAY. These are the most abundant white wines in Chile, with a style tending towards alcohol, maturity. Almost all pass through fermentation in the barrel but without the value of the terroir. The new models tend to reduce the alcoholic weight and to put forward more lightness and more integrated spicy aromas, such as those achieved in San Antonio and in the coastal zone of Casablanca. The more acidic chardonnays come from Bío Bío and Malleco they are located in the south, therefore, in colder latitudes.

WINES WITH SAUVIGNON BLANC. This has replaced chardonnay as the most elegant white grape in Chile and one of the best three in the world. It occupies 11% of the vineyards. The maritime climate with a certain freshness helps the vine to mature slowly without losing freshness. San Antonio has the most complex types, but they may also come from Aconcagua, Colchagua, Limarí and Bío Bío.

EXPORTATION

In a year in which the majority of wine producing countries have seen their grape harvests reduced and, consequently, the amount of wine, Chile was the country which increased its production most as compared to 2011. Its balance amounts to 12.5 million hectolitres, 20% more than the previous year, reaching 5th place in the wine producing countries, above Argentina and Australia. According to data provided by Wines of Chile, although there was an increase in comparison with the previous year, they maintained a more moderate increase.

Chile exported a total of 7.4 million hectolitres (13% more than in 2011) for a value amounting to $1,700,000,000 but at a lower average price, $2.39 per litre, 6% less.

© ProChile

By products, the most exported product was bottled Chilean wine which amounted to 4.3 million hectolitres (increased by 0.18%) with a value amounting to $1,420,000,000. Nevertheless, it was bulk wine which had the most important growth in 2012, achieving an increase in the total volume exported by 44%, reaching 2.7 million hectolitres and invoicing approximately $292,000,000 (47% more than in the previous financial year). The main countries importing Chilean wine in 2012 were the United Kingdom, the United States, Brazil, Japan, Holland, China, Canada, Russia, Ireland and Denmark.

Chile stood in the 5th position of wine producing countries in 2012, according to the International Organization of Vine and Wine (OIV), despite the fact that it currently stands in the 9th world position, with 205,000 hectares, the same as Rumania as regards surface area of vineyards and the 17th in consumption, with a total in 2012 of 2.7 million hectolitres (the figures fell 10% as compared to 2011).

DESCRIPTION

This is the region which coincides with the administrative region of Valparaíso where the highest peak in the southern hemisphere is located, the Aconcagua, which is 6,962 metres high. To the north it borders with the Region of Coquimbo, to the south with the Valle Central, to the east with the Andes and to the west with the Pacific Ocean. The capital is Valparaíso. The wines of this warm region of the valley are characterized by being mature, with low acidity and with a substantial amount of firm tannins, such as the most common cabernet sauvignon. Located here are the Córpora Group and the Errázuriz Winery which has opted for more modern, less alcoholic, blended wines, with syrah (which is booming here) and petit verdot, as well as applying the methods proximate to biodynamics.

NUMBER OF HECTARES: 8.523

ALTITUDES: Altitudes which reach 900 metres in the case of the more eastern wines, and those of the western coastal mountain chain.

PREDOMINANT VARIETIES: As regards white wines, chardonnay predominates and, to a lesser extent, *sauvignon blanc. Among the red grapes are syrah, cabernet sauvignon, carmenère and pinot noir.*

CLIMATOLOGY AND SOILS

Semi-desert climate with heat which leads to more mature wines which can become more elegant thanks to the inflow of the winds from the Andes. These differences regarding the proximity of the sea and the mountain sides lead to the lengthening or shortening of the harvests. Sand and rock soils near the hills and the River Aconcagua. Limestone soil in the valley.

PRODUCER ZONES

1-Valle del Aconcagua. 1.007 hectares

2-Valle de Casablanca. 5.710 hectares. This is located in the territories of Santiago and Valparaíso. It does not have uniform soils. In the middle of the coastal mountain chain, Casablanca receives the fresh breezes of the Humboldt Current. This phenomenon gives rise to mists due to the sea breeze striking the warm soil, which reduces the time of exposure to the sun together with more humidity, which leads to real headaches regarding cryptogamic diseases (see page 110). In San Antonio and Casablanca there is a greater contrast between the day and night owing to the lower altitude as compared to the zones located more in the interior. A more mature character can be perceived in wines of the Alto Casablanca unlike the more acid wines in Bajo Casablanca. The risk of freezing is lower on the slopes but it continues to be a complicated zone for planting long cycle grapes. It has been confirmed as an interesting zone for riesling, chardonnay and sauvignon blanc white wines. Sauvignon blanc offers more herbal, vegetable nuances than in other zones. Syrah has become an aromatic model, even more so in the deep soils with the granite minerals of the hills.

3-Valle de San Antonio. 1.806 hectares, To the south of the Valle de Casablanca, rather than a valley as it is called in Law, it is an area dominated by basins which take in the slopes of the west of the Sierra de la Costa, therefore, it is the zone nearest to the sea. The western strip of the Valle del Maipo can also be taken into consideration although it is inserted into the Denomination of Origin of Aconcagua. Its soils with gravel and granite contribute mineral tastes to the wines. The most successful are the short cycle wines which come from the cold areas such as chardonnay, pinot noir and of course, sauvignon blanc, due to their quality clones, the microclimate and the date of the harvest. Their history began in 2001 thanks to pioneer wineries such as Viña Leyda or Casa Marín. This includes the zones of Leyda, Rosario and Lo Abarca. The first is the most extensive, where new quality investments are concentrated due to the fact that it has the freshest climate in the wine growing zones of Chile.

BODEGA VILLARD

La Concepción 165, of. 507
Providencia (Santiago)
☎: +56 223 577 15
info@villard.cl
www.villard.cl

VILLARD EL NOBLE 2010 B
sauvignon blanc — Valle de San Casablanca

93 Colour: golden. Nose: powerfull, floral, honeyed notes, candied fruit, fragrant herbs. Palate: flavourful, sweet, fresh, fruity.

VILLARD GRAND VIN 2010 T
pinot noir — Valle de San Casablanca

91 Colour: bright cherry. Nose: ripe fruit, red berry notes, spicy, scrubland. Palate: flavourful, fruity.

VILLARD TANAGRA 2010 T
syrah — Valle de San Casablanca

90 Colour: bright cherry. Nose: ripe fruit, sweet spices, creamy oak. Palate: flavourful, fruity, toasty, round tannins.

CASA MARÍN

Lo Abarca, s/n
Cartagena (V Región)
☎: +56 223 342 986 - Fax:+562 334 9723
marketing@casamarin.cl
www.casamarin.cl

CASA MARÍN PINOT NOIR 2009 T
pinot noir — Valle de San Antonio

90 Colour: bright cherry. Nose: ripe fruit, sweet spices, creamy oak. Palate: flavourful, fruity, toasty, round tannins.

CASA MARÍN SAUVIGNON BLANC 2011 B
sauvignon blanc — Valle de San Antonio

90 Colour: bright straw. Nose: fresh, fresh fruit, white flowers, expressive, creamy oak. Palate: flavourful, fruity, good acidity, balanced.

GARCÍA + SCHWADERER CO.

Merced 838 A Of. 111
(Santiago)
☎: +56 228 954 140
bravado@bravadowines.com
www.garciaschwaderer.cl

MARINA GARCIA SCHWADERER 2012 B
100% sauvignon blanc — Valle de San Casablanca

90 Colour: bright straw. Nose: medium intensity, balsamic herbs, fresh fruit, grassy. Palate: flavourful, fruity, balanced, good acidity.

LOMA LARGA

Fundo Loma Larga
Casablanca (Valparaíso)
☎: +56 226 572 217 - Fax:+562 26 572 223
info@lomalarga.com
www.lomalarga.com

LOMA DEL VALLE SYRAH 2010 T
syrah — Valle de San Casablanca

90 Colour: very deep cherry. Nose: spicy, ripe fruit, red berry notes. Palate: good acidity, ripe fruit.

LOMA LARGA SAUVIGNON BLANC 2012 B
sauvignon blanc — Valle de San Casablanca

91 Colour: bright straw. Nose: fresh, fresh fruit, white flowers, varietal. Palate: flavourful, fruity, good acidity, balanced.

LOMAS DEL VALLE PINOT NOIR 2012 T
pinot noir — Valle de San Casablanca

92 Colour: deep cherry. Nose: mineral, fruit expression, red berry notes. Palate: balsamic, long, mineral, good acidity.

VIÑA CASABLANCA

Til Til 2228
7142250 (Santiago)
☎: +56 224 503 176 - Fax:+56 224 503 312
pmoreno@santacarolina.cl
www.casablancawinery.com

NIMBUS PINOT NOIR 2010 T
pinot noir — Valle de San Casablanca

90 Colour: bright cherry. Nose: ripe fruit, sweet spices, creamy oak, balsamic herbs, fragrant herbs. Palate: flavourful, fruity, toasty, round tannins, long.

VIÑA CONCHA Y TORO

Av. Nueva Tajamar 481, Torre Norte, Piso 15
7550099 Las Condes (Santiago)
☎: +56 247 650 00
maria.vallejo@conchaytoro.cl
www.conchaytoro.com

AMELIA CHARDONNAY 2011 B
100% chardonnay — Valle de San Casablanca

92 Color bright yellow. Aroma powerfull, ripe fruit, sweet spices, creamy oak, fragrant herbs. Taste rich, smoky aftertaste, flavourful, fresh, good acidity.

TRIO 2011 B
70% chardonnay, 15% pinot blanc, 15% pinot grigio
Valle de San Casablanca

90 Color bright straw. Aroma fresh, fresh fruit, white flowers, expressive. Taste flavourful, fruity, good acidity, balanced.

VIÑA CONO SUR

Av. Nueva Tajamar 481, Torre Sur, Of. 2101
Las Condes (Santiago)
☎: +56 224 765 090 - Fax:+56 222 036 732
www.conosur.com

CONO SUR 20 BARRELS LIMITED EDITION CHARDONNAY 2012 B
100% chardonnay — Valle de San Casablanca

91 Colour: bright yellow. Nose: floral, varietal, expressive. Palate: flavourful, balanced, fine bitter notes, good acidity, long.

CONO SUR OCIO PINOT NOIR 2011 T
100% pinot noir Valle de San Casablanca

90 Colour: cherry, garnet rim. Nose: toasty, spicy, powerfull. Palate: flavourful, spicy, good structure, round tannins.

CONO SUR SINGLE VINEYARD SYRAH Nº 25 2011 T
100% syrah Valle de San Antonio

91 Colour: deep cherry, garnet rim. Nose: candied fruit, sweet spices, powerfull, toasty. Palate: flavourful, good structure.

VIÑA ECHEVERRIA LTDA.

El Trovador 4280, Oficina 1202
750075 Las Condes (Santiago)
☎: +56 223 425 358
info@echewine.com
www.echewine.com

ECHEVERRÍA SYRAH 2010 TR
100% syrah Valle de Aconcagua

92 Colour: cherry, garnet rim. Nose: ripe fruit, spicy, creamy oak, earthy notes. Palate: powerful, flavourful, toasty, round tannins.

VIÑA GARCÉS SILVA LTDA.

Avda. El Golf 99, - Of. 801
Las Condes (Región Metropolitana)
☎: +56 224 288 080 - Fax:+56 224 288 081
fvargas@vgs.cl
www.amayna.cl

AMAYNA CHARDONNAY 2010 B
Valle de San Antonio

91 Colour: bright yellow. Nose: balanced, white flowers, ripe fruit, sweet spices. Palate: balanced, fine bitter notes, rich.

AMAYNA PINOT NOIR 2011 T
pinot noir Valle de San Antonio

90 Colour: deep cherry. Nose: ripe fruit, fruit expression, sweet spices, balsamic herbs. Palate: flavourful, fruity, fresh.

VIÑA MONTES

Avda. Del Valle, 945- Of. 2611, Ciudad Empresarial
Huechuraba (Santiago)
☎: +56 222 484 805 - Fax:+56 222 484 790
monteswines@monteswines.com
www.monteswines.com

OUTER LIMITS PINOT NOIR 2011 T
100% pinot noir Valle de Aconcagua

94 Colour: cherry, garnet rim. Nose: ripe fruit, complex, varietal, balsamic herbs. Palate: powerful, flavourful, toasty, round tannins.

OUTER LIMITS SAUVIGNON BLANC 2011 B
100% sauvignon blanc Valle de Aconcagua

92 Colour: bright straw. Nose: fresh, fresh fruit, white flowers, varietal. Palate: flavourful, fruity, good acidity, balanced.

VIÑA QUINTAY

Ruta 68, Km. 62,5
2480000 Casablanca (Valparaíso)
☎: +56 226 567 369
ventas@quintay.com
www.quintay.com

QUINTAY Q PINOT NOIR 2011 T
pinot noir Valle de San Casablanca

92 Colour: bright cherry. Nose: ripe fruit, sweet spices, creamy oak, expressive, characterful, earthy notes. Palate: flavourful, fruity, toasty, round tannins.

QUINTAY Q SAUVIGNON BLANC 2012 B
sauvignon blanc Valle de San Casablanca

90 Colour: bright straw. Nose: expressive, fruit expression, grassy, earthy notes. Palate: flavourful, correct, easy to drink.

QUINTAY Q SYRAH 2011 T
syrah Valle de San Casablanca

91 Colour: cherry, garnet rim. Nose: ripe fruit, spicy, creamy oak, toasty, red berry notes. Palate: powerful, flavourful, toasty, round tannins.

VIÑA TERRANOBLE

Av. El Bosque Norte 500, piso 24
7550092 Las Condes (Santiago)
☎: +56 226 301 511 - Fax:+56 226 301 520
tizquierdo@santacamila.cl
www.terranoble.cl

TERRANOBLE RESERVA TERROIR CHARDONNAY 2012 B
chardonnay Valle de San Casablanca

92 Colour: bright yellow. Nose: fresh, fresh fruit, white flowers, expressive, floral, varietal. Palate: flavourful, fruity, good acidity, balanced.

VIÑA VENTISQUERO

Camino La Estrella 401, Of. 5
Punta de Cortés (Rancagua)
☎: +56 722 444 300
nahumada@ventisquero.com
www.ventisquero.com

HERU 2010 T
100% pinot noir Valle de San Casablanca

92 Colour: bright cherry. Nose: ripe fruit, red berry notes, spicy. Palate: flavourful, long, mineral.

DESCRIPTION

This has a northern border with the Region of Antofagasta, to the south it has a border with the Region of Coquimbo, to the west with the provinces of Catamarca, La Rioja and San Juan in the Republic of Argentina and to the west with the Pacific Ocean. Its capital is Copiapó, 806 kilometres north of the capital of Chile, Santiago. 90% of the production is dessert grapes. The transversal valleys which unite the mountain ranges of the Coast and the Andes are fluvial.

NUMBER OF HECTARES: 11,61

ALTITUDES: Some valleys reach as far as 1,000 metres, but the Andes in this region reach 5,000 metres.

PREDOMINANT VARIETIES: The main dessert grape is the Thomson variety, which is intended mainly for the United States, Holland and Mexico. Red Globe is commercialized manly in Asia, in countries such as Japan, Korea, Singapore and Hong Kong. There is more abundance of red grape vine in bottled wines, but the muscat of Alexandria is the grape with the highest volume.

CLIMATOLOGY AND SOILS

There is a predominance of the desert attenuated from north to south by rainfall. Near the coast there is substantial mist.

PRODUCER ZONES

The cultivation of grapes takes place in the southern zone, in the sub-zones of Copiapó and Huasco, valleys created by a river which crosses from east to west.

VIÑA ARMIDITA

El Transito, comuna de Alto del Carmen
1610000 El Transito, Alto del Carmen (Vallenar)
☎: +56 516 192 53
molinosantaalicia@gmail.com
www.armidita.cl

VIÑA ARMIDITA 2011 MOSCATEL
moscatel — Valle del Huasco

91 Colour: golden. Nose: powerfull, floral, honeyed notes, candied fruit. Palate: flavourful, sweet, fruity, good acidity, long.

DESCRIPTION

Its northern border is with the Region of Atacama, to the south it borders with the region of Coquimbo, to the east with the Andes and to the west with the Pacific Ocean. This is the narrowest zone in all the territory of Chile.

NUMBER OF HECTARES: 2.155

ALTITUDES: In the interior of the region, 800 metres. In the Andes mountain range, 3,000 metres.

PREDOMINANT VARIETIES: As regards white grapes, chardonnay predominates and., to a lesser extent, sauvignon blanc. With regard to red grapes, syrah, cabernet sauvignon, carmenère and pinot noir.

CLIMATOLOGY AND SOILS

There are a variety of climates such as the coastal steppe or cloudy, warm steppe and high altitude cold temperate. This is a zone half-way between the desert and the Mediterranean climate of the south. Despite the semi-desert climate conditions, Coquimbo benefits from more moderate temperatures due to the influence of the Pacific.

PRODUCER ZONES

Puritaque has the best white wines and Ovalle the best red wines. In this region there are three valleys where production is concentrated:

1-Valle del Limarí. This is an ideal zone for fine wines, with substantial ventilation, near to the sea but with humid sub-zones beside the ocean, regions with sun and night-time cold and extremely hot zones where there is little rainfall and more balanced wines are produced, especially the white wines. Water is the big problem in this area. Gravel and sand soils with a limestone component which provide minerals to the wines which tend to have earth and organic aromas. The pioneer winery was Francisco de Aguirre which bought Concha y Toro. The producers decided for the potential of chardonnay and syrah in the coastal vineyards.

2-Valle de Elqui. A dry climate with little rainfall and a high incidence of sun. A fresher region with the influence of the Pacific Ocean and the winds from the Andes, with the possibility to make fresher and more herbaceous wines (syrah, carmenère, sauvignon blanc). Healthy wines are produced which have to be assisted with an irrigation system in the flattest sunny areas. The most common grape is cabernet sauvignon. Alluvial and decomposed granite soils in the hills. The pioneer winery was Falernia.

3-Valle de Choapa. With 134 hectares. The smallest of the three regions, where syrah has been most successful.

MIGUEL TORRES CHILE

Longitudinal Sur, Km. 195
3340000 (Curicó)
☎: +56 755 641 00 - Fax:+56 755 641 15
cmarquez@migueltorres.cl
www.migueltorres.cl

CORDILLERA CHARDONNAY 2012 B
chardonnay — Limarí

92 Colour: bright straw. Nose: expressive, balanced, dried flowers, mineral, fruit expression. Palate: flavourful, fine bitter notes, good acidity.

VIÑA CONCHA Y TORO

Av. Nueva Tajamar 481, Torre Norte, Piso 15
7550099 Las Condes (Santiago)
☎: +56 247 650 00
maria.vallejo@conchaytoro.cl
www.conchaytoro.com

MARQUES DE CASA CONCHA CHARDONNAY 2011 B
100% chardonnay — Limarí

90 Colour: bright yellow. Nose: powerfull, ripe fruit, sweet spices, fragrant herbs. Palate: rich, flavourful, fresh, good acidity.

VIÑA DALBOSCO

Cienfuegos 361
(La Serena)
☎: +56 537 314 56 - Fax:+56 537 314 56
laslluvias@dalboscohnos.cl
www.dalboscowines.cl

DALBOSCO 2011 TGR
syrah, carmenère — Limarí

93 Colour: cherry, garnet rim. Nose: ripe fruit, spicy, creamy oak, toasty, complex, earthy notes. Palate: powerful, flavourful, toasty, round tannins.

DALBOSCO CARMENÈRE 2012 T
carmenère — Limarí

91 Colour: cherry, purple rim. Nose: balanced, red berry notes, violet drops. Palate: flavourful, fruity, fine bitter notes, good acidity.

DALBOSCO ENSAMBLAJE 2012 TR
syrah, carmenère, merlot — Limarí

92 Colour: dark-red cherry. Nose: mineral, ripe fruit, red berry notes, fruit expression, sweet spices. Palate: flavourful, good acidity, round tannins.

DALBOSCO SYRAH 2012 TR
syrah — Limarí

90 Colour: bright cherry, purple rim. Nose: expressive, fruit expression, balanced. Palate: flavourful, fruity, good acidity.

DALBOSCO VIOGNIER 2011 B
viognier — Limarí

90 Colour: bright straw. Nose: ripe fruit, citrus fruit. Palate: flavourful, fruity.

VIÑA MAYCAS DEL LIMARI

Av. Nueva Tajamar, 481 Torre Sur, Oficina 1001
Las Condes (Santiago)
☎: +56 224 762 015
info@maycasdellimari.com
www.maycasdellimari.com

MAYCAS DEL LIMARÍ QUEBRADA SECA 2010 B
100% chardonnay — Limarí

91 Colour: bright yellow, greenish rim. Nose: expressive, ripe fruit, floral, spicy, mineral. Palate: balanced, round, long, rich.

MAYCAS DEL LIMARÍ RESERVA ESPECIAL CABERNET SAUVIGNON 2009 T
86% cabernet sauvignon, 14% syrah Limarí

91 Colour: cherry, garnet rim. Nose: ripe fruit, spicy, creamy oak, toasty, characterful. Palate: powerful, flavourful, toasty, round tannins.

MAYCAS DEL LIMARÍ RESERVA ESPECIAL CHARDONNAY 2009 B
100% chardonnay Limarí

92 Color bright yellow. Aroma powerfull, ripe fruit, sweet spices, creamy oak, fragrant herbs. Taste rich, smoky aftertaste, flavourful, fresh, good acidity.

MAYCAS DEL LIMARÍ RESERVA ESPECIAL PINOT NOIR 2011 T
100% pinot noir Limarí

93 Colour: bright cherry. Nose: fruit expression, red berry notes, spicy, scrubland. Palate: mineral, long, flavourful.

MAYCAS DEL LIMARÍ RESERVA ESPECIAL SAUVIGNON BLANC 2011 B
100% sauvignon blanc Limarí

91 Colour: bright straw. Nose: balanced, varietal, fresh, dried herbs, citrus fruit, earthy notes. Palate: fruity, good acidity, fine bitter notes.

MAYCAS DEL LIMARÍ RESERVA ESPECIAL SYRAH 2009 T
100% syrah Limarí

90 Colour: bright cherry, garnet rim. Nose: ripe fruit, spicy, warm, balanced. Palate: good structure, flavourful, full.

VIÑA OCHOTIERRAS

Parcela 44 B
184000 Ovalle (Limarí)
☎: +56 536 262 11 - Fax:+56 536 262 11
info@ochotierras.cl
www.ochotierras.cl

OCHOTIERRAS GRAN RESERVA ENSAMBLAJE 2010 T
60% cabernet sauvignon, 40% carmenère Limarí

90 Colour: cherry, garnet rim. Nose: ripe fruit, sweet spices, cocoa bean, dry stone. Palate: good structure, full, long.

OCHOTIERRAS GRAN RESERVA SYRAH 2010 T
100% syrah Limarí

92 Colour: cherry, garnet rim. Nose: ripe fruit, spicy, complex, sweet spices, new oak. Palate: powerful, flavourful, toasty, round tannins.

OCHOTIERRAS RESERVA SINGLE VINEYARD SYRAH 2011 T
100% syrah Limarí

92 Colour: bright cherry. Nose: ripe fruit, sweet spices, creamy oak, red berry notes. Palate: flavourful, fruity, toasty, round tannins.

VIÑA SUTIL

Fundo San Jorge Agrícola Reserva San Jorge, Parcelación San Miguel de Calleuque
Peralillo
☎: +56 226 582 256 - Fax:+56 226 582 251
marketing@topwinechile.cl
www.topwinechile.cl

AXEL SYRAH LA PLAYA 2011 T
85% syrah, 15% syrah colchagua Harvest Limarí

90 Color bright cherry. Aroma ripe fruit, sweet spices, creamy oak, expressive. Taste flavourful, fruity, toasty, round tannins.

VIÑA UNDURRAGA

Camino a Melipilla, km. 34
7550011 Talagante (Región Metropolitana)
☎: +56 223 722 800 - Fax:+56 237 229 58
info@undurraga.cl
www.undurraga.cl

T.H. SYRAH LIMARÍ 2010 T
100% syrah Limarí

90 Colour: bright cherry, garnet rim. Nose: balanced, spicy, ripe fruit. Palate: good structure, flavourful, sweet tannins.

DESCRIPTION

This is the second grand zone of Chilean wines. It belongs to the region of Maule in the VALLE CENTRAL. The nucleus of wineries is located to the east although it must be said that Curicó is no longer one of the more dynamic regions. Miguel Torres chose this area to build his winery in 1979.

NUMBER OF HECTARES: 15.284

ALTITUDES: an average 228 metres.

PREDOMINANT VARIETIES: : foreign varieties such as gewürztraminer, riesling, garró, garnacha, viognier have been developed together with tempranillo and cabernet sauvignon.

CLIMATOLOGY AND SOILS

With an ideal moderate climate which gives rise to more fruity and fresher wines as we ascend the Andes. It has borders with Colchagua to the north and Maule to the south, the sun predominates and the soils are fertile and tend to give volumes of wine. The soils in these valleys are quite uniform.

JUNTA WINERY

Av. La Dehesa 1201, of. 720
Lo Barnechea (Santiago)
☎: +56 229 549 755 - Fax:+56 229 549 756
vbarros@juntawinery.com
www.juntawinery.com

JUNTA CABERNET SAUVIGNON 2011 TGR
100% cabernet sauvignon Valle Central. Valle del Curicó

91 Colour: bright cherry. Nose: sweet spices, creamy oak, red berry notes, earthy notes, ripe fruit. Palate: flavourful, fruity, toasty, round tannins.

JUNTA CARMENERE 2010 TGR
100% carmenère Valle Central. Valle del Curicó

92 Colour: cherry, garnet rim. Nose: ripe fruit, spicy, toasty, characterful, creamy oak. Palate: powerful, flavourful, toasty, round tannins.

MIGUEL TORRES CHILE

Longitudinal Sur, Km. 195
3340000 (Curicó)
☎: +56 755 641 00 - Fax:+56 755 641 15
cmarquez@migueltorres.cl
www.migueltorres.cl

CONDE DE SUPERUNDA 2006 T
tempranillo, cabernet sauvignon, monastrell, carmenère
Valle Central. Valle del Curicó

92 Colour: cherry, garnet rim. Nose: spicy, creamy oak, toasty, characterful, ripe fruit. Palate: powerful, flavourful, toasty, round tannins, elegant.

CORDILLERA CARMENÈRE 2008 T
carmenère Valle Central. Valle del Curicó

91 Colour: cherry, garnet rim. Nose: ripe fruit, creamy oak, complex. Palate: powerful, flavourful, toasty, round tannins.

MANSO VELASCO 2009 T
cabernet sauvignon Valle Central. Valle del Curicó

92 Colour: cherry, garnet rim. Nose: ripe fruit, spicy, creamy oak, toasty, complex, scrubland, earthy notes. Palate: powerful, flavourful, toasty, round tannins.

NECTARIA 2009 B
riesling Valle Central. Valle del Curicó

93 Color golden. Aroma powerfull, floral, honeyed notes, candied fruit, fragrant herbs. Taste flavourful, sweet, fresh, fruity, good acidity, long.

VIÑA APALTAGUA

Málaga 50, Of. 31
7550133 Las Condes (Santiago)
☎: +56 223 651 539
info@apaltagua.com
www.apaltagua.com

TUTUNJIAN SINGLE VINEYARD 2011 T
cabernet sauvignon Valle Central. Valle del Curicó

93 Colour: cherry, garnet rim. Nose: ripe fruit, spicy, creamy oak, toasty, characterful, expressive. Palate: powerful, flavourful, toasty, round tannins.

VIÑA ECHEVERRIA LTDA.

El Trovador 4280, Oficina 1202
750075 Las Condes (Santiago)
☎: +56 223 425 358
info@echewine.com
www.echewine.com

ECHEVERRÍA SAUVIGNON BLANC 2007 B
100% sauvignon blanc Valle Central. Valle del Curicó

92 Colour: bright yellow. Nose: balanced, faded flowers, honeyed notes, expressive. Palate: fruity, rich, full.

VIÑA REQUINGUA

Av. Santa María, 2670 Of. 107
Providencia (Santiago)
☎: +56 222 310 033
mlong@requingua.com
www.requingua.com

POTRO DE PIEDRA 2010 T
cabernet sauvignon, cabernet franc — Valle Central. Valle del Curicó

92 Colour: bright cherry. Nose: ripe fruit, sweet spices, varietal, aromatic coffee. Palate: flavourful, fruity, toasty, round tannins.

TORO DE PIEDRA 2010 TGR
syrah, cabernet sauvignon — Valle Central. Valle del Curicó

91 Colour: cherry, garnet rim. Nose: ripe fruit, spicy, creamy oak, toasty, characterful, varietal. Palate: powerful, flavourful, toasty, round tannins.

VIÑA UNDURRAGA

Camino a Melipilla, km. 34
7550011 Talagante (Región Metropolitana)
☎: +56 223 722 800 - Fax:+56 23 722 958
info@undurraga.cl
www.undurraga.cl

ALIWEN SAUVIGNON BLANC 2012 B
100% sauvignon blanc — Valle Central. Valle del Curicó

91 Color bright straw. Aroma fresh, fresh fruit, white flowers, expressive. Taste flavourful, fruity, good acidity, balanced.

DESCRIPTION

This follows the course of the River Maipo. The zone is characterized by a long wine growing tradition. The Valle del Maipo has some communes of the Metropolitan Region. It is the only region surrounded by mountains with no coastline and which includes the capital, Santiago. Most of the classical original wineries in Chile are distributed at the foot of the Andes, where the grand cabernet sauvignon of the country are produced. Cabernet sauvignon and carmenère are planted where the temperatures are more moderate in deeper soils with alluvial stones, and the best samples are achieved in Isla de Maipo. The best vines of these wineries are cultivated towards the Alto Maipo, on the higher slopes of the Andes. For this reason, this region was the first to develop Chilean wine growing owing to the proximity of the capital. The coldest and nearest zone to the Andes, such as Pirque, have good harvests of chardonnay. The soils come from granite and material of a volcanic origin. Sede de Almaviva, Baron de Rothschild, Concha y Toro, and Santa Rita.

NUMBER OF HECTARES: 12.216

ALTITUDES: From the foot of the Andes mountain range there is an altitude of 1,500 metres which descends to 800 or 400 metres of the coastal range.

PREDOMINANT VARIETIES: Cabernet sauvignon is the queen of grapes, followed at some distance by merlot and syrah. As regards white wines, chardonnay and sauvignon blanc are important in number.

CLIMATOLOGY AND SOILS

The climate in the valley is warm temperate, with dry, warm summers (December -March) and cold, rainy winters (May and August). Its high temperatures and stony soils enable the best expression of the vines.

BODEGA ALMAVIVA

Avda. Santa Rosa, 821
Puente Alto (Región Metropolitana)
☎: +56 222 704 200 - Fax:+56 228 525 405
info@almavivawinery
www.almavivawinery.com

ALMAVIVA 2009 T
Valle del Maipo

95 Colour: cherry, garnet rim. Nose: spicy, creamy oak, toasty, complex, scrubland, expressive, powèrfull, characterfull. Palate: powerful, flavourful, toasty, round tannins.

CAROLINA WINE BRANDS

Til Til 2228
7142250 (Santiago)
☎: +56 224 503 176 - Fax:+56 24 503 312
pmoreno@santacarolina.cl
www.carolinawinebrands.com

SANTA CAROLINA CABERNET SAUVIGNON RESERVA DE LA FAMILIA 2010 TR
cabernet sauvignon Valle del Maipo

92 Colour: cherry, garnet rim. Nose: ripe fruit, spicy, creamy oak, toasty, complex, powerfull, varietal. Palate: powerful, flavourful, toasty, round tannins.

CLOS ANDINO

El Pregón, 16 Altos del Zapallar
Curicó (Maule)
☎: +56 751 975 525 - Fax:+56 751 975 526
info@closandino.cl
www.closandino.cl

CLOS ANDINO LES TERROIRS 2008 TR
85% cabernet sauvignon, 10% carmenère, 5% otras
Valle del Maipo

91 Colour: cherry, garnet rim. Nose: balanced, ripe fruit, sweet spices, violet drops. Palate: good structure, flavourful, good acidity, fine bitter notes.

COUSIÑO MACUL

Avda. Quilín 7100
Peñalolén (Santiago)
☎: +56 223 514 100
v.cousino@cousinomacul.cl
www.cousinomacul.com

ANTIGUAS RESERVAS CABERNET SAUVIGNON 2010 T
cabernet sauvignon Valle del Maipo

91 Colour: bright cherry, garnet rim. Nose: balanced, expressive, ripe fruit, creamy oak. Palate: good structure, fine tannins.

ANTIGUAS RESERVAS CHARDONNAY 2012 B
Valle del Maipo

91 Colour: bright straw. Nose: fresh, white flowers, characterful, ripe fruit. Palate: flavourful, fruity, good acidity, balanced.

ANTIGUAS RESERVAS MERLOT 2011 T
merlot Valle del Maipo

91 Colour: bright cherry, garnet rim. Nose: balanced, ripe fruit, spicy, wild herbs. Palate: balanced, fine bitter notes, good acidity.

ANTIGUAS RESERVAS SYRAH 2011 T
syrah Valle del Maipo

92 Colour: deep cherry, garnet rim. Nose: balanced, expressive, ripe fruit, sweet spices. Palate: good structure, flavourful, round tannins.

FINIS TERRAE 2009 T
cabernet sauvignon, merlot, syrah Valle del Maipo

92 Colour: cherry, garnet rim. Nose: ripe fruit, spicy, toasty, complex, scrubland. Palate: powerful, flavourful, toasty, round tannins.

VIÑA AQUITANIA

Avda. Consistorial, 5090
7940781 Peñalolén - Santiago (Región Metropolitana)
☎: +56 227 914 500 - Fax:+56 227 914 501
info@aquitania.cl
www.aquitania.cl

AQUITANIA 2011 TR
carmenère Valle del Maipo

93 Colour: cherry, garnet rim. Nose: spicy, creamy oak, toasty, fruit expression, earthy notes. Palate: powerful, flavourful, toasty, round tannins.

AQUITANIA CABERNET SAUVIGNON 2011 T
cabernet sauvignon Valle del Maipo

92 Colour: cherry, garnet rim. Nose: mineral, red berry notes, fruit expression, toasty, creamy oak. Palate: flavourful, fine bitter notes, good acidity.

AQUITANIA SYRAH 2011 T
100% syrah Valle del Maipo

93 Colour: bright cherry. Nose: spicy, red berry notes, expressive, complex. Palate: flavourful, fruity, spicy, long, good acidity, fine bitter notes.

LAZULI 2005 T
cabernet sauvignon Valle del Maipo

91 Colour: deep cherry. Nose: ripe fruit, roasted coffee, spicy, powerfull. Palate: flavourful, sweet tannins, good structure.

VIÑA CANEPA

Av. Nueva Tajamar 481, Torre Sur, Oficina 1001
Las Condes (Santiago)
☎: +56 224 762 015
info@canepawines.cl
www.canepawines.cl

CANEPA MAGNIFICUM 2007 T
97% cabernet sauvignon, 3% cabernet franc
Valle del Maipo

91 Colour: cherry, garnet rim. Nose: ripe fruit, spicy, creamy oak, characterful, roasted coffee. Palate: powerful, flavourful, toasty, round tannins.

VIÑA CONCHA Y TORO

Av. Nueva Tajamar 481, Torre Norte, Piso 15
7550099 Las Condes (Santiago)
☎: +56 247 650 00
maria.vallejo@conchaytoro.cl
www.conchaytoro.com

CARMIN DE PEUMO 2008 T
carmenère Valle del Maipo

94 Colour: bright cherry. Nose: expressive, dark chocolate, aged wood nuances, cocoa bean, fruit expression. Palate: flavourful, fruity, toasty, round tannins, good acidity, correct, elegant.

DON MELCHOR 2009 T
cabernet sauvignon Valle del Maipo

93 Colour: cherry, garnet rim. Nose: spicy, creamy oak, toasty, complex, scrubland, expressive, powerfull, characterfull. Palate: powerful, flavourful, toasty, round tannins.

MARQUES DE CASA CONCHA CABERNET SAUVIGNON 2010 T
100% cabernet sauvignon Valle del Maipo

91 Colour: cherry, garnet rim. Nose: spicy, creamy oak, toasty, characterful, varietal. Palate: powerful, flavourful, toasty, round tannins.

MARQUES DE CASA CONCHA SYRAH 2009 T
100% syrah Valle del Maipo

90 Colour: bright cherry, garnet rim. Nose: expressive, balanced, red berry notes, ripe fruit. Palate: good structure, fruity, good acidity.

RESERVA PRIVADA CASILLERO DEL DIABLO 2011 T
cabernet sauvignon, syrah Valle del Maipo

90 Colour: cherry, garnet rim. Nose: ripe fruit, wild herbs, medium intensity. Palate: good structure, powerful, correct, fine bitter notes.

TRIO 2011 TR
70% cabernet sauvignon, 15% cabernet franc, 15% syrah
Valle del Maipo

90 Colour: bright cherry. Nose: ripe fruit, sweet spices, creamy oak, characterful, powerfull. Palate: flavourful, fruity, toasty, round tannins.

VIÑA CONO SUR

Av. Nueva Tajamar 481, Torre Sur, Of. 2101
Las Condes (Santiago)
☎: +56 224 765 090 - Fax:+56 222 036 732
www.conosur.com

CONO SUR 20 BARRELS LIMITED EDITION CABERNET SAUVIGNON 2009 T
95% cabernet sauvignon, 4% syrah, 1% carmenère
Valle del Maipo

91 Colour: cherry, garnet rim. Nose: ripe fruit, spicy, toasty, complex, tobacco. Palate: powerful, flavourful, toasty, round tannins.

VIÑA ECHEVERRIA LTDA.

El Trovador 4280, Oficina 1202
750075 Las Condes (Santiago)
☎: +56 223 425 358
info@echewine.com
www.echewine.com

ECHEVERRÍA LIMITED EDITION CABERNET SAUVIGNON 2009 T
85% cabernet sauvignon, 10% syrah, 5% carmenère
Valle del Maipo

91 Colour: cherry, garnet rim. Nose: ripe fruit, spicy, creamy oak, toasty, complex, wild herbs. Palate: powerful, flavourful, toasty, round tannins.

ECHEVERRÍA SIGNATURA SYRAH 2009 T
100% syrah Valle del Maipo

92 Colour: cherry, garnet rim. Nose: ripe fruit, spicy, creamy oak, toasty, characterful, varietal. Palate: powerful, flavourful, toasty, round tannins.

VIÑA HARAS DE PIRQUE

Fundo La Rochuela s/n
Pirque (Santiago)
☎: +56 228 547 910
contact@harasdepirque.com
www.harasdepirque.com

ALBIS 2006 T
cabernet sauvignon, carmenère — Valle del Maipo

93 Colour: very deep cherry. Nose: fruit expression, ripe fruit, red berry notes, sweet spices, creamy oak. Palate: round, balanced, spicy.

VIÑA JARDÍN CORCORÁN GALLERY

Parcela 11, San Juan de Pirque
Pirque (Cordillera)
☎: +56 228 546 817 - Fax:+56 228 546 837
contacto@corcorangallery.cl
www.corcorangallery.cl

CORCORÁN GALLERY 2006 T
cabernet sauvignon — Valle del Maipo

90 Colour: cherry, garnet rim. Nose: ripe fruit, wild herbs. Palate: good structure, flavourful, spicy, fine bitter notes.

VIÑA MARTY SPA

Eliodoro Yánez 1649, Of. 802
7500662 Providencia (Santiago)
☎: +56 225 813 818 - Fax:+56 222 052 580
www.vinamarty.cl

CORAZÓN DEL INDIO 2010 T
cabernet sauvignon, carmenère, syrah — Valle del Maipo

92 Colour: cherry, garnet rim. Nose: balanced, spicy, red berry notes, ripe fruit, toasty. Palate: flavourful, good structure, sweet tannins, balanced.

LOVE RED 2011 T
cabernet sauvignon, carmenère — Valle del Maipo

92 Colour: cherry, garnet rim. Nose: spicy, creamy oak, toasty, ripe fruit. Palate: powerful, flavourful, toasty, round tannins.

PIRCA CARMENÈRE 2010 T
Valle del Maipo

90 Colour: deep cherry. Nose: powerfull, ripe fruit, toasty, spicy. Palate: flavourful, spicy, round tannins.

PIRCA CHARDONNAY 2010 B
chardonnay — Valle del Maipo

90 Colour: bright yellow, greenish rim. Nose: medium intensity, varietal, white flowers. Palate: flavourful, fruity, good acidity, fine bitter notes.

VIÑA PÉREZ CRUZ

Fundo Liguai De Huelquen, s/n Paine
Huelquén (Paine)
☎: +56 228 242 405
wines@perezcruz.com
www.perezcruz.com

CARMENERE LIMITED EDITION 2011 T
95% carmenère, 5% cabernet sauvignon
Valle del Maipo

92 Colour: deep cherry, garnet rim. Nose: spicy, scrubland, ripe fruit. Palate: balanced, round, ripe fruit, long, round tannins, good acidity.

CHASKI PETIT VERDOT 2010 T
95% petit verdot, 3% carmenère, 2% cot
Valle del Maipo

90 Colour: bright cherry. Nose: sweet spices, creamy oak, ripe fruit, fragrant herbs. Palate: flavourful, fruity, toasty, round tannins.

COT LIMITED EDITION 2011 T
92% cot, 4% petit verdot, 4% carmenère
Valle del Maipo

92 Colour: cherry, garnet rim. Nose: ripe fruit, spicy, creamy oak, toasty, characterful. Palate: powerful, flavourful, toasty, round tannins.

PÉREZ CRUZ CABERNET SAUVIGNON 2011 TR
95% cabernet sauvignon, 3% syrah, 2% carmenère
Valle del Maipo

91 Colour: cherry, garnet rim. Nose: ripe fruit, spicy, creamy oak, toasty. Palate: powerful, flavourful, toasty, round tannins.

SYRAH LIMITED EDITION 2011 T
93% syrah, 7% carmenere — Valle del Maipo

91 Colour: bright cherry. Nose: ripe fruit, sweet spices, creamy oak, expressive, raspberry. Palate: flavourful, fruity, toasty, round tannins.

VIÑA TRES PALACIOS

Magnere 1543
Providencia (Santiago)
☎: +56 222 359 852 - Fax:+56 222 359 852
m.pino@vinatrespalacios.cl
www.vinatrespalacios.cl

CHOLQUI PREMIUM CABERNET SAUVIGNON 2010 T
cabernet sauvignon — Valle del Maipo

93 Colour: cherry, garnet rim. Nose: ripe fruit, spicy, creamy oak, toasty, characterful. Palate: powerful, flavourful, toasty, round tannins.

CHOLQUI PREMIUM CARMENÈRE 2009 T
carmenère — Valle del Maipo

93 Colour: cherry, garnet rim. Nose: ripe fruit, spicy, creamy oak, toasty, complex, varietal, characterful. Palate: powerful, flavourful, toasty, round tannins.

VIÑA TRES PALACIOS CABERNET SAUVIGNON 2011 TR
cabernet sauvignon — Valle del Maipo

90 Colour: cherry, garnet rim. Nose: ripe fruit, creamy oak, spicy. Palate: flavourful, fruity, fresh, round tannins.

VIÑA TRES PALACIOS FAMILY VINTAGE CABERNET SAUVIGNON 2009 T
cabernet sauvignon — Valle del Maipo

92 Colour: cherry, garnet rim. Nose: spicy, creamy oak, toasty, fruit expression. Palate: powerful, flavourful, toasty, round tannins.

VIÑA TRES PALACIOS FAMILY VINTAGE MERLOT 2010 T
merlot — Valle del Maipo

92 Colour: light cherry, garnet rim. Nose: ripe fruit, medium intensity, balanced. Palate: flavourful, fruity, long, easy to drink.

VIÑA UNDURRAGA

Camino a Melipilla, km. 34
7550011 Talagante (Región Metropolitana)
☎: +56 223 722 800 - Fax:+56 23 722 958
info@undurraga.cl
www.undurraga.cl

FOUNDER'S COLLECTION CABERNET SAUVIGNON 2010 T
cabernet sauvignon — Valle del Maipo

93 Colour: cherry, garnet rim. Nose: spicy, creamy oak, toasty, complex, fruit expression. Palate: powerful, flavourful, toasty, round tannins.

VIÑA VALDIVIESO

Juan Mitjans, 200
Macul (Región Metropolitana)
☎: +56 223 819 200 - Fax:+56 222 382 383
info@valdiviesovineward.com
www.valdiviesovineyard.com

CABALLO LOCO Nº13 T
cabernet sauvignon, cabernet franc, merlot, malbec — Valle del Maipo

93 Colour: cherry, garnet rim. Nose: ripe fruit, spicy, creamy oak, toasty, complex, earthy notes. Palate: powerful, flavourful, toasty, round tannins.

VIÑA VENTISQUERO

Camino La Estrella 401, Of. 5
Punta de Cortés (Rancagua)
☎: +56 722 444 300
nahumada@ventisquero.com
www.ventisquero.com

QUEULAT 2010 TGR
carmenere — Valle del Maipo

92 Colour: cherry, garnet rim. Nose: ripe fruit, spicy, creamy oak. Palate: powerful, flavourful, toasty, round tannins.

RAMIRANA 2011 TR
cabernet sauvignon, carmenere — Valle del Maipo

91 Colour: cherry, garnet rim. Nose: ripe fruit, toasty, spicy. Palate: powerful, fine bitter notes, good acidity, sweet tannins.

RAMIRANA TRINIDAD 2010 T
64% syrah, 25% cabernet sauvignon, 11% carmenère
Valle del Maipo

92 Colour: cherry, garnet rim. Nose: ripe fruit, spicy, creamy oak, toasty, complex, fruit expression, earthy notes. Palate: powerful, flavourful, toasty, round tannins.

WILLIAM FÈVRE CHILE

Huelén, 56 - Of. B
7500617 Providencia (Santiago)
☎: +56 222 351 919 - Fax:+56 222 354 525
info@williamfevre.cl
www.williamfevre.cl

CHACAI BLANC 2011 B
chardonnay
Valle del Maipo

90 Color bright yellow. Aroma powerfull, ripe fruit, sweet spices, creamy oak, fragrant herbs. Taste rich, smoky aftertaste, flavourful, fresh, good acidity.

ESPINO 2011 T
85% cabernet sauvignon, 15% cabernet franc
Valle del Maipo

91 Colour: cherry, garnet rim. Nose: ripe fruit, spicy, creamy oak, toasty, characterful. Palate: powerful, flavourful, toasty, round tannins.

LAS MAJADAS ESPINO GRAN CUVÉE 2011 T
85% cabernet sauvignon, 15% cabernet franc
Valle del Maipo

92 Colour: bright cherry. Nose: sweet spices, creamy oak, expressive, fruit expression, violet drops. Palate: flavourful, fruity, toasty, round tannins, long.

ESPINO GRAN CUVÉE CARMÉNERE 2011 T
carmenère
Valle del Maipo

90 Colour: cherry, garnet rim. Nose: ripe fruit, creamy oak, toasty, varietal, expressive. Palate: powerful, flavourful, toasty, round tannins.

DESCRIPTION

This is the oldest zone, with the oldest vines, and is the most extensive in number of hectares in Chile. The vines of this zone have shaped the Wine Route, between San Javier and Villa Alegre. To the south of the province of Curicó, this becomes a wide depression irrigated by a multitude of rivers, including the Maule, which is 240 kilometres long. Here there are wineries such as Calina, Terranoble and Gillmore and, more recently, the Spanish companies Fournier and Torres, the latter in plots similar to Priorat. Maule has the wine with the highest points in the Guide with the torontel variety, the same torontel grape as in Argentina.

NUMBER OF HECTARES: 33.792

ALTITUDES: The differences are so radical that there are volcanoes over 3,000 metres high in the Andes, pre-mountain range reliefs of between 400 and 1,000 metres and coastal valleys (300-700 metres).

PREDOMINANT VARIETIES: A start has been made to recuperate older vineyards with cabernet sauvignon and merlot, as well as the fashionable grapes among Chilean oenologists: carignan and malbec. Their best versions are produced on slopes and come from old vines. Besides cabernet sauvignon, sauvignon blanc and chardonnay are the most abundant grapes.

CLIMATOLOGY AND SOILS

The climate of the region varies depending on the proximity of the sea and the altitude, with an annual average of mild temperatures (13-15 degrees centigrade). A warm environment, especially in the central areas with a certain geo-climatic diversity, where the new vineyards are being installed in the sheer zones of the west with higher rainfall (similar to the interior of Spain) and some slate soils, which makes it possible to cultivate vines with no artificial irrigation. The soils are deep, with alluvial deposits from the rivers, this provides a source of wines with a lighter body and higher acidity than the rest of Chilean wines.

BODEGA VOLCANES DE CHILE LTDA.

Av. Vitacura 2939
7550011 Las Condes (Santiago)
☎: +56 223 722 900
info@bodegavolcanesdechile.com
www.bodegavolcanesdechile.com

PARINACOTA 2010 T
70% syrah, 30% carignan — Valle del Maule

92 Colour: cherry, garnet rim. Nose: red berry notes, balanced, expressive, spicy. Palate: good structure, flavourful, good acidity, fine bitter notes.

VIÑA CREMASCHI FURLOTTI

Estado 359 4° Piso
(Santiago)
☎: +56 225 862 508
acremaschi@cf.cl
www.cf.cl

CREMASCHI FURLOTTI CARMENERE SINGLE VINEYARD 2010 T
100% carmenère — Valle del Maule

90 Colour: cherry, garnet rim. Nose: ripe fruit, spicy, toasty, complex. Palate: powerful, flavourful, toasty, round tannins.

CREMASCHI FURLOTTI CHARDONNAY SINGLE VINEYARD 2011 B
100% chardonnay Valle del Maule

90 Colour: bright yellow. Nose: sweet spices, mineral, balanced, expressive. Palate: full, fruity, toasty, spicy.

CREMASCHI FURLOTTI EDICIÓN LIMITADA DE FAMILIA 2011 T
60% cabernet sauvignon, 20% syrah, 20% carmenère
Valle del Maule

91 Colour: bright cherry. Nose: powerfull, red berry notes, creamy oak, cocoa bean. Palate: flavourful, fine bitter notes, good acidity, round tannins.

CREMASCHI FURLOTTI VÉNERE 2009 T
carmenère Valle del Maule

91 Colour: bright cherry. Nose: ripe fruit, sweet spices, creamy oak, expressive. Palate: flavourful, fruity, toasty, round tannins.

CASA DONOSO WINERY

Manuel Montt, 211
3460000 (Santiago)
☎: +56 222 357 373
sales@casadonoso.com
www.casadonoso.com

LEYENDA DE FAMILIA CACHOS DE ORO 2011 T
50% cabernet sauvignon, 50% carmenère
Valle del Maule

93 Colour: cherry, garnet rim. Nose: ripe fruit, toasty, complex, sweet spices, dark chocolate. Palate: powerful, flavourful, toasty, round tannins.

LEYENDA DE FAMILIA NOCHE DE LUNA 2011 T
40% cabernet sauvignon, 30% carmenère, 20% malbec, 10% cabernet franc
Valle del Maule

90 Colour: bright cherry. Nose: ripe fruit, sweet spices, creamy oak. Palate: flavourful, fruity, toasty, round tannins.

LEYENDAS DE FAMILIA CABERNET SAUVIGNON 2011 TR
85% cabernet sauvignon, 10% carmenère, 5% cabernet franc
Valle del Maule

90 Colour: cherry, garnet rim. Nose: sweet spices, ripe fruit, earthy notes. Palate: flavourful, good acidity, fine bitter notes.

SAN VICENTE CHUNGARA CARMENÈRE 2011 T
86% carmenère, 7% cabernet sauvignon, 7% malbec
Valle del Maule

90 Colour: cherry, garnet rim. Nose: ripe fruit, spicy, creamy oak, toasty, scrubland. Palate: powerful, flavourful, toasty, round tannins.

SAN VICENTE LUKAI 2009 T
40% cabernet sauvignon, 30% carmenère, 20% malbec, 10% cabernet franc
Valle del Maule

90 Colour: cherry, garnet rim. Nose: ripe fruit, spicy, creamy oak, toasty, characterful. Palate: powerful, flavourful, toasty, round tannins.

SAN VICENTE CORDILLERA LIRCAY 2011 T
50% cabernet sauvignon, 50% carmenère
Valle del Maule

91 Colour: bright cherry. Nose: ripe fruit, sweet spices, creamy oak, scrubland. Palate: flavourful, fruity, toasty, round tannins.

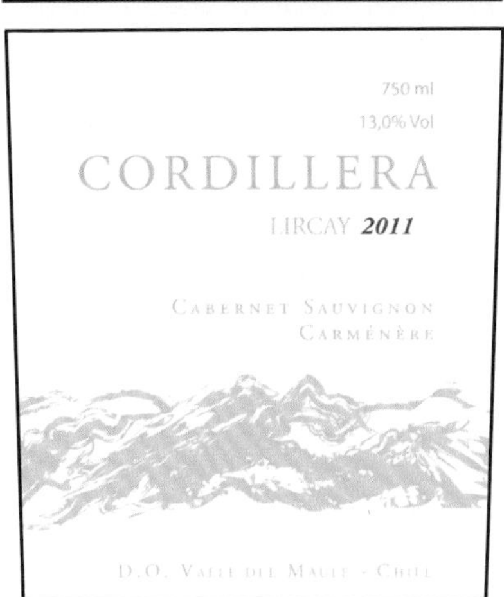

GARCÍA + SCHWADERER CO.

Merced 838 A Of. 111
(Santiago)
☎: +56 228 954 140
bravado@bravadowines.com
www.garciaschwaderer.cl

VIGNO BY GARCIA SCHWADERER 2010 T
100% carignan Valle del Maule

91 Colour: cherry, garnet rim. Nose: spicy, creamy oak, toasty, characterful, red berry notes. Palate: powerful, flavourful, toasty, round tannins.

GILLMORE

Camino a Constitución, Km. 20
San Javier (Linares)
☎: +56 731 975 539 - Fax:+567 31 975 538
daniela@tabonko.cl
www.gillmore.cl

HACEDOR DE MUNDOS GILLMORE CABERNET SAUVIGNON 2009 T
cabernet sauvignon Valle del Maule

90 Colour: cherry, garnet rim. Nose: ripe fruit, spicy, creamy oak, toasty, characterful, earthy notes. Palate: powerful, flavourful, toasty, round tannins.

HACEDOR DE MUNDOS GILLMORE MERLOT 2008 T
merlot Valle del Maule

91 Colour: cherry, garnet rim. Nose: ripe fruit, spicy, creamy oak, toasty, complex, balsamic herbs, scrubland. Palate: powerful, flavourful, toasty, round tannins.

J. BOUCHON

Evaristo Lillo 178 Of. 21
7580110 Las Condes (Santiago)
☎: +56 224 697 78 - Fax:+56 224 697 07
jbouchon@jbouchon.cl
www.jbouchon.cl

J. BOUCHON RESERVA ESPECIAL MALBEC 2010 T
100% malbec Valle del Maule

90 Colour: bright cherry, garnet rim. Nose: balanced, ripe fruit, spicy. Palate: good structure, spicy, good acidity.

LAS MERCEDES 2011 T
90% carmenère, 4% cabernet sauvignon, 3% syrah, 3% malbec
Valle del Maule

90 Colour: cherry, garnet rim. Nose: ripe fruit, creamy oak, toasty, balsamic herbs. Palate: powerful, flavourful, toasty, round tannins.

MINGRE 2008 T
32% syrah, 30% malbec, 20% carmenère, 18% cabernet sauvignon
Valle del Maule

91 Colour: cherry, garnet rim. Nose: ripe fruit, spicy, creamy oak, toasty, earthy notes, mineral. Palate: powerful, flavourful, toasty, round tannins.

MIGUEL TORRES CHILE

Longitudinal Sur, Km. 195
3340000 (Curicó)
☎: +56 755 641 00 - Fax:+56 755 641 15
cmarquez@migueltorres.cl
www.migueltorres.cl

CORDILLERA CARIGNAN VIGNO 2009 T
carignan — Valle del Maule

90 Colour: cherry, garnet rim. Nose: ripe fruit, spicy, balanced. Palate: good structure, flavourful, fine bitter notes, good acidity.

CORDILLERA SYRAH 2008 T
syrah — Valle del Maule

92 Colour: bright cherry. Nose: ripe fruit, sweet spices, creamy oak, powerfull, earthy notes. Palate: flavourful, fruity, toasty, round tannins.

O. FOURNIER

Camino Constitución, Km. 20
366000 San Javier (Maule)
☎: +54 926 146 710 35
info@ofournier.com
www.ofournier.com

ALFA CENTAURI RED BLEND 2008 T
cabernet sauvignon, merlot, carignan — Valle del Maule

92 Colour: cherry, garnet rim. Nose: ripe fruit, spicy, creamy oak, toasty, complex. Palate: powerful, flavourful, toasty, round tannins, balanced, elegant.

URBAN MAULE RED BLEND 2009 T
Valle del Maule

91 Colour: cherry, garnet rim. Nose: red berry notes, ripe fruit, mineral, creamy oak, expressive. Palate: flavourful, spicy, balanced.

VIÑA APALTAGUA

Málaga 50, Of. 31
7550133 Las Condes (Santiago)
☎: +56 223 651 539
info@apaltagua.com
www.apaltagua.com

APALTAGUA RESERVA SYRAH 2011 TR
Valle del Maule

91 Colour: cherry, garnet rim. Nose: spicy, ripe fruit, creamy oak, toasty. Palate: powerful, flavourful, toasty, round tannins.

VIÑA BOTALCURA

Rosario Norte 615, - Of. 2103
7561211 Las Condes (Santiago)
☎: +56 223 701 300 - Fax:+56 223 701 300
info@botalcura.cl
www.botalcura.cl

BOTALCURA EL DELIRIO 2012 T
60% syrah, 40% nebbiolo — Valle del Maule

90 Colour: cherry, garnet rim. Nose: spicy, creamy oak, toasty, fruit expression, red berry notes. Palate: powerful, flavourful, toasty, round tannins.

VIÑA CANEPA

Av. Nueva Tajamar 481, Torre Sur, Oficina 1001
Las Condes (Santiago)
☎: +56 224 762 015
info@canepawines.cl
www.canepawines.cl

CANEPA GENOVINO 2010 T
100% carignan — Valle del Maule

90 Colour: cherry, garnet rim. Nose: ripe fruit, spicy, toasty, characterful, roasted coffee. Palate: powerful, flavourful, toasty, round tannins.

VIÑA CONCHA Y TORO

Av. Nueva Tajamar 481, Torre Norte, Piso 15
7550099 Las Condes (Santiago)
☎: +56 24765 000
maria.vallejo@conchaytoro.cl
www.conchaytoro.com

GRAN RESERVA SERIE RIBERAS 2011 T
90% merlot, 10% cabernet sauvignon — Valle del Maule

92 Colour: cherry, garnet rim. Nose: ripe fruit, spicy, creamy oak, toasty, complex, expressive. Palate: powerful, flavourful, toasty, round tannins.

VIÑA EL AROMO

17 Oriente 931
3476000 (Talca)
☎: +56 712 655 87 - Fax:+56 712 655 83
exports@elaromo.cl
www.elaromo.com

AROMO BARREL SELECTION 2010 B
GRAN RESERVA
chardonnay — Valle del Maule

90 Colour: bright yellow. Nose: powerfull, ripe fruit, sweet spices, creamy oak. Palate: rich, smoky aftertaste, flavourful, fresh, good acidity.

AROMO RESERVA PRIVADA CABERNET SAUVIGNON 2011 TR
cabernet sauvignon — Valle del Maule

90 Colour: light cherry, garnet rim. Nose: spicy, ripe fruit, balanced, wild herbs. Palate: flavourful, fruity, fine bitter notes, good acidity.

AROMO RESERVA PRIVADA CHARDONNAY 2012 B
chardonnay — Valle del Maule

91 Color bright straw. Aroma fresh, fresh fruit, white flowers, expressive. Taste flavourful, fruity, good acidity, balanced.

AROMO RESERVA PRIVADA MERLOT 2010 T
merlot — Valle del Maule

90 Colour: bright cherry, garnet rim. Nose: sweet spices, balanced, toasty. Palate: flavourful, fruity, balanced.

AROMO RESERVA PRIVADA SYRAH 2010 T
syrah — Valle del Maule

91 Colour: cherry, garnet rim. Nose: ripe fruit, spicy, creamy oak, toasty, characterful, varietal. Palate: powerful, flavourful, toasty, round tannins.

AROMO WINEMAKER'S SELECTION 2010 TR
60% cabernet sauvignon, 40% syrah — Valle del Maule

90 Colour: cherry, garnet rim. Nose: ripe fruit, scrubland, spicy. Palate: balanced, fine bitter notes, fine tannins.

AROMO WINEMAKER'S SELECTION
PINOT NOIR 2011 TR
pinot noir — Valle del Maule

90 Colour: light cherry. Nose: floral, elegant, red berry notes, ripe fruit. Palate: balanced, fine bitter notes, ripe fruit.

VIÑA REQUINGUA

Av. Santa María, 2670 Of. 107
Providencia (Santiago)
☎: +56 222 310 033
mlong@requingua.com
www.requingua.com

TORO DE PIEDRA 2010 TGR
cabernet sauvignon, carmenère — Valle del Maule

90 Colour: bright cherry. Nose: sweet spices, creamy oak, ripe fruit, toasty. Palate: flavourful, fruity, toasty, round tannins.

TORO DE PIEDRA 2011 B GRAN RESERVA
chardonnay — Valle del Maule

90 Color bright straw. Aroma fresh, fresh fruit, white flowers, expressive. Taste flavourful, fruity, good acidity, balanced.

VIÑA TERRANOBLE

Av. El Bosque Norte 500, piso 24
7550092 Las Condes (Santiago)
☎: +56 226 301 511 - Fax:+56 226 301 520
tizquierdo@santacamila.cl
www.terranoble.cl

TERRANOBLE CARMENÈRE 2010 TGR
96% carmenère, 4% cabernet sauvignon — Valle del Maule

91 Colour: bright cherry, purple rim. Nose: expressive, red berry notes, ripe fruit, spicy, varietal. Palate: good structure, flavourful, fruity, good acidity.

TERRANOBLE CARMENÈRE 2010 TR
carmenère — Valle del Maule

90 Colour: cherry, garnet rim. Nose: ripe fruit, spicy, creamy oak, toasty, complex. Palate: powerful, flavourful, toasty, round tannins.

TERRANOBLE MERLOT 2010 TGR
85% merlot, 8% cabernet sauvignon — Valle del Maule

90 Colour: bright cherry. Nose: ripe fruit, sweet spices, creamy oak, toasty. Palate: flavourful, fruity, toasty, round tannins.

TERRANOBLE RESERVA TERROIR CARMENÈRE 2011 T
carmenere — Valle del Maule

91 Colour: cherry, garnet rim. Nose: medium intensity, varietal, ripe fruit, wild herbs. Palate: good structure, flavourful, fine bitter notes, fine tannins.

VIÑA UNDURRAGA

Camino a Melipilla, km. 34
7550011 Talagante (Región Metropolitana)
☎: +56 223 722 800 - Fax:+56 23 722 958
info@undurraga.cl
www.undurraga.cl

T.H. CARIGNAN MAULE 2010 T
100% carignan — Valle del Maule

93 Colour: cherry, garnet rim. Nose: ripe fruit, spicy, creamy oak, toasty, complex. Palate: powerful, flavourful, toasty, round tannins, great length.

DESCRIPTION

This is the central region of Chile, south of the capital, Santiago. This region includes the vineyards of Cachapoal in the north and Colchagua in the south, two of the most international wines with Denomination of Origin. It coincides with that of the Liberator General Bernardo O'Higgins. It receives its name from the River Cachapoal, which crosses the basin.

NUMBER OF HECTARES: 36.169

PREDOMINANT VARIETIES: Red is the official colour of this region where there are almost 15,000 hectares of cabernet sauvignon. Merlot and carmenère are good blends with the main wine. Chardonnay and sauvignon blanc, followed far behind by viogner and semillon are the most characteristic vines.

CLIMATOLOGY AND SOILS

This region is characterized by having the typical Mediterranean climate of the Chilean central valley: warm summers, temperate winters and substantial differencess between daytime and night-time temperatures. Its soils are by nature rich in minerals, deposited in sandy layers, together with the influence of lime and stones in some places.

1-Valle de Cachapoal. 10,282 hectares. This is one of the least known despite being located between Maipo and Colchagua. To the north of the Valle de Rapel, the wine growers have labelled their wines with less pretentiousness with this name. In the vineyards in the northernmost part of the Alto Maipo, fresh and elegant cabernet sauvignon is produced, aired by the winds of the Andes which lead to a drop of 10 degrees in temperature aided by poor soil as we ascend the Andes. In the proximity of Peumo, the temperatures are higher and the carmenère is the most interesting grape in the country. This is often confused with the local merlot.

2-Valle de Colchagua. 25,887 hectares. This lies around the city of Santa Cruz, where the most touristic wine route of Chile begins. It has the enormous climatic diversity of Chile because this is the most extensive territory with the highest level of evolution as regards the production of red wines. Most of the wineries are located near the coast but in a depression, between the coastal and the central mountain range, where the warmer climate is more predominant. The unfinished business is to control the maturity of the wine in order to prevent the excess of alcohol. The most representative grapes are carmenère and syrah, which require somewhat more sun and warmth although the other experiments have to do with blending. La Canepa, Cono Sur, Erraruriz, Los Vascos, Apalta Monte Alpha, Hacienda Araucano wineries were established in Colchagua.

CAROLINA WINE BRANDS

Til Til 2228
7142250 (Santiago)
☎: +56 224 503 176 - Fax:+56 24 503 312
pmoreno@santacarolina.cl
www.carolinawinebrands.com

SANTA CAROLINA BARRICA SELECTION CARMENÈRE 2010 T
carmenère Valle del Maule

91 Colour: cherry, garnet rim. Nose: ripe fruit, spicy, creamy oak, toasty, characterful, powerfull. Palate: powerful, flavourful, toasty, round tannins.

SANTA CAROLINA BARRICA SELECTION PETIT VERDOT 2011 T
petit verdot Valle del Maule

91 Colour: very deep cherry. Nose: powerfull, expressive, ripe fruit, toasty, aromatic coffee. Palate: powerful, flavourful, fine bitter notes.

SANTA CAROLINA RESERVA DE FAMILIA CARMENÈRE 2010 T
carmenère Valle del Maule

90 Colour: deep cherry, garnet rim. Nose: balanced, medium intensity, spicy, wild herbs. Palate: full, flavourful, good acidity, sweet tannins.

SANTA CAROLINA WILD SPIRIT MOUVEDRE 2010 T
Valle del Maule

90 Colour: bright cherry. Nose: ripe fruit, sweet spices, creamy oak, expressive. Palate: flavourful, fruity, toasty, round tannins.

CASA LAPOSTOLLE

Ruta I-50 Camino San Fernando a Pichilemu, km. 36
Cunaquito (Santa Cruz)
☎: +56 729 533 00
info@lapostolle.com
www.lapostolle.com

CLOS APALTA 2010 T
71% carmenère, 18% cabernet sauvignon, 11% merlot
Valle de Colchagua

93 Colour: deep cherry. Nose: powerfull, varietal, characterful, dark chocolate, aromatic coffee. Palate: long, ripe fruit, creamy.

CANTO DE APALTA 2011 T
45% carmenère, 25% merlot, 16% cabernet sauvignon, 14% syrah
Valle de Colchagua

91 Colour: very deep cherry. Nose: characterful, expressive, fruit expression, toasty. Palate: flavourful, complex, good acidity.

CLOS ANDINO

El Pregón, 16 Altos del Zapallar
Curicó (Maule)
☎: +75 197 55 25 - Fax:+75 197 5526
info@closandino.cl
www.closandino.cl

CLOS ANDINO LEE TERROIRS 2010 T
85% carmenère, 10% cabernet sauvignon, 5% otras
Valle del Rapel

90 Colour: bright cherry. Nose: ripe fruit, sweet spices, creamy oak, expressive, characterful, complex. Palate: flavourful, fruity, toasty, round tannins.

DONUM MASSENEZ VINEYARD

Longitudinal Sur, Km 110
2940000 Rengo (Cachapoal)
☎: +56 981 578 150
donum@donum.cl
www.donum.cl

DONUM MASSENEZ LIMITED EDITION – PINOT NOIR 2010 T
pinot noir Zona de producción: Valle del Rapel

90 Colour: bright cherry. Nose: ripe fruit, sweet spices, scrubland, balsamic herbs. Palate: flavourful, fruity, toasty, round tannins.

DONUM MASSENEZ LIMITED EDITION – RED ASSEMBLAGE 2008 T
78% cabernet sauvignon, 20% merlot, 2% cabernet franc
Valle del Rapel

92 Colour: cherry, garnet rim. Nose: spicy, creamy oak, toasty, complex, powerfull. Palate: powerful, flavourful, toasty, round tannins.

FLAVIATA CABERNET SAUVIGNON 2010 TGR
100% cabernet sauvignon Valle del Rapel

91 Colour: bright cherry, garnet rim. Nose: balanced, varietal, balsamic herbs, spicy. Palate: good structure, flavourful, fine tannins.

FLAVIATA GRAN RED ASSEMBLAGE 2010 T
33% cabernet sauvignon, 33% merlot, 33% syrah
Valle del Rapel

91 Colour: deep cherry, garnet rim. Nose: ripe fruit, sweet spices, cocoa bean. Palate: flavourful, full, round tannins, balanced.

FLAVIATA MERLOT 2010 TGR
100% merlot Valle del Rapel

90 Colour: bright cherry, garnet rim. Nose: wild herbs, ripe fruit, spicy. Palate: good structure, flavourful, varietal.

FRAVIATA CARMENERE 2010 T
100% carmenère Valle del Rapel

90 Colour: cherry, garnet rim. Nose: characterful, ripe fruit, sweet spices. Palate: flavourful, powerful, fine bitter notes.

EMILIANA

Avda. Nueva Tajamar, 481 - Of. 701 Torre Sur
7550000 Las Condes (Santiago)
☎: +56 223 539 130
jurrutia@emiliana.cl
www.emiliana.cl

ADOBE CARMENERE 2011 TR
carmenère Valle de Colchagua

90 Colour: bright cherry. Nose: ripe fruit, sweet spices, creamy oak, varietal, red berry notes. Palate: flavourful, fruity, toasty, round tannins.

COYAM 2010 T
38% syrah, 27% carmenère, 21% merlot, 12% cabernet sauvignon, 1% mouvedre, 1% petit verdot — Valle de Colchagua

93 Colour: deep cherry, garnet rim. Nose: balanced, medium intensity, red berry notes, ripe fruit, elegant. Palate: good structure, flavourful, fleshy, round tannins.

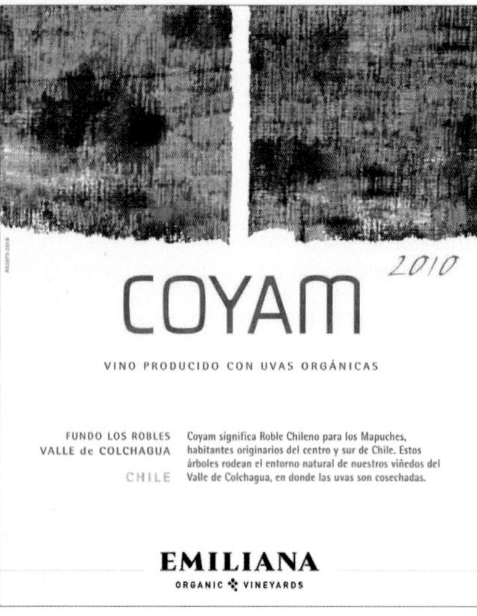

NOVAS 2009 TGR
carmenère, cabernet sauvignon — Valle de Colchagua

92 Colour: cherry, garnet rim. Nose: ripe fruit, spicy, creamy oak, toasty, varietal. Palate: powerful, flavourful, toasty, round tannins.

TORREÓN DE PAREDES

Fundo Santa Teresa, Camino a Las Nieves s/n
2940000 Rengo (Cachapoal)
☎: +56 725 125 51 - Fax:+56 725 125 51
torreon@torreon.cl
www.torreondeparedes.cl

DON AMADO 2007 T
90% cabernet sauvignon, 10% merlot — Cachapoal

90 Colour: bright cherry, garnet rim. Nose: expressive, ripe fruit, fragrant herbs. Palate: flavourful, spicy, ripe fruit, round tannins.

RESERVA PRIVADA TORREÓN DE PAREDES CABERNET SAUVIGNON 2009 T
100% cabernet sauvignon — Cachapoal

90 Colour: cherry, garnet rim. Nose: wild herbs, ripe fruit, warm, spicy. Palate: flavourful, fruity, spicy.

TORREÓN DE PAREDES RESERVA PRIVADA MERLOT 2009 T
merlot — Cachapoal

90 Colour: cherry, garnet rim. Nose: medium intensity, wild herbs, spicy, ripe fruit. Palate: flavourful, sweet tannins.

TREMONTE

Monte Rekewa
San Vicente De Tagua Tagua (San Vicente De Tagua Tagua)
☎: +56 994 520 291
ian@tremonte.cl
www.tremonte.cl

MONTE REKEWA 2011 TGR
45% cabernet sauvignon, 40% syrah, 15% malbec — Cachapoal

90 Colour: cherry, garnet rim. Nose: balanced, ripe fruit, wild herbs. Palate: flavourful, good structure, fine tannins.

TREMONTE ORO DE LOS COIPOS 2011 T
55% cabernet sauvignon, 45% malbec — Cachapoal

91 Colour: cherry, garnet rim. Nose: ripe fruit, spicy, creamy oak. Palate: powerful, flavourful, toasty, round tannins.

VIÑA ALTAÏR

Fundo Totihue, Camino Pimpinela s/n
Requínoa (VI Región)
☎: +56 224 775 598 - Fax:+56 224 775 599
clgomez@altairwines.com
www.altairwines.com

ALTAIR ICONO 2008 T
Cachapoal

94 Colour: bright cherry. Nose: ripe fruit, balanced, spicy, dark chocolate. Palate: good structure, flavourful, long, round tannins.

SIDERAL PREMIUM 2009 T
cabernet sauvignon, syrah, carmenère, petit verdot, petit syrah
Cachapoal

92 Colour: cherry, garnet rim. Nose: red berry notes, ripe fruit, spicy, balsamic herbs, mineral. Palate: elegant, fine bitter notes, fine tannins.

VIÑA APALTAGUA

Málaga 50, Of. 31
7550133 Las Condes (Santiago)
☎: +56 223 651 539
info@apaltagua.com
www.apaltagua.com

APALTAGUA ENVERO 2011 TGR
93% carmenère, 7% cabernet sauvignon
Valle de Colchagua

90 Colour: cherry, garnet rim. Nose: ripe fruit, scrubland, spicy. Palate: balanced, ripe fruit, good structure.

APALTAGUA GRIAL 2009 T
carmenère
Valle de Colchagua

90 Colour: deep cherry, garnet rim. Nose: balanced, balsamic herbs, spicy. Palate: good structure, fruity, flavourful, good acidity.

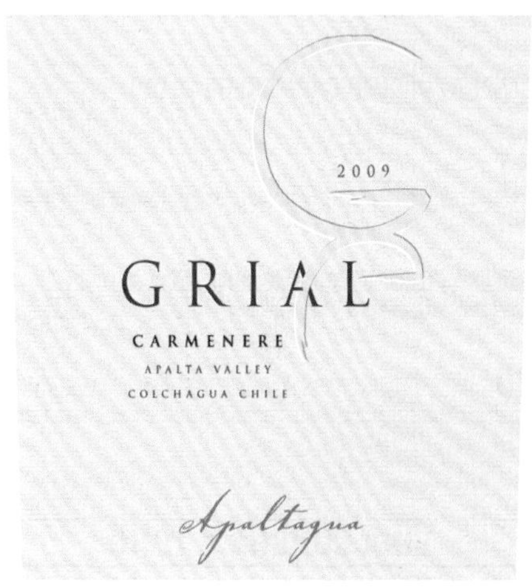

APALTAGUA RESERVA MALBEC 2012 TR
malbec
Valle de Colchagua

91 Colour: cherry, garnet rim. Nose: ripe fruit, spicy, creamy oak, toasty. Palate: powerful, flavourful, toasty, round tannins.

VIÑA CANEPA

Av. Nueva Tajamar 481, Torre Sur, Oficina 1001
Las Condes (Santiago)
☎: +56 224 762 015
info@canepawines.cl
www.canepawines.cl

CANEPA FINÍSIMO CARMENERE 2010 T
Valle del Rapel

91 Colour: cherry, garnet rim. Nose: ripe fruit, spicy, creamy oak, toasty, earthy notes. Palate: powerful, flavourful, toasty, round tannins.

CANEPA FINÍSIMO CARMENERE 2011 T
90% carmenère, 10% cabernet sauvignon
Valle del Rapel

90 Colour: bright cherry, garnet rim. Nose: medium intensity, balanced, ripe fruit, dried herbs. Palate: fine bitter notes, easy to drink, fine tannins.

VIÑA CONCHA Y TORO

Av. Nueva Tajamar 481, Torre Norte, Piso 15
7550099 Las Condes (Santiago)
☎: +56 247 650 00
maria.vallejo@conchaytoro.cl
www.conchaytoro.com

TERRUNYO 2009 T
90% carmenère, 10% cabernet sauvignon
Valle del Rapel

92 Colour: cherry, garnet rim. Nose: ripe fruit, spicy, creamy oak, toasty, characterful, varietal. Palate: powerful, flavourful, toasty, round tannins.

TRIO 2011 TR
70% merlot, 20% carmenère, 10% cabernet sauvignon
Valle del Rapel

90 Colour: cherry, purple rim. Nose: balanced, powerfull, red berry notes, ripe fruit, wild herbs. Palate: good structure, round tannins.

VIÑA GARCÉS SILVA LTDA.

Avda. El Golf 99, - Of. 801
Las Condes (Región Metropolitana)
☎: +56 224 288 080 - Fax:+56 224 288 081
fvargas@vgs.cl
www.amayna.cl

AMAYNA SAUVIGNON BLANC 2012 B
100% sauvignon blanc
Leyda

90 Colour: bright yellow. Nose: balanced, varietal, wild herbs, fresh. Palate: correct, flavourful, good acidity, fine bitter notes.

AMAYNA SYRAH 2011 T
100% syrah
Leyda

92 Colour: cherry, garnet rim. Nose: ripe fruit, spicy, creamy oak, toasty, complex, varietal, expressive, characterful. Palate: powerful, flavourful, toasty, round tannins.

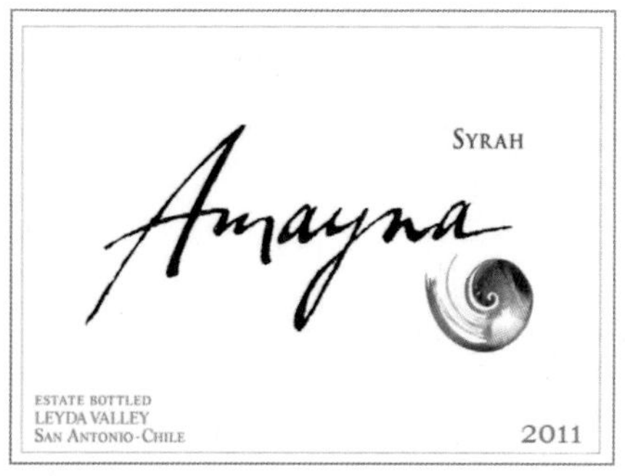

VIÑA KOYLE

Isidora Gooyenechea 360 of 1101
7550053 Las Condes (Santiago)
☎: +56 223 351 593 - Fax:+56 223 611 074
patricio@koyle.cl
www.koyle.cl

KOYLE COSTA SAUVIGNON BLANC 2012 B
100% sauvignon blanc Valle de Colchagua

90 Colour: bright straw. Nose: expressive, varietal, balsamic herbs, fresh fruit. Palate: balanced, easy to drink, good acidity.

KOYLE RESERVA CABERNET SAUVIGNON 2010 T
85% cabernet sauvignon, 8% syrah, 7% malbec
Valle de Colchagua

90 Colour: bright cherry. Nose: sweet spices, creamy oak, red berry notes. Palate: flavourful, fruity, toasty, round tannins.

KOYLE RESERVA SYRAH 2011 T
Valle de Colchagua

90 Colour: bright cherry. Nose: ripe fruit, sweet spices, creamy oak, varietal. Palate: flavourful, fruity, toasty, round tannins.

KOYLE ROYALE CABERNET SAUVIGNON 2009 T
85% cabernet sauvignon, 12% malbec, 3% tempranillo
Valle de Colchagua

90 Colour: deep cherry, garnet rim. Nose: ripe fruit, creamy oak, sweet spices. Palate: good structure, flavourful, sweet tannins.

KOYLE ROYALE CARMENÈRE 2010 T
85% syrah, 6% petit verdot, 5% malbec, 4% syrah
Valle de Colchagua

91 Colour: cherry, garnet rim. Nose: ripe fruit, spicy, creamy oak, toasty, characterful. Palate: powerful, flavourful, toasty, round tannins.

KOYLE ROYALE SYRAH 2009 T
94% syrah, 6% petit verdot Valle de Colchagua

91 Colour: bright cherry. Nose: sweet spices, creamy oak, characterful, candied fruit. Palate: flavourful, fruity, toasty, round tannins.

VIÑA LA RONCIERE

José Miguel Cousiño, s/n
Graneros (Cachapoal)
☎: +56 722 471 571 - Fax:+56 722 472 608
www.laronciere.com

MOUSAI CABERNET SAUVIGNON 2011 T
cabernet sauvignon Valle de Colchagua

91 Colour: bright cherry. Nose: ripe fruit, sweet spices, creamy oak, balsamic herbs. Palate: flavourful, fruity, toasty, round tannins.

MOUSAI MERLOT 2011 T
merlot Valle de Colchagua

92 Colour: bright cherry. Nose: ripe fruit, spicy, new oak, toasty. Palate: flavourful, fruity, toasty, round tannins.

QUIRON CABERNET SAUVIGNON 2010 T
cabernet sauvignon — Valle de Colchagua

92 Colour: cherry, garnet rim. Nose: ripe fruit, spicy, creamy oak, toasty, characterful, mineral. Palate: powerful, flavourful, toasty, round tannins.

QUIRON SYRAH 2010 T
syrah — Valle de Colchagua

91 Colour: cherry, garnet rim. Nose: ripe fruit, spicy, creamy oak, toasty, varietal, characterful. Palate: powerful, flavourful, toasty, round tannins.

VIÑA LAGAR DE BEZANA

Av. Los Leones, 1285
Providencia (Santiago)
☎: +56 227 544 400 - Fax:+56 223 416 727
eusabiaga@lagardebezana.cl
www.lagardebezana.cl

ALUVIÓN 2010 T
50% cabernet sauvignon, 35% syrah, 15% carmenère — Cachapoal

90 Colour: cherry, garnet rim. Nose: balanced, ripe fruit, dark chocolate, sweet spices. Palate: good structure, round tannins.

BEZANA GSM 2011 T
55% grenache, 27% syrah, 18% mouvedre — Cachapoal

90 Colour: cherry, garnet rim. Nose: ripe fruit, spicy, creamy oak, toasty. Palate: powerful, flavourful, toasty, round tannins.

SYRAH LIMITED EDITION 2010 T
syrah — Cachapoal

92 Colour: deep cherry, garnet rim. Nose: complex, balanced, ripe fruit, sweet spices. Palate: good structure, flavourful.

VIÑA LAS NIÑAS

Parcela 11 Millahue de Apalta Casilla 94
Apalta (Santa Cruz)
☎: +56 723 216 00
info@vinalasninas.cl
www.vinalasninas.cl

EL GUAPO 2012 T
carmenère, syrah — Valle de Colchagua

93 Colour: cherry, garnet rim. Nose: ripe fruit, spicy, toasty, sweet spices, cocoa bean, complex, expressive. Palate: powerful, flavourful, toasty, round tannins.

LAS NIÑAS APALTA 2012 T
cabernet sauvignon, merlot, carmenère — Valle de Colchagua

95 Colour: cherry, garnet rim. Nose: ripe fruit, spicy, toasty, complex, fruit expression, sweet spices. Palate: powerful, flavourful, toasty, round tannins.

LAS NIÑAS CABERNET SAUVIGNON 2012 T
100% cabernet sauvignon Valle de Colchagua

92 Colour: cherry, garnet rim. Nose: ripe fruit, spicy, creamy oak, toasty, complex. Palate: powerful, flavourful, toasty, round tannins.

LAS NIÑAS CARMENÈRE 2012 TR
carmenère Valle de Colchagua

90 Colour: bright cherry. Nose: ripe fruit, sweet spices, creamy oak, expressive. Palate: flavourful, fruity, round tannins.

VIÑA LOS VASCOS

Avda. Vitacura 2939, - Of. 1903 Edificio Millenium
Santiago (Las Condes)
☎: +56 722 350 900
visites@lafite.com
www.lafite.com

LE DIX DE LOS BASCOS 2010 T
cabernet sauvignon, syrah, merlot
Valle de Colchagua

93 Colour: cherry, garnet rim. Nose: ripe fruit, spicy, creamy oak, toasty, earthy notes, mineral, characterful. Palate: powerful, flavourful, toasty, round tannins.

VIÑA LUIS FELIPE EDWARDS LTDA.

Avda. Vitacura, 4130
6070170 Santiago (Región Metropolitana)
☎: +56 224 335 700 - Fax:+56 224 335 757
claudia.carcamo@lfewines.com
www.lfewines.com

DOÑA BERNARDA 2009 T
58% cabernet sauvignon, 22% carmenère, 15% syrah, 5% petit verdot Valle de Colchagua

93 Colour: cherry, garnet rim. Nose: spicy, complex, characterful. Palate: powerful, flavourful, toasty, round tannins.

LFE 900 BLEND 2010 T
36% syrah, 22% petit syrah, 20% cabernet sauvignon, 18% mouveane, 2% petit verdot, 2% malbec Valle de Colchagua

90 Colour: cherry, garnet rim. Nose: spicy, creamy oak, toasty, fruit expression. Palate: powerful, flavourful, toasty, round tannins.

LFE CARMENERE 2012 TR
100% carmenère Valle de Colchagua

90 Colour: bright cherry. Nose: ripe fruit, sweet spices, creamy oak, varietal, red berry notes, scrubland. Palate: flavourful, fruity, toasty, round tannins.

LFE SYRAH 2011 TGR
100% syrah Leyda

90 Colour: bright cherry. Nose: sweet spices, creamy oak, fruit expression, mineral. Palate: flavourful, fruity, toasty, round tannins.

MAREA CHARDONNAY 2012 B
100% chardonnay Leyda

90 Colour: bright yellow. Nose: balanced, floral, ripe fruit, expressive. Palate: flavourful, fruity, fine bitter notes.

MAREA PINOT NOIR 2011 T
100% pinot noir Leyda

91 Colour: bright cherry. Nose: ripe fruit, fruit expression, balsamic herbs. Palate: good acidity, fine bitter notes, fine tannins.

MAREA SAUVIGNON BLANC 2012 B
100% sauvignon blanc Leyda

90 Colour: bright straw. Nose: grassy, fresh fruit. Palate: fruity, fine bitter notes, good acidity, long.

VIÑA MONTES

Avda. Del Valle, 945- Of. 2611, Ciudad Empresarial
Huechuraba (Santiago)
☎: +56 222 484 805 - Fax:+56 222 484 790
monteswines@monteswines.com
www.monteswines.com

MONTES ALPHA CABERNET SAUVIGNON 2010 T
90% cabernet sauvignon, 10% merlot Valle de Colchagua

91 Colour: bright cherry, garnet rim. Nose: ripe fruit, scrubland, spicy. Palate: flavourful, good acidity, fine tannins.

MONTES ALPHA M 2010 T
80% cabernet sauvignon, 10% cabernet franc, 5% merlot, 5% petit verdot Valle de Colchagua

91 Colour: cherry, garnet rim. Nose: ripe fruit, spicy, creamy oak, cocoa bean. Palate: powerful, flavourful, toasty, round tannins.

MONTES ALPHA MALBEC 2011 T
90% malbec, 10% cabernet sauvignon — Valle de Colchagua

92 Colour: bright cherry, garnet rim. Nose: red berry notes, ripe fruit, sweet spices. Palate: good structure, flavourful, fine bitter notes.

MONTES PURPLE ANGEL 2010 T
92% carmenère, 8% petit verdot — Valle de Colchagua

94 Colour: cherry, garnet rim. Nose: ripe fruit, spicy, creamy oak, toasty, complex, varietal. Palate: powerful, flavourful, toasty, round tannins.

VIÑA QUINTAY

Ruta 68, Km. 62,5
2480000 Casablanca (Valparaíso)
☎: +56 226 567 369
ventas@quintay.com
www.quintay.com

QUINTAY CLAVA CARMENÈRE 2011 T
carmenere — Valle del Rapel

91 Colour: bright cherry. Nose: ripe fruit, sweet spices, creamy oak, fresh, varietal. Palate: flavourful, fruity, toasty, round tannins.

QUINTAY CLAVA PINOT NOIR 2011 T
pinot noir — Valle del Rapel

91 Colour: light cherry, garnet rim. Nose: medium intensity, floral, dried flowers. Palate: spicy, easy to drink, long, fruity.

VIÑA REQUINGUA

Av. Santa María, 2670 Of. 107
Providencia (Santiago)
☎: +56 222 310 033
mlong@requingua.com
www.requingua.com

TORO DE PIEDRA CABERNET SAUVIGNON 2010 T
cabernet sauvignon — Valle de Colchagua

90 Colour: bright cherry, garnet rim. Nose: fragrant herbs, sweet spices. Palate: flavourful, sweet tannins, fine bitter notes.

VIÑA SAN JOSÉ DE APALTA

Avda. Miguel Ramírez, 199
Rancagua (Cachapoal)
☎: +56 722 521 796 - Fax:+56 722 521 796
rbarros@sanjosedeapalta.cl
www.sanjosedeapalta.cl

SAN JOSÉ DE APALTA CABERNET SAUVIGNON SINGLE VINEYARD 2010 TR
cabernet sauvignon — Valle del Rapel

91 Colour: bright cherry. Nose: ripe fruit, sweet spices, creamy oak. Palate: flavourful, fruity, toasty, round tannins.

SAN JOSÉ DE APALTA CABERNET SAUVIGNON 2009 TGR
cabernet sauvignon | Valle del Rapel

90 Colour: cherry, garnet rim. Nose: medium intensity, ripe fruit. Palate: fruity, flavourful, balanced, long.

SAN JOSÉ DE APALTA CABERNET SAUVIGNON CARMENÈRE 2009 TGR
Valle del Rapel

92 Colour: cherry, garnet rim. Nose: ripe fruit, spicy, toasty, new oak, complex, scrubland. Palate: powerful, flavourful, toasty, round tannins.

SAN JOSÉ DE APALTA FRIEND'S COLLECTION VI 2009 T
cabernet sauvignon, syrah, carmenère | Valle del Rapel

91 Colour: cherry, garnet rim. Nose: ripe fruit, spicy, creamy oak, toasty, characterful. Palate: powerful, flavourful, toasty, round tannins.

SAN JOSÉ DE APALTA LATE HARVEST 2011 B
viognier | Valle del Rapel

90 Colour: bright straw. Nose: white flowers, candied fruit, balanced. Palate: fruity, flavourful, good acidity, sweetness.

SAN JOSÉ DE APALTA SYRAH SINGLE VINEYARD 2009 T
syrah | Valle del Rapel

91 Colour: bright cherry. Nose: sweet spices, creamy oak, expressive, balsamic herbs, ripe fruit. Palate: flavourful, fruity, toasty, round tannins.

VIÑA SIEGEL

Fundo San Elías, s/n Palmilla
3130000 Palmilla (Colchagua)
☎: +56 722 823 836 - Fax:+56 722 933 112
info@siegelvinos.com
www.siegelvinos.com

CRUCERO CARMENERE 2011 TR
carmenère | Valle de Colchagua

91 Colour: bright cherry. Nose: ripe fruit, sweet spices, creamy oak, expressive, red berry notes. Palate: flavourful, fruity, toasty, round tannins.

GRAN CRUCERO LIMITED EDITION 2010 T
45% cabernet sauvignon, 35% carmenère, 20% syrah
Valle de Colchagua

92 Colour: bright cherry. Nose: sweet spices, creamy oak, powerfull, characterful, fruit expression. Palate: flavourful, fruity, toasty, round tannins.

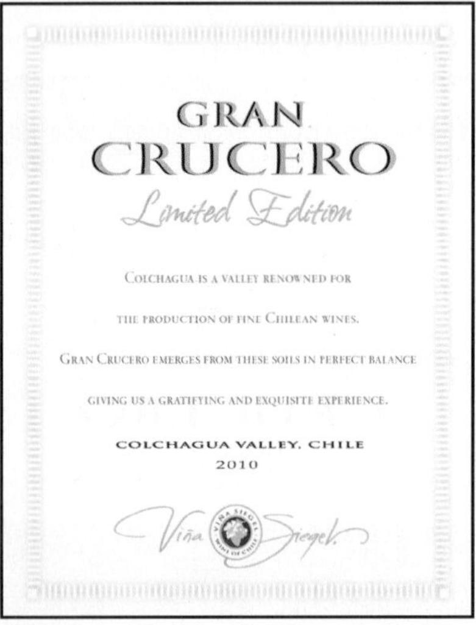

SIEGEL SINGLE VINEYARD CABERNET SAUVIGNON 2011 TGR
cabernet sauvignon
Valle de Colchagua

92 Colour: cherry, garnet rim. Nose: spicy, creamy oak, toasty, expressive, characterful. Palate: powerful, flavourful, toasty, round tannins.

SIEGEL SINGLE VINEYARD CARMENERE 2011 TGR
carmenere
Valle de Colchagua

90 Colour: very deep cherry. Nose: sweet spices, ripe fruit, creamy oak, spicy. Palate: flavourful, good acidity, round.

VIÑA SUTIL

Fundo San Jorge Agrícola Reserva San Jorge, Parcelación San Miguel de Calleuque
Peralillo
☎: +56 226 582 256 - Fax:+56 226 582 251
marketing@topwinechile.cl
www.topwinechile.cl

SUTIL PREMIUM BLEND ACRUX 2010 T
40% cabernet sauvignon, 24% carmenère, 20% petit verdot, 16% syrah — Valle de Colchagua

91 Color cherry, garnet rim. Aroma ripe fruit, spicy, creamy oak, toasty, complex. Taste powerful, flavourful, toasty, round tannins.

VIÑA TERRANOBLE

Av. El Bosque Norte 500, piso 24
7550092 Las Condes (Santiago)
☎: +56 226 301 511 - Fax:+56 226 301 520
tizquierdo@santacamila.cl
www.terranoble.cl

TERRANOBLE CABERNET SAUVIGNON 2010 T
90% cabernet sauvignon, carmenère — Valle de Colchagua

91 Colour: cherry, garnet rim. Nose: ripe fruit, balanced, sweet spices. Palate: flavourful, good structure, round tannins, fine bitter notes.

TERRANOBLE LOS CACTUS 2011 T
syrah — Valle del Rapel

90 Colour: bright cherry. Nose: ripe fruit, sweet spices. Palate: flavourful, fruity, toasty, round tannins.

VIÑA UNDURRAGA

Camino a Melipilla, km. 34
7550011 Talagante (Región Metropolitana)
☎: +56 223 722 800 - Fax:+56 23 722 958
info@undurraga.cl
www.undurraga.cl

ALIWEN CABERNET SYRAH 2011 TR
60% cabernet sauvignon, 40% syrah — Valle del Rapel

91 Colour: bright cherry. Nose: sweet spices, creamy oak, toasty, mineral. Palate: flavourful, fruity, toasty, round tannins.

FOUNDER'S COLLECTION CARMENÈRE 2009 T
100% camenère — Valle de Colchagua

92 Colour: deep cherry, garnet rim. Nose: balanced, ripe fruit, spicy, wild herbs. Palate: good structure, round tannins, long.

SIBARIS RESERVA ESPECIAL CABERNET SAUVIGNON 2011 T
100% cabernet sauvignon — Valle de Colchagua

90 Colour: bright cherry, garnet rim. Nose: powerfull, scrubland. Palate: good structure, flavourful, sweet tannins, spicy.

SIBARIS RESERVA ESPECIAL CARMENÈRE 2011 T
100% carmenère — Valle de Colchagua

90 Colour: cherry, garnet rim. Nose: earthy notes, ripe fruit, dried herbs. Palate: balanced, spicy, long, ripe fruit.

T.H. PINOT NOIR LEYDA 2011 T
100% pinot noir — Leyda

92 Colour: light cherry, garnet rim. Nose: spicy, medium intensity, ripe fruit. Palate: fruity, good acidity, spicy.

T.H. SAUVIGNON BLANC 2011 B
100% sauvignon blanc — Leyda

90 Colour: bright straw. Nose: grassy, fresh, balanced. Palate: good acidity, balanced, fine bitter notes, easy to drink.

VIÑA VALLE SECRETO

Longitudinal Sur Km 103
(Rengo)
☎: +56 72 552 195 - Fax:+56 725 521 80
yaedo@vallesecreto.cl
www.vallescreto.cl

VALLE SECRETO FIRST EDITION SYRAH 2010 T
syrah — Leyda

91 Colour: bright cherry, garnet rim. Nose: expressive, red berry notes, ripe fruit, spicy, balanced. Palate: good structure, balanced, fine bitter notes.

VIÑA VENTISQUERO

Camino La Estrella 401, Of. 5
Punta de Cortés (Rancagua)
☎: +56 722 444 300
nahumada@ventisquero.com
www.ventisquero.com

GREY 2010 T
syrah — Valle de Colchagua

91 Colour: cherry, garnet rim. Nose: ripe fruit, spicy, creamy oak, toasty, varietal. Palate: powerful, flavourful, toasty, round tannins.

PANGEA 2009 T
100% syrah — Valle de Colchagua

92 Colour: cherry, garnet rim. Nose: spicy, creamy oak, toasty, complex, earthy notes, mineral, fruit expression. Palate: powerful, flavourful, toasty, round tannins.

VÉRTICE 2008 T
carmenère, syrah — Valle de Colchagua

91 Colour: deep cherry, garnet rim. Nose: balanced, expressive, sweet spices, creamy oak. Palate: flavourful, ripe fruit, long, sweet tannins.

DESCRIPTION

These most innovative zones receive their names from their rivers and are integrated into the classification of southern regions with more temperate climatology due their latitudes. The southern zone of Chile includes the following regions: Araucanía, Los Ríos and Los Lagos. This area has one of the most uniform countryside.

NUMBER OF HECTARES: 3.421

ALTITUDES: To the south, the Patagonian Andes lose relative altitude, oscillating at approximately 1,500 metres on the north coast.

PREDOMINANT VARIETIES: The local país grape and muscat of Alexandria continue to be produced in the flatter, warmer strip, but the wineries (Viña Gracia, Viña Porta, Concha and Toro) plan to produce wines with grapes such as riesling, gewürztraminer and pinot noir although the most common grapes are cabernet and chardonnay.

CLIMATOLOGY AND SOILS

This sector is characterized by having a high level of rainfall and low temperatures in winter. The further south one goes, the climate involves more rainfall and freezing. In summer, the south is usually warm but there is rainfall all year round.

PRODUCER ZONES

1-Valles de Itata. (2,554 hectares). This has a similar climatology to Bío Bío and Malleco (cold winters, warm days and fresh nights) which means there are positive expectations for red wines. The muscat of Alejandria is the preferred grape followed by cabernet sauvignon.

2-Valle de Bío Bío. (850 hectares). The name is an onomatopoeia of a local bird or a form to define the "Rio Grande" Bío Bío, the second largest in Chile. The plantations are dominated by the país grape and muscat of Alexandria. The climate combines the Mediterranean conditions and the fresher climate of the south. There is no coastal influence in this central depression. Its soils are alluvial and sandy, formed by the rivers. The most successful tests have been with aromatic white grapes which contribute a slight mineral taste although the merlot has demonstrated its potential with a more fruity, fresh bouquet.

3-El valle del Malleco. (17 hectares). The most southerly vineyard in Chile has to combat 1,000 litres/m2 of rainfall annually but with fertile soil which rapidly increases production, but the summers are too moderate to give rise to a unique continental style microclimate. Chardonnay occupies almost all the plantations together with pinot noir.

ALTO LAS GREDAS

Km 8 Camino Perquenco-Quillem
Perquenco (Cautin)
☎: +56 991 004 757
mvpetermann@lasgredas.cl
www.altolasgredas.cl

ALTO LAS GREDAS 2011 B
chardonnay Valle del Malleco

90 Colour: bright yellow. Nose: ripe fruit, faded flowers, mineral. Palate: flavourful, fruity, good acidity, fine bitter notes.

VIÑA AQUITANIA

Avda. Consistorial, 5090
7940781 Peñalolén - Santiago (Región Metropolitana)
☎: +56 227 914 500 - Fax:+56 227 914 501
info@aquitania.cl
www.aquitania.cl

SOL DE SOL 2009 B
chardonnay Valle del Malleco

92 Colour: bright yellow. Nose: floral, ripe fruit, varietal, mineral. Palate: flavourful, balanced, fine bitter notes, long.

SOL DE SOL 2010 T
pinot noir Valle del Malleco

90 Colour: light cherry, garnet rim. Nose: varietal, medium intensity, floral. Palate: flavourful, fine bitter notes, correct, good finish.

WILLIAM FÈVRE CHILE

Huelén, 56 - Of. B
7500617 Providencia (Santiago)
☎: +56 222 351 919 - Fax:+56 222 354 525
info@williamfevre.cl
www.williamfevre.cl

PETIT QUINO BLANC 2012 B
sauvignon blanc Valle del Malleco

90 Colour: bright straw. Nose: medium intensity, fresh, wild herbs. Palate: easy to drink, fresh, fruity, fine bitter notes.

PEÑÍN GUIDE

TOP WINES FROM

SPAIN

DATA ON SPAIN:

POPULATION: 46,951,532 inhabitants
SURFACE AREA: 504.645 km²
SURFACE AREA OF VINEYARDS: 1.108.000 hectares
PREDOMINANT VARIETIES:
RED GRAPES: The main native grape is the tempranillo (18.9%), also called tinto fino in Ribera del Duero or tinta de Toro in Zamora. This is followed by the garnacha, bobal and monastrell. The French grapes are also very relevant in blends or singly, especially cabernet sauvignon and syrah.
WHITE GRAPES: Airén (is present in 26% of the vineyard) and macabeo (viura) are the most abundant, although in the bottled varietals are mainly verdejo and albariño. Also outstanding is the garnacha blanca. Grape harvests: The influence of an almost permanent anti-cyclone and the southern European latitude of Spain are offset by the higher average altitudes of its vineyards. The map shows plateaus and river valleys. The rivers mainly flow into the sea to the west and south west. In addition, the territory is crossed by mountain ranges in the directions southeast – northeast so that its vineyards lie on plains, in valleys, on slopes, terraces and plots, with different microclimates, orientations and altitudes, which makes it possible to have a wide range of harvest dates which start at the end of July and end in the first week of November. This fact, together with the wide variety of types of grapes which mature at different stages, enable the greatest number of wine styles in all of Europe.
CLIMATE: the warm climate of the Mediterranean is the pattern in all the country with the continental exceptions (warm daytime and fresh night-time) and more moderate influences of the Atlantic Ocean (facing north are the islands of Tenerife and La Palma in the Canary Islands, Galicia, Basque Country), Atlantic-Mediterranean (Huelva, Bierzo, Navarre, Rioja Alta),- Continental-Atlantic (Castile-León), Continental-Mediterranean (La Mancha, Extremadura, South Navarre, Rioja Baja and Aragón) and Mediterranean (Valencia, Alicante and Catalonia), among many other microclimates which give rise to many other wines.
PRODUCTION 2012: 29,6 millions hectolitres.
WINERIES: 4.000.
ALTITUDES: Spain has an average altitude of 660 metres above sea level. It is the second most mountainous country in Europe. One piece of relevant information is the fact that 18% of the land is above 1,000 metres high.

INTRODUCTION

In the last ten years, Spain has taken a gigantic step forward as compared with its neighbours France and Italy, and competes in the same league with the European countries producing quality wines except that, although it has half the vineyards on the continent, each hectare has less production than its neighbouring countries and, consequently, it achieves more quality. There is also the fact that the Spanish vineyards have a component of great value, which is the older age of the quality vineyards. This ensures a diversity of styles of wines protected by a group of native vines which are well adapted to Spanish soil such as garnacha, tempranillo, cariñena, bobal, mencía, verdejo and albariño. Moreover, the recuperation of unknown local varieties is in progress and this adds a rich and varied nursery for new tastes and for the approval of new geographical delimitations, which currently amount to 80 zones (Denominations of Origin and Single Estate Wines) and 52 production zones (Vinos de la Tierra or Local Wines and Quality Wines), with the same quality although protected by more flexible legislation than the others.

The pattern of Spanish wine has also changed direction in the last 20 years from the more classical "Rioja style", subjected to long periods of ageing in oak, which has extended as the model in almost all the Spanish areas, to the creation of a more fruity vine attached to the expression of the soil and the vine. The less institutional and corporate cooperatives, and more entrepreneurial and technical, were the precursors of a new variety of wine, which is balanced and has a good price. It comes from areas which were once undervalued such as Aragón, Extremadura and Levante, but which benefit from an ideal ecosystem for "terroir" wines.

MAP OF SPAIN'S DENOMINACIONES DE ORIGEN (DO) AND VINOS DE PAGO

A CORUÑA
LUGO
OVIEDO
PONTEVEDRA
DO Rías Baixas
DO Ribeira Sacra
DO Bierzo
LEÓN
DO Ribeiro
DO Valdeorras
OURENSE
DO Tierras de León
DO Monterrei
ZAMORA
DO Toro
VALLADOLID
DO Arribes
DO Rueda
DO Tierra del Vino de Zamora
SALAMANCA
ÁVILA
CÁCERES
DO Méntrida
BADAJOZ
DO Ribera del Guadiana
CÓRDOBA
DO Montilla-Moriles
SEVILLA
HUELVA
DO Condado de Huelva y Vino Naranja del Condado de Huelva
DO Jérez-Xérès-Sherry Manzanilla de Sanlúcar
MÁLAGA
CÁDIZ
Canary Islands
LANZAROTE
DO La Palma
LA PALMA
DO Valle del Güimar
DO Lanzarote
DO Tacoronte-Acentejo
DO Gran Canaria
DO Ycoden-Daute-Isora
LA GOMERA
TENERIFE
DO La Gomera
DO Abona
GRAN CANARIA
EL HIERRO
DO El Hierro
FUERTEVENTURA

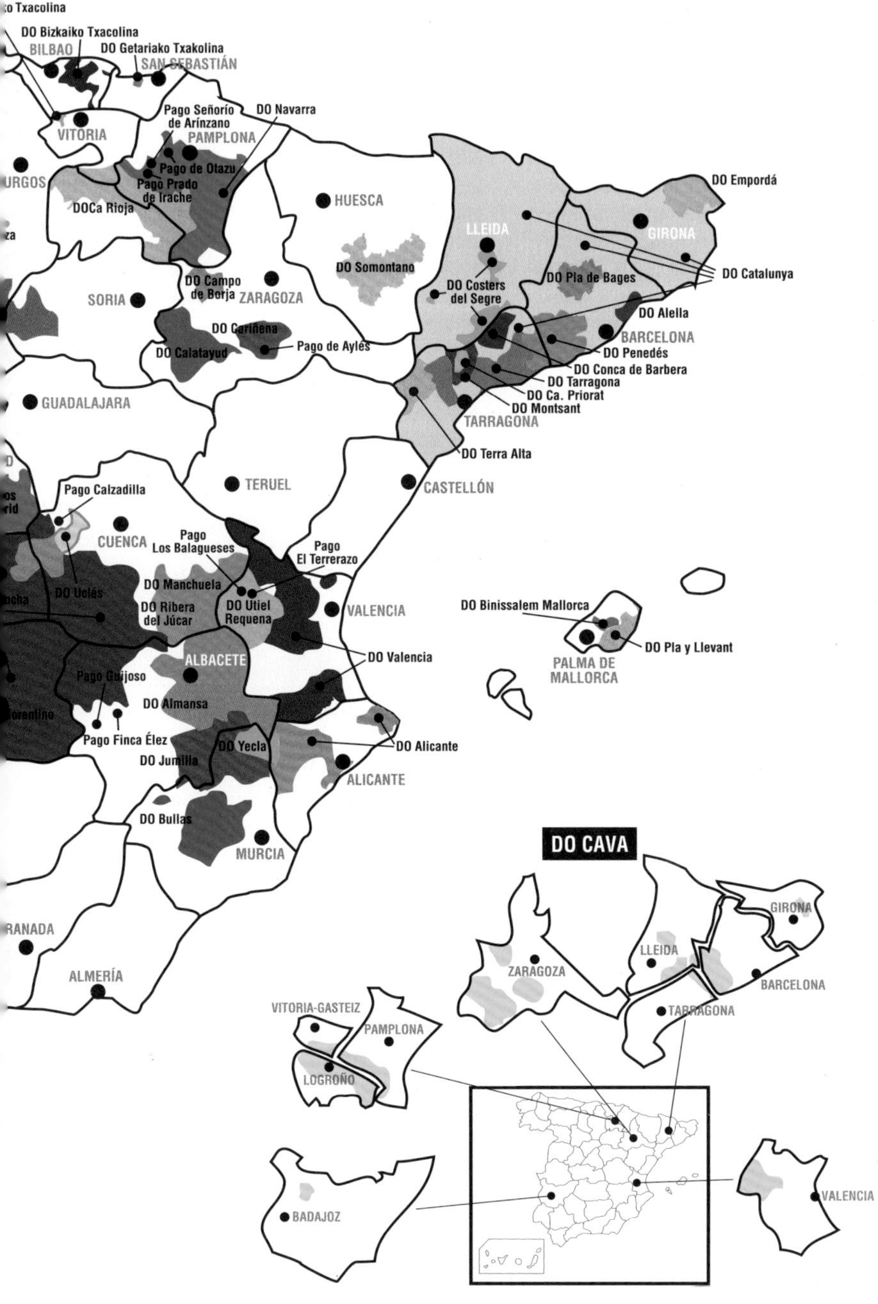
DO Bizkaiko Txacolina
BILBAO
DO Getariako Txakolina
SAN SEBASTIÁN
VITORIA
Pago Señorío de Arínzano
DO Navarra
PAMPLONA
Pago de Otazu
Pago Prado de Irache
DOCa Rioja
HUESCA
DO Somontano
DO Campo de Borja
ZARAGOZA
SORIA
DO Cariñena
DO Calatayud
Pago de Aylés
GUADALAJARA
LLEIDA
DO Costers del Segre
DO Empordá
GIRONA
DO Catalunya
DO Pla de Bages
DO Alella
BARCELONA
DO Penedés
DO Conca de Barbera
DO Tarragona
DO Ca. Priorat
DO Montsant
TARRAGONA
DO Terra Alta
CASTELLÓN
TERUEL
Pago Calzadilla
CUENCA
Pago Los Balagueses
Pago El Terrerazo
DO Manchuela
DO Uclés
DO Ribera del Júcar
DO Utiel Requena
VALENCIA
DO Valencia
ALBACETE
Pago Guijoso
DO Almansa
Pago Finca Élez
DO Jumilla
DO Yecla
DO Alicante
ALICANTE
DO Bullas
MURCIA
ALMERÍA
DO Binissalem Mallorca
DO Pla y Llevant
PALMA DE MALLORCA
DO CAVA
GIRONA
LLEIDA
ZARAGOZA
BARCELONA
TARRAGONA
VITORIA-GASTEIZ
PAMPLONA
LOGROÑO
BADAJOZ
VALENCIA

THE KEYS TO THE YEAR

Spain as a historical producer in Europe has big advantages over its competitors in the New World. Its long experience in the production of wine and in the creation of a wine industry have made it a country with the most extensive vital experience. However, as occurs with historical producers such as France and Italy, the legal baggage around wine is so complex and complicated that it slows up the natural growth of the industry. Thus, although the industry grows at a good pace, it does not attain the speed of countries such as Argentina and Chile, which are now involved in a pleasant oenological evolution. This includes the commercial evolution due to the simplicity of the message when addressing the non-specialized consumer.

Despite all this, wine growing and oenology in Spain is based on two important factors. One is the imposing varietal inheritance it has, with more than 200 native varieties distributed all over the country, a group of strains which guides the evolution of Spanish wine in the race to single out its products in a global wine market. The other is the diversity of climates and soils in all of Spain where historically wine has been a subsistence beverage and vineyards have proliferated in every corner of the land.

At tasting level, the main novelty of the year is the consolidation and expansion of the new trend in the production of red wine. Lighter and more expressive and, therefore, with a greater influence of balsamic and fruity nuances. These wines arise when the producers stop being obsessed by the phenolic maturing of all the components of the grape, which gave rise to wines about to become over mature, with a high level of alcohol and with less identification of their personalities. Fortunately, this practice tends to subside not only in the regions with excessive heat, but also in fresher areas, preventing delays to the grape harvesting, which gives red wines with elegant, delicate and sometimes more fragrant nuances. This trend is becoming more extended little by little and we find wines with this "taste" in very different regions and with such different climates as Navarra, Rioja, Madrid or Murcia. Obviously there are regions which are blessed with fresher, wetter climates, where these wines are obtained more easily, this explains the huge potential of the red wines from the northwest of Spain.

The other data which must be pointed out is the slow but sure growth of sparkling wines made with the traditional champagne method, including Cava, aged over a long period of time. A conception of cava proximate to the typology of a Grand Cru de Champagne, with long periods of ageing in stacks and with a common predominance of elegance, complexity and maturity as opposed to the freshness, simplicity and newness of the Cava produced in large volumes.

As regards the world of Spanish white wines, these are dominated by three opposing climatic influences. There are white wines of a continental type, specifically those produced in the central plateau, with Rueda and Rioja the leading types. Here the wines have nuances of fruit, freshness and green grass in contrast with the flower, fruit and acidity nuances of the Atlantic white wines, such as those from Galicia (Rías Baixas, Valdeorras and Ribeiro) or those from the Canary islands (Abona, Lanzarote and Ycoden, for example). The third style is conditioned by the purely Mediterranean climate, with wilder features, together with the ripeness of the fruit and they even have tropical hints and fuller sensations in the mouth. This is the case of the Denominations of Origin in Catalonia, the Balearic Islands and those located in Andalusia. A rich stylistic universe which few quality wine producing countries can match.

HISTORY

In Spain there are vestiges of wine since the times of the Phoenicians and Romans, since when Tarraco – the ancient name of the Spanish city of Tarragona– exported grand wines to all the empire. However, the monastic orders introduced French varieties as from the XII century which, with the passage of the centuries, became native grapes, such as tempranillo. Three centuries later, Navarre and Jerez became the most important wine growing engines. The full-bodied wines of Jerez, Alicante, Málaga and the Canary Islands soon reached the height of their fame, especially Canary Sack from the Canary Islands, one of the wines most appreciated by the English as from the XVII

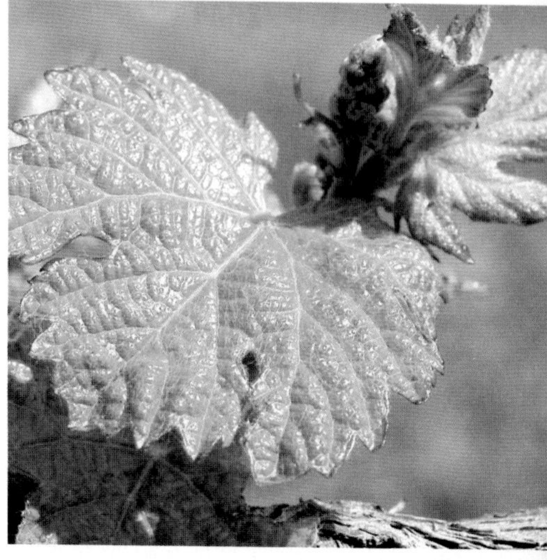

century. The new trade with the British, Dutch and French gave rise to new investments in Jerez, which would lead to the appearance of the warehouse owner and the first wineries in Jerez. The launch of Rioja wine onto the market took place at the end of the XIX century when the red grape plagues were devastating France and this forced the French to find new quality vineyards in the north of Spain in order to produce their wines with the Bordeaux label. In this glorious epoch for Spanish wine, there arose the main historical wineries of the country, such as Cune, López de Heredia and Marqués de Riscal. Until well into the twenties in the XX century, there were no regulations such as Denominations of Origin and the first cooperatives, which became family winery groups produced wine in bulk after the Spanish Civil War and the post-war period. In the seventies in the last century, Rioja went from being an elitist area of producers in barrels who acquired the wine from the harvesters to taking a more industrial approach with large wineries for production focussed on "socializing" Rioja wine in the catering industry. A Rioja wine with less colour and body but maintaining its relation with the taste of oak became the official style of Spanish wine and is appreciated by foreign consumers. The Spanish wineries were late to renew their installations and control systems in the vineyard. However, it was in the nineties when the boom occurred in Spanish oenology, when the oenologist appeared, as well as the controlled use of wood and the appearance of new Denominations of Origin.

REGULATION OF THE WINE GROWING ZONES

When Spain joined the European Union in 1986, Spanish wines were adapted to the legislation on the classification of its wines in two categories as in the rest of the wine producing countries: Table Wines and Quality Wines Produced in Specific Regions. The Spanish wine system is regulated by the Law on Wine of 2003, and the system is complicated by subdivisions in both groups, depending on the requirements regarding the quality of the wines and the origin of their production.

QUALITY WINES PRODUCED IN SPECIFIC REGIONS. This is the maximum category of Spanish wines and is divided into three labels:

1- ESTATE WINES.

These wines have very defined climate and soil characteristics and have the same requisites as wines with Qualified Denomination of Origin. Estate wines must be at least ten years as permanent quality wines on the market and also be produced and bottled in the winery of the estate or property where the grapes grow. Currently 13 Estate Wines are approved: eight in Castile-La Mancha (Calzadilla, Campo de la Guardia, Dehesa del Carrizal, Pago Florentino, Finca Élez, Pago del Guijoso, Dominio de Valdepusa, Casa del Blanco), three in Navarre (Señorío de Arínzano, Prado de Irache and Pago de Otazu) and two in the Autonomous Community of Valencia (El Terrerazo and Los Balagueses).

2- WINES WITH QUALIFIED DENOMINATION OF ORIGIN.

This designation was included in the Law when Rioja was granted this label after producing wines with the maximum quality standards for ten years once the Denomination of Origin was achieved. Other parameters required to achieve this status are that the wines be bottled in the wineries located in the same production zone or that they undergo a rigorous quality control. At the present time, there are only two Qualified Denominations of Origin: Rioja and Priorat.

3- WINES WITH DENOMINATION OF ORIGIN.

The first Denomination of Origin was Rioja in 1926, and it was also the first to receive the "Qualified" category in 1991. Today, Spain has 67 zones with Denomination of Origin which guarantees that the wines are from a specific geographical area and certifies a quality process and a type of soil or variety of grape, control of yield per hectare, or specific production methods and periods of ageing of the wines. These requirements are regulated by a Regulator Board with the participation of a specific number of wineries and wine growers. Before obtaining the Denomination of Origin, the region will have to have been recognized as a producer of quality wines for at least five years.

QUALITY WINES WITH GEOGRAPHICAL INDICATION. This is a recent classification which recognizes the wines produced in a specific region with grapes from the same region and whose quality, reputation or characteristics are due to the "geographical environment, to the human factor or to both, as regards the production of the grapes, the production of the wine or its ageing". To date, only six zones are recognized as such: Cangas, Valles de Benavente, Valtiendas, Granada, Lebrija and Sierra de Salamanca.

TABLE WINES. This is a step below the Quality Wines Produced in Specific Regions, but it does not indicate wines of a lower quality, but wines which entail freedom of movement for the oenologists who wish to produce without the conditioning imposed by the Denomination of Origin. This group includes table Wines and, according to national Law, Regional Wines. The latter are from specific areas of Spain where wine with notable local characteristics is produced, and the rules are more flexible than those for wines with Denomination of Origin. At present, 46 Regional Wines have been recognized in almost all the Autonomous Communities of Spain except for the Principality of Asturias, the Basque Country and Catalonia. They are equivalent to the French vins de pays and the Italian IGT.

Besides the aforementioned categories, Spanish wines may have the following classifications depending on ageing. These vary depending on the zones but we can list the most common ones which appear on all the labels with Denomination of Origin:

AGED WINE. Red wines with a minimum ageing period of 24 months with at least 6 months in oak wood.

RESERVA. Red wine with a minimum period of ageing amounting to 36 months with at least 12 months in wood and the rest in the bottle.

GRAN RESERVA. These are the red wines with a minimum of 60 months ageing with at least 18 months in wood.

WITH REGARD TO CAVAS the labels may bear the words gran reserva, used when this sparkling wine has undergone a period of 30 months ageing from tirage until disgorging. The amount of sugar in the tirage liqueur or wine in order to refill the cavas are the keys to differentiating between Brut Nature (up to 3 grams of sugar per litre), Extra Brut (up to 6 grams) or Brut (up to 12 grams). d zones with sweet wines, a variety of new types has appeared.

There are other types of denominations which are little by little falling into disuse. Among local wines and depending on the wine growing area, it is still possible to find traditional de-

signations associated to the time the wine has spent in the barrel such as: noble, aged wine, old wine , etc. and in the case of Jerez and zones with sweet wines, a variety of new types has appeared.

In almost all the continental area of the north of Spain with contrasting temperatures, fruity wines, with good acidity and very suited to ageing in barrels are produced. The aged and reserve wines are those preferred by the consumer, especially the Rioja wines which have a variety of outstanding styles (new, estate, short and long ageing) and a quality which is difficult to beat. The red wines of Toro, made from a clone of tempranillo adapted to the region of Zamora, are warmer wines with more potent tannins, a zone which is somewhat warmer than Ribera del Duero. In this Denomination of Origin, the wines are produced with the fine red variety which has a good structure and elegance in the barrel.

GENERAL CHARACTERISTICS OF THE WINES

Generally speaking, it is much easier to identify wines by their relation with the vine rather than by zone. The differences in taste owing to the territory as regards a variety is more reduced and only the climate makes a difference.

TYPOLOGIES OF RED WINES

TEMPRANILLO WINES. This is the most international wine in the country and occupies half the vineyards. It is part of the essential single varieties of Rioja, Ribera del Duero and La Mancha. It originated in the north of La Rioja where, due to its preference for fresh areas, it was better acclimatized. It is a variety which matures early, the reason for its name.

WINES WITH GARNACHA. Before choosing tempranillo, the Spanish vineyards were filled with this variety which grew with a good colour and alcohol, level in La Rioja, Navarre, Aragón and Catalonia. New oenology has made it possible to extract fine wines from garnacha in more mineral soils and from older vines which provide much more complex wines, with colours which have a variety of intensities, smoother tannins and more alcohol, but with new techniques to maintain the tendency of this variety to oxidization. The precursor of this grape was priorat and its earth wines produced with the taste of slate soils or slate of Tarragona, wines which are among the most valued in the world due to their character and mineral peculiarity. At a lower level are the cooperatives of Aragon, leaders due to their modern view of exportation, including those of Calatayud and Campo de Borja, which have recovered from the relegation of this variety in the highly mineralized soils. The garnacha wines from the area of Toledo and the west of Madrid have more balsamic sensations and smoother tannins in recent years.

WINES WITH MONASTRELL. This is the mourvèdre variety of France but is adapted to the warmer Mediterranean zones of Spain. It tends to give rise to more alcoholic wines, which are rich in volume but do not lose their variety identification. The most balanced wines as a variety or as a blend with less oxidizing grapes (syrah), are produced in Alicante and Murcia where mature wines with aromas of black fruits and sweet tannins although somewhat weak are achieved.

WINES WITH MENCÍA. Newer among the quality wines, these are produced between the Atlantic and the continental climates: exactly at the borders of the provinces of León and Zamora, although they also take in the province of Lugo and the north of Ourense (Denomination of Origin Bierzo and Denomination of Origin Ribeira Sacra). Their style is similar to the French grape cabernet franc, however, in the Atlantic strip of Spain wines with lively colours and aromatic potency are achieved and if the yield is reduced, wines with excellent complexity are achieved.

TIPOLOGIES OF WHITE WINES

WINES WITH ALBARIÑO. This is a first cousin of the German riesling. This vine is used to produce aromatic wines, with aromas of flowers and fine herbs, the fruit of vines which grow in wet less sunny areas of Galicia. Its oily hints in the mouth distinguish it from the other white wines, although this is offset with its good acidity which makes this wine ideal for ageing in bottles. Its promotion in English speaking countries has led to this wine becoming a sales record holder in the United States.

WINES WITH VERDEJO. Another of the native white grapes with more personality. It is very adapted to Valladolid and to the older, stony soils of Rueda, these wines are defined by their very fresh herbaceous aromas, as well as for their bitter hints. The latest novelties of Rueda wines are wines aged on lees in the style of albariño wines.

WINES WITH GODELLO. The best productions in vineyards with slate soils have become popular in all the world due to their oily taste and elegance. They originated from the zone of Valdeorras, the godellos – also from Monterrei or Bierzo- evoke fine ,herbs and flowers and become very complex with correct use in the barrel and careful work with the lees.

EXPORTATION

In 2012, Spanish wine invoiced €264,000,000 more abroad than in 2011, reaching over €2.500,000,000, which entails a 12% growth in value, according to the data of the Inland Revenue. However, the volume of exports fell by 8% as the average sales price increased considerably, by 22% up to €1.21 per litre. The ten main importing countries of Spanish wine are: Germany, the United Kingdom, the United States, France, Switzerland, the Netherlands, Belgium, China, Canada and Italy.

If we consider the types of wines, the exportations of bulk wines fell in 2012 as regards volume, but they increased in value. The sales which dropped most were those bulk wines with no Denomination of Origin (-20%) although they managed to increase their value by 9% due to the increase in the average price

A UNIQUE STYLE IN SPAIN

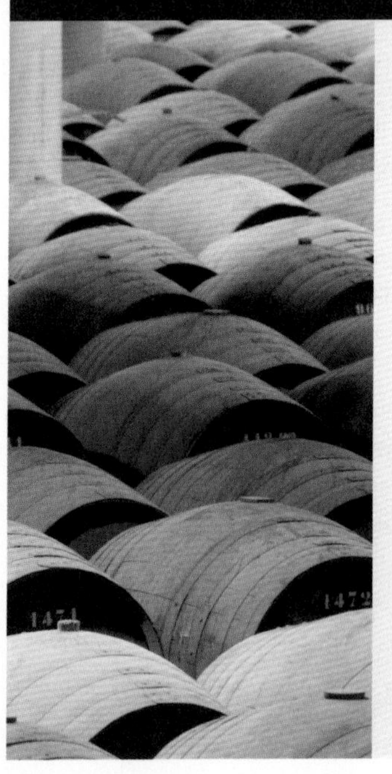

SHERRY WINE. The neutral palomino grape gives rise to some of the most special wines in the world: white wines with added alcohol which age in the particular system of criaderas (young) and soleras (vintage) in 550 litre American oak casks. From the final soleras, located nearest the ground, up to four final wine styls are extracted in four levels of barrels piled in rows.

FINOS AND MANZANILLAS. These are the wines with the best quality /price relation in the Spanish market, despite their complicated production: they are wines with 15 degrees of alcohol on which a flower or veil constituted by microscopic fungus is formed and this maintains the wine pale in colour with no contact with the air. It has curious aromas with saline nuances, its tactile sensation is oily and bitter. The manzanillas are the same types of wines as those which come from the humid environment of Sanlúcar de Barrameda. This is where the proximity of the sea contributes a greater thickness to the veil and a certain consistency in the mouth.

(it went up by 36%, going from 12 cents to 45 cents per litre). In this regard, bulk wine with no Denomination of Origin continues to be the product most exported by Spain and represents 45% of the total amount of sales abroad. The exportations of bulk wines with denomination of Origin also fell as regards volume, but by a lower percentage (-8%) and increased in value by approximately 4%.

As concerns bottled wines, in 2012 those which invoiced most were again wines with Denomination of Origin, whose sales supposed 40% (€1,013,000,000) of the total of exported wine. They were also the wines which grew most in volume (10%) and in terms of value, they increased by 10%, achieving a stable average price of €2.95 per litre. The sales of bottled wines with no Denomination of Origin were those which increased most in terms of value (18%), although the volume commercialized did not increase to the same extent (6%).

Spain, with a production in 2012 amounting to 29.6 million hectolitres (Mhl) of wine, continues to be the third wine producing country in the world, after France (42.2 Mhl) and Italy (40 Mhl), according to data of the International Organization of Vine and Wine (OIV) included in its Note on the World Situation presented in March 2013.

AMONTILLADOS. These are finos which lose the veil flower and oxidize. Wines with strong, salty aromas, and with a more oily taste which absorbs the toasted, more complex nuances of the barrel.

OLOROSOS. Wines which are produced from ageing racks which are leading wines with added alcohol up to 19 degrees which age by oxidation.

CREAM. Wines which are a blend of olorosos and sweet wines, designed for the British consumer.

PALOS CORTADOS. These are wines which came about by chance, not always due to the work of man. They combine the fineness of amontillado and the structure of oloroso on the palate.

PEDRO XIMÉNEZ. In Jerez and in Montilla-Moriles, these are dark mahogany coloured wines with extract of syrup from sun toasted and dehydrated grapes with the same name.

DESCRIPTION

In the south of the island of Tenerife, Abona includes vineyards with a multitude of micro-climates as these expand over the slopes of the Teide towards the coast. This is the Spanish brand of wines which has the vineyards at the highest altitude of all those with Spanish Denomination of Origin (up to 1,700 metres). The dominant wines are white with volcanic ash aromas.

NUMBER OF HECTARES: 1.086 **ALTITUDES:** 300 m. – 1.750 m.

PREDOMINANT VARIETIES:

White grapes: bastardo blanco, bermejuela, forastera blanca, güal, listán blanca (majority), malvasía, muscatel, pedro ximénez, sabro, torrontés, verdello and vijariego.

Red grapes: bastardo negro, cabernet sauvignon, castellana negra, listán negro, listán prieto, malvasía rosada, muscatel negro, negramoll, pinot noir, rubí cabernet, syrah, tempranillo, tintilla and vijariego negro.

CLIMATOLOGY AND SOILS

Mediterranean with the influence of the trade winds which refresh the air as they penetrate the island. The soils go from sandy on the coast to clay and well drained in the higher zones owing to their volcanic condition.

CUMBRES DE ABONA

Bajada El Vizo, s/n
38580 Arico - (Santa Cruz de Tenerife)
☎: +34 922 768 604 - Fax: +34 922 768 234
bodega@cumbresdeabona.es
www.cumbresabona.com

FLOR DE CHASNA 2011 T BARRICA

91 Colour: bright cherry, purple rim. Nose: balanced, red berry notes, ripe fruit, spicy, creamy oak. Palate: good structure, fruity, fresh.

TESTAMENTO MALVASÍA ESENCIA 2008 B

90 Colour: old gold. Nose: candied fruit, honeyed notes, faded flowers, complex. Palate: flavourful, fruity, good acidity.

DESCRIPTION

This is one of the smallest denominations in Spain due to its geographical limitation near Barcelona. Its characteristic wines are white from pansa blanca grapes, cultivated in vineyards near to the sea in sandy almost white soil (sauló) which helps to mature the grapes.

NUMBER OF HECTARES: 314 **ALTITUDES:** 60 m. – 400 m.

PREDOMINANT VARIETIES:

White grapes: pansa blanca, garnatxa blanca, pansa rosada, picapoll, malvasía, macabeo, parellada, chardonnay, sauvignon blanc and chenin blanc.

Red grapes: monastrell, garnatxa, ull de llebre, merlot, pinot noir, syrah, cabernet sauvignon, sumoll and mataró.

CLIMATOLOGY AND SOILS

Mediterranean climate. The soils in the interior are clay, while those located near the sea are almost white and are distinguished by their substantial permeability and their capacity to retain the rays of the sun, which helps to improve the maturing of the grape.

ALELLA VINÍCOLA

Angel Guimerà, 62
8328 Alella - (Barcelona)
☎: +34 935 403 842 - Fax: +34 935 401 648
xavi@alellavinicola.com
www.alellavinicola.com

MARFIL GENEROSO SEC 1976 B
100% pansa blanca

90 Colour: light mahogany. Nose: acetaldehyde, dry nuts, spicy, pattiserie. Palate: good finish, flavourful, toasty.

MARFIL GENEROSO SEMI 1976 B
100% pansa blanca

91 Colour: old gold, amber rim. Nose: powerfull, varnish, sweet spices, candied fruit. Palate: balanced, flavourful, spicy, long, good acidity.

MARFIL MOLT DOLÇ 2003 B
100% pansa blanca

93 Colour: old gold, amber rim. Nose: floral, honeyed notes, caramel. Palate: rich, spirituous, toasty, balanced, sweetness.

MARFIL MOSCATEL 2009 ESP
100% moscatel

90 Colour: bright straw. Nose: candied fruit, white flowers, grapey, fresh. Palate: fresh, fruity, flavourful, good acidity, sweet.

MARFIL VIOLETA 2003 T
100% garnacha

91 Colour: bright cherry, garnet rim. Nose: balsamic herbs, fruit preserve, spicy, dark chocolate. Palate: powerful, flavourful, fruity, toasty.

ALTA ALELLA BLANC DE NEU 2009 BFB
chardonnay, pansa blanca, viognier

90 Colour: bright golden. Nose: acetaldehyde, ripe fruit, citrus fruit, honeyed notes, sweet spices. Palate: long, full, flavourful, complex.

ALTA ALELLA DOLÇ MATARÓ 2010 TINTO DULCE
monastrell

91 Colour: cherry, garnet rim. Nose: acetaldehyde, ripe fruit, fruit liqueur notes, dark chocolate, spicy. Palate: powerful, flavourful, rich, balanced.

ALTA ALELLA LANIUS 2011 BFB
pansa blanca, chardonnay, sauvignon blanc, viognier, moscatel

90 Colour: bright yellow. Nose: ripe fruit, honeyed notes, fragrant herbs, sweet spices. Palate: flavourful, complex, long, spicy.

ALTA ALELLA ORBUS 2007 TC
syrah

90 Color cherry, garnet rim. Aroma ripe fruit, spicy, creamy oak, toasty, complex. Taste powerful, flavourful, toasty, round tannins.

ALTA ALELLA SYRAH DOLÇ 2006 T
syrah

90 Colour: cherry, garnet rim. Nose: ripe fruit, fruit liqueur notes, aromatic coffee, sweet spices, toasty. Palate: powerful, flavourful, complex, long.

BODEGAS CASTILLO DE SAJAZARRA

Del Río, s/n
26212 Sajazarra - (La Rioja)
☎: +34 941 320 066 - Fax: +34 941 320 251
bodega@castillodesajazarra.com
www.castillodesajazarra.com

IN VITA 2010 B
60% pansa blanca, 40% sauvignon blanc

91 Colour: bright straw. Nose: floral, balanced, fresh fruit, fragrant herbs. Palate: flavourful, fruity, good acidity.

IN VITA ELVIWINES KOSHER 2011 B
60% pansa blanca, 40% sauvignon blanc

90 Colour: bright straw. Nose: fresh, fresh fruit, white flowers, fragrant herbs. Palate: flavourful, fruity, good acidity, balanced.

MARQUÉS DE ALELLA

Torrente, 38
8391 Tiana - (Barcelona)
☎: +34 933 950 811 - Fax: +34 933 955 500
info@parxet.es
www.parxet.es

MARQUÉS DE ALELLA ALLIER 2009 BFB
100% chardonnay

90 Colour: bright golden. Nose: ripe fruit, dry nuts, powerfull, toasty, sweet spices. Palate: flavourful, fruity, spicy, toasty, long.

DESCRIPTION

In the province of Alicante and in a small part of Murcia there are full bodied, balsamic red grapes of the monastrell variety, one of the native, sweet grapes with a historical tradition. The muscatel grapes of La Marina are harvested from vineyards very near to the sea, in over-ripe bunches and from the famous fondillon of Alicante, which are monastrell red grapes, which is harvested over-ripe from the vine and go through an oxidizing ageing process.

NUMBER OF HECTARES: 12.570 **ALTITUDES:** 30 m. – 900 m.

PREDOMINANT VARIETIES:

White grapes: merseguera, muscat of Alexandria, macabeo, planta fina, verdil, airén, chardonnay and sauvignon blanc.

Red grapes: monastrell, garnacha, garnacha tintorera, bobal, tempranillo, cabernet sauvignon, merlot, pinot noir, syrah and petit verdot.

CLIMATOLOGY AND SOILS

In the coastal zone the climate is Mediterranean and somewhat wetter than in the interior. The soils are brown-limestone with low clay content and little organic material.

BODEGA COOPERATIVA SANT VICENTE FERRER

Avda. Las Palmas, 32
3725 Teulada - (Alicante)
☎: +34 965 740 051 - Fax: +34 965 740 489
bodega@coop-santvicent.com
www.coop-santvicent.com

TEULADA MOSCATEL RESERVA B RESERVA
moscatel

90 Colour: light mahogany. Nose: powerfull, characterful, overripe fruit, dried fruit, acetaldehyde, pattiserie. Palate: powerful, sweet, fine bitter notes.

BODEGA NUESTRA SEÑORA DE LAS VIRTUDES COOP. V.

Ctra. de Yecla, 9
3400 Villena - (Alicante)
☎: +34 965 802 187
coopvillena@coopvillena.com
www.coopvillena.com

TESORO DE VILLENA RESERVA ESPECIAL FONDILLÓN FONDILLÓN SOLERA
100% monastrell

90 Colour: light mahogany. Nose: fruit liqueur notes, acetaldehyde, dried fruit, aromatic coffee, roasted almonds, caramel. Palate: powerful, spirituous, fine bitter notes, spirituous.

BODEGA VINESSENS

Historiador Sebastian Garcia, 15
3400 Villena - (Alicante)
☎: +34 965 800 265
comercial@vinessens.es
www.vinessens.es

EL TELAR 2009 TC
100% monastrell

92 Colour: cherry, garnet rim. Nose: spicy, creamy oak, toasty, complex, varietal, warm. Palate: powerful, flavourful, toasty, round tannins.

ESSENS 2011 BFB
chardonnay

92 Color bright yellow. Aroma powerfull, ripe fruit, sweet spices, creamy oak, fragrant herbs. Taste rich, smoky aftertaste, flavourful, fresh, good acidity.

SEIN 2009 TC
monastrell, syrah

92 Colour: cherry, garnet rim. Nose: spicy, creamy oak, toasty, characterful, ripe fruit, mineral. Palate: powerful, flavourful, toasty, round tannins.

SEIN 2010 TC
60% monastrell, 40% syrah

92 Colour: cherry, garnet rim. Nose: spicy, creamy oak, toasty, complex, mineral, overripe fruit. Palate: powerful, flavourful, toasty, round tannins.

BODEGAS BERNABÉ NAVARRO

Ctra. Villena-Cañada, Km. 3
3400 Villena - (Alicante)
☎: +34 966 770 353 - Fax: +34 966 770 353
info@bodegasbernabenavarro.com
www.bodegasbernabenavarro.com

BERYNA 2010 T
monastrell, otras

92 Colour: cherry, garnet rim. Nose: mineral, powerfull, characterful, candied fruit, ripe fruit, toasty. Palate: powerful, concentrated, sweetness, fine bitter notes.

CASA BALAGUER 2008 T
monastrell, otras

92 Colour: bright cherry. Nose: sweet spices, creamy oak, expressive, overripe fruit. Palate: flavourful, fruity, toasty, round tannins.

CURRO 2010 T
60% cabernet sauvignon, 40% monastrell

95 Colour: cherry, garnet rim. Nose: ripe fruit, spicy, creamy oak, toasty, complex, earthy notes, powerfull. Palate: powerful, flavourful, toasty, round tannins.

BODEGAS E. MENDOZA

Partida El Romeral, s/n
3580 Alfaz del Pi - (Alicante)
☎: +34 965 888 639 - Fax: +34 965 889 232
bodegas-mendoza@bodegasmendoza.com
www.bodegasmendoza.com

ENRIQUE MENDOZA CABERNET - SHIRAZ 2008 TR
50% cabernet sauvignon, 50% syrah

91 Colour: bright cherry. Nose: ripe fruit, sweet spices, creamy oak. Palate: flavourful, fruity, toasty, round tannins.

ENRIQUE MENDOZA MOSCATEL DE MENDOZA 2009 B
100% moscatel

94 Colour: bright straw. Nose: powerfull, varietal, characterful, complex, ripe fruit, citrus fruit, honeyed notes. Palate: flavourful, powerful, sweet, good acidity.

ENRIQUE MENDOZA PETIT VERDOT 2010 TC
petit verdot

93 Colour: cherry, garnet rim. Nose: ripe fruit, spicy, creamy oak, toasty, balsamic herbs, earthy notes. Palate: flavourful, toasty, round tannins, balanced.

ENRIQUE MENDOZA SANTA ROSA 2007 TR
70% cabernet sauvignon, 15% merlot, 15% syrah

93 Colour: cherry, garnet rim. Nose: fruit expression, sweet spices, creamy oak, toasty, dark chocolate. Palate: powerful, spicy, ripe fruit, fine bitter notes.

ENRIQUE MENDOZA SANTA ROSA 2008 TR
cabernet sauvignon, merlot, syrah

93 Colour: cherry, garnet rim. Nose: ripe fruit, spicy, creamy oak, balsamic herbs, earthy notes. Palate: powerful, flavourful, toasty, round tannins, balanced, elegant.

ENRIQUE MENDOZA SHIRAZ 2009 TC
100% syrah

92 Colour: cherry, garnet rim. Nose: fruit expression, red berry notes, toasty, sweet spices, new oak. Palate: powerful, flavourful, harsh oak tannins.

ESTRECHO MONASTRELL 2007 T
100% monastrell

92 Colour: cherry, garnet rim. Nose: spicy, creamy oak, toasty, characterful, warm, ripe fruit. Palate: powerful, flavourful, toasty, round tannins.

LA TREMENDA 2009 T
100% monastrell

92 Colour: bright cherry. Nose: ripe fruit, sweet spices, creamy oak, mineral, smoky. Palate: flavourful, fruity, toasty, round tannins.

LAS QUEBRADAS 2010 T
100% monastrell

94 Colour: cherry, garnet rim. Nose: ripe fruit, spicy, creamy oak, toasty, complex, earthy notes. Palate: powerful, flavourful, toasty, balanced.

BODEGAS FRANCISCO GÓMEZ

Ctra. Villena - Pinoso, Km. 8,8
3400 Villena - (Alicante)
☎: +34 965 979 195 - Fax: +34 965 979 196
info@bodegasfranciscogomez.es
www.bodegasfranciscogomez.es

BOCA NEGRA 2007 TC
monastrell

90 Colour: bright cherry, garnet rim. Nose: powerfull, ripe fruit, spicy, mineral, balanced. Palate: warm, powerful, flavourful, round tannins.

BODEGAS GUTIÉRREZ DE LA VEGA

Les Quintanes, 1
3792 Parcent - (Alicante)
☎: +34 966 403 871 - Fax: +34 966 405 257
info@castadiva.es
www.castadiva.es

CASTA DIVA 2001 FONDILLÓN

93 Colour: pale ruby, brick rim edge. Nose: acetaldehyde, varnish, aged wood nuances, dried fruit, expressive, toasty. Palate: long, ripe fruit, sweetness, spicy, toasty.

CASTA DIVA ESENCIAL "A LUCRECIA BORI" B
100% moscatel de alejandría

97 Colour: iodine, amber rim. Nose: citrus fruit, floral, fragrant herbs, sweet spices, creamy oak, pattiserie. Palate: powerful, flavourful, creamy, long, ripe fruit, balanced.

CASTA DIVA FONDILLÓN SOLERA 1987 FONDILLÓN
100% monastrell

96 Colour: dark-red cherry. Nose: dry nuts, dried fruit, dark chocolate, sweet spices, creamy oak, toasty, acetaldehyde. Palate: fine bitter notes, flavourful, long, toasty, balanced, elegant.

CASTA DIVA RECÓNDITA ARMONÍA 2009 T

93 Colour: cherry, garnet rim. Nose: overripe fruit, ripe fruit, scrubland, mineral, spicy, creamy oak. Palate: powerful, flavourful, complex, long, balsamic.

CASTA DIVA RESERVA REAL 2002 B RESERVA
100% moscatel de alejandría

95 Colour: bright golden. Nose: ripe fruit, faded flowers, mineral, acetaldehyde, sweet spices, cocoa bean, toasty. Palate: powerful, flavourful, balanced, long, toasty.

BODEGAS GUTIÉRREZ DE LA VEGA

Les Quintanes, 1
3792 Parcent - (Alicante)
☎: +34 966 403 871 - Fax: +34 966 405 257
info@castadiva.es
www.castadiva.es

FURTIVA LÁGRIMA 2010 B

93 Colour: golden. Nose: candied fruit, white flowers, citrus fruit, honeyed notes. Palate: flavourful, sweet, fresh, fruity, long.

LA DIVA 2010 BC
moscatel

92 Color golden. Aroma powerfull, floral, honeyed notes, candied fruit, fragrant herbs. Taste flavourful, sweet, fresh, fruity, good acidity, long.

PRÍNCIPE DE SALINAS 2009 TC
monastrell

90 Colour: cherry, garnet rim. Nose: ripe fruit, medium intensity, earthy notes, complex, varietal. Palate: good structure, fruity, full.

BODEGAS MURVIEDRO

Ampliación Pol. El Romeral, s/n
46340 Requena - (Valencia)
☎: +34 962 329 003 - Fax: +34 962 329 002
murviedro@murviedro.es
www.murviedro.es

CUEVA DEL PERDÓN 2009 T
60% monastrell, 40% syrah

90 Colour: bright cherry. Nose: sweet spices, creamy oak, expressive, ripe fruit. Palate: flavourful, fruity, toasty, round tannins.

BODEGAS SIERRA DE CABRERAS

Mollenta, 27
3638 Salinas - (Alicante)
☎: +34 647 515 590
info@carabibas.com
www.carabibas.com

CARABIBAS VS 2010 T
65% cabernet sauvignon, 30% merlot, 5% monastrell

91 Colour: bright cherry. Nose: sweet spices, creamy oak, expressive, overripe fruit, mineral. Palate: flavourful, fruity, toasty, round tannins.

BODEGAS SIERRA SALINAS

Paraje del Puerto, s/n (Ctra. Villena-Pinoso, km. 16)
30400 Villena - (Alicante)
☎: +34 968 791 271 - Fax: +34 968 791 900
office@sierrasalinas.com
www.sierrasalinas.com

MIRA SALINAS 2009 T
50% monastrell, 20% cabernet sauvignon, 20% garnacha tintorera, 10% petit verdot

93 Colour: cherry, garnet rim. Nose: spicy, creamy oak, toasty, complex, earthy notes, dry stone, fruit expression. Palate: powerful, flavourful, toasty, round tannins.

MO SALINAS MONASTRELL 2010 T
85% monastrell, 10% cabernet sauvignon, 5% garnacha tintorera

90 Colour: bright cherry. Nose: ripe fruit, sweet spices, creamy oak, expressive, dark chocolate. Palate: flavourful, fruity, toasty, round tannins.

PUERTO SALINAS 2008 T
65% monastrell, 20% cabernet sauvignon, 15% garnacha tintorera

90 Colour: cherry, garnet rim. Nose: dark chocolate, creamy oak, toasty, overripe fruit. Palate: spirituous, powerful, fine bitter notes.

SALINAS 1237 2007 T
20% monastrell, 40% cabernet sauvignon, 40% garnacha tintorera

93 Colour: black cherry. Nose: powerfull, characterful, complex, creamy oak, toasty, new oak, ripe fruit. Palate: powerful, concentrated, good structure, harsh oak tannins.

BODEGAS VOLVER

Pza. de Grecia, 1 Local 1B
45005 Toledo - (Toledo)
☎: +34 925 167 493 - Fax: +34 925 167 059
export@bodegasvolver.com
www.bodegasvolver.com

TARIMA HILL 2009 T
100% monastrell

90 Colour: cherry, garnet rim. Nose: spicy, creamy oak, toasty, complex, overripe fruit. Palate: powerful, flavourful, toasty, round tannins.

BODEGAS XALÓ

Ctra. Xaló Alcalali, s/n
3727 Xaló - (Alicante)
☎: +34 966 480 034 - Fax: +34 966 480 808
comercial@bodegasxalo.com
www.bodegasxalo.com

BAHÍA DE DENIA 2011 B JOVEN
100% moscatel

90 Colour: bright straw. Nose: fresh, white flowers, varietal, ripe fruit. Palate: flavourful, fruity, good acidity, balanced.

RIU RAU 2010 MISTELA
100% moscatel

90 Colour: light mahogany. Nose: dried fruit, toasty, caramel, sweet spices. Palate: powerful, flavourful, sweetness, toasty.

BODEGAS Y VIÑEDOS EL SEQUÉ

El Sequé, 59
3650 Pinoso - (Alicante)
☎: +34 945 600 119 - Fax: +34 945 600 850
elseque@artadi.com

EL SEQUÉ 2010 T
100% monastrell

94 Colour: bright cherry. Nose: sweet spices, creamy oak, expressive, scrubland, red berry notes, toasty. Palate: flavourful, fruity, toasty, round tannins.

COMERCIAL GRUPO FREIXENET S.A.

Joan Sala, 2
8770 Sant Sadurní D'Anoia - (Barcelona)
☎: +34 938 917 000 - Fax: +34 938 183 095
freixenet@freixenet.es
www.freixenet.es

NAUTA 2006 TC
100% monastrell

90 Colour: light cherry, garnet rim. Nose: ripe fruit, creamy oak, sweet spices. Palate: powerful, flavourful, toasty, long.

IBERICA BRUNO PRATS

Ctra. Monovar - Salinas CV 830, km. 3,2
3640 Monovar - (Alicante)
☎: +34 645 963 122
stephanepoint@hotmail.com
www.fideliswines.com

ALFYNAL 2009 T
100% monastrell

90 Colour: black cherry. Nose: powerfull, varietal, characterful, overripe fruit, creamy oak, toasty. Palate: powerful, flavourful, concentrated, good acidity.

MOSYCA 2009 T
30% syrah, 25% monastrell, 25% cabernet sauvignon, 20% petit verdot

91 Colour: cherry, garnet rim. Nose: ripe fruit, spicy, creamy oak, toasty, varietal. Palate: powerful, flavourful, toasty, round tannins.

LA BODEGA DE PINOSO

Paseo de la Constitución, 82
3650 Pinoso - (Alicante)
☎: +34 965 477 040 - Fax: +34 966 970 149
dptocomercial@labodegadepinoso.com
www.labodegadepinoso.com

VERGEL SELECCIÓN BARRICAS 2010 T
70% monastrell, 20% syrah, 10% merlot

90 Colour: cherry, garnet rim. Nose: ripe fruit, fruit expression, creamy oak, sweet spices. Palate: powerful, good structure, fine bitter notes.

PRIMITIVO QUILES

Mayor, 4
3640 Monóvar - (Alicante)
☎: +34 965 470 099 - Fax: +34 966 960 235
info@primitivoquiles.com
www.primitivoquiles.com

GRAN IMPERIAL GE
100% moscatel

92 Colour: dark mahogany. Nose: powerfull, warm, fruit liqueur notes, fruit liqueur notes, sweet spices, aromatic coffee, dark chocolate. Palate: powerful, sweet, good acidity, fine bitter notes, spirituous.

PRIMITIVO QUILES FONDILLÓN 1948 GE
100% monastrell

91 Colour: light mahogany. Nose: acetaldehyde, fruit liqueur notes, fruit liqueur notes, aromatic coffee, caramel. Palate: flavourful, powerful, spirituous, spicy, long.

RAMBLIS DULCE 2010 T
monastrell

91 Colour: black cherry. Nose: powerfull, characterful, overripe fruit, candied fruit. Palate: powerful, sweet, concentrated, complex.

VINS DEL COMTAT

Turballos, 1 - 3
3820 Cocentaina - (Alicante)
☎: +34 965 593 194 - Fax: +34 965 593 590
info@vinsdelcomtat.com
www.vinsdelcomtat.com

CRISTAL.LI B
100% moscatel de alejandría

91 Colour: bright straw. Nose: fresh, fresh fruit, white flowers. Palate: flavourful, fruity, good acidity, balanced.

VIÑEDO Y BODEGA HERETAT DE CESILIA

Paraje Alcaydias, 4
3660 Novelda - (Alicante)
☎: +34 965 605 385 - Fax: +34 965 604 763
administracion@heretatdecesilia.com
www.heretatdecesilia.com

CESILIA BLANC 2011 B
50% moscatel, 50% malvasía

90 Colour: bright straw. Nose: fresh, fresh fruit, white flowers, dried herbs, citrus fruit. Palate: flavourful, fruity, good acidity, balanced.

VIÑEDOS CULTURALES

Plaza Constitución, 8 - 1º
3380 Bigastro - (Alicante)
☎: +34 966 770 353 - Fax: +34 966 770 353
vinedosculturales@gmail.com
vinedosculturales.blogspot.com.es

LOS CIPRESES DE USALDÓN 2011 T
100% garnacha peluda

93 Colour: cherry, purple rim. Nose: expressive, fresh fruit, floral, fragrant herbs. Palate: flavourful, fruity, good acidity, round tannins.

DESCRIPTION

This is the most eastern area of La Mancha, in transition towards Levante, it has borders with Yecla and Alicante. In the past it produced bulk wine and now has new expectations with new wines from garnacha tintorera, a grape has always served to give colour to volume wines. The new techniques and ageing processes achieve full bodied, potent and fruity wines.

NUMBER OF HECTARES: 7.600 **ALTITUDES:** 700 m.

PREDOMINANT VARIETIES:

White grapes: airén, verdejo and sauvignon blanc.
Red grapes: garnacha tintorera, monastrell, cencibel and syrah.

CLIMATOLOGY AND SOILS

This is of a continental type, somewhat less extreme than in La Mancha. The soil in these flatland vineyards is limestone, poor in organic material and with some clay areas.

BODEGA SANTA CRUZ DE ALPERA

Cooperativa, s/n
2690 Alpera - (Albacete)
☎: +34 967 330 108 - Fax: +34 967 330 903
comercial@bodegasantacruz.com
www.bodegasantacruz.com

SANTA CRUZ DE ALPERA 2011 T
100% garnacha tintorera

90 Colour: bright cherry, purple rim. Nose: fresh, red berry notes, balanced, violets. Palate: flavourful, fruity, good acidity.

BODEGAS ALMANSEÑAS

Ctra. de Alpera, CM 3201 Km. 98,6 (Apdo. de Correos 324)
2640 Almansa - (Albacete)
☎: +34 967 098 116 - Fax: +34 967 098 121
adaras@ventalavega.com
www.ventalavega.com

ADARAS 2007 T
garnacha tintorera

92 Colour: black cherry, garnet rim. Nose: ripe fruit, sweet spices, cocoa bean, dark chocolate. Palate: powerful, flavourful, toasty, balanced.

LA HUELLA DE ADARAS 2009 T
garnacha tintorera, monastrell, syrah

90 Colour: cherry, garnet rim. Nose: damp earth, dry stone, ripe fruit, floral, scrubland. Palate: powerful, flavourful, long, balanced.

BODEGAS ATALAYA

Ctra. Almansa - Ayora, Km. 1
2640 Almansa - (Albacete)
☎: +34 968 435 022 - Fax: +34 968 716 051
info@orowines.com
www.orowines.com

ALAYA 2010 T
100% garnacha tintorera

91 Colour: black cherry. Nose: powerfull, fruit liqueur notes, raspberry, sweet spices, dark chocolate, toasty, varietal. Palate: powerful, flavourful, sweetness, fine bitter notes, fine bitter notes.

LA ATALAYA 2010 T
85% garnacha tintorera, 15% monastrell

90 Colour: black cherry. Nose: roasted coffee, dark chocolate, ripe fruit. Palate: spicy, ripe fruit, fine bitter notes, round tannins.

LAYA 2010 T
70% garnacha tintorera, 30% monastrell

91 Colour: bright cherry. Nose: ripe fruit, sweet spices, creamy oak, expressive, red berry notes, fruit expression. Palate: flavourful, fruity, toasty, round tannins.

DESCRIPTION

This is located in the north of Spain, specifically in Vitoria – Gasteiz, in the northwest of the province of Álava, coinciding with the basin of the River Nervión. Within this Denomination of Origin is chacolí , a pale or greenish fresh white wine, which is acidic and with hints of fresh herbs. Unlike the chacolís of Bizkaiko Txakolina, very little of this wine is exported and is mostly consumed in the local market of the Basque Country.

NUMBER OF HECTARES: 100 **ALTITUDES:** 300 m. – 400 m.

PREDOMINANT VARIETIES:
White grapes: hondarrabi zuri.

CLIMATOLOGY AND SOILS

This is a production zone with less humidity and more freshness than the neighbouring Denomination of Origin, Bizkaiko Txakolina. The main risk in the zone lies in the spring frost. It has a diversity of soils, from clay to gravelly, the latter is where the grape matures best.

OKENDO TXAKOLINA BODEGA SEÑORÍO DE ASTOBIZA

Barrio Jandiola, 16 (Caserío Aretxabala)
1409 Okondo - (Álava)
☎: +34 945 898 516 - Fax: +34 945 898 447
comercial@senoriodeastobiza.com
www.senoriodeastobiza.com

MALKOA TXAKOLI 2011 B
100% hondarrabi zuri

90 Colour: bright straw. Nose: medium intensity, fresh fruit, citrus fruit, white flowers. Palate: rich, flavourful, fruity.

DESCRIPTION

This takes in from the central area of the province of Burgos to the south, with Lerma as its centre of operations. Its tempranillo wines differ from the neighbouring wines of La Ribera in that they are more aromatic and smoother. They become more intense as the altitude drops towards the west.

NUMBER OF HECTARES: 450 **ALTITUDES:** 800 m. – 1.200 m.

PREDOMINANT VARIETIES:

White grapes: albillo and viura.
Red grapes: tempranillo, garnacha and mencía.

CLIMATOLOGY AND SOILS

This is of a continental type. The soils have a clay-sandy texture.

BODEGA LA COLEGIADA

Ctra. Madrid-Irún, Km. 202,5
9340 Lerma - (Burgos)
☎: +34 947 177 030 - Fax: +34 947 177 004
info@tintolerma.com
www.tintolerma.com

GRAN LERMA 2009 TC
tempranillo

91 Color cherry, garnet rim. Aroma ripe fruit, spicy, creamy oak, toasty, complex. Taste powerful, flavourful, toasty, round tannins.

NABAL 2009 TC
tempranillo

90 Colour: bright cherry. Nose: ripe fruit, sweet spices, creamy oak. Palate: flavourful, fruity, toasty, round tannins.

BODEGAS ARLANZA

Ctra. Madrid-Irún km 203,800
9390 Villalmanzo - (Burgos)
☎: +34 947 172 070 - Fax: +34 947 170 259
comercial@bodegasarlanza.com
www.bodegasarlanza.com

DOMINIO DE MANCILES 2011 RD BARRICA
tempranillo, garnacha

90 Colour: rose, purple rim. Nose: red berry notes, ripe fruit, balsamic herbs, floral, fresh, sweet spices, creamy oak. Palate: rich, powerful, flavourful, fruity.

BODEGAS MONTE AMÁN

Ctra. Santo Domingo de Silos, s/n
9348 Castrillo de Solarana - (Burgos)
☎: +34 947 173 304 - Fax: +34 947 173 308
bodegas@monteaman.com
www.monteaman.com

MONTE AMÁN 2011 T
100% tempranillo

90 Colour: cherry, purple rim. Nose: fresh fruit, red berry notes, floral, balsamic herbs. Palate: flavourful, fruity, good acidity, round tannins.

BUEZO

Paraje Valdeazadón, s/n
9342 Mahamud - (Burgos)
☎: +34 947 616 899 - Fax: +34 947 616 885
rfranco@buezo.com
www.buezo.com

BUEZO NATTAN 2004 TR

90 Colour: cherry, garnet rim. Nose: ripe fruit, creamy oak, toasty, expressive, sweet spices, fine reductive notes. Palate: flavourful, toasty, round tannins, balanced.

BUEZO NATTAN 2005 TR

91 Colour: cherry, garnet rim. Nose: balanced, toasty, spicy, ripe fruit. Palate: flavourful, good structure, round tannins.

BUEZO PETIT VERDOT TEMPRANILLO 2005 TR
50% petit verdot, 50% tempranillo

91 Colour: cherry, garnet rim. Nose: ripe fruit, spicy, fine reductive notes, mineral. Palate: powerful, flavourful, toasty, round tannins, balanced.

DESCRIPTION

This is to the southwest of Zamora and to the northwest of Salamanca. It is a zone to be explored by those who are looking for exceptional local grapes with special qualities. In this case, the grapes are juan garcía and rufete in the main area (Fermoselle) which grow on vines located in slate soils, a prolongation of the Portuguese Douro area.

NUMBER OF HECTARES: 595 **ALTITUDES:** 700 m.

PREDOMINANT VARIETIES:

White grapes: malvasía, verdejo, albillo and puesta en cruz.
Red grapes: juan garcía, rufete, tempranillo, mencía and garnacha.

CLIMATOLOGY AND SOILS

The climate has Mediterranean influences due to the abrupt drop in altitude. The soils are sandy and shallow with an abundance of loose stones and quartz.

BODEGAS ARRIBES DEL DUERO

Ctra. Masueco, s/n
37251 Corporario - Aldeadavila - (Salamanca)
☎: +34 923 169 195 - Fax: +34 923 169 195
secretaria@bodegasarribesdelduero.com
www.bodegasarribesdelduero.com

SECRETO DEL VETTON 2006 T
juan garcía

90 Colour: cherry, garnet rim. Nose: ripe fruit, spicy, creamy oak, toasty, expressive. Palate: powerful, flavourful, balanced, long, spicy.

BODEGAS RIBERA DE PELAZAS

Camino de la Ermita, s/n
37175 Pereña de la Ribera - (Salamanca)
☎: +34 902 108 031 - Fax: +34 987 218 751
bodega@bodegasriberadepelazas.com
www.bodegasriberadepelazas.com

BRUÑAL 2007 T
100% bruñal

90 Colour: cherry, garnet rim. Nose: ripe fruit, spicy, creamy oak, scrubland, earthy notes. Palate: powerful, flavourful, toasty, round tannins, elegant.

GRAN ABADENGO 2005 TR
juan garcía

90 Colour: pale ruby, brick rim edge. Nose: spicy, wet leather, aged wood nuances, fruit liqueur notes, scrubland, earthy notes. Palate: spicy, long, round tannins, flavourful.

LA SETERA

Calzada, 7
49232 Fornillos de Fermoselle - (Zamora)
☎: +34 980 612 925 - Fax: +34 980 612 925
lasetera@lasetera.com
www.lasetera.com

LA SETERA SELECCIÓN ESPECIAL 2009 T ROBLE
touriga

92 Colour: bright cherry. Nose: ripe fruit, sweet spices, creamy oak, fragrant herbs. Palate: flavourful, fruity, toasty, round tannins, balanced.

OCELLUM DURII

San Juan 56 - 57
49220 Fermoselle - (Zamora)
☎: +34 983 390 606
ocellumdurii@hotmail.com

CONDADO DE FERMOSEL 2011 T
juan garcía, tempranillo, bruñal, rufete

92 Colour: bright cherry. Nose: ripe fruit, sweet spices, creamy oak, balsamic herbs. Palate: flavourful, fruity, toasty, round tannins.

TRANSITIUM DURII 2006 T
juan garcía, tempranillo, bruñal

90 Colour: cherry, garnet rim. Nose: mineral, red berry notes, ripe fruit, fragrant herbs, spicy. Palate: flavourful, fresh, long, spicy, good finish.

TRANSITIUM DURII 2007 T
juan garcía, tempranillo, bruñal

90 Colour: cherry, garnet rim. Nose: ripe fruit, spicy, creamy oak, toasty, balsamic herbs. Palate: flavourful, toasty, balanced, long.

TRANSITIUM DURII 2008 T
juan garcía, tempranillo, bruñal

91 Colour: bright cherry. Nose: ripe fruit, sweet spices, creamy oak, dark chocolate, cocoa bean, expressive. Palate: flavourful, fruity, toasty, round tannins.

DESCRIPTION

Geographically it is a transition zone between Galicia, León and Asturias. it lies on a plateau at a lower level than the plateau of León, which gives it a hotter climate and it is conditioned by the humidity of Galicia. The Denomination of Origin wines are those of the mencía variety, with an Atlantic balsamic style. The best are obtained from slate terraces at a good height.

NUMBER OF HECTARES: 3.969

ALTITUDES: 400 m. – 800 m.

PREDOMINANT VARIETIES:

White grapes: dona blanca, palomino, malvasía and godello.
Red grapes: mencía and garnacha tintorera.

CLIMATOLOGY AND SOILS

The climate is temperate with humid influences from Galicia and dry influences from Castile, the mountain soils are constituted by a mixture of fine components, quartzite, slate, and the meadows which are formed in the valleys continually receive components from the slopes. In El Bierzo, the vineyards are fundamentally located in moist brown soil, which is slightly acidic and lacks carbonate, which is typical of wet climates.

AKILIA

Nicolás de Brujas, 27
24400 Ponferrada - (León)
☎: +34 902 848 127
info@akiliawines.com
www.akiliawines.com

AKILIA 2011 T
mencía

92 Colour: dark-red cherry. Nose: fine lees, smoky, cocoa bean, spicy, fruit expression. Palate: good structure, powerful, flavourful, rich, creamy, balsamic.

BERNARDO ÁLVAREZ

San Pedro, 75
24530 Villadecanes - (León)
☎: +34 987 562 129 - Fax: +34 987 562 129
migarron@bodegasbernardoalvarez.e.telefonica.net

CAMPO REDONDO GODELLO 2011 B
100% godello

90 Colour: bright straw. Nose: fruit expression, ripe fruit, fragrant herbs. Palate: rich, full, powerful, flavourful, sweetness.

BODEGA ALBERTO LEDO

Estación, 6
24500 Villafranca del Bierzo - (León)
☎: +34 636 023 676
aallrs@msn.com
www.albertoledo.com

LEDO CLUB DE BARRICAS 2007 T
mencía

90 Colour: cherry, garnet rim. Nose: ripe fruit, spicy, creamy oak, toasty, mineral. Palate: powerful, flavourful, toasty, round tannins, balanced.

BODEGA DEL ABAD

Ctra. N-VI, km. 396
24549 Carracedelo - (León)
☎: +34 987 562 417 - Fax: +34 987 562 428
vinos@bodegadelabad.com
www.gotindelrisc.com

CARRACEDO 2008 TC
100% mencía

91 Colour: very deep cherry. Nose: dark chocolate, spicy, ripe fruit, fruit preserve. Palate: sweetness, spirituous, powerful, flavourful, ripe fruit, creamy, balsamic.

GOTÍN DEL RISC ESSENCIA 2007 TC
100% mencía

90 Colour: cherry, garnet rim. Nose: ripe fruit, spicy, creamy oak, roasted coffee. Palate: powerful, flavourful, toasty, round tannins.

GOTÍN DEL RISC GODELLO LÍAS 2008 B
100% godello

91 Colour: bright golden. Nose: macerated fruit, faded flowers, varietal, powerfull, complex, ripe fruit. Palate: slightly acidic, powerful, complex, reductive nuances.

BODEGA Y VIÑEDOS LUNA BEBERIDE

Ant. Ctra. Madrid - Coruña, Km. 402
24540 Cacabelos - (León)
☎: +34 987 549 002 - Fax: +34 987 549 214
info@lunabeberide.es
www.lunabeberide.es

ART LUNA BEBERIDE 2010 T
mencía

90 Colour: very deep cherry. Nose: fruit preserve, smoky, cedar wood. Palate: spirituous, sweetness, powerful, flavourful, creamy, ripe fruit.

FINCA LA CUESTA LUNA BEBERIDE 2010 T ROBLE
mencía

91 Colour: dark-red cherry, garnet rim. Nose: complex, expressive, varietal, red clay notes, red berry notes, ripe fruit, aromatic coffee, spicy, toasty. Palate: flavourful, powerful, mineral, toasty, ripe fruit.

BODEGA Y VIÑEDOS MAS ASTURIAS

Fueros de Leon nº 1
24400 Ponferrada - (León)
☎: +34 650 654 492
jose_mas_asturias@hotmail.com
www.bodegamasasturias.com

MASSURIA 2008 T
100% mencía

91 Colour: deep cherry. Nose: complex, varietal, elegant, fresh fruit, fruit expression, spicy. Palate: flavourful, powerful, full, spirituous, complex.

BODEGAS ADRIÁ

Antigua Ctra. Madrid - Coruña, Km. 408
24500 Villafranca del Bierzo - (León)
☎: +34 987 540 907 - Fax: +34 987 540 347
info@bodegasadria.com
www.bodegasadria.com

VEGA MONTÁN ECLIPSE 2005 T
mencía

93 Colour: pale ruby, brick rim edge. Nose: earthy notes, fine reductive notes, ripe fruit, spicy, creamy oak. Palate: correct, flavourful, long, fine tannins.

BODEGAS ALMÁZCARA MAJARA

Las Eras, 5
24398 Almázcara - (León)
☎: +34 609 322 194 - Fax: +34 937 952 859
javier.alvarez@es.coimgroup.com
www.almazcaramajara.com

DEMASIADO CORAZÓN 2010 B
godello

90 Colour: bright yellow. Nose: smoky, ripe fruit, wild herbs. Palate: flavourful, rich, fruity.

JARABE DE ALMÁZCARA MAJARA 2009 T
mencía

90 Colour: cherry, garnet rim. Nose: ripe fruit, spicy, creamy oak, toasty, complex. Palate: powerful, flavourful, toasty, balanced.

BODEGAS CUATRO PASOS

Santa María, 43
24540 Cacabelos - (León)
☎: +34 987 548 089 - Fax: +34 986 526 901
bierzo@martincodax.com
www.cuatropasos.es

MARTÍN SARMIENTO 2010 T
100% mencía

92 Colour: deep cherry, garnet rim. Nose: complex, varietal, fruit expression, cocoa bean, creamy oak. Palate: spirituous, round, warm, powerful, flavourful.

BODEGAS GODELIA

Antigua Ctra. N-VI, Km. 403,5
24547 Pieros (Cacabelos) - (León)
☎: +34 987 546 279 - Fax: +34 987 548 026
info@godelia.es
www.godelia.es

GODELIA 12 MESES 2010 T ROBLE
100% mencía

93 Colour: bright cherry. Nose: ripe fruit, sweet spices, creamy oak, cocoa bean, dark chocolate, expressive. Palate: flavourful, fruity, toasty, complex, balanced, elegant.

GODELIA BLANCO SELECCIÓN 2010 B
100% godello

90 Colour: bright golden. Nose: fine lees, floral, fragrant herbs, citrus fruit, balanced. Palate: powerful, flavourful, spicy, long, fresh, fruity.

GODELIA TINTO SELECCIÓN 2009 T
100% mencía

94 Colour: cherry, garnet rim. Nose: ripe fruit, spicy, creamy oak, toasty, fragrant herbs, complex. Palate: powerful, flavourful, toasty, complex, round, long, spicy, balanced, elegant.

BODEGAS PEIQUE

El Bierzo, s/n
24530 Valtuille de Abajo - (León)
☎: +34 987 562 044 - Fax: +34 987 562 044
bodega@bodegaspeique.com
www.bodegaspeique.com

PEIQUE SELECCIÓN FAMILIAR 2006 T
mencía

93 Colour: deep cherry. Nose: damp earth, fruit expression, fine reductive notes, spicy, cedar wood. Palate: spirituous, powerful, flavourful, full, round, soft tannins.

PEIQUE VIÑEDOS VIEJOS 2008 T ROBLE
mencía

92 Colour: dark-red cherry. Nose: undergrowth, varietal, closed, fruit liqueur notes, ripe fruit, creamy oak, toasty. Palate: balsamic, creamy, mineral, powerful, flavourful, fruity, spirituous.

BODEGAS Y VIÑEDO MENGOBA

Ctra. de Cacabelos, 11
24540 Sorribas - (León)
☎: +34 649 940 800
gregory@mengoba.com
www.mengoba.com

BREZO GODELLO Y DOÑA BLANCA 2011 B
godello, dona blanca

94 Colour: bright straw. Nose: ripe fruit, wild herbs, smoky, complex. Palate: spirituous, sweetness, powerful, flavourful, full.

BREZO MENCÍA 2011 T
mencía, alicante bouchet

90 Colour: dark-red cherry. Nose: smoky, ripe fruit, fruit expression, maceration notes. Palate: spirituous, powerful, flavourful, sweetness, balsamic.

MENGOBA GODELLO SOBRE LÍAS 2010 B
godello

95 Colour: bright straw. Nose: spicy, candied fruit, smoky, complex, expressive, varietal. Palate: elegant, round, full, rich, complex.

MENGOBA MENCÍA DE ESPANILLO 2009 T
mencía, alicante bouchet

92 Colour: deep cherry. Nose: balsamic herbs, powerfull, varietal, complex, ripe fruit. Palate: creamy, balsamic, powerful, flavourful, spirituous, sweetness.

BODEGAS Y VIÑEDOS BERGIDENSES

Antigua N-VI Km. 400. Apdo. Correos, 62
24540 Cacabelos - (León)
☎: +34 987 546 725 - Fax: +34 987 546 725
bergidenses@tegula.e.telefonica.net

TÉGULA 2007 TR

93 Colour: cherry, garnet rim. Nose: spicy, creamy oak, toasty, complex, earthy notes, mineral. Palate: powerful, flavourful, toasty, round tannins.

BODEGAS Y VIÑEDOS CASTRO VENTOSA

Finca El Barredo, s/n
24530 Valtuille de Abajo - (León)
☎: +34 987 562 148 - Fax: +34 987 562 191
info@castroventosa.com
www.castroventosa.com

CASTRO VENTOSA"VINTAGE" 2008 T
100% mencía

90 Colour: cherry, garnet rim. Nose: ripe fruit, spicy, creamy oak, earthy notes. Palate: powerful, flavourful, round tannins.

EL CASTRO DE VALTUILLE 2008 T
mencía

92 Colour: deep cherry. Nose: macerated fruit, ripe fruit, spicy, creamy oak, toasty. Palate: powerful, flavourful, spirituous, spicy.

VALTUILLE CEPAS CENTENARIAS 2008 T ROBLE
mencía

94 Colour: deep cherry. Nose: damp earth, truffle notes, ripe fruit, smoky, spicy, creamy oak. Palate: powerful, flavourful, spirituous, sweetness.

BODEGAS Y VIÑEDOS GANCEDO

Vistalegre, s/n
24548 Quilós - (León)
☎: +34 987 134 980 - Fax: +34 987 563 278
info@bodegasgancedo.com
www.bodegasgancedo.com

GANCEDO 2010 T
mencía

91 Colour: dark-red cherry. Nose: wild herbs, red berry notes, complex, characterful. Palate: round, powerful, flavourful, varietal.

GANCEDO 2011 T
mencía

90 Colour: very deep cherry. Nose: fruit preserve, violet drops, fruit liqueur notes, powerfull, caramel. Palate: powerful, flavourful, fruity, spirituous, sweetness, sweet tannins.

BODEGAS Y VIÑEDOS GANCEDO

Vistalegre, s/n
24548 Quilós - (León)
☎: +34 987 134 980 - Fax: +34 987 563 278
info@bodegasgancedo.com
www.bodegasgancedo.com

HERENCIA DEL CAPRICHO 2008 BFB
90% godello, 10% dona blanca

93 Colour: bright yellow. Nose: candied fruit, honeyed notes, fruit liqueur notes. Palate: creamy, spicy, ripe fruit, reductive nuances.

HERENCIA DEL CAPRICHO 2009 BFB
90% godello, 10% dona blanca

94 Colour: bright yellow. Nose: complex, characterful, elegant, fruit expression, candied fruit. Palate: fresh, full, powerful, rich.

VAL DE PAXARIÑAS "CAPRICHO" 2011 B
85% godello, 15% dona blanca

92 Colour: bright straw. Nose: white flowers, fresh fruit, varietal, powerfull, fresh, expressive. Palate: rich, powerful, sweetness, spirituous.

XESTAL 2008 T
mencía

91 Colour: very deep cherry. Nose: mineral, undergrowth, fruit expression, fruit liqueur notes, ripe fruit. Palate: sweet tannins, powerful, flavourful, fruity, sweetness.

BODEGAS Y VIÑEDOS PAIXAR

Ribadeo, 56
24500 Villafranca del Bierzo - (León)
☎: +34 987 549 002 - Fax: +34 987 549 214
info@lunabeberide.es

PAIXAR MENCÍA T
mencía

91 Colour: deep cherry. Nose: spicy, aromatic coffee, creamy oak. Palate: fruity, spirituous, sweetness, powerful, flavourful, balsamic.

CASAR DE BURBIA

Travesía la Constitución, s/n
24459 Carracedelo - (León)
☎: +34 987 562 910 - Fax: +34 987 562 850
info@casardeburbia.com
www.casardeburbia.com

CASAR DE BURBIA 2010 T
97% mencía, 3% garnacha

91 Colour: cherry, garnet rim. Nose: red berry notes, ripe fruit, earthy notes, dry stone, sweet spices, creamy oak. Palate: flavourful, fresh, fruity.

CASAR GODELLO 2011 B
100% godello

91 Colour: bright yellow. Nose: white flowers, fragrant herbs, citrus fruit, fresh fruit, mineral. Palate: fresh, fruity, light-bodied, flavourful, balanced.

HOMBROS 2009 T
100% mencía

93 Colour: cherry, garnet rim. Nose: dry stone, balsamic herbs, ripe fruit, complex, toasty, creamy oak. Palate: powerful, flavourful, fruity, spicy, long, balanced.

TEBAIDA 2010 T
100% mencía

94 Colour: cherry, garnet rim. Nose: ripe fruit, spicy, balsamic herbs, creamy oak, earthy notes. Palate: long, spicy, powerful, flavourful.

TEBAIDA NEMESIO 2009 T
100% mencía

92 Colour: cherry, garnet rim. Nose: ripe fruit, fragrant herbs, mineral, complex, spicy, creamy oak. Palate: good acidity, flavourful, fresh, fruity, balanced, elegant.

TEBAIDA NEMESIO MAGNUM 2009 T
100% mencía

94 Colour: cherry, garnet rim. Nose: ripe fruit, spicy, creamy oak, toasty, mineral, balanced. Palate: powerful, flavourful, toasty, round tannins, long, spicy, elegant.

DESCENDIENTES DE J. PALACIOS

Avda. Calvo Sotelo, 6
24500 Villafranca del Bierzo - (León)
☎: +34 987 540 821 - Fax: +34 987 540 851
info@djpalacios.com

LA FARAONA 2009 T
mencía

96 Colour: very deep cherry. Nose: expressive, complex, elegant, ripe fruit, creamy oak, mineral, scrubland. Palate: flavourful, round, fine bitter notes.

LAS LAMAS 2009 T
mencía

94 Colour: cherry, garnet rim. Nose: ripe fruit, earthy notes, toasty. Palate: flavourful, powerful, fine bitter notes, good acidity, spicy, ripe fruit.

MONCERBAL 2009 T
mencía

96 Colour: very deep cherry. Nose: ripe fruit, sweet spices, scrubland, balsamic herbs. Palate: long, spicy, ripe fruit, balsamic, fine tannins.

PÉTALOS DEL BIERZO 2010 T
mencía

94 Colour: deep cherry. Nose: fresh fruit, balsamic herbs, scrubland, creamy oak. Palate: spicy, ripe fruit, fine bitter notes, good acidity.

VILLA DE CORULLÓN 2009 T
mencía

95 Colour: deep cherry. Nose: fruit expression, ripe fruit, floral, mineral, toasty. Palate: spicy, fine bitter notes, good acidity.

DOMINIO DE LOS CEREZOS

Camino de las Salgueras, s/n
24413 Molinaseca - (León)
☎: +34 639 202 403
vangusvana@gmail.com

VAN GUS VANA 2009
mencía

90 Colour: cherry, garnet rim. Nose: fruit expression, cocoa bean, new oak, complex. Palate: fruity, fresh, powerful, flavourful, elegant.

ESTEFANÍA

Ctra. Dehesas - Posada del Bierzo, s/n
24390 Ponferrada - (León)
☎: +34 987 420 015 - Fax: +34 987 420 015
info@tilenus.com
www.tilenus.com

TILENUS 2006 TC
100% mencía

92 Colour: dark-red cherry, orangey edge. Nose: fine reductive notes, old leather, fruit preserve, sweet spices, cedar wood. Palate: elegant, round, good acidity.

TILENUS PAGOS DE POSADA 2004 T
100% mencía

90 Colour: dark-red cherry, orangey edge. Nose: spicy, cocoa bean, creamy oak, toasty, tobacco, fine reductive notes. Palate: flavourful, powerful, creamy, spicy, toasty, smoky aftertaste, reductive nuances.

TILENUS PIEROS 2003 T
100% mencía

90 Colour: dark-red cherry, orangey edge. Nose: fine reductive notes, tobacco, old leather, powerfull, complex. Palate: ripe fruit, spicy, reductive nuances, roasted-coffee aftertaste.

LOSADA VINOS DE FINCA

Ctra. a Villafranca LE-713, Km. 12
24540 Cacabelos - (León)
☎: +34 987 548 053 - Fax: +34 987 548 069
bodega@losadavinosdefinca.com
www.losadavinosdefinca.com

ALTOS DE LOSADA 2008 T
100% mencía

92 Colour: very deep cherry. Nose: ripe fruit, smoky, sweet spices, aged wood nuances, dark chocolate. Palate: sweetness, spirituous, powerful, flavourful.

LA BIENQUERIDA 2008 T
95% mencía, 5% otras

93 Colour: very deep cherry. Nose: complex, candied fruit, smoky, spicy, cedar wood. Palate: creamy, ripe fruit, mineral, flavourful, powerful, spirituous, spicy.

LOSADA 2009 T
100% mencía

91 Colour: dark-red cherry. Nose: fresh fruit, wild herbs, varietal, powerfull, expressive. Palate: fruity, full, powerful, flavourful.

OTERO SANTÍN

Ortega y Gasset, 10
24402 Ponferrada - (León)
☎: +34 987 410 101 - Fax: +34 987 418 544
oterobenito@gmail.com

OTERO SANTÍN 2011 B
godello

90 Colour: bright straw. Nose: fresh, fresh fruit, white flowers. Palate: flavourful, fruity, good acidity, balanced.

PÉREZ CARAMÉS

Peña Picón, s/n
24500 Villafranca del Bierzo - (León)
☎: +34 987 540 197 - Fax: +34 987 540 314
enoturismo@perezcarames.com
www.perezcarames.com

EL VINO DE LOS CÓNSULES DE ROMA 2011 T
100% mencía

90 Colour: very deep cherry. Nose: fruit preserve, fruit liqueur notes, fruit expression, varietal, powerfull, warm. Palate: balsamic, powerful, flavourful, spirituous, sweetness, pruney.

VALDAIGA X 2011 T
100% mencía

90 Colour: very deep cherry. Nose: earthy notes, damp earth, ripe fruit, fruit liqueur notes, fruit expression. Palate: fruity, flavourful, complex, sweetness, balsamic.

PRADA A TOPE

La Iglesia, s/n
24546 Canedo - (León)
☎: +34 987 563 366 - Fax: +34 987 567 000
info@pradaatope.es
www.pradaatope.es

PICANTAL 2008 T
mencía

90 Colour: dark-red cherry. Nose: ripe fruit, fruit liqueur notes, powerfull, warm, smoky, spicy, cedar wood, creamy oak. Palate: creamy, flavourful, powerful, spirituous, sweetness, round tannins, spicy.

PRADA A TOPE 2006 TR
mencía

92 Colour: pale ruby, brick rim edge. Nose: spicy, fine reductive notes, wet leather, aged wood nuances, toasty. Palate: spicy, long, round tannins.

PRADA GODELLO 2011 B
godello

91 Colour: bright straw. Nose: white flowers, jasmine, fragrant herbs. Palate: flavourful, powerful, full, rich, fruity, varietal.

RODRÍGUEZ SANZO

Manuel Azaña, 9
47014 - (Valladolid)
☎: +34 983 150 150 - Fax: +34 983 150 151
comunicacion@valsanzo.com
www.rodriguezsanzo.com

TERRAS DE JAVIER RODRÍGUEZ 2009 T
100% mencía

93 Colour: cherry, garnet rim. Nose: powerfull, varietal, complex, expressive, red berry notes, lactic notes, fragrant herbs. Palate: flavourful, spicy, ripe fruit, long, round tannins.

SOTO DEL VICARIO

Ctra. Cacabelos- San Clemente, Pol. Ind. 908 Parcela 155
24547 San Clemente - (León)
☎: +34 670 983 534 - Fax: +34 926 666 029
sandra.luque@pagodelvicario.com
www.sotodelvicario.com

GO DE GODELLO 2009 BFB
100% godello

92 Colour: bright golden. Nose: ripe fruit, dry nuts, scrubland. Palate: elegant, round, spirituous, powerful, flavourful, complex, spicy.

SOTO DEL VICARIO MEN 2009 T
100% mencía

91 Colour: deep cherry. Nose: toasty, creamy oak, fruit expression, complex. Palate: mineral, fruity, powerful, flavourful, sweetness, spirituous.

SOTO DEL VICARIO MEN SELECCIÓN 2008 T
100% mencía

90 Colour: deep cherry. Nose: creamy oak, roasted coffee, ripe fruit. Palate: powerful, flavourful, sweetness, grainy tannins.

VINOS VALTUILLE

La Fragua, s/n
24530 Valtuille de Abajo - (León)
☎: +34 987 562 165 - Fax: +34 987 549 425
pagodevaldoneje@yahoo.es

PAGO DE VALDONEJE VIÑAS VIEJAS 2008 T
mencía

92 Colour: cherry, garnet rim. Nose: ripe fruit, mineral, earthy notes, spicy, creamy oak. Palate: powerful, flavourful, long, balanced.

VIÑEDOS Y BODEGAS DOMINIO DE TARES

P.I. Bierzo Alto, Los Barredos, 4
24318 San Román de Bembibre - (León)
☎: +34 987 514 550 - Fax: +34 987 514 570
info@dominiodetares.com
www.dominiodetares.com

BEMBIBRE 2008 T
100% mencía

90 Colour: very deep cherry. Nose: fruit liqueur notes, fruit liqueur notes, ripe fruit. Palate: creamy, spicy, mineral, flavourful, powerful, full.

DOMINIO DE TARES CEPAS VIEJAS 2009 TC
100% mencía

91 Colour: deep cherry. Nose: spicy, toasty, new oak, ripe fruit. Palate: fruity, powerful, spicy, toasty.

DOMINIO DE TARES GODELLO 2011 BFB
100% godello

92 Colour: pale. Nose: fruit expression, fragrant herbs, creamy oak. Palate: powerful, flavourful, full, fruity, smoky aftertaste.

TARES P. 3 2008 T ROBLE
100% mencía

93 Colour: very deep cherry. Nose: damp earth, cocoa bean, spicy, sweet spices. Palate: powerful, flavourful, fruity, spirituous, sweetness, spicy, roasted-coffee aftertaste.

VIÑEDOS Y BODEGAS PITTACUM

De la Iglesia, 11
24546 Arganza - (León)
☎: +34 987 548 054 - Fax: +34 987 548 028
pittacum@pittacum.com
www.pittacum.com

LA PROHIBICIÓN 2008 T
garnacha tintorera

93 Colour: bright cherry. Nose: ripe fruit, sweet spices, creamy oak, expressive. Palate: flavourful, fruity, toasty, round tannins, balanced.

PITTACUM 2008 T BARRICA
mencía

92 Colour: deep cherry. Nose: smoky, cocoa bean, sweet spices, fruit expression, ripe fruit, damp earth. Palate: complex, spirituous, good structure, powerful, flavourful, spicy, ripe fruit.

PITTACUM AUREA 2008 TC
mencía

93 Colour: very deep cherry. Nose: smoky, aged wood nuances, cocoa bean, fruit expression, ripe fruit. Palate: powerful, flavourful, fruity, sweetness, creamy, spicy, toasty.

DESCRIPTION

The central zone of Mallorca is the oldest wine growing region on the island, and is known for its red wines made from the local callet and manto negro grapes which the new producers have fortified with a blend of French grapes. In recent year, they have shown an interest in original white grapes of the prensal blanc variety.

NUMBER OF HECTARES: 618 **ALTITUDES:** 75 m. – 220 m.

PREDOMINANT VARIETIES:

White grapes: prensal blanc, macabeo, parellada, muscatel and chardonnay.
Red grapes: manto negro, callet, syrah, merlot, cabernet sauvignon and tempranillo.

CLIMATOLOGY AND SOILS

Mild Mediterranean, soils with sand, limestone and gypsum which lie on clay and loam.

BODEGUES MACIÀ BATLE

Camí Coanegra, s/n
7320 Santa María del Camí - (Illes Balears)
☎: +34 971 140 014 - Fax: +34 971 140 086
correo@maciabatle.com
www.maciabatle.com

MACIÀ BATLE RESERVA PRIVADA 2008 TR
manto negro, merlot, cabernet sauvignon, syrah

90 Colour: bright cherry. Nose: balsamic herbs, scrubland, ripe fruit, spicy. Palate: balanced, good acidity, round tannins.

P. DE MARÌA 2009 T

93 Colour: bright cherry. Nose: complex, powerfull, ripe fruit, scrubland, dark chocolate. Palate: flavourful, good acidity, round tannins.

CELLER TIANNA NEGRE

Camí des Mitjans. Desvio a la izquierda en el km. 1,5 de la Ctra. Binissalem-Inca
7350 Binissalem - (Illes Balears)
☎: +34 971 886 826 - Fax: +34 971 226 201
info@tiannanegre.com
www.tiannanegre.com

SES NINES SELECCIO 2010 T
manto negro, cabernet sauvignon, syrah, merlot, callet, monastrell

90 Colour: bright cherry, purple rim. Nose: expressive, fruit expression, balsamic herbs. Palate: flavourful, fruity, fresh, balanced.

TIANNA NEGRE BOCCHORIS 2010 T
manto negro, cabernet sauvignon, syrah, merlot, callet, monastrell

93 Colour: bright cherry, garnet rim. Nose: elegant, expressive, red berry notes, sweet spices. Palate: fruity, flavourful, balanced, round tannins.

JAUME DE PUNTIRÓ

Pza. Nova, 23
7320 Santa María del Camí - (Illes Balears)
☎: +34 971 620 023 - Fax: +34 971 620 023
pere@vinsjaumedepuntiro.com
www.vinsjaumedepuntiro.com

DAURAT 2011 BFB
prensal

90 Colour: bright yellow. Nose: sweet spices, creamy oak, fresh fruit. Palate: fruity, flavourful, balanced, fine bitter notes.

JAUME DE PUNTIRÓ CARMESÍ 2009 T
manto negro, callet

90 Colour: cherry, garnet rim. Nose: spicy, balsamic herbs, ripe fruit, expressive. Palate: full, fruity, good acidity.

JOSÉ L. FERRER

Conquistador, 103
7350 Binissalem - (Illes Balears)
☎: +34 971 511 050 - Fax: +34 971 870 084
info@vinosferrer.com
www.vinosferrer.com

JOSÉ L. FERRER 2009 TC
manto negro, tempranillo, cabernet sauvignon, callet

90 Colour: cherry, garnet rim. Nose: powerfull, dark chocolate, sweet spices, candied fruit. Palate: flavourful, rich, sweet tannins.

VINYES I VINS CA SA PADRINA

Camí dels Horts, s/n
7140 Sencelles - (Illes Balears)
☎: +34 660 211 939 - Fax: +34 971 874 370
cellermantonegro@gmail.com

MOLLET SUÑER BIBILONI 2011 B JOVEN
prensal, chardonnay

91 Colour: bright straw. Nose: expressive, ripe fruit, fruit expression, citrus fruit, floral. Palate: flavourful, fruity, good acidity, fine bitter notes.

MONTENEGRO SUÑER BIBILONI 2010 T ROBLE
manto negro, cabernet sauvignon, merlot, callet

91 Colour: ruby red, garnet rim. Nose: mineral, ripe fruit, sweet spices, creamy oak. Palate: long, powerful, flavourful.

DESCRIPTION

This is where the chacolís or white wines of the Basque province of Bizkaia are produced. White wines which, unlike those of Guetaria, are somewhat more tasty and herbaceous. The majority of the vineyards are located in more internal areas rather than on the coast. The professionalization of the Denomination of Origin has given rise to more complex wines with less notable acidity. Red wines and some newly inspired sweet wines are also produced.

NUMBER OF HECTARES: 334 **ALTITUDES:** 150 m.

PREDOMINANT VARIETIES:

White grapes: hondarrabi beltza, hondarrabí zuri and folle blanche.

CLIMATOLOGY AND SOILS

It is quite wet and temperate due to the influence of the Bay of Biscay which makes the temperatures milder; the soil is clay and slightly acidic.

ABIO TXAKOLINA

Barrio Elexalde, 5 Caserío Basigo
48130 Bakio - (Bizkaia)
☎: +34 946 194 345

ABIO TXACOLINA 2011 B

90 Colour: bright straw. Nose: fresh, white flowers, fresh fruit. Palate: flavourful, fruity, good acidity, balanced.

DONIENE GORRONDONA TXAKOLINA

Gibelorratzagako San Pelaio, 1
48130 Bakio - (Bizkaia)
☎: +34 946 194 795 - Fax: +34 946 195 831
gorrondona@donienegorrondona.com
www.donienegorrondona.com

DONIENE 2010 B
hondarrabi zuri

90 Colour: bright straw. Nose: scrubland, balsamic herbs, ripe fruit, citrus fruit. Palate: flavourful, good acidity.

DONIENE 2010 BFB
hondarrabi zuri

91 Colour: bright yellow. Nose: powerfull, ripe fruit, sweet spices, creamy oak. Palate: rich, smoky aftertaste, flavourful, fresh, good acidity.

ITSASMENDI

Barrio Arane, 3
48300 Gernika - (Bizkaia)
☎: +34 946 270 316 - Fax: +34 946 251 032
info@bodegasitsasmendi.com
www.bodegasitsasmendi.com

ITSAS MENDI 2011 B
hondarrabi zuri

90 Colour: bright straw. Nose: fresh, white flowers, ripe fruit, grassy. Palate: flavourful, fruity, good acidity, balanced.

ITSAS MENDI UREZTI 2008 B
hondarrabi zuri

93 Colour: golden. Nose: powerfull, floral, honeyed notes, fragrant herbs, lactic notes. Palate: fresh, fruity, good acidity, long, sweetness.

ITURRIALDE

Barrio Legina, s/n
48195 Larrabetzu - (Bizkaia)
☎: +34 946 742 706 - Fax: +34 946 741 221
txakoli@gorkaizagirre.com
www.gorkaizagirre.com

GORKA IZAGIRRE 2011 B
50% hondarrabi zuri, hondarrabi zerratia

90 Colour: bright straw. Nose: fresh, white flowers, expressive, scrubland, ripe fruit. Palate: flavourful, fruity, good acidity, balanced.

GORKA IZAGIRRE ARIMA 2010 B
100% hondarrabi zerratia

90 Colour: golden. Nose: powerfull, floral, candied fruit, fragrant herbs. Palate: flavourful, sweet, fresh, fruity, good acidity, long.

MARKO 2011 B

92 Colour: bright straw. Nose: fresh, fresh fruit, white flowers, expressive, balsamic herbs, scrubland. Palate: flavourful, fruity, good acidity, balanced.

UIXAR 2011 B
100% hondarrabi zerratia

90 Colour: bright straw. Nose: fresh, white flowers, mineral, varietal. Palate: flavourful, fruity, good acidity, balanced.

OTXANDURI TXAKOLINA

Otxanduri, 41
48498 Arrankudiaga - (Bizkaia)
☎: +34 946 481 769
otxanduri@euskalnet.net

ARTZAI 2009 B

90 Colour: bright straw. Nose: cocoa bean, ripe fruit, toasty. Palate: fine bitter notes, sweetness, spicy.

OTXANDURI 2011 B

90 Colour: bright straw. Nose: white flowers, ripe fruit. Palate: flavourful, fruity, good acidity, balanced.

VIRGEN DE LOREA

Barrio de Lorea
48860 Otxaran-Zalla - (Bizkaia)
☎: +34 944 242 680 - Fax: +34 946 670 521
virgendelorea@spankor.com
www.bodegasvirgendelorea.com

SEÑORÍO DE OTXARAN 2011 B
80% hondarrabi zuri, 20% folle blanch

91 Colour: bright straw. Nose: fresh, white flowers, ripe fruit, grassy. Palate: flavourful, fruity, good acidity, balanced.

DESCRIPTION

The smallest of the brands from Murcia has taken a gigantic leap forward as regards quality, and has set aside its past as a bulk supplier of North European countries. With regard to the rest of the zones of Murcia, Bullas provides fresher and smoother monastrell grapes thanks to the higher altitude and soil which contribute to greater balance in the wines. The wines from cooperatives and private wineries are outstanding for their good prices.

NUMBER OF HECTARES: 2.563 **ALTITUDES:** 400 m. – 810 m.

PREDOMINANT VARIETIES:

White grapes: macabeo, airén, chardonnay, malvasía, muscatel, small grained muscatel and sauvignon blanc. Red grapes: monastrell, tempranillo, cabernet sauvignon, syrah, merlot, garnacha and petit verdot.

CLIMATOLOGY AND SOILS

Mediterranean climate, with strong storms in summer. The soil is brown-limestone with a limestone, alluvial crust.

BODEGA MONASTRELL

Paraje El Aceniche
30150 Bullas - (Murcia)
☎: +34 968 653 708 - Fax: +34 968 653 708
info@bodegamonastrell.com
www.bodegamonastrell.com

VALCHE 2006 TC
100% monastrell

92 Colour: cherry, garnet rim. Nose: ripe fruit, mineral, aromatic coffee, sweet spices. Palate: long, flavourful, toasty, balanced.

BODEGA TERCIA DE ULEA

Tercia de Ulea, s/n
30440 Moratalla - (Murcia)
☎: +34 968 433 213 - Fax: +34 968 433 965
info@terciadeulea.com
www.terciadeulea.com

TERCIA DE ULEA TC
76% monastrell, 24% tempranillo

90 Colour: cherry, garnet rim. Nose: spicy, toasty, red berry notes, floral. Palate: powerful, flavourful, toasty, round tannins.

BODEGAS DEL ROSARIO

Avda. de la Libertad, s/n
30180 Bullas - (Murcia)
☎: +34 968 652 075 - Fax: +34 968 653 765
info@bodegasdelrosario.com
www.bodegasdelrosario.com

3000 AÑOS 2009 T
50% monastrell, 50% syrah

92 Colour: bright cherry. Nose: sweet spices, creamy oak, overripe fruit. Palate: flavourful, fruity, toasty, round tannins.

MOLINO Y LAGARES DE BULLAS

Paraje Venta del Pino, s/n - Parcela 38
30430 Cehegin - (Murcia)
☎: +34 638 046 694 - Fax: +34 968 654 494
lavia@bodegaslavia.com
www.bodegaslavia.com

LAVIA MONASTRELL SYRAH 2008 TC
70% monastrell, 30% syrah

94 Colour: bright cherry. Nose: ripe fruit, lactic notes, scrubland, balsamic herbs, spicy. Palate: flavourful, fruity, fine bitter notes, good acidity.

LAVIA+ 2007 TC
100% monastrell

92 Colour: cherry, garnet rim. Nose: spicy, creamy oak, toasty, warm, overripe fruit. Palate: powerful, flavourful, toasty, round tannins.

DESCRIPTION

This is located in the western part of the province of Zaragoza (Aragón), the foothills of the Iberian System. Calatayud is a very dry area owing to the altitude, but with strong contrasts of temperature between daytime and night-time. For this Denomination of Origin garnacha tinta is the most characteristic grape variety and the vines reach old age at 100, producing wines with strong mineral complexity and international success. A large part of the wine from Calatayud (85%) is sold abroad as a result of the entrepreneurial, dynamic spirit of the cooperatives in the zone, which have known how to promote it with fantastic prices and modern aesthetics.

NUMBER OF HECTARES: 3.966 **ALTITUDES:** 550 m. – 800 m.

PREDOMINANT VARIETIES:
White grapes: macabeo and malvasía. Red grapes: garnacha tinta, tempranillo and mazuela.

CLIMATOLOGY AND SOILS

Semi-arid and dry, with soils which have high limestone content and is very uneven.

AGUSTÍN CUBERO

La Charluca, s/n
50300 Calatayud - (Zaragoza)
☎: +34 976 882 332 - Fax: +34 976 887 512
calatayud@bodegascubero.com
www.bodegascubero.com

STYLO 2010 T
100% garnacha

91 Colour: cherry, garnet rim. Nose: powerfull, sweet spices, toasty, ripe fruit, fragrant herbs. Palate: spicy, ripe fruit, long.

STYLO 2011 T
100% garnacha

90 Colour: cherry, purple rim. Nose: ripe fruit, sweet spices, dry stone, complex. Palate: balanced, ripe fruit, long.

ALIANZA DE GARAPITEROS

Plaza España, 6 Planta 1ª Oficina B
50001 - (Zaragoza)
☎: +34 976 094 033 - Fax: +34 976 094 033
info@alianzadegarapiteros.es
www.alianzadegarapiteros.es

NIETRO GARNACHA VIÑAS VIEJAS 2011 T
garnacha

90 Colour: cherry, garnet rim. Nose: ripe fruit, scrubland, spicy, earthy notes. Palate: powerful, complex, flavourful, balanced.

BODEGA COOPERATIVA VIRGEN DE LA SIERRA

Avda. de la Cooperativa, 21-23
50310 Villarroya de la Sierra - (Zaragoza)
☎: +34 976 899 015 - Fax: +34 976 899 032
oficina@bodegavirgendelasierra.com
www.bodegavirgendelasierra.com

CRUZ DE PIEDRA SELECCIÓN ESPECIAL 2010 T
garnacha

92 Colour: cherry, garnet rim. Nose: mineral, balsamic herbs, complex, red berry notes, sweet spices. Palate: good structure, flavourful, complex, round tannins.

BODEGA SAN GREGORIO

Ctra. Villalengua, s/n
50312 Cervera de la Cañada - (Zaragoza)
☎: +34 976 899 206 - Fax: +34 976 896 240
tresojos@bodegasangregorio.com
www.bodegasangregorio.com

ARMANTES SELECCIÓN ESPECIAL 2009 T
60% garnacha, 22% tempranillo, 6% syrah, 6% merlot, 6% cabernet sauvignon

90 Colour: bright cherry, garnet rim. Nose: complex, balanced, ripe fruit, dry stone. Palate: flavourful, fruity, round tannins.

BODEGAS ATECA

Ctra. N-II, s/n
50200 Ateca - (Zaragoza)
☎: +34 968 435 022 - Fax: +34 968 716 051
info@orowines.com
www.orowines.com

ATTECA 2010 T
100% garnacha

91 Colour: bright cherry. Nose: sweet spices, creamy oak, expressive, powerfull. Palate: flavourful, fruity, toasty, round tannins.

ATTECA ARMAS 2009 T
100% garnacha

93 Colour: black cherry. Nose: mineral, earthy notes, powerfull, ripe fruit, fruit expression. Palate: flavourful, powerful, concentrated, toasty, harsh oak tannins.

HONORO VERA GARNACHA 2011 T
100% garnacha

90 Colour: cherry, purple rim. Nose: red berry notes, ripe fruit, mineral, spicy. Palate: powerful, flavourful, fruity, balanced.

BODEGAS AUGUSTA BILBILIS

Carramiedes, s/n
50331 Mara - (Zaragoza)
☎: +34 677 547 127
bodegasaugustabilbilis@hotmail.com
www.bodegasaugustabilbilis.com

SAMITIER 2008 T
100% garnacha

90 Colour: cherry, garnet rim. Nose: ripe fruit, spicy, creamy oak, toasty, complex, dry stone. Palate: powerful, flavourful, toasty, balanced.

BODEGAS LANGA

Ctra. Nacional II, Km. 241,700
50300 Calatayud - (Zaragoza)
☎: +34 976 881 818 - Fax: +34 976 884 463
info@bodegas-langa.com
www.bodegas-langa.com

LANGA EMOCIÓN 2010 T
50% cabernet sauvignon, 50% syrah

90 Colour: cherry, garnet rim. Nose: ripe fruit, creamy oak, sweet spices. Palate: rich, flavourful, balanced, mineral, long.

LANGA TRADICIÓN 2010 T
100% garnacha

90 Colour: cherry, garnet rim. Nose: medium intensity, ripe fruit, varnish, sweet spices, earthy notes. Palate: complex, good structure, powerful, flavourful, good acidity.

REAL DE ARAGÓN 2009 T
garnacha

92 Colour: cherry, garnet rim. Nose: toasty, creamy oak, sweet spices. Palate: good structure, balanced, round, round tannins.

BODEGAS SAN ALEJANDRO

Ctra. Calatayud - Cariñena, Km. 16
50330 Miedes de Aragón - (Zaragoza)
☎: +34 976 892 205 - Fax: +34 976 890 540
contacto@san-alejandro.com
www.san-alejandro.com

BALTASAR GRACIÁN 2009 TC
70% garnacha, 20% tempranillo, 10% syrah

92 Colour: cherry, garnet rim. Nose: ripe fruit, spicy, creamy oak, toasty, complex. Palate: powerful, flavourful, toasty, round tannins, long.

BALTASAR GRACIÁN 2008 TR
70% garnacha, 20% tempranillo, 10% cabernet sauvignon

92 Colour: cherry, garnet rim. Nose: ripe fruit, spicy, toasty, complex, dark chocolate, cocoa bean. Palate: powerful, flavourful, toasty, round tannins.

BALTASAR GRACIÁN GARNACHA VIÑAS VIEJAS 2009 T
100% garnacha

92 Colour: cherry, garnet rim. Nose: balanced, complex, mineral, ripe fruit. Palate: spicy, balanced, good acidity, round tannins.

BALTASAR GRACIÁN GARNACHA VIÑAS VIEJAS 2010 T
100% garnacha

90 Colour: cherry, purple rim. Nose: ripe fruit, sweet spices, creamy oak, earthy notes. Palate: flavourful, fruity, toasty, round tannins.

LAS ROCAS GARNACHA 2010 T
100% garnacha

92 Colour: bright cherry, garnet rim. Nose: ripe fruit, sweet spices, creamy oak, mineral. Palate: flavourful, toasty, round tannins, balanced.

LAS ROCAS GARNACHA VIÑAS VIEJAS 2010 T
100% garnacha

93 Colour: cherry, garnet rim. Nose: complex, elegant, red berry notes, ripe fruit. Palate: spicy, balsamic, balanced, round tannins.

BODEGAS Y VIÑEDOS DEL JALÓN

Avda. José Antonio, 61
50340 Maluenda - (Zaragoza)
☎: +34 976 893 017 - Fax: +34 976 546 969
info@castillodemaluenda.com
www.castillodemaluenda.com

ALTO LAS PIZARRAS 2010 T
garnacha

90 Colour: cherry, garnet rim. Nose: medium intensity, balanced, sweet spices, ripe fruit, mineral, warm. Palate: flavourful, good structure, spicy.

TEOREMA 2010 T
garnacha

90 Colour: cherry, garnet rim. Nose: balanced, expressive, dry stone. Palate: flavourful, ripe fruit, balanced.

EL ESCOCÉS VOLANTE

Barrio La Rosa Bajo, 16
50300 Calatayud - (Zaragoza)
☎: +34 637 511 133
norrelrobertson@hotmail.com
www.escocesvolante.es

DOS DEDOS DE FRENTE 2010 T
96% syrah, 4% viognier

93 Colour: cherry, garnet rim. Nose: ripe fruit, sweet spices, cocoa bean, mineral, expressive. Palate: powerful, flavourful, fresh, fruity, spicy.

EL PUÑO BLANCO 2010 BFB
100% viognier

93 Colour: bright yellow. Nose: dried flowers, citrus fruit, ripe fruit, dried herbs, scrubland, mineral, earthy notes, creamy oak. Palate: powerful, flavourful, spicy, balanced.

EL PUÑO GARNACHA 2009 T
100% garnacha

92 Color cherry, garnet rim. Aroma ripe fruit, spicy, creamy oak, toasty, complex. Taste powerful, flavourful, toasty, round tannins.

MANGA DEL BRUJO 2010 T
65% garnacha, 15% syrah, 15% tempranillo, 2,5% mazuelo, 2,5% monastrell

94 Colour: bright cherry. Nose: ripe fruit, creamy oak, dry stone, dark chocolate, balsamic herbs. Palate: flavourful, fruity, good structure, good acidity, long, spicy.

ESPIAGO-ALONSO VINEYARDS

Avda. Cooperativa, 7
50310 Villarroya De La Sierra - (Zaragoza)
☎: +34 676 929 994
manuelespiago@yahoo.es
www.espiagoalonso.com

ALDA V 2010 B
100% viognier

90 Colour: bright yellow. Nose: powerfull, ripe fruit, sweet spices, fragrant herbs, mineral. Palate: rich, flavourful, good acidity, elegant. Personality.

PAGOS ALTOS DE ACERED

Avda. Río Jalón, 62
50300 Calatayud - (Zaragoza)
☎: +34 976 887 496 - Fax: +34 976 885 912
secretario@docalatayud.com
www.lajas.es

LAJAS 2007 T
garnacha

92 Colour: cherry, garnet rim. Nose: expressive, complex, sweet spices, ripe fruit, mineral. Palate: flavourful, good structure, good acidity.

LAJAS 2008 T
garnacha

92 Colour: cherry, garnet rim. Nose: fruit preserve, warm, mineral, dark chocolate. Palate: balanced, spicy, ripe fruit, long.

LAJAS 2009 T
garnacha

94 Colour: cherry, garnet rim. Nose: closed, mineral, complex, sweet spices. Palate: balanced, long, round tannins.

DESCRIPTION

This lies to the northwest of the province of Zaragoza, among the large producer zones of Rioja and Cariñena. The small wineries have boosted the new quality wines from these vineyards with garnacha grapes cultivated at the foot of the Moncayo mountain. The freshness and character of these wines are influenced by the strong healthy wind of the Cierzo which comes from the mountains.

NUMBER OF HECTARES: 7.414 **ALTITUDES:** 350 m. – 700 m.

PREDOMINANT VARIETIES:

White grapes: macabeo, garnacha blanca, muscatel, chardonnay, sauvignon blanc and verdejo.
Red grapes: garnacha, tempranillo, mazuela, cabernet sauvignon, merlot and syrah.

CLIMATOLOGY AND SOILS

In the lower zones, with altitudes between 350 and 450 metres, there are brown limestone soils and garnacha grapes which mature early. The intermediate zone is characterized by having the largest concentration and density of vineyards at altitudes between 450 and 550 metres. The soil is gravelly and clay-ferrous. The upper zone of the Denomination of Origin, whose vineyards go from 550 to 700 metres high, corresponds to the foothills of the Moncayo mountain, the region of the garnacha grape which gives the most elegant and freshest wines.

BODEGAS ALTO MONCAYO

Ctra. CV-606 Borja - El Buste, Km. 1,700
50540 Borja - (Zaragoza)
☎: +34 976 867 116 - Fax: +34 976 867 752
info@bodegasaltomoncayo.com
www.bodegasaltomoncayo.com

ALTO MONCAYO 2009 T
100% garnacha

95 Colour: very deep cherry. Nose: ripe fruit, fruit preserve, sweet spices, cocoa bean, dark chocolate, mineral. Palate: powerful, flavourful, concentrated, complex.

ALTO MONCAYO VERATÓN 2009 T
100% garnacha

93 Colour: cherry, garnet rim. Nose: ripe fruit, spicy, creamy oak, toasty, characterful, powerfull. Palate: powerful, flavourful, toasty, round tannins.

AQUILÓN 2009 T
100% garnacha

96 Colour: black cherry. Nose: cocoa bean, dark chocolate, sweet spices, ripe fruit, characterful, powerfull. Palate: round tannins, long, mineral, good finish, fruity, powerful, flavourful.

BODEGAS ARAGONESAS

Ctra. Magallón, s/n
50529 Fuendejalón - (Zaragoza)
☎: +34 976 862 153 - Fax: +34 976 862 363
info@bodegasaragonesas.com
www.bodegasaragonesas.com

ARAGONIA SELECCIÓN ESPECIAL 2009 T
100% garnacha

90 Colour: bright cherry. Nose: ripe fruit, sweet spices, creamy oak, expressive, elegant. Palate: flavourful, fruity, toasty, round tannins.

ARAGUS 2011 T
85% garnacha, 15% cabernet sauvignon

90 Colour: cherry, purple rim. Nose: red berry notes, ripe fruit, balsamic herbs. Palate: flavourful, good acidity, round tannins, correct, long.

ARAGUS ECOLÓGICO 2011 T
90% garnacha, 10% syrah

90 Colour: cherry, garnet rim. Nose: red berry notes, ripe fruit, floral, spicy, mineral. Palate: flavourful, complex, spicy, long.

COTO DE HAYAS 2008 TR
100% garnacha

90 Colour: cherry, garnet rim. Nose: complex, balanced, dark chocolate, spicy, ripe fruit. Palate: balanced, long, flavourful.

COTO DE HAYAS GARNACHA CENTENARIA 2011 T
100% garnacha

92 Colour: cherry, purple rim. Nose: red berry notes, ripe fruit, sweet spices, creamy oak, dark chocolate. Palate: powerful, flavourful, complex, long, toasty.

COTO DE HAYAS MISTELA 2011
VINO DULCE NATURAL
100% garnacha

90 Colour: pale ruby, brick rim edge. Nose: ripe fruit, sweet spices, aromatic coffee, dark chocolate, toasty. Palate: powerful, flavourful, toasty, balanced.

COTO DE HAYAS SOLO 10 2011 T
100% syrah

90 Colour: cherry, purple rim. Nose: expressive, red berry notes, ripe fruit. Palate: flavourful, fruity, balanced, complex.

FAGUS 10º ANIVERSARIO 2009 T
100% garnacha

94 Colour: bright cherry. Nose: ripe fruit, sweet spices, creamy oak, expressive, mineral. Palate: flavourful, fruity, toasty, round tannins. Personality.

FAGUS DE COTO DE HAYAS 2010 T
100% garnacha

93 Colour: deep cherry, garnet rim. Nose: powerfull, expressive, ripe fruit, cocoa bean, creamy oak. Palate: good structure, round tannins, full.

OXIA 2006 TC
100% garnacha

93 Colour: cherry, garnet rim. Nose: candied fruit, expressive, dark chocolate, tobacco, aromatic coffee, mineral. Palate: long, balanced, spicy.

OXIA 2008 T
100% garnacha

93 Colour: cherry, garnet rim. Nose: complex, mineral, ripe fruit, dark chocolate. Palate: full, fruity, round tannins, spicy.

BODEGAS BORSAO

Ctra. N- 122, Km. 63
50540 Borja - (Zaragoza)
☎: +34 976 867 116 - Fax: +34 976 867 752
info@bodegasborsao.com
www.bodegasborsao.com

BORSAO BEROLA 2008 T
80% garnacha, 20% syrah,

90 Colour: cherry, garnet rim. Nose: ripe fruit, spicy, creamy oak, toasty, balsamic herbs, mineral. Palate: powerful, flavourful, toasty, balanced.

BORSAO SELECCIÓN 2011 T
70% garnacha, 20% syrah, 10% tempranillo

90 Colour: deep cherry, purple rim. Nose: red berry notes, ripe fruit, scrubland, varietal. Palate: fresh, fruity, flavourful, easy to drink.

BORSAO TRES PICOS 2010 T
100% garnacha

92 Colour: cherry, garnet rim. Nose: fruit liqueur notes, floral, fragrant herbs, mineral, sweet spices, creamy oak. Palate: flavourful, fruity, spicy, balanced.

CRIANZAS Y VIÑEDOS SANTO CRISTO

Ctra. Tabuenca, s/n
50570 Ainzón - (Zaragoza)
☎: +34 976 869 696 - Fax: +34 976 868 097
info@bodegas-santo-cristo.com
www.bodegas-santo-cristo.com

CAYUS SELECCIÓN 2010 T ROBLE
100% garnacha

92 Colour: deep cherry, garnet rim. Nose: complex, expressive, cocoa bean, sweet spices, creamy oak, ripe fruit. Palate: flavourful, round tannins.

MOSCATEL AINZÓN 90 DÍAS 2010 B BARRICA
100% moscatel

92 Colour: bright yellow. Nose: expressive, varietal, honeyed notes, sweet spices, candied fruit. Palate: rich, flavourful, balanced.

TERRAZAS DEL MONCAYO GARNACHA 2009 T ROBLE
100% garnacha

90 Colour: cherry, garnet rim. Nose: spicy, creamy oak, toasty, complex, candied fruit. Palate: powerful, flavourful, toasty, round tannins.

PAGOS DEL MONCAYO

Ctra. Z-372, Km. 1,6
50580 Vera de Moncayo - (Zaragoza)
☎: +34 976 229 222
info@pagosdelmoncayo.com
www.pagosdelmoncayo.com

PAGOS DEL MONCAYO GARNACHA 2010 T
100% garnacha

92 Colour: bright cherry, purple rim. Nose: complex, balanced, ripe fruit, mineral. Palate: good structure, round tannins, long.

PAGOS DEL MONCAYO GARNACHA SYRAH 2011 T
65% garnacha, 35% syrah

90 Colour: bright cherry, purple rim. Nose: balanced, red berry notes, ripe fruit, violets. Palate: flavourful, fruity, round tannins.

PAGOS DEL MONCAYO SYRAH 2010 T
100% syrah

92 Colour: very deep cherry, purple rim. Nose: complex, balanced, sweet spices, aromatic coffee. Palate: flavourful, spicy, fine bitter notes.

DESCRIPTION

This has an exceptional geographical situation as it lies in the valley of the Ebro River 42 kilometres to the south of Zaragoza, in the nucleus of the Autonomous Community of Aragón. Cariñena became a source of supply for France at the time of the phylloxera plague in the XIX century. Currently, the young wines made from garnacha and tempranillo dominate. These are wines with good colour and structure.

NUMBER OF HECTARES: 15.059 **ALTITUDES:** 400 m. – 800 m.

VARIEDADES PREDOMINANTES:

White grapes: macabeo, garnacha blanca, muscat of Alexandria, perellada and chardonnay.
Red grapes: garnacha tinta, tempranillo and cariñena.

CLIMATOLOGY AND SOILS

Continental with brown-limestone soil on rocky deposits.

BIOENOS

Mayor, 88 Bajos
50400 Cariñena - (Zaragoza)
☎: +34 976 620 045 - Fax: +34 976 622 082
bioenos@bioenos.com
www.bioenos.com

GORYS CRESPIELLO 2007 T
95% vidadilo, 5% garnacha

93 Colour: cherry, garnet rim. Nose: ripe fruit, spicy, creamy oak, toasty, complex, mineral. Palate: powerful, flavourful, toasty, balanced.

PULCHRUM CRESPIELLO 2006 T
95% vidadillo, 5% garnacha

91 Colour: cherry, purple rim. Nose: candied fruit, sweet spices, ripe fruit, balanced. Palate: complex, good structure, round tannins.

BODEGAS AÑADAS

Ctra. Aguarón, km 47,100
50400 Cariñena - (Zaragoza)
☎: +34 976 793 016 - Fax: +34 976 620 448
bodega@carewines.com
www.carewines.com

CARE 2011 T ROBLE
50% garnacha, 50% syrah

90 Colour: cherry, purple rim. Nose: red berry notes, sweet spices, creamy oak, cocoa bean. Palate: powerful, flavourful, long, toasty.

CARE FINCA BANCALES 2008 TR
100% garnacha

92 Colour: cherry, garnet rim. Nose: ripe fruit, scrubland, earthy notes, expressive. Palate: powerful, complex, flavourful, long, toasty.

BODEGAS PANIZA

Ctra. Valencia, Km. 53
50480 Paniza - (Zaragoza)
☎: +34 976 622 515 - Fax: +34 976 622 958
info@bodegaspaniza.com
www.bodegasvirgenaguila.com

JABALÍ GARNACHA-SYRAH 2011 T
garnacha, syrah

90 Colour: bright cherry, purple rim. Nose: ripe fruit, violets, powerfull, balanced. Palate: fruity, good structure, flavourful.

BODEGAS PRINUR

Ctra. N-330, Km. 449,150
50400 Cariñena - (Zaragoza)
☎: +34 976 621 039 - Fax: +34 976 620 714
antonio@grupoprinur.com
www.bodegasprinur.com

PRINUR SELECCIÓN CALAR 2005 T
tempranillo, cabernet sauvignon, garnacha

91 Colour: cherry, garnet rim. Nose: ripe fruit, spicy, creamy oak, complex, earthy notes. Palate: powerful, flavourful, toasty, long, mineral.

PRINUR VIÑAS VIEJAS 2006 T
tempranillo, cabernet sauvignon, syrah, cariñena

92 Colour: cherry, garnet rim. Nose: complex, spicy, ripe fruit, toasty, mineral. Palate: good structure, flavourful, long, full.

BODEGAS SAN VALERO

Ctra. Nacional 330, Km. 450
50400 Cariñena - (Zaragoza)
☎: +34 976 620 400 - Fax: +34 976 620 398
bsv@sanvalero.com
www.sanvalero.com

SIERRA DE VIENTO GARNACHA GRAN SELECCIÓN 2006 T
garnacha

91 Colour: deep cherry, garnet rim. Nose: powerfull, dark chocolate, sweet spices, creamy oak, fruit preserve. Palate: rich, powerful, round tannins.

SIERRA DE VIENTO MOSCATEL VENDIMIA TARDÍA B
moscatel de alejandría

92 Colour: old gold, amber rim. Nose: honeyed notes, dry nuts, candied fruit, sweet spices. Palate: rich, flavourful, complex, elegant, long.

SIERRA DE VIENTO OLD VINES GARNACHA 2009 T
garnacha

90 Colour: cherry, garnet rim. Nose: ripe fruit, balsamic herbs, mineral, spicy, creamy oak. Palate: full, powerful, flavourful, spicy.

BODEGAS VICTORIA

Camino Virgen de Lagunas, s/n Apdo. Correos 47
50400 Cariñena - (Zaragoza)
☎: +34 976 621 007 - Fax: +34 976 621 106
comercial@bodegasvictoria.com
www.bodegasvictoria.com

DOMINIO DE LONGAZ PREMIUM 2006 T
syrah, merlot, cabernet sauvignon

90 Colour: ruby red, orangey edge. Nose: mineral, earthy notes, ripe fruit, spicy, creamy oak, fine reductive notes. Palate: powerful, flavourful, long, spicy, balanced.

LONGUS 2006 T

90 Colour: cherry, garnet rim. Nose: ripe fruit, spicy, creamy oak, toasty, waxy notes, cigar, old leather. Palate: powerful, flavourful, toasty, round tannins.

LONGUS 2007 T
40% syrah, 30% merlot, 30% cabernet sauvignon

91 Colour: cherry, garnet rim. Nose: sweet spices, cocoa bean, creamy oak, candied fruit. Palate: flavourful, balanced, ripe fruit, spicy.

COVINCA S. COOP.

Ctra, Valencia, s/n
50460 Longares - (Zaragoza)
☎: +34 976 142 653 - Fax: +34 976 142 402
info@covinca.es
www.covinca.es

TERRAI S10 2010 T
100% syrah

90 Colour: bright cherry. Nose: ripe fruit, sweet spices, creamy oak, expressive, toasty. Palate: flavourful, fruity, toasty, round tannins.

TORRELONGARES LICOR DE GARNACHA S/C VINO DE LICOR
garnacha

91 Colour: cherry, garnet rim. Nose: powerfull, dried fruit, fruit liqueur notes, sweet spices. Palate: flavourful, rich.

FINCA AYLÉS

Finca Aylés. Ctra. A-1101, Km. 24
50152 Mezalocha - (Zaragoza)
☎: +34 976 140 473 - Fax: +34 976 140 268
info@pagoayles.com
www.pagoayles.com

ALDEYA DE AYLÉS GARNACHA 2011 T
garnacha

90 Colour: cherry, purple rim. Nose: expressive, ripe fruit, balsamic herbs, sweet spices, creamy oak. Palate: flavourful, fruity, good acidity, toasty, smoky aftertaste.

AYLÉS "TRES DE 3000" 2008 T
garnacha, merlot, cabernet sauvignon

93 Colour: black cherry, garnet rim. Nose: ripe fruit, mineral, earthy notes, spicy, creamy oak, complex. Palate: powerful, flavourful, round, spicy, mineral.

SERENDIPIA GARNACHA DE AYLÉS 2009 T
garnacha

90 Colour: cherry, garnet rim. Nose: medium intensity, candied fruit. Palate: powerful, flavourful, toasty.

SERENDIPIA MERLOT DE AYLÉS 2009 T
merlot

93 Color cherry, garnet rim. Aroma ripe fruit, spicy, creamy oak, toasty, complex. Taste powerful, flavourful, toasty, round tannins.

GRANDES VINOS Y VIÑEDOS

Ctra. Valencia Km 45,700
50400 Cariñena - (Zaragoza)
☎: +34 976 621 261 - Fax: +34 976 621 253
info@grandesvinos.com
www.grandesvinos.com

ANAYÓN 2009 T BARRICA
tempranillo, cabernet sauvignon, syrah

90 Color cherry, garnet rim. Aroma ripe fruit, spicy, creamy oak, toasty, complex. Taste powerful, flavourful, toasty, round tannins.

ANAYÓN CHARDONNAY 2009 B BARRICA
chardonnay

90 Colour: bright golden. Nose: ripe fruit, dry nuts, powerfull, toasty. Palate: flavourful, fruity, spicy, toasty, long.

ANAYÓN GARNACHA SELECCIÓN 2008 T
garnacha

92 Colour: very deep cherry. Nose: creamy oak, dark chocolate, ripe fruit, spicy, mineral. Palate: good structure, rich, flavourful.

CORONA DE ARAGÓN DISPARATES CARIÑENA 2010 T
cariñena

90 Colour: black cherry, purple rim. Nose: balanced, ripe fruit, medium intensity, sweet spices. Palate: correct, spicy, ripe fruit.

HACIENDA MOLLEDA

Ctra. Belchite, km 29,3
50154 Tosos - (Zaragoza)
☎: +34 976 620 702 - Fax: +34 976 620 102
hm@haciendamolleda.com
www.haciendamolleda.com

GHM GARNACHA HACIENDA MOLLEDA 2008 T
100% garnacha

92 Color cherry, garnet rim. Aroma ripe fruit, spicy, creamy oak, toasty, complex. Taste powerful, flavourful, toasty, round tannins.

GHM GRAN HACIENDA MOLLEDA 2009 T ROBLE
100% mazuelo

90 Colour: cherry, garnet rim. Nose: ripe fruit, spicy, toasty, creamy oak. Palate: fine bitter notes, powerful, flavourful, balanced.

HACIENDA MOLLEDA GARNACHA 2007 T ROBLE
100% garnacha

90 Colour: bright cherry, purple rim. Nose: balsamic herbs, ripe fruit, spicy. Palate: balanced, spicy, long, round tannins.

SOLAR DE URBEZO

San Valero, 14
50400 Cariñena - (Zaragoza)
☎: +34 976 621 968 - Fax: +34 976 620 549
info@solardeurbezo.es
www.solardeurbezo.es

ALTIUS GARNACHA 2011 T
garnacha

90 Colour: cherry, purple rim. Nose: expressive, fresh fruit, red berry notes, floral, lactic notes. Palate: flavourful, fruity, good acidity, easy to drink.

URBEZO 2009 TC
syrah, merlot, cabernet sauvignon

90 Colour: deep cherry, garnet rim. Nose: complex, ripe fruit, sweet spices, cocoa bean, balsamic herbs. Palate: good structure, fruity.

VIÑA URBEZO 2011 T MACERACIÓN CARBÓNICA
garnacha, tempranillo

90 Colour: cherry, purple rim. Nose: expressive, fresh fruit, red berry notes, floral. Palate: flavourful, fruity, good acidity.

VIÑEDOS Y BODEGAS PABLO

Avda. Zaragoza, 16
50108 Almonacid de la Sierra - (Zaragoza)
☎: +34 976 627 037 - Fax: +34 976 627 102
granviu@granviu.com
www.granviu.com

GRAN VÍU GARNACHA DEL TERRENO 2006 T
garnacha

91 Colour: cherry, garnet rim. Nose: ripe fruit, spicy, creamy oak, complex, scrubland. Palate: powerful, flavourful, toasty, round tannins.

MENGUANTE GARNACHA BLANCA 2011 B
garnacha blanca

90 Colour: bright yellow. Nose: medium intensity, balanced, fragrant herbs, expressive. Palate: balanced, fruity, good acidity.

DESCRIPTION

This takes in the traditional Catalonian wine producing zones and corresponds practically to the existing Denominations of Origin. It began as an export brand which used the full name of Catalonia which served as a catch word for the production of wines with varieties not authorized in each zone, and to provide outlets for the cheaper wines of large wineries. With the passage of time, this label was competing in quality with the superior wines of the Denominations of Origin it had drawn together.

NUMBER OF HECTARES: 49.883

PREDOMINANT VARIETIES:

White grapes: chardonnay, garnacha blanca, macabeo, muscat, parellada, riesling, xarel.lo, gewürztraminer, subirat parent, malvasía de Sitges, chenin and picapoll blanc.
Red grapes: cabernet franc, cabernet sauvignon, garnacha negra, garnacha peluda, merlot, monastrell, pinot noir, samsó, sumoll, syrah, trepat and tempranillo

CLIMATOLOGY AND SOILS

As this takes in almost all of Catalonia, it is impossible to specify one type of climate and one type of soil.

BODEGAS PUIGGRÒS

Ctra. de Manresa, Km. 13
8711 Odena - (Barcelona)
☎: +34 629 853 587
bodegaspuiggros@telefonica.net
www.bodegaspuiggros.com

SENTITS BLANCS 2011 B
garnacha blanca

92 Colour: bright straw. Nose: powerfull, fine lees, ripe fruit, citrus fruit, lactic notes. Palate: flavourful, sweetness, good acidity.

SENTITS NEGRES 2010 T
garnacha

93 Colour: deep cherry. Nose: ripe fruit, earthy notes, mineral, toasty, spicy. Palate: flavourful, fine bitter notes, good acidity, long.

SIGNES 2010 T
80% sumoll, 20% garnacha

91 Colour: bright cherry. Nose: ripe fruit, sweet spices, creamy oak, red berry notes. Palate: flavourful, fruity, toasty, round tannins.

CA N'ESTRUC

Ctra. C-1414, Km. 1,05
8292 Esparreguera - (Barcelona)
☎: +34 937 777 017 - Fax: +34 937 771 108
canestruc@vilaviniteca.es
www.canestruc.com

IDOIA BLANC 2010 BFB
xarel.lo, macabeo, chardonnay, garnacha

93 Colour: bright yellow. Nose: sweet spices, fruit expression, fresh fruit. Palate: flavourful, ripe fruit, fine bitter notes.

L'EQUILIBRISTA 2010 T
syrah, garnacha, cariñena

92 Colour: bright cherry. Nose: sweet spices, creamy oak, fruit expression, red berry notes, earthy notes. Palate: flavourful, fruity, toasty, round tannins.

L'EQUILIBRISTA 2011 B
xarel.lo

93 Colour: bright straw. Nose: candied fruit, ripe fruit, white flowers, mineral. Palate: ripe fruit, fine bitter notes, good acidity.

L'EQUILIBRISTA GARNATXA 2010 T
100% garnacha

93 Colour: bright cherry. Nose: sweet spices, creamy oak, expressive, fruit expression, lactic notes. Palate: flavourful, fruity, toasty, round tannins.

CAVAS BOHIGAS

Finca Can Maciá s/n
8711 Ódena - (Barcelona)
☎: +34 938 048 100 - Fax: +34 938 032 366
comercial@bohigas.es
www.bohigas.es

BOHIGAS BLANC DE BLANCS 2011 B
xarel.lo

90 Colour: bright straw. Nose: fresh fruit, white flowers, mineral, dried herbs. Palate: flavourful, fruity, good acidity, balanced.

FERMÍ DE FERMÍ BOHIGAS 2008 TR
syrah

90 Colour: cherry, garnet rim. Nose: balanced, ripe fruit, sweet spices, toasty. Palate: powerful, flavourful, long, spicy, round tannins, balsamic.

CLOS D'AGON

Afores, s/n
17251 Calonge - (Girona)
☎: +34 972 661 486 - Fax: +34 972 661 462
info@closdagon.com
www.closdagon.com

CLOS D'AGON 2010 T
45% cabernet franc, 30% syrah, 10% merlot, 10% petit verdot, 5% cabernet sauvignon

93 Colour: black cherry, purple rim. Nose: fruit preserve, creamy oak, dark chocolate, expressive. Palate: good structure, powerful, round tannins.

CLOS D'AGON 2011 B
39% viognier, 39% roussanne, 22% marsanne

92 Colour: bright yellow. Nose: candied fruit, faded flowers, citrus fruit, spicy. Palate: flavourful, ripe fruit, good structure, long.

GRAU VELL

Can Grau Vell, s/n
8784 Hostalets de Pierola - (Barcelona)
☎: +34 676 586 933 - Fax: +34 932 684 965
info@grauvell.cat

ALCOR 2008 T
syrah, cabernet sauvignon, garnacha

93 Colour: cherry, garnet rim. Nose: ripe fruit, spicy, creamy oak, toasty, characterful. Palate: powerful, flavourful, toasty, round tannins.

ALCOR 2009 T

93 Colour: cherry, garnet rim. Nose: red berry notes, ripe fruit, dry stone, balsamic herbs, balanced, sweet spices, creamy oak. Palate: flavourful, fresh, long, round tannins.

ALCOR 2010 T
40% syrah, 25% garnacha, 15% monastrell, 10% marselan, 10% cabernet sauvignon

93 Colour: bright cherry. Nose: ripe fruit, sweet spices, expressive, earthy notes, roasted coffee. Palate: flavourful, fruity, toasty, round tannins.

MASET DEL LLEÓ

C-244, Km. 32,5
8792 La Granada del Penedès - (Barcelona)
☎: +34 902 200 250 - Fax: +34 938 921 333
info@maset.com
www.maset.com

MASET DEL LLEÓ GRAN ROBLE 2006 TR
tempranillo

90 Color cherry, garnet rim. Aroma ripe fruit, spicy, creamy oak, toasty, complex. Taste powerful, flavourful, toasty, round tannins.

MASET DEL LLEÓ SYRAH 2008 TR

92 Colour: cherry, garnet rim. Nose: ripe fruit, spicy, creamy oak, complex, dark chocolate. Palate: powerful, flavourful, toasty, round tannins.

PORTAL DEL MONTSANT

Carrer de Dalt, s/n
43775 Marça - (Tarragona)
☎: +34 933 950 811 - Fax: +34 933 955 500
info@parxet.es
www.parxet.es

SANTES ROSÉ 2010 RD
merlot, cabernet sauvignon

90 Colour: onion pink. Nose: elegant, candied fruit, dried flowers, fragrant herbs, red berry notes, mineral. Palate: light-bodied, flavourful, long, spicy, elegant. Personality.

DESCRIPTION

The Cava region is not restricted only to Catalonia, which is the fundamental source of cava, but to La Rioja, Aragón, Navarre, Valencia and Badajoz, taking in seven Autonomous Communities. Cava is the only Denomination of Origin which is formed around a production style and not a geographical area. The characteristics of cavas depend on the different combinations of varieties (normally the local varieties of each zone), years and also the different ageing periods and the amount of sugar added to the tirage liqueur during ageing. Cavas spend a minimum of nine months ageing, while reserve cava spends a minimum of 15 months and the grand reserve cavas up to 30 months. Cava follows the champagne production method of the French wineries, but it is made with Catalonian grapes (xarel.lo, parellada and macabeo) together with chardonnay, and it has an excellent quality/price ratio, to such an extent that it has ousted champagne as regards sales in recent years.

NUMBER OF HECTARES: 31.061 **ALTITUDES:** 400 m. – 800 m.

PREDOMINANT VARIETIES:

White grapes: macabeo, xare.lo, parellada, subirat and chardonnay.
Red grapes: garnacha tinta, monastrell, trepat and pinot noir.

CLIMATOLOGY AND SOILS

Depending on the zone, there is a diversity of climates and soils. The most characteristic (Tarragona and Barcelona) is Mediterranean.

1 + 1 = 3

Masía Navinés
8736 Guardiola de Font-Rubí - (Barcelona)
☎: +34 938 974 069 - Fax: +34 938 974 724
umesu@umesufan3.com
www.umesufan3.com

1 + 1 = 3 GRAN RESERVA ESPECIAL 2006
BN GRAN RESERVA
pinot noir, xarel.lo

91 Colour: bright yellow, greenish rim. Nose: ripe fruit, dried herbs, complex. Palate: flavourful, good structure, fine bitter notes, good acidity.

CYGNUS 1 + 1 = 3 2008 BN RESERVA
macabeo, xarel.lo, parellada

90 Colour: bright straw. Nose: fresh fruit, dried herbs, fine lees, floral. Palate: fresh, fruity, flavourful.

CYGNUS 1 + 1 = 3 2009 BR
macabeo, xarel.lo, parellada

90 Colour: bright yellow. Nose: white flowers, fragrant herbs, fruit expression. Palate: good acidity, fine bead, flavourful.

AGUSTÍ TORELLÓ MATA

La Serra, s/n PO Box 35
8770 Sant Sadurní D'Anoia - (Barcelona)
☎: +34 938 911 173 - Fax: +34 938 912 616
comunicacio@agustitorellomata.com
www.agustitorellomata.com

AGUSTÍ TORELLÓ MATA 2008 BN GRAN RESERVA
38% macabeo, 28% xarel.lo, 34% parellada

90 Colour: bright yellow. Nose: expressive, dry nuts, fine lees, dried flowers, medium intensity. Palate: long, ripe fruit, good acidity.

AGUSTÍ TORELLÓ MATA GRAN RESERVA BARRICA 2008 BN
100% macabeo

92 Colour: bright straw. Nose: elegant, balanced, dry nuts, dried flowers, spicy. Palate: fine bitter notes, good acidity, ripe fruit.

AGUSTÍ TORELLÓ MATA MAGNUM 2006 BN GRAN RESERVA
45% macabeo, 25% xarel.lo, 30% parellada

92 Colour: bright straw. Nose: dried herbs, fine lees, floral, ripe fruit, citrus fruit. Palate: fresh, fruity, flavourful, good acidity.

AGUSTÍ TORELLÓ MATA ROSAT TREPAT 2010 BR RESERVA
100% trepat

90 Colour: light cherry. Nose: medium intensity, red berry notes, rose petals, elegant. Palate: good acidity, balanced, fine bitter notes, fine bead.

BAYANUS 375ML 2008 BN GRAN RESERVA
40% macabeo, 30% xarel.lo, 30% parellada

90 Colour: bright straw. Nose: complex, expressive, fine lees, ripe fruit, dry nuts. Palate: flavourful, good structure, spicy.

KRIPTA 2006 BN GRAN RESERVA
45% macabeo, 35% parellada, 20% xarel.lo

92 Color bright golden. Aroma fine lees, dry nuts, fragrant herbs, complex. Taste powerful, flavourful, good acidity, fine bead, fine bitter notes.

ALBET I NOYA

Can Vendrell de la Codina, s/n
8739 Sant Pau D'Ordal - (Barcelona)
☎: +34 938 994 812 - Fax: +34 938 994 930
albetinoya@albetinoya.cat
www.albetinoya.cat

ALBET I NOYA 2008 BN GRAN RESERVA
macabeo, xarel.lo, parellada, chardonnay

90 Colour: bright yellow, greenish rim. Nose: fine lees, dry nuts, fragrant herbs. Palate: powerful, flavourful, good acidity, fine bead, fine bitter notes.

ALBET I NOYA BRUT 21 BR
57% chardonnay, 43% parellada

90 Colour: bright yellow, greenish rim. Nose: dried herbs, faded flowers, fine lees, fresh fruit. Palate: fine bitter notes, good acidity.

ALBET I NOYA BRUT 21 BARRICA BR
chardonnay, pinot noir

91 Colour: bright yellow. Nose: complex, balanced, sweet spices, expressive, faded flowers. Palate: balanced, fine bitter notes, full.

ALSINA SARDÁ

Barrio Les Tarumbas, s/n
8733 Pla del Penedès - (Barcelona)
☎: +34 938 988 132 - Fax: +34 938 988 671
alsina@alsinasarda.com
www.alsinasarda.com

ALSINA & SARDÁ GRAN CUVÉE VESTIGIS 2006 BN GRAN RESERVA
20% macabeo, 20% xarel.lo, 20% parellada, 20% chardonnay, 20% pinot noir

90 Colour: bright yellow. Nose: fine lees, dry nuts, fragrant herbs, complex. Palate: flavourful, fine bead, fine bitter notes.

ALSINA & SARDÁ MAS D'ALSINA BN RESERVA
65% chardonnay, 10% macabeo, 10% xarel.lo, 15% parellada

90 Color bright straw. Aroma medium intensity, fresh fruit, dried herbs, fine lees, floral. Taste fresh, fruity, flavourful, good acidity.

ALTA ALELLA

Camí Baix de Tiana - Finca Can Genis
8391 Tiana - (Barcelona)
☎: +34 934 693 720 - Fax: +34 934 691 343
altaalella@altaalella.cat
www.altaalella.cat

ALTA ALELLA MIRGIN 2007 BN GRAN RESERVA
chardonnay, pinot noir, pansa blanca

90 Colour: bright yellow. Nose: balanced, complex, fine lees, ripe fruit. Palate: balanced, fine bitter notes, spicy, long, toasty.

PRIVAT OPUS EVOLUTIUM 2007 BN GRAN RESERVA
chardonnay, pinot noir

92 Colour: bright golden. Nose: fine lees, dry nuts, candied fruit, jasmine. Palate: powerful, flavourful, good acidity, fine bead, fine bitter notes.

AVINYÓ CAVAS

Masia Can Fontanals
8793 Avinyonet del Penedès - (Barcelona)
☎: +34 938 970 055 - Fax: +34 938 970 691
avinyo@avinyo.com
www.avinyo.com

AVINYÓ SELECCIÓ LA TICOTA 2006
BN GRAN RESERVA
65% xarel.lo, 35% macabeo

90 Colour: yellow, greenish rim. Nose: balanced, lees reduction notes, faded flowers, dry nuts. Palate: balanced, fine bitter notes, good acidity.

BODEGA SEBIRAN

Pérez Galdos, 1
46352 Campo Arcis - Requena - (Valencia)
☎: +34 962 301 326 - Fax: +34 962 303 966
info@bodegasebiran.com
www.bodegasebiran.com

COTO D´ARCIS ESPECIAL BR

90 Color bright straw. Aroma medium intensity, fresh fruit, dried herbs, fine lees, floral. Taste fresh, fruity, flavourful, good acidity.

BODEGAS CAPITÀ VIDAL

Ctra. Villafranca-Igualada, Km. 21
8733 Pla del Penedès - (Barcelona)
☎: +34 938 988 630 - Fax: +34 938 988 625
capitavidal@capitavidal.com
www.capitavidal.com

FUCHS DE VIDAL CUVÉE BN RESERVA
40% xarel.lo, 35% macabeo, 25% parellada

90 Colour: bright yellow. Nose: petrol notes, fine lees, dried flowers, dry nuts. Palate: powerful, flavourful, complex, long.

BODEGAS HISPANO SUIZAS

Ctra. N-322, Km. 451,7 El Pontón
46357 Requena - (Valencia)
☎: +34 661 894 200
info@bodegashispanosuizas.com
www.bodegashispanosuizas.com

TANTUM ERGO CHARDONNAY PINOT NOIR 2009 BN
chardonnay, pinot noir

92 Colour: bright yellow. Nose: ripe fruit, spicy. Palate: balanced, fruity, flavourful, good acidity, fine bitter notes.

TANTUM ERGO PINOT NOIR ROSÉ 2010 BN
pinot noir

93 Colour: salmon. Nose: candied fruit, faded flowers, fine lees, balanced. Palate: good acidity, balanced, fine bitter notes, fine bead.

TANTUM ERGO VINTAGE 2007
chardonnay, pinot noir

93 Colour: bright yellow. Nose: ripe fruit, jasmine, complex, expressive, powerfull, fine lees. Palate: good structure, flavourful, long, fine bitter notes.

BODEGAS SIGNAT

Escultor Llimona, s/n
8328 Alella - (Barcelona)
☎: +34 935 403 400 - Fax: +34 935 401 471
signat@signat.es
www.signat.es

SIGNAT 5 ESTRELLAS BR RESERVA

91 Colour: bright straw. Nose: candied fruit, dry nuts, fine lees. Palate: flavourful, fine bitter notes, good acidity.

BODEGUES SUMARROCA

Barrio El Rebato, s/n
8739 Subirats - (Barcelona)
☎: +34 938 911 092 - Fax: +34 938 911 778
info@sumarroca.com
www.sumarroca.com

NÚRIA CLAVEROL 2008 BR
xarel.lo, chardonnay, parellada

93 Colour: bright straw. Nose: fresh fruit, dried herbs, fine lees, floral, medium intensity, complex, fresh. Palate: fresh, fruity, flavourful, good acidity.

SUMARROCA 2008 BN GRAN RESERVA
parellada, macabeo, xarel.lo, chardonnay

91 Colour: bright golden. Nose: lees reduction notes, pattiserie, dried flowers, ripe fruit, elegant. Palate: powerful, flavourful, balanced, long.

SUMARROCA 2009 BR RESERVA
parellada, macabeo, xarel.lo, chardonnay

90 Colour: bright straw. Nose: fresh fruit, fine lees, floral, fragrant herbs. Palate: fresh, fruity, flavourful, good acidity, balanced.

SUMARROCA CUVÉE 2008 BN GRAN RESERVA
chardonnay, parellada

90 Colour: bright golden. Nose: faded flowers, ripe fruit, dry nuts, pattiserie. Palate: good acidity, fine bitter notes, powerful, flavourful.

SUMARROCA GRAN BRUT BR GRAN RESERVA

91 Colour: bright yellow. Nose: white flowers, fresh fruit, fragrant herbs, expressive. Palate: balanced, powerful, flavourful, long.

SUMARROCA GRAN BRUT ALLIER
2009 BR GRAN RESERVA
chardonnay, pinot noir, parellada

93 Colour: bright yellow. Nose: toasty, dried flowers, fragrant herbs, spicy, aromatic coffee. Palate: complex, flavourful, fine bitter notes, balanced, long. Personality.

CANALS & MUNNÉ

Ctra. de Sant Sadurni a Vilafranca, km. 0,5
8770 Sant Sadurní D'Anoia - (Barcelona)
☎: +34 938 910 318 - Fax: +34 938 911 945
info@canalsimunne.com
www.canalsimunne.com

CANALS & MUNNÉ GRAN DUC
2007 BN GRAN RESERVA
40% pinot noir, 30% chardonnay, 30% xarel.lo

90 Colour: bright golden. Nose: roasted almonds, toasty, faded flowers, dry nuts. Palate: long, spicy, fine bead, fine bitter notes.

CANALS & MUNNÉ MAGNUM
2006 BN GRAN RESERVA
40% xarel.lo, 20% macabeo, 20% chardonnay, 20% parellada

91 Colour: bright golden. Nose: fine lees, dry nuts, fragrant herbs. Palate: powerful, flavourful, good acidity, fine bead, fine bitter notes.

CANALS NADAL

Ponent, 2
8733 El Pla del Penedès - (Barcelona)
☎: +34 938 988 081 - Fax: +34 938 989 050
cava@canalsnadal.com
www.canalsnadal.com

CANALS NADAL GRAN VINTAGE 2009 BR RESERVA
40% chardonnay, 30% macabeo, 20% xarel.lo, 10% parellada

90 Colour: bright yellow. Nose: fine lees, dry nuts, fragrant herbs, complex. Palate: powerful, flavourful, good acidity, fine bead, fine bitter notes.

CANALS NADAL ROSÉ 2010 BR RESERVA
100% trepat

90 Colour: raspberry rose. Nose: red berry notes, fine lees, floral, fresh, expressive. Palate: fresh, fruity, powerful, flavourful, easy to drink.

CASTELL SANT ANTONI

Passeig del Parc, 13
8770 Sant Sadurní D'Anoia - (Barcelona)
☎: +34 938 183 099 - Fax: +34 938 184 451
cava@castellsantantoni.com
www.castellsantantoni.com

CASTELL SANT ANTONI 37.5 BRUT BR

90 Colour: bright straw. Nose: medium intensity, dried herbs, fine lees, floral, candied fruit, dry nuts. Palate: fresh, fruity, flavourful, good acidity.

CASTELL SANT ANTONI 37.5 BRUT NATURE BN

91 Colour: bright straw. Nose: medium intensity, dried herbs, fine lees, floral, candied fruit, sweet spices, toasty. Palate: fresh, good acidity, flavourful, long.

CASTELL SANT ANTONI CAMÍ DEL SOT BN RESERVA

91 Colour: bright straw. Nose: dried herbs, fine lees, floral, candied fruit. Palate: fresh, fruity, flavourful, good acidity.

CASTELL SANT ANTONI CAMÍ DEL
SOT MAGNUM BN RESERVA

91 Colour: bright straw. Nose: fresh fruit, dried herbs, fine lees, floral, characterful. Palate: fresh, fruity, flavourful, good acidity.

CASTELL SANT ANTONI GRAN BARRICA BN GRAN RESERVA

91 Colour: bright golden. Nose: fine lees, dry nuts, fragrant herbs, complex, spicy. Palate: powerful, flavourful, good acidity, fine bead, fine bitter notes.

CASTELL SANT ANTONI GRAN BRUT BR GRAN RESERVA

92 Color bright golden. Aroma fine lees, dry nuts, fragrant herbs, complex. Taste powerful, flavourful, good acidity, fine bead, fine bitter notes.

CASTELL SANT ANTONI GRAN BRUT MAGNUM BR RESERVA

91 Colour: bright yellow. Nose: candied fruit, fruit liqueur notes, lees reduction notes, sweet spices. Palate: flavourful, powerful, fine bitter notes.

CASTELL SANT ANTONI GRAN RESERVA 2005 BN GRAN RESERVA

91 Colour: bright yellow. Nose: dry nuts, lees reduction notes, fragrant herbs, pattiserie. Palate: powerful, flavourful, spicy, long.

CASTELL SANT ANTONI GRAN RESERVA MAGNUM 2005 BN

93 Colour: bright straw. Nose: expressive, elegant, fine lees, dry nuts. Palate: balanced, fine bitter notes, good acidity, fine bead.

CASTELL SANT ANTONI TORRE DE L'HOMENATGE 1999 BN GRAN RESERVA

94 Colour: bright golden. Nose: dry nuts, fragrant herbs, complex, lees reduction notes, candied fruit. Palate: powerful, flavourful, good acidity, fine bead, fine bitter notes.

CASTELL SANT ANTONI TORRE DE L'HOMENATGE 2003 BN

93 Colour: bright golden. Nose: fine lees, dry nuts, fragrant herbs, complex, ripe fruit. Palate: powerful, flavourful, good acidity, fine bead, fine bitter notes.

CASTELLBLANCH

Avda. Casetes Mir, 2
8770 Sant Sadurní D'Anoia - (Barcelona)
☎: +34 938 917 025 - Fax: +34 938 910 126
castellblanch@castellblanch.es
www.castellblanch.es

CASTELLBLANCH GRAN CUVEÉ 2008 BN RESERVA
40% parellada, 30% macabeo, 30% xarel.lo

90 Colour: bright straw. Nose: medium intensity, dried herbs, fine lees, floral, toasty. Palate: fresh, fruity, flavourful, good acidity.

CASTILLO PERELADA VINOS Y CAVAS

Avda. Barcelona, 78
8720 Vilafranca del Penedès - (Barcelona)
☎: +34 938 180 676 - Fax: +34 938 180 926
perelada@castilloperalada.com
www.castilloperelada.com

CASTILLO PERELADA CUVÉE ESPECIAL 2009 BN
macabeo, parellada, xarel.lo, chardonnay

90 Colour: bright yellow. Nose: white flowers, fresh fruit, fragrant herbs. Palate: correct, fine bitter notes, flavourful, easy to drink.

GRAN CLAUSTRO CUVÉE ESPECIAL DE CASTILLO PERELADA 2007 BN GRAN RESERVA
chardonnay, pinot noir, parellada

90 Colour: bright golden. Nose: white flowers, ripe fruit, dry nuts, fragrant herbs, pattiserie. Palate: fine bitter notes, powerful, flavourful.

CAVA BERDIÉ

Les Conilleres (La Conillera Gran)
8732 Castellví de la Marca - (Barcelona)
☎: +34 902 800 229 - Fax: +34 938 919 735
info@cavaberdie.com
www.cavaberdie.com

BERDIÉ AMOR 2009 BR RESERVA
macabeo, xarel.lo, parellada, garnacha

90 Colour: onion pink. Nose: floral, fruit expression, fragrant herbs. Palate: good acidity, balanced, flavourful, long.

CAVA CRISTINA COLOMER BERNAT

Diputació, 58-60
8770 Sant Sadurní D'Anoia - (Barcelona)
☎: +34 938 910 804 - Fax: +34 938 913 034
ccolomer@cavescolomer.com
www.cavescolomer.com

COLOMER COSTA 2010 BN RESERVA
xarel.lo, macabeo, parellada

90 Colour: bright straw. Nose: medium intensity, fresh fruit, dried herbs, fine lees. Palate: fresh, fruity, flavourful, good acidity.

COLOMER PRESTIGE 2008 BN GRAN RESERVA
xarel.lo, chardonnay, macabeo, pinot noir, parellada

91 Colour: bright yellow. Nose: dry nuts, white flowers, dried herbs, expressive. Palate: complex, powerful, flavourful.

CAVA JOSEP M. FERRET GUASCH

Barri L'Alzinar, 68
8739 Font-Rubí - (Barcelona)
☎: +34 938 979 037 - Fax: +34 938 979 414
ferretguasch@ferretguasch.com
www.ferretguasch.com

FERRET GUASCH COUPAGE SARA
2004 BN GRAN RESERVA
10% macabeo, 50% xarel.lo, 20% parellada, 20% chardonnay

90 Colour: bright yellow. Nose: fine lees, dry nuts, fragrant herbs. Palate: powerful, flavourful, good acidity, fine bead, fine bitter notes.

CAVA MARÍA CASANOVAS

Montserrat, 117
8770 Sant Sadurní D'Anoia - (Barcelona)
☎: +34 938 910 812 - Fax: +34 938 911 572
mariacasanovas@brutnature.com
www.mariacasanovas.com

MARÍA CASANOVAS 2009 BN GRAN RESERVA
chardonnay, pinot noir, xarel.lo, macabeo, parellada

91 Color bright golden. Aroma fine lees, dry nuts, fragrant herbs, complex. Taste powerful, flavourful, good acidity, fine bead, fine bitter notes.

CAVA REVERTÉ

Paseo Tomás García Rebull, 4
43885 Salomó - (Tarragona)
☎: +34 630 929 380 - Fax: +34 977 629 246
enricreverte@terra.es
www.cavareverte.com

CAVA REVERTÉ "ELECTE" 2008 BN
40% xarel.lo, 20% macabeo, 20% parellada, 20% chardonnay

90 Colour: bright yellow. Nose: fine lees, floral, citrus fruit, dried herbs, expressive. Palate: good acidity, fine bead, fine bitter notes, flavourful.

CAVA VIDAL I FERRÉ

Nou, 2
43815 Les Pobles - (Tarragona)
☎: +34 977 638 554 - Fax: +34 977 638 554
vidaliferre@vidaliferre.com
www.vidaliferre.com

VIDAL I FERRÉ BN GRAN RESERVA
xarel.lo, parellada, macabeo

91 Colour: bright golden. Nose: dried flowers, dry nuts, fragrant herbs, fine lees. Palate: powerful, flavourful, balanced, fine bitter notes.

CAVAS BERTHA

Lavernó, 14
8770 Sant Sadurní D'Anoia - (Barcelona)
☎: +34 938 911 091
cavabertha@cavabertha.com
www.cavabertha.com

BERTHA SEGLE XXI BN GRAN RESERVA
macabeo, xarel.lo, parellada, chardonnay

90 Colour: bright yellow. Nose: fine lees, dry nuts, fragrant herbs, complex. Palate: powerful, flavourful, good acidity, fine bead, fine bitter notes.

CAVAS BOHIGAS

Finca Can Maciá s/n
8711 Ódena - (Barcelona)
☎: +34 938 048 100 - Fax: +34 938 032 366
comercial@bohigas.es
www.bohigas.es

NOA BN
pinot noir, xarel.lo

90 Colour: bright yellow. Nose: fragrant herbs, fine lees, fresh fruit, expressive. Palate: fine bead, powerful, flavourful.

CAVAS FERRET

Avda. de Catalunya, 36
8736 Guardiola de Font-Rubí - (Barcelona)
☎: +34 938 979 148 - Fax: +34 938 979 285
ferret@cavasferret.com
www.cavasferret.com

FERRET BR RESERVA
40% macabeo, 40% parellada, 20% xarel.lo

90 Colour: bright straw. Nose: fresh fruit, dried herbs, fine lees, floral. Palate: fresh, fruity, flavourful, good acidity, fine bead.

FERRET 2007 BN GRAN RESERVA
macabeo, xarel.lo, parellada

90 Colour: bright yellow. Nose: candied fruit, white flowers, fragrant herbs. Palate: fine bitter notes, powerful, flavourful.

CAVAS LAVERNOYA

Finca La Porxada
8729 Sant Marçal - (Barcelona)
☎: +34 938 912 202 - Fax: +34 938 919 948
lavernoya@lavernoya.com
www.lavernoya.com

LÁCRIMA BACCUS SUMMUM BN GRAN RESERVA

90 Colour: bright golden. Nose: white flowers, fragrant herbs, pattiserie, dry nuts. Palate: powerful, flavourful, good acidity, fine bead.

CAVAS MESTRES

Plaça Ajuntament, 8
8770 Sant Sadurní D'Anoia - (Barcelona)
☎: +34 938 910 043 - Fax: +34 938 911 611
cava@mestres.es
www.mestres.es

MESTRE CLOS NOSTRE SENYOR
2002 BN GRAN RESERVA
60% xarel.lo, 20% macabeo, 20% parellada,

91 Colour: bright yellow. Nose: sweet spices, dark chocolate, ripe fruit, fine lees, complex. Palate: good structure, ripe fruit, fine bitter notes.

MESTRES CUPAGE 50 AÑOS DE
"CAVA" 2006 BR GRAN RESERVA
25% macabeo, 50% xarel.lo, 25% parellada

91 Colour: bright yellow. Nose: dried flowers, fragrant herbs, complex, balanced. Palate: flavourful, full, ripe fruit, long.

MESTRES CUPAGE 80 ANIVERSARIO
2006 BR GRAN RESERVA
60% xarel.lo, 25% macabeo, 15% parellada

90 Colour: bright straw, greenish rim. Nose: medium intensity, dried herbs, dried flowers, fine lees. Palate: flavourful, fruity, balanced, fine bitter notes.

MESTRES CUPAGE BARCELONA
2007 BR GRAN RESERVA
40% macabeo, 30% xarel.lo, 30% parellada

91 Color bright golden. Aroma fine lees, dry nuts, fragrant herbs, complex. Taste powerful, flavourful, good acidity, fine bead, fine bitter notes.

MESTRES MAS VÍA 2000 BR GRAN RESERVA
75% xarel.lo, 15% macabeo, 10% parellada

92 Colour: bright golden. Nose: fine lees, dry nuts, complex, petrol notes. Palate: powerful, flavourful, good acidity, fine bead, fine bitter notes.

MESTRES VISOL 2006 BN GRAN RESERVA
40% xarel.lo, 35% macabeo, 25% parellada

90 Nose: fine lees, dry nuts, fragrant herbs, complex. Palate: powerful, flavourful, good acidity, fine bead, fine bitter notes.

CAVES CONDE DE CARALT S.A.

Ctra. Sant Sadurní-Sant Pere de Riudebitlles, Km. 5
8775 Torrelavit - (Barcelona)
☎: +34 938 917 070 - Fax: +34 938 996 006
condedecaralt@condedecaralt.com
www.condedecaralt.com

CONDE DE CARALT BLANC DE BLANCS BR
60% macabeo, 20% xarel.lo, 20% parellada

90 Colour: bright straw. Nose: white flowers, dried herbs, expressive, fine lees, elegant. Palate: powerful, flavourful, full, long, balanced.

CAVES NAVERÁN

Can Parellada - Sant Martí Sadevesa
8775 Torrelavit - (Barcelona)
☎: +34 938 988 400 - Fax: +34 938 989 027
sadeve@naveran.com
www.naveran.com

NAVERAN PERLES BLANQUES 2009 BR
pinot noir, chardonnay

92 Colour: bright yellow. Nose: expressive, complex, ripe fruit, white flowers, elegant. Palate: fruity, full, long, good acidity, fine bitter notes.

NAVERÁN PERLES ROSES PINOT NOIR 2010 RD
pinot noir

91 Colour: ochre. Nose: fine lees, fragrant herbs, wild herbs, fresh fruit, expressive. Palate: correct, powerful, flavourful, complex.

ODISEA NAVERÁN 2010 BN

91 Colour: bright straw. Nose: fresh fruit, dried herbs, fine lees, white flowers. Palate: fresh, fruity, flavourful, good acidity, fine bead, balanced.

CELLER CARLES ANDREU

Sant Sebastià, 19
43423 Pira - (Tarragona)
☎: +34 977 887 404 - Fax: +34 977 887 427
celler@cavandreu.com
www.cavandreu.com

CAVA RESERVA BARRICA BRUT NATURE CARLES ANDREU 2009
parellada, macabeo, chardonnay

90 Colour: bright yellow. Nose: faded flowers, ripe fruit, toasty, creamy oak. Palate: flavourful, powerful, toasty, roasted-coffee aftertaste.

CHOZAS CARRASCAL

Vereda San Antonio Pol. Ind. Catastral, 16 Parcelas 136-138
46340 San Antonio de Requena - (Valencia)
☎: +34 963 410 395 - Fax: +34 963 168 067
chozas@chozascarrascal.es
www.chozascarrascal.es

EL CAVA DE CHOZAS CARRASCAL 2008 BN RESERVA
chardonnay, macabeo

93 Colour: bright yellow. Nose: dry nuts, faded flowers, dried herbs, lees reduction notes. Palate: good acidity, fine bitter notes, correct.

CODORNÍU

Avda. Jaume Codorníu, s/n
8770 Sant Sadurní D'Anoia - (Barcelona)
☎: +34 938 183 232 - Fax: +34 938 910 822
s.martin@codorniu.es
www.codorniu.com

GRAN PLUS ULTRA BN RESERVA
chardonnay, parellada

91 Colour: bright yellow. Nose: white flowers, fresh fruit, fine lees, balanced. Palate: fruity, fine bitter notes, flavourful.

JAUME CODORNÍU BR
chardonnay, pinot noir

92 Colour: bright yellow. Nose: complex, balanced, ripe fruit, dried flowers, dried herbs. Palate: balanced, fine bitter notes, good acidity.

REINA Mª CRISTINA BLANC DE NOIRS 2008 BR RESERVA
87% pinot noir, 13% chardonnay

91 Colour: bright straw. Nose: medium intensity, floral, fresh. Palate: flavourful, fruity, complex, good acidity, fine bead, balanced.

DOMINIO DE LA VEGA

Ctra. Madrid - Valencia, Km. 270,6
46390 San Antonio. - (Valencia)
☎: +34 962 320 570 - Fax: +34 962 320 330
info@dominiodelavega.com
www.dominiodelavega.com

ARTEMAYOR IV CAVA BN
chardonnay, macabeo

91 Colour: bright yellow. Nose: faded flowers, sweet spices, toasty, fragrant herbs. Palate: powerful, flavourful, rich, good acidity.

DOMINIO DE LA VEGA RESERVA ESPECIAL BR RESERVA
macabeo, chardonnay

90 Colour: bright golden. Nose: ripe fruit, faded flowers, dry nuts, expressive. Palate: fine bitter notes, good acidity, flavourful, long. Personality.

EMENDIS

Barrio de Sant Marçal, 67
8732 Castellet i La Gornal - (Barcelona)
☎: +34 938 186 119 - Fax: +34 938 918 169
avalles@emendis.es
www.emendis.es

EMENDIS IMUM 2009 BN RESERVA
50% xarel.lo, 25% macabeo, 25% parellada

91 Colour: bright straw. Nose: complex, floral, fragrant herbs, fresh fruit. Palate: powerful, flavourful, fresh, fruity, balanced.

FERRE I CATASUS

Ctra. de Sant Sadurní, Km. 8- Masía Can Gustems
8792 La Granada - (Barcelona)
☎: +34 938 974 558 - Fax: +34 938 974 708
maracalvo@ferreicatasus.com
www.castelldelmirall.com

FERRÉ I CATASÚS 2008 BN RESERVA
55% xarel.lo, 35% macabeo, 10% parellada

91 Colour: bright golden. Nose: fine lees, dry nuts, fragrant herbs, complex, toasty. Palate: powerful, flavourful, good acidity, fine bead, fine bitter notes.

FINCA VALLDOSERA

Masia Les Garrigues, Urb. Can Trabal s/n
8734 Olèrdola - (Barcelona)
☎: +34 938 143 047 - Fax: +34 938 935 590
general@fincavalldosera.com
www.fincavalldosera.com

CAVA SUBIRAT PARENT 2009 BN
100% subirat parent

91 Colour: bright straw. Nose: dried flowers, candied fruit, citrus fruit, fine lees. Palate: flavourful, fine bitter notes, good acidity.

FREIXENET

Joan Sala, 2
8770 Sant Sadurní D'Anoia - (Barcelona)
☎: +34 938 917 000 - Fax: +34 938 183 095
freixenet@freixenet.es
www.freixenet.es

BRUT BARROCO BR GRAN RESERVA
parellada, macabeo, xarel.lo

91 Colour: bright yellow. Nose: ripe fruit, white flowers, dried herbs, fine lees. Palate: powerful, flavourful, rich, fine bitter notes.

MERITUM 2007 BR GRAN RESERVA
xarel.lo, macabeo, parellada

92 Colour: bright yellow. Nose: dried flowers, dry nuts, fragrant herbs, balanced. Palate: elegant, flavourful, complex, long.

RESERVA REAL BR RESERVA
macabeo, xarel.lo, parellada

94 Colour: bright straw. Nose: fragrant herbs, white flowers, dried flowers, expressive. Palate: good acidity, fine bead.

TREPAT 2010 BR
trepat

90 Colour: ochre. Nose: white flowers, fragrant herbs, fine lees, fresh fruit. Palate: powerful, flavourful, complex, balanced, long.

GASTÓN COTY S.A.

Avernó, 28-30
8770 Sant Sadurní D'Anoia - (Barcelona)
☎: +34 938 183 602 - Fax: +34 938 913 461
lorigan@lorigancava.com
www.lorigancava.com

AIRE DE L'O DE L'ORIGAN 2008 BN
50% macabeo, 30% xarel.lo, 10% parellada, 10% chardonnay

90 Colour: bright straw. Nose: powerfull, ripe fruit, sweet spices, candied fruit. Palate: flavourful, good acidity, fine bitter notes.

L'ORIGAN MAGNUM 2005 BN
30% xarel.lo, 40% macabeo, 20% chardonnay, 10% parellada

93 Color bright golden. Aroma fine lees, dry nuts, fragrant herbs, complex. Taste powerful, flavourful, good acidity, fine bead, fine bitter notes.

GIRÓ RIBOT

Finca El Pont, s/n
8792 Santa Fe del Penedès - (Barcelona)
☎: +34 938 974 050 - Fax: +34 938 974 311
giroribot@giroribot.es
www.giroribot.es

GIRÓ RIBOT AVANT BR RESERVA
45% xarel.lo, 40% chardonnay, 15% macabeo

93 Colour: bright yellow. Nose: lees reduction notes, dry nuts, pattiserie, toasty, creamy oak, complex. Palate: powerful, flavourful, fine bitter notes, toasty. Personality.

GIRÓ RIBOT DIVINIS MAGNUM 2008 BN RESERVA
90% chardonnay, 10% parellada

92 Colour: bright yellow. Nose: white flowers, fine lees, citrus fruit, ripe fruit, dried herbs. Palate: powerful, flavourful, fresh, fruity, good acidity.

GIRÓ RIBOT MARE 2007 BN GRAN RESERVA
50% xarel.lo, 30% macabeo, 20% parellada

93 Colour: bright golden. Nose: dry nuts, fragrant herbs, complex, expressive, pattiserie. Palate: powerful, flavourful, good acidity, fine bead, fine bitter notes, balanced.

GRAMONA

Industria, 34-36
8770 Sant Sadurní D'Anoia - (Barcelona)
☎: +34 938 910 113 - Fax: +34 938 183 284
comunicacion@gramona.com
www.gramona.com

GRAMONA ARGENT 2008 BR RESERVA
100% chardonnay

93 Colour: bright straw. Nose: balanced, elegant, fine lees, citrus fruit, spicy. Palate: rich, complex, fine bitter notes, fresh.

GRAMONA ARGENT ROSÉ 2008 RD GRAN RESERVA
100% pinot noir

90 Colour: coppery red. Nose: closed, toasty, fruit liqueur notes, fruit preserve, lees reduction notes. Palate: flavourful, fine bitter notes, powerful, fine bead.

GRAMONA CELLER BATLLE 2000 BR GRAN RESERVA
70% xarel.lo, 30% macabeo

98 Colour: yellow. Nose: complex, expressive, dry nuts, spicy, faded flowers, fine lees, candied fruit. Palate: flavourful, complex, fine bitter notes, good acidity.

GRAMONA CELLER BATLLE 2001 BR GRAN RESERVA
70% xarel.lo, 30% macabeo

96 Colour: bright golden. Nose: dry nuts, fragrant herbs, complex. Palate: powerful, flavourful, good acidity, fine bead, fine bitter notes, spicy.

GRAMONA CELLER BATLLE 2002 BR GRAN RESERVA
70% xarel.lo, 30% macabeo

94 Colour: bright golden. Nose: lees reduction notes, floral, fragrant herbs, pattiserie, sweet spices. Palate: powerful, flavourful, good acidity, fine bead, long, toasty.

GRAMONA COLECCIÓN DE ARTE
2000 BR GRAN RESERVA
100% chardonnay

95 Colour: bright golden. Nose: candied fruit, dry nuts, honeyed notes, dried herbs, sweet spices. Palate: sweetness, fresh, fine bitter notes, good acidity, fine bead.

GRAMONA III LUSTROS 2004 BN GRAN RESERVA
70% xarel.lo, 30% macabeo

94 Colour: bright yellow. Nose: candied fruit, spicy, lees reduction notes, dry nuts, complex, dried herbs. Palate: balanced, spicy, elegant.

GRAMONA III LUSTROS 2005 BN
70% xarel.lo, 30% macabeo

92 Colour: bright yellow. Nose: dried flowers, dry nuts, balanced, complex, faded flowers. Palate: balanced, long, good acidity.

GRAMONA IMPERIAL 2006 BR GRAN RESERVA
50% xarel.lo, 40% macabeo, 10% chardonnay

91 Colour: bright yellow. Nose: balanced, expressive, fresh, floral, fine lees. Palate: fine bitter notes, balanced, good acidity.

HACIENDAS DE ESPAÑA

Monistrol D'Anoia, s/n
8770 Sant Sadurní D'Anoia - (Barcelona)
☎: +34 914 365 900
iruiz@haciendas-espana.com
www.haciendas-espana.com

MM PREMIUM CUVÉE MILLESIME (MARQUÉS DE LA CONCORDIA FAMILY OF WINES) 2008 BN
35% chardonnay, 25% macabeo, 15% xarel.lo, 25% parellada

90 Colour: bright yellow. Nose: fine lees, white flowers, fragrant herbs, expressive. Palate: correct, fine bitter notes, fine bead, good acidity.

HERETAT MAS TINELL

Ctra. de Vilafranca a St. Martí Sarroca, Km. 0,5
8720 Vilafranca del Penedès - (Barcelona)
☎: +34 938 170 586 - Fax: +34 938 170 500
info@mastinell.com
www.mastinell.com

MAS TINELL BRUT ROSÉ 2007 BR RESERVA
100% trepat

91 Colour: onion pink. Nose: floral, red berry notes, ripe fruit, elegant, balanced, expressive. Palate: complex, powerful, flavourful, long, fine bitter notes.

MAS TINELL CARPE DIEM RESERVA ESPECIAL 2006 BN RESERVA
40% chardonnay, 30% xarel.lo, 30% parellada

90 Colour: bright yellow. Nose: expressive, faded flowers, ripe fruit, fragrant herbs. Palate: long, good acidity, fine bead, flavourful.

JANÉ VENTURA

Ctra. Calafell, 2
43700 El Vendrell - (Tarragona)
☎: +34 977 660 118 - Fax: +34 977 661 239
janeventura@janeventura.com
www.janeventura.com

JANÉ VENTURA DE L'ORGUE 2006 BN GRAN RESERVA
32% macabeo, 38% xarel.lo, 30% parellada

92 Colour: bright yellow. Nose: expressive, powerfull, white flowers, ripe fruit, dried herbs. Palate: rich, powerful, flavourful, good acidity.

JANÉ VENTURA RESERVA DE LA MÚSICA 2009 BN RESERVA
38% xarel.lo, 32% macabeo, 30% parellada

90 Colour: bright straw. Nose: fresh fruit, dried herbs, fine lees, fresh, powerfull, dried flowers. Palate: fresh, fruity, flavourful, easy to drink, fine bitter notes.

JANÉ VENTURA VINTAGE 2008 BN GRAN RESERVA
29% macabeo, 51% xarel.lo, 20% parellada

90 Colour: bright yellow. Nose: fine lees, white flowers, fragrant herbs, spicy. Palate: powerful, flavourful, complex, long.

JAUME GIRÓ I GIRÓ

Montaner i Oller, 5
8770 Sant Sadurní D'Anoia - (Barcelona)
☎: +34 938 910 165 - Fax: +34 938 911 271
cavagiro@cavagiro.com
www.cavagiro.com

CAN FESTIS 2009 BN RESERVA
xarel.lo, chardonnay, parellada, macabeo

90 Colour: bright yellow. Nose: jasmine, white flowers, fragrant herbs, fresh. Palate: correct, fine bitter notes, flavourful.

JAUME GIRÓ I GIRÓ GRANDALLA 2007 BR GRAN RESERVA

90 Colour: bright straw. Nose: fine lees, white flowers, fruit expression, expressive. Palate: balanced, good acidity, powerful, flavourful.

JAUME GIRÓ I GIRÓ GRANDALLA DE LUXE 2004 GRAN RESERVA

90 Colour: bright golden. Nose: dry nuts, ripe fruit, fragrant herbs, complex. Palate: powerful, flavourful, good acidity, fine bead, fine bitter notes.

JAUME GIRÓ I GIRÓ SELECTE 2006
BN GRAN RESERVA

91 Colour: bright yellow. Nose: complex, candied fruit, fine lees, faded flowers, expressive. Palate: correct, flavourful, fine bead, good acidity.

JAUME LLOPART ALEMANY

Font Rubí, 9
8736 Font-Rubí - (Barcelona)
☎: +34 938 979 133 - Fax: +34 938 979 133
info@jaumellopartalemany.com
www.jaumellopartalemany.com

JAUME LLOPART ALEMANY 2007 BN GRAN RESERVA
macabeo, xarel.lo, parellada

90 Colour: bright yellow. Nose: dried herbs, faded flowers, ripe fruit, dry nuts. Palate: good acidity, rich, flavourful.

JAUME LLOPART ALEMANY VINYA
D'EN FERRAN 2008 BN GRAN RESERVA
pinot noir, chardonnay

92 Colour: bright golden. Nose: ripe fruit, balanced, elegant, dry nuts. Palate: good structure, flavourful, good acidity, fine bitter notes.

JOSEP Mª RAVENTÓS I BLANC

Plaça del Roure, s/n
8770 Sant Sadurní D'Anoia - (Barcelona)
☎: +34 938 183 262 - Fax: +34 938 912 500
raventos@raventos.com
www.raventos.com

RAVENTÓS I BLANC GRAN RESERVA
PERSONAL M.R.N. 1998 BN

96 Colour: bright golden. Nose: dry nuts, fragrant herbs, complex, lees reduction notes, characterful, toasty. Palate: powerful, flavourful, good acidity, fine bead, fine bitter notes.

RAVENTÓS I BLANC GRAN RESERVA
PERSONAL M.R.N. 1999 BN GRAN RESERVA

95 Colour: bright golden. Nose: fine lees, fragrant herbs, complex, sweet spices, dry nuts. Palate: powerful, flavourful, good acidity, fine bead, fine bitter notes.

RAVENTÓS I BLANC GRAN RESERVA PERSONAL
M.R.N. 2000 BN GRAN RESERVA

95 Colour: bright golden. Nose: fine lees, dry nuts, fragrant herbs, complex, candied fruit, ripe fruit, toasty. Palate: powerful, flavourful, good acidity, fine bead, fine bitter notes.

RAVENTÓS I BLANC LA FINCA MAGNUM BN

92 Colour: bright straw. Nose: medium intensity, fresh fruit, dried herbs, floral. Palate: fresh, fruity, flavourful, good acidity.

RAVENTÓS I BLANC DE NIT 2010 BR
55% macabeo, 30% xarel.lo, 10% parellada, 5% monastrell

90 Colour: raspberry rose. Nose: medium intensity, elegant, red berry notes, fruit expression. Palate: good acidity, ripe fruit, fine bead.

JUVÉ Y CAMPS

Sant Venat, 1
8770 Sant Sadurní D'Anoia - (Barcelona)
☎: +34 938 911 000 - Fax: +34 938 912 100
juveycamps@juveycamps.com
www.juveycamps.com

GRAN JUVÉ CAMPS 2009 BR GRAN RESERVA
40% xarel.lo, 26% macabeo, 25% chardonnay, 9% parellada

91 Colour: bright yellow. Nose: fine lees, fragrant herbs, complex. Palate: powerful, flavourful, good acidity, fine bead, fine bitter notes.

GRAN JUVÉ CAMPS SELECCIÓN XAREL.LO
BR GRAN RESERVA
xarel.lo

94 Colour: bright golden. Nose: fine lees, dry nuts, fragrant herbs, characterful, fresh. Palate: powerful, flavourful, good acidity, fine bead, fine bitter notes.

JUVÉ & CAMPS MILESIMÉ CHARDONNAY
2009 BR RESERVA
100% chardonnay

91 Colour: bright straw. Nose: dry nuts, fragrant herbs, complex. Palate: powerful, flavourful, good acidity, fine bead, fine bitter notes.

JUVÉ & CAMPS MILESIMÉ MAGNUM
2009 BR RESERVA
100% chardonnay

91 Colour: bright yellow. Nose: powerfull, reduction notes, fruit preserve, citrus fruit. Palate: flavourful, good acidity, fine bitter notes.

JUVÉ & CAMPS MILLESIMÉ 2006 BR GRAN RESERVA
chardonnay

92 Color bright golden. Aroma fine lees, dry nuts, fragrant herbs, complex. Taste powerful, flavourful, good acidity, fine bead, fine bitter notes.

JUVÉ & CAMPS RESERVA DE LA
FAMILIA 2009 BN GRAN RESERVA
30% macabeo, 50% xarel.lo, 10% parellada, 10% chardonnay

90 Colour: bright golden. Nose: fine lees, dry nuts, fragrant herbs, citrus fruit. Palate: powerful, flavourful, good acidity, fine bead, fine bitter notes.

JUVÉ & CAMPS RESERVA DE LA
FAMILIA MAGNUM 2009 BN RESERVA
30% macabeo, 50% xarel.lo, 10% parellada, 10% chardonnay

93 Colour: bright golden. Nose: fine lees, dry nuts, fragrant herbs. Palate: powerful, flavourful, good acidity, fine bead, fine bitter notes.

LLOPART

Ctra. de Sant Sadurni - Ordal, Km. 4
8739 Subirats (Els Casots) - (Barcelona)
☎: +34 938 993 125 - Fax: +34 938 993 038
llopart@llopart.com
www.llopart.com

LLOPART EX-VITE 2006 BR GRAN RESERVA
60% xarel.lo, 40% macabeo

90 Colour: bright yellow. Nose: floral, dry nuts, sweet spices, fine lees, complex, expressive. Palate: good acidity, flavourful, good structure, long.

LLOPART LEOPARDI 2007 BN GRAN RESERVA
40% macabeo, 40% xarel.lo, 10% parellada, 10% chardonnay

92 Colour: bright straw. Nose: fine lees, dry nuts, fragrant herbs. Palate: powerful, flavourful, good acidity, fine bead, fine bitter notes.

LLOPART MAGNUM IMPERIAL
2008 BR GRAN RESERVA
50% xarel.lo, 40% macabeo, 10% parellada

90 Color bright straw. Aroma medium intensity, fresh fruit, dried herbs, fine lees, floral. Taste fresh, fruity, flavourful, good acidity.

LOXAREL

Can Mayol, s/n
8735 Vilobí del Penedès - (Barcelona)
☎: +34 938 978 001 - Fax: +34 938 978 111
loxarel@loxarel.com
www.loxarel.com

LOXAREL RESERVA FAMILIA BN GRAN RESERVA

90 Colour: bright yellow. Nose: fine lees, dry nuts, fragrant herbs, balanced. Palate: powerful, flavourful, good acidity, fine bead, fine bitter notes.

MARQUÉS DE GELIDA - L'ALZINAR

Can Llopart de Les Alzines
8770 Sant Sadurní D'Anoia - (Barcelona)
☎: +34 938 912 353 - Fax: +34 938 183 956
info@elcep.com
www.elcep.com

MARQUÉS DE GELIDA 2007 BN GRAN RESERVA
25% macabeo, 35% xarel.lo, 20% parellada, 20% chardonnay

90 Colour: bright golden. Nose: fine lees, dry nuts, fragrant herbs, complex. Palate: flavourful, good acidity, fine bead.

MARRUGAT

Doctor Pasteur, 6
8720 Vilafranca del Penedès - (Barcelona)
☎: +34 938 903 066 - Fax: +34 938 170 979
pinord@pinord.com
www.pinord.com

MARRUGAT RIMA 32 2007 BN RESERVA
pinot noir, chardonnay

90 Colour: bright yellow. Nose: dried flowers, fine lees, dry nuts, pattiserie. Palate: long, good acidity, flavourful, fine bitter notes.

MARTÍ SERDÀ

Camí Mas del Pont s/n
8792 Santa Fe del Penedès - (Barcelona)
☎: +34 938 974 411 - Fax: +34 938 974 405
info@martiserda.com
www.martiserda.com

MARTÍ SERDÀ CUVÉE REAL 2006 BN GRAN RESERVA
25% xarel.lo, 50% macabeo, 25% vino de reserva

91 Colour: bright yellow. Nose: fine lees, dry nuts, fragrant herbs, complex. Palate: powerful, flavourful, good acidity, fine bead, fine bitter notes.

MATA I COLOMA

Montserrat, 73
8770 Sant Sadurní D'Anoia - (Barcelona)
☎: +34 938 183 968 - Fax: +34 938 183 968
info@matacoloma.com
www.matacoloma.com

PERE MATA RESERVA FAMILIA
2007 BN GRAN RESERVA
40% macabeo, 30% xarel.lo, 30% parellada

90 Colour: bright yellow. Nose: dry nuts, fragrant herbs, sweet spices, toasty, ripe fruit. Palate: powerful, flavourful, good acidity, fine bitter notes.

MIQUEL PONS

Baix Llobregat, 5
8792 La Granada - (Barcelona)
☎: +34 938 974 541 - Fax: +34 938 974 710
miquelpons@cavamiquelpons.com
www.cavamiquelpons.com

MIQUEL PONS 2007 BN GRAN RESERVA
macabeo, xarel.lo, parellada

90 Colour: bright yellow. Nose: petrol notes, lees reduction notes, spicy, faded flowers. Palate: round, powerful, flavourful, complex.

MONT MARÇAL

Finca Manlleu
8732 Castellví de la Marca - (Barcelona)
☎: +34 938 918 281 - Fax: +34 938 919 045
mrivas@mont-marcal.com
www.mont-marcal.com

AUREUM DE MONT MARÇAL BN RESERVA
50% xarel.lo, 30% chardonnay, 10% pinot noir, 10% parellada

90 Colour: bright yellow. Nose: dried flowers, pattiserie, fine lees, fragrant herbs, expressive. Palate: powerful, flavourful, good acidity, fine bitter notes.

MONT MARÇAL EXTREMARIUM ROSADO BN
100% pinot noir

90 Colour: light cherry. Nose: balanced, red berry notes, medium intensity, dried flowers. Palate: flavourful, fine bitter notes, good acidity, long.

MONT-FERRANT

Abat Escarré, 1
17300 Blanes - (Girona)
☎: +34 934 191 000 - Fax: +34 934 193 170
jcivit@montferrant.com
www.montferrant.com

AGUSTÍ VILARET 2006 GRAN RESERVA
70% chardonnay, 10% xarel.lo, 10% macabeo, 10% parellada

90 Colour: bright yellow. Nose: white flowers, jasmine, balanced, fresh, fine lees. Palate: correct, good acidity, balanced.

BERTA BOUZY 2008 BR RESERVA
24% macabeo, 15% chardonnay, 36% xarel.lo, 25% parellada

91 Colour: bright straw. Nose: fresh fruit, dried herbs, fine lees, floral, expressive. Palate: fresh, fruity, flavourful, good acidity, balanced.

PAGO DE THARSYS

Ctra. Nacional III, km. 274
46340 Requena - (Valencia)
☎: +34 962 303 354 - Fax: +34 962 329 000
pagodetharsys@pagodetharsys.com
www.pagodetharsys.com

PAGO DE THARSYS MILLESIME 2009 BR RESERVA
macabeo, parellada, chardonnay

90 Colour: bright yellow. Nose: ripe fruit, white flowers, balanced. Palate: fine bitter notes, good acidity, flavourful, complex.

PAGO DE THARSYS MILLÉSIME ROSÉ RESERVA 2009 BR
100% garnacha

90 Colour: salmon. Nose: medium intensity, red berry notes, floral, balanced. Palate: fruity, fresh, balanced, easy to drink, good acidity.

PARATÓ

Can Respall de Renardes
8733 - (Barcelona)
☎: +34 938 988 182 - Fax: +34 938 988 510
info@parato.es
www.parato.es

ELIAS I TERNS 2004 BN GRAN RESERVA
35% macabeo, 55% xarel.lo, 10% chardonnay, parellada

90 Colour: bright yellow. Nose: complex, balanced, fine lees, floral. Palate: complex, good acidity, balanced.

PARÉS BALTÀ

Masía Can Baltá, s/n
8796 Pacs del Penedès - (Barcelona)
☎: +34 938 901 399 - Fax: +34 938 901 143
paresbalta@paresbalta.com
www.paresbalta.com

BLANCA CUSINÉ BR

92 Colour: bright straw. Nose: medium intensity, fresh fruit, dried herbs, fine lees, floral, rose petals. Palate: fresh, fruity, flavourful, balanced.

PARÉS BALTÀ SELECTIO BR

90 Colour: bright straw. Nose: medium intensity, fresh fruit, floral, lees reduction notes. Palate: fresh, fruity, flavourful, good acidity.

ROSA CUSINE 2008 RD

90 Colour: brilliant rose. Nose: floral, fresh fruit, red berry notes, fragrant herbs. Palate: flavourful, fruity, fresh, good acidity, fine bitter notes.

PARXET

Torrent, 38
8391 Tiana - (Barcelona)
☎: +34 933 950 811 - Fax: +34 933 955 500
info@parxet.es
www.parxet.es

GRAN RESERVA MARÍA CABANE 2008 EXTRA BRUT GRAN RESERVA

90 Colour: bright golden. Nose: fine lees, dry nuts, fragrant herbs, complex, fresh fruit. Palate: powerful, flavourful, fine bead, fine bitter notes, balanced.

PARXET ANIVERSARIO 2008 BN

92 Colour: bright yellow. Nose: elegant, floral, spicy, fragrant herbs, complex, characterful. Palate: powerful, flavourful, long, balanced, round.

TITIANA PANSA BLANCA 2010 BR
pansa blanca

91 Colour: bright straw. Nose: white flowers, fresh fruit, grassy, spicy. Palate: flavourful, fine bitter notes, good acidity.

RECAREDO

Tamarit, 10 Apartado 15
8770 Sant Sadurní D'Anoia - (Barcelona)
☎: +34 938 910 214 - Fax: +34 938 911 697
cava@recaredo.es
www.recaredo.es

RECAREDO BRUT DE BRUT 2004 BN GRAN RESERVA
67% macabeo, 33% xarel.lo

92 Colour: bright yellow. Nose: medium intensity, dry nuts, fine lees. Palate: flavourful, fine bitter notes, fine bead, good acidity.

RECAREDO BRUT NATURE 2008 BN GRAN RESERVA
46% xarel.lo, 40% macabeo, 14% parellada

93 Colour: bright yellow. Nose: dried flowers, fine lees, fragrant herbs, powerfull, complex. Palate: fine bitter notes, flavourful, long, good structure.

RECAREDO INTENS ROSAT 2008 BN GRAN RESERVA
90% pinot noir, 10% monastrell

90 Colour: light cherry. Nose: fine lees, rose petals, red berry notes, expressive. Palate: good acidity, fine bitter notes, flavourful, fruity, long.

RECAREDO RESERVA PARTICULAR 2002 BN GRAN RESERVA
72% macabeo, 28% xarel.lo

96 Colour: bright yellow. Nose: ripe fruit, spicy, dry nuts, dried flowers, lees reduction notes. Palate: flavourful, complex, elegant, fine bitter notes.

RECAREDO SUBTIL 2007 BN GRAN RESERVA
62% xarel.lo, 30% chardonnay, 8% macabeo

93 Colour: bright yellow. Nose: complex, balanced, dry nuts, spicy, fragrant herbs. Palate: good structure, flavourful, complex.

TURO D'EN MOTA 2002 BN RESERVA
100% xarel.lo

93 Colour: bright golden. Nose: aromatic coffee, pattiserie, toasty, candied fruit, petrol notes. Palate: long, good acidity, powerful, flavourful. Personality.

REXACH BAQUES

Santa María, 12
8736 Guardiola de Font-Rubí - (Barcelona)
☎: +34 938 979 170
info@rexachbaques.com
www.rexachbaques.com

REXACH BAQUES 100 ANIVERSARI 2006 BR GRAN RESERVA
35% xarel.lo, 25% macabeo, 30% parellada, 10% pinot noir

90 Colour: bright yellow. Nose: white flowers, dry nuts, dried herbs, spicy. Palate: correct, powerful, flavourful, complex.

RIMARTS

Avda. Cal Mir, 44
8770 Sant Sadurní D'Anoia - (Barcelona)
☎: +34 938 912 775 - Fax: +34 938 912 775
rimarts@rimarts.net
www.rimarts.net

RIMARTS CHARDONNAY 2008 BN RESERVA ESPECIAL
chardonnay

90 Colour: bright straw. Nose: medium intensity, dried herbs, fine lees, floral, varietal. Palate: fresh, fruity, good acidity, elegant.

ROGER GOULART

Major, s/n
8635 Sant Esteve Sesrovires - (Barcelona)
☎: +34 934 191 000 - Fax: +34 934 193 170
jcivit@montferrant.com
www.rogergoulart.com

COMPTE ARNAU 2008 BR RESERVA
40% xarel.lo, 30% macabeo, 30% parellada

90 Color bright straw. Aroma medium intensity, fresh fruit, dried herbs, fine lees, floral. Taste fresh, fruity, flavourful, good acidity.

ROSELL & FORMOSA

Rambla de la Generalitat, 14
8770 Sant Sadurní D'Anoia - (Barcelona)
☎: +34 938 911 013 - Fax: +34 938 911 967
rformosa@roselliformosa.com
www.roselliformosa.com

DAURAT "BRUT DE BRUTS" 2006 BR GRAN RESERVA
45% macabeo, 30% xarel.lo, 25% parellada

90 Colour: bright golden. Nose: lees reduction notes, ripe fruit, dried herbs, pattiserie, lactic notes. Palate: powerful, flavourful, long.

ROVELLATS

Finca Rovellats - Bº La Bleda
8731 Sant Marti Sarroca - (Barcelona)
☎: +34 934 880 575 - Fax: +34 934 880 819
rovellats@cavasrovellats.com
www.cavasrovellats.com

ROVELLATS COL.LECCIÓ 2007
58% parellada, 42% xarel.lo

90 Colour: bright golden. Nose: fine lees, dry nuts, fragrant herbs, complex. Palate: powerful, flavourful, fine bead, fine bitter notes.

ROVELLATS MAGNUM 2007 BN
60% xarel.lo, 26% macabeo, 14% parellada

90 Colour: bright golden. Nose: fine lees, dry nuts, complex, dried herbs. Palate: flavourful, good acidity, fine bead, fine bitter notes.

SEGURA VIUDAS

Ctra. Sant Sadurní a St. Pere de Riudebitlles, Km. 5
8775 Torrelavit - (Barcelona)
☎: +34 938 917 070 - Fax: +34 938 996 006
seguraviudas@seguraviudas.es
www.seguraviudas.com

SEGURA VIUDAS RESERVA HEREDAD
2008 BR GRAN RESERVA
67% macabeo, 33% parellada

92 Colour: bright yellow. Nose: fine lees, dry nuts, fragrant herbs, complex. Palate: powerful, flavourful, good acidity, fine bead, fine bitter notes.

TORRE GALIMANY 2007 BN GRAN RESERVA
xarel.lo

90 Colour: bright straw. Nose: floral, citrus fruit, fresh fruit, fragrant herbs, fine lees. Palate: good acidity, fine bead, fine bitter notes, fresh, fruity, flavourful.

TORELLÓ

Can Martí de Baix, Ctra. de Sant Sadurni a Gélida - Apdo. Correos 8
8770 Sant Sadurní D'Anoia - (Barcelona)
☎: +34 938 910 793 - Fax: +34 938 910 877
torello@torello.es
www.torello.com

GRAN TORELLÓ 2007 BN GRAN RESERVA
macabeo, xarel.lo, parellada

91 Colour: bright golden. Nose: fine lees, dry nuts, complex, dried herbs. Palate: powerful, flavourful, good acidity, fine bead, fine bitter notes.

GRAN TORELLÓ MAGNUM 2007 BN GRAN RESERVA
macabeo, xarel.lo, parellada

91 Color bright straw. Aroma medium intensity, fresh fruit, dried herbs, fine lees, floral. Taste fresh, fruity, flavourful, good acidity.

JEROBOAM TORELLÓ 2008 BN GRAN RESERVA

94 Colour: bright straw. Nose: dried herbs, fine lees, overripe fruit, expressive, powerfull, fresh, white flowers. Palate: fruity, flavourful, good acidity, elegant, fresh, balanced.

TORELLÓ 225 2008 BN GRAN RESERVA
macabeo, xarel.lo, parellada

92 Colour: bright yellow, greenish rim. Nose: dry nuts, dried herbs, dried flowers. Palate: good acidity, balanced, fine bitter notes.

TORELLÓ BY CUSTO BARCELONA
2007 BR GRAN RESERVA
macabeo, xarel.lo, parellada

92 Colour: bright golden. Nose: fine lees, dry nuts, balanced. Palate: powerful, flavourful, good acidity, fine bead, fine bitter notes.

VILARNAU

Ctra. d'Espiells, Km. 1,4 Finca "Can Petit"
8770 Sant Sadurní D'Anoia - (Barcelona)
☎: +34 938 912 361 - Fax: +34 938 912 913
vilarnau@vilarnau.es
www.vilarnau.es

ALBERT DE VILARNAU GLOP
2008 BN GRAN RESERVA
50% chardonnay, 50% pinot noir

91 Colour: bright golden. Nose: fine lees, dry nuts, fragrant herbs, complex, varietal. Palate: powerful, flavourful, good acidity, fine bead, fine bitter notes.

ALBERT DE VILARNAU GLOP FERMENTADO EN BARRICA 2008 BN GRAN RESERVA
60% chardonnay, 20% macabeo, 20% parellada

93 Colour: bright golden. Nose: fine lees, dry nuts, complex, sweet spices. Palate: powerful, flavourful, good acidity, fine bead, fine bitter notes.

VINÍCOLA DE NULLES S.C.C.L.

Estació, s/n
43887 Nulles - (Tarragona)
☎: +34 977 602 622 - Fax: +34 977 602 622
botiga@vinicoladenulles.com
www.vinicoladenulles.com

ADERNATS 2008 BN GRAN RESERVA
40% macabeo, 30% xarel.lo, 30% chardonnay

90 Colour: bright yellow. Nose: expressive, dried herbs, dried flowers, ripe fruit. Palate: balanced, powerful, flavourful, long.

ADERNATS XC 2006 BR GRAN RESERVA
100% xarel.lo

92 Colour: bright golden. Nose: petrol notes, ripe fruit, sweet spices, complex, expressive. Palate: good acidity, fine bitter notes, powerful, flavourful, long.

VINÍCOLA DE SARRAL Í SELECCIÓ DE CREDIT

Avinguda de la Conca, 33
43424 Sarral - (Tarragona)
☎: +34 977 890 031 - Fax: +34 977 890 136
cavaportell@covisal.es
www.cava-portell.com

PORTELL SUBLIM ROSADO 2009 BN
100% trepat

90 Colour: light cherry. Nose: jasmine, sweet spices, red berry notes, fruit expression. Palate: balanced, fruity, flavourful. Personality.

DESCRIPTION

This Denomination of Origin extends from the heart of Valladolid to the north of the province, and also takes in a small part of Palencia. It has been considered the ugly duckling of the region of Valladolid watered by the River Duero. It is distinguished by the use of tempranillo grapes from very old vines and by having contrasting temperatures which favour wines with colour and concentration.

NUMBER OF HECTARES: 2.400 **ALTITUDES:** 750 m.

PREDOMINANT VARIETIES:
White grapes: verdejo, albillo and viura.
Red grapes: tempranillo, garnacha and garnacha gris.

CLIMATOLOGY AND SOILS

Continental type with Atlantic influences, the soils are formed by sand, limestone and white clay, which lie on clay and loam.

BODEGA CÉSAR PRÍNCIPE

Ctra. Fuensaldaña-Mucientes, s/n
47194 Fuensaldaña - (Valladolid)
☎: +34 983 663 123
cesarprincipe@cesarprincipe.es
www.cesarprincipe.es

CÉSAR PRÍNCIPE 2009 TC
100% tempranillo

93 Colour: black cherry. Nose: ripe fruit, varietal, powerfull, characterful, mineral, toasty. Palate: powerful, fine bitter notes, spicy, long.

BODEGA HIRIART

Los Cortijos, 38
47270 Cigales - (Valladolid)
☎: +34 983 580 094 - Fax: +34 983 100 701
ines@bodegahiriart.es
www.bodegahiriart.es

HIRIART 2009 TC
100% tinta del país

90 Colour: bright cherry. Nose: ripe fruit, dark chocolate, aromatic coffee. Palate: flavourful, fruity, toasty, round tannins.

BODEGA VALDELOSFRAILES

Camino de Cubillas, s/n
47290 Cubillas de Santa Marta - (Valladolid)
☎: +34 983 485 028 - Fax: +34 983 485 028
valdelosfrailes@matarromera.es
www.valdelosfrailes.es

SELECCIÓN PERSONAL CARLOS MORO VALDELOSFRAILES RESERVA ESPECIAL 2006 T
100% tinta del país

90 Colour: deep cherry. Nose: powerfull, varietal, characterful, fruit preserve, toasty, dark chocolate. Palate: powerful, sweetness, spicy, ripe fruit.

VALDELOSFRAILES PRESTIGIO 2006 TR
100% tinta del país

90 Colour: very deep cherry. Nose: powerfull, ripe fruit, toasty, dark chocolate, scrubland. Palate: powerful, spicy, ripe fruit.

BODEGAS FERNÁNDEZ CAMARERO

Condes de Torreanaz, 45- 1ºA
28028 - (Madrid)
☎: +34 677 682 426
javier.fernandez@balvinar.com
www.balvinar.com

BALVINAR PAGOS SELECCIONADOS 2007 TC
100% tempranillo

92 Colour: cherry, garnet rim. Nose: ripe fruit, spicy, creamy oak, toasty, complex, mineral. Palate: powerful, flavourful, toasty, round tannins.

BODEGAS LEZCANO-LACALLE

Ctra. Valoria, 2
47282 Trigueros del Valle - (Valladolid)
☎: +34 629 280 515
info@lezcano-lacalle.com
www.lezcano-lacalle.com

LEZCANO-LACALLE DÚ 2006 T
tempranillo, merlot, cabernet sauvignon

91 Colour: deep cherry. Nose: powerfull, ripe fruit, sweet spices, toasty. Palate: flavourful, spicy, ripe fruit, fine bitter notes.

BODEGAS Y VIÑEDOS ALFREDO SANTAMARÍA

Poniente, 18
47290 Cubillas de Santa Marta - (Valladolid)
☎: +34 983 585 006 - Fax: +34 983 440 770
info@bodega-santamaria.com
www.bodega-santamaria.com

TRASCASAS 2007 TR
tempranillo

90 Colour: deep cherry. Nose: earthy notes, ripe fruit, toasty, sweet spices. Palate: flavourful, spicy, ripe fruit.

BODEGAS Y VIÑEDOS SINFORIANO

San Pedro, 12
47194 Mucientes - (Valladolid)
☎: +34 983 663 008 - Fax: +34 983 587 789
sinfo@sinforianobodegas.com
www.sinforianobodegas.com

SINFORIANO 2008 TR
100% tempranillo

90 Colour: cherry, garnet rim. Nose: ripe fruit, spicy, creamy oak, toasty, characterful. Palate: powerful, flavourful, toasty, round tannins.

SINFORIANO 2009 TC
100% tempranillo

90 Color cherry, garnet rim. Aroma ripe fruit, spicy, creamy oak, toasty, complex. Taste powerful, flavourful, toasty, round tannins.

CONCEJO BODEGAS

Ctra. Valoria, Km. 3.6
47200 Valoria La Buena - (Valladolid)
☎: +34 983 502 263 - Fax: +34 983 502 253
info@concejobodegas.com
www.concejobodegas.com

CARREDUEÑAS 2011 RD FERMENTADO EN BARRICA
100% tempranillo

91 Color bright cherry. Aroma ripe fruit, sweet spices, creamy oak, expressive. Taste flavourful, fruity, toasty, round tannins.

CARREDUEÑAS DOLCE 2011 RD
100% tempranillo

90 Colour: rose, purple rim. Nose: powerfull, ripe fruit, red berry notes, floral, expressive. Palate: , fruity, fresh, sweetness.

FINCA MUSEUM

Ctra. Cigales - Corcos, Km. 3
47270 Cigales - (Valladolid)
☎: +34 983 581 029 - Fax: +34 983 581 030
info@bodegasmuseum.com
www.bodegasmuseum.com

MUSEUM REAL 2009 TR
tempranillo

90 Colour: cherry, garnet rim. Nose: powerfull, characterful, ripe fruit, sweet spices, aromatic coffee. Palate: powerful, spicy, ripe fruit.

VINEA 2009 TC
100% tinta del país

91 Colour: cherry, garnet rim. Nose: spicy, creamy oak, toasty, complex, red berry notes. Palate: powerful, flavourful, toasty, round tannins.

LA LEGUA

Ctra. Cigales, km. 1
47194 Fuensaldaña - (Valladolid)
☎: +34 983 583 244 - Fax: +34 983 583 172
lalegua@lalegua.com
www.lalegua.com

LA LEGUA CAPRICHO 2007 T
tempranillo

90 Colour: deep cherry. Nose: ripe fruit, roasted coffee, dark chocolate. Palate: spicy, fine bitter notes, round tannins.

OVIDIO GARCÍA

Malpique, s/n
47270 Cigales - (Valladolid)
☎: +34 628 509 475 - Fax: +34 983 474 085
info@ovidiogarcia.com
www.ovidiogarcia.com

OVIDIO GARCÍA ESENCIA 2006 TC
100% tempranillo

90 Colour: cherry, garnet rim. Nose: powerfull, characterful, ripe fruit, toasty, dark chocolate. Palate: powerful, flavourful, concentrated.

TRASLANZAS

Barrio de las Bodegas, s/n
47194 Mucientes - (Valladolid)
☎: +34 639 641 123
traslanzas@traslanzas.com
www.traslanzas.com

TRASLANZAS 2008 T
100% tinta del país

91 Colour: deep cherry. Nose: candied fruit, fruit expression, scrubland, spicy, cocoa bean. Palate: flavourful, good acidity, fine bitter notes.

DESCRIPTION

This is located in the north of the province of Tarragona, in the northeast of Spain, with a production zone which takes in 14 towns.

NUMBER OF HECTARES: 5.600 **ALTITUDES:** 350m.- 600 m.

PREDOMINANT VARIETIES:

White grapes: macabeo, perellada, chardonnay and sauvignon blanc. Red grapes: trepat, ull de llebre, garnacha, cabernet sauvignon, merlot, syrah and pinot noir.

CLIMATOLOGY AND SOILS

Mediterranean and continental influences, most of the soils are brown-limestone.

BODEGA SANSTRAVÉ

De la Conca, 10
43412 Solivella - (Tarragona)
☎: +34 977 892 165 - Fax: +34 977 892 073
bodega@sanstrave.com
www.sanstrave.com

SANSTRAVÉ PARTIDA DELS JUEUS 2009 TC
merlot, tempranillo, cabernet sauvignon, garnacha, trepat

90 Colour: cherry, garnet rim. Nose: ripe fruit, spicy, creamy oak, balsamic herbs. Palate: powerful, flavourful, toasty, round tannins.

BODEGAS BELLOD

Avda. Mare de Déu de Montserrat, 6
8970 Sant Joan Despí - (Barcelona)
☎: +34 933 731 151 - Fax: +34 933 731 354
bodegasbellod@bodegasbellod.com
www.bodegasbellod.com

MAS DEL NEN 2009 T
50% cabernet sauvignon, 50% syrah

90 Colour: deep cherry, purple rim. Nose: creamy oak, dark chocolate, fragrant herbs, candied fruit. Palate: good structure, flavourful, ripe fruit.

BODEGAS TORRES

Miguel Torres i Carbó, 6
8720 Vilafranca del Penedès - (Barcelona)
☎: +34 938 177 400 - Fax: +34 938 177 444
mailadmin@torres.es
www.torres.es

GRANS MURALLES 2008 TR
garnacha, cariñena, monastrell, garró, samsó

93 Colour: deep cherry, purple rim. Nose: tobacco, ripe fruit, powerfull, scrubland, balsamic herbs, toasty. Palate: long, spirituous, spicy, ripe fruit, round tannins.

MILMANDA 2009 B
100% chardonnay

90 Colour: bright yellow. Nose: powerfull, ripe fruit, sweet spices, creamy oak, fragrant herbs. Palate: rich, smoky aftertaste, flavourful, fresh, good acidity.

CELLER MAS FORASTER

Camino Ermita de Sant Josep, s/n
43400 Montblanc - (Tarragona)
☎: +34 977 860 229 - Fax: +34 977 875 037
info@josepforaster.com
www.josepforaster.com

JOSEP FORASTER SELECCIÓ 2007 TR
90% cabernet sauvignon, 10% ull de llebre

90 Colour: very deep cherry. Nose: complex, powerfull, ripe fruit, spicy, creamy oak. Palate: good structure, full, good acidity.

CELLER TINTORÉ DE VIMBODÍ I POBLET

Copèrnic, 44
8021 - (Barcelona)
☎: +34 932 096 101 - Fax: +34 934 145 236
oriol@tinto-re.com

RE 2009 T
garnacha, cariñena, cabernet sauvignon

90 Colour: cherry, garnet rim. Nose: ripe fruit, creamy oak, toasty, fragrant herbs. Palate: powerful, flavourful, toasty, round tannins.

CLOS MONTBLANC

Ctra. Montblanc-Barbera, s/n
43422 Barberà de la Conca - (Tarragona)
☎: +34 977 887 030 - Fax: +34 977 887 032
club@closmontblanc.com
www.closmontblanc.com

CLOS MONTBLANC MASÍA LES COMES 2007 TR
60% cabernet sauvignon, 40% merlot

90 Colour: very deep cherry. Nose: dry stone, ripe fruit, candied fruit, dark chocolate, creamy oak. Palate: ripe fruit, long.

GATZARA VINS

Josep M. Tossas, 47. 1º-2º
43400 Montblanc - (Tarragona)
☎: +34 977 861 175 - Fax: +34 977 861 175
info@gatzaravins.com
viverdecelleristes.concadebarbera.cat

GATZARA 2009 TC
50% merlot, 30% cabernet sauvignon, 20% ull de llebre

92 Colour: cherry, garnet rim. Nose: complex, balanced, candied fruit, dark chocolate, sweet spices. Palate: full, round tannins.

GATZARA 2011 T
100% trepat

90 Colour: cherry, purple rim. Nose: fresh fruit, red berry notes, floral, fragrant herbs, mineral. Palate: flavourful, fruity, good acidity, round tannins, balanced.

RENDÉ MASDÉU

Avda. Catalunya, 44
43440 L'Espluga de Francolí - (Tarragona)
☎: +34 977 871 361 - Fax: +34 977 871 361
rendemasdeu@terra.es
www.rendemasdeu.com

MANUELA VENTOSA 2009 T
70% cabernet sauvignon, 30% syrah

90 Colour: bright cherry, garnet rim. Nose: cocoa bean, tobacco, candied fruit, sweet spices. Palate: flavourful, fruity, good finish.

ROSA MARÍA TORRES

Avda. Anguera, 2
43424 Sarral - (Tarragona)
☎: +34 977 890 013 - Fax: +34 977 890 173
info@rosamariatorres.com
www.rosamariatorres.com

SUSEL 2011 RD
cabernet sauvignon

90 Colour: light cherry. Nose: fresh, red berry notes, fragrant herbs. Palate: flavourful, ripe fruit, balanced.

DESCRIPTION

This takes in a wide zone situated to the southeast of the province of Huelva, in the south of Spain. The city of Huelva is in the far south of the Denomination of Origin. The Regulating Board has its headquarters in Bollullos del Condado, where 11 of the 27 wineries in the zone are located. The full-bodied wines which have historical labels such as "Condado" have lost their importance in favour of newer white and red wines. There are some curiosities such as the excellent orange wines, liqueur wines which are aged in barrels in contact with dehydrated orange peel from Doñana.

NUMBER OF HECTARES: 4.000

ALTITUDES: < 100 m.

PREDOMINANT VARIETIES:

White grapes: zalema, palomino and listán de Huelva.
Red grapes: merlot, tempranillo and syrah.

CLIMATOLOGY AND SOILS

Mediterranean-Atlantic with neutral, loam soils providing intermediate fertility.

BODEGAS OLIVEROS

Rábida, 12
21710 Bollullos Par del Condado - (Huelva)
☎: +34 959 410 057 - Fax: +34 959 410 057
oliveros@bodegasoliveros.com
www.bodegasoliveros.com

OLIVEROS PEDRO XIMÉNEZ PX

90 Color dark mahogany. Aroma complex, fruit liqueur notes, dried fruit, pattiserie, toasty. Taste sweet, rich, unctuous, powerful.

BODEGAS SAUCI

Doctor Fleming, 1
21710 Bollullos del Condado - (Huelva)
☎: +34 959 410 524 - Fax: +34 959 410 331
sauci@bodegassauci.es
www.bodegassauci.es

S' PX SOLERA 1989 VINO DE LICOR
100% pedro ximénez

91 Colour: mahogany. Nose: sweet spices, fruit liqueur notes, complex, expressive, caramel. Palate: creamy, balanced, fruity, flavourful.

CONVENTO DE MORAÑINA

Avda. de la Paz, 43
21710 Bollullos Par del Condado - (Huelva)
☎: +34 959 412 250
bodega@bodegasconvento.com
www.bodegasconvento.com

CONVENTO PX RESERVA
100% pedro ximénez

91 Color dark mahogany. Aroma complex, fruit liqueur notes, dried fruit, pattiserie, toasty. Taste sweet, rich, unctuous, powerful.

SECRETO DEL CONVENTO 1960 CR
palomino, zalema, pedro ximénez

90 Colour: mahogany. Nose: powerfull, expressive, acetaldehyde, sweet spices, varnish. Palate: flavourful, spicy, ripe fruit, balanced.

DESCRIPTION

This is situated to the south of Lerida and some municipalities of Tarragona and takes in a wide range of soils and climates affecting up to seven sub-regions. A very dry climate with higher temperatures favour long cycle varieties such as cabernet sauvignon, garnacha and macabeo. This label includes the wines of Raimat, the first vineyard which followed the Australian concepts regarding volume and quality, with the support of the Codorníu Group.

NUMBER OF HECTARES: 4.696 **ALTITUDES:** 200 m. – 400 m.

PREDOMINANT VARIETIES:

White grapes: macabeo, xare.lo, parellada, riesling, sauvignon blanc, muscat of Alexandria, malvasía and gewürztraminer.
Red grapes: garnacha negra, Ull de llebre, cabernet sauvignon, merlot, monastrell, trepat, samsó, pinot noir and syrah.

CLIMATOLOGY AND SOILS

Continental climate. The soils are limestone and granite, poor in organic material, brown-limestone, with a high percentage of limestone and a scarcity of clay.

BODEGAS COSTERS DEL SIÓ

Ctra. de Agramunt, Km. 4,2
25600 Balaguer - (Lleida)
☎: +34 973 424 062 - Fax: +34 973 424 112
comunicacio@costersio.com
www.costersio.com

ALTO SIÓS 2007 T
60% syrah, 40% tempranillo

90 Colour: deep cherry, garnet rim. Nose: candied fruit, sweet spices, cocoa bean. Palate: ripe fruit, flavourful, round tannins.

SIÓS SELECCIÓN 2009 T
40% syrah, 25% garnacha, 25% tempranillo, 10% cabernet sauvignon

90 Colour: black cherry. Nose: creamy oak, toasty, complex, candied fruit, fruit preserve, dark chocolate. Palate: powerful, flavourful, toasty, round tannins.

CASTELL D'ENCUS

Ctra. Tremp a Santa Engracia, Km. 5
25630 Talarn - (Lleida)
☎: +34 973 252 974
celler@encus.org
www.encus.org

ACUSP 2010 T
100% pinot noir

92 Colour: deep cherry. Nose: candied fruit, violet drops, scrubland. Palate: fruity, rich, flavourful.

QUEST 2010 T
cabernet sauvignon, cabernet franc, merlot, petit verdot

91 Colour: very deep cherry. Nose: spicy, ripe fruit, sweet spices, creamy oak. Palate: round tannins, spicy, ripe fruit.

TALEIA 2011 B
85% sauvignon blanc, 15% semillón

94 Colour: straw, greenish rim. Nose: powerfull, ripe fruit, sweet spices, fragrant herbs. Palate: rich, flavourful, fresh, good acidity, mineral.

THALARN 2010 T
100% syrah

96 Colour: deep cherry. Nose: powerfull, complex, ripe fruit, fruit expression, creamy oak, sweet spices. Palate: flavourful, good acidity, fine bitter notes, long.

CASTELL DEL REMEI

Finca Castell del Remei, s/n
25300 Castell del Remei - (Lleida)
☎: +34 973 580 200 - Fax: +34 973 718 312
info@castelldelremei.com
www.castelldelremei.com

CASTELL DEL REMEI 1780 2006 T

91 Colour: cherry, garnet rim. Nose: toasty, sweet spices, earthy notes. Palate: flavourful, powerful, fine bitter notes.

CASTELL DEL REMEI ODA BLANC 2011 BFB
55% macabeo, 45% chardonnay

90 Colour: bright yellow. Nose: roasted coffee, creamy oak, ripe fruit. Palate: powerful, flavourful, fine bitter notes.

CÉRVOLES CELLER

Avda. Les Garrigues, 26
25471 La Pobla de Cèrvoles - (Lleida)
☎: +34 973 175 101 - Fax: +34 973 718 312
info@cervoles.com
www.cervoles.com

CÉRVOLES 2011 BFB
54% macabeo, 46% chardonnay

92 Colour: bright straw. Nose: citrus fruit, ripe fruit, creamy oak, toasty. Palate: flavourful, fine bitter notes, good acidity, round.

CÉRVOLES COLORS 2011 B
70% macabeo, 30% chardonnay

90 Colour: bright straw. Nose: ripe fruit, fruit expression, white flowers. Palate: flavourful, ripe fruit, fine bitter notes.

CÉRVOLES ESTRATS 2006 T
42% cabernet sauvignon, 36% tempranillo, 17% garnacha, 5% merlot

94 Colour: very deep cherry. Nose: toasty, sweet spices, ripe fruit. Palate: flavourful, complex, sweetness.

CÉRVOLES NEGRE 2007 T

90 Colour: cherry, garnet rim. Nose: spicy, creamy oak, toasty, complex, mineral. Palate: powerful, flavourful, toasty, round tannins.

CLOS PONS

Ctra. LV-7011, km. 4,5
25155 L'Albagés - (Lleida)
☎: +34 973 070 737
clospons@grup-pons.com
www.clospons.com

CLOS PONS ROC NU 2009 TC
tempranillo, garnacha, cabernet sauvignon

90 Colour: cherry, garnet rim. Nose: ripe fruit, spicy, toasty, earthy notes, balsamic herbs. Palate: powerful, flavourful, toasty, round tannins, balanced.

LAGRAVERA

Ctra. de Tamarite, 9
25120 Alfarrás - (Lleida)
☎: +34 973 761 374 - Fax: +34 973 760 218
info@lagravera.com
www.lagravera.com

ÒNRA 2010 T
garnacha, merlot, cabernet sauvignon

90 Colour: cherry, garnet rim. Nose: medium intensity, ripe fruit, dry stone. Palate: flavourful, rich, fruity, good structure.

ÓNRA MOLTA HONRA 2010 T
garnacha, cabernet sauvignon

91 Colour: cherry, purple rim. Nose: cocoa bean, sweet spices, candied fruit, neat. Palate: good structure, flavourful, round tannins.

ÒNRA VI DE PEDRA SOLERA
garnacha blanca

93 Colour: bright golden. Nose: candied fruit, honeyed notes, white flowers, creamy oak. Palate: good structure, rich, flavourful, good acidity.

MAS BLANCH I JOVÉ

Paratge Llinars. Pol. Ind. 9- Parc. 129
25471 La Pobla de Cérvoles - (Lleida)
☎: +34 973 050 018 - Fax: +34 973 391 151
sara@masblanchijove.com
www.masblanchijove.com

SAÓ ABRIVAT 2008 T
40% tempranillo, 35% garnacha, 15% cabernet sauvignon

90 Colour: cherry, garnet rim. Nose: medium intensity, balanced, cocoa bean, spicy, ripe fruit. Palate: fruity, good finish, easy to drink.

SAÓ EXPRESSIU 2007 T
55% garnacha, 25% cabernet sauvignon, 20% tempranillo

92 Colour: cherry, garnet rim. Nose: complex, expressive, cocoa bean, creamy oak, ripe fruit. Palate: good structure, ripe fruit, round tannins.

OLIVERA

La Plana, s/n
25268 Vallbona de les Monges - (Lleida)
☎: +34 973 330 276 - Fax: +34 973 330 276
olivera@olivera.org
www.olivera.org

EIXADERS 2009 BFB

92 Colour: bright yellow. Nose: balanced, complex, ripe fruit, creamy oak, sweet spices. Palate: rich, flavourful, balanced.

MISSENYORA 2010 BFB

91 Colour: bright yellow. Nose: candied fruit, creamy oak, sweet spices, expressive. Palate: flavourful, full, ripe fruit, long.

VALLISBONA 89 2010 B

92 Colour: bright yellow. Nose: powerfull, creamy oak, sweet spices, candied fruit. Palate: rich, ripe fruit, balanced.

RAIMAT

Ctra. Lleida, s/n
25111 - (Lleida)
☎: +34 973 724 000 - Fax: +34 935 051 567
info@raimat.es
www.raimat.es

RAIMAT GRAN BRUT BR
60% chardonnay, 40% pinot noir

90 Colour: bright straw. Nose: fresh fruit, wild herbs, medium intensity. Palate: flavourful, correct, fine bitter notes, fresh.

RAIMAT TERRA 2011 B
100% chardonnay

91 Colour: bright yellow. Nose: ripe fruit, floral, balanced, expressive. Palate: flavourful, fruity, good acidity.

TOMÁS CUSINÉ

Plaça Sant Sebastià, 13
25457 El Vilosell - (Lleida)
☎: +34 973 176 029 - Fax: +34 973 175 945
info@tomascusine.com
www.tomascusine.com

AUZELLS 2011 B
31% macabeo, 27% sauvignon blanc, 16% chardonnay, 16% riesling, 5% albariño, 5% otras

94 Colour: bright straw. Nose: expressive, floral, grassy, ripe fruit. Palate: spicy, ripe fruit, round, good acidity.

FINCA COMABARRA 2009 T
50% cabernet sauvignon, 25% syrah, 25% garnacha

92 Colour: cherry, garnet rim. Nose: ripe fruit, spicy, creamy oak, complex, sweet spices, aromatic coffee. Palate: powerful, flavourful, toasty, round tannins.

GEOL 2008 T
44% merlot, 30% cabernet sauvignon, 9% cabernet franc, 6% garnacha, 6% cariñena, 6% marselan

92 Colour: cherry, garnet rim. Nose: earthy notes, ripe fruit, sweet spices. Palate: flavourful, powerful, fine bitter notes.

MACABEU FINCA RACONS 2010 B
100% macabeo

92 Colour: bright straw. Nose: scrubland, ripe fruit, white flowers. Palate: flavourful, fine bitter notes, good acidity.

VILOSELL 2009 T
55% tempranillo, 18% syrah, 12% merlot, 11% cabernet sauvignon, 4% cariñena

92 Colour: cherry, garnet rim. Nose: spicy, creamy oak, toasty, characterful. Palate: powerful, flavourful, toasty, round tannins.

VINYA VILARS

Camí de Puiggrós, s/n
25140 Arbeca - (Lleida)
☎: +34 973 149 144 - Fax: +34 973 160 719
vinyaelsvilars@vinyaelsvilars.com
www.vinyaelsvilars.com

LEIX 2009 T
100% syrah

91 Colour: cherry, garnet rim. Nose: complex, expressive, elegant, ripe fruit. Palate: flavourful, spicy, round tannins.

DESCRIPTION

The zone is located in the northeast of the province of Gerona. Its closeness to the Mediterranean Sea influences the style of the wines. This proximity generates a high level of humidity, which is mitigated by a drying wind, the Tramontana. Its red wines are very tasty, with a strong character and complexity, even more so if they are made with the local varieties.

NUMBER OF HECTARES: 2.001

ALTITUDES: < 300 m.

PREDOMINANT VARIETIES:

White grapes: macabeo, garnacha blanca, muscat of Alexandria, picapoll, xarel.lo, sauvignon blanc and gewürztraminer.

Red grapes: cariñena, garnacha tinta, cabernet sauvignon, cabernet franc, merlot, monastrell, tempranillo and syrah.

CLIMATOLOGY AND SOILS

The climate is conditioned by the Tramontana, a strong wind from the north which affects the crops. The soils are poor, granite type in the mountains, alluvial on the plains and slate on the coast.

AGRÍCOLA DE GARRIGUELLA

Ctra. de Roses, s/n
17780 Garriguella - (Girona)
☎: +34 972 530 002 - Fax: +34 972 531 747
lluis@cooperativagarriguella.com
www.cooperativagarriguella.com

DOLÇ DE GERISENA 2005 VINO DE LICOR
75% garnacha, 25% mazuelo

90 Colour: mahogany. Nose: acetaldehyde, pattiserie, sweet spices, candied fruit. Palate: flavourful, good finish.

CASTILLO PERELADA VINOS Y CAVAS

Pl. del Carmen, 1
17491 Perelada - (Girona)
☎: +34 972 538 011 - Fax: +34 972 538 277
perelada@castilloperelada.com
www.castilloperelada.com

CASTILLO DE PERELADA 5 FINCAS 2007 TR
20% merlot, 25% cabernet sauvignon, 25% garnacha, 15% syrah, 15% samsó

92 Colour: black cherry, garnet rim. Nose: complex, balanced, expressive, balsamic herbs, sweet spices. Palate: flavourful, good structure, round tannins, long.

CASTILLO DE PERELADA EX EX 9 S/C T
50% sangiovese, 50% nero D'Avola

94 Colour: deep cherry, purple rim. Nose: red berry notes, ripe fruit, scrubland, spicy. Palate: good structure, flavourful, long, ripe fruit. Personality.

CASTILLO PERELADA FINCA ESPOLLA 2009 T
60% monastrell, 40% syrah

90 Colour: very deep cherry. Nose: expressive, balanced, balsamic herbs, dark chocolate, toasty. Palate: full, flavourful, fine bitter notes, round tannins.

CASTILLO PERELADA FINCA MALAVEÏNA 2008 T
50% merlot, 30% cabernet sauvignon, 10% syrah, 10% garnacha

90 Colour: cherry, garnet rim. Nose: ripe fruit, spicy, creamy oak, toasty, complex, balsamic herbs. Palate: powerful, flavourful, toasty, round tannins.

CASTILLO PERELADA FINCA MALAVEÏNA 2009 T
40% merlot, 30% cabernet sauvignon, 20% syrah, 10% garnacha

91 Colour: cherry, garnet rim. Nose: complex, ripe fruit, sweet spices, balsamic herbs. Palate: long, good acidity, round tannins, spicy.

CASTILLO PERELADA GARNATXA DE L'EMPORDÀ B
80% garnacha roja, 20% garnacha blanca

92 Colour: amber. Nose: creamy oak, caramel, roasted almonds, sweet spices. Palate: rich, full, spicy.

CASTILLO PERELADA GRAN CLAUSTRO 2005 T
50% cabernet sauvignon, 20% merlot, 15% garnacha, 15% samsó

92 Colour: deep cherry, garnet rim. Nose: complex, balanced, elegant, mineral, creamy oak, wild herbs. Palate: full, flavourful, complex, round tannins, long.

CASTILLO PERELADA GRAN CLAUSTRO 2006 T
40% cabernet sauvignon, 30% merlot, 15% garnacha, 15% samsó

91 Colour: deep cherry, garnet rim. Nose: cocoa bean, sweet spices, ripe fruit, balsamic herbs, complex, expressive. Palate: fruity, good structure, elegant, fine bitter notes.

CASTILLO PERELADA LA GARRIGA 2008 T
100% samsó

90 Colour: bright cherry, garnet rim. Nose: mineral, spicy, complex, expressive, ripe fruit. Palate: long, fruity, rich, good acidity.

CASTILLO PERELADA LA GARRIGA 2011 B
40% cariñena blanca, 40% chardonnay, 20% sauvignon blanc

90 Colour: bright yellow. Nose: ripe fruit, floral, powerfull. Palate: rich, spicy, ripe fruit, long.

FINCA GARBET 2006 T
90% syrah, 10% cabernet sauvignon

91 Colour: deep cherry, garnet rim. Nose: sweet spices, cocoa bean, candied fruit, balsamic herbs, closed. Palate: complex, spicy, long, round tannins.

FINCA GARBET 2009 T
60% syrah, 40% cabernet sauvignon

92 Colour: black cherry, purple rim. Nose: complex, elegant, mineral, cocoa bean, ripe fruit, warm. Palate: round, complex, good structure, round tannins.

CELLER CAN SAIS

Raval de Dalt, 10
17253 Vall-Llobrega - (Girona)
☎: +34 647 443 873
correu@cellercansais.com
www.facebook.com/cellercansais

CAN SAIS PRIVILEGI 2009 T
100% garnacha

90 Colour: cherry, garnet rim. Nose: expressive, candied fruit, fruit liqueur notes, varnish, balsamic herbs. Palate: flavourful, balanced, good finish.

CELLER MARIÀ PAGÈS

Pujada, 6
17750 Capmany - (Girona)
☎: +34 972 549 160 - Fax: +34 972 549 160
info@cellermpages.com
www.cellermpages.com

CELLER MARÍÀ PAGÈS GARNACHA 2010 B
50% garnacha, 50% garnacha blanca

91 Colour: light mahogany. Nose: candied fruit, roasted almonds, sweet spices, caramel, varnish. Palate: flavourful, sweet, rich.

CELLER MARTÍ FABRA

Barrio Vic, 26
17751 Sant Climent Sescebes - (Girona)
☎: +34 972 563 011 - Fax: +34 972 563 867
info@cellermartifabra.com

MASÍA CARRERAS BLANC 2010 BFB
40% cariñena blanca, 30% cariñena rosada, 10% garnacha blanca, 10% garnacha rosada, 10% picapoll

91 Colour: bright yellow. Nose: ripe fruit, sweet spices, creamy oak, fragrant herbs. Palate: rich, smoky aftertaste, flavourful, fresh, good acidity.

MASÍA PAIRAL CAN CARRERAS MOSCAT 2007 B
100% moscatel

90 Color golden. Aroma powerfull, floral, honeyed notes, candied fruit, fragrant herbs. Taste flavourful, sweet, fresh, fruity, good acidity, long.

CLOS D'AGON

Afores, s/n
17251 Calonge - (Girona)
☎: +34 972 661 486 - Fax: +34 972 661 462
info@closdagon.com
www.closdagon.com

AMIC DE CLOS D'AGON 2011 B
garnacha blanca

90 Color bright straw. Aroma fresh, fresh fruit, white flowers, expressive. Taste flavourful, fruity, good acidity, balanced.

AMIC DE CLOS D'AGON 2011 T
66% garnacha, 21% cabernet sauvignon, 9% merlot, 4% syrah

90 Colour: cherry, purple rim. Nose: medium intensity, ripe fruit, balsamic herbs, spicy. Palate: flavourful, powerful, fruity aftestaste, long.

ESPELT VITICULTORS

Mas Espelt
17493 Vilajuiga - (Girona)
☎: +34 972 531 727 - Fax: +34 972 531 741
info@espeltviticultors.com
www.espeltviticultors.com

TERRAMALA VINYES VELLES 2010 T
cariñena

90 Colour: very deep cherry, purple rim. Nose: toasty, dark chocolate, sweet spices, ripe fruit. Palate: fruity, flavourful, round tannins.

LAVINYETA

Ctra. de Mollet de Peralada a Masarac, s/n
17752 Mollet de Peralada - (Girona)
☎: +34 647 748 809 - Fax: +34 972 505 323
celler@lavinyeta.es
www.lavinyeta.es

HEUS NEGRE 2011 T
31% syrah, 26% garnacha, 24% merlot, 19% cariñena

90 Colour: deep cherry, purple rim. Nose: medium intensity, ripe fruit, lactic notes. Palate: fruity, flavourful, fine bitter notes.

MICROVINS NEGRE 2010 T ROBLE
100% cariñena

90 Color bright cherry. Aroma ripe fruit, sweet spices, creamy oak, expressive. Taste flavourful, fruity, toasty, round tannins.

MAS LLUNES

Ctra. de Roses, s/n
17780 Garriguella - (Girona)
☎: +34 972 552 684 - Fax: +34 972 530 112
masllunes@masllunes.es
www.masllunes.es

RHODES 2007 T
63% samsó, 37% syrah

90 Colour: bright cherry, garnet rim. Nose: medium intensity, ripe fruit, cocoa bean, sweet spices. Palate: balanced, fine bitter notes.

MAS OLLER

Ctra. GI-652, Km. 0,23
17123 Torrent - (Girona)
☎: +34 972 300 001 - Fax: +34 972 300 001
info@masoller.es
www.masoller.es

MAS OLLER BLAU 2011 T
syrah

90 Colour: cherry, purple rim. Nose: red berry notes, ripe fruit, scrubland, earthy notes.

MAS OLLER MAR 2011 B
picapoll, malvasía

91 Colour: bright straw. Nose: fresh, fresh fruit, white flowers, expressive, fragrant herbs, mineral. Palate: flavourful, fruity, good acidity, balanced, elegant.

MAS OLLER PLUS 2010 T
syrah, garnacha

92 Colour: cherry, garnet rim. Nose: ripe fruit, spicy, creamy oak, toasty, balsamic herbs, earthy notes. Palate: powerful, flavourful, toasty, long, spicy.

MAS OLLER PUR 2011 T
syrah, garnacha, cabernet sauvignon

91 Colour: cherry, purple rim. Nose: expressive, fresh fruit, red berry notes, floral, fragrant herbs, mineral. Palate: flavourful, fruity, good acidity, round tannins.

MASIA SERRA

Dels Solés, 20
17708 Cantallops - (Girona)
☎: +34 689 703 687
masiaserra@masiaserra.com
www.masiaserra.com

AROA 2006 T
garnacha roja, marselan

90 Colour: cherry, garnet rim. Nose: ripe fruit, spicy, creamy oak, toasty, characterful. Palate: powerful, flavourful, toasty, round tannins.

CTÒNIA 2011 BFB
garnacha blanca

90 Colour: bright yellow. Nose: powerfull, ripe fruit, sweet spices. Palate: rich, smoky aftertaste, flavourful, fresh, good acidity.

INO GARNATXA DE L'EMPORDÀ
VINO DULCE NATURAL
garnacha roja

94 Colour: light mahogany. Nose: candied fruit, dry nuts, acetaldehyde, sweet spices, cocoa bean, dark chocolate, toasty. Palate: powerful, flavourful, spicy, balanced, elegant.

IO MASIA SERRA 2008 T
marselan, merlot, cabernet franc, garnacha

90 Colour: cherry, garnet rim. Nose: ripe fruit, spicy, creamy oak, toasty. Palate: powerful, flavourful, toasty, round tannins.

OLIVER CONTI

Puignau, s/n
17550 Capmany - (Girona)
☎: +34 972 193 161 - Fax: +34 972 193 040
dolors@oliverconti.com
www.oliverconti.com

ENOC TINTO 2009 TR
70% cabernet sauvignon, 20% merlot, 10% cabernet franc

90 Colour: bright cherry. Nose: ripe fruit, sweet spices, creamy oak, expressive, scrubland. Palate: flavourful, fruity, round tannins, fruity aftestaste.

OLIVER CONTI ARA 2009 T
20% garnacha, 22% cabernet franc, 58% cabernet sauvignon, merlot

90 Colour: cherry, garnet rim. Nose: varietal, balanced, scrubland, ripe fruit, earthy notes. Palate: correct, ripe fruit, long.

OLIVER CONTI CARLOTA 2009 T
75% cabernet franc, 25% cabernet sauvignon

90 Colour: bright cherry, garnet rim. Nose: ripe fruit, wild herbs, balanced, spicy. Palate: correct, balanced, fine bitter notes, good acidity.

SOTA ELS ÀNGELS

Apdo. Correos 27
17100 La Bisbal - (Girona)
info@sotaelsangels.com
www.sotaelsangels.com

SOTA ELS ÀNGELS 2010 BFB
picapoll, viognier

90 Colour: bright yellow. Nose: balanced, ripe fruit, white flowers, sweet spices. Palate: fruity, correct, fine bitter notes.

VINYES D'OLIVARDOTS

Paratge Olivadots, s/n
17750 Capmany - (Girona)
☎: +34 650 395 627
vdo@olivardots.com
www.olivardots.com

GRESA 2008 T
30% garnacha, 30% cariñena, 30% syrah, 10% cabernet sauvignon

92 Colour: cherry, garnet rim. Nose: balanced, earthy notes, ripe fruit, candied fruit, sweet spices. Palate: good structure, complex, fine bitter notes, elegant, ripe fruit.

VD'O 1.08 2008 T
100% cariñena

91 Colour: cherry, garnet rim. Nose: dark chocolate, candied fruit, medium intensity, spicy, mineral. Palate: full, complex, long, creamy.

VD'O 2.08 2008 T
100% cariñena

92 Colour: cherry, garnet rim. Nose: medium intensity, expressive, sweet spices, creamy oak. Palate: ripe fruit, round tannins, spicy.

VD'O 4.09 2009 T
100% cabernet sauvignon

93 Colour: very deep cherry, purple rim. Nose: complex, balsamic herbs, cocoa bean, creamy oak, mineral. Palate: full, good structure, elegant, fine bitter notes, round tannins.

DESCRIPTION

This lies in the coastal zone of the province of Gipuzkoa, in the north of Spain. The vineyards are just 25 kilometres from San Sebastián. As happens with its neighbouring Denominations of Origin, white wines called chacolís are also produced here.

NUMBER OF HECTARES: 402 **ALTITUDES:** 100 m.

PREDOMINANT VARIETIES:
White grapes: hondarrabi zuri, gros manseng and riesling.
Red grapes: hondarrabi beltza.

CLIMATOLOGY AND SOILS

It has a mild annual temperature, with approximately 13ºC and abundant rainfall. The vineyards are located in small valleys and on gently sloping hillsides which may rise to an altitude of 200 metres. The soils are limestone and rich in organic material.

BODEGA REZABAL

Itsas Begi Etxea, 628
20800 Zarautz - (Gipuzkoa)
☎: +34 943 580 899 - Fax: +34 943 580 775
info@txakolirezabal.com
www.txakolirezabal.com

TXAKOLI REZABAL 2011 B
hondarrabi zuri

90 Colour: bright straw. Nose: fresh, fresh fruit, white flowers, grassy. Palate: flavourful, fruity, good acidity, balanced.

K5

Apdo. Correos 258
20800 Zarautz - (Gipuzkoa)
☎: +34 943 240 005
bodega@txakolina-k5.com
www.txakolina-k5.com

K5 ARGUIÑANO 2011 B
hondarrabi zuri

90 Colour: bright straw. Nose: fresh, fresh fruit, citrus fruit, dried flowers, dried herbs. Palate: flavourful, fruity, good acidity, balanced.

TXOMIN ETXANIZ

Txomin Etxaniz
20808 Getaria - (Gipuzkoa)
☎: +34 943 140 702 - Fax: +34 943 140 462
txakoli@txominetxaniz.com
www.txominetxaniz.com

TXOMÍN ETXANÍZ BEREZIA 2011 B
90% hondarrabi zuri, 10% hondarrabi beltza

90 Colour: bright straw. Nose: white flowers, fruit expression, complex, balanced. Palate: light-bodied, fresh, fruity, flavourful.

DESCRIPTION

The production zone takes in the totality of the island of Gran Canaria as the climate and conditions of the terrain make it possible to cultivate on the lowest levels, sea level, to the highest summits.

NUMBER OF HECTARES: 236 **ALTITUDES:** 700 m. (50 – 1.200 m.)

PREDOMINANT VARIETIES:

White grapes: malvasía, gal, marmajuelo, vijariego, albillo and muscatel.
Red grapes: listán negro, negramoll, tintilla and malvasía rosada.

CLIMATOLOGY AND SOILS

The differences in altitude as regards the vineyards means that there are a variety of microclimates on the island. However, the climate is conditioned by the influence of the trade winds from the east.

BODEGA LOS BERRAZALES

León y Castillo, 43
35480 Agaete - (Las Palmas)
☎: +34 628 922 588 - Fax: +34 928 898 154
lugojorge3@hotmail.com
www.bodegalosberrazales.com

LOS BERRAZALES DULCE VENDIMIA NOCTURNA 2010 B
moscatel

90 Colour: bright straw. Nose: white flowers, balanced, ripe fruit, honeyed notes. Palate: fruity, flavourful, long.

DESCRIPTION

Jerez is situated in the northeast of the province of Cadiz, and is the most southerly denomination in the Iberian Peninsula. This region produces some of the most singular wines in the world, beginning with the fact that the wines are not vintages and are a combination of red grape harvests, through a system of casks piled up in rows of three or four levels called criaderas (agers) and soleras (the oldest). The wines are classified depending on whether they go through a process of ageing, which may be biological (those under a velum of flor yeast are manzanillas or finos, with the difference that the former are only produced in Sanlúcar de Barrameda), or oxidative ageing, with no velum of flor yeast and with added alcohol. The finos and manzanillas can boast of being the wines with the best prices and quality excellence in the country thanks to the proximity of the sea and the local whitish soil called "albariza". Besides fortified wines which include finos, manzanillas, amontillados, olorosos and palos cortados, under the Sherry Brand a large number of natural sweet wines are produced based on pedro ximénez and muscatel, fortified liqueurs (pale cream, medium and cream) and very old wines, genuine treasures in some wineries as they are over 20 and 30 years old.

NUMBER OF HECTARES: 9.100 **ALTITUDES:** 200 m. – 400 m.

PREDOMINANT VARIETIES:

White grapes: palomino, pedro ximénez, muscatel, palomino fino and palomino de Jerez.

CLIMATOLOGY AND SOILS

Warm with Atlantic influences and substantial changes in humidity depending on the wind. The soils are practically white and are rich in calcium carbonate, clay and silica.

ALVARO DOMECQ

Madre de Dios s/n
11401 Jerez de la Frontera - (Cádiz)
☎: +34 956 339 634 - Fax: +34 956 340 402
alvarodomecqsl@alvarodomecq.com
www.alvarodomecq.com

1730 VORS OL
palomino

92 Colour: light mahogany. Nose: acetaldehyde, cocoa bean, dark chocolate, spicy, toasty. Palate: powerful, flavourful, complex, long.

ALBUREJO OL
palomino

91 Colour: mahogany. Nose: spicy, acetaldehyde, varnish, cocoa bean, expressive. Palate: powerful, flavourful, spicy.

PEDRO XIMÉNEZ 1730 PX
pedro ximénez

93 Colour: dark mahogany. Nose: dried fruit, spicy, cocoa bean, dark chocolate, aged wood nuances, complex, expressive. Palate: long, spicy, powerful, flavourful, toasty.

BODEGAS BARBADILLO

Luis de Eguilaz, 11
11540 Sanlúcar de Barrameda - (Cádiz)
☎: +34 956 385 500 - Fax: +34 956 385 501
barbadillo@barbadillo.com
www.barbadillo.com

BARBADILLO AMONTILLADO VORS AM
palomino

95 Colour: light mahogany. Nose: powerfull, warm, acetaldehyde, toasty, sweet spices. Palate: flavourful, powerful, concentrated, spirituous.

BARBADILLO OLOROSO SECO VORS OL

90 Colour: iodine, amber rim. Nose: sweet spices, powerfull, characterful. Palate: powerful, good acidity, fine bitter notes, spicy.

BARBADILLO PALO CORTADO VORS PC
palomino

93 Colour: light mahogany. Nose: powerfull, candied fruit, fruit liqueur notes, toasty, sweet spices. Palate: powerful, sweetness, concentrated, fine bitter notes.

CUCO OLOROSO SECO OL

90 Colour: iodine, amber rim. Nose: powerfull, complex, dry nuts, toasty. Palate: rich, fine bitter notes, , long, spicy.

EVA CREAM CR
palomino

90 Colour: light mahogany. Nose: balanced, toasty, sweet spices, dark chocolate. Palate: flavourful, balanced, long, sweetness.

MANZANILLA EN RAMA SACA DE INVIERNO MZ
palomino

96 Colour: bright golden. Nose: faded flowers, dry nuts, powerfull, flor yeasts, saline. Palate: powerful, flavourful, fine bitter notes.

MANZANILLA EN RAMA SACA DE PRIMAVERA 2012 MZ
palomino

95 Colour: bright yellow. Nose: complex, expressive, pungent, saline, dry nuts, dried herbs, spicy, iodine notes. Palate: rich, powerful, fresh, fine bitter notes, flavourful, spicy, balanced, elegant.

OBISPO GASCÓN PC
palomino

92 Colour: light mahogany. Nose: sweet spices, acetaldehyde, expressive, dry nuts. Palate: good structure, balanced, long, spicy.

PRÍNCIPE AM
palomino

92 Colour: iodine, amber rim. Nose: powerfull, complex, elegant, toasty, dark chocolate. Palate: rich, fine bitter notes, long, confected.

RELIQUIA AM
palomino

96 Colour: light mahogany. Nose: powerfull, complex, elegant, dry nuts, toasty, acetaldehyde. Palate: rich, fine bitter notes, , long, spicy, powerful, concentrated.

RELIQUIA OL
palomino

94 Colour: iodine, amber rim. Nose: powerfull, complex, dry nuts, toasty, expressive. Palate: rich, fine bitter notes, , long, spicy.

RELIQUIA PC
palomino

94 Colour: iodine, amber rim. Nose: powerfull, complex, elegant, dry nuts, toasty, acetaldehyde. Palate: rich, fine bitter notes, , long, spicy, powerful.

RELIQUIA PX
pedro ximénez

96 Colour: dark mahogany. Nose: complex, expressive, fruit liqueur notes, dried fruit, dark chocolate, cocoa bean. Palate: unctuous, fine bitter notes, complex.

SOLEAR MZ
palomino

90 Nose: complex, pungent, saline, dry nuts. Palate: rich, powerful, fine bitter notes, complex.

BODEGAS BARÓN

Molinillo 2a 2 y 3
11540 Sanlúcar de Barrameda - (Cádiz)
☎: +34 956 360 796 - Fax: +34 956 363 256
baron.as@terra.es
www.bodegasbaron.net

ATALAYA AM

90 Colour: iodine, amber rim. Nose: powerfull, dry nuts, toasty, cocoa bean, dark chocolate. Palate: rich, fine bitter notes, , long, spicy.

MANZANILLA PASADA BARÓN MZ
palomino

92 Colour: bright yellow. Nose: saline, acetaldehyde, dried herbs, expressive. Palate: fine bitter notes, flavourful, complex, rich.

P.X. BARÓN PX
15% pedro ximénez

92 Colour: dark mahogany. Nose: acetaldehyde, spicy, aromatic coffee, dark chocolate, creamy oak. Palate: flavourful, complex, rich, long.

P.X. BARÓN VIEJO PX
pedro ximénez

92 Colour: dark mahogany. Nose: complex, fruit liqueur notes, dried fruit, pattiserie, toasty, acetaldehyde. Palate: sweet, rich, unctuous, powerful.

BODEGAS DIEZ MÉRITO

Ctra. Morabita, Km. 2
11407 Jerez de la Frontera - (Cádiz)
☎: +34 956 186 112 - Fax: +34 956 303 500
paternina@paternina.com
www.paternina.com

BERTOLA FI
100% palomino

90 Colour: bright yellow. Nose: powerfull, complex, dried flowers, pungent, saline. Palate: long, fine bitter notes, balanced.

BERTOLA 12 AÑOS AM
100% palomino

90 Colour: light mahogany. Nose: balanced, sweet spices, complex, expressive. Palate: flavourful, rich, balanced, spicy.

FINO IMPERIAL 30 AÑOS VORS AM
100% palomino

92 Colour: iodine, amber rim. Nose: acetaldehyde, mineral, dry nuts, spicy. Palate: powerful, flavourful, complex, toasty.

VIEJA SOLERA 30 AÑOS VORS PX
100% pedro ximénez

92 Colour: dark mahogany. Nose: expressive, varnish, spicy, aged wood nuances, acetaldehyde, aromatic coffee. Palate: long, rich, powerful, flavourful, complex.

BODEGAS GARVEY JEREZ

Ctra. Circunvalación, s/n
11407 Jerez de la Frontera - (Cádiz)
☎: +34 956 319 650 - Fax: +34 956 319 824
marketing@grupogarvey.com
www.bodegasgarvey.com

ASALTO AMOROSO B
palomino, pedro ximénez

90 Colour: mahogany. Nose: balanced, dried fruit, acetaldehyde, cocoa bean. Palate: flavourful, good structure, sweetness, full.

FLOR DEL MUSEO CR
palomino, pedro ximénez

92 Colour: mahogany. Nose: complex, expressive, powerfull, acetaldehyde, spicy, dry nuts. Palate: good structure, flavourful, complex, fine bitter notes.

GARVEY 1780 VORS OL
palomino

92 Colour: light mahogany. Nose: dry nuts, expressive, balanced, powerfull, toasty. Palate: good structure, complex, spirituous, long.

GARVEY 1780 VORS PX
pedro ximénez

92 Colour: dark mahogany. Nose: complex, fruit liqueur notes, dried fruit, pattiserie, toasty, acetaldehyde, dark chocolate, spicy, creamy oak. Palate: sweet, rich, unctuous, powerful, long, flavourful.

GARVEY 1780 VOS OL
palomino

90 Colour: mahogany. Nose: powerfull, complex, spicy, balanced. Palate: fine bitter notes, spicy, long, spirituous.

GARVEY 1780 VOS PX
pedro ximénez

91 Colour: dark mahogany. Nose: complex, fruit liqueur notes, dried fruit, pattiserie, toasty, dark chocolate. Palate: sweet, rich, unctuous, powerful, balanced.

GRAN ORDEN PX
pedro ximénez

95 Colour: dark mahogany. Nose: complex, fruit liqueur notes, dried fruit, acetaldehyde, spicy. Palate: sweet, rich, unctuous, powerful.

JAUNA PC
palomino

91 Colour: light mahogany. Nose: spicy, creamy oak, candied fruit, balanced. Palate: rich, flavourful, complex, spicy.

OÑANA AM
palomino

93 Colour: bright golden. Nose: sweet spices, acetaldehyde, varnish. Palate: fine bitter notes, spirituous, round.

PEDRO XIMENEZ ZOILO RUIZ MATEOS PX
pedro ximénez

95 Colour: dark mahogany. Nose: expressive, elegant, spicy, caramel, dark chocolate, toasty, creamy oak. Palate: long, spicy, complex, rich, powerful, flavourful.

PUERTA REAL OL
palomino

90 Colour: light mahogany. Nose: cocoa bean, sweet spices, dried fruit. Palate: powerful, good structure, long, fine bitter notes, spirituous.

SAN PATRICIO FI
palomino

90 Colour: bright straw. Nose: saline, flor yeasts, expressive. Palate: flavourful, complex, fine bitter notes.

BODEGAS GUTIÉRREZ COLOSÍA

Avda. Bajamar, 40
11500 El Puerto de Santa María - (Cádiz)
☎: +34 956 852 852 - Fax: +34 956 542 936
info@gutierrezcolosia.com
www.gutierrezcolosia.com

GUTIÉRREZ COLOSÍA AM
palomino

91 Colour: light mahogany. Nose: acetaldehyde, fruit liqueur notes, cocoa bean, spicy, creamy oak. Palate: fine bitter notes, powerful, flavourful, long.

GUTIÉRREZ COLOSÍA FI
palomino

90 Colour: bright golden. Nose: powerfull, pungent, saline, acetaldehyde, dry nuts. Palate: flavourful, fine bitter notes, long, balanced.

GUTIÉRREZ COLOSÍA MZ
palomino

91 Colour: bright straw. Nose: balanced, medium intensity, saline, dry nuts. Palate: powerful, flavourful.

GUTIÉRREZ COLOSÍA SOLERA FAMILIAR AM
palomino

91 Colour: iodine, amber rim. Nose: powerfull, complex, dry nuts, toasty, dark chocolate. Palate: rich, fine bitter notes, long, spicy.

GUTIÉRREZ COLOSÍA SOLERA FAMILIAR OL
palomino

92 Colour: mahogany. Nose: elegant, balanced, dry nuts, sweet spices, caramel. Palate: rich, powerful, complex.

GUTIÉRREZ COLOSÍA SOLERA FAMILIAR PC
palomino

90 Colour: iodine, amber rim. Nose: aromatic coffee, toasty, varnish, expressive. Palate: balanced, powerful, flavourful.

GUTIÉRREZ COLOSÍA SOLERA FAMILIAR PX
pedro ximénez

90 Colour: dark mahogany. Nose: varnish, acetaldehyde, spicy, dark chocolate, aged wood nuances. Palate: sweetness, powerful, flavourful, complex.

BODEGAS HARVEYS

Pintor Muñoz Cebrián, s/n
11402 Jerez de la Frontera - (Cádiz)
☎: +34 956 346 000 - Fax: +34 956 349 427
visitas@bodegasharveys.com
www.bodegasharveys.com

HARVEYS VORS AM
100% palomino

92 Colour: iodine, amber rim. Nose: dry nuts, acetaldehyde, spicy, creamy oak. Palate: complex, flavourful, rich, spicy.

HARVEYS VORS PC
98% palomino, 2% pedro ximénez

93 Colour: amber. Nose: sweet spices, caramel, acetaldehyde, candied fruit. Palate: long, spicy, flavourful.

HARVEYS VORS PX
100% pedro ximénez

90 Color dark mahogany. Aroma complex, fruit liqueur notes, dried fruit, pattiserie, toasty. Taste sweet, rich, unctuous, powerful.

HARVEYS VORS RICH OLD OL
90% palomino, 10% pedro ximénez

94 Colour: light mahogany. Nose: expressive, elegant, cocoa bean, dark chocolate, spicy, creamy oak. Palate: fine bitter notes, powerful, flavourful, complex.

BODEGAS HIDALGO-LA GITANA

Banda de Playa, 42
11540 Sanlúcar de Barrameda - (Cádiz)
☎: +34 956 385 304 - Fax: +34 956 363 844
bodegashidalgo@lagitana.es
www.lagitana.es

FARAÓN 30 AÑOS VORS 50 CL. OL
100% palomino

92 Colour: iodine, amber rim. Nose: dry nuts, varnish, spicy, toasty. Palate: correct, fine bitter notes, toasty, long.

LA GITANA MZ
100% palomino

92 Colour: bright straw. Nose: saline, dried flowers, balanced, expressive. Palate: complex, fresh, flavourful, elegant.

NAPOLEÓN 30 AÑOS VORS 50 CL. AM
100% palomino

93 Colour: light mahogany. Nose: complex, expressive, dry nuts, acetaldehyde, spicy. Palate: full, flavourful, balanced, fine bitter notes.

PASTRANA MANZANILLA PASADA MZ
100% palomino

94 Colour: bright golden. Nose: saline, pungent, dry nuts, roasted almonds, expressive. Palate: rich, powerful, flavourful, balanced.

TRIANA PX
100% pedro ximénez

90 Colour: dark mahogany. Nose: spicy, caramel, dark chocolate, dried fruit. Palate: rich, powerful, flavourful.

TRIANA 30 AÑOS VORS PX
100% pedro ximénez

92 Colour: dark mahogany. Nose: creamy oak, dark chocolate, aromatic coffee, toasty, expressive. Palate: long, sweet, rich, flavourful.

WELLINGTON 30 AÑOS VORS PC
100% palomino

91 Colour: mahogany. Nose: powerfull, expressive, complex, spicy, pungent, acetaldehyde. Palate: full, good structure, long, spicy.

WELLINGTON JEREZ CORTADO 20 AÑOS VOS PC
100% palomino

90 Colour: light mahogany. Nose: medium intensity, sweet spices. Palate: light-bodied, correct, balanced, spirituous.

BODEGAS LA CIGARRERA

Pza. Madre de Dios, s/n
11540 Sanlúcar de Barrameda - (Cádiz)
☎: +34 956 381 285 - Fax: +34 956 383 824
lacigarrera@bodegaslacigarrera.com
www.bodegaslacigarrera.com

LA CIGARRERA AM
100% palomino

91 Colour: golden. Nose: powerfull, complex, elegant, dry nuts, toasty, acetaldehyde. Palate: rich, fine bitter notes, , long, spicy.

LA CIGARRERA MOSCATEL
100% moscatel

92 Colour: light mahogany. Nose: dried fruit, acetaldehyde, aromatic coffee, spicy, toasty. Palate: sweetness, powerful, flavourful, complex, balanced.

BODEGAS OSBORNE

Fernán Caballero, 7
11500 El Puerto de Santa María - (Cádiz)
☎: +34 956 869 000 - Fax: +34 925 869 026
comunicacion@osborne.es
www.osborne.es

AMONTILLADO 51-1ª V.O.R.S AM
100% palomino

93 Colour: light mahogany. Nose: powerfull, acetaldehyde, dark chocolate, aromatic coffee, varnish. Palate: powerful, good acidity, fine bitter notes, spicy.

CAPUCHINO V.O.R.S PC
100% palomino

94 Colour: iodine, amber rim. Nose: powerfull, characterful, ripe fruit, toasty. Palate: good acidity, flavourful, powerful.

COQUINERO FI
100% palomino

92 Colour: bright yellow. Nose: dry nuts, sweet spices, white flowers. Palate: long, fine bitter notes, flavourful.

FINO QUINTA FI
100% palomino

93 Colour: bright straw. Nose: complex, balanced, pungent, saline. Palate: flavourful, dry, elegant, long, fine bitter notes.

OSBORNE 1827 PX
100% pedro ximénez

91 Colour: dark mahogany. Nose: fruit liqueur notes, dried fruit, toasty, dark chocolate, aged wood nuances. Palate: complex, powerful, flavourful.

OSBORNE RARE SHERRY AOS AM
palomino

96 Colour: iodine, amber rim. Nose: powerfull, complex, elegant, dry nuts, toasty, acetaldehyde. Palate: rich, , spicy, long, fine bitter notes.

OSBORNE RARE SHERRY PX VORS PX
pedro ximénez

93 Colour: dark mahogany. Nose: acetaldehyde, powerfull, expressive, varnish, aromatic coffee, toasty, complex. Palate: long, powerful, flavourful, sweet, spicy, spirituous.

OSBORNE RARE SHERRY SOLERA BC 200 OL
pedro ximénez, palomino

97 Colour: iodine, amber rim. Nose: powerfull, complex, dry nuts, toasty, acetaldehyde. Palate: rich, fine bitter notes, long, spicy.

OSBORNE RARE SHERRY SOLERA INDIA OL
pedro ximénez, palomino

94 Colour: iodine, amber rim. Nose: fruit liqueur notes, fruit liqueur notes, pattiserie. Palate: spicy, spirituous, fine bitter notes.

OSBORNE RARE SHERRY SOLERA PAP PC
pedro ximénez, palomino

93 Colour: light mahogany. Nose: powerfull, fruit liqueur notes, toasty, acetaldehyde. Palate: powerful, spicy, good acidity, fine bitter notes, sweetness.

SIBARITA V.O.R.S. OL
98% palomino, 2% pedro ximénez

95 Colour: iodine, amber rim. Nose: powerfull, complex, elegant, dry nuts, toasty. Palate: rich, fine bitter notes, , long, good acidity.

VENERABLE VORS PX
100% pedro ximénez

97 Colour: dark mahogany. Nose: acetaldehyde, varnish, aromatic coffee, caramel, dark chocolate, toasty, aged wood nuances, expressive. Palate: powerful, flavourful, sweet, spirituous, balanced, elegant.

BODEGAS PEDRO ROMERO

Trasbolsa, 84
11540 Sanlúcar de Barrameda - (Cádiz)
☎: +34 956 360 736 - Fax: +34 956 361 027
pedroromero@pedroromero.es
www.pedroromero.es

DON PEDRO ROMERO VORS PRESTIGE AM
100% palomino

94 Colour: iodine, amber rim. Nose: acetaldehyde, toasty, creamy oak, varnish, expressive, pungent. Palate: powerful, flavourful, complex, spicy.

HIJO DE PEDRO ROMERO VILLAREAL VORS PRESTIGE PC
100% palomino

93 Colour: iodine, amber rim. Nose: spicy, creamy oak, balanced, acetaldehyde. Palate: unctuous, round, flavourful, complex, long.

BODEGAS TERESA RIVERO

Puerto, 21
11540 Sanlúcar de Barrameda - (Cádiz)
☎: +34 956 361 491 - Fax: +34 956 368 369
info@bodegasteresarivero.com
www.grupogarvey.com

BAJO DE GUÍA MZ
palomino

90 Colour: bright straw. Nose: dried herbs, pungent, saline, flor yeasts. Palate: flavourful, dry, balanced, long.

LA SANLUQUEÑA MZ
palomino

90 Colour: bright straw. Nose: medium intensity, fresh, dried herbs, pungent. Palate: flavourful, dry, long.

BODEGAS TERRY

Toneleros, s/n
11500 El Puerto de Santa María - (Cádiz)
☎: +34 956 151 500 - Fax: +34 956 858 474
visitas@bodegasterry.com
www.bodegasterry.com

TERRY AMONTILLADO AM
100% palomino

90 Colour: light mahogany. Nose: sweet spices, dry nuts, acetaldehyde. Palate: flavourful, powerful, spirituous.

TERRY FINO FI
100% palomino

91 Colour: bright straw. Nose: pungent, fine lees, white flowers. Palate: powerful, fine bitter notes, long.

TERRY PEDRO XIMÉNEZ PX
100% pedro ximénez

90 Color dark mahogany. Aroma complex, fruit liqueur notes, dried fruit, pattiserie, toasty. Taste sweet, rich, unctuous, powerful.

BODEGAS TRADICIÓN

Cordobeses, 3
11408 Jerez de la Frontera - (Cádiz)
☎: +34 956 168 628 - Fax: +34 956 331 963
mllanos@bodegastradicion.com
www.bodegastradicion.com

AMONTILLADO TRADICIÓN VORS AM
palomino

93 Colour: light mahogany. Nose: expressive, balanced, dry nuts, acetaldehyde. Palate: flavourful, dry, complex, full.

OLOROSO TRADICIÓN VORS OL
palomino

94 Colour: light mahogany. Nose: complex, elegant, spicy, expressive, toasty. Palate: flavourful, spirituous, fine bitter notes.

PALO CORTADO TRADICIÓN VORS PC
palomino

91 Colour: light mahogany. Nose: acetaldehyde, dark chocolate, spicy, creamy oak. Palate: fine bitter notes, complex, flavourful, spicy.

PEDRO XIMÉNEZ TRADICIÓN VOS PX
pedro ximénez

91 Colour: dark mahogany. Nose: complex, fruit liqueur notes, pattiserie, toasty, sweet spices, dark chocolate. Palate: sweet, rich, unctuous, powerful, long, flavourful.

BODEGAS VALDIVIA

Zoilo Ruiz Mateo, s/n
11408 Jerez de la Frontera - (Cádiz)
☎: +34 956 314 358 - Fax: +34 956 169 657
info@bodegasvaldivia.com
www.bodegasvaldivia.com

SACROMONTE 15 AÑOS AM
palomino

90 Colour: iodine, amber rim. Nose: powerfull, toasty, acetaldehyde, sweet spices. Palate: rich, fine bitter notes, , long, spicy.

SACROMONTE 15 AÑOS OL
palomino

91 Colour: iodine, amber rim. Nose: acetaldehyde, dry nuts, dark chocolate, sweet spices. Palate: complex, powerful, flavourful, spicy.

SACROMONTE 15 AÑOS PX
pedro ximénez

90 Colour: dark mahogany. Nose: complex, fruit liqueur notes, dried fruit, pattiserie, toasty, aromatic coffee, cocoa bean. Palate: sweet, rich, unctuous, powerful.

VALDIVIA FI
palomino

91 Colour: bright straw. Nose: balanced, powerfull, complex, pungent, saline. Palate: long, flavourful, full.

VALDIVIA ATRUM CR
palomino

91 Colour: light mahogany. Nose: dried fruit, sweet spices, dark chocolate, expressive. Palate: long, flavourful, spicy, complex.

VALDIVIA PRUNE OL
palomino

90 Colour: old gold, amber rim. Nose: spicy, toasty, dry nuts. Palate: rich, flavourful, long, balanced.

VALDIVIA SUN PALE CREAM PCR
palomino

90 Colour: bright yellow. Nose: complex, fresh, saline. Palate: balanced, fine bitter notes, easy to drink, sweetness, good acidity.

CÉSAR L. FLORIDO ROMERO

Padre Lerchundi, 35-37
11550 Chipiona - (Cádiz)
☎: +34 956 371 285 - Fax: +34 956 370 222
florido@bodegasflorido.com
www.bodegasflorido.com

CÉSAR FLORIDO MOSCATEL ESPECIAL MOSCATEL
100% moscatel

91 Colour: dark mahogany. Nose: powerfull, sweet spices, pattiserie, candied fruit, dark chocolate. Palate: good structure, rich, full, flavourful.

FINO CÉSAR FI
100% palomino

91 Colour: bright yellow. Nose: complex, expressive, pungent, saline. Palate: rich, powerful, fresh, fine bitter notes, complex.

DELGADO ZULETA

Avda. Rocío Jurado, s/n
11540 Sanlúcar de Barrameda - (Cádiz)
☎: +34 956 360 133 - Fax: +34 956 360 780
direccioncomercial@delgadozuleta.com
www.delgadozuleta.com

MONTEAGUDO AM
100% palomino

90 Colour: iodine, amber rim. Nose: expressive, caramel, spicy, toasty. Palate: fine bitter notes, flavourful, long.

QUO VADIS AM
100% palomino

90 Colour: old gold, amber rim. Nose: acetaldehyde, roasted almonds, expressive. Palate: spicy, long, flavourful.

DIOS BACO

Tecnología, A-14
11407 Jerez de la Frontera - (Cádiz)
☎: +34 956 333 337 - Fax: +34 956 333 825
info@bodegasdiosbaco.com
www.bodegasdiosbaco.com

BACO DE ÉLITE MEDIUM OL
palomino

90 Colour: light mahogany. Nose: toasty, aged wood nuances, spicy. Palate: spirituous, sweetness, rich, balanced.

DIOS BACO CR
palomino, pedro ximénez

91 Colour: mahogany. Nose: dried fruit, caramel, pattiserie, powerfull, fruit liqueur notes. Palate: rich, flavourful, balanced.

DIOS BACO OL
18% palomino

91 Colour: light mahogany. Nose: expressive, spicy, aged wood nuances. Palate: flavourful, long, fine bitter notes, rich.

OXFORD 1970 PX
pedro ximénez

90 Colour: dark mahogany. Nose: varietal, warm, fruit liqueur notes, dark chocolate, fruit liqueur notes. Palate: correct, balanced, good structure.

EL MAESTRO SIERRA

Pza. de Silos, 5
11403 Jerez de la Frontera - (Cádiz)
☎: +34 956 342 433 - Fax: +34 956 342 433
info@maestrosierra.com
www.maestrosierra.com

EL MAESTRO SIERRA FI
palomino

92 Colour: bright yellow. Nose: balanced, spicy, dried herbs, pungent. Palate: rich, full, fine bitter notes.

EL MAESTRO SIERRA OLOROSO 1/14 OL
palomino

94 Colour: mahogany. Nose: dark chocolate, cocoa bean, spicy, toasty, expressive. Palate: long, spicy, powerful, flavourful, complex.

EMILIO LUSTAU

Arcos, 53
11402 Jerez de la Frontera - (Cádiz)
☎: +34 956 341 597 - Fax: +34 956 859 204
lustau@lustau.es
www.lustau.es

LA INA FI
palomino

96 Colour: bright straw. Nose: expressive, complex, pungent, saline, flor yeasts. Palate: complex, flavourful, long, fine bitter notes.

LUSTAU AÑADA 1997 OLOROSO DULCE OL
palomino

92 Colour: iodine, amber rim. Nose: sweet spices, pattiserie, dried fruit, honeyed notes. Palate: powerful, flavourful, complex, sweetness.

LUSTAU EAST INDIA CR
palomino, pedro ximénez

90 Colour: mahogany. Nose: powerfull, dried fruit, spicy, pattiserie, dark chocolate, expressive. Palate: sweetness, powerful, flavourful.

LUSTAU EMILÍN MOSCATEL
100% moscatel

91 Colour: light mahogany. Nose: acetaldehyde, dried fruit, cocoa bean, sweet spices. Palate: rich, flavourful, complex, toasty, long.

LUSTAU ESCUADRILLA AM
palomino

90 Colour: iodine, amber rim. Nose: powerfull, complex, dry nuts, toasty. Palate: rich, fine bitter notes, , long, spicy.

LUSTAU JARANA FI
100% palomino

91 Colour: bright straw. Nose: powerfull, complex, white flowers, pungent. Palate: long, fine bitter notes, good acidity.

LUSTAU PAPIRUSA MZ SOLERA
palomino

94 Colour: bright yellow. Nose: saline, flor yeasts, pungent, faded flowers. Palate: complex, flavourful, rich.

LUSTAU PENÍSULA PC
palomino

90 Colour: iodine, amber rim. Nose: powerfull, pungent, spicy, toasty. Palate: flavourful, powerful, fine bitter notes.

LUSTAU SAN EMILIO PX
pedro ximénez

93 Colour: mahogany. Nose: powerfull, varietal, candied fruit, dark chocolate, aromatic coffee. Palate: full, complex, good acidity, fine bitter notes.

MACARENA MZ
100% palomino

90 Colour: bright straw. Nose: powerfull, characterful, pungent, flor yeasts. Palate: flavourful, good acidity, full.

PUERTO FINO FI
palomino

93 Colour: bright yellow. Nose: expressive, pungent, saline. Palate: rich, powerful, fresh, fine bitter notes.

RÍO VIEJO OL
palomino

92 Colour: iodine, amber rim. Nose: sweet spices, dark chocolate, fruit liqueur notes. Palate: long, spicy, powerful.

EQUIPO NAVAZOS

Cartuja, 1 - módulo 6
11401 Jerez de la Frontera - (Cádiz)
equipo@navazos.com
www.equiponavazos.com

LA BOTA DE AMONTILLADO (BOTA Nº 37) AM

95 Colour: light mahogany. Nose: powerfull, acetaldehyde, varnish, sweet spices, roasted almonds. Palate: concentrated, balanced, spicy, long.

LA BOTA DE CREAM Nº 38 CR

96 Colour: light mahogany. Nose: caramel, varnish, pattiserie, sweet spices, complex. Palate: long, rich, fine bitter notes.

LA BOTA DE DULCE Nº33 COLOR SOLERA

95 Colour: dark mahogany. Nose: complex, fruit liqueur notes, dried fruit, pattiserie, toasty, varnish, aromatic coffee, dark chocolate. Palate: sweet, rich, unctuous, powerful, slightly acidic.

LA BOTA DE FINO (BOTA Nº 35) FI

99 Colour: bright golden. Nose: complex, elegant, dry nuts, pungent, balsamic herbs, flor yeasts. Palate: long, spicy, complex, fine bitter notes.

LA BOTA DE MANZANILLA PASADA
(BOTA NO) Nº39 MZ

99 Colour: bright golden. Nose: complex, expressive, dry nuts, pungent. Palate: fine bitter notes, elegant, spicy, lacks balance. Personality.

LA BOTA DE MANZANILLA PASADA
(BOTA NO) Nº40 MZ

99 Colour: bright golden. Nose: powerfull, expressive, candied fruit, acetaldehyde, spicy, dry nuts, honeyed notes. Palate: rich, flavourful, long, powerful.

LA BOTA DE PALO CORTADO (BOTA Nº 34) PC

94 Colour: light mahogany. Nose: medium intensity, dry nuts, roasted almonds, sweet spices, pattiserie. Palate: balanced, spicy.

LA BOTA DE PEDRO XIMENEZ Nº36 BOTA NO PX
pedro ximénez

96 Colour: mahogany. Nose: balanced, medium intensity, candied fruit, pattiserie, neat. Palate: unctuous, full.

MANZANILLA I THINK MZ

92 Colour: bright straw. Nose: fresh fruit, flor yeasts, saline, powerfull, complex, slightly evolved, dry nuts. Palate: flavourful, long, fine bitter notes, balanced.

ESPÍRITUS DE JEREZ

Pza. Cocheras, 3
11403 Jerez de la Frontera - (Cádiz)
direccion@espiritusdejerez.com

COLECCIÓN ROBERTO AMILLO AMONTILLADO AM
palomino

95 Colour: iodine, amber rim. Nose: complex, dry nuts, toasty, acetaldehyde, pungent, expressive. Palate: rich, fine bitter notes, long, spicy.

COLECCIÓN ROBERTO AMILLO OLOROSO OL
palomino

95 Colour: iodine, amber rim. Nose: dry nuts, toasty, pattiserie, expressive. Palate: rich, fine bitter notes, long, spicy.

COLECCIÓN ROBERTO AMILLO PALO CORTADO PC
palomino

96 Colour: iodine, amber rim. Nose: elegant, dry nuts, toasty, expressive, warm, varnish, acetaldehyde. Palate: rich, fine bitter notes, long, spicy.

COLECCIÓN ROBERTO AMILLO PEDRO XIMÉNEZ PX
pedro ximénez

95 Colour: dark mahogany. Nose: dried fruit, fruit liqueur notes, pattiserie, toasty, tar, varnish, characterful. Palate: rich, unctuous, powerful, spicy, long, spirituous.

FERNANDO DE CASTILLA

San Fco. Javier, 3
11404 Jerez de la Frontera - (Cádiz)
☎: +34 956 182 454 - Fax: +34 956 182 222
bodegas@fernandodecastilla.com
www.fernandodecastilla.com

FERNANDO DE CASTILLA "AMONTILLADO ANTIQUE" AM
100% palomino

94 Color iodine, amber rim. Aroma powerfull, complex, elegant, dry nuts, toasty. Taste rich, fine bitter notes, fine solera notes, long, spicy.

FERNANDO DE CASTILLA "FINO ANTIQUE" FI
100% palomino

94 Colour: bright yellow. Nose: powerfull, complex, characterful, pungent, dry nuts. Palate: powerful, complex, long, creamy.

FERNANDO DE CASTILLA "OLOROSO ANTIQUE" OL
100% palomino

92 Colour: iodine, amber rim. Nose: powerfull, dry nuts, toasty. Palate: rich, fine bitter notes, , long, spicy.

FERNANDO DE CASTILLA "P.X. ANTIQUE" PX
100% pedro ximénez

94 Colour: dark mahogany. Nose: complex, varietal, dried fruit, dark chocolate, sweet spices, spicy. Palate: balanced, spirituous, unctuous.

FERNANDO DE CASTILLA "PALO CORTADO ANTIQUE" PC
100% palomino

94 Colour: light mahogany. Nose: powerfull, dry nuts, fruit liqueur notes, creamy oak, dark chocolate, pungent. Palate: spicy, fine bitter notes, long.

FERNANDO DE CASTILLA "PX PREMIUM" PX
100% pedro ximénez

91 Colour: mahogany. Nose: balanced, dried fruit, dark chocolate, sweet spices, pattiserie. Palate: flavourful, sweetness, easy to drink.

FERNANDO DE CASTILLA FINO CLASSIC FI
100% palomino

90 Color bright yellow. Aroma complex, expressive, pungent, saline. Taste rich, powerful, fresh, fine bitter notes.

GONZÁLEZ BYASS JEREZ

Manuel María González, 12
11403 Jerez de la Frontera - (Cádiz)
☎: +34 956 357 000 - Fax: +34 956 357 043
elrincondegb@gonzalezbyass.es
www.gonzalezbyass.es

AMONTILLADO DEL DUQUE VORS AM
100% palomino

93 Colour: mahogany. Nose: complex, powerfull, spicy, dry nuts. Palate: rich, long, fine bitter notes, spirituous.

APÓSTOLES VORS PC
palomino, pedro ximénez

92 Colour: light mahogany. Nose: honeyed notes, dark chocolate, sweet spices, toasty, acetaldehyde. Palate: round, powerful, flavourful, complex, sweetness.

GONZALEZ BYASS AÑADA 1982 PC
100% palomino

95 Colour: iodine. Nose: complex, elegant, expressive, acetaldehyde. Palate: good structure, rich, complex, fine bitter notes, balanced.

LEONOR PC
100% palomino

90 Nose: sweet spices, caramel, dry nuts, aromatic coffee. Palate: flavourful, spicy, long.

MATUSALEM VORS CR
palomino, pedro ximénez

92 Colour: iodine, amber rim. Nose: sweet spices, dark chocolate, dry nuts. Palate: flavourful, powerful, fine bitter notes.

NÉCTAR PX
100% pedro ximénez

90 Colour: light mahogany. Nose: cocoa bean, dark chocolate, toasty, dried fruit. Palate: flavourful, rich, concentrated, complex.

NOÉ PX
100% pedro ximénez

94 Colour: dark mahogany. Nose: complex, fruit liqueur notes, pattiserie, toasty, caramel, spicy. Palate: sweet, rich, unctuous, long, flavourful, complex.

TÍO PEPE FI
100% palomino

93 Colour: bright yellow. Nose: pungent, saline, fresh, flor yeasts. Palate: rich, powerful, fresh, fine bitter notes.

VIÑA AB AM
100% palomino

90 Colour: golden. Nose: powerfull, pungent, acetaldehyde, iodine notes. Palate: flavourful, rich, long, complex.

HEREDEROS DE ARGÜESO S.A.

Mar, 8
11540 Sanlúcar de Barrameda - (Cádiz)
☎: +34 956 385 116 - Fax: +34 956 368 169
argueso@argueso.es
www.argueso.es

ARGÜESO AMONTILLADO VIEJO AM
100% palomino

91 Colour: light mahogany. Nose: powerfull, dry nuts, acetaldehyde. Palate: powerful, spirituous, fine bitter notes.

LAS MEDALLAS DE ARGÜESO MZ
100% palomino

91 Colour: bright straw. Nose: saline, flor yeasts, floral, expressive. Palate: rich, powerful, flavourful.

SAN LEÓN "CLÁSICA" MZ
100% palomino

92 Color bright yellow. Aroma complex, expressive, pungent, saline. Taste rich, powerful, fresh, fine bitter notes.

SAN LEÓN RESERVA DE FAMILIA MZ
100% palomino

95 Colour: bright yellow. Nose: complex, expressive, pungent, saline, powerfull, dry nuts. Palate: rich, powerful, fresh, fine bitter notes.

HIDALGO

Clavel, 29
11402 Jerez de la Frontera - (Cádiz)
☎: +34 956 341 078 - Fax: +34 956 320 922
emiliohidalgo@emiliohidalgo.es
www.hidalgo.com

EL TRESILLO 1874 AMONTILLADO VIEJO AM
palomino

93 Colour: old gold, amber rim. Nose: balanced, expressive, spicy, acetaldehyde, pungent. Palate: good structure, complex, fine bitter notes.

GOBERNADOR OL
palomino

90 Colour: light mahogany. Nose: balanced, expressive, dry nuts, acetaldehyde, spicy. Palate: long, flavourful, fine bitter notes.

LA PANESA ESPECIAL FINO FI
palomino

95 Colour: bright yellow. Nose: complex, expressive, pungent, saline, dry nuts. Palate: powerful, fresh, fine bitter notes, complex, full.

MARQUÉS DE RODIL PC
palomino

91 Colour: old gold, amber rim. Nose: medium intensity, acetaldehyde, sweet spices, pungent. Palate: fine bitter notes, balanced, flavourful.

VILLAPANÉS OL
palomino

94 Colour: iodine, amber rim. Nose: complex, elegant, dry nuts, toasty. Palate: rich, fine bitter notes, , long, spicy, complex, full.

LUIS CABALLERO

San Francisco, 24
11500 El Puerto de Santa María - (Cádiz)
☎: +34 956 851 751 - Fax: +34 956 853 802
marketing@caballero.es
www.caballero.es

CABALLERO OLOROSO REAL OL
palomino

90 Colour: light mahogany. Nose: medium intensity, sweet spices, caramel. Palate: balanced, spicy, long.

PAVÓN PUERTO FINO FI SOLERA
palomino

90 Colour: bright straw. Nose: mineral, faded flowers, flor yeasts, saline. Palate: long, rich, flavourful, fresh.

REAL TESORO

Ctra. Nacional IV, Km. 640
11406 Jerez de la Frontera - (Cádiz)
☎: +34 956 321 004 - Fax: +34 956 340 829
visitas@grupoestevez.com
www.grupoestevez.es

DEL PRÍNCIPE AM

95 Colour: iodine, amber rim. Nose: powerfull, complex, elegant, dry nuts, toasty, acetaldehyde. Palate: rich, fine bitter notes, , long, spicy.

SACRISTÍA AB

Sevilla, 2 1º Izq.
11540 Sanlúcar de Barrameda - (Cádiz)
☎: +34 607 920 337
www.sacristiaab.com

SACRISTÍA AB MZ

95 Colour: bright straw. Nose: pungent, dry nuts, toasty, pattiserie. Palate: flavourful, spirituous, fine bitter notes, long.

SÁNCHEZ ROMATE

Lealas, 26
11404 Jerez de la Frontera - (Cádiz)
☎: +34 956 182 212 - Fax: +34 956 185 276
comercial@romate.com
www.romate.com

CARDENAL CISNEROS PX
100% pedro ximénez

91 Colour: dark mahogany. Nose: aromatic coffee, cocoa bean, toasty, fruit liqueur notes, fruit liqueur notes. Palate: long, toasty, flavourful, concentrated, complex.

DON JOSÉ OL
100% palomino

91 Colour: mahogany. Nose: cocoa bean, dark chocolate, balanced. Palate: good structure, rich, full, spicy, flavourful.

FINO PERDIDO 1/15 FI
palomino

92 Colour: bright golden. Nose: dried flowers, saline, woody, aged wood nuances. Palate: fine bitter notes, rich, flavourful, long.

NPU AM
100% palomino

91 Colour: light mahogany. Nose: saline, dried herbs, spicy, roasted almonds. Palate: rich, flavourful, spicy, long.

OLD & PLUS AMONTILLADO VORS AM
100% palomino

92 Colour: light mahogany. Nose: acetaldehyde, roasted almonds, spicy, toasty. Palate: complex, flavourful, fine bitter notes, spicy.

OLD & PLUS OLOROSO OL
100% palomino

94 Colour: iodine. Nose: expressive, balanced, complex, spicy. Palate: good structure, rich, fine bitter notes, complex.

OLD & PLUS P.X. PX
100% pedro ximénez

93 Colour: dark mahogany. Nose: complex, fruit liqueur notes, dried fruit, pattiserie, toasty, dark chocolate, aromatic coffee, spicy. Palate: sweet, rich, unctuous, powerful, long, flavourful.

REGENTE PC
100% palomino

90 Colour: iodine, amber rim. Nose: acetaldehyde, fruit liqueur notes, spicy, toasty. Palate: powerful.

SANDEMAN JEREZ

Porrera, 3 of. 8
11403 Jerez de la Frontera - (Cádiz)
☎: +34 956 151 700 - Fax: +34 956 303 534
jose.moreno@sogrape.pt
www.sandeman.eu

SANDEMAN ROYAL AMBROSANTE VOS PX
100% pedro ximénez

92 Colour: dark mahogany. Nose: complex, fruit liqueur notes, dried fruit, toasty, aromatic coffee, fruit preserve. Palate: sweet, rich, unctuous, powerful, flavourful.

SANDEMAN ROYAL CORREGIDOR VOS OL
85% palomino, 15% pedro ximénez

91 Colour: light mahogany. Nose: powerfull, sweet spices, dark chocolate, acetaldehyde. Palate: spicy, long, sweetness.

SANDEMAN ROYAL ESMERALDA VOS AM
100% palomino

94 Colour: iodine, amber rim. Nose: powerfull, complex, elegant, dry nuts, toasty, varnish, pattiserie. Palate: rich, fine bitter notes, , long, spicy.

VALDESPINO

Ctra. Nacional IV, Km.640
11406 Jerez de la Frontera - (Cádiz)
☎: +34 956 321 004 - Fax: +34 956 340 829
visitas@grupoestevez.com
www.grupoestevez.es

DON GONZALO VOS OL

96 Colour: iodine, amber rim. Nose: powerfull, complex, elegant, dry nuts, toasty, characterful, acetaldehyde. Palate: rich, fine bitter notes, , long, spicy.

SOLERA 1842 VOS OL

94 Colour: iodine, amber rim. Nose: acetaldehyde, toasty, dark chocolate. Palate: long, fine bitter notes, powerful.

SOLERA SU MAJESTAD VORS OL

96 Colour: light mahogany. Nose: complex, elegant, expressive, spicy, dry nuts. Palate: good structure, rich, flavourful, complex, fine bitter notes.

YNOCENTE FI

95 Colour: bright yellow. Nose: complex, expressive, pungent, saline, dry nuts. Palate: rich, powerful, fresh, fine bitter notes.

WILLIAMS & HUMBERT S.A.

Ctra. N-IV, Km. 641,75
11408 Jerez de la Frontera - (Cádiz)
☎: +34 956 353 400 - Fax: +34 956 353 412
secretaria@williams-humbert.com
www.williams-humbert.com

DON GUIDO SOLERA ESPECIAL 20 AÑOS VOS PX
pedro ximénez

93 Colour: dark mahogany. Nose: complex, fruit liqueur notes, dried fruit, pattiserie, toasty, acetaldehyde, varnish. Palate: sweet, rich, unctuous, powerful, spicy, long.

DOS CORTADOS PC
palomino

92 Colour: iodine, amber rim. Nose: pattiserie, acetaldehyde, powerfull, sweet spices. Palate: flavourful, correct, fine bitter notes, spicy.

DRY SACK "SOLERA ESPECIAL" 15 AÑOS OL
palomino, pedro ximénez

91 Colour: mahogany. Nose: acetaldehyde, dark chocolate, aromatic coffee, toasty. Palate: powerful, flavourful, sweetness.

DRY SACK FINO FI
palomino

90 Colour: bright yellow. Nose: flor yeasts, saline, pungent, roasted almonds. Palate: powerful, flavourful, long, complex.

JALIFA VORS "30 YEARS" AM

92 Colour: iodine, amber rim. Nose: powerfull, complex, elegant, dry nuts, toasty, sweet spices. Palate: rich, fine bitter notes, , long, spicy.

ZOILO RUIZ-MATEOS

Pizarro 12 y 14
11403 Jerez de la Frontera - (Cádiz)
☎: +34 956 310 014 - Fax: +34 956 310 014
gael.barowman@zoiloruizmateos.com
www.grupogarvey.com

AMONTILLADO ZOILO RUIZ MATEOS AM
palomino

95 Colour: light mahogany. Nose: elegant, expressive, balanced, acetaldehyde, varnish. Palate: complex, flavourful, long, spicy.

DESCRIPTION

This is the kingdom of the monastrell rape as it is one of the zones most cultivated with this grape in Levante. It also has the title of being the most densely cultivated region after Burgundy and La Rioja. The climate is almost continental and its poor soils ensure textbook monastrell wines, rounded, full bodied red wines with a certain amount of strength. Petit verdot and syrah long cycle grapes are also having good and unexpected results.

NUMBER OF HECTARES: 2.200 **ALTITUDES:** 400 m. – 800 m.

PREDOMINANT VARIETIES:

White grapes: airén, macabeo, malvasía, chardonnay, sauvignon blanc, small grained muscatel and pedro ximénez.

Red grapes: monastrell, garnacha, garnacha tintorera, cencibel, cabernet sauvignon, merlot, petit verdot and syrah.

CLIMATOLOGY AND SOILS

The climate is continental with Mediterranean influences. It is characterized by its aridity and low rainfall; the soils are brown, brown/limestone and limestone, poor in organic matter and with an excellent capacity to retain water.

BARÓN DEL SOLAR

Paraje El Jurado
30520 Jumilla - (Murcia)
☎: +34 679 874 590 - Fax: +34 968 716 197
pepita@barondelsolar.com
www.barondelsolar.com

BARÓN DEL SOLAR MANOS COLECCIÓN PRIVADA 2008 T
100% monastrell

91 Colour: cherry, garnet rim. Nose: ripe fruit, sweet spices, cocoa bean, dark chocolate, fine reductive notes. Palate: flavourful, toasty, long, spicy.

BODEGAS CARCHELO

Casas de la Hoya, s/n
30520 Jumilla - (Murcia)
☎: +34 968 435 137 - Fax: +34 968 435 200
administracion@carchelo.com
www.carchelo.com

ALTICO SYRAH 2009 T
100% syrah

91 Colour: bright cherry. Nose: ripe fruit, sweet spices, creamy oak. Palate: flavourful, fruity, toasty, round tannins.

CANALIZO 2008 TC
40% monastrell, 40% syrah, 10% tempranillo

90 Colour: cherry, garnet rim. Nose: ripe fruit, spicy, creamy oak, toasty, characterful. Palate: powerful, flavourful, toasty, round tannins.

SIERVA 2010 T
monastrell, cabernet sauvignon, syrah

91 Colour: deep cherry, garnet rim. Nose: balanced, ripe fruit, wild herbs, spicy. Palate: balanced, fine bitter notes, round tannins.

BODEGAS EL NIDO

Ctra. de Fuentealamo - Paraje de la Aragona
30520 Jumilla - (Murcia)
☎: +34 968 435 022 - Fax: +34 968 435 653
info@bodegaselnido.com
www.orowines.com

CLÍO 2009 T
70% monastrell, 30% cabernet sauvignon

94 Colour: cherry, garnet rim. Nose: ripe fruit, spicy, creamy oak, toasty, characterful. Palate: powerful, flavourful, toasty, round tannins.

EL NIDO 2009 T
30% monastrell, 70% cabernet sauvignon

96 Colour: black cherry. Nose: creamy oak, dark chocolate, aromatic coffee, fruit liqueur notes, ripe fruit. Palate: fine bitter notes, powerful, concentrated, good acidity.

BODEGAS HACIENDA DEL CARCHE

Ctra. del Carche, Km. 8,3- Apdo. Correos 257
30520 Jumilla - (Murcia)
☎: +34 968 108 248 - Fax: +34 968 975 935
info@haciendadelcarche.com
www.haciendadelcarche.com

TAVS 2011 T
70% monastrell, 20% syrah, 10% garnacha

90 Colour: cherry, purple rim. Nose: expressive, fresh fruit, ripe fruit. Palate: flavourful, fruity, good acidity, round tannins.

BODEGAS JUAN GIL

Ctra. Fuentealamo - Paraje de la Aragona
30520 Jumilla - (Murcia)
☎: +34 968 435 022 - Fax: +34 968 716 051
info@juangil.es
www.juangil.es

HONORO VERA ORGANIC 2011 T
100% monastrell

90 Colour: cherry, purple rim. Nose: red berry notes, floral, ripe fruit. Palate: flavourful, fruity, good acidity, round tannins.

JUAN GIL 12 MESES 2010 T
100% monastrell

93 Colour: very deep cherry. Nose: ripe fruit, powerfull, characterful, sweet spices, creamy oak, fruit expression, earthy notes. Palate: powerful, round tannins, long.

JUAN GIL 18 MESES 2009 T
60% monastrell, 30% cabernet sauvignon, 10% syrah

92 Colour: cherry, garnet rim. Nose: spicy, creamy oak, toasty, characterful, fruit expression. Palate: powerful, flavourful, toasty, round tannins.

JUAN GIL 4 MESES 2010 T
100% monastrell

90 Color bright cherry. Aroma ripe fruit, sweet spices, creamy oak, expressive. Taste flavourful, fruity, toasty, round tannins.

JUAN GIL MOSCATEL 2011 B
100% moscatel

90 Color bright straw. Aroma fresh, fresh fruit, white flowers, expressive. Taste flavourful, fruity, good acidity, balanced.

BODEGAS LUZÓN

Ctra. Jumilla-Calasparra, Km. 3,1
30520 Jumilla - (Murcia)
☎: +34 968 784 135 - Fax: +34 968 781 911
info@bodegasluzon.com
www.bodegasluzon.com

ALMA DE LUZÓN 2007 T
70% monastrell, 10% syrah, 20% cabernet sauvignon

93 Colour: cherry, garnet rim. Nose: ripe fruit, spicy, creamy oak, complex, mineral, roasted coffee. Palate: powerful, flavourful, toasty, round tannins.

ALTOS DE LUZÓN 2008 T
50% monastrell, 25% tempranillo, 25% cabernet sauvignon

90 Colour: cherry, garnet rim. Nose: ripe fruit, wild herbs, earthy notes, dark chocolate. Palate: flavourful, long, correct.

LUZÓN 2011 T
70% monastrell, 30% syrah

91 Colour: bright cherry. Nose: ripe fruit, sweet spices, expressive. Palate: flavourful, fruity, toasty, round tannins.

LUZÓN VERDE ORGANIC 2011 T
100% monastrell

90 Colour: cherry, purple rim. Nose: fresh fruit, red berry notes, floral, expressive, varietal. Palate: flavourful, fruity, good acidity, round tannins.

PORTÚ 2008 T
80% monastrell, 20% cabernet sauvignon

93 Color cherry, garnet rim. Aroma ripe fruit, spicy, creamy oak, toasty, complex. Taste powerful, flavourful, toasty, round tannins.

BODEGAS MADROÑO

Ctra., Jumilla-Ontur, km. 16
30520 Jumilla - (Murcia)
☎: +34 662 380 985
gmartinez@vinocrapula.com

MADROÑO 2009 T
monastrell, syrah, cabernet sauvignon

91 Colour: cherry, garnet rim. Nose: ripe fruit, spicy, creamy oak, toasty, characterful. Palate: powerful, flavourful, toasty, round tannins.

BODEGAS OLIVARES

Vereda Real, s/n
30520 Jumilla - (Murcia)
☎: +34 968 780 180 - Fax: +34 968 756 474
correo@bodegasolivares.com
www.bodegasolivares.com

OLIVARES DULCE MONASTRELL 2008 T
100% monastrell

90 Colour: cherry, garnet rim. Nose: dark chocolate, spicy, dried fruit. Palate: good acidity, powerful, flavourful, complex, long.

BODEGAS PÍO DEL RAMO

Ctra. Almanza, s/n
2652 Ontur - (Albacete)
☎: +34 967 323 230
info@piodelramo.com
www.piodelramo.com

CHARDONNAY PÍO DEL RAMO 2011 B BARRICA
chardonnay

91 Color bright yellow. Aroma powerfull, ripe fruit, sweet spices, creamy oak, fragrant herbs. Taste rich, smoky aftertaste, flavourful, fresh, good acidity.

PÍO DEL RAMO 2008 TC
syrah, monastrell, cabernet sauvignon, petit verdot

91 Colour: cherry, garnet rim. Nose: ripe fruit, spicy, creamy oak, toasty. Palate: powerful, flavourful, toasty, round tannins.

BODEGAS SILVANO GARCÍA

Avda. de Murcia, 29
30520 Jumilla - (Murcia)
☎: +34 968 780 767 - Fax: +34 968 716 125
bodegas@silvanogarcia.com
www.silvanogarcia.com

SILVANO GARCÍA MOSCATEL 2010 B
100% moscatel

90 Color golden. Aroma powerfull, floral, honeyed notes, candied fruit, fragrant herbs. Taste flavourful, sweet, fresh, fruity, good acidity, long.

BODEGAS Y VIÑEDOS CASA DE LA ERMITA

Ctra. El Carche, Km. 11,5
30520 Jumilla - (Murcia)
☎: +34 968 783 035 - Fax: +34 968 716 063
bodega@casadelaermita.com
www.casadelaermita.com

CASA DE LA ERMITA ECOLÓGICO MONASTRELL 2011 T
100% monastrell

90 Color cherry, purple rim. Aroma expressive, fresh fruit, red berry notes, floral. Taste flavourful, fruity, good acidity, round tannins.

CRAPULA WINES, S.L.

Avda. de la Asunción, 42 2D
30520 Jumilla - (Murcia)
☎: +34 968 781 855
gmartinez@vinocrapula.com

CÁRMINE 2009 T
monastrell, syrah

93 Colour: cherry, garnet rim. Nose: spicy, creamy oak, toasty, complex, red berry notes. Palate: powerful, flavourful, toasty, round tannins, long. Personality.

CÁRMINE 3 MESES 2010 T
monastrell

90 Color bright cherry. Aroma ripe fruit, sweet spices, creamy oak, expressive. Taste flavourful, fruity, toasty, round tannins.

CELEBRE 2009 T
monastrell, syrah

92 Colour: cherry, garnet rim. Nose: powerfull, varietal, fruit expression, mineral. Palate: powerful, flavourful, fruity, complex.

CELEBRE 2010 T
monastrell, syrah, petit verdot

93 Colour: bright cherry. Nose: sweet spices, creamy oak, expressive, fruit expression. Palate: flavourful, fruity, toasty, round tannins.

CRÁPULA 2009 T
85% monastrell, 15% otras

91 Colour: bright cherry. Nose: ripe fruit, sweet spices, creamy oak, expressive, aromatic coffee. Palate: flavourful, fruity, toasty, balanced.

CRÁPULA PETIT VERDOT 2010 T
petit verdot

90 Colour: very deep cherry. Nose: powerfull, characterful, ripe fruit, violet drops. Palate: powerful, flavourful, fine bitter notes, spicy, long.

NDQ (NACIDO DEL QUORUM) 2009 T
monastrell, syrah, cabernet sauvignon

93 Colour: cherry, garnet rim. Nose: red berry notes, expressive, dark chocolate, sweet spices, aromatic coffee. Palate: good structure, flavourful, complex, long, toasty.

EGO BODEGAS

Plaza Santa Gertrudis, Nº 1, Entresuelo A
30001 - (Murcia)
☎: +34 968 964 326
esther@gsdwines.com
www.egobodegas.com

EGO MONASTRELL 2009 T
60% monastrell, 40% cabernet sauvignon

90 Colour: cherry, garnet rim. Nose: ripe fruit, spicy, toasty, roasted coffee. Palate: powerful, flavourful, toasty, round tannins.

PEDRO LUIS MARTÍNEZ

Barrio Iglesias, 55
30520 Jumilla - (Murcia)
☎: +34 968 780 142 - Fax: +34 968 716 256
plmsa@alceno.com
www.alceno.com

ALCEÑO 12 MESES 2009 T
85% monastrell, 15% syrah

91 Colour: cherry, garnet rim. Nose: spicy, creamy oak, toasty, characterful, fruit expression. Palate: powerful, flavourful, toasty, round tannins.

ALCEÑO DULCE 2010 T
100% monastrell

90 Colour: bright cherry. Nose: sweet spices, creamy oak, expressive, candied fruit. Palate: flavourful, fruity, toasty, sweet tannins.

ALCEÑO PREMIUM 2011 T
85% syrah, 15% monastrell

92 Colour: cherry, purple rim. Nose: expressive, red berry notes, floral, ripe fruit. Palate: flavourful, fruity, good acidity, round tannins.

PROPIEDAD VITÍCOLA CASA CASTILLO

Ctra. Jumilla - Hellín, RM-428, Km. 8
30520 Jumilla - (Murcia)
☎: +34 968 781 691 - Fax: +34 968 716 238
info@casacastillo.es
www.casacastillo.es

CASA CASTILLO MONASTRELL 2011 T
100% monastrell

92 Colour: cherry, garnet rim. Nose: fresh fruit, fruit expression, scrubland, spicy. Palate: balanced, good acidity, fine bitter notes.

CASA CASTILLO PIE FRANCO 2008 T
100% monastrell

95 Colour: cherry, garnet rim. Nose: creamy oak, toasty, complex, mineral, elegant. Palate: powerful, flavourful, toasty, round tannins.

EL MOLAR 2010 T
100% garnacha

91 Colour: bright cherry. Nose: complex, elegant, mineral, spicy, scrubland. Palate: powerful, flavourful, spicy, balsamic.

LAS GRAVAS 2009 T
80% monastrell, 15% garnacha, 5% syrah

95 Colour: cherry, garnet rim. Nose: spicy, creamy oak, toasty, complex, mineral, fruit expression. Palate: powerful, flavourful, toasty, round tannins.

VALTOSCA 2010 T
100% syrah

92 Colour: bright cherry. Nose: ripe fruit, sweet spices, creamy oak, mineral. Palate: flavourful, fruity, toasty, round tannins.

RED BOTTLE INTERNATIONAL

Rosales, 6
9400 Aranda de Duero - (Burgos)
☎: +34 947 515 884 - Fax: +34 947 515 886
rbi@redbottleint.com

CASPER 2009 T BARRICA
100% monastrell

90 Colour: cherry, garnet rim. Nose: ripe fruit, spicy, creamy oak, toasty, characterful. Palate: powerful, flavourful, toasty, round tannins.

VIÑAS DE LA CASA DEL RICO

Poeta Andrés Bolarin, 1-5ºB
30011- (Murcia)
☎: +34 639 957 687
vino@gorgocil.com
www.gorgocil.com

GORGOCIL MONASTRELL 2009 T
monastrell

90 Colour: cherry, garnet rim. Nose: spicy, creamy oak, toasty, earthy notes, overripe fruit. Palate: powerful, flavourful, toasty, round tannins.

GORGOCIL TEMPRANILLO 2009 T
100% tempranillo

93 Colour: bright cherry. Nose: ripe fruit, sweet spices, creamy oak, fragrant herbs. Palate: flavourful, fruity, toasty, round tannins.

DESCRIPTION

This is one of the islands in the Canary Island archipelago. The largest extension of vineyards is in the north of the island, in the municipalities of Vallehermoso and Hermigua.

NUMBER OF HECTARES: 125 **ALTITUDES:** 100 – 1,300 m.

PREDOMINANT VARIETIES:

Red grapes: Listán negra, negramoll, listán negro.

White grapes: forastera gomera, listán blanco, marmajuelo, malvasía and pedro ximénez.

CLIMATOLOGY AND SOILS

The island is benefited by a subtropical climate added to by higher levels of the Garajonay peak, with its permanent humidity termed "the sea of clouds", caused by the trade winds. This humid air from the north strikes the mountain systems, creating horizontal rainfall, which in turn creates a particular ecosystem made up of luxuriant valleys. The soil in the higher part of the mountain is deep and made up of clay, while lower down Mediterranean style scrubland appears, with an abundance of stones and terraces similar to those of Priorat.

None of the wines tasted achieve the minimum required scoring

DESCRIPTION

This is the great southern plateau within the provinces of Albacete, Ciudad Real, Cuenca and Toledo. It is the most extensive wine growing region in Spain and in the world. The emblematic grape is the cencibel, which is the local tempranillo, used to produce the most singular wines in the zone chosen by the best wineries as an identification of La Mancha. In the recent past the production of bulk wines and alcohol was eliminated, and it was decided that the Denomination of Origin would be a laboratory for all types of international vines with volume and good prices. Other national varieties are also imported such as the verdejo grape of Rueda.

NUMBER OF HECTARES: 170.963

ALTITUDES: 700 m.

PREDOMINANT VARIETIES:

White grapes: airén, macabeo, pardilla, chardonnay, sauvignon blanc, verdejo, muscatel de grano menudo, gewürztraminer, parellada, pedro ximénez, riesling and torrontés.

Red grapes: cencibel, garnacha, moravia, cabernet sauvignon, merlot, syrah, petit verdot, bobal, cabernet franc, graciano, malbec, mencía, monastrell and pinot noir.

CLIMATOLOGY AND SOILS

The climate is extreme continental and the soils are sandy, limestone and clay. The temperatures are extreme, oscillating between -15ºC in the cold winter and 45ºC in summer. Dryness is another of its marked characteristics since, due to its microclimate, the wet winds are prevented from entering, therefore, there is little rainfall.

BODEGAS CAMPOS REALES

Castilla La Mancha, 4
16670 El Provencio - (Cuenca)
☎: +34 967 166 066 - Fax: +34 967 165 032
info@bodegascamposreales.com
www.bodegascamposreales.com

CÁNFORA PIE FRANCO 2009 T
tempranillo

92 Colour: cherry, garnet rim. Nose: ripe fruit, spicy, scrubland, creamy oak, toasty, fine reductive notes. Palate: powerful, flavourful, complex, spicy.

GLADIUM VIÑAS VIEJAS 2009 TC
tempranillo

91 Colour: cherry, garnet rim. Nose: ripe fruit, balsamic herbs, earthy notes, mineral, dark chocolate, creamy oak, toasty. Palate: flavourful, good structure, spicy, round tannins.

BODEGAS VOLVER

Pza. de Grecia, 1 Local 1B
45005 Toledo - (Toledo)
☎: +34 925 167 493 - Fax: +34 925 167 059
export@bodegasvolver.com
www.bodegasvolver.com

VOLVER 2009 T
100% tempranillo

90 Colour: cherry, garnet rim. Nose: balanced, ripe fruit, sweet spices, expressive. Palate: ripe fruit, long, round tannins, toasty.

VOLVER 2010 T
100% tempranillo

90 Colour: bright cherry. Nose: ripe fruit, sweet spices, creamy oak, varietal, characterful, earthy notes. Palate: flavourful, fruity, toasty, round tannins.

FINCA ANTIGUA

Ctra. Quintanar - Los Hinojosos, Km. 11,5
16417 Los Hinojosos - (Cuenca)
☎: +34 969 129 700 - Fax: +34 969 129 496
info@fincaantigua.com
www.familiamartinezbujanda.com

CLAVIS VIÑEDO PICO GARBANZO 2006 TR

91 Colour: deep cherry, garnet rim. Nose: sweet spices, creamy oak, cocoa bean, ripe fruit. Palate: round, balanced, long, ripe fruit, spicy.

FINCA ANTIGUA MOSCATEL 2011 B
100% moscatel

90 Colour: bright golden. Nose: jasmine, ripe fruit, citrus fruit, fragrant herbs. Palate: long, powerful, flavourful, sweetness.

FINCA ANTIGUA SYRAH 2010 T
100% syrah

91 Colour: cherry, purple rim. Nose: balanced, powerfull, sweet spices, ripe fruit. Palate: good structure, flavourful, good acidity.

VIÑEDOS Y BODEGAS MUÑOZ

Ctra. Villarrubia, 11
45350 Noblejas - (Toledo)
☎: +34 925 140 070 - Fax: +34 925 141 334
info@bodegasmunoz.com
www.bodegasmunoz.com

BLAS MUÑOZ CHARDONNAY 2010 BFB
100% chardonnay

91 Colour: bright golden. Nose: sweet spices, ripe fruit, fragrant herbs, citrus fruit, creamy oak. Palate: powerful, flavourful, spicy, toasty, balanced.

DESCRIPTION

The production zone takes in the island of San Miguel de La Palma where most of the production is concentrated in a single winery: Noroeste de la Palma. On the so called "Pretty Island" the predominant wine is sweet wine produced from overripe malvasía grapes, together with interesting red wines with negramoll grapes, a variety which provides wines with floral and mineral expression.

NUMBER OF HECTARES: 755 **ALTITUDES:** 100 m. – 1.900 m.

PREDOMINANT VARIETIES:

White grapes: malvasía, güal and verdillo.

Red grapes: bastardo negro, listán negro, listán prieto, malvasía rosada, muscatel negro, negramoll, tintilla, vijariego negro and castellana negra.

CLIMATOLOGY AND SOILS

Mediterranean on the coastal strip, but fresher towards the interior owing to the influence of the trade winds. The soils depend a lot on the altitude and the orientation of the vineyard, but the creeping vines grow on volcanic stone or "picón granado" (volcanic ash).

BODEGAS CARBALLO

Ctra. a Las Indias de la Palma, 74
38740 Fuencaliente de La Palma - (Santa Cruz de Tenerife)
☎: +34 922 444 140 - Fax: +34 922 211 744
info@bodegascarballo.com
www.bodegascarballo.com

MALVASÍA DULCE CARBALLO 1997 B
malvasía

97 Colour: light mahogany. Nose: complex, expressive, candied fruit, floral, acetaldehyde, caramel, pattiserie, aromatic coffee. Palate: concentrated, balanced, unctuous.

MALVASÍA DULCE CARBALLO 2009 B
malvasía

93 Colour: old gold, amber rim. Nose: spicy, candied fruit, tobacco, white flowers. Palate: flavourful, unctuous, balanced, long.

BODEGAS NOROESTE DE LA PALMA

Bellido Alto, s/n
38780 Tijarafe - (Santa Cruz de Tenerife)
☎: +34 922 491 075 - Fax: +34 922 491 075
administracion@vinosveganorte.com
www.vinosveganorte.com

VEGA NORTE ALBILLO 2011 B

90 Colour: bright straw. Nose: fresh, fresh fruit, white flowers, expressive. Palate: flavourful, fruity, good acidity, balanced, fine bitter notes.

BODEGAS TAMANCA S.L.

Ctra. Gral. Tamanca, 75
38750 El Paso - (Santa Cruz de Tenerife)
☎: +34 922 494 155 - Fax: +34 922 494 296
bioaad@telefonica.net

TAMANCA MALVASÍA 2008 B

90 Colour: old gold, amber rim. Nose: medium intensity, balanced, floral, candied fruit, varietal. Palate: flavourful, fruity.

BODEGAS TENEGUÍA

Los Canarios, s/n
38740 Fuencaliente de La Palma - (Santa Cruz de Tenerife)
☎: +34 922 444 078 - Fax: +34 922 444 394
enologia@vinosteneguia.com
www.vinosteneguia.com

TENEGUÍA MALVASÍA BOTRYTIS PARCIAL 2008 B
malvasía

92 Colour: old gold, amber rim. Nose: balanced, sweet spices, candied fruit, honeyed notes, cocoa bean. Palate: flavourful, balanced, long.

TENEGUÍA MALVASÍA DULCE 1996 B RESERVA

95 Colour: light mahogany. Nose: candied fruit, pattiserie, caramel, sweet spices, acetaldehyde, dark chocolate. Palate: flavourful, full, good structure, balanced.

BODEGAS TENEGUÍA

Los Canarios, s/n
38740 Fuencaliente de La Palma - (Santa Cruz de Tenerife)
☎: +34 922 444 078 - Fax: +34 922 444 394
enologia@vinosteneguia.com
www.vinosteneguia.com

TENEGUÍA MALVASÍA DULCE 2006 B RESERVA
malvasía

93 Colour: light mahogany. Nose: neat, expressive, candied fruit, acetaldehyde, sweet spices, pattiserie, cocoa bean. Palate: balanced, flavourful, unctuous, long.

TENEGUÍA SABRO DULCE 2011 B

91 Colour: old gold, amber rim. Nose: candied fruit, dry nuts, faded flowers, toasty. Palate: flavourful, rich, full, good acidity.

EUFROSINA PÉREZ RODRÍGUEZ

Briesta, 3- El Castillo
38787 El Castillo - (La Palma)
☎: +34 922 400 447
adali_12@msn.com

EL NÍSPERO 2011 B

91 Colour: bright straw. Nose: fresh fruit, neat, varietal, citrus fruit, white flowers. Palate: powerful, flavourful, fruity, balanced, fine bitter notes.

JUAN MATÍAS TORRES

Ciudad Real, 10- Los Canarios
38740 Fuentecaliente de la Palma - (Santa Cruz de Tenerife)
☎: +34 922 444 219
bodega@matiasitorres.com
www.matiastorres.com

MATIAS I TORRES MALVASÍA AROMÁTICA 2010 B
malvasía

93 Colour: old gold, amber rim. Nose: dried fruit, expressive, balanced, varietal, honeyed notes. Palate: flavourful, balanced, long.

MATÍAS TORRES ALBILLO 2011 B
albillo

90 Colour: bright straw. Nose: expressive, fragrant herbs, fresh fruit, balanced, floral. Palate: balanced, fine bitter notes, easy to drink, good acidity.

VID SUR DULCE 2006 B
malvasía

93 Colour: old gold, amber rim. Nose: balanced, expressive, toasty, honeyed notes. Palate: good structure, flavourful, full.

VID SUR DULCE 2008 B
malvasía

93 Colour: old gold, amber rim. Nose: expressive, candied fruit, honeyed notes, complex, varietal. Palate: balanced, good acidity, complex.

DESCRIPTION

This is the most easterly island of those which compose the Canary Island Archipelago. In the region of La Geria, the most original cultivation in Spain takes place: circular holes under ash from the volcano where the vines are planted. Around the volcanic mass, the layer of ash permits the rapid absorption of water and prevents its evaporation. Moreover, this favours the constant maintenance of the temperature of the soil and an extra contribution of aromatic minerals. On the island, sublime sweet wines are produced from malvasía grapes, a vestige of the historical Canary Sack.

NUMBER OF HECTARES: 1.995

ALTITUDES: < 670 m.

PREDOMINANT VARIETIES:

White grapes: malvasía, pedro ximénez, diego, listán blanco, muscatel and burrablanca breval. Red grapes: listán negra and negramoll

CLIMATOLOGY AND SOILS

Subtropical dry, with volcanic sandy soil.

BODEGA STRATVS

Ctra. La Geria, Km. 18
35570 Yaiza - (Las Palmas)
☎: +34 928 809 977 - Fax: +34 928 524 651
bodega@stratvs.com
www.stratvs.com

STRATVS 2010 T
40% tinta conejera, 60% listán negro

90 Colour: cherry, garnet rim. Nose: balanced, expressive, ripe fruit, scrubland. Palate: balanced, fine bitter notes, balsamic.

STRATVS MALVASÍA NATURALMENTE DULCE S/C B
100% malvasía

94 Colour: old gold. Nose: elegant, expressive, faded flowers, candied fruit, sweet spices, honeyed notes. Palate: rich, flavourful, long.

STRATVS MALVASÍA SECO 2010
100% malvasía

91 Colour: bright yellow. Nose: white flowers, ripe fruit, balanced, varietal, expressive. Palate: flavourful, rich, fruity, balanced, fine bitter notes, good acidity.

STRATVS MOSCATEL DULCE 2010 B
moscatel de alejandría

90 Colour: bright yellow. Nose: medium intensity, citrus fruit, floral, varietal. Palate: balanced, good acidity, long.

STRATVS MOSCATEL LICOR S/C B
moscatel de alejandría

92 Colour: light mahogany. Nose: candied fruit, expressive, powerfull, sweet spices, pattiserie, caramel. Palate: balanced, unctuous, complex.

STRATVS MOSCATEL SEMIDULCE 2010 B
85% moscatel, 15% diego

91 Colour: bright yellow. Nose: white flowers, expressive, varietal, neat. Palate: good acidity.

BODEGA VULCANO DE LANZAROTE

Victor Fernández Gopar, 5
35572 Tías - (Las Palmas)
☎: +34 928 834 456 - Fax: +34 928 524 384
info@bodegavulcano.es
www.bodegavulcano.es

VULCANO DOLCE 2011 B
moscatel de alejandría

90 Colour: bright yellow. Nose: candied fruit, honeyed notes, varietal, pattiserie. Palate: flavourful, balanced, unctuous.

BODEGAS LOS BERMEJOS

Camino a Los Bermejos, 7
35550 San Bartolomé de Lanzarote - (Las Palmas)
☎: +34 928 522 463 - Fax: +34 928 522 641
bodegas@losbermejos.com
www.losbermejos.com

BERMEJO MALVASIA NATURALMENTE DULCE S/C B
malvasía

93 Colour: bright yellow. Nose: complex, expressive, balanced, toasty, candied fruit, acetaldehyde. Palate: balanced, good structure, flavourful.

BODEGAS RUBICÓN

Ctra. Teguise - Yaiza, 2
35570 La Geria - Yaiza - (Las Palmas)
☎: +34 928 173 708
bodegasrubicon@gmail.com
www.vinosrubicon.com

SWEET GOLD 2009 B

91 Colour: bright yellow. Nose: balanced, expressive, white flowers, sweet spices, honeyed notes. Palate: rich, flavourful, full.

EL GRIFO

Lugar de El Grifo, s/n
35550 San Bartolomé - (Las Palmas de Gran Canaria)
☎: +34 928 524 036 - Fax: +34 928 832 634
malvasia@elgrifo.com
www.elgrifo.com

ARIANA 2010 T
60% listán negro, 40% syrah

93 Colour: deep cherry, purple rim. Nose: red berry notes, ripe fruit, wild herbs, sweet spices. Palate: flavourful, fruity, correct.

EL GRIFO CANARI DULCE DE LICOR S/C B
100% malvasía

95 Colour: old gold, amber rim. Nose: pattiserie, complex, expressive, candied fruit, acetaldehyde, floral, sweet spices. Palate: flavourful, elegant, rich, full.

DESCRIPTION

This is in the province of Málaga, in the south of Spain and is composed of five regions with different microclimates, outstanding among which is Axarquía, an interesting eastern zone with slate soils where complex sweet wines are produced with muscatel grapes, and the Sierra de Ronda, at an altitude of over 750 metres, where interesting red wines are produced with long cycle and Mediterranean grapes. These wines are the new generation of an ancient region which has always been outstanding for its sweet Málaga wines produced from the local variety of pedro ximénez dehydrated grapes.

NUMBER OF HECTARES: 1.320 **ALTITUDES:** 0 m. – 1.000 m.

PREDOMINANT VARIETIES:

Red grapes DO Sierras de Málaga: romé, cabernet sauvignon, merlot, syrah, tempranillo and petit verdot. White grapes Denomination of Origin Málaga: pedro ximénez and muscatel. Denomination of Origin Sierras de Málaga: chardonnay, muscatel, pedro ximénez, macabeo and sauvignon blanc.

CLIMATOLOGY AND SOILS

Dry-sub-humid, with mainly red soils with slate.

BODEGA ANTIGUA CASA DE GUARDIA

Ctra. Olias - Comares- El Romerillo
29197 - (Málaga)
☎: +34 952 030 714 - Fax: +34 952 252 150
info@casadeguardia.com
www.casadeguardia.com

ISABEL II TRASAÑEJO
100% moscatel de alejandría

93 Colour: mahogany. Nose: aromatic coffee, creamy oak, sweet spices, roasted almonds, candied fruit. Palate: flavourful, full, long.

VERDIALES CONARTE VINO DE LICOR DULCE
70% pedro ximénez, 30% moscatel de alejandría

90 Colour: mahogany. Nose: sweet spices, creamy oak, pattiserie, dark chocolate. Palate: flavourful, sweet, rich, spicy.

BODEGA KIENINGER

Los Frontones, 67
29400 Ronda - (Málaga)
☎: +34 952 879 554
martin@bodegakieninger.com
www.bodegakieninger.com

VINANA CUVÉE COUPAGE 2010 T
cabernet sauvignon, cabernet franc, pinot noir, merlot

91 Color cherry, garnet rim. Aroma ripe fruit, spicy, creamy oak, toasty, complex. Taste powerful, flavourful, toasty, round tannins.

BODEGA LOS BUJEOS

Ctra. Ronda El Burgo, Km 1
29400 Ronda - (Málaga)
☎: +34 610 269 422 - Fax: +34 952 161 160
bodegapasoslargos@gmail.com
www.bodegapasoslargos.com

A PASOS 2008 T

90 Color bright cherry. Aroma ripe fruit, sweet spices, creamy oak, expressive. Taste flavourful, fruity, toasty, round tannins.

PASOS LARGOS 2005 T ROBLE
cabernet sauvignon, petit verdot, merlot, syrah

91 Colour: cherry, garnet rim. Nose: dark chocolate, aromatic coffee, ripe fruit. Palate: flavourful, good structure, round tannins, spicy.

BODEGA VETAS

Camino Nador " El Baco", s/n
29350 Arriate - (Málaga)
☎: +34 647 177 620
info@bodegavetas.com
www.bodegavetas.com

VETAS PETIT VERDOT 2004 T
100% petit verdot

92 Colour: cherry, garnet rim. Nose: expressive, medium intensity, ripe fruit, spicy, mineral. Palate: flavourful, balanced, spicy.

VETAS PETIT VERDOT 2006 T
100% petit verdot,

93 Colour: deep cherry, garnet rim. Nose: elegant, balanced, creamy oak, sweet spices, dried herbs. Palate: good structure, round tannins, long.

VETAS SELECCIÓN 2005 T
cabernet franc, cabernet sauvignon, petit verdot

93 Colour: cherry, garnet rim. Nose: medium intensity, ripe fruit, scrubland, sweet spices, earthy notes. Palate: balanced, powerful.

VETAS SELECCIÓN 2006 T
cabernet franc, cabernet sauvignon, petit verdot

93 Colour: black cherry, garnet rim. Nose: balanced, expressive, ripe fruit, cocoa bean, creamy oak. Palate: flavourful, good structure, fruity, long, round tannins.

BODEGAS BENTOMIZ

Finca Almendro - Pago Cuesta Robano
29752 Sayalonga - (Málaga)
☎: +34 658 845 285
info.bodegasbentomiz@gmail.com
www.bodegasbentomiz.com

ARIYANAS NATURALMENTE DULCE
2008 BLANCO DULCE
100% moscatel de alejandría

92 Colour: bright yellow. Nose: candied fruit, faded flowers, dried herbs. Palate: balanced, rich, long.

ARIYANAS TERRUÑO PIZARROSO 2008 B
moscatel de alejandría

94 Colour: old gold. Nose: candied fruit, honeyed notes, white flowers, sweet spices, citrus fruit. Palate: flavourful, balanced, complex.

BODEGAS GOMARA

Diseminado Maqueda Alto, 59
29590 Maqueda - Campanillas - (Málaga)
☎: +34 952 434 195 - Fax: +34 952 626 312
bodegas@gomara.com
www.gomara.com

GRAN GOMARA TRASAÑEJO SOLERA
70% pedro ximénez, 30% moscatel de alejandría

92 Colour: mahogany. Nose: acetaldehyde, varnish, dark chocolate, sweet spices, fruit liqueur notes. Palate: full, flavourful, complex, long, balanced.

MÁLAGA TRASAÑEJO GOMARA TRASAÑEJO
100% pedro ximénez

90 Colour: dark mahogany. Nose: balanced, cocoa bean, pattiserie, candied fruit. Palate: flavourful, long, spirituous, complex.

BODEGAS JORGE ORDÓÑEZ & CO

Bartolome Esteban Murillo, 11
29700 Velez-Málaga - (Málaga)
☎: +34 952 504 706 - Fax: +34 951 284 796
office@jorge-ordonez.es
www.jorge-ordonez.es

JORGE ORDÓÑEZ & CO BOTANI 2011 B
100% moscatel de alejandría

92 Colour: bright straw. Nose: fresh, fresh fruit, white flowers, expressive. Palate: flavourful, fruity, balanced, good acidity, round.

JORGE ORDÓÑEZ & CO Nº 1 SELECCIÓN
ESPECIAL 2010 B
moscatel de alejandría

93 Colour: bright straw. Nose: white flowers, fragrant herbs, candied fruit, citrus fruit, elegant. Palate: fresh, fruity, rich, flavourful, round.

JORGE ORDÓÑEZ & CO Nº 2 VICTORIA
2010 BLANCO DULCE
moscatel de alejandría

94 Colour: bright yellow. Nose: pattiserie, candied fruit, honeyed notes, floral, mineral, expressive. Palate: fruity, complex, flavourful, good acidity, unctuous, long, sweet, elegant.

JORGE ORDÓÑEZ & CO. Nº3 VIÑAS VIEJAS 2008 B
moscatel de alejandría

96 Colour: golden. Nose: powerfull, floral, honeyed notes, candied fruit, fragrant herbs. Palate: flavourful, sweet, fresh, fruity, good acidity, long, balanced.

BODEGAS MÁLAGA VIRGEN

Autovía A-92, Málaga-Sevilla, Km. 132
29520 Fuente de Piedra - (Málaga)
☎: +34 952 319 454 - Fax: +34 952 359 819
didier.bricout@bodegasmalagavirgen.com
www.bodegasmalagavirgen.com

CHORRERA CREAM AÑEJO

91 Colour: mahogany. Nose: cocoa bean, roasted almonds, pattiserie, candied fruit, complex. Palate: flavourful, rich, good structure, long.

DON JUAN TRASAÑEJO

93 Colour: dark mahogany. Nose: complex, expressive, aromatic coffee, caramel, creamy oak, pattiserie. Palate: flavourful, creamy, long.

MOSCATEL 30 AÑOS MOSCATEL

93 Colour: mahogany. Nose: complex, expressive, candied fruit, fruit liqueur notes, honeyed notes, varnish, pattiserie, tobacco. Palate: unctuous, long, spicy, toasty.

PEDRO XIMÉNEZ RESERVA DE FAMILIA PX

91 Colour: light mahogany. Nose: candied fruit, medium intensity, cocoa bean, varietal. Palate: long, flavourful, sweet, correct.

SECO TRASAÑEJO B

93 Colour: old gold. Nose: toasty, fruit liqueur notes, candied fruit, honeyed notes, sweet spices, acetaldehyde. Palate: full, flavourful, spicy, elegant, fine bitter notes.

COMPAÑÍA DE VINOS TELMO RODRÍGUEZ

El Monte
1308 Lanciego - (Álava)
☎: +34 945 628 315 - Fax: +34 945 628 314
contact@telmorodriguez.com
www.telmorodriguez.com

MOLINO REAL 2008 B
100% moscatel

96 Color golden. Aroma powerfull, floral, honeyed notes, candied fruit, fragrant herbs. Taste flavourful, sweet, fresh, fruity, good acidity, long.

MOUNTAIN 2010 B
moscatel

93 Colour: bright straw. Nose: fresh, fresh fruit, white flowers, varietal. Palate: flavourful, fruity, good acidity, balanced.

MR 2010 B
100% moscatel

93 Colour: bright yellow. Nose: candied fruit, fruit expression, citrus fruit, white flowers. Palate: flavourful, sweet, fruity, fresh.

CORTIJO LOS AGUILARES

Ctra. Ronda a Campillo, km. 5
29400 Ronda - (Málaga)
☎: +34 952 874 457 - Fax: +34 951 166 000
info@cortijolosaguilares.com
www.cortijolosaguilares.com

CORTIJO LOS AGUILARES PAGO EL ESPINO 2008 T
25% tempranillo, 25% merlot, 29% petit verdot, 21% cabernet sauvignon

91 Colour: cherry, garnet rim. Nose: sweet spices, creamy oak, ripe fruit, cocoa bean. Palate: good structure, ripe fruit, long, good acidity.

CORTIJO LOS AGUILARES PINOT NOIR 2011 T
pinot noir

93 Colour: bright cherry, purple rim. Nose: floral, red berry notes, expressive. Palate: flavourful, fruity, good acidity, fine bitter notes. Personality.

CORTIJO LOS AGUILARES TADEO 2008 T
petit verdot

94 Colour: deep cherry, garnet rim. Nose: complex, elegant, expressive, sweet spices. Palate: full, good structure, ripe fruit, long, round tannins.

CORTIJO LOS AGUILARES TADEO 2009 T
100% petit verdot

94 Colour: cherry, garnet rim. Nose: fruit preserve, sweet spices, cocoa bean, creamy oak. Palate: balanced, long, round tannins.

DESCALZOS VIEJOS

Finca Descalzos Viejos- Partido de los Molinos, s/n
29400 Ronda - (Málaga)
☎: +34 952 874 696 - Fax: +34 952 874 696
info@descalzosviejos.com
www.descalzosviejos.com

DV CONARTE 2007 TC
petit verdot, cabernet sauvignon, syrah, merlot

92 Colour: deep cherry, garnet rim. Nose: medium intensity, creamy oak, sweet spices, ripe fruit. Palate: complex, good structure, flavourful, long, round tannins.

FINCA LA MELONERA

Paraje Los Frontones, Camino Ronda-Setenil s/n
29400 Ronda - (Malaga)
☎: +34 932 097 514 - Fax: +34 932 011 068
info@lamelonera.com
www.lamelonera.com

PAYOYA NEGRA 2009 T
garnacha, tintilla de rota

92 Colour: cherry, garnet rim. Nose: balanced, cocoa bean, ripe fruit, earthy notes. Palate: good structure, fruity, long, good acidity, round tannins.

LA DONAIRA

Pza. Portugal, 23
29400 Ronda - (Málaga)
☎: +34 678 733 286
info@mapa7g.com
www.ladonaira.com

LA DONAIRA PETIT VERDOT CABERNET FRANC 2009 T
petit verdot, cabernet franc

91 Colour: deep cherry, garnet rim. Nose: sweet spices, creamy oak, cocoa bean, fruit preserve. Palate: full, ripe fruit, toasty, long.

DESCRIPTION

This is situated to the southeast of the province of Cuenca and to the northeast of Albacete. The influence of the sea forms the temperatures of the vines and especially favours maturing, leading to more tasty and complex wines. The most relevant grape is the bobal, the promising new Spanish wine after having eliminated its past bulk wine production. It produces a volume of litres which can compete with La Mancha and Ribera del Guadiana in Extremadura.

NUMBER OF HECTARES: 4.139 **ALTITUDES:** 600 m. – 700 m.

PREDOMINANT VARIETIES:

White grapes: albillo, chardonnay, macabeo, sauvignon blanc, verdejo, pardillo, viognier and small grained muscatel.

Red grapes: cencibel, garnacha, moravia dulce, moravia agría, cabernet sauvignon, merlot, syrah, petit verdot, cabernet franc, graciano, malbec, rojal, frasco and pinot noir.

CLIMATOLOGY AND SOILS

The predominant climate is continental, with clay-limestone soils.

ALTOLANDÓN

Ctra. N-330, km. 242
16330 Landete - (Cuenca)
☎: +34 962 300 662 - Fax: +34 962 300 662
altolandon@altolandon.com
www.altolandon.com

ALTOLANDÓN 2010 BFB
petit manseng, chardonnay

92 Colour: bright golden. Nose: white flowers, fruit expression, citrus fruit, sweet spices, creamy oak. Palate: elegant, fruity, flavourful, balanced.

RAYUELO 2009 T
80% bobal, 20% malbec, monastrell

92 Colour: cherry, purple rim. Nose: floral, red berry notes, citrus fruit, scrubland, spicy, creamy oak. Palate: flavourful, fruity, long, toasty.

BODEGA CIEN Y PICO

San Francisco, 19
2240 Mahora - (Albacete)
☎: +34 967 494 336 - Fax: +34 967 494 336
luisjimenaz@gmail.com
www.cienypico.com

CIEN Y PICO KNIGHTS-ERRANT 2008 T
100% garnacha tintorera

90 Color cherry, garnet rim. Aroma ripe fruit, spicy, creamy oak, toasty, complex. Taste powerful, flavourful, toasty, round tannins.

BODEGA INIESTA

C/ Andres Iniesta, 2
2260 Fuentealbilla - (Albacete)
☎: +34 967 090 650 - Fax: +34 967 090 651
info@bodegainiesta.com
www.bodegainiesta.com

FINCA EL CARRIL 2010 T ROBLE
tempranillo, petit verdot

90 Colour: bright cherry. Nose: ripe fruit, sweet spices, expressive, dark chocolate, mineral. Palate: flavourful, fruity, toasty, round tannins.

BODEGAS Y VIÑEDOS PONCE

La Virgen, 34
16235 Iniesta - (Cuenca)
☎: +34 677 434 523 - Fax: +34 967 220 876
bodegasponce@gmail.com

CLOS LOJEN 2011 T
100% bobal

92 Colour: cherry, purple rim. Nose: red berry notes, raspberry, floral, balsamic herbs, expressive. Palate: light-bodied, fresh, fruity, flavourful, easy to drink.

LA CASILLA (ESTRECHA) 2010 T
100% bobal

92 Colour: cherry, garnet rim. Nose: balanced, red berry notes, ripe fruit, violets, scrubland. Palate: fruity, good structure.

P.F. 2010 T
100% bobal

93 Colour: cherry, garnet rim. Nose: powerfull, ripe fruit, scrubland, spicy. Palate: good structure, fruity, fine bitter notes, harsh oak tannins.

PINO 2010 T
bobal

94 Colour: cherry, garnet rim. Nose: mineral, ripe fruit, sweet spices, expressive. Palate: flavourful, fruity, round tannins.

FINCA SANDOVAL

Ctra. CM-3222, Km. 26,800
16237 Ledaña - (Cuenca)
☎: +34 616 444 805
fincasandoval@gmail.com
www.grandespagos.com

FINCA SANDOVAL 2008 T
77% syrah, 16% monastrell, 7% bobal

94 Colour: cherry, garnet rim. Nose: ripe fruit, spicy, creamy oak, toasty, complex, mineral. Palate: powerful, flavourful, toasty, round tannins.

FINCA SANDOVAL CUVEE TNS MAGNUM 2008 T
67% touriga nacional, 33% syrah

95 Colour: cherry, garnet rim. Nose: earthy notes, red berry notes, ripe fruit, sweet spices, creamy oak, balanced, expressive. Palate: elegant, flavourful, complex, long, fine tannins.

SALIA 2009 T

93 Colour: cherry, garnet rim. Nose: red berry notes, ripe fruit, aromatic coffee, spicy, expressive. Palate: powerful, flavourful, complex, long, toasty.

SIGNO BOBAL 2009 T
bobal

93 Colour: cherry, garnet rim. Nose: red berry notes, earthy notes, spicy, balanced, expressive. Palate: powerful, flavourful, complex, long, toasty.

SIGNO GARNACHA 2010 T
garnacha

93 Colour: cherry, garnet rim. Nose: red berry notes, ripe fruit, mineral, sweet spices, creamy oak. Palate: powerful, flavourful, complex, long, toasty.

DESCRIPTION

This is located in the northern zone of the province of Toledo, it borders to the north with the provinces of Ávila and Madrid. These were the most popular wines in the taverns of Madrid until they were replaced by the wines of Ribera del Duero and La Mancha in the XIX century. Until only a few years ago, the garnacha which had an excess of alcohol and oxidation has become more refined thanks to new wine growers who chose vineyards at a higher altitude and ageing periods which evoke French wines.

NUMBER OF HECTARES: 8.833 **ALTITUDES:** 400 m. – 700 m.

PREDOMINANT VARIETIES:

White grapes: albillo, viura, sauvignon blanc and chardonnay.
Red grapes: garnacha, cencibel, cabernet sauvignon, merlot, syrah and petit verdot.

CLIMATOLOGY AND SOILS

This is a continental type which is dry and extreme, the soil is sand-clay with medium to loose texture.

ALONSO CUESTA

Pza. de la Constitución, 4
45920 La Torre de Esteban Hambrán - (Toledo)
☎: +34 925 795 742 - Fax: +34 925 795 742
comercial@alonsocuesta.com
www.alonsocuesta.com

ALONSO CUESTA 2009 T
garnacha, tempranillo, cabernet sauvignon

93 Color cherry, garnet rim. Aroma ripe fruit, spicy, creamy oak, toasty, complex. Taste powerful, flavourful, toasty, round tannins.

BODEGAS ARRAYÁN

Finca La Verdosa
45513 Santa Cruz del Retamar - (Toledo)
☎: +34 916 633 131 - Fax: +34 916 632 796
comercial@arrayan.es
www.arrayan.es

ARRAYÁN PETIT VERDOT 2009 T
100% petit verdot

90 Colour: cherry, garnet rim. Nose: ripe fruit, fruit expression, scrubland. Palate: toasty, fine bitter notes, good acidity.

ARRAYÁN PREMIUM 2008 T
syrah, merlot, cabernet sauvignon, petit verdot

91 Colour: deep cherry. Nose: spicy, fruit liqueur notes, ripe fruit, toasty, dark chocolate. Palate: flavourful, good acidity, fine bitter notes.

ESTELA DE ARRAYÁN 2008 T
syrah, merlot, cabernet sauvignon, petit verdot

93 Colour: very deep cherry. Nose: powerfull, characterful, ripe fruit, toasty, sweet spices. Palate: spicy, ripe fruit, fine bitter notes, good acidity.

BODEGAS CANOPY

Avda. Barber, 71
45004 - (Toledo)
☎: +34 619 244 878 - Fax: +34 925 283 681
achacon@bodegascanopy.com

CONGO 2009 T
100% garnacha

93 Colour: bright cherry. Nose: red berry notes, overripe fruit, balsamic herbs, scrubland. Palate: flavourful, light-bodied, good acidity.

LA VIÑA ESCONDIDA 2008 T
garnacha

94 Colour: cherry, garnet rim. Nose: balsamic herbs, scrubland, ripe fruit, warm, characterful. Palate: flavourful, powerful, fine bitter notes, good acidity.

LOCO 2011 B
garnacha blanca

93 Colour: bright straw. Nose: white flowers, ripe fruit, fine lees. Palate: flavourful, powerful, good acidity, long, round.

MALPASO 2008 T
syrah

94 Colour: very deep cherry. Nose: sweet spices, mineral, balsamic herbs, scrubland, floral. Palate: flavourful, fine bitter notes, good acidity, round tannins.

TRES PATAS 2008 T
90% garnacha, 10% syrah

93 Colour: cherry, garnet rim. Nose: expressive, red berry notes, sweet spices, scrubland, mineral. Palate: flavourful, powerful, fine bitter notes, good acidity.

BODEGAS JIMÉNEZ LANDI

Avda. Solana, 39-41
45930 Méntrida - (Toledo)
☎: +34 918 178 213 - Fax: +34 918 178 213
jose@jimenezlandi.com
www.jimenezlandi.com

ATAULFOS 2010 T
garnacha

96 Colour: light cherry. Nose: dried flowers, candied fruit, fruit liqueur notes, cocoa bean, dark chocolate, sweet spices, mineral. Palate: flavourful, long, round, balanced, ripe fruit, sweetness.

PIÉLAGO 2010 T
garnacha

94 Colour: cherry, garnet rim. Nose: dry stone, wild herbs, balsamic herbs, spicy, creamy oak, expressive. Palate: complex, flavourful, spicy, mineral, elegant, balanced.

SOTORRONDERO 2010 T
garnacha, syrah

93 Colour: cherry, garnet rim. Nose: ripe fruit, fruit preserve, balsamic herbs, mineral. Palate: long, spicy, flavourful, fine bitter notes, balanced.

THE END 2010 T
garnacha

95 Colour: ruby red, orangey edge. Nose: scrubland, red berry notes, ripe fruit, earthy notes, mineral, creamy oak. Palate: elegant, round, good acidity, flavourful, fresh, fruity, complex.

DO MONDÉJAR

DESCRIPTION

This Denomination of Origin is composed of only two exclusive wineries. It is located in the southwest of the province of Guadalajara, and belongs to the Autonomous Community of Castile La Mancha.

NUMBER OF HECTARES: 600 **ALTITUDES:** 800 m.

PREDOMINANT VARIETIES:
White grapes: malvar.
Red grapes: cencibel.

CLIMATOLOGY AND SOILS

It has a temperate Mediterranean climate with average temperatures of around 18ºC. Its soils vary between red with silt-clay sediment with gravel (south zone) and brown-limestone on loam and sandstone (north zone).

None of the wines tasted achieve the minimum required scoring

DESCRIPTION

The Denomination of Origin Monterrei is a zone of white wines, similar to its Galicia family. However, red wines have come to predominate over the native varieties. Geographically it is situated to the southeast of the province of Ourense, a zone where the vineyards share the freshness of the wines of Galicia and the full bodied wines of the climate of Castile - León.

NUMBER OF HECTARES: 400 **ALTITUDES:** 400 m. – 700 m.

PREDOMINANT VARIETIES:

White grapes: dona blanca, verdello and treixadura.

Red grapes: mencía, merenzao, arauxa, caiño tinto and sousón.

CLIMATOLOGY AND SOILS

Atlantic - continental. The soils are mainly clay, deep, rather heavy and in some places quite sandy.

ALMA ATLÁNTICA

Ctra. N- 525
36618 Albarellos de Monterrei - (Ourense)
☎: +34 986 526 040 - Fax: +34 986 526 901
comercial@martincodax.com
www.almaatlantica.com

MARA MARTIN GODELLO 2011 B
100% godello

90 Colour: bright straw. Nose: fresh, fresh fruit, white flowers, fragrant herbs, expressive. Palate: flavourful, fruity, good acidity, balanced.

BODEGA GARGALO

Rua Do Castelo, 59
32619 Pazos Verín - (Ourense)
☎: +34 988 590 203 - Fax: +34 988 590 295
gargalo@verino.es
www.gargalo.es

GARGALO ALBARIÑO & TREIXADURA 2011 B
albariño, treixadura

90 Colour: bright straw. Nose: fresh, expressive, ripe fruit, citrus fruit, grassy. Palate: flavourful, fruity, good acidity, balanced.

GARGALO GODELLO 2011 B
godello

91 Colour: bright straw. Nose: fresh, white flowers, ripe fruit, mineral. Palate: flavourful, fruity, good acidity, balanced.

TERRA DO GARGALO SOBRE LÍAS 2011 B
godello, treixadura

91 Colour: bright straw. Nose: fresh, white flowers, expressive, lactic notes, ripe fruit. Palate: flavourful, fruity, good acidity, balanced.

BODEGAS ABANICO

Pol. Ind Ca l'Avellanet - Susany, 6
8553 Seva - (Barcelona)
☎: +34 938 125 676 - Fax: +34 938 123 213
info@exportiberia.com
www.bodegasabanico.com

VIÑA TOEN 2011 B
50% godello, 50% treixadura

90 Colour: bright straw. Nose: white flowers, fresh fruit, dried herbs, expressive. Palate: balanced, fine bitter notes, flavourful, fruity, long.

BODEGAS Y VIÑEDOS QUINTA DA MURADELLA

Avda. Luis Espada, 99- Entresuelo, dcha.
32600 Verín - (Ourense)
☎: +34 988 411 724 - Fax: +34 988 590 427
muradella@verin.net

GORVIA 2010 T
100% mencía

92 Colour: bright cherry. Nose: mineral, earthy notes, balsamic herbs, scrubland, fruit expression. Palate: flavourful, fruity, fresh, good acidity.

GORVIA FERMENTADO EN BARRICA 2010 BFB
100% dona blanca

92 Colour: bright golden. Nose: balanced, floral, wild herbs, spicy, creamy oak, expressive. Palate: round, fine bitter notes, powerful, flavourful, balanced.

MURADELLA 2010 T
mencía, bastardo, sousón

91 Colour: deep cherry. Nose: mineral, fruit expression, spicy, floral. Palate: flavourful, fruity, fine bitter notes, good acidity.

MURADELLA 2011 B
treixadura, dona blanca

91 Colour: bright yellow. Nose: spicy, creamy oak, dried herbs, floral, ripe fruit, mineral. Palate: balsamic, long, powerful, flavourful, spicy.

CREGO E MONAGUILLO S.L.

Rua Nova, 24
32618 Salgueira - (Ourense)
☎: +34 988 418 164 - Fax: +34 988 418 164
tito@cregoemonaguillo.com
www.cregoemonaguillo.com

CREGO E MONAGUILLO 2011 T
mencía, arauxa

90 Colour: cherry, purple rim. Nose: red berry notes, floral, ripe fruit. Palate: flavourful, good acidity, ripe fruit.

MAROVA 2010 B
treixadura, godello

90 Colour: bright straw. Nose: ripe fruit, citrus fruit, sweet spices. Palate: flavourful, fruity, fine bitter notes, good acidity.

MANUEL GUERRA JUSTO

Ctra. Albarellos, 61
32618 Villaza (Monterrei) - (Ourense)
☎: +34 687 409 618
viaarxentea@viaarxentea.com

VÍA ARXÉNTEA 2011 B
treixadura, godello

91 Colour: bright yellow. Nose: white flowers, fragrant herbs, citrus fruit, fresh fruit, balanced. Palate: powerful, flavourful, fruity, complex.

PAZO BLANCO S.L. (TAPIAS-MARIÑÁN)

Ctra. N-525, Km. 170,4
32619 Pazos - (Ourense)
☎: +34 988 411 693 - Fax: +34 988 411 693
pazoblanco@yahoo.es
www.tapiasmarinhan.com

QUINTAS DAS TAPIAS 2011 B
treixadura, godello, albariño

90 Colour: bright straw. Nose: floral, fresh fruit, citrus fruit, grassy. Palate: flavourful, fruity, fresh, full.

PAZOS DEL REY

Carrero Blanco, 33- Albarellos
32618 Monterrei - (Ourense)
☎: +34 988 425 959 - Fax: +34 988 425 949
info@pazosdelrey.com
www.pazosdelrey.com

PAZO DE MONTERREY 2011 B
godello

90 Colour: bright straw. Nose: expressive, ripe fruit, citrus fruit, grassy, balsamic herbs. Palate: flavourful, fruity, fresh.

DESCRIPTION

This extends over a large part of the south of the province of Córdoba. Amontillado was created in Montilla. This is a wine which comes from the name of this Denomination of Origin and, according to historical information, it was probably the origin of the wines created by the system of criaderas and soleras in Jerez. 90% of the vineyards are occupied by the pedro ximénez variety, which gives rise to the most characteristic wines of Montilla. They are different from the sweet Sherry wines because the full bodied wines of this zone are not fortified with alcohol and their aromas are direct and natural.

NUMBER OF HECTARES: 6.250 **ALTITUDES:** 125 m. – 640 m.

PREDOMINANT VARIETIES:

White grapes: pedro ximénez, airén, baladí, muscatel, torrontés and verdejo.
Red grapes: tempranillo, syrah and cabernet sauvignon.

CLIMATOLOGY AND SOILS

Semi-continental Mediterranean with loam and loam-sand soils. In the higher zones, the soils are of a limestone type.

ALVEAR

María Auxiliadora, 1
14550 Montilla - (Córdoba)
☎: +34 957 650 100 - Fax: +34 957 650 135
alvearsa@alvear.es
www.alvear.es

ALVEAR DULCE VIEJO PX RESERVA
100% pedro ximénez

94 Colour: dark mahogany. Nose: dried fruit, complex, varietal, expressive, aromatic coffee, tobacco. Palate: concentrated, rich, good structure.

ALVEAR FINO EN RAMA 2006 FI
100% pedro ximénez

90 Colour: bright yellow. Nose: complex, expressive, saline, pungent, faded flowers. Palate: fresh, easy to drink, long, fine bitter notes.

ALVEAR PX 1830 PX RESERVA
100% pedro ximénez

98 Colour: dark mahogany. Nose: complex, dried fruit, pattiserie, toasty, acetaldehyde, tobacco. Palate: sweet, rich, unctuous, powerful.

ALVEAR PX 1927 S/C PX SOLERA
100% pedro ximénez

90 Colour: dark mahogany. Nose: fruit liqueur notes, pattiserie, toasty, acetaldehyde, varnish, dry nuts, dried fruit. Palate: sweet, rich, unctuous, flavourful, long, toasty.

ALVEAR PX COSECHA 2008 PX
100% pedro ximénez

90 Colour: light mahogany. Nose: fruit liqueur notes, fruit liqueur notes, expressive, powerfull, caramel, pattiserie. Palate: balanced, unctuous.

ALVEAR SOLERA CREAM CR
100% pedro ximénez

90 Colour: light mahogany. Nose: spicy, dry nuts, acetaldehyde, candied fruit, cocoa bean. Palate: complex, flavourful, long, elegant, balanced.

ALVEAR SOLERA FUNDACIÓN AM
100% pedro ximénez

94 Colour: light mahogany. Nose: complex, powerfull, neat, caramel, acetaldehyde, sweet spices. Palate: good structure, rich, full, fine bitter notes.

ASUNCIÓN OL
100% pedro ximénez

91 Colour: light mahogany. Nose: elegant, candied fruit, sweet spices, caramel. Palate: complex, rich, full, fine bitter notes.

C.B. FI
100% pedro ximénez

90 Colour: bright straw. Nose: pungent, saline, floral, dry nuts, complex, expressive. Palate: flavourful, long, fine bitter notes, elegant.

CARLOS VII AM
100% pedro ximénez

90 Colour: old gold. Nose: balanced, sweet spices, candied fruit. Palate: balanced, fine bitter notes, flavourful.

BODEGAS CRUZ CONDE

Ronda Canillo, 4
14550 Montilla - (Córdoba)
☎: +34 957 651 250 - Fax: +34 957 653 619
info@bodegascruzconde.es
www.bodegascruzconde.es

CRUZ CONDE SOLERA FUNDACIÓN 1902 PX
pedro ximénez

92 Colour: mahogany. Nose: complex, tobacco, dark chocolate, pattiserie, dried fruit. Palate: flavourful, balanced, unctuous, spicy.

BODEGAS DELGADO

Cosano, 2
14500 Puente Genil - (Córdoba)
☎: +34 957 600 085 - Fax: +34 957 604 571
fino@bodegasdelgado.com
www.bodegasdelgado.com

DELGADO 1874 PX
pedro ximénez

94 Colour: dark mahogany. Nose: complex, powerfull, dark chocolate, pattiserie, expressive, varnish. Palate: fruity, flavourful, spicy, creamy.

DELGADO 1874 AMONTILLADO NATURAL MUY VIEJO AM
100% pedro ximénez

90 Colour: old gold, amber rim. Nose: acetaldehyde, sweet spices, cocoa bean, caramel. Palate: long, spicy, rich, flavourful.

BODEGAS LA AURORA

Avda. de Europa, 7
14550 Montilla - (Córdoba)
☎: +34 957 650 362 - Fax: +34 957 654 642
administracion@bodegaslaaurora.com
www.bodegaslaaurora.com

SOLERA 1981 PX

91 Colour: mahogany. Nose: toasty, sweet spices, fruit liqueur notes, fruit liqueur notes, dark chocolate. Palate: flavourful, unctuous.

BODEGAS MORENO

Fuente de la Salud, 2
14006 - (Córdoba)
☎: +34 957 767 605 - Fax: +34 957 279 907
moreno@morenosa.com
www.morenosa.com

MUSA OL
100% pedro ximénez

90 Colour: light mahogany. Nose: medium intensity, sweet spices, cocoa bean, candied fruit. Palate: flavourful, spicy, fine bitter notes.

PLATINO SOLERA OLOROSA OL
100% pedro ximénez

90 Color iodine, amber rim. Aroma powerfull, complex, elegant, dry nuts, toasty. Taste rich, fine bitter notes, fine solera notes, long, spicy.

VIRGILIO PX
100% pedro ximénez

90 Colour: dark mahogany. Nose: dried fruit, honeyed notes, caramel, aromatic coffee, dark chocolate. Palate: rich, flavourful.

BODEGAS ROBLES

Ctra. Córdoba-Málaga, Km. 44,7
14550 Montilla - (Córdoba)
☎: +34 957 650 063 - Fax: +34 957 653 140
info@bodegasrobles.com
www.bodegasrobles.com

SELECCIÓN ROBLES 1927 PX PX

90 Colour: dark mahogany. Nose: complex, dried fruit, toasty, fruit liqueur notes, dark chocolate, aromatic coffee. Palate: sweet, rich, unctuous, powerful.

CÍA. VINÍCOLA DEL SUR - TOMÁS GARCÍA

Avda. Luis de Góngora y Argote, s/n
14550 Montilla - (Córdoba)
☎: +34 957 650 204 - Fax: +34 957 652 335
info@vinicoladelsur.com
www.vinicoladelsur.com

MONTE CRISTO OL
100% pedro ximénez

92 Colour: iodine, amber rim. Nose: powerfull, toasty, sweet spices. Palate: rich, fine bitter notes, , balanced, long.

EQUIPO NAVAZOS

Cartuja, 1 - módulo 6
11401 Jerez de la Frontera - (Cádiz)
equipo@navazos.com
www.equiponavazos.com

CASA DEL INCA 2010 PX
pedro ximénez

95 Colour: mahogany. Nose: candied fruit, dried fruit, balanced, sweet spices, pattiserie. Palate: rich, concentrated, long, balanced.

GRACIA HERMANOS

Avda. Marqués de la Vega de Armijo, 103
14550 Montilla - (Córdoba)
☎: +34 957 650 162 - Fax: +34 957 652 335
info@bodegasgracia.com
www.bodegasgracia.com

TAUROMAQUIA PX
100% pedro ximénez

90 Color dark mahogany. Aroma complex, fruit liqueur notes, dried fruit, pattiserie, toasty. Taste sweet, rich, unctuous, powerful.

PÉREZ BARQUERO S.A.

Avda. Andalucía, 27
14550 Montilla - (Córdoba)
☎: +34 957 650 500 - Fax: +34 957 650 208
info@perezbarquero.com
www.perezbarquero.com

GRAN BARQUERO AM
100% pedro ximénez

91 Colour: old gold. Nose: neat, sweet spices, caramel, candied fruit. Palate: flavourful, balanced, spicy.

GRAN BARQUERO OL
100% pedro ximénez

90 Colour: old gold. Nose: candied fruit, sweet spices, caramel, medium intensity. Palate: ripe fruit, balanced, fine bitter notes.

GRAN BARQUERO PX
100% pedro ximénez

90 Colour: mahogany. Nose: pattiserie, toasty, dark chocolate, powerfull, dried fruit. Palate: flavourful, sweet, correct, balanced.

LA CAÑADA PX
100% pedro ximénez

96 Color dark mahogany. Aroma complex, fruit liqueur notes, dried fruit, pattiserie, toasty. Taste sweet, rich, unctuous, powerful.

TORO ALBALÁ

Avda. Antonio Sánchez Romero, 1
14920 Aguilar de la Frontera - (Córdoba)
☎: +34 957 660 046 - Fax: +34 957 661 494
info@toroalbala.com
www.toroalbala.com

DON P.X. 1985 PX GRAN RESERVA
100% pedro ximénez

94 Colour: dark mahogany. Nose: complex, expressive, floral, balsamic herbs, balanced, dried fruit, fruit liqueur notes. Palate: full, flavourful, elegant, unctuous.

DON P.X. 2008 PX
100% pedro ximénez

90 Colour: mahogany. Nose: cocoa bean, sweet spices, fruit liqueur notes, honeyed notes. Palate: spirituous, flavourful, toasty, spicy, balanced.

DESCRIPTION

This is the youngest of the denominations of Origin of Catalonia, an excision from the Denomination of Origin of Tarragona although Montsant is almost synonymous with the red wines which are produced in the Denomination of Origin Ca. Priorat. The difference with these wines is that, in this region to the south of Priorat and a part of the River Ebro, vines are not cultivated in slate or fine slate soil. In addition, the temperatures are milder. In this ecosystem, wines are produced from garnacha and cariñena grapes which are much more delicate and fruity than the potent, mineral priorats. Moreover, the international grapes and the better prices as compared with priorats makes Montsant attractive for many importers.

NUMBER OF HECTARES: 1.903

ALTITUDES: 0 m. – 700 m.

PREDOMINANT VARIETIES:

White grapes: chardonnay, garnacha blanca, macabeo, muscatel de grano pequeño, pansal and parellada.

Red grapes: cabernet sauvignon, cariñena, garnacha tinta, garnacha peluda, merlot, monastrell, picapoll, syrah, tempranillo and mazuela.

CLIMATOLOGY AND SOILS

The climate is marked by the uneven profile of the mountains, the influences of the River Ebro and the sea winds. There are three types of soils: compact limestone with small stones in the periphery of the Denomination of Origin, granite sand in the zone of Falset; and silica slate in certain areas.

ACÚSTIC CELLER

Progrés s/n
43775 Marça - (Tarragona)
☎: +34 672 432 691 - Fax: +34 977 660 867
acustic@acusticceller.com
www.acusticceller.com

ACÚSTIC 2009 T ROBLE
35% garnacha, 65% cariñena

91 Colour: bright cherry. Nose: sweet spices, creamy oak, overripe fruit. Palate: flavourful, fruity, toasty, round tannins.

ACÚSTIC 2010 B
60% garnacha, 10% garnacha roja, 25% macabeo, pansa

91 Colour: bright yellow. Nose: floral, toasty, sweet spices, fresh fruit. Palate: balanced, good acidity, rich, flavourful, long.

ACÚSTIC 2010 T ROBLE
35% garnacha, 65% cariñena

91 Colour: black cherry, purple rim. Nose: ripe fruit, balsamic herbs, elegant, spicy. Palate: balanced, good acidity, ripe fruit, long.

ACÚSTIC 2011 BFB
60% garnacha, 10% garnacha roja, 25% macabeo, 5% pansal

90 Colour: bright yellow. Nose: balanced, expressive, wild herbs, spicy. Palate: flavourful, good acidity, balanced, fine bitter notes, full.

AUDITORI 2009 T
100% garnacha

94 Colour: cherry, garnet rim. Nose: spicy, creamy oak, toasty, characterful, mineral. Palate: powerful, flavourful, toasty, round tannins.

AUDITORI 2010 T
100% garnacha

93 Colour: deep cherry, purple rim. Nose: balanced, complex, scrubland, expressive. Palate: good structure, flavourful, round tannins.

BRAÓ 2009 T
55% cariñena, 45% garnacha

93 Colour: cherry, garnet rim. Nose: ripe fruit, spicy, creamy oak, toasty, complex, dark chocolate, mineral, scrubland. Palate: powerful, flavourful, toasty, round tannins.

BRAÓ 2010 T
55% cariñena, 45% garnacha

92 Colour: deep cherry, garnet rim. Nose: sweet spices, creamy oak, elegant, balanced, ripe fruit. Palate: good structure, long, round tannins.

AGRÍCOLA D'ULLDEMOLINS SANT JAUME

Avda. Verge de Montserrat, s/n
43363 Ulldemolins - (Tarragona)
☎: +34 977 561 613 - Fax: +34 977 561 613
coopulldemolins@ono.com
www.coopulldemolins.com

LES PEDRENYERES 2009 T
garnacha

90 Colour: cherry, garnet rim. Nose: ripe fruit, mineral, earthy notes, creamy oak, sweet spices. Palate: powerful, flavourful, long, spicy.

ALFREDO ARRIBAS

Sort dels Capellans, 5
43730 Falset - (Tarragona)
☎: +34 932 531 760 - Fax: +34 934 173 591
info@portaldelpriorat.com
www.portaldelpriorat.com

TROSSOS SANTS 2011 B
90% garnacha blanca, 10% garnacha gris

93 Colour: bright straw. Nose: floral, fragrant herbs, mineral, spicy, creamy oak. Palate: rich, flavourful, fruity, long, spicy, balanced.

TROSSOS TROS BLANC 2010 B
garnacha blanca

92 Colour: bright yellow. Nose: ripe fruit, sweet spices, creamy oak, fragrant herbs, white flowers, mineral, expressive. Palate: rich, flavourful, fresh, good acidity, long, balanced.

TROSSOS TROS BLANC MAGNUM 2009 B
garnacha blanca

96 Colour: bright yellow. Nose: dried flowers, ripe fruit, mineral, wild herbs, sweet spices, creamy oak, balanced. Palate: long, spicy, flavourful, fresh, mineral, elegant.

TROSSOS TROS NEGRE 2009 T
garnacha

95 Colour: light cherry, garnet rim. Nose: balanced, cocoa bean, sweet spices, expressive. Palate: flavourful, fruity, round tannins.

TROSSOS TROS NEGRE MAGNUM 2008 T
garnacha

95 Colour: light cherry, orangey edge. Nose: complex, elegant, balanced, wild herbs, sweet spices. Palate: good structure, flavourful, elegant, fine bitter notes.

BUIL & GINÉ

Ctra. de Gratallops - Vilella Baixa, Km. 11,5
43737 Gratallops - (Tarragona)
☎: +34 977 839 810 - Fax: +34 977 839 811
info@builgine.com
www.builgine.com

BABOIX 2008 T
garnacha, cariñena, tempranillo, cabernet sauvignon

90 Colour: very deep cherry. Nose: sweet spices, ripe fruit, mineral. Palate: flavourful, spicy, good acidity.

CELLER COOPERATIU CORNUDELLA

Comte de Rius, 2
43360 Cornudella de Montsant - (Tarragona)
☎: +34 977 821 329 - Fax: +34 977 821 329
info@cornudella.net
www.cornudella.net

CASTELL DE SIURANA GARNATXA DEL MONTSANT 2010
100% garnacha roja

90 Colour: light mahogany. Nose: fruit liqueur notes, fruit liqueur notes, caramel, pattiserie, toasty, varnish. Palate: powerful, flavourful, long, spicy.

CASTELL DE SIURANA SELECCIÓ DE COSTERS 2009 T
70% garnacha, 30% cariñena

90 Colour: cherry, garnet rim. Nose: ripe fruit, spicy, creamy oak, earthy notes. Palate: powerful, flavourful, toasty.

LES TROIES 2011 T
50% garnacha, 50% cariñena

91 Colour: dark-red cherry, garnet rim. Nose: fresh, ripe fruit, balsamic herbs, mineral, earthy notes. Palate: powerful, flavourful, complex, spicy.

CELLER DE CAPÇANES

Celler de Capçanes
43776 Capçanes - (Tarragona)
☎: +34 977 178 319 - Fax: +34 977 178 319
cellercapcanes@cellercapcanes.com
www.cellercapcanes.com

CABRIDA VIÑAS VIEJAS 2009 T
100% garnacha

91 Colour: cherry, garnet rim. Nose: wild herbs, ripe fruit, sweet spices. Palate: flavourful, good structure, good acidity.

COSTERS DEL GRAVET 2010 TC
60% cabernet sauvignon, 30% garnacha, 10% cariñena

92 Colour: deep cherry, purple rim. Nose: expressive, red berry notes, ripe fruit, balsamic herbs, sweet spices. Palate: good structure, good acidity, fine bitter notes, round tannins.

FLOR DE PRIMAVERA PERAJ HA'ABIB KOSHER 2010 T
33% cabernet sauvignon, 33% cariñena, 33% garnacha

91 Colour: cherry, garnet rim. Nose: complex, expressive, balanced, ripe fruit, creamy oak. Palate: good structure, flavourful, full.

LASENDAL GARNATXA 2010 T BARRICA
85% garnacha, 15% syrah

90 Colour: deep cherry, purple rim. Nose: spicy, balsamic herbs, ripe fruit. Palate: correct, ripe fruit, good finish.

MAS PICOSA 2011 T
garnacha, merlot, tempranillo

90 Colour: cherry, purple rim. Nose: powerfull, ripe fruit, fruit expression. Palate: powerful, flavourful, ripe fruit.

MAS TORTÓ 2010 TC
70% garnacha, 10% syrah, 10% merlot, 10% cabernet sauvignon

91 Colour: cherry, purple rim. Nose: complex, balanced, ripe fruit, spicy, scrubland. Palate: good structure, flavourful, complex.

PANSAL DEL CALÀS VINO DE POSTRE 2008 T
70% garnacha, 30% cariñena

90 Colour: cherry, garnet rim. Nose: ripe fruit, fruit liqueur notes, dark chocolate, cocoa bean, sweet spices, toasty. Palate: powerful, flavourful, long, balanced.

VALL DEL CALÀS 2009 T
50% merlot, 30% garnacha, 20% tempranillo

90 Colour: cherry, garnet rim. Nose: ripe fruit, spicy, creamy oak, complex. Palate: powerful, flavourful, toasty, round tannins.

CELLER DOSTERRAS

Ctra. Falset a Marça, Km. 2
43775 Marça - (Tarragona)
☎: +34 678 730 596
jgrau@dosterras.com
www.dosterras.com

DOSTERRAS 2010 T
garnacha

92 Colour: bright cherry. Nose: sweet spices, creamy oak, expressive, red berry notes, ripe fruit. Palate: flavourful, fruity, toasty, round tannins.

CELLER EL MASROIG

Passeig de L'Arbre, 3
43736 El Masroig - (Tarragona)
☎: +34 977 825 026
celler@cellermasroig.com
www.cellermasroig.com

CASTELL DE LES PINYERES 2009 T
40% garnacha, 40% mazuelo, 20% cabernet sauvignon, merlot, tempranillo

91 Colour: cherry, garnet rim. Nose: ripe fruit, spicy, toasty, complex, mineral, earthy notes. Palate: powerful, flavourful, toasty, balanced.

ETNIC 2010 BFB
100% garnacha blanca

90 Color bright yellow. Aroma powerfull, ripe fruit, sweet spices, creamy oak, fragrant herbs. Taste rich, smoky aftertaste, flavourful, fresh, good acidity.

LES SORTS VINYES VELLES 2007 TC
60% samsó, 30% garnacha, 10% cabernet sauvignon

90 Colour: deep cherry, garnet rim. Nose: cocoa bean, sweet spices, ripe fruit. Palate: good structure, balanced, fine bitter notes, good acidity.

CELLER ELS GUIAMETS

Avinguda Ctra., 23
43777 Els Guiamets - (Tarragona)
☎: +34 977 413 018
eguasch@cellerelsguiamets.com
www.cellerelsguiamets.com

GRAN METS 2008 TC
cabernet sauvignon, merlot, ull de llebre

92 Colour: cherry, garnet rim. Nose: ripe fruit, spicy, creamy oak, toasty, complex, balsamic herbs. Palate: powerful, flavourful, toasty, round tannins, balanced.

CELLER LAURONA S.A.

Ctra. Bellmunt, s/n
43730 Falset - (Tarragona)
☎: +34 977 830 221 - Fax: +34 977 831 797
laurona@cellerlaurona.com
www.cellerlaurona.com

6 VINYES DE LAURONA 2006 T
garnacha, cariñena

92 Colour: cherry, garnet rim. Nose: creamy oak, toasty, complex, earthy notes, mineral. Palate: powerful, flavourful, toasty, round tannins.

LAURONA 2007 T
garnacha, cariñena, merlot, syrah, cabernet sauvignon

91 Color cherry, garnet rim. Aroma ripe fruit, spicy, creamy oak, toasty, complex. Taste powerful, flavourful, toasty, round tannins.

CELLER VERMUNVER

Dalt, 29
43775 Marçà - (Tarragona)
☎: +34 977 178 288 - Fax: +34 977 178 288
info@genesi.cat
www.genesi.cat

GÈNESI SELECCIÓ 2007 T
garnacha, cariñena

90 Colour: cherry, garnet rim. Nose: ripe fruit, scrubland, earthy notes, spicy, fine reductive notes. Palate: powerful, flavourful, complex, long, toasty.

GÈNESI VARIETAL 2009 T
100% samsó

95 Colour: cherry, garnet rim. Nose: ripe fruit, spicy, creamy oak, toasty, complex, mineral, elegant. Palate: powerful, flavourful, toasty, round tannins, balanced, elegant.

CELLERS BARONÍA DEL MONTSANT S.L.

Comte de Rius, 1
43360 Cornudella de Montsant - (Tarragona)
☎: +34 977 821 483 - Fax: +34 977 821 483
englora@baronia-m.com
www.baronia-m.com

CLOS D'ENGLORA AV 14 2008 T
38% garnacha, 18% cariñena, 14% merlot, 11% cabernet sauvignon, 11% syrah, 8% otras

91 Colour: deep cherry. Nose: candied fruit, spicy, toasty. Palate: flavourful, spicy, ripe fruit.

ENGLORA 2009 TC
49% garnacha, 24% cariñena, 7% syrah, 19% cabernet sauvignon, 1% ull de llebre

92 Color cherry, garnet rim. Aroma ripe fruit, spicy, creamy oak, toasty, complex. Taste powerful, flavourful, toasty, round tannins.

CELLERS CAN BLAU

Ctra. Bellmunt, s/n
43730 Falset - (Tarragona)
☎: +34 629 261 379 - Fax: +34 968 716 051
info@orowines.com
www.orowines.com

BLAU 2010 T
50% cariñena, 25% syrah, 25% garnacha

91 Colour: deep cherry. Nose: sweet spices, red berry notes, ripe fruit, toasty, creamy oak. Palate: flavourful, balsamic, spicy, ripe fruit.

MAS DE CAN BLAU 2009 T
50% mazuelo, 30% garnacha, 20% syrah

94 Colour: cherry, garnet rim. Nose: creamy oak, dark chocolate, ripe fruit, earthy notes. Palate: powerful, flavourful, concentrated, fine bitter notes, good acidity.

CELLERS SANT RAFEL

Ctra. La Torre, Km. 1,7
43774 Pradell de la Teixeta - (Tarragona)
☎: +34 689 792 305 - Fax: +34 977 323 078
info@solpost.com
www.solpost.com

JOANA 2009 T
80% garnacha, 10% merlot, 10% cabernet sauvignon

90 Colour: bright cherry. Nose: ripe fruit, sweet spices, expressive, dark chocolate. Palate: flavourful, fruity, toasty, round tannins.

SOLPOST 2007 TC
50% garnacha, 35% cariñena, 15% cabernet sauvignon

92 Colour: cherry, garnet rim. Nose: ripe fruit, balsamic herbs, mineral, earthy notes, creamy oak, sweet spices. Palate: round, powerful, flavourful, complex, toasty.

SOLPOST FRESC 2009 TC
80% garnacha, 35% cariñena, 15% cabernet sauvignon

90 Colour: cherry, garnet rim. Nose: ripe fruit, spicy, toasty, mineral. Palate: powerful, flavourful, toasty, round tannins.

CINGLES BLAUS

Finca Mas de les Moreres (Afueras de Cornudella)
43360 Cornudella de Montsant - (Tarragona)
☎: +34 977 326 080 - Fax: +34 977 323 928
cinglesblaus@cinglesblaus.com
www.cinglesblaus.com

CINGLES BLAUS OCTUBRE 2010 T
60% garnacha, 20% cariñena, 20% syrah

92 Colour: very deep cherry. Nose: scrubland, ripe fruit, red berry notes, violet drops. Palate: flavourful, powerful, fine bitter notes, good acidity.

COCA I FITÓ

Avda. 11 de Setembre s/n
43736 El Masroig - (Tarragona)
☎: +34 619 776 948 - Fax: +34 935 457 092
info@cocaifito.cat
www.cocaifito.com

COCA I FITÓ NEGRE 2009 T
50% syrah, 30% garnacha, 20% cariñena

93 Colour: cherry, garnet rim. Nose: ripe fruit, spicy, creamy oak, toasty, complex, earthy notes, mineral. Palate: powerful, flavourful, toasty, round tannins.

JASPI MARAGDA 2010 T
55% garnacha, 25% cariñena, 20% syrah

90 Colour: cherry, garnet rim. Nose: red berry notes, ripe fruit, balsamic herbs, sweet spices, creamy oak, mineral. Palate: powerful, flavourful, long, spicy.

JASPI NEGRE 2010 T
45% garnacha, 25% cariñena, 15% cabernet sauvignon, 15% syrah

90 Colour: bright cherry. Nose: ripe fruit, sweet spices, creamy oak, mineral. Palate: flavourful, fruity, spicy.

COOPERATIVA FALSET - MARÇA

Miquel Barceló, 31
43730 Falset - (Tarragona)
☎: +34 977 830 105 - Fax: +34 977 830 363
info@etim.es
www.etim.cat

CASTELL DE FALSET 2009 BFB
100% garnacha blanca

90 Colour: bright yellow. Nose: powerfull, sweet spices, toasty. Palate: rich, flavourful, toasty, good acidity.

ÈTIM RANCI
garnacha, cariñena

92 Colour: bright golden. Nose: complex, balanced, varnish, roasted almonds, acetaldehyde. Palate: long, balanced.

ÈTIM SELECTION SYRAH 2006 T
syrah

90 Colour: black cherry, garnet rim. Nose: toasty, sweet spices, ripe fruit. Palate: flavourful, powerful, fine bitter notes, round tannins.

ÈTIM VEREMA TARDANA BLANC 2009 B
garnacha blanca

90 Colour: bright yellow. Nose: candied fruit, white flowers, balanced. Palate: flavourful, rich, sweet, balanced, good acidity.

ÈTIM VEREMA TARDANA NEGRE 2009 T
garnacha

91 Colour: cherry, garnet rim. Nose: sweet spices, cocoa bean, candied fruit. Palate: fruity, long, good acidity.

DIT CELLER

Avda. Setembre, s/n Baixos
43736 El Masroig - (Tarragona)
☎: +34 619 777 419
tonicoca@gmail.com
www.ditceller.com

CABIROL 10 2010 T ROBLE
garnacha, tempranillo

90 Colour: cherry, garnet rim. Nose: red berry notes, ripe fruit, balsamic herbs, sweet spices, creamy oak. Palate: powerful, flavourful, long, toasty.

SELENITA TERRER 2009 T
garnacha, cariñena

91 Colour: cherry, garnet rim. Nose: ripe fruit, sweet spices, creamy oak, earthy notes. Palate: powerful, flavourful, complex, toasty.

EDICIONES I-LIMITADAS

Claravall n.2
8022 - (Barcelona)
info@edicionesi.limitadas.com
www.edicionesi.limitadas.com

FAUNUS 2010 T
ull de llebre, syrah, merlot, cariñena

91 Colour: cherry, garnet rim. Nose: balanced, ripe fruit, expressive, spicy. Palate: good structure, balanced, elegant.

NÚVOL 2011 B
garnacha blanca, macabeo

91 Colour: bright straw. Nose: dried flowers, fragrant herbs, tropical fruit, fruit expression, creamy oak. Palate: powerful, flavourful, long, spicy.

SIURALTA 2008 T
cariñena

91 Colour: deep cherry, garnet rim. Nose: balanced, elegant, ripe fruit, spicy, creamy oak. Palate: balanced, fine bitter notes, round tannins.

ESPECTACLE VINS

Camí Manyetes, s/n
43737 Gratallops - (Tarragona)
☎: +34 977 839 171 - Fax: +34 977 839 426
jordi@espectaclevins.com
www.espectaclevins.com

ESPECTACLE 2009 T
garnacha

96 Colour: bright cherry. Nose: red berry notes, fruit expression, floral, scrubland, balsamic herbs, sweet spices. Palate: good acidity, fine bitter notes, elegant, fine tannins.

LA COVA DELS VINS

Hermenegild Pallejà, 6
43730 Falset - (Tarragona)
☎: +34 636 395 386
info@lacovadelsvins.com
www.lacovadelsvins.cat

TERRÒS 2009 T
garnacha, cariñena, syrah

90 Colour: cherry, garnet rim. Nose: ripe fruit, spicy, earthy notes, balsamic herbs, creamy oak. Palate: powerful, flavourful, complex.

MAS D'EN CANONGE

Pol. Ind. 7, Parc. 27
43775 Marça - (Tarragona)
☎: +34 977 054 071 - Fax: +34 977 054 971
celler@masdencanonge.com
www.masdencanonge.com

RESSONS CLOT DE LA VELLA 2009 TC
garnacha

90 Colour: cherry, garnet rim. Nose: ripe fruit, balanced, sweet spices, cocoa bean. Palate: ripe fruit, long, good acidity.

MAS PERINET

Finca Mas Perinet, s/n
43660 Cornudella de Montsant - (Tarragona)
☎: +34 977 827 113 - Fax: +34 977 827 180
info@masperinet.com
www.masperinet.com

GOTIA 2005 T

93 Colour: cherry, garnet rim. Nose: ripe fruit, spicy, creamy oak, toasty, complex, earthy notes. Palate: powerful, flavourful, toasty, round tannins.

GOTIA 2006 T

93 Colour: bright cherry. Nose: sweet spices, creamy oak, fruit liqueur notes. Palate: flavourful, fruity, toasty, round tannins.

NOGUERALS

Tou, 5
43360 Cornudella de Montsant - (Tarragona)
☎: +34 650 033 546 - Fax: +34 934 419 879
noguerals@hotmail.com
www.noguerals.com

CORBATERA 2009 T
70% garnacha, 30% cabernet sauvignon

91 Colour: cherry, garnet rim. Nose: ripe fruit, spicy, creamy oak. Palate: powerful, flavourful, toasty, round tannins.

ORTO VINS

Major, 10
43736 El Masroig - (Tarragona)
☎: +34 629 171 246
info@ortovins.com

BLANC D'ORTO BRISAT 2011 B
garnacha blanca

91 Colour: bright golden. Nose: ripe fruit, fragrant herbs, dried flowers, mineral, sweet spices, creamy oak. Palate: rich, flavourful, complex, spicy, long, toasty.

DOLÇ D'ORTO 2011 DULCE NATURAL
80% garnacha blanca, 20% macabeo, tripó de gat, mamella de monja, trobat

92 Colour: bright golden. Nose: faded flowers, honeyed notes, candied fruit, citrus fruit. Palate: flavourful, sweet, long.

LA CARRERADA 2010 T
100% samsó

93 Colour: cherry, garnet rim. Nose: ripe fruit, spicy, creamy oak, toasty, complex, mineral, earthy notes. Palate: powerful, flavourful, toasty, round tannins.

LES PUJOLES 2010 TC
100% ull de llebre

90 Colour: very deep cherry. Nose: scrubland, ripe fruit, sweet spices. Palate: flavourful, powerful, fine bitter notes.

LES TALLADES DE CAL NICOLAU 2010 TC
picapoll negro

92 Colour: very deep cherry. Nose: spicy, fruit liqueur notes, scrubland, earthy notes. Palate: flavourful, spicy, ripe fruit, fine bitter notes. Personality.

PALELL 2010 TC
100% garnacha peluda

93 Colour: bright cherry. Nose: ripe fruit, sweet spices, creamy oak, earthy notes. Palate: flavourful, fruity, toasty, round tannins.

PORTAL DEL MONTSANT

Carrer de Dalt, s/n
43775 Marça - (Tarragona)
☎: +34 933 950 811 - Fax: +34 933 955 500
info@parxet.es
www.parxet.es

BRUBERRY 2011 B
100% garnacha blanca

90 Colour: bright straw. Nose: fresh, fresh fruit, white flowers, expressive, complex. Palate: flavourful, fruity, good acidity, balanced.

BRUNUS 2009 T
cariñena, garnacha, syrah, cabernet sauvignon

90 Colour: bright cherry. Nose: ripe fruit, sweet spices, creamy oak, mineral, expressive. Palate: flavourful, fruity, toasty, round tannins.

BRUNUS ROSÉ 2011 RD
garnacha

90 Colour: rose, purple rim. Nose: powerfull, ripe fruit, red berry notes, floral, mineral, balanced. Palate: , powerful, fruity, fresh, fine bitter notes.

SANTBRU 2008 T
cariñena, garnacha, syrah

93 Colour: bright cherry, garnet rim. Nose: expressive, balanced, ripe fruit, spicy, scrubland. Palate: good structure, fine bitter notes, round tannins.

SANTBRU BLANC 2010 B
garnacha

92 Colour: bright straw. Nose: fresh, fresh fruit, white flowers, scrubland, spicy, mineral. Palate: flavourful, fruity, good acidity, balanced.

RONADELLES

Finca La Plana, s/n
43360 Cornudella del Montsant - (Tarragona)
☎: +34 977 821 104 - Fax: +34 977 274 913
info@ronadelles.com
www.ronadelles.com

PETIT BLANC 2009 B
garnacha blanca, macabeo

90 Colour: bright yellow. Nose: fine lees, ripe fruit, dried herbs, earthy notes, dried flowers. Palate: powerful, flavourful, complex, fine bitter notes.

PETIT NEGRE 2009 T
garnacha, cariñena

90 Colour: deep cherry, garnet rim. Nose: balanced, wild herbs, ripe fruit, spicy. Palate: good structure, good acidity.

VENUS LA UNIVERSAL

Ctra. Porrera, s/n
43730 Falset - (Tarragona)
☎: +34 699 435 154 - Fax: +34 639 121 244
info@venuslauniversal.com
www.venuslauniversal.com

DIDO 2010 T

91 Colour: cherry, purple rim. Nose: ripe fruit, dried flowers. Palate: good structure, ripe fruit, good acidity, balanced, fine bitter notes.

DIDO 2011 B
macabeo, garnacha blanca

92 Colour: bright straw. Nose: ripe fruit, faded flowers, dried herbs, earthy notes, mineral, toasty, creamy oak. Palate: powerful, flavourful, rich, spicy, good acidity.

VENUS 2008 T

92 Colour: bright cherry, garnet rim. Nose: expressive, balanced, spicy, complex, cocoa bean, mineral. Palate: good structure, full, balanced, fine bitter notes, round tannins.

VINYES D'EN GABRIEL

Ctra. Darmós - La Serra, s/n
43746 Darmós - (Tarragona)
☎: +34 609 989 345
info@vinyesdengabriel.com
www.vinyesdengabriel.com

DOLCET DE MIREIA 2011 T

90 Colour: black cherry, purple rim. Nose: candied fruit, pattiserie, fruit liqueur notes, sweet spices, cocoa bean. Palate: flavourful, fruity.

MANS DE SAMSÓ 2010 T
samsó

90 Colour: black cherry, purple rim. Nose: sweet spices, fruit liqueur notes, fruit preserve, red berry notes. Palate: warm, sweetness, concentrated.

VINYES DOMÈNECH

Camí del Collet, km. 3,8
43776 Capçanes - (Tarragona)
☎: +34 670 297 395 - Fax: +34 932 127 759
jidomenech@vinyesdomenech.com
www.vinyesdomenech.com

BANCAL DEL BOSC 2010 T
60% garnacha, 20% syrah, 20% cabernet sauvignon

90 Colour: cherry, garnet rim. Nose: medium intensity, balanced, scrubland, fruit expression. Palate: long, ripe fruit, round tannins.

BANCAL RITA 2011 B
80% garnacha blanca, 20% macabeo

90 Colour: bright straw. Nose: white flowers, ripe fruit, balanced, expressive. Palate: rich, flavourful, ripe fruit, spicy.

FURVUS 2009 T
85% garnacha, 15% merlot

92 Colour: cherry, garnet rim. Nose: ripe fruit, spicy, creamy oak, toasty, characterful. Palate: powerful, flavourful, toasty, round tannins.

TEIXAR 2009 T
100% garnacha peluda

94 Colour: cherry, garnet rim. Nose: mineral, earthy notes, ripe fruit, spicy. Palate: fine bitter notes, good acidity, long, spicy, ripe fruit.

TEIXAR 2010 T
100% garnacha peluda

95 Colour: bright cherry. Nose: sweet spices, creamy oak, expressive, varietal, mineral, ripe fruit, fragrant herbs. Palate: flavourful, fruity, toasty, round tannins.

DESCRIPTION

More than 15,000 hectares mean that it is a very diverse zone which is composed of five sub-zones with different climates and soils: Low Mountain, Tierra Estella and Valdizarbe with the influence of the Atlantic, and Ribera Alta and Ribera Baja, with Mediterranean influence. It was once a region known almost exclusively for its rosé wines, but the Denomination of Origin has taken a giant leap forward to become a producer of quality red wines, exploiting the singular nature of cabernet sauvignon and garnacha in the region. In the rearguard, there are grand white wines made from chardonnay and excellent sweet muscatels.

NUMBER OF HECTARES: 15.280

ALTITUDES: 400 m. – 800 m.

PREDOMINANT VARIETIES:

White grapes: chardonnay, garnacha blanca, malvasía, small grained muscatel, viura and sauvignon blanc.

Red grapes: cabernet sauvignon, garnacha tinta, graciano, mazuelo, merlot, tempranillo, syrah and pinot noir.

CLIMATOLOGY AND SOILS

The climate is dry sub-humid in the northern strip. A transition climate in the middle zone which evolves towards more arid conditions in the southern areas. The soils are reddish or yellowish and are gravelly in the low mountain area, brown-limestone and limestone in Valdizarbe and Tierra de Estella, loam-limestone and alluvial in Ribera Alta, and brown, grey, brown-limestone and alluvial in Ribera Baja.

AROA BODEGAS

Apalaz, 13
31292 Gorozin-Zurukoain - (Navarra)
☎: +34 948 921 867
info@aroawines.com
www.aroawines.com

AROA GORENA 18M 2008 TR
70% cabernet sauvignon, 30% merlot

90 Colour: cherry, garnet rim. Nose: spicy, balsamic herbs, varietal, ripe fruit. Palate: balanced, ripe fruit, long, toasty.

AZUL Y GARANZA BODEGAS

San Juan, 19
31310 Carcastillo - (Navarra)
☎: +34 636 406 939 - Fax: +34 948 725 677
info@azulygaranza.com
www.azulygaranza.com

DESIERTO DE AZUL Y GARANZA 2008 T
cabernet sauvignon

91 Colour: bright cherry. Nose: ripe fruit, fragrant herbs, sweet spices, varietal, expressive. Palate: flavourful, good acidity, spicy, long.

VIURA DE AZUL Y GARANZA 2011 B
viura

90 Colour: bright straw. Nose: fresh, fresh fruit, expressive, fragrant herbs. Palate: flavourful, fruity, good acidity, balanced.

BODEGA DE SARRÍA

Finca Señorío de Sarría, s/n
31100 Puente La Reina - (Navarra)
☎: +34 948 202 200 - Fax: +34 948 202 202
info@taninia.com
www.bodegadesarria.com

SEÑORÍO DE SARRÍA 2001 TGR
merlot, cabernet sauvignon

90 Colour: pale ruby, brick rim edge. Nose: elegant, spicy, fine reductive notes, aged wood nuances, fruit liqueur notes. Palate: spicy, fine tannins, elegant, long.

SEÑORÍO DE SARRÍA RESERVA ESPECIAL 2004 TR
cabernet sauvignon

90 Colour: cherry, garnet rim. Nose: balanced, varietal, ripe fruit, balsamic herbs, spicy. Palate: good structure, round tannins.

SEÑORÍO DE SARRÍA VIÑEDO Nº 3 2009 BFB
chardonnay

91 Colour: bright yellow. Nose: ripe fruit, jasmine, fragrant herbs, sweet spices, toasty, creamy oak. Palate: rich, flavourful, fruity, spicy.

BODEGA INURRIETA

Ctra. Falces-Miranda de Arga, km. 30
31370 Falces - (Navarra)
☎: +34 948 737 309 - Fax: +34 948 737 310
info@bodegainurrieta.com
www.bodegainurrieta.com

ALTOS DE INURRIETA 2008 TR
graciano, garnacha, syrah

91 Color cherry, garnet rim. Aroma ripe fruit, spicy, creamy oak, toasty, complex. Taste powerful, flavourful, toasty, round tannins.

INURRIETA "SUR" 2010 T ROBLE
garnacha, graciano

90 Colour: very deep cherry. Nose: creamy oak, sweet spices, cocoa bean. Palate: good structure, ripe fruit, round tannins.

INURRIETA CUATROCIENTOS 2009 TC
cabernet sauvignon, merlot

90 Colour: cherry, garnet rim. Nose: ripe fruit, powerfull, sweet spices, toasty. Palate: powerful, flavourful, balanced, toasty.

INURRIETA ORCHÍDEA 2011 B
sauvignon blanc

90 Colour: bright straw. Nose: floral, citrus fruit, fruit expression, fragrant herbs, balanced, expressive. Palate: light-bodied, fresh, fruity, flavourful, good acidity, balanced.

INURRIETA ORCHÍDEA CUVÉE 2009 B
sauvignon blanc

92 Color bright yellow. Aroma powerfull, ripe fruit, sweet spices, creamy oak, fragrant herbs. Taste rich, smoky aftertaste, flavourful, fresh, good acidity.

INURRIETA PV 2009 T

92 Colour: deep cherry, garnet rim. Nose: complex, balanced, ripe fruit, sweet spices. Palate: good structure, flavourful.

LADERAS DE INURRIETA 2009 T
graciano

91 Colour: cherry, garnet rim. Nose: ripe fruit, earthy notes, aromatic coffee, sweet spices. Palate: balanced, round, powerful, flavourful.

BODEGA MARQUÉS DE MONTECIERZO

San José, 62
31590 Castejón - (Navarra)
☎: +34 948 814 414 - Fax: +34 948 814 420
info@marquesdemontecierzo.com
www.marquesdemontecierzo.com

MARQUES DE MONTECIERZO MERLOT SELECCIÓN 2005 TC
100% merlot

90 Colour: deep cherry, garnet rim. Nose: powerfull, ripe fruit, sweet spices, tobacco, fragrant herbs. Palate: flavourful, ripe fruit, long.

BODEGA OTAZU

Señorío de Otazu, s/n
31174 Etxauri - (Navarra)
☎: +34 948 329 200 - Fax: +34 948 329 353
otazu@otazu.com
www.otazu.com

OTAZU CHARDONNAY 2010 B
chardonnay

90 Colour: bright straw. Nose: white flowers, expressive, ripe fruit, fragrant herbs. Palate: flavourful, fruity, good acidity.

OTAZU PREMIUM CUVEE 2007 T
cabernet sauvignon, tempranillo, merlot

92 Colour: cherry, garnet rim. Nose: spicy, creamy oak, toasty, dark chocolate, ripe fruit. Palate: powerful, flavourful, toasty, round tannins.

PALACIO DE OTAZU CHARDONNAY 2009 BFB

91 Colour: bright yellow. Nose: powerfull, ripe fruit, sweet spices, fragrant herbs, new oak. Palate: rich, smoky aftertaste, flavourful, fresh, good acidity.

BODEGA TÁNDEM

Ctra. Pamplona - Logroño Km. 35,9
31292 Lácar - (Navarra)
☎: +34 948 536 031 - Fax: +34 948 536 068
bodega@tandem.es
www.tandem.es

ARS MÁCULA 2005 T
cabernet sauvignon, merlot

90 Colour: pale ruby, brick rim edge. Nose: spicy, fine reductive notes, aged wood nuances, cocoa bean, dark chocolate. Palate: spicy, fine tannins, long.

BODEGA Y VIÑAS VALDELARES

Ctra. Eje del Ebro, km. 60
31579 Carcar - (Navarra)
☎: +34 656 849 602
valdelares@terra.es
www.valdelares.com

VALDELARES 2009 TC
tempranillo, cabernet sauvignon, merlot

90 Colour: cherry, garnet rim. Nose: red berry notes, ripe fruit, cocoa bean, sweet spices, toasty. Palate: balanced, powerful, flavourful.

BODEGAS CAMILO CASTILLA

Santa Bárbara, 40
31591 Corella - (Navarra)
☎: +34 948 780 006 - Fax: +34 948 780 515
info@bodegascamilocastilla.com
www.bodegascamilocastilla.com

CAPRICHO DE GOYA VINO DE LICOR
100% moscatel grano menudo

91 Colour: dark mahogany. Nose: dark chocolate, caramel, sweet spices, creamy oak, dry nuts, acetaldehyde. Palate: rich, powerful, flavourful, spirituous.

BODEGAS CASTILLO DE MONJARDÍN

Viña Rellanada, s/n
31242 Villamayor de Monjardín - (Navarra)
☎: +34 948 537 412 - Fax: +34 948 537 436
sonia@monjardin.es
www.monjardin.es

CASTILLO DE MONJARDÍN CHARDONNAY 2009 BFB
chardonnay

93 Colour: bright yellow. Nose: powerfull, ripe fruit, creamy oak, fragrant herbs, citrus fruit, toasty. Palate: rich, flavourful, fresh, good acidity.

ESENCIA MONJARDÍN 2007 B
chardonnay

93 Colour: bright golden. Nose: elegant, expressive, candied fruit, dried flowers, sweet spices. Palate: balanced, spicy.

BODEGAS CAUDALIA

San Francisco, 7
Najera - (La Rioja)
☎: +34 670 833 340 - Fax: +34 941 145 394
info@bodegascaudalia.com
www.bodegascaudalia.com

PAAL 01 2011 T
100% syrah

92 Colour: cherry, purple rim. Nose: powerfull, varietal, ripe fruit, fruit expression, scrubland. Palate: flavourful, powerful, spicy, ripe fruit.

BODEGAS CORELLANAS

Santa Bárbara, 29
31591 Corella - (Navarra)
☎: +34 948 780 029 - Fax: +34 948 781 542
info@bodegascorellanas.com
www.bodegascorellanas.com

VIÑA RUBICÁN ÚNICO 2007 T
15% tempranillo, 85% garnacha

90 Colour: cherry, garnet rim. Nose: ripe fruit, spicy, creamy oak, toasty, complex. Palate: powerful, flavourful, toasty, fine tannins.

BODEGAS DE LA CASA DE LÚCULO

Ctra. Larraga, s/n
31150 Mendigorría - (Navarra)
☎: +34 948 343 148 - Fax: +34 948 343 148
bodega@luculo.es
www.luculo.es

JARDÍN DE LÚCULO 2008 T
garnacha

91 Colour: light cherry, garnet rim. Nose: fruit liqueur notes, earthy notes, spicy, fine reductive notes. Palate: elegant, balanced, round, powerful, flavourful.

BODEGAS FERNÁNDEZ DE ARCAYA

La Serna, 31
31210 Los Arcos - (Navarra)
☎: +34 948 640 811 - Fax: +34 948 441 060
info@fernandezdearcaya.com
www.fernandezdearcaya.com

FERNÁNDEZ DE ARCAYA 2008 TR
100% cabernet sauvignon

90 Colour: cherry, garnet rim. Nose: spicy, creamy oak, fragrant herbs. Palate: toasty, flavourful, ripe fruit.

BODEGAS GRAN FEUDO

Calle de la Ribera 32
31592 Cintruénigo - (Navarra)
☎: +34 948 811 000
info@bodegaschivite.com

GRAN FEUDO 2008 TR
tempranillo, garnacha, cabernet sauvignon

90 Colour: cherry, garnet rim. Nose: ripe fruit, spicy, toasty, complex, elegant. Palate: powerful, flavourful, toasty, round tannins.

GRAN FEUDO EDICIÓN CHARDONNAY SOBRE LÍAS 2011 B
100% chardonnay

91 Colour: bright straw. Nose: fresh, fresh fruit, white flowers, floral, mineral. Palate: flavourful, fruity, good acidity, balanced.

GRAN FEUDO EDICIÓN DULCE DE MOSCATEL 2011 B
moscatel

92 Colour: golden. Nose: powerfull, floral, candied fruit, fragrant herbs. Palate: flavourful, sweet, fruity, good acidity.

GRAN FEUDO EDICIÓN SELECCIÓN ESPECIAL 2008 TC
tempranillo, merlot, cabernet sauvignon

91 Colour: cherry, garnet rim. Nose: ripe fruit, toasty, complex, sweet spices, mineral. Palate: powerful, flavourful, toasty, round tannins.

BODEGAS LOGOS

Avda. de los Fueros, 18
31522 Monteagudo - (Navarra)
☎: +34 948 843 102 - Fax: +34 948 843 161
inma@bodegasescudero.com
www.familiaescudero.com

LOGOS I 2004 T
40% garnacha, 30% tempranillo, 30% cabernet sauvignon

91 Colour: bright cherry, garnet rim. Nose: macerated fruit, candied fruit, cocoa bean, sweet spices. Palate: good structure, full, ripe fruit, long.

BODEGAS OCHOA

Alcalde Maillata, 2
31390 Olite - (Navarra)
☎: +34 948 740 006 - Fax: +34 948 740 048
info@bodegasochoa.com
www.bodegasochoa.com

OCHOA MOSCATEL 2011 BLANCO DULCE
moscatel grano menudo

90 Colour: bright yellow. Nose: candied fruit, citrus fruit, white flowers, balanced, expressive. Palate: rich, flavourful, elegant.

BODEGAS PIEDEMONTE

Rua Romana, s/n
31390 Olite - (Navarra)
☎: +34 948 712 406 - Fax: +34 948 740 090
bodega@piedemonte.com
www.piedemonte.com

PIEDEMONTE MOSCATEL 2011 B
moscatel grano menudo

90 Colour: golden. Nose: powerfull, floral, honeyed notes, candied fruit. Palate: flavourful, sweet, fresh, fruity, long.

BODEGAS PRÍNCIPE DE VIANA

Mayor, 191
31521 Murchante - (Navarra)
☎: +34 948 838 640 - Fax: +34 948 818 574
info@principedeviana.com
www.principedeviana.com

PRÍNCIPE DE VIANA EDICIÓN LIMITADA 2008 TC
50% merlot, 25% tempranillo, 25% cabernet sauvignon

90 Colour: cherry, garnet rim. Nose: ripe fruit, spicy, creamy oak. Palate: powerful, flavourful, toasty, round tannins.

BODEGAS URABAIN

Ctra. Estella, 21
31262 Allo - (Navarra)
☎: +34 948 523 011 - Fax: +34 948 523 409
vinos@bodegasurabain.com
www.bodegasurabain.com

UN PASO MÁS 2009 T
tempranillo, cabernet sauvignon, merlot

91 Colour: deep cherry, garnet rim. Nose: creamy oak, cocoa bean, sweet spices. Palate: good structure, full, ripe fruit.

BODEGAS VALCARLOS

Ctra. Circunvalación, s/n
31210 Los Arcos - (Navarra)
☎: +34 948 640 806
info@bodegasvalcarlos.com
www.bodegasvalcarlos.com

ÉLITE DE FORTIUS 2004 TR
merlot, cabernet sauvignon

90 Colour: pale ruby, brick rim edge. Nose: ripe fruit, fragrant herbs, earthy notes, spicy, fine reductive notes. Palate: elegant, good structure, flavourful.

BODEGAS VEGA DEL CASTILLO

Rua Romana, 3
31390 Olite - (Navarra)
☎: +34 948 740 012
info@vegadelcastillo.com
www.vegadelcastillo.com

DUBHE 2007 T ROBLE
50% merlot, 25% cabernet sauvignon, 25% tempranillo

90 Colour: cherry, garnet rim. Nose: complex, sweet spices, cocoa bean, creamy oak. Palate: full, toasty, round tannins.

VEGA DEL CASTILLO 2007 TR
25% merlot, 50% tempranillo, 25% cabernet sauvignon

90 Colour: cherry, garnet rim. Nose: ripe fruit, balsamic herbs, sweet spices, toasty. Palate: spicy, long, powerful, flavourful.

BODEGAS VIÑA MAGAÑA

San Miguel, 9
31523 Barillas - (Navarra)
☎: +34 948 850 034 - Fax: +34 948 851 536
bodegas@vinamagana.com
www.vinamagana.com

BARÓN DE MAGAÑA 2009 TC

91 Colour: cherry, garnet rim. Nose: ripe fruit, creamy oak, toasty, balsamic herbs, wild herbs. Palate: powerful, flavourful, toasty, balanced.

MAGAÑA CALCHETAS 2008 T

92 Colour: cherry, garnet rim. Nose: ripe fruit, earthy notes, spicy, balsamic herbs, expressive, creamy oak. Palate: powerful, flavourful, complex, long, spicy.

MAGAÑA DIGNUS 2007 TC

90 Colour: cherry, garnet rim. Nose: ripe fruit, spicy, creamy oak, toasty, complex, fine reductive notes. Palate: powerful, flavourful, toasty, round tannins.

MAGAÑA MERLOT 2009 TR
merlot

91 Colour: cherry, garnet rim. Nose: creamy oak, mineral, fragrant herbs, ripe fruit, spicy, balanced. Palate: long, spicy, flavourful, fresh, fruity, round tannins.

BODEGAS Y VIÑEDOS ARTAZU

Mayor, 3
31109 Artazu - (Navarra)
☎: +34 945 600 119 - Fax: +34 945 600 850
artazu@artadi.com

SANTA CRUZ DE ARTAZU 2010 T
garnacha

95 Colour: cherry, purple rim. Nose: floral, fragrant herbs, balsamic herbs, toasty, spicy, mineral. Palate: round, good acidity, powerful, round tannins.

DISTRIBUCIONES B. IÑAKI NÚÑEZ

Ctra. de Ablitas a Ribafora, Km. 5
31523 Ablitas - (Navarra)
☎: +34 948 386 210 - Fax: +34 629 354 190
bodegasin@pagodecirsus.com
www.pagodecirsus.com

PAGO DE CIRSUS CHARDONNAY 2010 BFB
100% chardonnay

91 Colour: bright yellow. Nose: balanced, expressive, ripe fruit, white flowers. Palate: flavourful, spicy, ripe fruit, long.

PAGO DE CIRSUS DE IÑAKI NÚÑEZ
SELECCIÓN DE FAMILIA 2007 T
tempranillo, syrah

92 Colour: cherry, purple rim. Nose: powerfull, cocoa bean, creamy oak, ripe fruit. Palate: full, flavourful, long, good acidity.

PAGO DE CIRSUS DE IÑAKI NUÑEZ VENDIMIA SELECCIONADA 2009 TC
tempranillo, merlot, syrah

90 Colour: cherry, garnet rim. Nose: closed, ripe fruit, spicy, aromatic coffee. Palate: balanced, good structure, round tannins.

PAGO DE CIRSUS MOSCATEL VENDIMIA TARDÍA 2007 BFB
100% moscatel grano menudo

91 Colour: golden. Nose: honeyed notes, candied fruit, elegant, faded flowers, sweet spices. Palate: flavourful, sweet, fruity, long, rich.

PAGO DE CIRSUS OPUS 11 2008 T
syrah, tempranillo

92 Colour: dark-red cherry, garnet rim. Nose: powerfull, fruit preserve, sweet spices. Palate: good structure, rich, complex, round tannins.

DOMAINES LUPIER

Monseñor Justo Goizueta, 4
31495 San Martín de Unx - (Navarra)
☎: +34 639 622 111
info@domaineslupier.com
www.domaineslupier.com

DOMAINES LUPIER EL TERROIR 2009 T
100% garnacha

94 Colour: cherry, garnet rim. Nose: balanced, ripe fruit, floral, fragrant herbs, spicy, cocoa bean, creamy oak. Palate: fresh, fruity, flavourful, long, toasty.

DOMAINES LUPIER LA DAMA VIÑAS VIEJAS 2009 T
100% garnacha

93 Colour: cherry, garnet rim. Nose: ripe fruit, balsamic herbs, varietal, mineral, sweet spices, creamy oak. Palate: long, balanced, fresh, fruity, flavourful, round tannins.

FINCA ALBRET

Ctra. Cadreita-Villafranca, s/n
31515 Cadreita - (Navarra)
☎: +34 948 406 806 - Fax: +34 948 406 699
info@fincaalbret.com
www.fincaalbret.com

JUAN DE ALBRET 2009 T
50% tempranillo, 30% cabernet sauvignon, 20% merlot

90 Colour: cherry, garnet rim. Nose: ripe fruit, sweet spices, creamy oak. Palate: flavourful, complex, rich, balanced.

GARCÍA BURGOS

Finca La Cantera de Santa Ana, s/n
31521 Murchante - (Navarra)
☎: +34 948 847 734 - Fax: +34 948 847 734
info@bodegasgarciaburgos.com
www.bodegasgarciaburgos.com

FINCA LA CANTERA DE SANTA ANA 2007 T
100% cabernet sauvignon

92 Colour: bright cherry, garnet rim. Nose: complex, elegant, balanced, sweet spices, creamy oak. Palate: full, good acidity, round tannins.

GARCÍA BURGOS SH 2009 T
100% syrah

91 Color bright cherry. Aroma ripe fruit, sweet spices, creamy oak, expressive. Taste flavourful, fruity, toasty, round tannins.

GARCÍA BURGOS VENDIMIA SELECCIONADA 2009 T
40% cabernet sauvignon, 40% merlot, 20% syrah

90 Colour: cherry, garnet rim. Nose: ripe fruit, fragrant herbs, expressive, creamy oak. Palate: round, powerful, flavourful.

LOLA GARCÍA AS RESERVA 2007 TR
100% merlot

91 Colour: cherry, garnet rim. Nose: spicy, creamy oak, toasty, ripe fruit, earthy notes. Palate: powerful, flavourful, toasty, round tannins, elegant.

J. CHIVITE PAGOS & ESTATES

Ribera, 34
31592 Cimtruénigo - (Navarra)
☎: +34 948 555 285
info@bodegaschivite.com
www.bodegaschivite.com

CHIVITE BIOLÓGICO MERLOT 2008 T
merlot

90 Colour: cherry, garnet rim. Nose: ripe fruit, spicy, creamy oak, toasty, balsamic herbs. Palate: powerful, flavourful, toasty, round tannins.

CHIVITE COLECCIÓN 125 2006 TR
tempranillo, merlot, cabernet sauvignon

92 Colour: cherry, garnet rim. Nose: toasty, aromatic coffee, scrubland, ripe fruit. Palate: flavourful, fine bitter notes, good acidity, spicy, long.

CHIVITE COLECCIÓN 125 2007 RD

92 Colour: onion pink. Nose: scrubland, red berry notes, ripe fruit, sweet spices, toasty. Palate: flavourful, ripe fruit, creamy, fine bitter notes.

CHIVITE COLECCIÓN 125 2009 BFB
chardonnay

95 Colour: bright yellow. Nose: powerfull, ripe fruit, sweet spices, fragrant herbs, mineral. Palate: rich, smoky aftertaste, flavourful, fresh, good acidity.

CHIVITE COLECCIÓN 125 VENDIMIA TARDÍA B
moscatel

95 Colour: golden. Nose: powerfull, honeyed notes, candied fruit, fragrant herbs, balanced, expressive. Palate: flavourful, sweet, fresh, fruity, good acidity, long, balanced.

CHIVITE FINCA DE VILLATUERTA 2010 B
chardonnay

93 Colour: bright straw. Nose: fresh fruit, ripe fruit, mineral, sweet spices, white flowers. Palate: flavourful, good acidity, fine bitter notes, spicy, long.

CHIVITE FINCA DE VILLATUERTA SYRAH 2010 T
100% syrah

93 Colour: cherry, garnet rim. Nose: ripe fruit, spicy, toasty, red berry notes, fruit expression, creamy oak, cocoa bean. Palate: powerful, flavourful, toasty, round tannins.

LA CALANDRIA. PURA GARNACHA

Camino de Aspra, s/n
31521 Murchante - (Navarra)
☎: +34 630 904 327
luis@lacalandria.org
www.lacalandria.org

CIENTRUENOS 2011 T BARRICA
100% garnacha

91 Colour: light cherry, purple rim. Nose: elegant, red berry notes, scrubland, mineral. Palate: flavourful, balanced, complex, spicy.

LADERAS DE MONTEJURRA

Paraje de Argonga, s/n
31263 Dicastillo - (Navarra)
☎: +34 638 218 727
info@laderasdemontejurra.com
www.laderasdemontejurra.com

EMILIO VALERIO LADERAS DE MONTEJURRA 2010 T

91 Colour: dark-red cherry, garnet rim. Nose: ripe fruit, dried flowers, fragrant herbs, earthy notes. Palate: fresh, fruity, flavourful, spicy, long, balsamic.

USUARAN 2010 T

91 Colour: cherry, garnet rim. Nose: spicy, creamy oak, red berry notes, ripe fruit, earthy notes, balsamic herbs. Palate: powerful, flavourful, toasty, spicy.

VIÑA DE LEORÍN 2010 T

92 Colour: black cherry, garnet rim. Nose: earthy notes, fruit liqueur notes, spicy, balsamic herbs, balanced. Palate: powerful, flavourful, spicy, long, fine bitter notes.

VIÑA DE SAN MARTÍN 2010 T

93 Colour: bright cherry. Nose: ripe fruit, sweet spices, creamy oak, expressive, balsamic herbs, mineral. Palate: flavourful, fruity, toasty, good acidity, balanced.

MARCO REAL

Ctra. Pamplona-Zaragoza, Km. 38
31390 Olite - (Navarra)
☎: +34 948 712 193 - Fax: +34 948 712 343
info@familiabelasco.com
www.familiabelasco.com

MARCO REAL COLECCIÓN PRIVADA 2009 TC
tempranillo, cabernet sauvignon, merlot, graciano

91 Colour: bright cherry, garnet rim. Nose: expressive, balanced, elegant, cocoa bean, ripe fruit, dry stone. Palate: flavourful, good structure, good acidity.

MARCO REAL RESERVA DE FAMILIA 2007 TR
tempranillo, cabernet sauvignon, merlot, graciano

91 Colour: cherry, garnet rim. Nose: complex, balanced, sweet spices. Palate: good structure, flavourful, round tannins.

NEKEAS

Las Huertas, s/n
31154 Añorbe - (Navarra)
☎: +34 948 350 296 - Fax: +34 948 350 300
nekeas@nekeas.com
www.nekeas.com

NEKEAS CEPA X CEPA (CXC) 2010 T
100% garnacha

90 Colour: bright cherry, garnet rim. Nose: balanced, medium intensity, scrubland, spicy. Palate: good structure, fruity, round tannins.

NEKEAS CHARDONNAY 2011 B
100% chardonnay

90 Colour: bright straw. Nose: fresh, fresh fruit, white flowers, expressive. Palate: flavourful, fruity, good acidity, balanced, elegant.

PAGO DE LARRÁINZAR

Camino de la Corona, s/n
31240 Ayegui - (Navarra)
☎: +34 948 550 421 - Fax: +34 948 556 210
info@pagodelarrainzar.com
www.pagodelarrainzar.com

PAGO DE LARRAINZAR 2007 T
40% merlot, 40% cabernet sauvignon, 15% tempranillo, 5% garnacha

93 Colour: bright cherry. Nose: complex, spicy, creamy oak, cocoa bean, ripe fruit. Palate: flavourful, fruity, round tannins.

RASO DE LARRAINZAR 2008 T
43% tempranillo, merlot, 23% cabernet sauvignon, 3% garnacha

91 Colour: cherry, garnet rim. Nose: ripe fruit, spicy, creamy oak, toasty. Palate: powerful, flavourful, toasty, round tannins.

PAGO DE SAN GABRIEL

Paraje La Sarda. N-232, Km. 83,4
31590 Castejón - (Navarra)
☎: +34 659 620 209
socoymanu@hotmail.com
www.pagosangabriel.com

ZUBIOLA 2009 T
90% cabernet sauvignon, 5% merlot, 5% cabernet franc

90 Colour: cherry, garnet rim. Nose: elegant, balanced, sweet spices, ripe fruit, scrubland. Palate: good structure, flavourful.

ZUBIOLA EDICIÓN LIMITADA 2007 T
95% cabernet sauvignon, 5% merlot

92 Colour: cherry, garnet rim. Nose: ripe fruit, mineral, sweet spices, creamy oak, elegant. Palate: powerful, flavourful, long, balanced.

SEÑORÍO DE ANDIÓN

Ctra. Pamplona-Zaragoza, Km. 38
31390 Olite - (Navarra)
☎: +34 948 712 193 - Fax: +34 948 712 343
info@familiabelasco.com
www.familiabelasco.com

SEÑORÍO DE ANDIÓN 2005 T
tempranillo, merlot, cabernet sauvignon, graciano

92 Colour: cherry, garnet rim. Nose: neat, toasty, sweet spices, ripe fruit. Palate: flavourful, ripe fruit, spicy, round tannins.

SEÑORÍO DE ANDIÓN MOSCATEL
VENDIMIA TARDÍA 2007 B
100% moscatel grano menudo

93 Colour: golden. Nose: powerfull, floral, honeyed notes, candied fruit, fragrant herbs, citrus fruit, spicy. Palate: flavourful, sweet, fresh, fruity, good acidity, long.

VIÑEDOS DE CALIDAD

Ctra. Tudela, s/n
31591 Corella - (Navarra)
☎: +34 948 782 014 - Fax: +34 948 782 164
inf@vinosalex.com
www.vinosalex.com

ONTINAR 14 BARRICAS 2009 T
50% tempranillo, 50% merlot

90 Colour: cherry, garnet rim. Nose: creamy oak, toasty, new oak. Palate: flavourful, good structure, ripe fruit, good acidity, long.

DESCRIPTION

In the province of Barcelona, this is the best known Denomination of Origin in Catalonia. It is situated between the pre-coastal mountain range of Catalonia and the plains which extend to the Mediterranean coast. The classical wines of this zone, which has one of the greatest concentrations of wineries (161) in Spain, are wines made from local grapes, pleasant to drink in the year. The white wines are aged in barrels and have more quality, as well as the red wines from any unimaginable native or foreign variety.

NUMBER OF HECTARES: 25.620

ALTITUDES: 0 m. – 800 m.

PREDOMINANT VARIETIES:

White grapes: macabeo, xarel.lo, parellada, chardonnay, riesling, gewürztraminer, chenin blanc, muscat of Alexandria and garnacha blanca.

Red grapes: garnacha, merlot, cariñena, ull de llebre, pinot noir, monastrell, cabernet sauvignon, syrah and sumoll.

CLIMATOLOGY AND SOILS

Mediterranean, generally warm and mild; warmer in the area of Bajo Penedés due to the influence of the Mediterranean, with slightly lower temperatures in the Middle Penedès and in the Upper Penedès, where the climate is pre-coastal.

1 + 1 = 3

Masía Navinés
8736 Guardiola de Font-Rubí - (Barcelona)
☎: +34 938 974 069 - Fax: +34 938 974 724
umesu@umesufan3.com
www.umesufan3.com

DÉFORA 1 + 1 = 3 2009 T
75% garnacha, 25% cariñena

90 Color cherry, garnet rim. Aroma ripe fruit, spicy, creamy oak, toasty, complex. Taste powerful, flavourful, toasty, round tannins.

AGUSTÍ TORELLÓ MATA

La Serra, s/n PO Box 35
8770 Sant Sadurní D'Anoia - (Barcelona)
☎: +34 938 911 173 - Fax: +34 938 912 616
comunicacio@agustitorellomata.com
www.agustitorellomata.com

APTIÀ D'AGUSTÍ TORELLÓ MATA "COL.LECCIÓ TERRERS" 2011 B
100% macabeo

93 Colour: bright straw. Nose: fresh, fresh fruit, white flowers, expressive, creamy oak. Palate: flavourful, fruity, good acidity, balanced.

XAREL.LO D'AGUSTÍ TORELLÓ MATA "COL.LECCIÓ TERRERS" 2011 B
100% xarel.lo

91 Colour: bright straw. Nose: ripe fruit, powerfull, expressive. Palate: good acidity, powerful, light-bodied, ripe fruit.

XII SUBIRAT PARENT D'AGUSTÍ TORELLÓ MATA "COL.LECCIÓ TERRERS" 2011 B
100% subirat parent

90 Colour: bright straw. Nose: mineral, ripe fruit, fruit expression, citrus fruit, earthy notes. Palate: flavourful, fruity, good acidity.

ALBET I NOYA

Can Vendrell de la Codina, s/n
8739 Sant Pau D'Ordal - (Barcelona)
☎: +34 938 994 812 - Fax: +34 938 994 930
albetinoya@albetinoya.cat
www.albetinoya.cat

ALBET I NOYA 3 MACABEUS 2011 B
macabeo

90 Colour: bright straw. Nose: white flowers, fresh fruit, mineral, balsamic herbs. Palate: fresh, fruity, flavourful, balanced.

ALBET I NOYA COL.LECCIÓ CHARDONNAY 2011 B
chardonnay

92 Colour: bright yellow. Nose: ripe fruit, sweet spices, creamy oak, fragrant herbs. Palate: rich, smoky aftertaste, flavourful, good acidity.

ALBET I NOYA COL.LECCIÓ SYRAH 2008 T
syrah

92 Colour: cherry, garnet rim. Nose: ripe fruit, spicy, creamy oak, toasty, earthy notes. Palate: powerful, flavourful, toasty, round tannins.

ALBET I NOYA EL BLANC XXV "ECOLÓGICO" 2011 B

91 Colour: bright yellow. Nose: ripe fruit, dried flowers, mineral, dry stone, wild herbs. Palate: powerful, flavourful, rich, long, balanced.

ALBET I NOYA LIGNUM 2010 T
cabernet sauvignon, garnacha, merlot, ull de llebre, syrah

90 Color bright cherry. Aroma ripe fruit, sweet spices, creamy oak, expressive. Taste flavourful, fruity, toasty, round tannins.

ALBET I NOYA LIGNUM 2011 B
chardonnay, sauvignon blanc, xarel.lo

90 Colour: bright yellow. Nose: white flowers, sweet spices, creamy oak, balsamic herbs, mineral. Palate: long, balanced, elegant, flavourful.

ALBET I NOYA RESERVA MARTÍ 2007 T

93 Colour: cherry, garnet rim. Nose: ripe fruit, spicy, creamy oak, toasty, characterful. Palate: powerful, flavourful, toasty, round tannins.

ALBET I NOYA TEMPRANILLO CLÀSSIC 2011 T
tempranillo

90 Color cherry, purple rim. Aroma expressive, fresh fruit, red berry notes, floral. Taste flavourful, fruity, good acidity, round tannins.

ALBET I NOYA XAREL-LO CLÀSSIC 2011 B
xarel.lo

90 Color bright straw. Aroma fresh, fresh fruit, white flowers, expressive. Taste flavourful, fruity, good acidity, balanced.

BELAT 2008 T
belat

93 Colour: cherry, garnet rim. Nose: ripe fruit, spicy, complex, mineral. Palate: powerful, flavourful, toasty, round tannins.

FINCA LA MILANA 2006 T
caladoc, ull de llebre, cabernet sauvignon, merlot

91 Colour: cherry, garnet rim. Nose: creamy oak, toasty, characterful, ripe fruit. Palate: powerful, flavourful, toasty, round tannins.

ALEMANY I CORRIO

Melió, 78
8720 Vilafranca del Penedès - (Barcelona)
☎: +34 938 922 746 - Fax: +34 938 172 587
sotlefriec@sotlefriec.com

PAS CURTEI 2010 T

92 Colour: very deep cherry. Nose: ripe fruit, overripe fruit, sweet spices. Palate: flavourful, powerful, good acidity, fine bitter notes.

SOT LEFRIEC 2007 T
cabernet sauvignon, cariñena, merlot

96 Colour: cherry, garnet rim. Nose: spicy, creamy oak, toasty, complex, earthy notes, ripe fruit. Palate: powerful, flavourful, toasty, round tannins.

ALSINA SARDÁ

Barrio Les Tarumbas, s/n
8733 Pla del Penedès - (Barcelona)
☎: +34 938 988 132 - Fax: +34 938 988 671
alsina@alsinasarda.com
www.alsinasarda.com

ALSINA & SARDÁ FINCA LA BOLTANA 2011 B
100% xarel.lo

90 Colour: bright straw. Nose: expressive, ripe fruit, white flowers. Palate: flavourful, fruity, fresh, good acidity, fine bitter notes.

BODEGAS CA N'ESTELLA

Masia Ca N'Estella, s/n
8635 Sant Esteve Sesrovires - (Barcelona)
☎: +34 934 161 387 - Fax: +34 934 161 620
j.rodriguez@fincacanestella.com
www.fincacanestella.com

GRAN CLOT DELS OMS 2006 TR
40% merlot, 60% cabernet sauvignon

90 Color cherry, garnet rim. Aroma ripe fruit, spicy, creamy oak, toasty, complex. Taste powerful, flavourful, toasty, round tannins.

GRAN CLOT DELS OMS XAREL.LO 2008 BFB
xarel.lo

90 Colour: bright yellow. Nose: ripe fruit, faded flowers, fragrant herbs, sweet spices, creamy oak. Palate: fruity, flavourful, spicy, long.

BODEGAS TORRE DEL VEGUER

Urb. Torre de Veguer, s/n
8810 Sant Pere de Ribes - (Barcelona)
☎: +34 938 963 190 - Fax: +34 938 962 967
torredelveguer@torredelveguer.com
www.torredelveguer.com

TORRE DEL VEGUER DULCE VENDIMIA TARDÍA 2011 B
90% moscatel de frontignan, 10% chardonnay

92 Colour: golden. Nose: powerfull, floral, candied fruit, fragrant herbs, complex, citrus fruit. Palate: flavourful, sweet, fresh, fruity, good acidity, long.

BODEGAS TORRES

Miguel Torres i Carbó, 6
8720 Vilafranca del Penedès - (Barcelona)
☎: +34 938 177 400 - Fax: +34 938 177 444
mailadmin@torres.es
www.torres.es

ATRIUM CHARDONNAY 2011 B
85% chardonnay, 15% parellada

92 Color bright straw. Aroma fresh, fresh fruit, white flowers, expressive. Taste flavourful, fruity, good acidity, balanced.

ATRIUM MERLOT 2010 T
100% merlot

90 Colour: cherry, garnet rim. Nose: red berry notes, ripe fruit, fragrant herbs, expressive. Palate: powerful, flavourful, spicy, long.

FRANSOLA 2011 B
95% sauvignon blanc, 5% parellada

91 Colour: bright straw. Nose: floral, citrus fruit, candied fruit, balsamic herbs, wild herbs. Palate: light-bodied, fresh, fruity, flavourful, easy to drink.

MAS LA PLANA CABERNET SAUVIGNON 2008 TR
100% cabernet sauvignon

93 Colour: deep cherry, garnet rim. Nose: complex, elegant, spicy, scrubland. Palate: balanced, fine bitter notes, round tannins.

RESERVA REAL 2003 TGR
cabernet sauvignon, merlot, cabernet franc

90 Color pale ruby, brick rim edge. Aroma elegant, spicy, fine reductive notes, wet leather, aged wood nuances, fruit liqueur notes. Taste spicy, fine tannins, elegant, long.

BODEGUES SUMARROCA

Barrio El Rebato, s/n
8739 Subirats - (Barcelona)
☎: +34 938 911 092 - Fax: +34 938 911 778
info@sumarroca.com
www.sumarroca.com

BÒRIA 2008 T
syrah, cabernet sauvignon, merlot

91 Colour: bright cherry. Nose: ripe fruit, sweet spices, creamy oak, characterful, mineral. Palate: flavourful, fruity, toasty, round tannins.

SUMARROCA SANTA CREU DE CREIXÀ 2009 T
syrah, garnacha, cabernet sauvignon, cabernet franc

90 Colour: cherry, garnet rim. Nose: sweet spices, cocoa bean, red berry notes, ripe fruit. Palate: flavourful, powerful, fine bitter notes.

SUMARROCA TEMPS DE FRUITS Nº 2 2011 T

90 Colour: cherry, purple rim. Nose: red berry notes, ripe fruit, balsamic herbs, mineral, floral. Palate: light-bodied, fresh, fruity, flavourful, balanced.

TERRAL 2009 T
syrah, cabernet franc, merlot, cabernet sauvignon

92 Colour: very deep cherry. Nose: sweet spices, ripe fruit, fruit expression, toasty, mineral. Palate: fruity, flavourful, fine bitter notes, good acidity.

CAL RASPALLET VITICULTORS

Barri Sabanell, 11
8736 Font Rubí - (Barcelona)
☎: +34 607 262 779
calraspallet@vinifera.cat

IMPROVISACIÓ 2010 B
xarel.lo

91 Colour: bright straw. Nose: candied fruit, citrus fruit, spicy. Palate: flavourful, ripe fruit, fine bitter notes, good acidity.

NUN VINYA DELS TAUS 2010 B
xarel.lo

94 Colour: bright yellow. Nose: characterful, expressive, varietal, ripe fruit, citrus fruit. Palate: good acidity, fine bitter notes, round.

CAN CREDO

Tamarit, 10 Apartado 15
8770 Sant Sadurní D'Anoia - (Barcelona)
☎: +34 938 910 214 - Fax: +34 938 911 697
cava@recaredo.es
www.recaredo.es

CAN CREDO 2010 B
100% xarel.lo

90 Colour: bright yellow. Nose: candied fruit, citrus fruit, spicy. Palate: flavourful, spicy, ripe fruit.

CAN FEIXES (HUGUET)

Finca Can Feixes, s/n
8718 Cabrera D'Anoia - (Barcelona)
☎: +34 937 718 227 - Fax: +34 937 718 031
canfeixes@canfeixes.com
www.canfeixes.com

CAN FEIXES CHARDONNAY 2007 BFB
chardonnay

91 Colour: bright golden. Nose: ripe fruit, dry nuts, powerfull, toasty, honeyed notes. Palate: flavourful, fruity, spicy, toasty, long, balanced.

CAN RÀFOLS DELS CAUS

Can Rafols del Caus s/n
8792 Avinyonet del Penedès - (Barcelona)
☎: +34 938 970 013 - Fax: +34 938 970 370
canrafolsdelscaus@canrafolsdelscaus.com
www.canrafolsdelscaus.com

EL ROCALLÍS 2009 BFB
Incrozio manzoni

90 Colour: bright yellow. Nose: candied fruit, toasty, spicy, honeyed notes. Palate: rich, flavourful, good structure, spicy, long.

VINYA LA CALMA 2009 BFB
chenin blanc

93 Colour: bright yellow. Nose: elegant, complex, petrol notes, ripe fruit, sweet spices, creamy oak. Palate: fruity, flavourful, complex. Personality.

CASTELLROIG - FINCA SABATÉ I COCA

Ctra. Sant Sadurní d'Anoia a Vilafranca del Penedès, Km. 1
8739 Subirats - (Barcelona)
☎: +34 938 911 927 - Fax: +34 938 914 055
info@castellroig.com
www.castellroig.com

CASTELLROIG SELECCIÓ 2010 B
xarel.lo, chardonnay

90 Colour: bright straw. Nose: powerfull, ripe fruit, spicy. Palate: flavourful, powerful, complex, long.

TERROJA DE SABATÉ I COCA 2011 B
xarel.lo

91 Colour: bright straw. Nose: fresh, white flowers, fresh fruit. Palate: flavourful, fruity, good acidity, balanced.

CAVAS FERRET

Avda. de Catalunya, 36
8736 Guardiola de Font-Rubí - (Barcelona)
☎: +34 938 979 148 - Fax: +34 938 979 285
ferret@cavasferret.com
www.cavasferret.com

ABAC 2011 B
100% xarel.lo

90 Colour: yellow, greenish rim. Nose: saline, ripe fruit, floral, fragrant herbs. Palate: light-bodied, fresh, fruity, flavourful.

CAVES GRAMONA

Industria, 36
8770 Sant Sadurní D'Anoia - (Barcelona)
☎: +34 938 910 113 - Fax: +34 938 183 284
comunicacion@gramona.com
www.gramona.com

GRAMONA MAS ESCORPÍ CHARDONNAY 2011 B
100% chardonnay

92 Colour: bright yellow. Nose: ripe fruit, floral, citrus fruit, wild herbs, complex, mineral. Palate: flavourful, rich, fruity, long, elegant.

GRAMONA SAUVIGNON BLANC 2011 BFB
100% sauvignon blanc

94 Colour: bright yellow. Nose: elegant, white flowers, citrus fruit, fruit expression, sweet spices, mineral. Palate: balanced, fresh, fruity, flavourful, complex. Personality.

GRAMONA XAREL.LO FONT JUI 2010 B
100% xarel.lo

93 Colour: bright yellow. Nose: ripe fruit, sweet spices, creamy oak, fragrant herbs, complex, expressive. Palate: rich, smoky aftertaste, flavourful, fresh, good acidity.

VI DE GLASS GEWÜRZTRAMINER 0,375 2010 B
100% gewürztraminer

90 Colour: bright yellow. Nose: powerfull, candied fruit, honeyed notes, white flowers. Palate: flavourful, sweet, good acidity.

VI DE GLASS GEWÜRZTRAMINER 0,75 2007 BC
100% gewürztraminer

94 Colour: bright yellow. Nose: powerfull, floral, honeyed notes, candied fruit, fragrant herbs. Palate: flavourful, sweet, fresh, fruity, good acidity, long.

VI DE GLASS RIESLING 2010 B
100% riesling

90 Colour: bright straw. Nose: powerfull, candied fruit, fruit preserve, citrus fruit. Palate: flavourful, sweet, fruity.

CAVES NAVERÁN

Can Parellada - Sant Martí Sadevesa
8775 Torrelavit - (Barcelona)
☎: +34 938 988 400 - Fax: +34 938 989 027
sadeve@naveran.com
www.naveran.com

CLOS ANTONIA 2011 B
viognier

93 Colour: bright yellow. Nose: ripe fruit, sweet spices, creamy oak, fragrant herbs, elegant. Palate: rich, flavourful, fresh, good acidity. Personality.

NAVERÁN CLOS DELS ANGELS 2010 T
syrah, merlot, cabernet sauvignon

93 Colour: light cherry, garnet rim. Nose: red berry notes, ripe fruit, fragrant herbs, expressive. Palate: light-bodied, fresh, balsamic, elegant.

NAVERÁN DON PABLO 2005 TR
cabernet sauvignon

90 Colour: cherry, garnet rim. Nose: ripe fruit, spicy, creamy oak, balsamic herbs. Palate: powerful, flavourful, toasty, round tannins.

CELLERS AVGVSTVS FORVM

Ctra. Sant Vicenç, s/n
43700 El Vendrell - (Tarragona)
☎: +34 977 666 910 - Fax: +34 977 666 590
albert@avgvstvs.es
www.avgvstvs.es

AVGVSTVS CABERNET SAUVIGNON-MERLOT 2010 T ROBLE
cabernet sauvignon, merlot

90 Colour: very deep cherry. Nose: balanced, expressive, mineral, ripe fruit. Palate: good structure, complex, ripe fruit, spicy, round tannins.

AVGVSTVS CHARDONNAY 2011 BFB
100% chardonnay

92 Color bright yellow. Aroma powerfull, ripe fruit, sweet spices, creamy oak, fragrant herbs. Taste rich, smoky aftertaste, flavourful, fresh, good acidity.

AVGVSTVS CHARDONNAY MAGNUM 2010 B
100% chardonnay

94 Colour: bright straw. Nose: fragrant herbs, warm, complex, expressive, ripe fruit, citrus fruit. Palate: ripe fruit, fine bitter notes, good acidity, spicy.

AVGVSTVS TRAJANVS 2009 TR
cabernet sauvignon, merlot, cabernet franc, garnacha

90 Colour: deep cherry, garnet rim. Nose: closed, ripe fruit, spicy, scrubland. Palate: full, good structure, round tannins.

AVGVSTVS XAREL.LO 2011 BFB
100% xarel.lo

90 Colour: bright yellow. Nose: ripe fruit, sweet spices, creamy oak, fragrant herbs, mineral. Palate: rich, smoky aftertaste, flavourful, fresh.

COLET

Cami del Salinar, s/n
8739 Pacs del Penedès - (Barcelona)
☎: +34 938 170 809 - Fax: +34 938 170 809
info@colet.cat
www.colet.cat

COLET ASSEMBLAGE BLANC DE NOIR ESP
chardonnay, pinot noir

92 Colour: coppery red. Nose: powerfull, candied fruit, spicy, toasty, dry nuts. Palate: flavourful, fine bitter notes, good acidity, fine bead.

COLET GRAND CUVEÉ ESP
chardonnay, macabeo, xarel.lo

92 Colour: bright straw. Nose: ripe fruit, fine lees, pattiserie, spicy. Palate: flavourful, fine bitter notes, ripe fruit.

COLET NAVAZOS EXTRA BRUT 2008 EXTRA BRUT RESERVA
chardonnay

94 Colour: bright yellow. Nose: complex, expressive, candied fruit, pattiserie, saline. Palate: flavourful, long, spicy, fine bitter notes.

COLET NAVAZOS EXTRA BRUT 2009 EXTRA BRUT

92 Colour: bright straw. Nose: spicy, medium intensity, balanced, balsamic herbs, dry nuts. Palate: flavourful, long, fine bitter notes.

COLET TRADICIONAL ESP
55% xarel.lo, 40% macabeo, 5% parellada

92 Colour: bright straw. Nose: powerfull, expressive, characterful, fine lees. Palate: flavourful, powerful, sweetness, fine bitter notes, balanced.

VATUA ! ESP
moscatel, parellada, gewürztraminer

90 Color bright straw. Aroma medium intensity, fresh fruit, dried herbs, fine lees, floral. Taste fresh, fruity, flavourful, good acidity.

EMENDIS

Barrio de Sant Marçal, 67
8732 Castellet i La Gornal - (Barcelona)
☎: +34 938 186 119 - Fax: +34 938 918 169
avalles@emendis.es
www.emendis.es

EMENDIS DUET VARIETAL 2010 T

91 Color cherry, garnet rim. Aroma ripe fruit, spicy, creamy oak, toasty, complex. Taste powerful, flavourful, toasty, round tannins.

EMENDIS MATER 2006 TC
100% merlot

91 Colour: cherry, garnet rim. Nose: spicy, creamy oak, toasty, characterful. Palate: powerful, flavourful, toasty, round tannins.

FINCA VALLDOSERA

Masia Les Garrigues, Urb. Can Trabal s/n
8734 Olèrdola - (Barcelona)
☎: +34 938 143 047 - Fax: +34 938 935 590
general@fincavalldosera.com
www.fincavalldosera.com

FINCA VALLDOSERA 2008 T
merlot, cabernet sauvignon, tempranillo

91 Colour: cherry, garnet rim. Nose: dark chocolate, ripe fruit, powerfull, red berry notes. Palate: good structure, full, round tannins.

FINCA VALLDOSERA 2011 T
syrah, merlot, cabernet sauvignon

90 Colour: cherry, purple rim. Nose: fruit expression, expressive, balanced. Palate: correct, fruity, easy to drink.

FINCA VALLDOSERA SUBIRAT PARENT 2011 B
100% subirat parent

90 Colour: bright straw. Nose: expressive, candied fruit, powerfull. Palate: flavourful, sweetness, fine bitter notes. Personality.

FINCA VILADELLOPS

Celler Gran Viladellops
8734 Olérdola - (Barcelona)
☎: +34 938 188 371 - Fax: +34 938 188 371
md@viladellops.com
www.viladellops.com

TURÓ DE LES ABELLES 2008 T
50% garnacha, 50% syrah

91 Colour: cherry, garnet rim. Nose: ripe fruit, spicy, creamy oak, toasty, earthy notes. Palate: powerful, flavourful, toasty.

VILADELLOPS GARNATXA 2011 T
garnacha

92 Colour: cherry, garnet rim. Nose: ripe fruit, balsamic herbs, scrubland, fresh, expressive. Palate: powerful, flavourful, complex, balsamic, balanced.

GIRÓ DEL GORNER

Finca Giró del Gorner, s/n
8797 Puigdálber - (Barcelona)
☎: +34 938 988 032
gorner@girodelgorner.com
www.girodelgorner.com

XAREL.LO GORNER 2010 B
100% xarel.lo

90 Colour: bright yellow. Nose: dried flowers, wild herbs, ripe fruit, spicy. Palate: powerful, rich, flavourful, toasty.

GIRÓ RIBOT

Finca El Pont, s/n
8792 Santa Fe del Penedès - (Barcelona)
☎: +34 938 974 050 - Fax: +34 938 974 311
giroribot@giroribot.es
www.giroribot.es

GIRÓ RIBOT MUSCAT DE FRONTIGNAC 2011 B
100% moscatel de frontignan

90 Colour: bright straw. Nose: fresh, fresh fruit, white flowers, expressive, candied fruit. Palate: flavourful, fruity, good acidity, balanced.

HERETAT MAS TINELL

Ctra. de Vilafranca a St. Martí Sarroca, Km. 0,5
8720 Vilafranca del Penedès - (Barcelona)
☎: +34 938 170 586 - Fax: +34 938 170 500
info@mastinell.com
www.mastinell.com

MAS TINELL GISELE 2009 BFB
100% xarel.lo

91 Colour: bright yellow, yellow, greenish rim. Nose: dried flowers, dry nuts, scrubland, spicy. Palate: powerful, flavourful, round, long, complex.

HERETAT MONT-RUBÍ

L'Avellà, 1
8736 Font- Rubí - (Barcelona)
☎: +34 938 979 066 - Fax: +34 938 979 066
hmr@montrubi.com
www.montrubi.com

ADVENT SAMSÓ DULCE NATURAL 2010 RD
samsó

92 Colour: light mahogany. Nose: ripe fruit, fruit liqueur notes, varnish, cocoa bean, toasty, sweet spices. Palate: round, rich, flavourful.

ADVENT SUMOLL DULCE NATURAL 2009 RD
sumoll

94 Colour: coppery red. Nose: candied fruit, raspberry, floral, sweet spices, creamy oak, dark chocolate. Palate: powerful, flavourful, spicy, toasty, roasted-coffee aftertaste.

ADVENT XAREL.LO 2009 B
xarel.lo

90 Colour: bright golden. Nose: ripe fruit, dry nuts, citrus fruit, fragrant herbs, dried flowers. Palate: powerful, flavourful, concentrated, balanced, round.

BLACK HMR 2011 T
60% garnacha, 40% otras

91 Colour: cherry, purple rim. Nose: floral, raspberry, red berry notes, lactic notes, expressive. Palate: good acidity, powerful, flavourful, balanced.

DURONA 2007 T
sumoll, garnacha, cariñena

90 Colour: cherry, garnet rim. Nose: ripe fruit, spicy, creamy oak, toasty, earthy notes. Palate: powerful, flavourful, toasty, round tannins.

GAINTUS 2007 T
sumoll

91 Colour: cherry, garnet rim. Nose: spicy, creamy oak, toasty, expressive, characterful, ripe fruit. Palate: powerful, flavourful, toasty, round tannins.

JANÉ VENTURA

Ctra. Calafell, 2
43700 El Vendrell - (Tarragona)
☎: +34 977 660 118 - Fax: +34 977 661 239
janeventura@janeventura.com
www.janeventura.com

JANÉ VENTURA "FINCA ELS CAMPS"
MACABEU 2010 BFB

90 Colour: bright straw. Nose: wild herbs, elegant, ripe fruit, complex. Palate: fruity, good acidity, fine bitter notes.

JANÉ VENTURA "FINCA ELS CAMPS"
SERRA DEL MOMTMELL 2011 B
macabeo

91 Colour: bright straw. Nose: fresh, white flowers, expressive, ripe fruit. Palate: flavourful, fruity, good acidity, balanced.

JANÉ VENTURA "FINCA ELS CAMPS"
ULL DE LLEBRE 2007 T
ull de llebre

91 Color cherry, garnet rim. Aroma ripe fruit, spicy, creamy oak, toasty, complex. Taste powerful, flavourful, toasty, round tannins.

JANÉ VENTURA "MAS VILELLA"
COSTERS DEL ROTLLAN 2009 T
cabernet sauvignon

92 Colour: cherry, garnet rim. Nose: scrubland, ripe fruit, earthy notes, expressive, spicy, creamy oak. Palate: round, powerful, flavourful, long, balanced.

JANÉ VENTURA MALVASÍA DE
SITGES 2011 B BARRICA
malvasía

92 Colour: bright straw. Nose: elegant, complex, white flowers, ripe fruit, sweet spices. Palate: balanced, good acidity, fine bitter notes. Personality.

JEAN LEON

Pago Jean León, s/n
8775 Torrelavit - (Barcelona)
☎: +34 938 995 512 - Fax: +34 938 995 517
jeanleon@jeanleon.com
www.jeanleon.com

JEAN LEÓN CABERNET SAUVIGNON 2005 TR
85% cabernet sauvignon, 15% cabernet franc

92 Colour: dark-red cherry, orangey edge. Nose: ripe fruit, balsamic herbs, earthy notes, fine reductive notes. Palate: long, flavourful, spicy, balanced.

JEAN LEÓN PETIT CHARDONNAY 2011 B
100% chardonnay

90 Colour: bright yellow. Nose: expressive, ripe fruit, jasmine, powerfull, varietal. Palate: flavourful, rich, long, good acidity, balanced.

JEAN LEÓN VINYA LA SCALA CABERNET
SAUVIGNON 2001 TGR
100% cabernet sauvignon

92 Color pale ruby, brick rim edge. Aroma elegant, spicy, fine reductive notes, wet leather, aged wood nuances, fruit liqueur notes. Taste spicy, fine tannins, elegant, long.

JEAN LEÓN VINYA PALAU MERLOT 2007 TC
100% merlot

91 Colour: cherry, garnet rim. Nose: ripe fruit, spicy, creamy oak, toasty, wild herbs. Palate: powerful, flavourful, toasty, round tannins, elegant.

JEAN LEÓN VIÑA GIGI CHARDONNAY 2009 BC
100% chardonnay

90 Colour: bright yellow. Nose: elegant, balanced, candied fruit, creamy oak. Palate: flavourful, toasty, ripe fruit.

JOSEP Mª RAVENTÓS I BLANC

Plaça del Roure, s/n
8770 Sant Sadurní D'Anoia - (Barcelona)
☎: +34 938 183 262 - Fax: +34 938 912 500
raventos@raventos.com
www.raventos.com

SILENCIS 2011 B
100% xarel.lo

90 Colour: bright straw. Nose: white flowers, varietal, ripe fruit, balanced. Palate: flavourful, fruity, good acidity, balanced.

JUVÉ Y CAMPS

Sant Venat, 1
8770 Sant Sadurní D'Anoia - (Barcelona)
☎: +34 938 911 000 - Fax: +34 938 912 100
juveycamps@juveycamps.com
www.juveycamps.com

IOHANNES 2008 T
55% merlot, 45% cabernet sauvignon

91 Colour: cherry, garnet rim. Nose: scrubland, ripe fruit, spicy, balanced. Palate: long, balsamic, flavourful, round tannins.

MIRANDA D'ESPIELLS 2011 B
100% chardonnay

90 Color bright straw. Aroma fresh, fresh fruit, white flowers, expressive. Taste flavourful, fruity, good acidity, balanced.

MAS BERTRAN

Ctra. BP - 2121, km. 7,7
8731 St. Martí Sarroca - (Barcelona)
☎: +34 938 990 859 - Fax: +34 938 990 859
info@masbertran.com
www.masbertran.com

ARGILA 2007 BN GRAN RESERVA
xarel.lo

92 Color bright golden. Aroma fine lees, dry nuts, fragrant herbs, complex. Taste powerful, flavourful, good acidity, fine bead, fine bitter notes.

NUTT SUMOLL 2011 RD
100% sumoll

90 Colour: salmon, bright. Nose: floral, fruit expression, expressive, balanced. Palate: fruity, flavourful, long, good acidity.

MAS CAN COLOMÉ

Masies Sant Marçal s/n
8720 Castellet i La Gornal - (Barcelona)
☎: +34 938 918 203 - Fax: +34 938 918 203
info@mascancolome.com
www.mascancolome.com

SERENOR 2010 ESP
xarel.lo, chardonnay, parellada, macabeo

90 Colour: bright straw. Nose: fresh fruit, dried herbs, fine lees, floral, citrus fruit. Palate: fresh, fruity, flavourful, good acidity, complex.

MAS CANDÍ

Ctra. de Les Gunyoles, s/n
8793 Avinyonet - (Barcelona)
☎: +34 680 765 275
info@mascandi.com
www.mascandi.com

MAS CANDI PECAT NOBLE 2010 B
malvasía

92 Colour: bright yellow. Nose: citrus fruit, fruit liqueur notes, varnish, creamy oak, fragrant herbs. Palate: powerful, flavourful, fruity, sweet, balanced.

MAS CANDÍ QUATRE XAREL.LO QX 2010 BFB
100% xarel.lo

90 Colour: bright yellow. Nose: toasty, spicy, candied fruit, wild herbs. Palate: balanced, fruity, full.

MAS COMTAL

Mas Comtal, 1
8793 Avinyonet del Penedès - (Barcelona)
☎: +34 938 970 052 - Fax: +34 938 970 591
mascomtal@mascomtal.com
www.mascomtal.com

ANTISTIANA 2008 T
85% merlot, 15% cabernet sauvignon

90 Colour: cherry, garnet rim. Nose: ripe fruit, spicy, creamy oak, toasty, dark chocolate. Palate: powerful, flavourful, toasty, round tannins.

PÉTREA 2008 BFB
85% chardonnay, 15% xarel.lo

91 Colour: bright yellow. Nose: powerfull, ripe fruit, sweet spices, creamy oak, fragrant herbs. Palate: rich, flavourful, fresh, good acidity, long.

MAS RODÓ

Finca Mas Rodo, km. 2 Ctra. Sant Pere Sacarrera a Sant Joan de Mediona
8773 Sant Joan de Mediona - (Barcelona)
☎: +34 932 385 780 - Fax: +34 932 174 356
info@masrodo.com
www.masrodo.com

MAS RODÓ RIESLING 2011 BFB
85% riesling, 15% montonega

90 Colour: bright yellow. Nose: ripe fruit, sweet spices, creamy oak, fragrant herbs. Palate: rich, flavourful, fresh, good acidity, toasty.

MIQUEL PONS

Baix Llobregat, 5
8792 La Granada - (Barcelona)
☎: +34 938 974 541 - Fax: +34 938 974 710
miquelpons@cavamiquelpons.com
www.cavamiquelpons.com

MONTARGULL 2011 BFB
100% xarel.lo

90 Colour: bright yellow. Nose: powerfull, ripe fruit, sweet spices, creamy oak, floral. Palate: rich, smoky aftertaste, flavourful, fresh, good acidity.

ORIOL ROSSELL

Propietat Can Cassanyes, s/n
8732 St. Marçal - (Barcelona)
☎: +34 977 671 061 - Fax: +34 977 671 050
oriolrossell@oriolrossell.com
www.oriolrossell.com

VIROLET XAREL.LO 2011 B
100% xarel.lo

90 Colour: bright yellow. Nose: balanced, expressive, ripe fruit, wild herbs, faded flowers. Palate: balanced, rich, fine bitter notes, long.

PARATÓ

Can Respall de Renardes
8733 - (Barcelona)
☎: +34 938 988 182 - Fax: +34 938 988 510
info@parato.es
www.parato.es

FINCA RENARDES BLANC MACABEU + COUPAGE 2011 B
46% macabeo, 43% chardonnay, 11% xarel.lo

90 Color bright straw. Aroma fresh, fresh fruit, white flowers, expressive. Taste flavourful, fruity, good acidity, balanced.

PARDAS

Finca Can Comas, s/n
8775 Torrelavit - (Barcelona)
☎: +34 938 995 005
pardas@cancomas.com
www.pardas.net

PARDAS ASPRIU 2009 T
100% cabernet franc

94 Colour: deep cherry. Nose: toasty, spicy, earthy notes, ripe fruit, fruit expression, scrubland. Palate: flavourful, spicy, ripe fruit, fine bitter notes.

PARDAS ASPRIU 2010 B
100% xarel.lo

92 Colour: bright straw. Nose: faded flowers, ripe fruit, creamy oak, sweet spices. Palate: flavourful, sweetness, fine bitter notes, good acidity.

PARDAS NEGRE FRANC 2009 T
66% cabernet franc, 23% cabernet sauvignon, 11% sumoll

91 Colour: deep cherry. Nose: ripe fruit, sweet spices, mineral. Palate: flavourful, powerful, fine bitter notes, round tannins.

PARÉS BALTÀ

Masía Can Baltá, s/n
8796 Pacs del Penedès - (Barcelona)
☎: +34 938 901 399 - Fax: +34 938 901 143
paresbalta@paresbalta.com
www.paresbalta.com

ELECTIO XAREL.LO 2009 B
100% xarel.lo

90 Colour: bright yellow. Nose: faded flowers, fruit preserve, citrus fruit. Palate: flavourful, fine bitter notes, good acidity, long.

HISENDA MIRET GARNATXA 2009 T
100% garnacha

90 Colour: deep cherry. Nose: fruit preserve, toasty, spicy, aromatic coffee. Palate: flavourful, powerful, spicy, long.

INDÍGENA 2010 T
100% garnacha,

91 Colour: deep cherry. Nose: ripe fruit, spicy, toasty, mineral. Palate: round tannins, spicy, ripe fruit.

INDÍGENA 2011 B
100% garnacha blanca

94 Colour: bright straw. Nose: ripe fruit, citrus fruit, dried herbs. Palate: flavourful, good acidity, fine bitter notes, easy to drink, long.

MARTA DE BALTÀ 2007 T
100% syrah

91 Colour: cherry, garnet rim. Nose: spicy, toasty, complex, aromatic coffee, fruit expression. Palate: powerful, flavourful, toasty, round tannins.

MAS ELENA 2009 T
merlot, cabernet sauvignon, cabernet franc

91 Colour: cherry, garnet rim. Nose: spicy, creamy oak, toasty, characterful. Palate: powerful, flavourful, toasty, round tannins.

MAS IRENE 2007 T
72% merlot, 28% cabernet franc

92 Colour: cherry, garnet rim. Nose: ripe fruit, spicy, creamy oak, toasty, characterful. Palate: powerful, flavourful, toasty, round tannins.

PUIG ROMEU

Barri Piscina, 5
8779 La Llacuna - (Barcelona)
☎: +34 938 976 206 - Fax: +34 938 977 087
info@puig-romeu.com
www.puig-romeu.com

VINYA JORDINA 2011 B
50% viognier, 30% sauvignon blanc, 20% garnacha blanca

91 Colour: bright yellow. Nose: ripe fruit, floral, fragrant herbs, sweet spices, spicy. Palate: good acidity, correct, elegant, powerful, flavourful.

TORELLÓ

Can Martí de Baix, Ctra. de Sant Sadurni a Gélida - Apdo. Correos 8
8770 Sant Sadurní D'Anoia - (Barcelona)
☎: +34 938 910 793 - Fax: +34 938 910 877
torello@torello.es
www.torello.com

PETJADES 2011 RD
merlot

90 Colour: rose, purple rim. Nose: powerfull, ripe fruit, red berry notes, floral, expressive, mineral. Palate: , powerful, fruity, fresh.

VALL DOLINA

Plaça de la Creu, 1
8795 Olesa de Bonesvalls - (Barcelona)
☎: +34 938 984 181 - Fax: +34 938 984 181
info@valldolina.com
www.valldolina.com

VALL DOLINA XAREL.LO "ECOLÓGICO" 2011 B
xarel.lo

90 Colour: yellow, greenish rim. Nose: floral, ripe fruit, dried herbs, expressive, mineral. Palate: powerful, flavourful, balanced, good acidity.

DESCRIPTION

This is in the natural region of Bages, in the geographical centre of Catalonia. It borders to the south with the Montserrat mountain range, a line which separates it from Penedès. Despite its 10 wineries, the production of quality wines is concentrated in the hands of the Abadal company, the first to explore the possibilities of the picapoll variety. This grape which was given its name due to the skin "picada" (pitted), and produces fruity, very intense wines. The red wines of the region are made from French grapes.

NUMBER OF HECTARES: 500 **ALTITUDES:** 400 m.

PREDOMINANT VARIETIES:

White grapes: chardonnay, gewürztraminer, macabeo, picapoll, parellada and sauvignon blanc. Red grapes: sumoll, ull de llebre, merlot, cabernet franc, cabernet sauvignon, syrah and garnacha.

CLIMATOLOGY AND SOILS

Mediterranean at medium mountain height. The soils are silt- clay, silt – sand and silt – clay/sand.

ABADAL

Santa María d'Horta d'Avinyó
8279 Santa María D'Horta D'Avinyó - (Barcelona)
☎: +34 938 743 511 - Fax: +34 938 737 204
info@abadal.net
www.abadal.net

ABADAL 3.9 2008 TR
85% cabernet sauvignon, 15% syrah

93 Colour: cherry, garnet rim. Nose: ripe fruit, spicy, fine reductive notes, earthy notes, scrubland. Palate: powerful, flavourful, complex, balanced.

ABADAL PICAPOLL 2011 B
100% picapoll

91 Colour: bright straw. Nose: fresh, fresh fruit, white flowers, expressive, fragrant herbs, citrus fruit, mineral. Palate: flavourful, fruity, good acidity, balanced.

ABADAL SELECCIÓ 2007 TR
40% cabernet sauvignon, 40% cabernet franc, 15% syrah, 5% sumoll, 5% mandó

93 Colour: cherry, garnet rim. Nose: ripe fruit, spicy, toasty, aromatic coffee, earthy notes, scrubland. Palate: powerful, flavourful, toasty.

EL MOLI

Camí de Rajadell, Km. 3
8241 Manresa - (Barcelona)
☎: +34 931 021 965 - Fax: +34 931 021 965
collbaix@cellerelmoli.com
www.cellerelmoli.com

COLLBAIX SINGULAR 2008 T
100% cabernet sauvignon

91 Colour: cherry, garnet rim. Nose: ripe fruit, spicy, creamy oak, complex, wild herbs. Palate: powerful, flavourful, toasty, round tannins.

COLLBAIX SINGULAR 2011 B
90% macabeo, 10% picapoll

90 Colour: bright straw. Nose: floral, citrus fruit, spicy, expressive, ripe fruit. Palate: flavourful, rich, complex, long, good acidity, balanced.

HERETAT OLLER DEL MAS

Ctra. de Igualada (C-37), km. 91
8241 Manresa - (Barcelona)
☎: +34 938 768 315 - Fax: +34 932 056 949
info@ollerdelmas.com
www.ollerdelmas.com

ARNAU OLLER SELECCIÓ DE LA FAMILIA 2007 T
100% merlot

90 Colour: cherry, garnet rim. Nose: ripe fruit, earthy notes, fragrant herbs, spicy. Palate: complex, powerful, flavourful, balanced.

DO PLA I LLEVANT

DESCRIPTION

In the central and eastern zones of the Island of Mallorca, the name of this Denomination of Origin in Mallorcan means "flat, eastern coast". Its principal product is the wine made from the local callet variety and varieties of French grapes (pinot noir, chardonnay, merlot, cabernet sauvignon and syrah), processed with the same procedure as the Burgundy wines. The wines include an aroma between Mediterranean and a deep terroir as a result of the limestone soils.

NUMBER OF HECTARES: 349 **ALTITUDES:** 150 m.

PREDOMINANT VARIETIES:

White grapes: prensal blanc, macabeo, parellada, muscatel and chardonnay.
Red grapes: callet, manto negro, fogoneu, tempranillo, monastrell, cabernet sauvignon, merlot and syrah.

CLIMATOLOGY AND SOILS

Mediterranean, the soils are made up of limestone rocks which give them a limestone – clay character.

BODEGA JAUME MESQUIDA

Vileta, 7
7260 Porreres - (Illes Ballears)
☎: +34 971 647 106 - Fax: +34 971 168 205
info@jaumemesquida.com
www.jaumemesquida.com

JAUME MESQUIDA CABERNET SAUVIGNON 2006 TC
100% cabernet sauvignon

93 Colour: cherry, garnet rim. Nose: complex, spicy, earthy notes, ripe fruit, fragrant herbs, dark chocolate, elegant. Palate: balanced, good acidity.

JAUME MESQUIDA CABERNET SAUVIGNON 2007 TC
cabernet sauvignon

90 Colour: cherry, garnet rim. Nose: ripe fruit, spicy, toasty, complex. Palate: powerful, flavourful, toasty, round tannins.

MOLÍ DE VENT NEGRE 2009 T
callet, manto negro

90 Colour: bright cherry. Nose: ripe fruit, sweet spices, creamy oak, scrubland. Palate: flavourful, fruity, round tannins, good acidity.

VIÑA DEL ALBARICOQUE 2009 T

90 Colour: deep cherry, garnet rim. Nose: complex, balanced, ripe fruit, sweet spices, creamy oak. Palate: flavourful, spicy.

BODEGA MESQUIDA MORA

Vileta, 7
7260 Porreres - (Mallorca)
☎: +34 687 971 457
info@mesquidamora.com
www.mesquidamora.com

TRISPOL 2010 T

90 Colour: bright cherry, purple rim. Nose: powerfull, ripe fruit, spicy. Palate: powerful, flavourful, full, good acidity.

BODEGAS PERE SEDA

Cid Campeador, 22
7500 Manacor - (Illes Ballears)
☎: +34 971 605 087 - Fax: +34 971 604 856
pereseda@pereseda.com
www.pereseda.com

GVIVM MERLOT-CALLET 2009 T
70% merlot, 30% callet

90 Colour: bright cherry, garnet rim. Nose: ripe fruit, candied fruit, sweet spices. Palate: long, balanced, full.

PERE SEDA 2008 TC
cabernet sauvignon, merlot, syrah, callet

90 Colour: bright cherry. Nose: sweet spices, cocoa bean, balanced, red berry notes, ripe fruit. Palate: good structure, flavourful, long.

VINS MIQUEL GELABERT

Carrer d'en Sales, 50
7500 Manacor - (Illes Balears)
☎: +34 971 821 444 - Fax: +34 971 596 441
vinsmg@vinsmiquelgelabert.com
www.vinsmiquelgelabert.com

AUTÓCTON 2009 T
60% callet, 30% manto negro, 10% fogoneu

91 Colour: bright cherry, garnet rim. Nose: elegant, balanced, wild herbs, ripe fruit, mineral. Palate: long, round tannins, good acidity.

CHARDONNAY ROURE BFB
100% chardonnay

90 Colour: bright yellow. Nose: powerfull, ripe fruit, sweet spices, creamy oak. Palate: rich, smoky aftertaste, flavourful, fresh, good acidity.

GOLÓS 2009 T
callet, manto negro, fogoneu

92 Colour: bright cherry, garnet rim. Nose: balsamic herbs, wild herbs, ripe fruit, mineral, spicy. Palate: complex, good structure, flavourful, good acidity.

GRAN VINYA SON CAULES 2006 T
95% callet, 5% manto negro, fogoneu

90 Colour: bright cherry, orangey edge. Nose: powerfull, toasty, scrubland. Palate: ripe fruit, spicy, long, good acidity.

PETIT TORRENT 2005 T
70% cabernet sauvignon, 15% merlot, 15% callet

90 Colour: cherry, garnet rim. Nose: balsamic herbs, ripe fruit, balanced, sweet spices. Palate: flavourful, long.

TORRENT NEGRE SELECCIÓ PRIVADA SYRAH 2005 T
100% syrah

91 Colour: bright cherry. Nose: ripe fruit, creamy oak, sweet spices. Palate: flavourful, ripe fruit, long, round tannins.

VINYA DES MORÉ 2006 T
100% pinot noir

90 Colour: cherry, garnet rim. Nose: ripe fruit, spicy, creamy oak, dark chocolate. Palate: powerful, flavourful, toasty, round tannins.

VINS TONI GELABERT

Camí dels Horts de Llodrá Km. 1,3
7500 Manacor - (Illes Balears)
☎: +34 610 789 531
info@vinstonigelabert.com
www.vinstonigelabert.com

FANGOS NEGRE 2008 T
callet, merlot, cabernet sauvignon, syrah

90 Colour: cherry, garnet rim. Nose: powerfull, warm, ripe fruit, sweet spices. Palate: flavourful, round tannins.

NEGRE DE SA COLONIA 2010 T
100% callet

90 Colour: bright cherry. Nose: expressive, scrubland, ripe fruit. Palate: spicy, fruity, easy to drink, elegant.

SES HEREVES 2005 T
cabernet sauvignon, merlot, syrah

90 Colour: bright cherry, orangey edge. Nose: spicy, creamy oak, warm, scrubland, fruit liqueur notes. Palate: powerful, flavourful, toasty, round tannins.

TONI GELABERT CHARDONNAY 2011 BFB
100% chardonnay

90 Colour: bright yellow. Nose: creamy oak, roasted coffee. Palate: good structure, rich, flavourful, ripe fruit, spicy.

TONI GELABERT COLONIA U 2008 TC
cabernet sauvignon, otras

90 Colour: cherry, purple rim. Nose: balanced, scrubland, ripe fruit. Palate: full, flavourful, good structure.

TONI GELABERT NEGRE SELECCIO 2007 T
cabernet sauvignon, manto negro

91 Colour: bright cherry, garnet rim. Nose: complex, balsamic herbs, spicy, ripe fruit. Palate: full, flavourful, round tannins, long.

VINYES I BODEGUES MIQUEL OLIVER

Font, 26
7520 Petra-Mallorca - (Illes Ballears)
☎: +34 971 561 117 - Fax: +34 971 561 117
bodega@miqueloliver.com
www.miqueloliver.com

AIA 2009 T
100% merlot

91 Colour: bright cherry, garnet rim. Nose: ripe fruit, powerfull, expressive, scrubland. Palate: fruity, full, spicy, long.

SES FERRITGES 2008 TC
callet, cabernet sauvignon, merlot, syrah

92 Colour: bright cherry. Nose: cocoa bean, creamy oak, ripe fruit, balsamic herbs. Palate: balanced, good acidity, spicy, ripe fruit.

XPERIMENT 2009 T
100% callet

90 Colour: bright cherry, purple rim. Nose: ripe fruit, complex, balanced, cocoa bean. Palate: fruity, good acidity.

DESCRIPTION

This is in the province of Tarragona and occupies a small mountainous zone to the west of the city of Tarragona. Owing to the uneven orography, the garnacha and cariñena vines are cultivated on very steep slopes on layers of slate or fine slate. This material has given the mineral fame to these full bodied, concentrated wines, and it also serves as a natural barrier which prevents erosion and humidity. The red wines have become lighter with the mixture of new varieties such as syrah. The white wines have reached their zenith with the discovery of the potential of the expressive garnacha blanca.

NUMBER OF HECTARES: 1.925 **ALTITUDES:** 100 m. – 700 m.

PREDOMINANT VARIETIES:

White grapes: chenin, macabeo, garnacha blanca, pedro ximénez, muscat of Alexandria, muscatel de grano pequeño, xarel.lo, picapoll blanca and viognier.

Red grapes: cariñena, garnacha, mazuela, garnacha peluda, cabernet sauvignon, cabernet franc, ull de llebre, pinot noir, merlot, syrah and picapoll negra.

CLIMATOLOGY AND SOILS

It is temperate and dry with Mediterranean influences. The soils are the distinctive component of this zone. The poor soils and the volcanic constitution are formed by small sheets of slate and provide a notable mineral character to the wines.

ACÚSTIC CELLER

Progrés s/n
43775 Marça - (Tarragona)
☎: +34 672 432 691 - Fax: +34 977 660 867
acustic@acusticceller.com
www.acusticceller.com

RITME NEGRE 2010 T
70% cariñena, 30% garnacha

92 Colour: bright cherry. Nose: sweet spices, creamy oak, mineral, fruit expression. Palate: flavourful, fruity, toasty, round tannins.

AGNÈS DE CERVERA

Ctra. El Molar - El Lloar, Km. 10
43736 El Molar - (Tarragona)
☎: +34 977 054 851 - Fax: +34 977 054 851
comunicacion@agnesdecervera.com
www.agnesdecervera.com

KALOS 2010 T
85% mazuelo, 15% syrah

90 Colour: bright cherry. Nose: sweet spices, creamy oak, mineral. Palate: flavourful, fruity, toasty, round tannins.

LYTOS 2010 T
45% mazuelo, 30% garnacha, 15% syrah, 5% cabernet sauvignon

91 Colour: cherry, garnet rim. Nose: red berry notes, ripe fruit, mineral, creamy oak. Palate: spicy, powerful, flavourful, balanced.

ALVARO PALACIOS

Afores, s/n
43737 Gratallops - (Tarragona)
☎: +34 977 839 195 - Fax: +34 977 839 197
info@alvaropalacios.com

CAMINS DEL PRIORAT 2011 T
40% garnacha, 30% samsó, 5% syrah, 20% cabernet sauvignon, 5% merlot

90 Colour: bright cherry. Nose: ripe fruit, raspberry, scrubland. Palate: flavourful, fruity, toasty, round tannins.

FINCA DOFÍ 2010 TC
80% garnacha, 15% syrah, 5% cabernet sauvignon

95 Colour: deep cherry. Nose: expressive, complex, elegant, scrubland, sweet spices. Palate: flavourful, ripe fruit, spicy, good acidity, fine bitter notes.

GRATALLOPS VI DE LA VILA 2010 T
65% garnacha, 15% samsó, 10% syrah, 10% cabernet sauvignon

94 Colour: very deep cherry. Nose: sweet spices, ripe fruit, fruit expression, mineral. Palate: flavourful, spicy, ripe fruit, long, round tannins.

L'ERMITA 2010 TC
garnacha

97 Colour: very deep cherry. Nose: scrubland, characterful, expressive, ripe fruit, toasty, sweet spices. Palate: flavourful, fine bitter notes, spicy, fine tannins.

LES TERRASSES VINYES VELLES 2010 T
40% garnacha, 45% samsó, 10% cabernet sauvignon, 5% syrah

93 Colour: cherry, garnet rim. Nose: toasty, sweet spices, fruit expression, earthy notes. Palate: flavourful, spicy, fine bitter notes, good acidity.

AUTOR

Balandra, 6
43737 Torroja de Priorat - (Tarragona)
☎: +34 977 839 285
adminbodega@rotllantorra.com
www.rotllantorra.com

AUTOR 2008 TR
garnacha, mazuelo, cabernet sauvignon

91 Colour: deep cherry, garnet rim. Nose: balanced, expressive, cocoa bean, creamy oak. Palate: balanced, good acidity, fine bitter notes.

BLAI FERRÉ JUST

Piró, 28
43737 Gratallops - (Tarragona)
☎: +34 647 217 751 - Fax: +34 977 839 507
blaiferrejust@yahoo.es

DESNIVELL 2009 TC
80% garnacha, 20% cariñena

90 Colour: cherry, garnet rim. Nose: powerfull, warm, ripe fruit. Palate: flavourful, concentrated, sweetness.

BODEGAS MAS ALTA

Ctra. T-702, Km. 16,8
43375 La Vilella Alta - (Tarragona)
☎: +34 977 054 151 - Fax: +34 977 817 194
info@bodegasmasalta.com
www.bodegasmasalta.com

ARTIGAS 2009 T
garnacha, mazuelo, cabernet sauvignon

94 Colour: cherry, garnet rim. Nose: ripe fruit, spicy, creamy oak, toasty, mineral. Palate: powerful, flavourful, toasty, round tannins.

ARTIGAS 2011 BFB
garnacha blanca, macabeo, pedro ximénez

93 Colour: bright yellow. Nose: powerfull, ripe fruit, sweet spices, fragrant herbs. Palate: rich, flavourful, fresh, good acidity.

CIRERETS 2009 T

91 Colour: cherry, garnet rim. Nose: spicy, creamy oak, toasty, complex, mineral. Palate: powerful, flavourful, toasty, round tannins.

ELS PICS 2010 T

91 Colour: very deep cherry. Nose: characterful, ripe fruit, spicy, creamy oak. Palate: flavourful, powerful, fine bitter notes.

LA BASSETA 2009 T

92 Colour: very deep cherry. Nose: ripe fruit, sweet spices, toasty, mineral. Palate: flavourful, powerful, fine bitter notes, good acidity, round tannins.

LA CREU ALTA 2005 T
50% cariñena, 35% garnacha, 15% cabernet sauvignon

94 Colour: cherry, garnet rim. Nose: spicy, complex, fruit expression, new oak, earthy notes. Palate: powerful, flavourful, toasty, round tannins.

BUIL & GINÉ

Ctra. de Gratallops - Vilella Baixa, Km. 11,5
43737 Gratallops - (Tarragona)
☎: +34 977 839 810 - Fax: +34 977 839 811
info@builgine.com
www.builgine.com

PLERET BLANC DOLÇ 2010 B
macabeo, garnacha blanca, pedro ximénez

90 Colour: bright yellow. Nose: powerfull, fruit preserve, sweet spices. Palate: flavourful, sweetness, fine bitter notes.

BURGOS PORTA

Mas Sinén, s/n
43376 Poboleda - (Tarragona)
☎: +34 696 094 509
burgosporta@massinen.com
www.massinen.com

MAS SINÉN 2008 T
garnacha, cariñena, cabernet sauvignon, syrah

90 Colour: cherry, garnet rim. Nose: toasty, spicy, overripe fruit. Palate: spicy, ripe fruit, fine bitter notes.

CASA GRAN DEL SIURANA

Mayor, 3
43738 Bellmunt del Priorat - (Tarragona)
☎: +34 932 233 022 - Fax: +34 932 231 370
perelada@castilloperelada.com
www.castilloperelada.com

CRUOR 2008 T
30% garnacha, 20% syrah, 10% merlot, 20% cabernet sauvignon, 20% cariñena

91 Colour: bright cherry. Nose: sweet spices, creamy oak, expressive, overripe fruit. Palate: flavourful, fruity, toasty, round tannins.

GR-174 2011 T
42% garnacha, 38% cariñena, 20% cabernet sauvignon

90 Colour: bright cherry. Nose: sweet spices, expressive, fruit preserve. Palate: flavourful, fruity, toasty, round tannins.

GRAN CRUOR 2008 T
70% syrah, 20% cariñena, 10% garnacha

93 Colour: cherry, garnet rim. Nose: ripe fruit, spicy, creamy oak, complex, mineral, dark chocolate. Palate: powerful, flavourful, toasty, round tannins.

CASTELL D'OR

Mare Rafols, 3- 1º 4º
8720 Vilafranca del Penedès - (Barcelona)
☎: +34 938 905 446 - Fax: +34 938 905 446
castelldor@castelldor.com
www.castelldor.com

ABADÍA MEDITERRÀNIA 2010 TC
60% garnacha, 40% cariñena

90 Colour: cherry, purple rim. Nose: balanced, spicy, wild herbs. Palate: good structure, flavourful, long.

GRAN ABADÍA MEDITERRÀNIA 2009 TR
50% garnacha, 35% cariñena, 15% cabernet sauvignon

90 Colour: cherry, garnet rim. Nose: ripe fruit, spicy, creamy oak, toasty. Palate: powerful, flavourful, toasty, round tannins.

CELLER BARTOLOMÉ

Major, 23
43738 Bellmunt del Priorat - (Tarragona)
☎: +34 616 478 581 - Fax: +34 977 320 448
cellerbartolome@hotmail.com
www.cellerbartolome.com

CLOS BARTOLOME 2008 T
45% garnacha, 45% cariñena, 10% cabernet sauvignon

90 Colour: deep cherry, garnet rim. Nose: powerfull, expressive, cigar, dark chocolate, varnish. Palate: balanced, fine bitter notes, round tannins.

PRIMITIU DE BELLMUNT 2007 T
50% garnacha, 50% cariñena

91 Colour: cherry, garnet rim. Nose: cocoa bean, sweet spices, ripe fruit. Palate: good structure, flavourful, fruity, round tannins.

CELLER DE L'ABADÍA

De la Font, 38
43737 Gratallops - (Tarragona)
☎: +34 627 032 134
jeroni@cellerabadia.com
www.cellerabadia.com

ALICE 2007 T
30% garnacha, 40% cariñena, 10% syrah, 10% cabernet sauvignon

90 Colour: bright cherry. Nose: sweet spices, creamy oak, overripe fruit. Palate: flavourful, fruity, toasty, round tannins.

CLOS CLARA 2007 TC
40% garnacha, 40% cariñena, 10% syrah, 10% cabernet sauvignon

90 Colour: cherry, garnet rim. Nose: mineral, earthy notes, ripe fruit, fruit expression, toasty. Palate: mineral, long, spicy, ripe fruit.

CELLER DE L'ENCASTELL

Castell, 13
43739 Porrera - (Tarragona)
☎: +34 630 941 959
roquers@roquers.com
www.roquers.com

ROQUERS DE PORRERA 2009 TC

93 Colour: cherry, garnet rim. Nose: spicy, creamy oak, toasty, red berry notes, raspberry. Palate: powerful, flavourful, toasty, round tannins.

CELLER DEL PONT

Del Riu, 1- Baixos
43374 La Vilella Baixa - (Tarragona)
☎: +34 977 828 231 - Fax: +34 977 828 231
cellerdelpont@gmail.com
www.cellerdelpont.com

LO GIVOT 2008 T
33% garnacha, 32% mazuelo, 25% cabernet sauvignon, syrah

93 Colour: cherry, garnet rim. Nose: ripe fruit, spicy, toasty, complex, mineral. Palate: powerful, flavourful, toasty, round tannins, elegant.

CELLER DELS PINS VERS

Afores, s/n
43736 El Molar - (Tarragona)
☎: +34 977 825 458 - Fax: +34 977 825 458
info@lafuina.com
www.lafuina.com

ELS PINS VERS 2008 T
garnacha, samsó, cabernet sauvignon, syrah

90 Colour: cherry, garnet rim. Nose: spicy, creamy oak, toasty, complex, fruit preserve. Palate: powerful, flavourful, toasty, round tannins.

CELLER DEVINSSI

Masets, 1
43737 Gratallops - (Tarragona)
☎: +34 977 839 523
devinssi@il-lia.com
www.devinssi.com

CUPATGE 2009 T
garnacha, cariñena, cabernet sauvignon, merlot, syrah

90 Colour: cherry, garnet rim. Nose: overripe fruit, creamy oak, sweet spices. Palate: flavourful, powerful, ripe fruit.

ROCAPOLL 2008 T
cariñena

90 Colour: dark-red cherry, garnet rim. Nose: balanced, ripe fruit, expressive, spicy, scrubland. Palate: powerful, flavourful, long.

CELLER HIDALGO ALBERT

Finca Les Salanques, Pol. Ind. 14, Parc. 102
43376 Poboleda - (Tarragona)
☎: +34 977 842 064 - Fax: +34 977 842 064
hialmi@yahoo.es

1270 A VUIT 2007 T
garnacha, cariñena, merlot, syrah, cabernet sauvignon

92 Colour: cherry, garnet rim. Nose: ripe fruit, scrubland, earthy notes, spicy. Palate: powerful, flavourful, long, balsamic, spicy.

1270 A VUIT 2010 B
80% garnacha blanca, 20% viognier

90 Colour: bright yellow. Nose: expressive, candied fruit, floral, powerfull. Palate: flavourful, fruity, rich, balanced.

CELLER JORDI DOMENECH

Finca Les Comes
43376 Poboleda - (Tarragona)
☎: +34 646 169 210
jordidomenech@live.com
www.cellerjordidomenech.com

PETIT CLOS PENAT 2008 T
garnacha, syrah

91 Colour: cherry, garnet rim. Nose: spicy, creamy oak, toasty, overripe fruit. Palate: powerful, flavourful, toasty, round tannins.

CELLER MAS BASTE

Font, 38
43737 Gratallops - (Tarragona)
☎: +34 629 300 291
info@cellermasbaste.com
www.cellermasbaste.com

CLOS PEITES 2009 T
80% cariñena, 20% cabernet sauvignon

90 Colour: cherry, garnet rim. Nose: ripe fruit, balanced, expressive, balsamic herbs. Palate: fruity, flavourful, round tannins.

PEITES 2011 T
80% garnacha, 20% syrah

90 Colour: very deep cherry, purple rim. Nose: balanced, powerfull, balsamic herbs, ripe fruit. Palate: fruity, balanced.

CELLER MAS DE LES PERERES

Mas de Les Pereres, s/n
43376 Poboleda - (Tarragona)
☎: +34 977 827 257 - Fax: +34 977 827 257
dirk@nunci.com
www.nunci.com

NUNCI ABOCAT 2009 B
macabeo, garnacha, moscatel de alejandría, moscatel grano menudo

90 Colour: bright yellow. Nose: white flowers, fruit expression, tropical fruit, fragrant herbs. Palate: fresh, fruity, light-bodied, flavourful.

NUNCI BLANC 2008 BFB
garnacha, macabeo

91 Colour: bright yellow. Nose: powerfull, ripe fruit, creamy oak, dried herbs. Palate: rich, smoky aftertaste, flavourful, fresh.

NUNCI BLANC 2009 BFB
garnacha blanca, macabeo

90 Colour: bright yellow. Nose: powerfull, ripe fruit, sweet spices, creamy oak, fragrant herbs. Palate: rich, flavourful, fresh, good acidity.

NUNCI COSTERO 2006 T
55% mazuelo, 40% garnacha, 5% merlot

91 Colour: cherry, garnet rim. Nose: ripe fruit, spicy, creamy oak, toasty, earthy notes, expressive. Palate: powerful, flavourful, toasty, round tannins, balanced.

NUNCI NEGRE 2006 T
garnacha, syrah, mazuelo, cabernet franc, cabernet sauvignon

91 Colour: cherry, garnet rim. Nose: ripe fruit, spicy, creamy oak, complex. Palate: powerful, flavourful, toasty, round tannins.

NUNCITO 2008 T BARRICA
garnacha, syrah, mazuelo

91 Colour: cherry, garnet rim. Nose: powerfull, scrubland, ripe fruit. Palate: good structure, flavourful, full.

NUNCITO 2009 T BARRICA
garnacha, syrah, mazuelo

92 Colour: cherry, garnet rim. Nose: ripe fruit, spicy, creamy oak, scrubland, expressive. Palate: powerful, flavourful, toasty, round tannins.

CELLER MAS DOIX

Carme, 115
43376 Poboleda - (Tarragona)
☎: +34 639 356 172 - Fax: +34 933 216 790
info@masdoix.com
www.masdoix.com

DOIX 2010 TC
55% cariñena, 45% garnacha

94 Colour: cherry, garnet rim. Nose: sweet spices, ripe fruit, red berry notes, toasty. Palate: flavourful, good acidity, fine bitter notes, round tannins.

LES CRESTES 2010 T

91 Colour: bright cherry. Nose: sweet spices, creamy oak, ripe fruit. Palate: flavourful, fruity, toasty, round tannins.

SALANQUES 2010 T

92 Colour: cherry, garnet rim. Nose: earthy notes, fruit expression, ripe fruit, creamy oak, spicy. Palate: ripe fruit, good acidity, fine bitter notes.

CELLER PRIOR PONS

Rey, 4
43375 La Vilella Alta - (Tarragona)
☎: +34 606 547 865
info@priorpons.com
www.priorpons.com

PLANETS DE PRIOR PONS 2009 T
40% garnacha, 40% mazuelo, 10% cabernet sauvignon, 5% syrah, 5% merlot

90 Colour: cherry, garnet rim. Nose: ripe fruit, spicy, creamy oak, toasty, balsamic herbs. Palate: powerful, flavourful, toasty, balanced.

PRIOR PONS 2009 T
40% garnacha, 45% mazuelo, 15% cabernet sauvignon

91 Colour: cherry, garnet rim. Nose: ripe fruit, spicy, complex, mineral, earthy notes. Palate: powerful, flavourful, toasty, round tannins.

CELLER SABATÉ

Nou, 6
43374 La Vilella Baixa - (Tarragona)
☎: +34 977 839 209 - Fax: +34 977 839 209
cellersabate@cellersabate.com
www.cellersabate.com

MAS PLANTADETA 2009 T ROBLE
100% garnacha

90 Color bright cherry. Aroma ripe fruit, sweet spices, creamy oak, expressive. Taste flavourful, fruity, toasty, round tannins.

CELLER VALL-LLACH

Del Pont, 9
43739 Porrera - (Tarragona)
☎: +34 977 828 244 - Fax: +34 977 828 325
celler@vallllach.com
www.vallllach.com

EMBRUIX DE VALL-LLACH 2009 T

93 Colour: cherry, garnet rim. Nose: spicy, creamy oak, toasty, fruit expression. Palate: powerful, flavourful, toasty, round tannins.

CELLERS DE SCALA DEI

Rambla de la Cartoixa, s/n
43379 Scala Dei - (Tarragona)
☎: +34 977 827 027 - Fax: +34 977 827 044
codinfo@codorniu.es
www.grupocodorniu.com

SCALA DEI CARTOIXA 2007 TR
60% garnacha, 25% cariñena, 10% syrah, 5% cabernet sauvignon

91 Colour: cherry, garnet rim. Nose: ripe fruit, spicy, creamy oak, toasty. Palate: flavourful, toasty, round tannins.

CELLERS RIPOLL SANS - CAL BATLLET

Consolació, 16
43737 Gratallops - (Tarragona)
☎: +34 687 638 951
mripoll@closabatllet.com
www.closabatllet.com

ARTAI 2009 T
47% garnacha, 28% cariñena, 23% cabernet sauvignon, 2% syrah

90 Colour: cherry, garnet rim. Nose: ripe fruit, scrubland, sweet spices, cocoa bean. Palate: ripe fruit, spicy, fine bitter notes, round tannins.

GRATALLOPS 5 PARTIDES 2009 T
100% cariñena

92 Colour: cherry, garnet rim. Nose: ripe fruit, sweet spices, mineral, spicy, balsamic herbs, expressive. Palate: long, powerful, flavourful, complex, balanced.

GRATALLOPS ESCANYA VELLA 2010 B
100% escanya-vella

91 Colour: bright yellow. Nose: candied fruit, faded flowers, expressive, dried herbs. Palate: flavourful, fine bitter notes. Personality.

TORROJA RONÇAVALL 2009 T
cariñena

93 Colour: deep cherry. Nose: powerfull, varietal, ripe fruit, sweet spices, creamy oak. Palate: flavourful, powerful, good structure, long, mineral.

CELLERS UNIÓ

Joan Oliver, 16-24
43206 Reus - (Tarragona)
☎: +34 977 330 055 - Fax: +34 977 330 070
info@cellersunio.com
www.cellersunio.com

ROUREDA LLICORELLA VITIS 60 2006 T
40% garnacha, 40% cariñena, 10% cabernet sauvignon, 10% syrah

90 Color cherry, garnet rim. Aroma ripe fruit, spicy, creamy oak, toasty, complex. Taste powerful, flavourful, toasty, round tannins.

CLOS DE L'OBAC

Camí Manyetes, s/n
43737 Gratallops - (Tarragona)
☎: +34 977 839 276 - Fax: +34 977 839 371
info@obac.es
www.obac.es

CLOS DE L'OBAC 2008 TC
garnacha, cabernet sauvignon, cariñena, merlot, syrah

91 Colour: cherry, garnet rim. Nose: ripe fruit, spicy, scrubland. Palate: toasty, long, spicy, balanced.

KYRIE 2008 BC
garnacha blanca, macabeo, xarel.lo, moscatel

93 Colour: bright yellow. Nose: ripe fruit, sweet spices, creamy oak, fragrant herbs, dry stone. Palate: rich, flavourful, fresh, good acidity, balanced.

MISERERE 2008 TC
garnacha, cabernet sauvignon, tempranillo, cariñena, merlot

92 Colour: cherry, garnet rim. Nose: ripe fruit, spicy, toasty, mineral, fragrant herbs. Palate: flavourful, toasty, complex, spicy.

CLOS DEL PORTAL

Pista del Lloar a Bellmunt
43376 Solanes del Molar - (Tarragona)
☎: +34 932 531 760 - Fax: +34 934 173 591
info@portaldelpriorat.com
www.portaldelpriorat.com

GOTES DEL PRIORAT MAGNUM 2010 T
cariñena, garnacha

91 Colour: cherry, purple rim. Nose: expressive, fresh fruit, red berry notes, floral, mineral, cocoa bean, spicy. Palate: flavourful, fruity, balanced, spicy.

NEGRE DE NEGRES 2010 T
garnacha, cariñena, cabernet sauvignon

93 Colour: bright cherry. Nose: ripe fruit, sweet spices, creamy oak, mineral, balsamic herbs. Palate: flavourful, fruity, toasty, round tannins, good acidity, long.

NEGRE DE NEGRES MAGNUM 2009 T
garnacha, cariñena, cabernet sauvignon

93 Colour: cherry, garnet rim. Nose: dry stone, earthy notes, red berry notes, ripe fruit, cocoa bean, dark chocolate, spicy, balanced. Palate: good acidity, elegant, flavourful, fresh, fruity.

SOMNI 2010 T

92 Colour: bright cherry. Nose: ripe fruit, sweet spices, creamy oak, cocoa bean, dark chocolate, toasty, mineral. Palate: flavourful, fruity, toasty, round tannins.

SOMNI MAGNUM 2009 T
cariñena, syrah

93 Colour: cherry, garnet rim. Nose: red berry notes, ripe fruit, fragrant herbs, mineral, aromatic coffee, toasty. Palate: powerful, complex, fresh, fruity, flavourful.

TROS DE CLOS 2010 T
cariñena

94 Colour: bright cherry. Nose: ripe fruit, sweet spices, creamy oak, dark chocolate, cocoa bean, dry stone. Palate: flavourful, fruity, toasty, round tannins, balanced, elegant.

TROS DE CLOS MAGNUM 2009 T
cariñena

93 Colour: cherry, garnet rim. Nose: ripe fruit, spicy, creamy oak, toasty, balsamic herbs, complex. Palate: powerful, flavourful, toasty, round tannins, good acidity, balanced, elegant.

CLOS FIGUERAS

Carrer La Font, 38
43737 Gratallops - (Tarragona)
☎: +34 977 830 217 - Fax: +34 977 830 422
info@closfigueras.com
www.desfigueras.com

CLOS FIGUERES 2009 T

91 Colour: cherry, garnet rim. Nose: spicy, creamy oak, toasty, complex, earthy notes, overripe fruit. Palate: powerful, flavourful, toasty, round tannins.

SERRAS DEL PRIORAT 2010 T
65% garnacha, 15% mazuelo, 10% syrah, 10% cabernet sauvignon

91 Colour: bright cherry, garnet rim. Nose: powerfull, ripe fruit, spicy. Palate: good structure, round tannins, long.

CLOS MOGADOR

Camí Manyetes, s/n
43737 Gratallops - (Tarragona)
☎: +34 977 839 171 - Fax: +34 977 839 426
closmogador@closmogador.com
www.closmogador.com

CLOS MOGADOR 2009 T
garnacha, cariñena, cabernet sauvignon, syrah

93 Colour: cherry, garnet rim. Nose: earthy notes, overripe fruit, dark chocolate. Palate: powerful, flavourful, fine bitter notes, good acidity, round tannins.

MANYETES 2009 T
cariñena, garnacha

94 Colour: cherry, garnet rim. Nose: powerfull, ripe fruit, toasty, creamy oak, mineral. Palate: powerful, flavourful, fine bitter notes, good acidity, mineral, spicy.

NELIN 2010 B
garnacha, macabeo, viognier, escanyavelles

90 Colour: bright yellow. Nose: balanced, expressive, spicy, ripe fruit. Palate: rich, flavourful, fruity, fine bitter notes.

COMBIER-FISCHER-GERIN

Baixa Font, 18
43737 Torroja del Priorat - (Tarragona)
☎: +34 600 753 840 - Fax: +34 977 828 380
yalellamaremos@yahoo.es
www.trioinfernal.es

TRÍO INFERNAL Nº 2/3 2007 T
100% cariñena

91 Colour: very deep cherry, garnet rim. Nose: powerfull, dark chocolate, ripe fruit, fruit preserve, sweet spices. Palate: good structure, round tannins.

COSTERS DEL PRIORAT

Finca Sant Martí
43738 Bellmunt del Priorat - (Tarragona)
☎: +34 618 203 473
info@costersdelpriorat.com
www.costersdelpriorat.com

CLOS CYPRES 2010 T
90% cariñena, 10% garnacha

91 Colour: deep cherry. Nose: spicy, toasty, mineral, ripe fruit. Palate: flavourful, ripe fruit, fine bitter notes.

PISSARRES 2010 T
55% cariñena, 30% garnacha, 15% cabernet sauvignon, syrah

90 Colour: cherry, garnet rim. Nose: ripe fruit, spicy, toasty, mineral. Palate: powerful, flavourful, round tannins.

DE MULLER

Camí Pedra Estela, 34
43205 Reus - (Tarragona)
☎: +34 977 757 473 - Fax: +34 977 771 129
lab@demuller.es
www.demuller.es

DOM JOAN FORT 1865 SOLERA
moscatel de alejandría, garnacha, garnacha blanca

94 Colour: bright golden. Nose: dry nuts, saline, acetaldehyde, aged wood nuances, creamy oak. Palate: balanced, powerful, flavourful, spicy, long.

DOMINI DE LA CARTOIXA

Camino de la Solana, s/n
43736 El Molar - (Tarragona)
☎: +34 606 443 736 - Fax: +34 977 771 737
info@closgalena.com
www.closgalena.com

CLOS GALENA 2009 TC
garnacha, cariñena, syrah, cabernet sauvignon

93 Colour: cherry, garnet rim. Nose: ripe fruit, spicy, creamy oak, toasty, complex, earthy notes, mineral. Palate: powerful, flavourful, toasty, round tannins.

CROSSOS 2010 T
60% garnacha, 20% cabernet sauvignon, 20% cariñena

90 Colour: bright cherry. Nose: ripe fruit, sweet spices, creamy oak, scrubland, mineral. Palate: flavourful, fruity, toasty, round tannins.

FORMIGA DE VELLUT 2010 T

90 Colour: cherry, garnet rim. Nose: balanced, ripe fruit, powerfull, mineral. Palate: balanced, fine bitter notes, good structure.

GALENA 2009 T

91 Colour: cherry, garnet rim. Nose: ripe fruit, creamy oak, toasty, complex. Palate: powerful, flavourful, toasty, round tannins, balanced.

ELVIWINES

Finca "Clos Mesorah" Ctra. T-300 Falset Marça, Km. 1
43775 Marça Priorat - (Tarragona)
☎: +34 935 343 026 - Fax: +34 936 750 316
moises@elviwines.com
www.elviwines.com

EL26 2008 TR
40% cabernet sauvignon, 25% syrah, 20% garnacha, 15% cariñena

91 Color cherry, garnet rim. Aroma ripe fruit, spicy, creamy oak, toasty, complex. Taste powerful, flavourful, toasty, round tannins.

FERRER BOBET

Ctra. Falset a Porrera, Km. 6,5
43730 Falset - (Tarragona)
☎: +34 609 945 532 - Fax: +34 935 044 265
eguerre@ferrerbobet.com
www.ferrerbobet.com

FERRER BOBET SELECCIÓ ESPECIAL 2009 T
100% cariñena

96 Colour: cherry, garnet rim. Nose: ripe fruit, spicy, creamy oak, complex, mineral, new oak. Palate: powerful, flavourful, toasty, round tannins.

FERRER BOBET SELECCIÓ ESPECIAL 2010 T
100% cariñena,

94 Colour: bright cherry. Nose: ripe fruit, sweet spices, creamy oak, expressive, earthy notes. Palate: flavourful, fruity, toasty, round tannins.

FERRER BOBET VINYES VELLES 2009 T
70% cariñena, 30% garnacha

95 Colour: cherry, garnet rim. Nose: ripe fruit, spicy, creamy oak, toasty, mineral. Palate: powerful, flavourful, toasty, round tannins, fruity, good acidity, long.

FERRER BOBET VINYES VELLES 2010 T
70% cariñena, 30% garnacha

95 Colour: cherry, garnet rim. Nose: ripe fruit, spicy, creamy oak, toasty. Palate: powerful, flavourful, toasty, round tannins.

GRAN CLOS

Montsant, 2
43738 Bellmunt - (Tarragona)
☎: +34 977 830 675
cellersfuentes@granclos.com
www.granclos.com

CARTUS 2005 T
garnacha, 25% cariñena

91 Colour: very deep cherry. Nose: powerfull, fruit liqueur notes, overripe fruit, toasty, spicy. Palate: powerful, fine bitter notes, good acidity.

GRAN CLOS 2005 T
55% garnacha, 25% cariñena, 20% cabernet sauvignon

92 Colour: pale ruby, brick rim edge. Nose: elegant, spicy, fine reductive notes, aged wood nuances, fruit liqueur notes, earthy notes. Palate: spicy, fine tannins, elegant, long.

GRATAVINUM

Mas D'en Serres, s/n
43737 Gratallops - (Tarragona)
☎: +34 938 901 399 - Fax: +34 938 901 143
gratavinum@gratavinum.com
www.gratavinum.com

GRATAVINUM COSTER 2007 T
100% cariñena

92 Colour: black cherry, garnet rim. Nose: balanced, ripe fruit, tobacco, spicy. Palate: good structure, powerful, round tannins, balanced.

GRATAVINUM GV5 2009 T
cariñena, garnacha, cabernet sauvignon

92 Colour: cherry, garnet rim. Nose: ripe fruit, spicy, creamy oak, toasty, complex, mineral. Palate: powerful, flavourful, toasty, round tannins.

HUELLAS

De la Mora de Sant Pere, 26- 2º
8880 Cubelles - (Barcelona)
☎: +34 609 428 507
franckmassard@epicure-wines.com

AMIC 2011 T
garnacha, merlot, cabernet sauvignon

91 Colour: cherry, garnet rim. Nose: spicy, creamy oak, toasty, characterful, fruit expression. Palate: powerful, flavourful, toasty, round tannins.

JOAN AMETLLER

Ctra. La Morera de Monsant - Cornudella, km. 3,2
43361 La Morera de Monsant - (Tarragona)
☎: +34 933 208 439 - Fax: +34 933 208 437
ametller@ametller.com
www.ametller.com

CLOS CORRIOL 2009 T
garnacha, cabernet sauvignon, merlot

90 Colour: bright cherry, garnet rim. Nose: powerfull, fruit expression, balsamic herbs, spicy. Palate: fruity, flavourful.

CLOS MUSTARDÓ 2010 B
garnacha blanca

91 Colour: bright straw. Nose: fresh, fresh fruit, white flowers, characterful. Palate: flavourful, fruity, good acidity, balanced.

JOAN SIMÓ

11 de Setembre, 7
43739 Porrera - (Tarragona)
☎: +34 627 563 713 - Fax: +34 977 830 993
leseres@cellerjoansimo.com
www.cellerjoansimo.com

LES ERES 2008 T
60% cariñena, 30% garnacha, 10% cabernet sauvignon

92 Colour: cherry, garnet rim. Nose: ripe fruit, spicy, creamy oak, toasty. Palate: powerful, flavourful, toasty, round tannins.

LES ERES ESPECIAL DELS CARNERS 2007 T
75% garnacha, 25% cariñena

91 Colour: cherry, garnet rim. Nose: ripe fruit, balsamic herbs, mineral, sweet spices, creamy oak. Palate: powerful, flavourful, complex, long, spicy.

LA CONRERIA D'SCALA DEI

Carrer Mitja Galta, s/n - Finca Les Brugueres
43379 Scala Dei - (Tarragona)
☎: +34 977 827 055 - Fax: +34 977 827 055
laconreria@vinslaconreria.com
www.vinslaconreria.com

IUGITER SELECCIÓ VINYES VELLES 2007 TC
garnacha, cariñena, cabernet sauvignon

90 Colour: cherry, garnet rim. Nose: ripe fruit, spicy, creamy oak, toasty, characterful. Palate: powerful, flavourful, toasty, round tannins.

LES BRUGUERES 2011 B
garnacha blanca

90 Colour: bright straw. Nose: fresh, white flowers, ripe fruit. Palate: flavourful, fruity, good acidity, balanced.

LA PERLA DEL PRIORAT

Mas dels Frares, s/n
43736 El Molar - (Tarragona)
☎: +34 977 825 202
frares@laperladelpriorat.com
www.laperladelpriorat.com

CLOS LES FITES 2006 T
garnacha, carignan, cabernet sauvignon

91 Colour: light cherry, garnet rim. Nose: dry stone, ripe fruit, fragrant herbs, spicy, creamy oak. Palate: elegant, round, flavourful, spicy.

LLICORELLA VINS

Carrer de l'Era, 11
43737 Torroja del Priorat - (Tarragona)
☎: +34 977 839 049 - Fax: +34 977 839 049
comercial@llicorellavins.com
www.llicorellavins.com

AÒNIA 2009 T
garnacha, cariñena, cabernet sauvignon

92 Color cherry, garnet rim. Aroma ripe fruit, spicy, creamy oak, toasty, complex. Taste powerful, flavourful, toasty, round tannins.

GRAN NASARD 2008 TC
garnacha, cariñena

90 Colour: very deep cherry. Nose: dark chocolate, sweet spices, ripe fruit, fruit preserve. Palate: full, flavourful, ripe fruit, balanced, fine bitter notes, round tannins.

MAS SAURA 2008 TC
garnacha, cabernet sauvignon, syrah, cariñena

91 Colour: cherry, garnet rim. Nose: spicy, toasty, scrubland, ripe fruit, mineral. Palate: powerful, flavourful, toasty, round tannins, balanced.

MARCO ABELLA

Ctra. de Porrera a Cornudella del Montsant, Km. 0,7
43739 Porrera - (Tarragona)
☎: +34 933 712 407 - Fax: +34 933 712 407
admin@marcoabella.com
www.marcoabella.com

CLOS ABELLA 2005 T
40% cariñena, 40% garnacha, 10% cabernet sauvignon, 10% syrah

92 Colour: cherry, garnet rim. Nose: ripe fruit, spicy, creamy oak, toasty, characterful. Palate: powerful, flavourful, toasty, round tannins.

CLOS ABELLA 2006 T
40% cariñena, 40% garnacha, 15% cabernet sauvignon, 5% syrah

90 Colour: cherry, garnet rim. Nose: spicy, creamy oak, dried herbs, tobacco. Palate: flavourful, fruity, good structure.

MAS MARTINET

Ctra. Falset - Gratallops, Km. 6
43730 Falset - (Tarragona)
☎: +34 629 238 236 - Fax: +34 977 262 348
masmartinet@masmartinet.com
www.masmartinet.com

CAMI PESSEROLES 2009 T

93 Colour: deep cherry, garnet rim. Nose: complex, balanced, expressive, ripe fruit, creamy oak, varnish, dry stone. Palate: good structure, ripe fruit, long.

CLOS MARTINET 2009 T

92 Colour: cherry, garnet rim. Nose: ripe fruit, spicy, acetaldehyde, fragrant herbs, dried flowers, mineral. Palate: flavourful, toasty, long, mineral, elegant, fine tannins. Personality.

ELS ESCURÇONS 2009 T

94 Colour: deep cherry, garnet rim. Nose: complex, earthy notes, scrubland, ripe fruit. Palate: good structure, balanced, fine bitter notes, elegant.

MARTINET BRU 2009 T

90 Colour: cherry, garnet rim. Nose: warm, ripe fruit, scrubland, spicy, creamy oak, fine reductive notes. Palate: flavourful, complex, long, spicy, balsamic, round tannins.

MARTINET DEGUSTACIÓ 1 2004 T

92 Colour: cherry, garnet rim. Nose: creamy oak, toasty, scrubland, fruit liqueur notes, mineral, acetaldehyde. Palate: powerful, flavourful, toasty, balanced, round.

MAS MARTINET ASSESSORAMENTS

Vidal i Barraquer, 8
43739 Porrera - (Tarragona)
☎: +34 609 715 004 - Fax: +34 977 262 348
info@masmartinet-ass.com
www.masmartinet-ass.com

MARTINET DEGUSTACIÓ 2 2005 T

92 Colour: bright cherry. Nose: ripe fruit, sweet spices, creamy oak, aromatic coffee, balsamic herbs, mineral. Palate: flavourful, fruity, toasty, spicy, long, ripe fruit, elegant, fine tannins.

MAS PERINET

Finca Mas Perinet, s/n - T-702, Km. 1,6
43361 La Morera de Montsant - (Tarragona)
☎: +34 977 827 113 - Fax: +34 977 827 180
info@masperinet.com
www.masperinet.com

PERINET + PLUS 2006 T

94 Colour: cherry, garnet rim. Nose: spicy, creamy oak, toasty, mineral, earthy notes. Palate: powerful, flavourful, toasty, round tannins.

PERINET 2005 T

92 Colour: cherry, garnet rim. Nose: spicy, creamy oak, toasty, overripe fruit, earthy notes. Palate: powerful, flavourful, toasty, round tannins.

PERINET 2006 T

92 Colour: cherry, garnet rim. Nose: ripe fruit, creamy oak, toasty, characterful. Palate: powerful, flavourful, toasty, round tannins.

MASET DEL LLEÓ

C-244, Km. 32,5
8792 La Granada del Penedès - (Barcelona)
☎: +34 902 200 250 - Fax: +34 938 921 333
info@maset.com
www.maset.com

MAS VILÓ 2008 T

90 Colour: black cherry, garnet rim. Nose: medium intensity, cocoa bean, dried herbs. Palate: good structure, flavourful, round tannins.

MELIS

Balandra, 54
43737 Torroja del Priorat - (Tarragona)
☎: +34 937 313 021 - Fax: +34 937 312 371
javier@melispriorat.com
www.melispriorat.com

ELIX 2009 T

92 Colour: cherry, garnet rim. Nose: ripe fruit, balsamic herbs, floral, sweet spices, creamy oak, expressive. Palate: powerful, flavourful, spicy, long, balanced.

MELIS 2009 T

92 Colour: cherry, garnet rim. Nose: ripe fruit, scrubland, earthy notes, mineral, spicy, creamy oak. Palate: balanced, round, flavourful, long, elegant.

OBRADOR 2009 T

90 Colour: cherry, garnet rim. Nose: ripe fruit, spicy, creamy oak, fragrant herbs, mineral. Palate: powerful, flavourful, toasty, round tannins.

MERUM PRIORATI S.L.

Ctra. a Falset (T-740), km. 9,3
43739 Porrera - (Tarragona)
☎: +34 977 828 307 - Fax: +34 977 828 324
info@merumpriorati.com
www.merumpriorati.com

OSMIN 2007 T
garnacha, cariñena, cabernet sauvignon, syrah, merlot

90 Colour: deep cherry. Nose: creamy oak, earthy notes, overripe fruit, fruit liqueur notes. Palate: flavourful, powerful, fine bitter notes.

NOGUERALS

Tou, 5
43360 Cornudella de Montsant - (Tarragona)
☎: +34 650 033 546 - Fax: +34 934 419 879
noguerals@hotmail.com
www.noguerals.com

ABELLARS 2009 T
50% garnacha, 25% samsó, 15% cabernet sauvignon, 10% syrah

90 Colour: cherry, garnet rim. Nose: balanced, old leather, earthy notes. Palate: flavourful, fine bitter notes, long, round tannins.

R.TI 2 2009 T
garnacha, cabernet sauvignon, syrah

91 Colour: cherry, garnet rim. Nose: ripe fruit, creamy oak, toasty, earthy notes, mineral. Palate: powerful, flavourful, toasty, balanced.

ROCA DE LES DOTZE

Turó, 5
8328 Alella - (Barcelona)
☎: +34 662 302 214
info@rocadelesdotze.cat
www.rocadelesdotze.cat

NORAY 2007 T
garnacha, samsó, cabernet sauvignon, syrah

90 Colour: cherry, garnet rim. Nose: ripe fruit, balsamic herbs, spicy, creamy oak, mineral. Palate: correct, powerful, flavourful, long.

RODRÍGUEZ SANZO

Manuel Azaña, 9
47014 - (Valladolid)
☎: +34 983 150 150 - Fax: +34 983 150 151
comunicacion@valsanzo.com
www.rodriguezsanzo.com

NASSOS 2009 T
100% garnacha

93 Colour: cherry, garnet rim. Nose: spicy, creamy oak, toasty, earthy notes, mineral, ripe fruit. Palate: powerful, flavourful, toasty, round tannins.

ROTLLAN TORRA

Balandra, 6
43737 Torroja del Priorat - (Tarragona)
☎: +34 977 839 285 - Fax: +34 933 050 112
comercial@rotllantorra.com
www.rotllantorra.com

MISTIK 2008 T

90 Colour: cherry, garnet rim. Nose: ripe fruit, spicy, creamy oak, toasty, complex. Palate: powerful, flavourful, toasty, balanced.

SANGENÍS I VAQUÉ

Pl. Catalunya, 3
43739 Porrera - (Tarragona)
☎: +34 977 828 252
celler@sangenisivaque.com
www.sangenisivaque.com

LO COSTER BLANC 2010 B
garnacha blanca, macabeo

90 Colour: bright yellow. Nose: ripe fruit, fragrant herbs, floral, expressive. Palate: powerful, flavourful, complex, long.

SAÓ DEL COSTER

De Les Valls, 28
43737 Gratallops - (Priorat)
☎: +34 977 839 298
info@saodelcoster.com
www.saodelcoster.com

"S" 2009 T
garnacha, merlot, cabernet sauvignon, syrah

90 Colour: bright cherry, purple rim. Nose: fresh fruit, expressive, earthy notes. Palate: good structure, flavourful, balsamic, spicy.

PLANASSOS 2006 T
cariñena

90 Colour: pale ruby, brick rim edge. Nose: elegant, spicy, fine reductive notes, fruit liqueur notes, mineral. Palate: spicy, fine tannins, elegant, long.

TERRAM 2008 T
garnacha, cariñena, syrah, cabernet sauvignon

91 Colour: bright cherry. Nose: sweet spices, creamy oak, overripe fruit. Palate: flavourful, fruity, toasty, round tannins.

TERRES DE VIDALBA

Partida Foreses
43376 Poboleda - (Tarragona)
☎: +34 616 413 722
info@terresdevidalba.com

TOCS 2007 T
30% garnacha, 35% syrah, 35% cabernet sauvignon, 5% merlot

90 Colour: very deep cherry. Nose: powerfull, ripe fruit, sweet spices, aromatic coffee, dark chocolate, earthy notes, mineral. Palate: powerful, flavourful, fine bitter notes.

TERROIR AL LIMIT

Baixa Tont, 10
43737 Torroja del Priorat - (Tarragona)
☎: +34 699 732 707
vi@terroir-al-limit.com
www.terroir-al-limit.com

ARBOSSAR 2009 T
cariñena

95 Colour: cherry, garnet rim. Nose: powerfull, characterful, candied fruit. Palate: flavourful, powerful, good acidity, fine bitter notes, elegant, mineral, balsamic.

DITS DEL TERRA 2009 T
cariñena

92 Colour: very deep cherry. Nose: ripe fruit, characterful, powerfull, creamy oak. Palate: flavourful, good acidity, ripe fruit.

LES MANYES 2009 T
garnacha

93 Colour: cherry, garnet rim. Nose: balsamic herbs, ripe fruit, elegant. Palate: ripe fruit, long, good structure, round tannins.

LES TOSSES 2009 T
cariñena

94 Colour: cherry, garnet rim. Nose: expressive, elegant, red berry notes, scrubland. Palate: ripe fruit, long, fine bitter notes, elegant.

PEDRA DE GUIX 2009 B
garnacha blanca, macabeo, pedro ximénez

90 Colour: bright straw. Nose: mineral, ripe fruit, citrus fruit, dried herbs, faded flowers. Palate: spicy, ripe fruit, long.

TORROJA VI DE LA VILA 2009 T
50% garnacha, 50% cariñena

96 Colour: cherry, garnet rim. Nose: ripe fruit, spicy, creamy oak, toasty, complex, mineral, scrubland. Palate: powerful, flavourful, toasty, round tannins.

TORRES PRIORAT

Finca La Soleta, s/n
43737 El Lloar - (Tarragona)
☎: +34 938 177 400 - Fax: +34 938 177 444
admin@torres.es
www.torres.es

PERPETUAL 2009 TC
cariñena, garnacha

92 Colour: deep cherry. Nose: ripe fruit, creamy oak, toasty, spicy. Palate: flavourful, powerful, good acidity, round.

TROSSOS DEL PRIORAT

Ctra. Gratallops a La Vilella Baixa, Km. 10,65
43737 Gratallops - (Tarragona)
☎: +34 670 590 788 - Fax: +34 933 704 154
celler@trossosdelpriorat.com
www.trossosdelpriorat.com

ABRACADABRA 2010 B
70% garnacha blanca, 30% macabeo

90 Colour: bright straw. Nose: mineral, ripe fruit, citrus fruit, floral. Palate: flavourful, fruity, fresh.

LO MÓN 2009 T
garnacha, cariñena, cabernet sauvignon, syrah

92 Colour: cherry, garnet rim. Nose: spicy, creamy oak, toasty, complex, earthy notes, ripe fruit. Palate: powerful, flavourful, toasty, long.

UN PAM DE NAS 2009 T
garnacha, cariñena, cabernet sauvignon, syrah

92 Colour: cherry, garnet rim. Nose: complex, mineral, ripe fruit, spicy. Palate: good structure, balanced, fine bitter notes.

VINÍCOLA DEL PRIORAT

Piró, s/n
43737 Gratallops - (Tarragona)
☎: +34 977 839 167 - Fax: +34 977 839 201
info@vinicoladelpriorat.com
www.jordimirodiego.blogsopt.com

NADIU 2009 TC
garnacha, mazuelo, cabernet sauvignon, merlot, syrah

90 Color cherry, garnet rim. Aroma ripe fruit, spicy, creamy oak, toasty, complex. Taste powerful, flavourful, toasty, round tannins.

ÒNIX CLÁSSIC 2011 B
garnacha blanca, viura, pedro ximénez

90 Colour: bright straw, greenish rim. Nose: ripe fruit, balanced, floral. Palate: flavourful, ripe fruit, fine bitter notes.

ÒNIX CLÁSSIC 2011 T
garnacha, mazuelo

91 Colour: cherry, purple rim. Nose: expressive, fresh fruit, red berry notes. Palate: flavourful, fruity, good acidity, round tannins.

ÒNIX EVOLUCIÓ 2009 T
garnacha, mazuelo, cabernet sauvignon

90 Colour: cherry, garnet rim. Nose: ripe fruit, spicy, creamy oak, toasty. Palate: powerful, flavourful, toasty, round tannins.

ÒNIX FUSIÓ 2010 T
garnacha, syrah, mazuelo

92 Colour: cherry, garnet rim. Nose: spicy, toasty, red berry notes, ripe fruit, mineral. Palate: powerful, flavourful, toasty, round tannins.

VINYES ALTAIR

Consolacio, 26
43737 Gratallops - (Tarragona)
☎: +34 646 748 500
info@masperla.com
www.masperla.com

MASPERLA 2006 T
garnacha, cariñena, syrah, merlot, cabernet sauvignon

91 Colour: deep cherry. Nose: sweet spices, cocoa bean, toasty, spicy, earthy notes. Palate: flavourful, powerful, fine bitter notes, good acidity.

MASPERLA 2007 T
garnacha, cariñena, syrah, merlot, cabernet sauvignon

91 Colour: cherry, garnet rim. Nose: powerfull, characterful, complex, ripe fruit. Palate: flavourful, powerful, concentrated, fine bitter notes.

VITICULTORS MAS D'EN GIL

Finca Mas d'en Gil
43738 Bellmunt del Priorat - (Tarragona)
☎: +34 977 830 192 - Fax: +34 977 830 152
mail@masdengil.com
www.masdengil.com

CLOS FONTÀ 2009 T
60% cariñena, 30% garnacha peluda, 10% garnacha

91 Colour: cherry, garnet rim. Nose: ripe fruit, creamy oak, complex, mineral. Palate: powerful, flavourful, toasty, round tannins.

COMA BLANCA 2011 BC
50% macabeo, 50% garnacha blanca

91 Colour: bright straw. Nose: balanced, spicy, scrubland, toasty. Palate: rich, fruity, flavourful, ripe fruit, good acidity.

NUS 2010 DULCE NATURAL
80% garnacha, 15% syrah, 5% viognier

92 Colour: ruby red. Nose: ripe fruit, dark chocolate, sweet spices, creamy oak, toasty, expressive. Palate: powerful, flavourful, spicy, sweet, toasty.

DESCRIPTION

This is the most international zone of Galicia and one of the domestic white wines par excellence, which has made the albariño variety famous. It is a very fragmented zone, with an enormous number of wine growers, each one cultivating an average of one hectare. The largest amount of albariño is produced in Val do Salnés, one of the sub-regions which constitute the Rías Baixas together with the Condado de Tea, O' Rosal, Soutomaior and Ribera do Ulla. This type of vine has a strong capacity to age in the bottle despite the years, but the common denominators are the young fruity wines which evoke peach and tactile sensations with glyceride weight in the mouth.

NUMBER OF HECTARES: 3.698

ALTITUDES: 0 m. – 600 m.

PREDOMINANT VARIETIES:

White grapes: albariño, loureira blanca, treixadura, caiño blanco, torrotés and godello.
Red grapes: caiño tinto, espadeiro, loureira tinta, sousón, mencía and brancellao.

CLIMATOLOGY AND SOILS

Atlantic with mild, moderate temperatures owing to the influence of the sea, a high level of relative humidity with abundant rainfall. The soils are sandy, some with granite rock but they differ in the four sub-zones.

A. PAZOS DE LUSCO

Grixó - Alxén s/n
36458 Salvaterra do Miño - (Pontevedra)
☎: +34 987 514 550 - Fax: +34 987 514 570
info@lusco.es
www.lusco.es

LUSCO 2011 B
100% albariño

92 Colour: bright straw. Nose: elegant, varietal, fruit expression, ripe fruit. Palate: flavourful, fruity, good acidity, fine bitter notes.

PAZO DE PIÑEIRO 2010 B
100% albariño

95 Colour: bright straw. Nose: white flowers, scrubland, mineral, ripe fruit. Palate: flavourful, fine bitter notes, good acidity, spicy, ripe fruit.

ZIOS DE LUSCO 2011 B
100% albariño

91 Colour: bright straw. Nose: white flowers, fresh fruit, fragrant herbs, mineral. Palate: correct, fresh, fruity, flavourful, balanced.

ADEGA CONDES DE ALBAREI

Lugar a Bouza, 1 Castrelo
36639 Cambados - (Pontevedra)
☎: +34 986 543 535 - Fax: +34 986 524 251
inf@condesdealbarei.com
www.condesdealbarei.com

CARBALLO GALEGO 2010 BFB
100% albariño

92 Colour: bright yellow. Nose: powerfull, ripe fruit, sweet spices, fragrant herbs, dried flowers. Palate: rich, smoky aftertaste, flavourful, fresh, good acidity.

CONDES DE ALBAREI 2011 B
100% albariño

90 Colour: bright straw. Nose: ripe fruit, citrus fruit, white flowers. Palate: flavourful, fruity, fine bitter notes, good acidity.

ENXEBRE 2010 B
100% albariño

90 Colour: bright straw. Nose: white flowers, grassy, fresh fruit, citrus fruit. Palate: light-bodied, fresh, flavourful.

ADEGA DOS EIDOS

Padriñán, 65
36960 Sanxenxo - (Pontevedra)
☎: +34 986 690 009 - Fax: +34 986 720 307
info@adegaeidos.com
www.adegaeidos.com

CONTRAAPAREDE 2008 B
100% albariño

93 Colour: bright yellow. Nose: dry nuts, fragrant herbs, ripe fruit, complex, petrol notes. Palate: powerful, flavourful, long, balanced.

EIDOS DE PADRIÑÁN 2011 B
100% albariño

91 Colour: bright straw. Nose: fresh, fresh fruit, white flowers, expressive, dried herbs. Palate: flavourful, fruity, good acidity, balanced.

VEIGAS DE PADRIÑÁN 2010 B
100% albariño

91 Colour: bright straw. Nose: characterful, varietal, ripe fruit, grassy. Palate: flavourful, fine bitter notes, good acidity.

ADEGA VALDÉS

Santa Cruz de Rivadulla, s/n
15885 Vedra - (A Coruña)
☎: +34 981 512 439 - Fax: +34 981 509 226
ventas@gundian.com
www.adegavaldes.com

ALBARIÑO GUNDIAN 2011 B
100% albariño

90 Colour: bright straw. Nose: fresh, fresh fruit, white flowers, expressive, fine lees. Palate: flavourful, fruity, good acidity, balanced.

PAZO VILADOMAR 2011 B
treixadura, albariño

90 Color bright straw. Aroma fresh, fresh fruit, white flowers, expressive. Taste flavourful, fruity, good acidity, balanced.

XIRADELLA 2011 B
100% albariño

90 Color bright straw. Aroma fresh, fresh fruit, white flowers, expressive. Taste flavourful, fruity, good acidity, balanced.

ADEGAS AROUSA

Tirabao, 15 - Baión
36614 Vilanova de Arousa - (Pontevedra)
☎: +34 986 506 113 - Fax: +34 986 715 454
grupoarousaboucina@gmail.com
www.adegasarousa.com

PAZO DA BOUCIÑA 2011 B
albariño

91 Colour: bright straw. Nose: fresh, fresh fruit, white flowers, expressive, fragrant herbs. Palate: flavourful, fruity, good acidity, balanced.

ADEGAS CASTROBREY

Camanzo, s/n
36587 Vila de Cruces - (Pontevedra)
☎: +34 986 583 643 - Fax: +34 986 583 722
bodegas@castrobrey.com
www.castrobrey.com

SIN PALABRAS CASTRO VALDÉS 2011 B
100% albariño

92 Colour: bright straw. Nose: fresh, fresh fruit, white flowers, balsamic herbs, grassy. Palate: flavourful, fruity, good acidity, balanced.

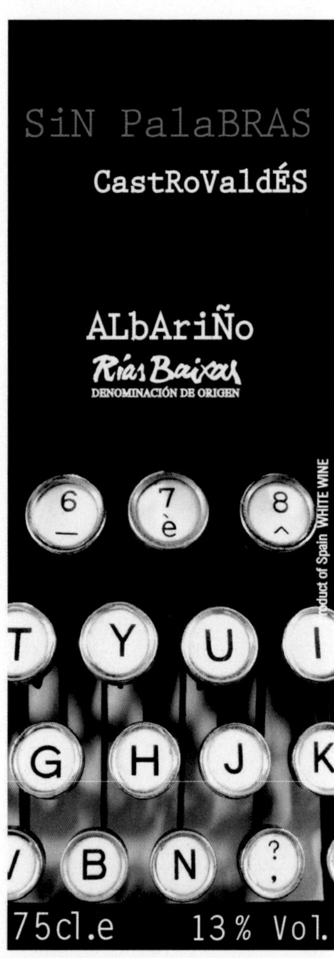

ADEGAS GALEGAS

Meder, s/n
36457 Salvaterra de Miño - (Pontevedra)
☎: +34 986 657 143 - Fax: +34 986 526 901
comercial@adegasgalegas.es
www.adegasgalegas.es

DON PEDRO SOUTOMAIOR 2011 B
100% albariño

91 Colour: bright straw. Nose: fresh, white flowers, ripe fruit, citrus fruit, dry stone. Palate: flavourful, fruity, good acidity, balanced.

ADEGAS GRAN VINUM

Fermín Bouza Brei, 9 - 5ºB
36600 Vilagarcía de Arousa - (Pontevedra)
☎: +34 986 555 742 - Fax: +34 986 555 742
info@adegasgranvinum.com
www.adegasgranvinum.com

ESENCIA DIVIÑA 2011 B
albariño

91 Colour: bright straw. Nose: fresh, fresh fruit, white flowers, expressive, fragrant herbs. Palate: flavourful, fruity, good acidity, balanced.

ADEGAS TOLLODOURO

Ctra. Tui-A Guarda, Km. 45
36760 O Rosal - (Pontevedra)
☎: +34 986 609 810 - Fax: +34 986 609 811
bodega@tollodouro.com
www.tollodouro.com

PONTELLÓN ALBARIÑO 2011 B
albariño

90 Colour: bright straw. Nose: fresh, white flowers, ripe fruit. Palate: flavourful, fruity, good acidity, balanced.

ADEGAS VALMIÑOR

A Portela, s/n - San Juan de Tabagón
36760 O'Rosal - (Pontevedra)
☎: +34 986 609 060 - Fax: +34 986 609 313
valminor@valminorebano.com
www.adegasvalminor.com

DÁVILA 2010 B
albariño, loureiro, treixadura

90 Colour: bright yellow. Nose: fine lees, ripe fruit, fragrant herbs, expressive. Palate: long, rich, flavourful, balanced.

DÁVILA L100 2010 B
loureiro

92 Colour: bright straw. Nose: ripe fruit, citrus fruit, grassy. Palate: flavourful, fine bitter notes, ripe fruit.

DÁVILA M.100 2009 B
albariño, loureiro, treixadura

90 Colour: bright straw. Nose: mineral, ripe fruit, grassy. Palate: easy to drink, ripe fruit, good acidity.

VALMIÑOR 2011 B
albariño

90 Colour: bright straw. Nose: ripe fruit, citrus fruit, white flowers. Palate: flavourful, fine bitter notes, good acidity.

ADEGAS VALTEA

Lg. Portela, 14
36429 Crecente - (Pontevedra)
☎: +34 986 666 344 - Fax: +34 986 644 914
vilarvin@vilarvin.com
www.vilarvin.com

VALTEA 2010 B
100% albariño

90 Colour: bright yellow. Nose: faded flowers, fragrant herbs, ripe fruit. Palate: powerful, flavourful, rich, long.

VALTEA 2011 B
100% albariño

90 Colour: bright yellow. Nose: fruit expression, fine lees, fragrant herbs, expressive. Palate: correct, fine bitter notes, powerful, flavourful.

ALBARIÑO BAIÓN

Lg. Abelleira 4,5,6 - Baión
36614 Vilanova de Arousa - (Pontevedra)
☎: +34 986 543 535 - Fax: +34 986 524 251
info@pazobaion.com
www.pazobaion.com

PAZO BAIÓN 2011 B
100% albariño

91 Colour: bright straw. Nose: fresh, white flowers, expressive, varietal, ripe fruit, mineral. Palate: flavourful, fruity, good acidity, balanced.

BODEGA CASTRO BAROÑA

Cabeiro - San Martín
36637 Meis - (Pontevedra)
☎: +34 981 134 847 - Fax: +34 981 174 030
castrobarona@castrobarona.com
www.castrobarona.com

CASTRO BAROÑA 2011 B
100% albariño

90 Colour: bright straw. Nose: fresh, white flowers, ripe fruit. Palate: flavourful, fruity, good acidity, balanced.

CASTRO BAROÑA SELECCIÓN ÚNICA 2010 B
100% albariño

91 Colour: bright yellow. Nose: floral, dried herbs, mineral, balanced. Palate: powerful, flavourful, complex, fine bitter notes, balanced.

LAGAR DO CASTELO 2011 B
100% albariño

90 Colour: bright straw. Nose: fresh, white flowers, ripe fruit, citrus fruit. Palate: flavourful, fruity, balanced.

BODEGA FORJAS DEL SALNÉS

As Covas, 5
36968 Meaño - (Pontevedra)
☎: +34 699 446 113 - Fax: +34 986 744 428
rodri@movistar.net

BASTIÓN DE LA LUNA 2010 T
espadeiro, loureiro, caíño

90 Colour: bright cherry. Nose: ripe fruit, sweet spices, creamy oak, wild herbs, roasted coffee. Palate: flavourful, fruity, toasty, round tannins, balsamic.

GOLIARDO ATELLEIRA 2010 B BARRICA
100% albariño

93 Colour: bright yellow. Nose: powerfull, ripe fruit, sweet spices, creamy oak, fragrant herbs, varnish, cocoa bean, dry stone. Palate: rich, flavourful, fresh, good acidity, long, elegant.

GOLIARDO CAIÑO 2010 T
caíño

92 Colour: cherry, garnet rim. Nose: ripe fruit, creamy oak, cocoa bean, dark chocolate, scrubland, toasty. Palate: powerful, flavourful, round tannins, balsamic.

GOLIARDO ESPADEIRO 2010 T
espadeiro

91 Colour: cherry, garnet rim. Nose: ripe fruit, fruit liqueur notes, balsamic herbs, spicy, creamy oak, mineral, floral. Palate: flavourful, long, fine bitter notes, round, good acidity.

GOLIARDO LOUREIRO 2010 T
loureiro

90 Colour: cherry, garnet rim. Nose: balsamic herbs, mineral, dried flowers, spicy, creamy oak. Palate: fresh, flavourful, long, spicy, balanced.

LEIRANA 2011 B
albariño

91 Colour: bright straw. Nose: saline, white flowers, fruit expression, fragrant herbs. Palate: elegant, flavourful, fresh, fruity, balanced.

LEIRANA FINCA GENOVEVA 2010 B
albariño

94 Colour: bright yellow. Nose: powerfull, ripe fruit, sweet spices, creamy oak, fragrant herbs, dried flowers, mineral. Palate: rich, flavourful, fresh, good acidity, complex, round, balanced.

BODEGA GRANBAZÁN

Tremoedo, 46
36628 Vilanova de Arousa - (Pontevedra)
☎: +34 986 555 562 - Fax: +34 986 555 799
agrodebazan@agrodebazansa.es
www.agrodebazansa.es

GRANBAZÁN DON ALVARO DE BAZÁN 2010 B
100% albariño

92 Colour: bright yellow. Nose: powerfull, ripe fruit, sweet spices, creamy oak, fragrant herbs. Palate: rich, flavourful, fresh, balanced.

GRANBAZÁN ETIQUETA ÁMBAR 2011 B
100% albariño

91 Colour: bright straw. Nose: wild herbs, ripe fruit, dried flowers, fresh. Palate: powerful, flavourful, rich, fine bitter notes, balanced.

GRANBAZÁN ETIQUETA VERDE 2011 B
100% albariño

90 Colour: bright straw. Nose: fresh, white flowers, fragrant herbs, ripe fruit. Palate: flavourful, fruity, good acidity.

GRANBAZÁN LIMOUSIN 2010 B
100% albariño

93 Colour: bright golden. Nose: powerfull, toasty, honeyed notes, ripe fruit, sweet spices. Palate: flavourful, fruity, spicy, toasty, long.

BODEGAS ALBAMAR

O Adro, 11 - Castrelo
36639 Cambados - (Pontevedra)
☎: +34 660 292 750 - Fax: +34 986 520 048
info@bodegasalbamar.com

ALBAMAR 2011 B
albariño

90 Colour: bright straw. Nose: fresh fruit, white flowers, fragrant herbs. Palate: flavourful, fruity, good acidity, fine bitter notes.

PEPE LUIS SOBRE LÍAS 2010 B
albariño

92 Color bright yellow. Aroma powerfull, ripe fruit, sweet spices, creamy oak, fragrant herbs. Taste rich, smoky aftertaste, flavourful, fresh, good acidity.

BODEGAS ALTOS DE TORONA

Vilachán s/n
36740 Tomiño - (Pontevedra)
☎: +34 986 288 212 - Fax: +34 986 401 185
info@reginaviarum.es
www.hgabodegas.com

ALTOS DE TORONA 2011 B
85% albariño, 10% caiño blanco, 5% loureiro

90 Colour: bright straw. Nose: white flowers, dried herbs, fresh fruit, expressive. Palate: powerful, flavourful, fresh, balanced.

BODEGAS AS LAXAS

As Laxas, 16
36430 Arbo - (Pontevedra)
☎: +34 986 665 444 - Fax: +34 986 665 554
info@bodegasaslaxas.com
www.bodegasaslaxas.com

BÁGOA DO MIÑO 2011 B
100% albariño

91 Colour: bright straw. Nose: fresh, fresh fruit, white flowers. Palate: flavourful, fruity, good acidity, balanced.

LAXAS 2011 B
100% albariño

91 Colour: bright straw. Nose: fruit expression, floral, fragrant herbs, mineral, balanced. Palate: powerful, flavourful, good structure, correct.

VAL DO SOSEGO 2011 B
100% albariño

90 Colour: bright straw. Nose: fresh, fresh fruit, white flowers, varietal, complex. Palate: flavourful, fruity, good acidity.

BODEGAS COTO REDONDO

Bouza do Rato, s/n - Rubiós
36449 As Neves - (Pontevedra)
☎: +34 986 667 212 - Fax: +34 986 648 279
info@bodegas-cotoredondo.com
www.bodegas-cotoredondo.com

SEÑORÍO DE RUBIÓS CONDADO BLANCO DO TEA 2011 B
treixadura, albariño, loureiro, godello, torrontés

91 Colour: bright yellow. Nose: powerfull, ripe fruit, citrus fruit, white flowers. Palate: flavourful, fruity, fresh.

SEÑORÍO DE RUBIÓS CONDADO DO TEA BARRICA 2007 B
treixadura, albariño, loureiro, godello, torrontés

91 Color bright yellow. Aroma powerfull, ripe fruit, sweet spices, creamy oak, fragrant herbs. Taste rich, smoky aftertaste, flavourful, fresh, good acidity.

SEÑORÍO DE RUBIÓS SOUSÓN 2011 T
100% sausón

90 Colour: cherry, purple rim. Nose: balsamic herbs, scrubland, red berry notes, fruit expression. Palate: fine bitter notes, balsamic.

BODEGAS DEL PALACIO DE FEFIÑANES

Pza. de Fefiñanes, s/n
36630 Cambados - (Pontevedra)
☎: +34 986 542 204 - Fax: +34 986 524 512
fefinanes@fefinanes.com
www.fefinanes.com

1583 ALBARIÑO DE FEFIÑANES 2011 BFB
100% albariño

92 Colour: bright yellow. Nose: faded flowers, candied fruit, citrus fruit. Palate: flavourful, fruity, ripe fruit.

ALBARIÑO DE FEFIÑANES 2011 B
100% albariño

92 Colour: bright straw. Nose: ripe fruit, citrus fruit, white flowers, varietal. Palate: flavourful, fruity, fine bitter notes, good acidity.

ALBARIÑO DE FEFIÑANES III AÑO 2009 B
100% albariño

95 Colour: bright yellow. Nose: spicy, candied fruit, characterful, powerfull. Palate: long, ripe fruit, spicy, fine bitter notes.

BODEGAS EIDOSELA

Eidos de Abaixo, s/n - Sela
36494 Arbo - (Pontevedra)
☎: +34 986 665 550 - Fax: +34 986 665 299
info@bodegaseidosela.com
www.bodegaseidosela.com

EIDOSELA 2011 B
100% albariño

91 Colour: bright straw. Nose: fresh, white flowers, ripe fruit. Palate: flavourful, fruity, good acidity, balanced.

ETRA CONDADO 2011 B
70% albariño, 20% treixadura, 10% loureiro

90 Colour: bright straw. Nose: fresh, fresh fruit, white flowers, fragrant herbs. Palate: flavourful, fruity, good acidity, balanced.

BODEGAS FILLABOA

Lugar de Fillaboa, s/n
36450 Salvaterra do Miño - (Pontevedra)
☎: +34 986 658 132
info@bodegasfillaboa.masaveu.com
www.bodegasfillaboa.com

FILLABOA 2011 B
albariño

91 Colour: bright straw. Nose: ripe fruit, white flowers, citrus fruit, mineral. Palate: flavourful, fruity, fresh, ripe fruit.

FILLABOA SELECCIÓN FINCA MONTEALTO 2010 B
albariño

92 Colour: bright yellow. Nose: grassy, fragrant herbs, ripe fruit, fruit expression, citrus fruit. Palate: flavourful, powerful, ripe fruit, fine bitter notes.

BODEGAS GERARDO MÉNDEZ

Galiñanes, 10 - Lores
36968 Meaño - (Pontevedra)
☎: +34 986 747 046 - Fax: +34 986 748 915
info@bodegasgerardomendez.com
www.bodegasgerardomendez.com

ALBARIÑO DO FERREIRO 2011 B
albariño

92 Colour: bright straw. Nose: grassy, fragrant herbs, dried flowers, mineral. Palate: powerful, flavourful, complex, long.

BODEGAS LA CANA

Bartolome Esteban Murillo, 11 - Pol Ind La Pañoleta
29700 Vélez - (Málaga)
☎: +34 952 504 706 - Fax: +34 951 284 796
office@jorge-ordonez.es
www.lacana.es

LA CANA 2011 B
100% albariño

92 Color bright straw. Aroma fresh, fresh fruit, white flowers, expressive. Taste flavourful, fruity, good acidity, balanced.

BODEGAS LA VAL

Lugar Muguiña, s/n - Arantei
36458 Salvaterra de Miño - (Pontevedra)
☎: +34 986 610 728 - Fax: +34 986 611 635
laval@bodegaslaval.com
www.bodegaslaval.com

LA VAL ALBARIÑO 2010 BFB
100% albariño

90 Colour: bright yellow. Nose: creamy oak, sweet spices, candied fruit, citrus fruit. Palate: flavourful, powerful, fine bitter notes, balanced.

LA VAL ALBARIÑO 2011 B
100% albariño

91 Colour: bright straw. Nose: dried flowers, fragrant herbs, mineral, expressive. Palate: rich, flavourful, correct, balanced.

LA VAL CRIANZA SOBRE LÍAS 2005 BC
100% albariño

92 Colour: bright yellow. Nose: powerfull, expressive, complex, candied fruit, citrus fruit, dried flowers. Palate: rich, powerful, flavourful, fine bitter notes, good acidity.

ORBALLO 2011 B
100% albariño

90 Colour: bright straw. Nose: fresh, white flowers, ripe fruit. Palate: flavourful, fruity, good acidity, balanced.

BODEGAS MAR DE FRADES

Lg. Arosa, 16 - Finca Valiñas
36637 Meis - (Pontevedra)
☎: +34 986 680 911 - Fax: +34 986 680 926
info@mardefrades.es
www.mardefrades.es

FINCA VALIÑAS "CRIANZA SOBRE LÍAS" 2010 B
albariño

93 Colour: bright yellow. Nose: citrus fruit, candied fruit, dried herbs, mineral, fragrant herbs. Palate: good acidity, flavourful, fresh, fruity, balanced, elegant.

BODEGAS MARQUÉS DE VIZHOJA

Finca La Moreira s/n
36438 Arbo - (Pontevedra)
☎: +34 986 665 825 - Fax: +34 986 665 960
marquesdevizhoja@marquesdevizhoja.com
www.marquesdevizhoja.com

TORRE LA MOREIRA 2011 B
100% albariño

90 Colour: bright straw. Nose: grassy, fruit expression, citrus fruit, fresh fruit. Palate: flavourful, good acidity.

BODEGAS MARTÍN CÓDAX

Burgans, 91
36633 Vilariño-Cambados - (Pontevedra)
☎: +34 986 526 040 - Fax: +34 986 526 901
comercial@martincodax.com
www.martincodax.com

ALBA MARTÍN 2011 B
100% albariño

91 Colour: bright straw. Nose: fresh, white flowers, varietal, ripe fruit, mineral. Palate: flavourful, fruity, good acidity, balanced.

ANXO MARTÍN 2011 B
85% albariño, 10% caiño blanco, 5% loureiro

93 Colour: bright straw. Nose: fresh, fresh fruit, white flowers, expressive, grassy, balsamic herbs, mineral. Palate: flavourful, fruity, good acidity, balanced.

BURGÁNS 2011 B
100% albariño

90 Colour: bright straw. Nose: fresh, white flowers, expressive, fruit expression. Palate: flavourful, fruity, good acidity.

MARTÍN CÓDAX GALLAECIA 2009 B
100% albariño

90 Colour: bright yellow. Nose: powerfull, ripe fruit, sweet spices, creamy oak. Palate: rich, smoky aftertaste, flavourful, fresh, good acidity.

MARTIN CODAX LÍAS 2008 B
100% albariño

90 Colour: bright yellow. Nose: powerfull, ripe fruit, sweet spices, fragrant herbs. Palate: rich, smoky aftertaste, flavourful, fresh, good acidity.

BODEGAS SANTIAGO ROMA

Catariño, 5 - Besomaño
36636 Ribadumia - (Pontevedra)
☎: +34 679 469 218
bodega@santiagoroma.com
www.santiagoroma.com

ALBARIÑO SANTIAGO ROMA SELECCIÓN ALBARIÑO 2011 B
100% albariño

91 Colour: bright yellow. Nose: ripe fruit, dried flowers, fragrant herbs, sweet spices. Palate: rich, fruity, flavourful, long.

COLLEITA DE MARTIS ALBARIÑO 2011 B
100% albariño

90 Colour: bright straw. Nose: white flowers, citrus fruit, dried herbs. Palate: flavourful, fruity, fine bitter notes, easy to drink.

BODEGAS SEÑORÍO DE VALEI

La Granja, s/n
36494 Sela - Arbo - (Pontevedra)
☎: +34 698 146 950 - Fax: +34 986 665 390
info@bodegasenoriodevalei.com
www.bodegasenoriodevalei.com

PAZO DE VALEI 2011 B
100% albariño

91 Colour: bright straw. Nose: fresh, fresh fruit, white flowers, citrus fruit. Palate: flavourful, fruity, good acidity, balanced.

SEÑORÍO DE VALEI 2011 B
100% albariño

90 Colour: bright straw. Nose: fresh, fresh fruit, white flowers. Palate: flavourful, fruity, good acidity, balanced.

BODEGAS TERRAS GAUDA

Ctra. Tui - A Guarda, Km. 55
36760 O´Rosal - (Pontevedra)
☎: +34 986 621 001 - Fax: +34 986 621 084
terrasgauda@terrasgauda.com
www.terrasgauda.com

ABADÍA DE SAN CAMPIO 2011 B
albariño

90 Colour: bright straw. Nose: fresh, fresh fruit, white flowers, expressive, grassy. Palate: flavourful, fruity, good acidity, balanced.

TERRAS GAUDA 2011 B
70% albariño, 18% loureiro, 12% caiño blanco

91 Colour: bright yellow. Nose: fresh, neat, varietal, complex, dry stone. Palate: fruity, full, fine bitter notes.

TERRAS GAUDA ETIQUETA NEGRA 2010 BFB
70% albariño, 20% loureiro, 10% caiño blanco

92 Colour: bright yellow. Nose: sweet spices, cocoa bean, ripe fruit, fruit expression, citrus fruit. Palate: long, ripe fruit, spicy.

BODEGAS VINUM TERRAE

Lugar de Axis - Simes, s/n
36968 Meaño - (Pontevedra)
☎: +34 986 747 566 - Fax: +34 986 747 621
pepa.formoso@vinumterrae.com
www.vinumterrae.com

AGNUSDEI ALBARIÑO 2011 B
100% albariño

90 Colour: bright straw. Nose: ripe fruit, floral, fragrant herbs. Palate: fruity, rich, flavourful, easy to drink.

YOU & ME WHITE EXPERIENCE 2011 B
100% albariño

91 Colour: bright straw. Nose: ripe fruit, citrus fruit, white flowers, fragrant herbs, expressive. Palate: rich, fresh, fruity, flavourful.

BODEGAS Y VIÑEDOS DON OLEGARIO

Refoxos, s/n - Corvillón
36634 Cambados - (Pontevedra)
☎: +34 986 520 886 - Fax: +34 986 520 886
info@donolegario.com
www.donolegario.com

DON OLEGARIO ALBARIÑO 2011 B
albariño

92 Colour: bright straw. Nose: grassy, balsamic herbs, citrus fruit, ripe fruit. Palate: good acidity, fine bitter notes, round.

BOUZA DO REI

Lugar de Puxafeita, s/n
36636 Ribadumia - (Pontevedra)
☎: +34 986 710 257 - Fax: +34 986 718 393
bouzadorei@bouzadorei.com
www.bouzadorei.com

ALBARIÑO BOUZA DO REI 2011 B
100% albariño

90 Color bright straw. Aroma fresh, fresh fruit, white flowers, expressive. Taste flavourful, fruity, good acidity, balanced.

CASTEL DE BOUZA 2011 B
100% albariño

90 Colour: bright straw. Nose: white flowers, fresh fruit, fragrant herbs, fresh, complex. Palate: flavourful, fruity, long.

CAMPOS DE CELTAS

Avda. Diagonal, 590, 5º 1ª
8021 - (Barcelona)
☎: +34 660 445 464
info@vinergia.com
www.vinergia.com

CAMPOS DE CELTAS 2011 B
100% albariño,

90 Color bright straw. Aroma fresh, fresh fruit, white flowers, expressive. Taste flavourful, fruity, good acidity, balanced.

COMERCIAL GRUPO FREIXENET S.A.

Joan Sala, 2
8770 Sant Sadurní D'Anoia - (Barcelona)
☎: +34 938 917 000 - Fax: +34 938 183 095
freixenet@freixenet.es
www.freixenet.es

VIONTA 2011 B
100% albariño

90 Colour: bright straw. Nose: fresh, fresh fruit, citrus fruit, fragrant herbs. Palate: flavourful, fruity, good acidity, fine bitter notes.

CRUCEIRO VELLO

Raul Alfonsin, 3 - Lugar Cruceiro Vello
36636 Ribadumia - (Pontevedra)
☎: +34 941 454 050 - Fax: +34 941 454 529
bodega@bodegasriojanas.com
www.bodegasriojanas.com

CRUCEIRO VELLO 2011 B
100% albariño

91 Colour: bright yellow. Nose: candied fruit, ripe fruit, faded flowers. Palate: flavourful, good acidity, ripe fruit.

DAVIDE

Serantes, 36 Bayón
36614 Vilanova de Arousa - (Pontevedra)
☎: +34 620 248 165 - Fax: +34 986 506 330
info@davide.es
www.davide.es

DAVIDE DUO 2011 B
50% albariño, 50% godello,

91 Colour: bright straw. Nose: fresh, fresh fruit, white flowers, expressive, fragrant herbs. Palate: flavourful, fruity, good acidity, balanced.

DAVIDE TRADICIÓN 2011 B
100% albariño

90 Colour: bright straw. Nose: fresh, fresh fruit, white flowers. Palate: flavourful, fruity, good acidity, balanced.

DOMECQ WINES

Vía Rápida do Salnés, Km. 5
36637 - (Pontevedra)
☎: +34 986 710 827 - Fax: +34 986 710 827
info@domecqbodegas.com
www.domecqbodegas.com

VILLAREI 2011 B
100% albariño

90 Color bright straw. Aroma fresh, fresh fruit, white flowers, expressive. Taste flavourful, fruity, good acidity, balanced.

GRUPO VINÍCOLA MARQUÉS DE VARGAS - PAZO DE SAN MAURO

Pombal, 3 - Lugar de Porto
36458 Salvaterra de Miño - (Pontevedra)
☎: +34 986 658 285 - Fax: +34 986 664 208
info@pazosanmauro.com
www.marquesdevargas.com

SANAMARO 2009 B
95% albariño, 5% loureiro

91 Colour: bright yellow. Nose: dried herbs, white flowers, mineral. Palate: balanced, powerful, flavourful.

LAGAR DE BESADA

Pazo, 11
36968 Xil-Meaño - (Pontevedra)
☎: +34 986 747 473 - Fax: +34 986 747 826
info@lagardebesada.com
www.lagardebesada.com

AÑADA DE BALADIÑA 2004 B
100% albariño

91 Colour: bright yellow. Nose: powerfull, characterful, candied fruit. Palate: ripe fruit, spicy, fine bitter notes, good acidity.

BALADIÑA 2011 B
100% albariño

90 Colour: bright straw. Nose: medium intensity, fresh fruit, citrus fruit. Palate: flavourful, full.

LAGAR DE COSTA

Sartaxes, 8 - Castrelo
36639 Cambados - (Pontevedra)
☎: +34 986 543 526 - Fax: +34 986 982 342
contacto@lagardecosta.com
www.lagardecosta.com

MAIO5 DE LAGAR COSTA 2010 B
100% albariño

91 Colour: bright straw. Nose: white flowers, fresh fruit, fragrant herbs, mineral, balanced. Palate: powerful, flavourful, long, balanced.

LAGAR DE FORNELOS

Barrio de Cruces - Fornelos
36770 O Rosal - (Pontevedra)
☎: +34 986 625 875 - Fax: +34 986 625 011
lagar@riojalta.com
www.riojalta.com

LAGAR DE CERVERA 2011 B
100% albariño

91 Colour: bright straw. Nose: white flowers, ripe fruit, fragrant herbs, expressive, varietal. Palate: powerful, flavourful, long.

LUAR DE MINARELLOS

Plaza de Matute 12, 3º
28012 - (Madrid)
☎: +34 609 119 248
info@miravinos.es
www.miravinos.es

MINARELLOS 2011 B
albariño

91 Colour: bright yellow. Nose: powerfull, mineral, candied fruit, citrus fruit. Palate: flavourful, ripe fruit, fine bitter notes.

M. CONSTANTINA SOTELO ARES

Castelo Castriño,
36639 Cambados - (Pontevedra)
☎: +34 639 835 073
adegasotelo@yahoo.es

ROSALÍA 2011 B
albariño

90 Colour: bright straw. Nose: fresh, fresh fruit, white flowers. Palate: flavourful, fruity, good acidity, balanced.

MAIOR DE MENDOZA

Rúa de Xiabre, 58
36613 Villagarcía de Arosa - (Pontevedra)
☎: +34 986 508 896 - Fax: +34 986 507 924
maiordemendoza@hotmail.es
www.maiordemendoza.com

FULGET 2011 B
100% albariño

90 Colour: bright straw. Nose: ripe fruit, white flowers, mineral. Palate: flavourful, fruity, fresh.

MAR DE ENVERO

Lugar Quintáns, 17
36638 Ribadumia - (Pontevedra)
☎: +34 981 577 083 - Fax: +34 981 569 552
bodega@mardeenvero.es
www.mardeenvero.es

MAR DE ENVERO 2009 B
albariño

91 Colour: bright yellow. Nose: dried flowers, fragrant herbs, ripe fruit, balanced. Palate: powerful, flavourful, long, correct.

TROUPE 2011 B

90 Colour: bright straw. Nose: fresh, fresh fruit, white flowers. Palate: flavourful, fruity, good acidity, balanced.

PACO & LOLA

Valdamor, 18 - XII
36968 Meaño - (Pontevedra)
☎: +34 986 747 779 - Fax: +34 986 748 940
internacional@pacolola.com
www.pacolola.com

FOLLAS NOVAS 2011 B
albariño,

90 Colour: bright straw. Nose: fresh, fresh fruit, white flowers. Palate: flavourful, fruity, good acidity, balanced.

PACO & LOLA 2011 B
albariño

92 Colour: bright straw. Nose: mineral, fragrant herbs, dried flowers, varietal. Palate: good acidity, flavourful, fruity.

PAZO DE BARRANTES

Finca Pazo de Barrantes
36636 Barrantes - (Pontevedra)
☎: +34 986 718 211 - Fax: +34 986 710 424
bodega@pazodebarrantes.com
www.pazodebarrantes.com

LA COMTESSE 2009 B
100% albariño

94 Colour: bright yellow. Nose: powerfull, ripe fruit, sweet spices, creamy oak, fragrant herbs, mineral. Palate: rich, flavourful, fresh, good acidity.

PAZO DE BARRANTES ALBARIÑO 2011 B
100% albariño

93 Colour: bright straw. Nose: fresh, white flowers, ripe fruit, varietal, expressive. Palate: flavourful, fruity, good acidity, balanced.

PAZO DE SEÑORANS

Vilanoviña,s/n
36616 Meis - (Pontevedra)
☎: +34 986 715 373 - Fax: +34 986 715 569
info@pazodesenorans.com
www.pazodesenorans.com

PAZO SEÑORANS 2011 B
100% albariño

92 Colour: bright straw. Nose: fresh, fresh fruit, white flowers, expressive, mineral. Palate: flavourful, fruity, good acidity, balanced.

PAZO SEÑORANS SELECCIÓN DE AÑADA 2005 B
100% albariño

96 Colour: bright yellow. Nose: mineral, ripe fruit, fruit expression, white flowers, complex, varietal. Palate: good acidity, flavourful, ripe fruit, long.

PRIMA VINIA

Soutelo, 3
36750 Goián - (Pontevedra)
☎: +34 902 100 723 - Fax: +34 986 620 071

GAUDILA 2009 B
albariño

92 Colour: bright yellow. Nose: ripe fruit, floral, fine lees, fragrant herbs, complex. Palate: powerful, flavourful, long, balanced.

LEIRA VELLA 2011 B
albariño

90 Color bright straw. Aroma fresh, fresh fruit, white flowers, expressive. Taste flavourful, fruity, good acidity, balanced.

QUINTA COUSELO

Barrio de Couselo, 13
36770 O'Rosal - (Pontevedra)
☎: +34 986 625 051 - Fax: +34 986 626 267
quintacouselo@quintacouselo.com
www.quintacouselo.com

QUINTA DE COUSELO 2011 B
albariño, loureiro

90 Colour: bright straw. Nose: fresh, fresh fruit, white flowers, varietal. Palate: flavourful, fruity, good acidity, balanced.

TVRONIA 2011 B
albariño

90 Colour: bright straw. Nose: fresh, white flowers, ripe fruit, varietal. Palate: flavourful, fruity, good acidity, balanced.

RED BOTTLE INTERNATIONAL

Rosales, 6
9400 Aranda de Duero - (Burgos)
☎: +34 947 515 884 - Fax: +34 947 515 886
rbi@redbottleint.com

ELAS 2011 B
100% albariño

90 Colour: bright straw. Nose: citrus fruit, floral, fragrant herbs, expressive. Palate: balanced, fresh, fruity, flavourful.

SANTIAGO RUIZ

Rua do Vinicultor Santiago Ruiz
36760 San Miguel de Tabagón - O Rosal - (Pontevedra)
☎: +34 986 614 083 - Fax: +34 986 614 142
info@bodegasantiagoruiz.com
www.bodegasantiagoruiz.com

SANTIAGO RUIZ 2011 B
albariño, loureiro, treixadura, caiño, godello

91 Colour: bright straw. Nose: fresh, fresh fruit, white flowers, fragrant herbs. Palate: flavourful, fruity, good acidity, balanced.

TERRA DE ASOREI

Rúa San Francisco, 2 - 1º C-D
36630 Cambados - (Pontevedra)
☎: +34 986 198 882 - Fax: +34 986 520 813
info@terradeasorei.com
www.terradeasorei.com

NAI 2011 B
albariño

90 Colour: bright straw. Nose: fresh, fresh fruit, white flowers. Palate: flavourful, fruity, good acidity.

VIÑA ALMIRANTE

Peroxa, 5
36658 Portas - (Pontevedra)
☎: +34 620 294 293 - Fax: +34 986 541 471
info@vinaalmirante.com
www.vinaalmirante.com

PIONERO MUNDI 2011 B
100% albariño

90 Colour: bright straw. Nose: balsamic herbs, grassy, ripe fruit, citrus fruit. Palate: flavourful, fruity, fresh.

VANIDADE 2011 B
100% albariño

90 Colour: bright straw. Nose: grassy, ripe fruit, citrus fruit, fruit expression. Palate: flavourful, fruity, ripe fruit.

VIÑA CARTIN

Baceiro, 1 - Lantaño
36657 Portas - (Pontevedra)
☎: +34 615 646 442
bodegas@montino.es
www.terrasdelantano.com

TERRAS DE LANTAÑO 2011 B
100% albariño

90 Colour: bright straw. Nose: ripe fruit, citrus fruit, white flowers. Palate: flavourful, good acidity, fine bitter notes.

VIÑA NORA

Bruñeiras, 7
36440 As Neves - (Pontevedra)
☎: +34 986 667 210 - Fax: +34 986 664 610
info@vinanora.com
www.vinanora.com

NORA 2011 B
albariño

90 Colour: bright straw. Nose: fresh, fresh fruit, white flowers, mineral. Palate: flavourful, fruity, good acidity, balanced.

NORA DA NEVE 2009 BFB
albariño

95 Colour: bright yellow. Nose: complex, characterful, candied fruit, fruit expression, mineral. Palate: fine bitter notes, good acidity, balanced, round.

DESCRIPTION

While Rías Baixas and Ribeiro are zones with white wines, Ribeira Sacra is a zone with red wines and local grapes which evoke the younger wines of El Bierzo. The difference with these is that they are more Atlantic and acidic wines in this part of the south of Lugo and the north of Ourense. This region is difficult to describe, taking into account the system of altitudes and terraces where the vines are cultivated and the complexity of the soils, in some cases mineral, which provides this zone with huge potential.

NUMBER OF HECTARES: 2.500 **ALTITUDES:** 400 m. – 500 m.

PREDOMINANT VARIETIES:

White grapes: albariño, loureira blanca, treixadura, dona blanca, torrontés and godello.
Red grapes: mencía, brancellao, merenzao, garnacha tintorera, tempranillo, sousón, caiño tinto and mouratón.

CLIMATOLOGY AND SOILS

A variable climate depending on the zones: slightly fresher with greater continental influence in the valley of the Sil, and with more Atlantic character in the valley of the Miño. The soils have a high level of acidity, and the vineyards are located on terraces on steep slopes.

VAL DE NORA 2011 B
albariño

90 Colour: bright straw. Nose: fresh, fresh fruit, white flowers, lactic notes. Palate: flavourful, fruity, good acidity, balanced.

VIÑEDOS SINGULARES

Cuzco, 26 - 28, Nave 8
8030 - (Barcelona)
☎: +34 609 168 191 - Fax: +34 934 807 076
info@vinedossingulares.com
www.vinedossingulares.com

LUNA CRECIENTE 2011 B
albariño

90 Colour: bright straw. Nose: fresh, fresh fruit, white flowers, citrus fruit, fragrant herbs. Palate: flavourful, fruity, good acidity, balanced.

ZÁRATE

Bouza, 23
36668 Padrenda - Meaño - (Pontevedra)
☎: +34 986 718 503 - Fax: +34 986 718 549
info@zarate.es
www.albarino-zarate.com

ZÁRATE CAIÑO TINTO 2010 T
caiño

90 Colour: deep cherry. Nose: stalky, ripe fruit, spicy, balsamic herbs. Palate: flavourful, fine bitter notes.

ZÁRATE EL BALADO 2010 B
albariño

90 Colour: bright straw. Nose: candied fruit, fruit expression, floral. Palate: flavourful, powerful, fine bitter notes.

ADEGAS MOURE

Buenos Aires, 12 - Bajo
27540 Escairón - (Lugo)
☎: +34 982 452 031 - Fax: +34 982 452 700
abadiadacova@adegasmoure.com
www.adegasmoure.com

ABADÍA DA COVA 2010 T BARRICA
mencía

92 Colour: cherry, garnet rim. Nose: ripe fruit, spicy, creamy oak, toasty, red berry notes, characterful. Palate: powerful, flavourful, toasty, round tannins, mineral.

ABADÍA DA COVA 2011 T BARRICA
mencía

91 Colour: bright cherry. Nose: ripe fruit, sweet spices, expressive, toasty, mineral. Palate: flavourful, fruity, toasty, round tannins.

ABADÍA DA COVA ALBARIÑO 2011 B
85% albariño, 15% godello

91 Colour: bright straw. Nose: white flowers, expressive, ripe fruit. Palate: flavourful, fruity, good acidity, balanced.

ABADÍA DA COVA DE AUTOR 2011 T
mencía

94 Colour: cherry, purple rim. Nose: elegant, mineral, balsamic herbs, spicy. Palate: balanced, fine bitter notes, good finish, round tannins.

ABADÍA DA COVA MENCÍA 2011 T
100% mencía

90 Colour: cherry, garnet rim. Nose: red berry notes, balsamic herbs, mineral, medium intensity. Palate: light-bodied, fresh, fruity, easy to drink.

ALGUEIRA

Doade, s/n
27460 Sober - (Lugo)
☎: +34 629 208 917 - Fax: +34 982 410 299
info@adegaalgueira.com
www.adegaalgueira.com

ALGUEIRA FINCAS 2010 T ROBLE
caíño, sousón

94 Colour: bright cherry. Nose: ripe fruit, sweet spices, creamy oak, fragrant herbs. Palate: flavourful, fruity, toasty, round tannins, balanced, elegant.

ALGUEIRA MERENZAO 2010 T ROBLE
merenzao

95 Colour: bright cherry. Nose: ripe fruit, varietal, dry stone, floral, balsamic herbs, expressive. Palate: fruity, toasty, round tannins, round. Personality.

BODEGAS ALBAMAR

O Adro, 11 - Castrelo
36639 Cambados - (Pontevedra)
☎: +34 660 292 750 - Fax: +34 986 520 048
info@bodegasalbamar.com

FUSCO 2011 T
mencía

90 Colour: cherry, purple rim. Nose: medium intensity, fruit expression, fragrant herbs, mineral. Palate: flavourful, fruity, long, good acidity.

DOMINIO DO BIBEI

Langullo, s/n
32781 Manzaneda - (Ourense)
☎: +34 988 294 453 - Fax: +34 988 519 494
info@dominiodobibei.com
www.dominiodobibei.com

DOMINIO DE BIBEI MT 2008 T

93 Colour: deep cherry. Nose: scrubland, powerfull, ripe fruit, raspberry, sweet spices. Palate: flavourful, powerful, complex, round tannins.

DOMINIO DO BIBEI B 2008 T
brancellao

96 Colour: deep cherry. Nose: spicy, balsamic herbs, scrubland, fresh, complex, expressive. Palate: flavourful, fresh, fruity, light-bodied, long.

LACIMA 2009 T

94 Colour: cherry, garnet rim. Nose: creamy oak, sweet spices, ripe fruit, fruit expression, dried herbs. Palate: good acidity, fine bitter notes, spicy, powerful tannins.

LALAMA 2009 T

92 Colour: bright cherry. Nose: ripe fruit, red berry notes, fruit expression, balsamic herbs. Palate: flavourful, spicy, ripe fruit.

LAPENA 2009 B

93 Colour: bright yellow. Nose: candied fruit, citrus fruit, medium intensity, sweet spices. Palate: good acidity, balanced, round.

LAPOLA 2010 B

93 Colour: bright straw. Nose: mineral, ripe fruit, fruit expression, sweet spices. Palate: flavourful, ripe fruit, long.

PEDRO MANUEL RODRÍGUEZ PÉREZ

Sanmil, 43 - Santa Cruz de Brosmos
27425 Sober - (Lugo)
☎: +34 982 152 508 - Fax: +34 982 402 000
adegasguimaro@gmail.com

FINCA CAPELIÑOS 2010 T
100% mencía

93 Colour: bright cherry. Nose: ripe fruit, creamy oak, spicy, balsamic herbs, mineral. Palate: flavourful, fruity, toasty, fresh, balanced.

FINCA MEIXEMAN 2010 T
100% mencía

93 Colour: cherry, garnet rim. Nose: ripe fruit, spicy, dried flowers. Palate: powerful, flavourful, toasty, balsamic, round tannins.

GUIMARO MENCÍA 2011 T
100% mencía

91 Colour: cherry, garnet rim. Nose: ripe fruit, spicy, toasty, complex, balsamic herbs, scrubland. Palate: powerful, flavourful, round tannins.

PONTE DA BOGA

15178 Castro Caldelas - (Ourense)
☎: +34 988 203 306 - Fax: +34 988 203 299
ruben@pontedaboga.es
www.pontedaboga.es

PONTE DA BOGA BANCALES OLVIDADOS MENCÍA 2009 T
mencía

91 Colour: cherry, garnet rim. Nose: red berry notes, ripe fruit, scrubland, spicy. Palate: flavourful, long, balanced, balsamic.

PONTE DA BOGA BLANCO DE BLANCOS 2011 B
albariño, godello, dona blanca

91 Colour: bright straw. Nose: fresh, fresh fruit, white flowers, expressive, balsamic herbs, mineral. Palate: flavourful, fruity, good acidity, balanced.

PONTE DA BOGA CAPRICHO DE MERENZAO 2009 T
merenzao, brancellao, sousón

93 Colour: cherry, garnet rim. Nose: ripe fruit, spicy, scrubland, expressive, creamy oak. Palate: round, flavourful, long, spicy, elegant.

PONTE DA BOGA EXPRESIÓN HISTÓRICA 2010 T
mencía, merenzao, sausón, brancellao

91 Colour: cherry, garnet rim. Nose: spicy, complex, red berry notes, ripe fruit. Palate: powerful, flavourful, toasty, round tannins.

DESCRIPTION

The Denomination of Origin Ribeiro is situated in southern Galicia, in the western part of Ourense. The wines of Galicia associated to the white porcelain cup, the "taciña" have progressed much in order to compete with the wines of the Rías Baixas. This is achieved through production in the French style in order to obtain the splendour of the local treixadura, godello, loureira grapes, included in all kinds of blends.

NUMBER OF HECTARES: 2.767

ALTITUDES: 75 m. – 400 m.

PREDOMINANT VARIETIES:

White grapes: treixadura, torrontés, palomino, godello, macabeo, loureira and albariño.
Red grapes: caiño, sosuón, ferrón, mencía, tempranillo, brancellao and garnacha tintorera.

CLIMATOLOGY AND SOILS

The climate is favoured by the natural barriers of the geography and its location in the south of Galicia, which protects it from sub-Atlantic storms and gives rise to a transition eco-climate from oceanic to Mediterranean. The soils are fundamentally of granite origin, with a substantial presence of stones and gravel which improves the macro-structure of the soil and the insolation of the bunches. The predominant textures are silt - sand.

ADEGA MANUEL FORMIGO

Cabo de Vila, 49
32431 Beade - (Ourense)
☎: +34 627 569 885
info@fincateira.com
www.fincateira.com

FINCA TEIRA 2011 B
treixadura, godello, torrontés

90 Colour: bright straw. Nose: fresh, fresh fruit, white flowers, characterful, grassy. Palate: flavourful, fruity, good acidity, balanced.

TOSTADO DE TEIRA 2006 B
treixadura

94 Colour: golden. Nose: powerfull, honeyed notes, fragrant herbs, dark chocolate, cocoa bean. Palate: flavourful, sweet, fresh, fruity, good acidity, long.

ADEGAS VALDAVIA

Cuñas, s/n
32454 Cenlle - (Ourense)
☎: +34 669 892 681 - Fax: +34 986 367 016
comercial@adegasvaldavia.com
www.adegasvaldavia.com

CUÑAS DAVIA 2010 BFB
treixadura, albariño

92 Colour: bright straw. Nose: powerfull, ripe fruit, citrus fruit, white flowers, mineral. Palate: flavourful, ripe fruit, long, fine bitter notes, good acidity.

CUÑAS DAVIA 2011 B JOVEN
treixadura, albariño, godello, lado

91 Colour: bright straw. Nose: fresh, white flowers, fresh fruit, ripe fruit, citrus fruit. Palate: flavourful, fruity, good acidity, balanced.

BODEGA ALANÍS

Lg. Santa Cruz de Arrabaldo, s/n
32990 - (Ourense)
☎: +34 988 384 200 - Fax: +34 988 384 068
vinos@bodegasgallegas.com
www.bodegasgallegas.com

GRAN ALANÍS 2011 B
treixadura, godello

90 Colour: bright straw. Nose: fresh, fresh fruit, white flowers, expressive, complex, varietal, grassy. Palate: flavourful, fruity, good acidity, balanced.

BODEGA COOP. SAN ROQUE DE BEADE

Ctra. Ribadavia - Carballiño, Km. 4
32431 Beade - (Ourense)
☎: +34 988 471 522 - Fax: +34 988 471 502
adegas@terradocastelo.com
www.terradocastelo.com

TERRA DO CASTELO "SENSACIÓN" 2011 B
50% treixadura, 45% palomino, 5% godello

90 Colour: bright straw. Nose: white flowers, fresh fruit, fragrant herbs. Palate: correct, balanced, fresh, fruity.

BODEGAS CAMPANTE

Finca Reboreda, s/n
32941 Puga - (Ourense)
☎: +34 988 261 212 - Fax: +34 988 261 213
info@campante.com
www.campante.com

GRAN REBOREDA 2011 B
treixadura, godello, loureiro

90 Colour: bright straw. Nose: fresh, fresh fruit, white flowers, scrubland. Palate: flavourful, fruity, good acidity, balanced.

BODEGAS DOCAMPO

Lg. Sampaio
32414 Ribadavia - (Ourense)
☎: +34 988 470 258 - Fax: +34 988 470 421
admin@bodegasdocampo.com
www.bodegasdocampo.com

SEÑORÍO DA VILA 2010 B
treixadura

91 Colour: bright yellow. Nose: ripe fruit, citrus fruit, fragrant herbs. Palate: flavourful, fruity, rich, balanced.

BODEGAS EL PARAGUAS

Lugar de Esmelle, 111
15594 Ferrol - (A Coruña)
☎: +34 636 161 479
info@bodegaselparaguas.com
www.bodegaselparaguas.com

EL PARAGUAS ATLÁNTICO 2011 B
85% treixadura, 10% godello, 5% albariño

90 Colour: bright straw. Nose: fresh, fresh fruit, fragrant herbs, dried flowers. Palate: flavourful, fruity, good acidity, balanced.

BODEGAS NAIROA

A Ponte, 2
32417 Arnoia - (Ourense)
☎: +34 988 492 867
info@bodegasnairoa.com
www.bodegasnairoa.com

ALBERTE 2011 B
80% treixadura, 20% albariño

90 Colour: bright straw. Nose: ripe fruit, citrus fruit, grassy. Palate: ripe fruit, flavourful, powerful.

CASAL DE ARMÁN

Lugar O Cotiño, s/n. San Andrés de Camporredondo
32400 Ribadavia - (Ourense)
☎: +34 699 060 464 - Fax: +34 988 491 809
bodega@casaldearman.net
www.casaldearman.net

ARMAN FINCA OS LOUREIROS 2010 B
100% treixadura

90 Colour: bright straw. Nose: mineral, dry stone, floral, citrus fruit, ripe fruit. Palate: flavourful, round, sweetness.

CASAL DE ARMÁN 2011 B
90% treixadura, 5% albariño, 5% godello

92 Colour: bright straw. Nose: fresh, fresh fruit, white flowers, scrubland, varietal, mineral. Palate: flavourful, fruity, good acidity, balanced.

CASAL DE ARMÁN 2011 T
brancellao, sousón, caiño

91 Colour: cherry, purple rim. Nose: fruit expression, red berry notes, scrubland. Palate: flavourful, fruity, fresh, good acidity.

COTO DE GOMARIZ

Barrio de Gomariz
32429 Leiro - (Ourense)
☎: +34 671 641 982 - Fax: +34 988 488 174
gomariz@cotodegomariz.com
www.cotodegomariz.com

COTO DE GOMARIZ 2011 B
treixadura, godello, loureiro, torrontés

91 Colour: bright straw. Nose: fresh, white flowers, varietal, complex, citrus fruit, dried herbs. Palate: flavourful, fruity, good acidity, balanced.

GOMARIZ X 2011 B
95% albariño, 5% treixadura

91 Colour: bright straw. Nose: powerfull, varietal, characterful, ripe fruit. Palate: flavourful, powerful, good acidity, carbonic notes.

EDUARDO PEÑA

Carrero Blanco, s/n - Barral
Castelo de Miño - (Ourense)
☎: +34 629 872 130
bodega@bodegaeduardopenha.es
www.bodegaeduardopenha.es

EDUARDO PEÑA 2011 B

90 Colour: bright straw. Nose: ripe fruit, fruit expression, balsamic herbs, scrubland, mineral. Palate: flavourful, spicy, ripe fruit.

EMILIO DOCAMPO DIÉGUEZ

San Andrés, 57
32415 Ribadavia - (Ourense)
☎: +34 639 332 790 - Fax: +34 988 275 318
edocampodieguez@hotmail.com

CASAL DE PAULA 2011 B
treixadura, torrontés, albariño, godello

90 Colour: bright straw, greenish rim. Nose: white flowers, fresh fruit, fragrant herbs, mineral, citrus fruit. Palate: powerful, flavourful, rich, fruity.

EMILIO ROJO

Lugar de Remoiño, s/n
32233 Arnoia - (Ourense)
☎: +34 988 488 050
vinoemiliorojo@hotmail.com

EMILIO ROJO 2011 B

91 Colour: bright straw, greenish rim. Nose: citrus fruit, white flowers, fragrant herbs, sweet spices, creamy oak, mineral. Palate: fresh, fruity, flavourful, spicy, long.

FINCA VIÑOA

A Viñoa,s/n, Banga
32821 O Carballiño - (Ourense)
☎: +34 95 220 256 - Fax: +34 988 488 741
info@fincavinoa.com
www.fincavinoa.com

FINCA VIÑOA 2011 B
treixadura, godello, loureiro, albariño

91 Colour: bright straw. Nose: fresh, fresh fruit, floral, varietal, grassy. Palate: flavourful, fruity, good acidity, balanced.

LAGAR DO MERENS

Chaos
32430 Arnoia - (Ourense)
☎: +34 607 533 314
info@lagardomerens.com
www.lagardomerens.com

30 COPELOS 2010 T
sousón, brancellao, caiño, ferrón

90 Colour: cherry, purple rim. Nose: expressive, fresh fruit, red berry notes, floral, balsamic herbs. Palate: flavourful, fruity, good acidity, round tannins.

LAGAR DO MERENS 2010 B
treixadura, lado, torrontés

91 Colour: bright straw. Nose: candied fruit, fruit expression, dried herbs, balsamic herbs. Palate: flavourful, powerful, good acidity, fine bitter notes.

LAGAR DO MERENS 2010 BFB
treixadura, lado, torrontés

92 Colour: bright yellow. Nose: powerfull, ripe fruit, sweet spices, creamy oak, fragrant herbs. Palate: rich, flavourful, fresh, good acidity.

LUIS A. RODRÍGUEZ VÁZQUEZ

Laxa, 7
32417 Arnoia - (Ourense)
☎: +34 988 492 977 - Fax: +34 988 492 977

VIÑA DE MARTÍN "OS PASÁS" 2010 B
treixadura, lado, albariño, torrontés

91 Colour: bright straw. Nose: fresh, dried flowers, dried herbs, citrus fruit. Palate: flavourful, fruity, balanced, good acidity.

VIÑA DE MARTÍN ESCOLMA 2008 BFB
treixadura, albariño, lado, torrontés

92 Colour: bright yellow. Nose: creamy oak, candied fruit, fruit liqueur notes, toasty. Palate: powerful, sweetness, fine bitter notes, good acidity.

PRODUCCIONES A MODIÑO

Cubilledo-Gomariz
32420 Leiro - (Ourense)
☎: +34 686 961 681
sanclodiovino@gmail.com
www.vinosanclodio.com

SANCLODIO 2011 B
treixadura, godello, loureiro, albariño, torrontés

92 Colour: bright straw. Nose: white flowers, dry stone, mineral, fruit expression, fragrant herbs. Palate: flavourful, fresh, fruity, rich, balanced.

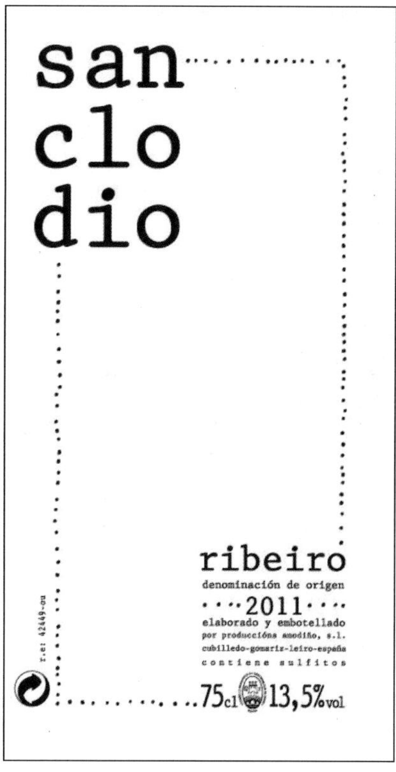

SAMEIRÁS

San Andrés, 98
32415 Ribadavia - (Ourense)
☎: +34 988 491 812 - Fax: +34 988 470 591
sameiras@terra.es

1040 SAMEIRÁS 2011 B

90 Colour: bright straw. Nose: fresh, fresh fruit, white flowers, expressive, creamy oak, spicy. Palate: flavourful, fruity, good acidity, balanced.

VIÑA MEIN S.L.

Mein, s/n
32420 Leiro - (Ourense)
☎: +34 617 326 248 - Fax: +34 988 488 732
info.bodega@vinamein.com
www.vinamein.com

VIÑA MEIN 2011 B

94 Colour: bright straw. Nose: fresh, fresh fruit, white flowers, fragrant herbs, mineral. Palate: flavourful, fruity, good acidity, balanced, elegant.

VIÑA MEIN 2011 BFB

91 Colour: bright yellow. Nose: ripe fruit, sweet spices, creamy oak, balsamic herbs, balanced. Palate: rich, flavourful, fresh, good acidity, spicy, long.

VIÑOS DE ENCOSTAS

Florentino Cuevillas Nº6, 1ºC
32500 O Carballiño - (Ourense)
☎: +34 647 468 464
xlsebio@gmail.com
vinosdeencostas.blogspot.com.es

HUSH 2009 T
100% sousón

92 Colour: cherry, garnet rim. Nose: earthy notes, mineral, fragrant herbs, ripe fruit, spicy, toasty. Palate: powerful, flavourful, long, spicy, balanced, elegant.

SALVAXE 2010 B
treixadura, albariño, lado, loureiro

92 Colour: bright yellow. Nose: floral, ripe fruit, dried herbs, dry stone, fine lees. Palate: rich, flavourful, fresh, long, balanced, elegant.

VITIVINÍCOLA DEL RIBEIRO VIÑA COSTEIRA

Valdepereira, s/n
32415 Ribadavia - (Ourense)
☎: +34 988 477 210 - Fax: +34 988 470 330
info@pazoribeiro.com
www.vinoribeiro.com

COLECCIÓN COSTEIRA TREIXADURA BARRICA 2011 BFB
treixadura

90 Colour: bright yellow. Nose: powerfull, ripe fruit, creamy oak, toasty. Palate: rich, smoky aftertaste, flavourful, good acidity.

COLECCIÓN COSTEIRA TREIXADURA DO RIBEIRO 2011 B
treixadura

90 Colour: bright straw. Nose: white flowers, fruit expression, fragrant herbs, expressive. Palate: flavourful, fruity, fresh, balanced.

DESCRIPTION

This is one of the most prestigious zones in Spain thanks to its distinctive wines made from fine red grapes (tempranillo) which grows in a climate with strong contrasts in temperature which favours slow maturing of the grape and a good degree of acidity. It is situated between the provinces of the south of Burgos, the east of Valladolid, the northwest of Segovia and western Soria. Two of the most emblematic and most international Spanish wineries are in Ribera del Duero: Vega Sicilia and Pingus.

NUMBER OF HECTARES: 20.956 **ALTITUDES:** 700 m. – 850 m.

PREDOMINANT VARIETIES:
White grapes: albillo.
Red grapes: tinta del país, garnacha tinta, cabernet sauvignon, malbec and merlot.

CLIMATOLOGY AND SOILS

Continental climate with slight Atlantic influences, the soils are loose, not very fertile and with a high content of limestone.

3 ASES

Carretera, 7
9315 Fuentemolinos - (Burgos)
☎: +34 670 601 118
info@3asesvino.com
www.3asesvino.com

3 ASES 2009 TC
tempranillo

90 Colour: cherry, garnet rim. Nose: spicy, creamy oak, toasty, characterful, mineral. Palate: powerful, flavourful, toasty, round tannins.

4U WINES

Aranda,11
9471 Fuentelcesped - (Burgos)
☎: +34 665 305 666
4uwines@gmail.com

4 U + 2009 T
tempranillo

91 Color cherry, garnet rim. Aroma ripe fruit, spicy, creamy oak, toasty, complex. Taste powerful, flavourful, toasty, round tannins.

4U 2008 T
tempranillo

91 Colour: cherry, garnet rim. Nose: ripe fruit, spicy, creamy oak, toasty, varietal. Palate: powerful, flavourful, toasty, round tannins.

4U VENDIMIA SELECCIONADA 2007 T
tempranillo

91 Colour: cherry, garnet rim. Nose: ripe fruit, spicy, creamy oak, toasty, characterful. Palate: powerful, flavourful, toasty, round tannins.

ALTO BODEGAS Y VIÑEDOS

Paraje Vallejo de Carril, s/n
47360 Quintanilla de Arriba - (Valladolid)
☎: +34 620 351 182 - Fax: +34 983 036 949
aalto@aalto.es
www.aalto.es

AALTO 2009 T
tempranillo

93 Colour: cherry, garnet rim. Nose: ripe fruit, creamy oak, toasty, sweet spices, expressive. Palate: powerful, flavourful, toasty, round tannins, balanced.

AALTO PS 2009 T
tempranillo

94 Colour: bright cherry. Nose: ripe fruit, sweet spices, creamy oak, cocoa bean, dark chocolate, mineral, expressive. Palate: flavourful, fruity, toasty, balanced, elegant.

ABADÍA DE ACÓN

Ctra. Hontangas, Km. 09400
9391 Castrillo de la Vega - (Burgos)
☎: +34 947 509 292 - Fax: +34 947 508 586
info@abadiadeacon.com
www.abadiadeacon.com

ABADÍA DE ACÓN VENDIMIA SELECCIONADA 2005 T
100% tempranillo

90 Colour: dark-red cherry, orangey edge. Nose: ripe fruit, powerfull, wet leather, tobacco, spicy, toasty. Palate: flavourful, powerful, spicy, long.

ACÓN 2007 TR
90% tempranillo, 10% cabernet sauvignon

91 Colour: bright cherry. Nose: sweet spices, creamy oak, earthy notes. Palate: flavourful, fruity, toasty, round tannins.

ACÓN 2009 TC
100% tempranillo

90 Colour: bright cherry. Nose: ripe fruit, sweet spices, creamy oak, varietal. Palate: flavourful, fruity, toasty, round tannins.

TARGÚM 2007 T
100% tempranillo

91 Colour: cherry, garnet rim. Nose: ripe fruit, balsamic herbs, spicy, dark chocolate, toasty, fine reductive notes. Palate: powerful, flavourful, long, spicy.

ALTOS DEL TERRAL

Barrionuevo, 11
9400 Aranda de Duero - (Burgos)
☎: +34 616 953 451
bodega@altosdelterral.com
www.altosdelterral.com

ALTOS DEL TERRAL T1 2009 T
100% tinto fino

93 Color cherry, garnet rim. Aroma ripe fruit, spicy, creamy oak, toasty, complex. Taste powerful, flavourful, toasty, round tannins.

CUVÉE JULIA ALTOS DEL TERRAL 2009 T
100% tinto fino

93 Colour: black cherry, garnet rim. Nose: red berry notes, ripe fruit, balsamic herbs, mineral, sweet spices, creamy oak. Palate: balanced, powerful, flavourful, complex, toasty.

ASTRALES

Ctra. Olmedillo, Km. 7
9313 Anguix - (Burgos)
☎: +34 947 554 222 - Fax: +34 947 554 222
administracion@astrales.es
www.astrales.es

ASTRALES 2009 T
tempranillo

91 Colour: cherry, garnet rim. Nose: ripe fruit, spicy, creamy oak, complex, mineral. Palate: powerful, flavourful, toasty, balanced.

ASTRALES CHRISTINA 2009 T
tempranillo

92 Colour: cherry, garnet rim. Nose: creamy oak, complex, sweet spices, red berry notes, ripe fruit. Palate: powerful, flavourful, toasty, round tannins, balanced.

BADEN NUMEN

Carreterilla, s/n
47359 San Bernardo Valbuena de Duero - (Valladolid)
☎: +34 615 995 552 - Fax: +34 983 683 041
bodega@badennumen.es
www.badennumen.es

BADEN NUMEN "N" 2009 TC

91 Colour: cherry, garnet rim. Nose: ripe fruit, balsamic herbs, sweet spices, creamy oak. Palate: powerful, flavourful, good structure, long, toasty.

BADEN NUMEN ORO "AU" 2009 T

92 Colour: cherry, garnet rim. Nose: ripe fruit, mineral, sweet spices, creamy oak, toasty. Palate: powerful, flavourful, spicy, toasty.

BODEGA CONVENTO SAN FRANCISCO

Calvario, 22
47300 Peñafiel - (Valladolid)
☎: +34 983 878 052 - Fax: +34 983 873 052
bodega@bodegaconvento.com
www.bodegaconvento.com

CONVENTO SAN FRANCISCO SELECCIÓN ESPECIAL 2005 T BARRICA
90% tinta del país, 10% cabernet sauvignon

91 Colour: dark-red cherry, cherry, garnet rim. Nose: ripe fruit, spicy, fine reductive notes, dark chocolate, earthy notes, expressive. Palate: powerful, flavourful, spicy.

BODEGA DE BLAS SERRANO

Ctra. Santa Cruz, s/n
9471 Fuentelcésped - (Burgos)
☎: +34 606 338 632
dbs@bodegasdeblasserrano.com
www.bodegasdeblasserrano.com

DE BLAS SERRANO BODEGAS 2008 T
100% tinta del país

90 Colour: bright cherry. Nose: ripe fruit, sweet spices, creamy oak, aromatic coffee. Palate: flavourful, fruity, toasty, balanced.

MATHIS 2007 T
100% tinta del país

91 Colour: cherry, garnet rim. Nose: ripe fruit, spicy, creamy oak, toasty, complex. Palate: powerful, flavourful, toasty, round tannins, elegant.

PHYLOS 2009 T
100% tinta del país

91 Colour: cherry, garnet rim. Nose: red berry notes, ripe fruit, sweet spices, cocoa bean, creamy oak, expressive. Palate: powerful, flavourful, long, toasty, balanced.

BODEGA MARQUÉS DE VELILLA

Ctra. de Sotillo de la Ribera, s/n
9311 La Horra - (Burgos)
☎: +34 947 542 166 - Fax: +34 947 542 165
bodega@marquesdevelilla.com
www.marquesdevelilla.com

DONCEL DE MATAPERRAS 2005 TC
100% tinta del país

93 Colour: cherry, garnet rim. Nose: spicy, creamy oak, toasty, fruit preserve, fine reductive notes. Palate: powerful, flavourful, toasty, round tannins, balanced.

MARQUÉS DE VELILLA FINCA LA MARÍA 2009 T
100% tinta del país

90 Colour: bright cherry. Nose: sweet spices, creamy oak, red berry notes, ripe fruit. Palate: flavourful, fruity, toasty, balanced.

BODEGA MATARROMERA

Ctra. Renedo-Pesquera, Km. 30
47359 Valbuena de Duero - (Valladolid)
☎: +34 902 430 170 - Fax: +34 902 430 189
matarromera@matarromera.es
www.grupomatarromera.com

MATARROMERA 2005 TGR
100% tempranillo

91 Colour: cherry, garnet rim. Nose: elegant, creamy oak, sweet spices, old leather. Palate: spicy, fine tannins, elegant, long.

MATARROMERA 2009 TC
100% tempranillo

90 Colour: cherry, garnet rim. Nose: spicy, creamy oak, toasty, ripe fruit. Palate: powerful, flavourful, toasty, round tannins.

MATARROMERA PRESTIGIO 2009 T
100% tempranillo

91 Colour: cherry, garnet rim. Nose: red berry notes, ripe fruit, balsamic herbs, sweet spices, toasty. Palate: long, powerful, flavourful.

BODEGA NEXUS

Santiago, 17 - 4º
47001 - (Valladolid)
☎: +34 983 360 284 - Fax: +34 983 345 546
info@bodegasfrontaura.es
www.bodegasfrontaura.es

NEXUS + 2006 T
100% tempranillo

93 Colour: very deep cherry. Nose: sweet spices, mineral, balanced, expressive. Palate: good structure, flavourful, good acidity, round tannins.

NEXUS 2006 TC
100% tempranillo

92 Colour: cherry, garnet rim. Nose: spicy, creamy oak, toasty. Palate: toasty, round tannins, flavourful.

NEXUS 2010 T
100% tempranillo

91 Colour: cherry, garnet rim. Nose: ripe fruit, spicy, creamy oak, toasty, varietal. Palate: powerful, flavourful, toasty, round tannins.

BODEGA RENACIMIENTO

Santa María, 36
47359 Olivares de Duero - (Valladolid)
☎: +34 902 430 170 - Fax: +34 902 430 189
emina@emina.es
www.grupomatarromera.com

RENTO 2005 TC
100% tempranillo

90 Colour: cherry, garnet rim. Nose: dark chocolate, toasty, fruit preserve. Palate: balanced, good structure, round tannins.

BODEGA S. ARROYO

Avda. del Cid, 99
9441 Sotillo de la Ribera - (Burgos)
☎: +34 947 532 444 - Fax: +34 947 532 444
info@tintoarroyo.com
www.tintoarroyo.com

TINTO ARROYO 2009 TC
100% tempranillo

90 Colour: cherry, garnet rim. Nose: ripe fruit, spicy, creamy oak, toasty, elegant. Palate: powerful, flavourful, toasty, good acidity, round.

BODEGA SAN MAMÉS

Ctra. Valladolid, s/n
9315 Fuentecén - (Burgos)
☎: +34 947 532 693 - Fax: +34 947 532 653
info@bodegasanmames.com
www.bodegasanmames.com

DOBLE R 2009 T
tempranillo

90 Colour: cherry, garnet rim. Nose: red berry notes, ripe fruit, mineral, sweet spices, creamy oak. Palate: powerful, flavourful, spicy.

BODEGA Y VIÑEDO FUENTECÉN S.L.

La Iglesia, 48
9315 Fuentecén - (Burgos)
☎: +34 947 532 718 - Fax: +34 947 532 768
info@bodegahemar.com
www.bodegahemar.com

LLANUM 2006 T
tempranillo

90 Colour: dark-red cherry, orangey edge. Nose: ripe fruit, earthy notes, fine reductive notes, aged wood nuances, sweet spices. Palate: long, powerful, flavourful, complex.

BODEGAS ABADÍA LA ARROYADA

La Tejera, s/n
9442 Terradillos de Esgueva - (Burgos)
☎: +34 947 545 309 - Fax: +34 947 545 309
bodegas@abadialaarroyada.es
www.abadialaarroyada.es

ABADÍA LA ARROYADA 2007 TC
tempranillo

90 Colour: cherry, garnet rim. Nose: ripe fruit, spicy, creamy oak, toasty, complex, balsamic herbs, violets. Palate: powerful, flavourful, toasty, round tannins. Personality.

BODEGAS ABANICO

Pol. Ind Ca l'Avellanet - Susany, 6
8553 Seva - (Barcelona)
☎: +34 938 125 676 - Fax: +34 938 123 213
info@exportiberia.com
www.bodegasabanico.com

CATHAR 2006 TR
100% tempranillo

90 Colour: ruby red, orangey edge. Nose: ripe fruit, fruit liqueur notes, balsamic herbs, spicy, creamy oak, fine reductive notes. Palate: balanced, powerful, flavourful, long, spicy.

BODEGAS ARROCAL S.L.

Eras de Santa María, s/n
9443 Gumiel de Mercado - (Burgos)
☎: +34 606 292 102 - Fax: +34 947 561 290
arrocal@arrocal.com
www.arrocal.com

ARROCAL ANGEL 2008 T
tempranillo

90 Colour: cherry, garnet rim. Nose: ripe fruit, creamy oak, toasty, mineral. Palate: flavourful, toasty, round tannins, long, balanced.

ARROCAL MÁXIMO 2006 T
tempranillo

92 Colour: cherry, garnet rim. Nose: ripe fruit, balsamic herbs, creamy oak, toasty, expressive. Palate: balanced, elegant, flavourful, spicy.

ARROCAL PASSIÓN 2009 T
tempranillo

90 Colour: cherry, garnet rim. Nose: red berry notes, ripe fruit, sweet spices, creamy oak. Palate: powerful, flavourful, long, toasty, balanced.

BODEGAS ARZUAGA NAVARRO

Ctra. N-122, Km. 325
47350 Quintanilla de Onésimo - (Valladolid)
☎: +34 983 681 146 - Fax: +34 983 681 147
bodeg@arzuaganavarro.com
www.arzuaganavarro.com

AMAYA ARZUAGA AUTOR 2007 T
95% tinto fino, 5% albillo

92 Colour: cherry, garnet rim. Nose: ripe fruit, spicy, aromatic coffee, sweet spices, toasty. Palate: long, powerful, flavourful, balanced.

AMAYA ARZUAGA AUTOR 2008 T
95% tinto fino, 5% albillo

92 Colour: bright cherry. Nose: ripe fruit, sweet spices, creamy oak, expressive, roasted coffee. Palate: flavourful, fruity, toasty, balanced.

AMAYA ARZUAGA AUTOR 2009 T
95% tinto fino, 5% albillo

90 Colour: very deep cherry. Nose: powerfull, overripe fruit, toasty, dark chocolate. Palate: flavourful, fine bitter notes, good acidity, spicy, toasty.

ARZUAGA 2010 TC
90% tinto fino, 7% cabernet sauvignon, 3% merlot

91 Colour: very deep cherry. Nose: sweet spices, aromatic coffee, ripe fruit, red berry notes. Palate: round, good acidity, spicy, ripe fruit.

ARZUAGA 2004 TGR
90% tinto fino, 10% cabernet sauvignon, merlot

90 Colour: cherry, garnet rim. Nose: creamy oak, sweet spices, ripe fruit. Palate: flavourful, powerful, spicy, ripe fruit.

ARZUAGA 2009 TC
90% tinto fino, 7% cabernet sauvignon, 3% merlot

90 Colour: bright cherry. Nose: ripe fruit, sweet spices, creamy oak, roasted coffee. Palate: flavourful, fruity, toasty, round tannins.

ARZUAGA 2009 TR
95% tinto fino, 5% cabernet sauvignon, merlot

92 Colour: cherry, garnet rim. Nose: ripe fruit, spicy, creamy oak, toasty, characterful, mineral. Palate: powerful, flavourful, toasty, round tannins.

ARZUAGA ECOLÓGICO 2010 TC
100% tinto fino

90 Colour: cherry, garnet rim. Nose: ripe fruit, spicy, creamy oak, characterful, roasted coffee. Palate: powerful, flavourful, toasty, round tannins.

ARZUAGA RESERVA ESPECIAL 2008 TR
95% tinto fino, 5% albillo

92 Colour: cherry, garnet rim. Nose: mineral, ripe fruit, red berry notes, fruit expression, creamy oak. Palate: ripe fruit, spicy, fine bitter notes.

ARZUAGA RESERVA ESPECIAL 2009 TR
95% tinto fino, 5% albillo

93 Colour: cherry, garnet rim. Nose: ripe fruit, fruit expression, spicy, balanced. Palate: flavourful, powerful, fruity.

GRAN ARZUAGA 2009 T
75% tinto fino, 25% cabernet sauvignon, albillo

94 Colour: cherry, garnet rim. Nose: spicy, creamy oak, toasty, characterful, ripe fruit. Palate: powerful, flavourful, toasty, round tannins.

BODEGAS ASENJO & MANSO

Ctra.. Palencia, km. 58,200
9311 La Horra - (Burgos)
☎: +34 636 972 421 - Fax: +34 947 505 269
info@asenjo-manso.com
www.asenjo-manso.com

A&M AUTOR 2006 T
100% tempranillo

92 Colour: cherry, garnet rim. Nose: ripe fruit, spicy, creamy oak, toasty, characterful, varietal. Palate: powerful, flavourful, toasty, round tannins.

BODEGAS BALBÁS

La Majada, s/n
9311 La Horra - (Burgos)
☎: +34 947 542 111 - Fax: +34 947 542 112
bodegas@balbas.es
www.balbas.es

ALITUS 2004 T
75% tempranillo, 20% cabernet sauvignon, 5% merlot

91 Colour: cherry, garnet rim. Nose: spicy, creamy oak, toasty, ripe fruit. Palate: powerful, flavourful, toasty, round tannins.

ARDAL 2006 TR
80% tempranillo, 20% cabernet sauvignon

91 Colour: bright cherry. Nose: sweet spices, creamy oak, red berry notes, ripe fruit. Palate: flavourful, fruity, toasty, round tannins.

RITUS 2009 T
75% tempranillo, 25% merlot

90 Colour: cherry, garnet rim. Nose: medium intensity, creamy oak, dark chocolate. Palate: balanced, ripe fruit, long.

BODEGAS BALUARTE

Calle de la Ribera 32
31592 Cintruénigo - (Navarra)
☎: +34 948 811 000
info@bodegaschivite.com

BALUARTE 2008 TC
tinta del país

91 Colour: cherry, garnet rim. Nose: ripe fruit, spicy, creamy oak, toasty, mineral, floral. Palate: powerful, flavourful, toasty, round tannins.

BODEGAS BRIEGO

Del Rosario, 32
47311 Fompedraza - (Valladolid)
☎: +34 983 892 156 - Fax: +34 983 892 156
info@bodegasbriego.com
www.bodegasbriego.com

BRIEGO VENDIMIA SELECCIONADA 2009 T ROBLE
100% tempranillo

92 Colour: very deep cherry. Nose: creamy oak, dark chocolate, ripe fruit, balanced. Palate: good structure, flavourful, good acidity, long.

SUPERNOVA ROBLE 2009 T ROBLE
100% tempranillo

92 Colour: cherry, garnet rim. Nose: spicy, creamy oak, toasty, characterful, ripe fruit. Palate: powerful, flavourful, toasty, round tannins.

BODEGAS CASTILLO DE GUMIEL

Avda. de Extremadura, 55
9400 Aranda de Duero - (Burgos)
☎: +34 947 510 839 - Fax: +34 947 510 839
castillodegumiel@hotmail.com
www.silenciovaldiruela.com

SILENCIO DE VALDIRUELA 2007 TR
tempranillo

90 Colour: ruby red, orangey edge. Nose: ripe fruit, creamy oak, sweet spices, fine reductive notes. Palate: correct, balanced, powerful, flavourful.

BODEGAS CASTILLO DE LA DUQUESA

Calle Mar, 116
12181 Benlloch - (Castellón)
☎: +34 693 299 449 - Fax: +34 964 339 958
info@banus.eu
www.banus.eu

QUINTADO TEMPRANILLO 2008 TR
94% tempranillo, 6% merlot

90 Colour: cherry, garnet rim. Nose: ripe fruit, spicy, creamy oak, toasty, fine reductive notes. Palate: powerful, flavourful, toasty, round tannins, balanced.

BODEGAS CEPA 21

Ctra. N-122, Km. 297
47318 Castrillo de Duero - (Valladolid)
☎: +34 983 484 083 - Fax: +34 983 480 017
bodega@cepa21.com
www.cepa21.com

CEPA 21 2009 T
100% tinto fino

92 Colour: cherry, garnet rim. Nose: spicy, creamy oak, toasty, ripe fruit. Palate: powerful, flavourful, toasty, round tannins.

MALABRIGO 2010 T
100% tinto fino

93 Colour: very deep cherry. Nose: powerfull, dark chocolate, roasted coffee, ripe fruit. Palate: powerful, fine bitter notes, good acidity, round tannins.

BODEGAS CRUZ DE ALBA

Síndico, 4 y 5
47350 Quintanilla de Onésimo - (Valladolid)
☎: +34 941 310 295 - Fax: +34 941 310 832
info@cruzdealba.es
www.cruzdealba.es

CRUZ DE ALBA 2009 TC
100% tempranillo

91 Colour: cherry, garnet rim. Nose: ripe fruit, creamy oak, toasty, sweet spices. Palate: powerful, flavourful, toasty, round tannins, balanced.

BODEGAS CUEVAS JIMÉNEZ - FERRATUS

Ctra. Madrid-Irún, A-I km. 165
9370 Gumiel de Izán - (Burgos)
☎: +34 947 679 999 - Fax: +34 947 613 873
bodega@ferratus.es
www.ferratus.es

FERRATUS 2007 T
100% tempranillo

93 Colour: cherry, garnet rim. Nose: spicy, creamy oak, toasty, ripe fruit, mineral. Palate: powerful, flavourful, toasty, round tannins.

FERRATUS 2008 T
100% tempranillo

94 Colour: bright cherry, garnet rim. Nose: balanced, ripe fruit, sweet spices. Palate: flavourful, good acidity, round tannins.

FERRATUS SENSACIONES 2006 T
100% tempranillo

93 Colour: cherry, garnet rim. Nose: spicy, creamy oak, toasty, characterful, ripe fruit, earthy notes. Palate: powerful, flavourful, toasty, round tannins.

FERRATUS SENSACIONES 2007 T
100% tempranillo

93 Colour: deep cherry, garnet rim. Nose: cocoa bean, creamy oak, complex. Palate: ripe fruit, long, good structure.

BODEGAS DE LOS RÍOS PRIETO

Ctra. Pesquera - Renedo, 1
47315 Pesquera de Duero - (Valladolid)
☎: +34 983 880 383 - Fax: +34 983 878 032
info@bodegasdelosriosprieto.com
www.bodegasdelosriosprieto.com

LARA PRIOS MAXIMUS VINO DE AUTOR 2006 T
100% tempranillo

90 Colour: cherry, garnet rim. Nose: ripe fruit, spicy, creamy oak, toasty, fragrant herbs, characterful. Palate: powerful, flavourful, toasty, round tannins.

BODEGAS EMILIO MORO

Ctra. Peñafiel - Valoria, s/n
47315 Pesquera de Duero - (Valladolid)
☎: +34 983 878 400 - Fax: +34 983 870 195
bodega@emiliomoro.com
www.emiliomoro.com

EMILIO MORO 2009 TC
100% tinto fino

93 Colour: cherry, garnet rim. Nose: ripe fruit, spicy, creamy oak, toasty, characterful. Palate: powerful, flavourful, toasty, round tannins.

FINCA RESALSO 2011 T
100% tinto fino

90 Colour: bright cherry. Nose: ripe fruit, sweet spices, creamy oak, varietal. Palate: flavourful, fruity, toasty, round tannins.

MALLEOLUS 2009 T
100% tinto fino

93 Colour: cherry, garnet rim. Nose: creamy oak, toasty, characterful, ripe fruit, spicy. Palate: powerful, flavourful, toasty, round tannins.

MALLEOLUS DE SANCHOMARTÍN 2008 T
100% tinto fino

94 Color cherry, garnet rim. Aroma ripe fruit, spicy, creamy oak, toasty, complex. Taste powerful, flavourful, toasty, round tannins.

MALLEOLUS DE VALDERRAMIRO 2008 T
100% tinto fino

93 Colour: cherry, garnet rim. Nose: ripe fruit, mineral, dark chocolate, cocoa bean, sweet spices, creamy oak. Palate: balanced, powerful, flavourful, toasty.

BODEGAS FÉLIX CALLEJO

Avda. del Cid, km. 16
9441 Sotillo de la Ribera - (Burgos)
☎: +34 947 532 312 - Fax: +34 947 532 304
callejo@bodegasfelixcallejo.com
www.bodegasfelixcallejo.com

FÉLIX CALLEJO SELECCIÓN 2009 TC
tempranillo

92 Colour: deep cherry, garnet rim. Nose: balanced, complex, spicy, ripe fruit. Palate: good structure, long, balanced.

GRAN CALLEJO 2006 TGR
tempranillo

91 Colour: cherry, garnet rim. Nose: ripe fruit, creamy oak, expressive. Palate: powerful, flavourful, toasty, round tannins.

MAJUELOS DE CALLEJO 2009 T
tempranillo

90 Colour: deep cherry, purple rim. Nose: medium intensity, red berry notes, ripe fruit, sweet spices. Palate: flavourful, good structure.

BODEGAS FUENTENARRO

Constitución, 32
9311 La Horra - (Burgos)
☎: +34 947 542 092 - Fax: +34 947 542 083
bodegas@fuentenarro.com
www.fuentenarro.com

FUENTENARRO 2006 TR
100% tempranillo

91 Colour: cherry, garnet rim. Nose: ripe fruit, spicy, fine reductive notes, cocoa bean. Palate: powerful, flavourful, toasty, round tannins.

FUENTENARRO 2009 TC
100% tempranillo

90 Color cherry, garnet rim. Aroma ripe fruit, spicy, creamy oak, toasty, complex. Taste powerful, flavourful, toasty, round tannins.

FUENTENARRO VENDIMIA SELECCIONADA 2010 T
100% tempranillo

91 Colour: cherry, garnet rim. Nose: spicy, creamy oak, toasty, characterful, ripe fruit. Palate: powerful, flavourful, toasty, round tannins.

BODEGAS FUENTESPINA

Camino Cascajo, s/n
9470 Fuentespina - (Burgos)
☎: +34 921 596 002 - Fax: +34 921 596 035
ana@avelinovegas.com
www.avelinovegas.com

CORONA DE CASTILLA PRESTIGIO 2009 TC
tempranillo

91 Colour: cherry, garnet rim. Nose: spicy, creamy oak, toasty, characterful, ripe fruit. Palate: powerful, flavourful, toasty, round tannins.

F DE FUENTESPINA 2004 TR
tempranillo

90 Colour: cherry, garnet rim. Nose: ripe fruit, creamy oak, dark chocolate. Palate: powerful, flavourful, toasty, round tannins.

FUENTESPINA SELECCIÓN 2009 T
tempranillo

90 Colour: cherry, garnet rim. Nose: ripe fruit, spicy, toasty, complex, mineral, cocoa bean, dark chocolate. Palate: powerful, flavourful, toasty, harsh oak tannins.

BODEGAS GARCÍA DE ARANDA

Ctra. de Soria, s/n
9400 Aranda de Duero - (Burgos)
☎: +34 947 501 817 - Fax: +34 947 506 355
bodega@bodegasgarcia.com
www.bodegasgarcia.com

PEDRO GARCÍA 2009 T
tempranillo

92 Color bright cherry. Aroma ripe fruit, sweet spices, creamy oak, expressive. Taste flavourful, fruity, toasty, round tannins.

BODEGAS HACIENDA MONASTERIO

Ctra. Pesquera - Valbuena, km. 38
47315 Pesquera de Duero - (Valladolid)
☎: +34 983 484 002 - Fax: +34 983 484 079
bmonasterio@haciendamonasterio.com
www.haciendamonasterio.com

HACIENDA MONASTERIO 2007 TR
80% tempranillo, 20% cabernet sauvignon

92 Colour: cherry, garnet rim. Nose: ripe fruit, spicy, creamy oak, toasty, complex, wet leather. Palate: powerful, flavourful, toasty, round tannins.

HACIENDA MONASTERIO 2009 T
80% tempranillo, 10% cabernet sauvignon, 10% merlot

92 Colour: cherry, garnet rim. Nose: ripe fruit, spicy, creamy oak, toasty, characterful, elegant. Palate: powerful, flavourful, toasty, round tannins.

HACIENDA MONASTERIO RESERVA ESPECIAL 2009 TR
80% tempranillo, 20% cabernet sauvignon

93 Colour: cherry, garnet rim. Nose: ripe fruit, spicy, creamy oak, toasty, complex, expressive. Palate: powerful, flavourful, toasty, round tannins.

BODEGAS HERMANOS PÉREZ PASCUAS

Ctra. Roa, s/n
9314 Pedrosa de Duero - (Burgos)
☎: +34 947 530 100 - Fax: +34 947 530 002
vinapedrosa@perezpascuas.com
www.perezpascuas.com

PÉREZ PASCUAS GRAN SELECCIÓN 2006 TGR

93 Colour: pale ruby, brick rim edge. Nose: ripe fruit, balsamic herbs, dark chocolate, sweet spices, creamy oak, expressive, elegant. Palate: spicy, long, flavourful, balanced, elegant, good acidity.

VIÑA PEDROSA 2006 TGR
90% tinta del país, 10% cabernet sauvignon

92 Colour: pale ruby, brick rim edge. Nose: elegant, spicy, fine reductive notes, wet leather, aged wood nuances, ripe fruit. Palate: spicy, fine tannins, elegant, long, balanced.

VIÑA PEDROSA 2009 TR
90% tinta del país, 10% cabernet sauvignon

94 Colour: cherry, garnet rim. Nose: ripe fruit, spicy, creamy oak, toasty, characterful, varietal. Palate: flavourful, toasty, round tannins, good acidity, elegant.

VIÑA PEDROSA 2010 TC
100% tinta del país

90 Colour: cherry, garnet rim. Nose: sweet spices, creamy oak, cocoa bean, ripe fruit. Palate: long, powerful, flavourful, fruity, balsamic, spicy.

VIÑA PEDROSA LA NAVILLA 2009 T
100% tinta del país

95 Colour: cherry, garnet rim. Nose: creamy oak, toasty, red berry notes, ripe fruit, sweet spices, mineral. Palate: powerful, flavourful, toasty, round tannins, balanced.

BODEGAS HERMANOS SASTRE

San Pedro, s/n
9311 La Horra - (Burgos)
☎: +34 947 542 108 - Fax: +34 947 542 108
sastre@vinasastre.com
www.vinasastre.com

REGINA VIDES 2009 T
100% tinta del país

97 Colour: bright cherry, garnet rim. Nose: complex, creamy oak, spicy, cocoa bean, ripe fruit. Palate: good structure, full, round tannins.

VIÑA SASTRE 2009 TC
tinta del país

93 Colour: cherry, garnet rim. Nose: spicy, creamy oak, toasty, characterful, ripe fruit, mineral. Palate: powerful, flavourful, toasty, round tannins.

VIÑA SASTRE PAGO DE SANTA CRUZ 2009 T
100% tinta del país

95 Colour: cherry, garnet rim. Nose: ripe fruit, spicy, creamy oak, toasty, mineral. Palate: powerful, flavourful, toasty, round tannins.

VIÑA SASTRE PESUS 2009 T
80% tinta del país, 10% merlot, 10% cabernet sauvignon

96 Colour: cherry, garnet rim. Nose: spicy, creamy oak, characterful, fruit expression, toasty, cocoa bean. Palate: powerful, flavourful, toasty, round tannins.

BODEGAS IMPERIALES

Ctra. Madrid - Irun, Km. 171
9370 Gumiel de Izán - (Burgos)
☎: +34 947 544 070 - Fax: +34 947 525 759
direccion@bodegasimperiales.com
www.bodegasimperiales.com

ABADÍA DE SAN QUIRCE 2001 TGR
100% tinta del país

91 Colour: pale ruby, brick rim edge. Nose: elegant, spicy, wet leather, aged wood nuances, fruit liqueur notes. Palate: spicy, elegant, balanced, fine bitter notes.

ABADÍA DE SAN QUIRCE 2005 TR
100% tinta del país

90 Colour: cherry, garnet rim. Nose: complex, balanced, powerfull, warm, ripe fruit, old leather. Palate: flavourful, fruity.

ABADÍA DE SAN QUIRCE 2009 TC
100% tinta del país

92 Colour: cherry, garnet rim. Nose: red berry notes, ripe fruit, balsamic herbs, sweet spices, toasty, mineral. Palate: powerful, flavourful, complex, toasty.

ABADÍA DE SAN QUIRCE 2010 T
100% tinta del país

90 Colour: deep cherry. Nose: powerfull, ripe fruit, toasty, spicy. Palate: flavourful, spicy, ripe fruit, fine bitter notes.

FINCA HELENA AUTOR 2006 T
100% tinta del país

92 Colour: cherry, garnet rim. Nose: spicy, ripe fruit, aromatic coffee, creamy oak. Palate: flavourful, good structure, fruity.

BODEGAS ISMAEL ARROYO - VALSOTILLO

Los Lagares, 71
9441 Sotillo de la Ribera - (Burgos)
☎: +34 947 532 309 - Fax: +34 947 532 487
bodega@valsotillo.com
www.valsotillo.com

VALSOTILLO 2004 TGR
100% tinta del país

91 Colour: cherry, garnet rim. Nose: spicy, creamy oak, toasty, complex, animal reductive notes, fine reductive notes. Palate: powerful, flavourful, toasty, round tannins.

VALSOTILLO 2009 TC
100% tinta del país

91 Colour: cherry, garnet rim. Nose: spicy, creamy oak, toasty, ripe fruit. Palate: powerful, flavourful, toasty, round tannins.

VALSOTILLO VS 2001 TR
100% tinta del país

92 Colour: cherry, garnet rim. Nose: spicy, creamy oak, toasty, wet leather, ripe fruit, fine reductive notes. Palate: powerful, flavourful, round tannins, spicy.

VALSOTILLO VS 2004 TR
100% tinta del país

90 Colour: cherry, garnet rim. Nose: spicy, creamy oak, toasty, complex, characterful, ripe fruit. Palate: powerful, flavourful, toasty, round tannins.

BODEGAS LA HORRA

Camino de Anguix, s/n
9311 La Horra - (Burgos)
☎: +34 947 613 963 - Fax: +34 947 613 963
rodarioja@roda.es
www.bodegaslahorra.es

CORIMBO 2010 T
tempranillo,

91 Colour: cherry, garnet rim. Nose: ripe fruit, fruit expression, toasty, new oak. Palate: flavourful, ripe fruit, spicy, long.

CORIMBO I 2009 T
tempranillo

92 Colour: cherry, garnet rim. Nose: creamy oak, toasty, ripe fruit, mineral. Palate: powerful, flavourful, toasty, round tannins.

CORIMBO I 2010 T
tinta del país

93 Colour: cherry, garnet rim. Nose: ripe fruit, spicy, creamy oak, toasty, characterful. Palate: powerful, flavourful, toasty, round tannins.

BODEGAS LÓPEZ CRISTÓBAL

Barrio Estación, s/n
9300 Roa de Duero - (Burgos)
☎: +34 947 561 139 - Fax: +34 947 540 606
info@lopezcristobal.com
www.lopezcristobal.com

BAGÚS VENDIMIA SELECCIONADA 2009 T
100% tempranillo

91 Colour: bright cherry, garnet rim. Nose: toasty, new oak, powerfull, ripe fruit. Palate: good structure, full, flavourful, round tannins.

LÓPEZ CRISTOBAL 2009 TC
95% tempranillo, 5% merlot

92 Colour: cherry, garnet rim. Nose: red berry notes, ripe fruit, sweet spices, creamy oak. Palate: powerful, flavourful, long, spicy.

LÓPEZ CRISTOBAL 2011 T ROBLE
95% tinta del país, 5% merlot

91 Colour: bright cherry. Nose: ripe fruit, sweet spices, creamy oak, expressive, red berry notes. Palate: flavourful, fruity, toasty, round tannins.

BODEGAS PASCUAL

Ctra. de Aranda, Km. 5
9471 Fuentelcesped - (Burgos)
☎: +34 947 557 351 - Fax: +34 947 557 312
export@bodegaspascual.com
www.bodegaspascual.com

BURÓ SELECCIÓN 2009 T
100% tempranillo

92 Colour: cherry, garnet rim. Nose: ripe fruit, balsamic herbs, earthy notes, spicy, toasty. Palate: powerful, flavourful, spicy, long, toasty.

BODEGAS PINGÓN

Ctra. N-122, Km. 311
47300 Peñafiel - (Valladolid)
☎: +34 983 880 623 - Fax: +34 983 880 623
carramimbre@bodegaspingon.com
www.bodegaspingon.com

ALTAMIMBRE 2009 T
100% tinto fino

92 Colour: cherry, garnet rim. Nose: ripe fruit, mineral, sweet spices, creamy oak. Palate: powerful, flavourful, complex, long, toasty.

CARRAMIMBRE 2009 TC
95% tinto fino, 5% cabernet sauvignon

91 Colour: cherry, garnet rim. Nose: ripe fruit, creamy oak, toasty, balsamic herbs. Palate: powerful, flavourful, toasty, round tannins.

BODEGAS PORTIA

Antigua Ctra. N-I, km. 170
9370 Gumiel de Izán - (Burgos)
☎: +34 947 102 700 - Fax: +34 947 107 004
info@bodegasportia.com
www.bodegasportia.com

PORTIA PRIMA 2010 T
tempranillo

92 Colour: cherry, garnet rim. Nose: balanced, expressive, sweet spices, ripe fruit, cocoa bean. Palate: flavourful, good structure, round tannins.

TRIENNIA 2010 T
tempranillo

91 Colour: cherry, garnet rim. Nose: mineral, spicy, ripe fruit, toasty. Palate: flavourful, ripe fruit, good acidity, round tannins.

BODEGAS RESALTE DE PEÑAFIEL

Ctra. N-122, Km. 312
47300 Peñafiel - (Valladolid)
☎: +34 983 878 160 - Fax: +34 983 880 601
info@resalte.com
www.resalte.com

PEÑA ROBLE 2004 TR
100% tempranillo

90 Colour: dark-red cherry, orangey edge. Nose: elegant, spicy, fine reductive notes, aged wood nuances. Palate: spicy, fine tannins, elegant, long.

RESALTE 2005 TR
100% tempranillo

90 Colour: ruby red, orangey edge. Nose: ripe fruit, scrubland, earthy notes, cocoa bean, dark chocolate, creamy oak. Palate: powerful, flavourful, long, spicy.

BODEGAS RODERO

Ctra. Boada, s/n
9314 Pedrosa de Duero - (Burgos)
☎: +34 947 530 046 - Fax: +34 947 530 097
rodero@bodegasrodero.com
www.bodegasrodero.com

CARMELO RODERO 2009 TC
90% tempranillo, 10% cabernet sauvignon

91 Colour: cherry, garnet rim. Nose: creamy oak, sweet spices, tobacco. Palate: flavourful, full, round tannins, complex.

CARMELO RODERO 2009 TR
90% tempranillo, 10% cabernet sauvignon

93 Colour: cherry, garnet rim. Nose: ripe fruit, spicy, creamy oak, toasty, characterful, varietal. Palate: powerful, flavourful, toasty, round tannins.

CARMELO RODERO TSM 2006 T
75% tempranillo, 10% cabernet sauvignon, 15% merlot

93 Colour: cherry, garnet rim. Nose: ripe fruit, spicy, creamy oak, toasty, dark chocolate. Palate: powerful, flavourful, toasty, round tannins.

PAGO DE VALTARREÑA 2005 T
100% tempranillo

94 Colour: cherry, garnet rim. Nose: ripe fruit, spicy, creamy oak, toasty, complex, fine reductive notes. Palate: powerful, flavourful, toasty, round tannins, balanced, elegant.

BODEGAS SANTA EULALIA

Malpica, s/n
9311 La Horra - (Burgos)
☎: +34 983 586 868 - Fax: +34 947 580 180
bodegasfrutosvillar@bodegasfrutosvillar.com
www.bodegasfrutosvillar.com

CONDE DE SIRUELA 2008 TC
100% tinta del país

90 Colour: cherry, garnet rim. Nose: balanced, creamy oak, overripe fruit. Palate: flavourful, round tannins.

BODEGAS SEÑORÍO DE NAVA

Ctra. Valladolid - Soria, s/n
9318 Nava de Roa - (Burgos)
☎: +34 987 209 712 - Fax: +34 947 550 003
snava@senoriodenava.es
www.senoriodenava.es

SEÑORÍO DE NAVA 2008 TC
100% tinta del país

90 Colour: cherry, garnet rim. Nose: ripe fruit, earthy notes, scrubland, fine reductive notes, aged wood nuances, toasty. Palate: powerful, flavourful, balanced, long, spicy.

SEÑORÍO DE NAVA FINCA SAN COBATE 2005 TR
100% tinta del país

90 Colour: ruby red, orangey edge. Nose: ripe fruit, spicy, aged wood nuances, varnish, creamy oak, tobacco, old leather. Palate: powerful, flavourful, spicy, round.

BODEGAS TAMARAL

Ctra. N-122, Km. 310,6
47300 Peñafiel - (Valladolid)
☎: +34 983 878 017 - Fax: +34 983 878 089
exterior@tamaral.com
www.tamaral.com

TAMARAL 2008 TR

92 Colour: deep cherry. Nose: powerfull, characterful, ripe fruit. Palate: flavourful, powerful, concentrated, ripe fruit, long.

TAMARAL FINCA LA MIRA 2005 T

90 Colour: deep cherry, garnet rim. Nose: overripe fruit, fragrant herbs, sweet spices. Palate: flavourful, long.

BODEGAS TARSUS

Ctra. de Roa - Anguix, Km. 3
9313 Anguix - (Burgos)
☎: +34 947 554 218 - Fax: +34 947 541 804
tarsus@pernod-ricard.com
www.domecqbodegas.com

QUINTA DE TARSUS 2009 TC
100% tempranillo

90 Colour: cherry, garnet rim. Nose: balanced, expressive, ripe fruit, neat. Palate: flavourful, full, good acidity.

TARSUS 2006 TR
98% tempranillo, 2% cabernet sauvignon

91 Colour: cherry, garnet rim. Nose: spicy, creamy oak, toasty, complex, dark chocolate. Palate: powerful, flavourful, toasty, round tannins.

TARSUS 2010 T ROBLE
100% tinta del país

90 Colour: cherry, garnet rim. Nose: ripe fruit, dark chocolate, spicy, creamy oak. Palate: powerful, flavourful, toasty, long.

BODEGAS TIONIO

Ctra. de Valoria, Km. 7
47315 Pesquera de Duero - (Valladolid)
☎: +34 933 950 811 - Fax: +34 983 870 185
info@parxet.es
www.parxet.es

TIONIO 2009 T
100% tinto fino

91 Colour: cherry, garnet rim. Nose: ripe fruit, creamy oak, toasty. Palate: powerful, flavourful, toasty, round tannins.

BODEGAS TORREDEROS

Ctra. Valladolid, Km. 289,300
9318 Fuentelisendo - (Burgos)
☎: +34 947 532 627 - Fax: +34 947 532 731
administracion@torrederos.com
www.torrederos.com

TORREDEROS 2009 TC
100% tempranillo

90 Colour: cherry, garnet rim. Nose: spicy, creamy oak, toasty, characterful, ripe fruit. Palate: powerful, flavourful, toasty, round tannins.

TORREDEROS SELECCIÓN 2009 T
100% tempranillo

90 Colour: cherry, garnet rim. Nose: ripe fruit, spicy, creamy oak, toasty, complex, aromatic coffee. Palate: powerful, flavourful, toasty, good acidity.

TORREMORÓN 2009 TC
100% tempranillo

91 Colour: cherry, garnet rim. Nose: spicy, creamy oak, toasty, characterful, ripe fruit. Palate: powerful, flavourful, toasty, round tannins, fine bitter notes.

BODEGAS TRUS

Ctra. Pesquera - Encinas, Km. 3
47316 Piñel de Abajo - (Valladolid)
☎: +34 913 872 033 - Fax: +34 902 302 340
trus@bodegastrus.com
www.bodegastrus.com

KREL 2009 T ROBLE
100% tinto fino

90 Colour: bright cherry, purple rim. Nose: creamy oak, sweet spices, ripe fruit, cocoa bean. Palate: good structure, flavourful, fruity.

KREL 2010 T ROBLE
100% tinto fino

91 Colour: cherry, garnet rim. Nose: ripe fruit, red berry notes, toasty, spicy. Palate: flavourful, powerful, spicy, ripe fruit.

TRUS 2005 TR
100% tinto fino

92 Colour: very deep cherry. Nose: dark chocolate, creamy oak, ripe fruit, candied fruit. Palate: good structure, flavourful, full.

BODEGAS VALDAYA

Ctra. de Burgos, s/n
9441 Sotillo de la Ribera - (Burgos)
☎: +34 947 532 450 - Fax: +34 947 532 476
info@valdaya.com
www.valdaya.com

VALDAYA VENDIMIA SELECCIONADA 2009 TC
100% tinto fino

90 Colour: cherry, garnet rim. Nose: ripe fruit, spicy, creamy oak, toasty, expressive. Palate: powerful, flavourful, toasty, round tannins.

BODEGAS VALDEVIÑAS

Ctra. Nacional 122, Km. 245
42320 Langa de Duero - (Soria)
☎: +34 975 186 000 - Fax: +34 975 186 012
info@valdevinas.es
www.valdevinas.es

MIRAT 2004 TR
100% tempranillo

90 Colour: cherry, garnet rim. Nose: earthy notes, powerfull, ripe fruit, sweet spices. Palate: flavourful, fruity, good acidity.

BODEGAS VALDUBÓN

Antigua N-I, Km. 151
9460 Milagros - (Burgos)
☎: +34 947 546 251 - Fax: +34 947 546 250
valdubon@valdubon.es
www.valdubon.es

HONORIS DE VALDUBÓN 2006 T
85% tempranillo, 9% merlot, 6% cabernet sauvignon

92 Colour: ruby red, garnet rim. Nose: ripe fruit, balsamic herbs, spicy, creamy oak, expressive. Palate: powerful, flavourful, spicy, long, balanced.

VALDUBÓN DIEZ T
100% tempranillo

91 Colour: cherry, garnet rim. Nose: ripe fruit, spicy, creamy oak, toasty, complex, mineral, balsamic herbs. Palate: powerful, flavourful, toasty, balanced.

BODEGAS VEGA SICILIA

Ctra. N-122, Km. 323
47359 Valbuena de Duero - (Valladolid)
☎: +34 983 680 147 - Fax: +34 983 680 263
vegasicilia@vega-sicilia.com
www.vega-sicilia.com

VALBUENA 5º 2008 T
93% tinto fino, 7% merlot, malbec

94 Colour: cherry, garnet rim. Nose: creamy oak, sweet spices, cocoa bean, mineral, ripe fruit. Palate: rich, flavourful, full, complex.

VEGA SICILIA RESERVA ESPECIAL 94/99/00 T

97 Colour: cherry, garnet rim. Nose: complex, fruit preserve, spicy, dark chocolate, elegant. Palate: spicy, classic aged character, good acidity, balanced, fine bitter notes, round.

VEGA SICILIA ÚNICO 2003 T
92% tinto fino, 8% cabernet sauvignon

96 Colour: deep cherry, garnet rim. Nose: sweet spices, balanced, ripe fruit, toasty, fine reductive notes. Palate: rich, good acidity, elegant, fine bitter notes, long.

BODEGAS VITULIA

Sendín, 49
9400 Aranda de Duero - (Burgos)
☎: +34 947 515 051 - Fax: +34 947 515 051
bvitulia@bodegasvitulia.com
www.bodegasvitulia.com

VITULIA 2009 TC
90% tinto fino, 10% otras

90 Colour: cherry, garnet rim. Nose: red berry notes, ripe fruit, sweet spices, creamy oak. Palate: powerful, flavourful, harsh oak tannins.

BODEGAS VIZCARRA

Finca Chirri, s/n
9317 Mambrilla de Castrejón - (Burgos)
☎: +34 947 540 340 - Fax: +34 947 540 340
bodegas@vizcarra.es
www.vizcarra.es

CELIA VIZCARRA 2010 T
90% tinto fino, 10% garnacha

95 Colour: cherry, garnet rim. Nose: ripe fruit, creamy oak, toasty, earthy notes, mineral, sweet spices. Palate: powerful, flavourful, toasty, round tannins, long, balanced.

INÉS VIZCARRA 2010 T
90% tinto fino, 10% merlot

96 Colour: cherry, garnet rim. Nose: red berry notes, ripe fruit, mineral, sweet spices, aromatic coffee, balsamic herbs. Palate: powerful, flavourful, long, toasty, balanced.

VIZCARRA 2010 T
100% tinto fino

92 Colour: bright cherry. Nose: ripe fruit, sweet spices, creamy oak, dark chocolate. Palate: flavourful, fruity, toasty, round tannins.

VIZCARRA SENDA DEL ORO 2011 T
100% tinto fino

90 Colour: cherry, purple rim. Nose: expressive, fresh fruit, red berry notes, floral. Palate: flavourful, fruity, good acidity, balanced.

VIZCARRA TORRALVO 2010 T
100% tinto fino

94 Colour: bright cherry. Nose: ripe fruit, creamy oak, dark chocolate, caramel, mineral. Palate: flavourful, fruity, toasty, round, long, spicy.

BODEGAS Y VIÑEDOS ACEÑA

Avda. Valladolid, 4
42330 San Esteban de Gormaz - (Soria)
☎: +34 667 784 220
bodega@terraesteban.com
www.terraesteban.com

TERRAESTEBAN 2009 TC
100% tempranillo

91 Colour: cherry, garnet rim. Nose: expressive, elegant, mineral, earthy notes. Palate: flavourful, good acidity, spicy.

BODEGAS Y VIÑEDOS ALIÓN

Ctra. N-122, Km. 312,4 Padilla de Duero
47300 Peñafiel - (Valladolid)
☎: +34 983 881 236 - Fax: +34 983 881 246
imartin@bodegasalion.com
www.bodegasalion.com

ALIÓN 2009 T
100% tinto fino

95 Colour: deep cherry, garnet rim. Nose: expressive, balanced, complex, ripe fruit, sweet spices. Palate: long, ripe fruit, round tannins, fine bitter notes.

BODEGAS Y VIÑEDOS DEL JARO

Ctra. Pesquera - Valbuena, s/n. Finca El Quiñón
47315 Pesquera de Duero - (Valladolid)
☎: +34 900 505 855 - Fax: +34 956 852 339
vinos@gvitivinicola.com
www.grupohebe.com

CHAFANDÍN 2009 T

92 Colour: bright cherry. Nose: ripe fruit, sweet spices, creamy oak, toasty. Palate: flavourful, fruity, toasty, round tannins, balanced.

SED DE CANÁ 2009 T

93 Colour: cherry, garnet rim. Nose: ripe fruit, spicy, dark chocolate, cocoa bean, earthy notes. Palate: powerful, flavourful, toasty, long, spicy, good acidity, balanced.

BODEGAS Y VIÑEDOS ESCUDERO

Camino El Ramo, s/n
9311 Olmedillo de Roa - (Burgos)
☎: +34 629 857 575 - Fax: +34 947 551 070
info@costaval.com
www.costaval.com

COSTAVAL 2005 TR
100% tempranillo

90 Colour: bright cherry, orangey edge. Nose: ripe fruit, fruit liqueur notes, spicy, fine reductive notes. Palate: long, spicy, powerful, flavourful.

BODEGAS Y VIÑEDOS GALLEGO ZAPATERO

Segunda Travesía de la Olma, 4
9312 Anguix - (Burgos)
☎: +34 648 180 777
info@bodegasgallegozapatero.com
www.bodegasgallegozapatero.com

YOTUEL FINCA SAN MIGUEL 2008 T
100% tinta del país

90 Colour: cherry, garnet rim. Nose: scrubland, spicy, ripe fruit, expressive. Palate: powerful, flavourful, long, toasty.

YOTUEL FINCA VALDEPALACIOS 2007 T
100% tinta del país

92 Colour: cherry, garnet rim. Nose: spicy, creamy oak, toasty, complex, fragrant herbs, candied fruit. Palate: powerful, flavourful, toasty, round tannins.

YOTUEL SELECCIÓN 2009 T
100% tinta del país

90 Colour: cherry, garnet rim. Nose: spicy, creamy oak, toasty, characterful, ripe fruit. Palate: powerful, flavourful, toasty, round tannins.

BODEGAS Y VIÑEDOS LLEIROSO

Ctra. Monasterio, s/n
47359 Valbuena del Duero - (Valladolid)
☎: +34 983 683 300 - Fax: +34 983 683 301
enologia@bodegaslleiroso.com
www.bodegaslleiroso.com

LVZMILLAR 2009 TC
tempranillo

90 Colour: black cherry, garnet rim. Nose: red berry notes, ripe fruit, dark chocolate, aromatic coffee, creamy oak. Palate: long, powerful, flavourful, toasty.

BODEGAS Y VIÑEDOS MARTÍN BERDUGO

Ctra. de la Colonia, s/n
9400 Aranda de Duero - (Burgos)
☎: +34 947 506 331 - Fax: +34 947 506 602
bodega@martinberdugo.com
www.martinberdugo.com

MB MARTÍN BERDUGO 2006 T
tempranillo

92 Colour: cherry, garnet rim. Nose: medium intensity, dark chocolate, sweet spices. Palate: ripe fruit, long, round tannins.

BODEGAS Y VIÑEDOS MONTEABELLÓN

Calvario, s/n
9318 Nava de Roa - (Burgos)
☎: +34 947 550 000 - Fax: +34 947 550 219
info@monteabellon.com
www.monteabellon.com

MONTEABELLÓN 14 MESES EN BARRICA 2009 T
tempranillo

91 Colour: cherry, garnet rim. Nose: creamy oak, toasty, characterful, ripe fruit, sweet spices. Palate: powerful, flavourful, toasty, round tannins.

MONTEABELLÓN 24 MESES EN BARRICA 2007 T
tempranillo

92 Colour: cherry, garnet rim. Nose: spicy, creamy oak, toasty, complex, scrubland, balsamic herbs. Palate: powerful, flavourful, toasty, round tannins.

MONTEABELLÓN FINCA LA BLANQUERA 2006 T
tempranillo,

90 Colour: black cherry. Nose: warm, overripe fruit, fruit preserve, aromatic coffee, dark chocolate. Palate: powerful, sweetness.

BODEGAS Y VIÑEDOS NEO

Ctra. N-122, Km. 274,5
9391 Castrillo de la Vega - (Burgos)
☎: +34 947 514 393 - Fax: +34 947 515 445
info@bodegasconde.com
www.bodegasneo.com

NEO 2009 T
100% tempranillo

90 Colour: cherry, garnet rim. Nose: ripe fruit, creamy oak, toasty, sweet spices, dark chocolate. Palate: powerful, flavourful, toasty, round tannins, long.

NEO PUNTA ESENCIA 2009 T
100% tempranillo

92 Colour: cherry, garnet rim. Nose: red berry notes, ripe fruit, spicy, creamy oak, mineral, elegant. Palate: round, flavourful, long, fine tannins, balanced.

SENTIDO 2010 T
100% tempranillo

90 Colour: bright cherry. Nose: ripe fruit, sweet spices, mineral, balsamic herbs, creamy oak. Palate: flavourful, fruity, toasty, balanced.

BODEGAS Y VIÑEDOS ORTEGA FOURNIER

Finca El Pinar, s/n
9316 Berlangas de Roa - (Burgos)
☎: +34 947 533 006 - Fax: +34 947 533 010
jmortega@ofournier.com
www.ofournier.com

ALFA SPIGA 2006 T
100% tinta del país

93 Colour: cherry, garnet rim. Nose: spicy, creamy oak, toasty, characterful, mineral, ripe fruit. Palate: powerful, flavourful, toasty, round tannins.

SPIGA 2007 T
100% tinta del país

90 Colour: cherry, garnet rim. Nose: spicy, creamy oak, toasty, sweet spices, fragrant herbs. Palate: powerful, flavourful, toasty, round tannins.

BODEGAS Y VIÑEDOS QUMRÁN

Pago de las Bodegas, s/n
47300 Padilla de Duero - (Valladolid)
☎: +34 983 882 103 - Fax: +34 983 881 514
info@bodegasqumran.es
www.bodegasqumran.es

PROVENTUS 2009 T
100% tempranillo

90 Colour: cherry, garnet rim. Nose: ripe fruit, spicy, varietal. Palate: powerful, flavourful, toasty, round tannins.

QUMRÁN 2008 TC
100% tempranillo

90 Colour: bright cherry. Nose: ripe fruit, sweet spices, creamy oak. Palate: flavourful, fruity, toasty, round tannins.

BODEGAS Y VIÑEDOS RECOLETAS

Ctra. Quintanilla, s/n
47359 Olivares de Duero - (Valladolid)
☎: +34 983 687 017 - Fax: +34 983 687 017
bodegas@gruporecoletas.com
www.bodegasrecoletas.com

RECOLETAS VENDIMIA SELECCIONADA 2005 T
tempranillo

92 Colour: cherry, garnet rim. Nose: ripe fruit, dark chocolate, aromatic coffee, creamy oak, toasty, fine reductive notes. Palate: powerful, flavourful, long, round.

BODEGAS Y VIÑEDOS ROBEAL

Ctra. Anguix, s/n
9300 Roa - (Burgos)
☎: +34 947 484 606 - Fax: +34 947 482 817
info@bodegasrobeal.com
www.bodegasrobeal.com

VALNOGAL 16 MESES 2009 T BARRICA
tempranillo

91 Colour: cherry, garnet rim. Nose: balanced, ripe fruit, sweet spices. Palate: good structure, fruity, flavourful, round tannins.

BODEGAS Y VIÑEDOS TÁBULA

Ctra. de Valbuena, km. 2
47359 Olivares de Duero - (Valladolid)
☎: +34 608 219 019 - Fax: +34 983 107 300
armando@bodegastabula.es
www.bodegastabula.es

CLAVE DE TÁBULA 2009 T
100% tempranillo

93 Colour: cherry, garnet rim. Nose: ripe fruit, spicy, creamy oak, complex. Palate: powerful, flavourful, toasty, round tannins.

DAMANA 2009 TC
100% tempranillo

91 Colour: bright cherry. Nose: ripe fruit, sweet spices, creamy oak. Palate: flavourful, fruity, toasty, round tannins.

GRAN TÁBULA 2008 T
100% tempranillo

92 Colour: cherry, purple rim. Nose: characterful, ripe fruit, creamy oak, sweet spices, varietal. Palate: flavourful, fine bitter notes, round tannins.

TÁBULA 2009 T
100% tempranillo

93 Colour: cherry, garnet rim. Nose: spicy, creamy oak, toasty, characterful, varietal, red berry notes. Palate: powerful, flavourful, toasty, round tannins.

BODEGAS Y VIÑEDOS VALDERIZ

Ctra. Pedrosa, km 1
9300 Roa - (Burgos)
☎: +34 947 540 460 - Fax: +34 947 541 032
bodega@valderiz.com
www.valderiz.com

VALDEHERMOSO 2010 TC
tinto fino

90 Colour: cherry, garnet rim. Nose: neat, balanced, ripe fruit, spicy. Palate: good structure, complex, full, flavourful, good acidity, balanced.

VALDERIZ 2010 T
tinto fino

91 Colour: cherry, garnet rim. Nose: closed, expressive, mineral, ripe fruit, cocoa bean, scrubland, roasted coffee. Palate: good structure, round tannins, long.

VALDERIZ JUEGALOBOS 2010 T
tinto fino

93 Colour: dark-red cherry, garnet rim. Nose: red berry notes, ripe fruit, red clay notes, mineral, expressive, medium intensity, sweet spices, creamy oak. Palate: complex, flavourful, round, round tannins.

BODEGAS Y VIÑEDOS VEGA DE YUSO S.L.

Basilón, 9 - Cañada Real, s/n
47350 Quintanilla de Onésimo - (Valladolid)
☎: +34 983 680 054 - Fax: +34 983 680 294
bodega@vegadeyuso.com
www.vegadeyuso.com

TRES MATAS 2009 TC
100% tempranillo

91 Colour: cherry, garnet rim. Nose: spicy, creamy oak, toasty, characterful, ripe fruit. Palate: powerful, flavourful, toasty, round tannins.

TRES MATAS VENDIMIA SELECCIONADA 2009 T
100% tempranillo

91 Colour: cherry, garnet rim. Nose: ripe fruit, spicy, creamy oak, toasty, complex. Palate: powerful, flavourful, toasty, round tannins, elegant.

CINEMA WINES

Felipe Gómez, 1
47140 Laguna de Duero - (Valladolid)
☎: +34 983 544 696 - Fax: +34 983 545 539
info@cinemawines.es
www.cinemawines.es

CINEMA 2009 TC
100% tempranillo

91 Colour: cherry, garnet rim. Nose: spicy, creamy oak, toasty, ripe fruit. Palate: powerful, flavourful, toasty, round tannins.

COMENGE BODEGAS Y VIÑEDOS

Camino del Castillo, s/n
47316 Curiel de Duero - (Valladolid)
☎: +34 983 880 363 - Fax: +34 983 880 717
admin@comenge.com
www.comenge.com

DON MIGUEL COMENGE 2009 T
tempranillo

96 Colour: cherry, garnet rim. Nose: ripe fruit, spicy, creamy oak, toasty, complex, earthy notes, mineral. Palate: powerful, flavourful, toasty, round tannins.

COMPAÑÍA DE VINOS TELMO RODRÍGUEZ

El Monte
1308 Lanciego - (Álava)
☎: +34 945 628 315 - Fax: +34 945 628 314
contact@telmorodriguez.com
www.telmorodriguez.com

M2 DE MATALLANA 2009 T
100% tinta del país

92 Colour: cherry, garnet rim. Nose: sweet spices, ripe fruit, earthy notes, mineral, toasty. Palate: flavourful, powerful, round tannins.

MATALLANA 2007 T
100% tinto fino

92 Colour: cherry, garnet rim. Nose: ripe fruit, spicy, creamy oak, toasty. Palate: powerful, flavourful, toasty, round tannins.

CONVENTO DE OREJA

Avda. Palencia, 1
47010 - (Valladolid)
☎: +34 685 990 596 - Fax: +34 913 710 098
convento@conventooreja.es
www.conventooreja.net

CONVENTO OREJA 2009 TC
100% tinta del país

90 Colour: cherry, garnet rim. Nose: medium intensity, balanced, ripe fruit, sweet spices. Palate: flavourful, fruity, good acidity.

CONVENTO OREJA MEMORIA 2007 TR
100% tinta del país

92 Colour: cherry, garnet rim. Nose: ripe fruit, spicy, creamy oak, toasty, complex, mineral. Palate: powerful, flavourful, toasty, round tannins, balanced.

DEHESA DE LOS CANÓNIGOS S.A.

Ctra. Renedo - Pesquera, Km. 39
47315 Pesquera de Duero - (Valladolid)
☎: +34 983 484 001 - Fax: +34 983 484 040
bodega@dehesacanonigos.com
www.bodegadehesadeloscanonigos.com

DEHESA DE LOS CANÓNIGOS 2005 TR
85% tempranillo, 12% cabernet sauvignon, 3% albillo

90 Colour: dark-red cherry, orangey edge. Nose: ripe fruit, spicy, creamy oak. Palate: elegant, flavourful, spicy, long.

DEHESA VALDELAGUNA

Ctra. Valoria, Km. 16
Pesquera de Duero - (Valladolid)
☎: +34 619 460 308 - Fax: +34 921 142 325
montelaguna@montelaguna.es
www.montelaguna.es

MONTELAGUNA 2009 TC
tempranillo

90 Colour: cherry, garnet rim. Nose: ripe fruit, aromatic coffee, sweet spices, creamy oak. Palate: powerful, flavourful, spicy, toasty.

MONTELAGUNA SELECCIÓN 2009 T
tempranillo

92 Colour: bright cherry, garnet rim. Nose: ripe fruit, sweet spices, creamy oak, expressive. Palate: flavourful, fruity, toasty, round tannins, balanced.

DEHESA VALDELAGUNA

Ctra. Valoria, Km. 16
Pesquera de Duero - (Valladolid)
☎: +34 619 460 308 - Fax: +34 921 142 325
montelaguna@montelaguna.es
www.montelaguna.es

RA 08 2008 TR
tempranillo

91 Colour: cherry, garnet rim. Nose: ripe fruit, spicy, creamy oak, toasty, expressive. Palate: powerful, flavourful, toasty, round tannins, elegant.

DÍAZ BAYO HERMANOS

Camino de los Anarinos, s/n
9471 Fuentelcésped - (Burgos)
☎: +34 947 561 020 - Fax: +34 947 561 204
info@bodegadiazbayo.com
www.bodegadiazbayo.com

DIAZ BAYO MAJUELO DE LA HOMBRÍA 2009 T BARRICA
100% tempranillo

93 Colour: cherry, garnet rim. Nose: ripe fruit, spicy, creamy oak, toasty, complex, mineral. Palate: powerful, flavourful, toasty, round tannins. Personality.

FDB 2006 T BARRICA
tempranillo

91 Colour: cherry, garnet rim. Nose: powerfull, fruit preserve, toasty, dark chocolate, aromatic coffee. Palate: flavourful, ripe fruit, fine bitter notes, good acidity.

NUESTRO 12 MESES 2010 T BARRICA
tempranillo

91 Color bright cherry. Aroma ripe fruit, sweet spices, creamy oak, expressive. Taste flavourful, fruity, toasty, round tannins.

NUESTRO 20 MESES 2006 T BARRICA
tempranillo

92 Colour: cherry, garnet rim. Nose: spicy, creamy oak, toasty, complex, overripe fruit. Palate: powerful, flavourful, toasty, round tannins.

NUESTRO CRIANZA 2008 TC
tempranillo

91 Colour: black cherry, garnet rim. Nose: mineral, ripe fruit, citrus fruit, fragrant herbs, spicy, creamy oak. Palate: powerful, flavourful, balanced, long.

DOMINIO DE ATAUTA

Ctra. a Morcuera, s/n
42345 Atauta - (Soria)
☎: +34 975 351 349
dominiodeatauta.ribera@arrakis.es
www.dominiodeatauta.com

DOMINIO DE ATAUTA 2009 TC
100% tinto fino

93 Colour: cherry, garnet rim. Nose: ripe fruit, spicy, creamy oak, toasty, characterful. Palate: powerful, flavourful, toasty, round tannins.

DOMINIO DE ATAUTA LA MALA 2009 TC
100% tinto fino

93 Colour: cherry, garnet rim. Nose: spicy, creamy oak, toasty, characterful, fruit expression. Palate: powerful, flavourful, toasty, round tannins.

DOMINIO DE ATAUTA LLANOS DEL ALMENDRO 2009 T
100% tinto fino

96 Colour: cherry, garnet rim. Nose: expressive, ripe fruit, mineral, sweet spices. Palate: flavourful, fine bitter notes, good acidity, elegant.

DOMINIO DE ATAUTA VALDEGATILES 2009 T
100% tinto fino

94 Colour: cherry, garnet rim. Nose: spicy, creamy oak, toasty, complex, expressive, overripe fruit. Palate: powerful, flavourful, toasty, round tannins.

PARADA DE ATAUTA 2009 T
100% tinto fino

94 Colour: cherry, garnet rim. Nose: spicy, creamy oak, toasty, characterful, fruit expression. Palate: powerful, flavourful, toasty, round tannins.

TORRE DE GOLBAN 2009 TC
100% tinto fino

90 Colour: cherry, garnet rim. Nose: ripe fruit, spicy, creamy oak, toasty, dark chocolate. Palate: powerful, flavourful, toasty, round tannins.

DOMINIO DE PINGUS S.L.

Hospital, s/n - Apdo. 93, Peñafiel
47350 Quintanilla de Onésimo - (Valladolid)
☎: +34 639 833 854
www.dominiopingus.com

FLOR DE PINGUS 2010 T
100% tinto fino

95 Colour: cherry, garnet rim. Nose: spicy, creamy oak, toasty, complex, scrubland, fruit expression, red berry notes. Palate: powerful, flavourful, toasty, powerful tannins, good acidity.

PINGUS 2010 T
100% tinto fino

97 Colour: cherry, garnet rim. Nose: ripe fruit, spicy, toasty, complex, sweet spices, earthy notes, mineral, fruit expression. Palate: powerful, flavourful, toasty, round tannins, round, fine bitter notes.

PSI 2010 T
100% tinto fino

92 Colour: bright cherry. Nose: sweet spices, creamy oak, varietal, red berry notes. Palate: flavourful, fruity, toasty, round tannins.

DOMINIO ROMANO

Los Lagares, s/n
47319 Rábano - (Valladolid)
☎: +34 983 871 661 - Fax: +34 938 901 143
dominioromano@dominioromano.com
www.dominioromano.com

CAMINO ROMANO 2009 T
tinto fino

90 Colour: cherry, garnet rim. Nose: expressive, ripe fruit, fruit expression, toasty, spicy. Palate: flavourful, spicy, ripe fruit.

DOMINIO ROMANO 2009 T
tinto fino

90 Colour: bright cherry. Nose: sweet spices, creamy oak, expressive, fruit preserve. Palate: flavourful, fruity, toasty, round tannins.

ÉBANO VIÑEDOS Y BODEGAS

Ctra. N-122 Km., 299,6 Pol. Ind. 1 Parcela 32
47318 Castrillo de Duero - (Valladolid)
☎: +34 983 106 440 - Fax: +34 986 609 313
ebano@valminorebano.com
www.ebanovinedosybodegas.com

ÉBANO 2008 T
100% tempranillo

90 Colour: cherry, garnet rim. Nose: medium intensity, balanced, ripe fruit. Palate: flavourful, correct.

EL LAGAR DE ISILLA

Camino Real, 1
9471 La Vid - (Burgos)
☎: +34 947 530 434 - Fax: +34 947 504 316
bodegas@lagarisilla.es
www.lagarisilla.es

EL LAGAR DE ISILLA VENDIMIA SELECCIONADA 2009 T
100% tinta del país

91 Colour: cherry, garnet rim. Nose: spicy, creamy oak, toasty, ripe fruit. Palate: powerful, flavourful, toasty, round tannins.

FINCA TORREMILANOS BODEGAS PEÑALBA LÓPEZ

Finca Torremilanos, s/n
9400 Aranda de Duero - (Burgos)
☎: +34 947 510 377 - Fax: +34 947 512 856
torremilanos@torremilanos.com
www.torremilanos.com

CYCLO 2008 T
tempranillo, garnacha, blanca del pais

91 Colour: cherry, garnet rim. Nose: spicy, creamy oak, cocoa bean, dark chocolate, balsamic herbs, mineral, ripe fruit. Palate: powerful, flavourful, long, spicy.

CYCLO 2009 T
85% tempranillo, 10% garnacha, 5% blanca del pais,

92 Colour: cherry, garnet rim. Nose: ripe fruit, spicy, creamy oak, complex, sweet spices, earthy notes. Palate: powerful, flavourful, toasty, round tannins, balanced.

LOS CANTOS DE TORREMILANOS 2009 T
100% tempranillo

92 Colour: cherry, garnet rim. Nose: ripe fruit, spicy, creamy oak, mineral. Palate: powerful, flavourful, toasty, round tannins, good acidity, balanced.

TORREMILANOS COLECCIÓN 2006 T
100% tempranillo

90 Colour: cherry, garnet rim. Nose: ripe fruit, spicy, creamy oak, toasty, balsamic herbs. Palate: powerful, flavourful, round tannins, spicy, balanced.

FINCA VILLACRECES

Ctra. N-122 Km. 322
47350 Quintanilla de Onésimo - (Valladolid)
☎: +34 983 680 437 - Fax: +34 983 683 314
villacreces@villacreces.com
www.villacreces.com

FINCA VILLACRECES 2007 T
86% tinto fino, 10% cabernet sauvignon, 4% merlot

91 Colour: cherry, garnet rim. Nose: spicy, toasty, complex, overripe fruit, dark chocolate. Palate: powerful, flavourful, toasty, round tannins.

PRUNO 2010 T
90% tinto fino, 10% cabernet sauvignon

92 Colour: cherry, garnet rim. Nose: creamy oak, red berry notes, fruit expression, cocoa bean. Palate: flavourful, good acidity, fine bitter notes, round.

GRUPO VINÍCOLA MARQUÉS DE VARGAS - CONDE SAN CRISTÓBAL

Ctra. Valladolid a Soria, Km. 303
47300 Peñafiel - (Valladolid)
☎: +34 983 878 055 - Fax: +34 983 878 196
bodega@condesancristobal.com
www.marquesdevargas.com

CONDE DE SAN CRISTÓBAL 2009 T
80% tinto fino, 10% merlot, 10% cabernet sauvignon

90 Colour: cherry, garnet rim. Nose: powerfull, balanced, ripe fruit, scrubland. Palate: fruity, good structure, round tannins.

CONDE DE SAN CRISTÓBAL RAÍCES 2007 T RESERVA ESPECIAL
90% tinto fino, 10% merlot

91 Colour: cherry, garnet rim. Nose: ripe fruit, toasty, wet leather, earthy notes. Palate: spicy, balanced, toasty, long.

GRUPO YLLERA

Autovía A-6, Km. 173, 5
47490 Rueda - (Valladolid)
☎: +34 983 868 097 - Fax: +34 983 868 177
grupoyllera@grupoyllera.com
www.grupoyllera.com

BRACAMONTE 2006 TC
tempranillo

90 Colour: pale ruby, brick rim edge. Nose: scrubland, spicy, ripe fruit, creamy oak. Palate: powerful, flavourful, spicy, long.

HACIENDA SOLANO

La Solana, 6
9370 La Aguilera - (Burgos)
☎: +34 947 545 582 - Fax: +34 947 545 582
administracion@haciendasolano.com
www.haciendasolano.com

HACIENDA ERNESTINA SOLANO 12 MESES SELECCIÓN VIÑAS VIEJAS 2009 TC
100% tempranillo

92 Colour: cherry, garnet rim. Nose: ripe fruit, spicy, creamy oak, toasty, lactic notes. Palate: powerful, flavourful, toasty, round tannins.

HACIENDAS DE ESPAÑA

Hacienda Abascal, N-122, Km. 321,5
47360 Quintanilla de Onésimo - (Valladolid)
☎: +34 914 365 924
comunicacion@arcoinvest-group.com
www.haciendas-espana.com

HACIENDA ABASCAL PREMIUM (MARQUÉS DE LA CONCORDIA FAMILY OF WINES) 2008 T
100% tempranillo

91 Colour: cherry, garnet rim. Nose: ripe fruit, spicy, toasty, cocoa bean, expressive. Palate: powerful, flavourful, toasty, round tannins.

HORNILLOS BALLESTEROS

Camino Tenerías, 9
9300 Roa de Duero - (Burgos)
☎: +34 947 541 071 - Fax: +34 947 541 071
hornillosballesteros@telefonica.net
www.hornillosballesteros.es

PERFIL 2009 T
100% tempranillo

91 Colour: cherry, garnet rim. Nose: cocoa bean, sweet spices, ripe fruit. Palate: good structure, complex, flavourful, ripe fruit.

LA VIÑA DEL LOCO

Plaza de Matute 12, - 3º
28012 - (Madrid)
☎: +34 609 119 248
info@miravinos.es
www.miravinos.es

TOGA 2010 T
tinto fino

94 Colour: cherry, garnet rim. Nose: spicy, complex, new oak, earthy notes, fruit expression, ripe fruit. Palate: powerful, flavourful, toasty, round tannins.

VENTA EL LOCO 2009 T
tinto fino

91 Colour: bright cherry. Nose: ripe fruit, sweet spices, creamy oak, characterful, varietal. Palate: flavourful, fruity, toasty, round tannins.

LEGARIS

Ctra. Peñafiel - Encinas de Esgueva, km. 4,3
47316 Curiel de Duero - (Valladolid)
☎: +34 983 878 088 - Fax: +34 983 881 034
info@legaris.com
www.grupocodorniu.com

LEGARIS 2006 TR
100% tinto fino

91 Colour: cherry, garnet rim. Nose: ripe fruit, spicy, creamy oak, toasty, complex, elegant. Palate: powerful, flavourful, toasty, round tannins, balanced.

LEGARIS 2009 TC
100% tinto fino

90 Colour: cherry, garnet rim. Nose: ripe fruit, spicy, creamy oak, toasty, complex. Palate: powerful, flavourful, toasty, long, balanced.

LOESS

C/ Burgohondo, 4
28023 - (Madrid)
☎: +34 983 664 898 - Fax: +34 983 406 579
loess@loess.es
www.loess.es

LOESS 2009 T
100% tempranillo

90 Colour: cherry, garnet rim. Nose: ripe fruit, spicy, creamy oak, complex. Palate: flavourful, round tannins, balanced, good acidity.

LOESS COLLECTION 2009 T
100% tempranillo

92 Colour: deep cherry, garnet rim. Nose: ripe fruit, creamy oak, sweet spices, balanced. Palate: fine bitter notes, round tannins.

LYNUS VIÑEDOS Y BODEGAS

Camino de las Pozas, s/n
47350 Quintanilla de Onésimo - (Valladolid)
☎: +34 661 879 016 - Fax: +34 983 680 224
info@lynus.es
www.lynus.es

LYNUS ÁUREA 2007 TR
100% tempranillo

91 Colour: bright cherry, garnet rim. Nose: warm, ripe fruit, dark chocolate. Palate: fruity, round tannins.

MONTEBACO

Finca Montealto
47359 Valbuena de Duero - (Valladolid)
☎: +34 983 485 128 - Fax: +34 983 485 033
montebaco@bodegasmontebaco.com
www.bodegasmontebaco.com

MONTEBACO 2009 TC
tempranillo

92 Color cherry, garnet rim. Aroma ripe fruit, spicy, creamy oak, toasty, complex. Taste powerful, flavourful, toasty, round tannins.

MONTEBACO 2010 TC
tempranillo

91 Colour: cherry, garnet rim. Nose: ripe fruit, spicy, creamy oak, toasty, complex, varietal. Palate: powerful, flavourful, toasty, round tannins.

MONTEBACO VENDIMIA SELECCIONADA 2008 T
tempranillo

91 Colour: cherry, garnet rim. Nose: powerfull, varietal, ripe fruit, creamy oak. Palate: flavourful, fine bitter notes, good acidity.

SEMELE 2010 TC
90% tempranillo, 10% merlot

91 Colour: cherry, garnet rim. Nose: ripe fruit, spicy, creamy oak, toasty. Palate: powerful, flavourful, toasty, round tannins.

MONTEGAREDO

Ctra. Boada a Pedrosa, s/n
9314 Boada de Roa - (Burgos)
☎: +34 947 530 003 - Fax: +34 947 530 140
info@montegaredo.com
www.montegaredo.com

PIRÁMIDE 2010 T
tinto fino

91 Colour: bright cherry. Nose: ripe fruit, sweet spices, creamy oak, expressive. Palate: flavourful, fruity, toasty, balanced, long.

PAGO DE CARRAOVEJAS

Camino de Carraovejas, s/n
47300 Peñafiel - (Valladolid)
☎: +34 983 878 020 - Fax: +34 983 878 022
administracion@pagodecarraovejas.com
www.pagodecarraovejas.com

PAGO DE CARRAOVEJAS 2009 TC
96% tinto fino, 4% cabernet sauvignon

93 Colour: cherry, garnet rim. Nose: ripe fruit, fruit expression, red berry notes, lactic notes, creamy oak. Palate: flavourful, powerful, complex, creamy, round tannins.

PAGO DE CARRAOVEJAS 2010 TC
95% tinto fino, 5% cabernet sauvignon

92 Colour: cherry, garnet rim. Nose: ripe fruit, creamy oak, sweet spices. Palate: good structure, flavourful, full, toasty.

PAGO DE CARRAOVEJAS EL ANEJÓN DE LA CUESTA DE LAS LIEBRES 2009 T
93% tinto fino, 6% cabernet sauvignon, 1% merlot

96 Colour: cherry, garnet rim. Nose: spicy, creamy oak, toasty, characterful, ripe fruit, mineral. Palate: powerful, flavourful, toasty, round tannins.

PAGO DE LOS CAPELLANES

Camino de la Ampudia, s/n
9314 Pedrosa de Duero - (Burgos)
☎: +34 947 530 068 - Fax: +34 947 530 111
bodega@pagodeloscapellanes.com
www.pagodeloscapellanes.com

PAGO DE LOS CAPELLANES 2008 TR
100% tempranillo

91 Colour: cherry, garnet rim. Nose: fruit preserve, balanced, sweet spices. Palate: balanced, spicy, ripe fruit, long.

PAGO DE LOS CAPELLANES 2009 TC
100% tempranillo

93 Colour: cherry, garnet rim. Nose: ripe fruit, spicy, creamy oak, toasty, complex, mineral, earthy notes. Palate: powerful, flavourful, toasty, round tannins.

PAGO DE LOS CAPELLANES 2011 T ROBLE
100% tempranillo

90 Colour: deep cherry, purple rim. Nose: toasty, creamy oak, sweet spices. Palate: balanced, ripe fruit, good acidity.

PAGO DE LOS CAPELLANES PARCELA EL NOGAL 2006 T
100% tempranillo

92 Colour: cherry, garnet rim. Nose: spicy, creamy oak, toasty, characterful, overripe fruit. Palate: powerful, flavourful, toasty, round tannins.

PAGO DE LOS CAPELLANES PARCELA EL PICÓN 2006 T
100% tempranillo

93 Colour: cherry, garnet rim. Nose: creamy oak, characterful, overripe fruit. Palate: powerful, flavourful, toasty, round tannins.

PAGOS DE MATANEGRA

Ctra. Santa María, 27
9311 Olmedillo de Roa - (Burgos)
☎: +34 947 551 310 - Fax: +34 947 551 309
info@pagosdematanegra.es
www.pagosdematanegra.es

MATANEGRA 2009 TC
100% tempranillo

90 Colour: bright cherry. Nose: ripe fruit, sweet spices, roasted coffee, dark chocolate. Palate: flavourful, fruity, toasty.

MATANEGRA VENDIMIA SELECCIONADA 2009 T
tempranillo

91 Colour: cherry, garnet rim. Nose: ripe fruit, creamy oak, roasted coffee. Palate: flavourful, toasty, long, balanced.

MATANEGRA VENDIMIA SELECCIONADA MM 2009 T
100% tempranillo

93 Colour: cherry, garnet rim. Nose: red berry notes, ripe fruit, elegant, cocoa bean, dark chocolate, toasty. Palate: balanced, powerful, flavourful, long, toasty.

PAGOS DEL REY

Ctra. Palencia-Aranda, Km. 53
9311 Olmedillo de Roa - (Burgos)
☎: +34 947 551 111 - Fax: +34 947 551 311
pdr@pagosdelrey.com
www.pagosdelrey.com

CONDADO DE ORIZA 2006 TGR
100% tempranillo

90 Colour: ruby red, garnet rim. Nose: ripe fruit, sweet spices, creamy oak, powerfull, fine reductive notes. Palate: long, spicy, flavourful, fruity.

CONDADO DE ORIZA 2010 TC
100% tempranillo

90 Colour: bright cherry. Nose: ripe fruit, sweet spices, creamy oak, dark chocolate. Palate: flavourful, fruity, toasty.

CONDADO DE ORIZA 409 2008 T
100% tempranillo

91 Colour: cherry, garnet rim. Nose: sweet spices, creamy oak, ripe fruit, candied fruit. Palate: powerful, flavourful, fruity, balanced.

LA ÚNICA AUTOR S/C T
100% tempranillo

92 Colour: bright cherry, garnet rim. Nose: elegant, expressive, cocoa bean, sweet spices. Palate: good structure, good acidity, ripe fruit, long.

PÁRAMO DE GUZMÁN

Ctra. Circunvalación R-30, s/n
9300 Roa - (Burgos)
☎: +34 947 541 191 - Fax: +34 947 541 192
paramodeguzman@paramodeguzman.es
www.paramodeguzman.es

RAÍZ 2008 TR
tempranillo

90 Colour: deep cherry, orangey edge. Nose: creamy oak, aromatic coffee, fine reductive notes, fruit liqueur notes. Palate: spicy, ripe fruit, round tannins.

RAÍZ 2009 TC
tempranillo

92 Colour: cherry, garnet rim. Nose: ripe fruit, spicy, creamy oak, toasty, characterful, expressive. Palate: powerful, flavourful, toasty, round tannins.

RAÍZ 2011 RD
tempranillo

90 Color rose, purple rim. Aroma powerfull, ripe fruit, red berry notes, floral, expressive. Taste fleshy, powerful, fruity, fresh.

RAÍZ 2011 T ROBLE
100% tempranillo

90 Color bright cherry. Aroma ripe fruit, sweet spices, creamy oak, expressive. Taste flavourful, fruity, toasty, round tannins.

RAÍZ DE GUZMÁN 2007 T
100% tempranillo

94 Colour: dark-red cherry, garnet rim. Nose: ripe fruit, earthy notes, mineral, aromatic coffee, creamy oak. Palate: powerful, flavourful, spicy, long, balanced, round tannins.

RAÍZ VINO DE AUTOR 2009 T
tempranillo

94 Colour: cherry, garnet rim. Nose: ripe fruit, spicy, creamy oak, toasty, complex, mineral, earthy notes. Palate: powerful, flavourful, toasty, round tannins.

PICO CUADRO

Del Río, 22
47350 Quintanilla de Onésimo - (Valladolid)
☎: +34 620 547 057
picocuadro@picocuadro.com
www.picocuadro.com

PICO CUADRO ORIGINAL 2009 T
tinto fino

93 Colour: cherry, garnet rim. Nose: red berry notes, ripe fruit, wild herbs, sweet spices, creamy oak. Palate: balanced, long, powerful, flavourful.

PICO CUADRO VENDIMIA SELECCIONADA 2009 T
tinto fino

92 Colour: cherry, garnet rim. Nose: red berry notes, ripe fruit, balsamic herbs, spicy, aromatic coffee, mineral. Palate: powerful, flavourful, long, toasty, balanced.

PICO CUADRO WILD 2009 T
tinto fino

92 Colour: bright cherry. Nose: ripe fruit, sweet spices, creamy oak, expressive, dark chocolate, roasted coffee, new oak. Palate: flavourful, fruity, toasty, balanced.

PINNA FIDELIS

Camino Llanillos, s/n
47300 Peñafiel - (Valladolid)
☎: +34 983 878 034 - Fax: +34 983 878 035
info@pinnafidelis.com
www.pinnafidelis.com

PINNA FIDELIS 2004 TGR
100% tinta del país

90 Colour: pale ruby, brick rim edge. Nose: spicy, wet leather, fruit liqueur notes, scrubland. Palate: spicy, fine tannins, long.

PINNA FIDELIS ROBLE ESPAÑOL 2007 T
100% tinta del país

90 Colour: cherry, garnet rim. Nose: ripe fruit, earthy notes, spicy, medium intensity. Palate: powerful, flavourful, long, toasty.

PINNA FIDELIS VENDIMIA SELECCIONADA 2006 T
100% tinta del país

90 Colour: cherry, garnet rim. Nose: ripe fruit, spicy, creamy oak, toasty. Palate: powerful, flavourful, toasty, fine tannins.

PROTOS BODEGAS RIBERA DUERO DE PEÑAFIEL

Bodegas Protos, 24-28
47300 Peñafiel - (Valladolid)
☎: +34 983 878 011 - Fax: +34 983 878 012
bodega@bodegasprotos.com
www.bodegasprotos.com

PROTOS 2006 TR
100% tinto fino

92 Colour: very deep cherry. Nose: powerfull, elegant, ripe fruit, toasty, sweet spices. Palate: flavourful, good acidity, fine bitter notes.

PROTOS 2010 TC
100% tinta del país

91 Colour: cherry, garnet rim. Nose: ripe fruit, spicy, toasty, characterful, new oak. Palate: powerful, flavourful, toasty, round tannins.

PROTOS 2005 TGR
100% tinto fino

91 Colour: deep cherry, garnet rim. Nose: powerfull, characterful, complex, ripe fruit, creamy oak, toasty. Palate: flavourful, powerful, good acidity, fine bitter notes.

PROTOS 2010 T ROBLE
100% tinta del país

91 Colour: bright cherry. Nose: sweet spices, creamy oak, ripe fruit. Palate: flavourful, fruity, toasty, round tannins.

PROTOS SELECCIÓN FINCA EL GRAJO VIEJO 2009 T
100% tinta del país

95 Colour: very deep cherry. Nose: mineral, varietal, powerfull, characterful, ripe fruit, sweet spices, dark chocolate, creamy oak. Palate: flavourful, powerful, concentrated, good acidity, fine bitter notes.

QUINTA MILÚ

Camino El Val, s/n
La Aguilera - (Burgos)
☎: +34 661 328 504
info@quintamilu.com
www.quintamilu.com

QUINTA MILÚ EL MALO 2009 TC
tinta del país

90 Colour: cherry, garnet rim. Nose: spicy, creamy oak, toasty, complex, fragrant herbs, red berry notes. Palate: powerful, flavourful, toasty, round tannins.

REAL SITIO DE VENTOSILLA

Ctra. CL-619 (Magaz Aranda) Km. 66,1
9443 Gumiel del Mercado - (Burgos)
☎: +34 947 546 900 - Fax: +34 947 546 999
bodega@pradorey.com
www.pradorey.com

ADARO DE PRADOREY 2010 TC
100% tempranillo

93 Colour: cherry, garnet rim. Nose: ripe fruit, creamy oak, toasty, complex, expressive, mineral. Palate: powerful, flavourful, toasty, round tannins.

PRADOREY 2004 TGR
95% tinto fino, 3% cabernet sauvignon, 2% merlot

92 Colour: cherry, garnet rim. Nose: balanced, expressive, ripe fruit, dark chocolate, sweet spices. Palate: good structure, flavourful, round tannins.

PRADOREY 2009 TC
95% tinto fino, 3% cabernet sauvignon, 2% merlot

90 Colour: cherry, garnet rim. Nose: medium intensity, balanced, spicy, ripe fruit. Palate: good structure, good acidity, round tannins.

PRADOREY ÉLITE 2009 T
100% tinto fino

94 Colour: cherry, garnet rim. Nose: spicy, creamy oak, toasty, complex, fruit expression, characterful. Palate: powerful, flavourful, toasty, round tannins.

PRADOREY ÉLITE 2010 T
100% tinto fino

95 Colour: cherry, garnet rim. Nose: ripe fruit, spicy, creamy oak, toasty, complex, varietal, expressive, mineral. Palate: powerful, flavourful, toasty, round tannins.

RED BOTTLE INTERNATIONAL

Rosales, 6
9400 Aranda de Duero - (Burgos)
☎: +34 947 515 884 - Fax: +34 947 515 886
rbi@redbottleint.com

ADMIRACIÓN 2009 T
100% tempranillo

90 Color cherry, garnet rim. Aroma ripe fruit, spicy, creamy oak, toasty, complex. Taste powerful, flavourful, toasty, round tannins.

RODRÍGUEZ SANZO

Manuel Azaña, 9
47014 - (Valladolid)
☎: +34 983 150 150 - Fax: +34 983 150 151
comunicacion@valsanzo.com
www.rodriguezsanzo.com

VALL SANZO 2009 TC
tempranillo

91 Colour: very deep cherry. Nose: characterful, ripe fruit, dark chocolate, sweet spices, creamy oak. Palate: ripe fruit, spicy, round tannins.

RUDELES

Trasterrera, 10
42345 Peñalba de San Esteban - (Soria)
☎: +34 618 644 633 - Fax: +34 975 350 582
jmartin@rudeles.com
www.rudeles.com

RUDELES "23" 2009 T
95% tempranillo, 5% garnacha

92 Colour: cherry, garnet rim. Nose: ripe fruit, balsamic herbs, aromatic coffee, sweet spices, toasty, mineral. Palate: powerful, flavourful, toasty, balanced.

RUDELES CERRO EL CUBERILLO 2009 T
100% tempranillo

90 Colour: cherry, garnet rim. Nose: spicy, creamy oak, balanced, dark chocolate. Palate: flavourful, full, fine bitter notes.

RUDELES SELECCIÓN 2006 T
97% tempranillo, 3% garnacha

90 Colour: cherry, garnet rim. Nose: ripe fruit, spicy, creamy oak, toasty, complex, sweet spices, varnish. Palate: powerful, flavourful, toasty, round tannins.

SELECCIÓN CÉSAR MUÑOZ

Acera de Recoletos, 14
47004 - (Valladolid)
☎: +34 666 548 751
info@cesarmunoz.es
www.cesarmunoz.es

MAGALLANES 2009 TC
tempranillo

90 Colour: cherry, garnet rim. Nose: ripe fruit, warm, powerfull, closed. Palate: flavourful, powerful, good structure, round tannins.

SELECCIÓN TORRES

Del Rosario, 56
47311 Fompedraza - (Valladolid)
☎: +34 938 177 400 - Fax: +34 938 177 444
mailadmin@torres.es
www.torres.es

CELESTE 2009 TC
100% tinto fino

90 Colour: cherry, garnet rim. Nose: ripe fruit, dark chocolate, sweet spices, creamy oak. Palate: powerful, flavourful, long, toasty.

TOMÁS POSTIGO

Estación, 12
47300 Peñafiel - (Valladolid)
☎: +34 983 873 019 - Fax: +34 983 880 258
administracion@tomaspostigo.es

TOMÁS POSTIGO 2009 TC
85% tinto fino, 10% cabernet sauvignon, 5% merlot

93 Colour: cherry, garnet rim. Nose: red berry notes, sweet spices, toasty, balanced, expressive. Palate: powerful, flavourful, spicy, complex, elegant.

TORRES DE ANGUIX

Camino La Tejera, s/n
9312 Anguix - (Burgos)
☎: +34 947 554 008 - Fax: +34 947 554 129
enologia@torresdeanguix.com
www.torresdeanguix.com

T D'ANGUIX 2004 TR
tinta del país

90 Colour: cherry, garnet rim. Nose: creamy oak, toasty. Palate: powerful, flavourful, toasty, round tannins.

UVAS FELICES

Agullers, 7
8003 Barcelona - (Barcelona)
☎: +34 902 327 777
www.vilaviniteca.es

VENTA LAS VACAS 2010 T
tempranillo

91 Color bright cherry. Aroma ripe fruit, sweet spices, creamy oak, expressive. Taste flavourful, fruity, toasty, round tannins.

VALTRAVIESO

Finca La Revilla, s/n
47316 Piñel de Arriba - (Valladolid)
☎: +34 983 484 030 - Fax: +34 983 484 037
valtravieso@valtravieso.com
www.valtravieso.com

GRAN VALTRAVIESO 2006 TR
100% tinto fino

93 Colour: cherry, garnet rim. Nose: ripe fruit, spicy, creamy oak, toasty, characterful, dark chocolate. Palate: powerful, flavourful, toasty, round tannins.

VALTRAVIESO VT VENDIMIA SELECCIONADA 2009 T
75% tinto fino, 15% cabernet sauvignon, 10% merlot

90 Colour: cherry, garnet rim. Nose: ripe fruit, spicy, creamy oak, toasty, characterful. Palate: powerful, flavourful, toasty, round tannins.

VEGA CLARA

Ctra. N-122 Km 328 (Entrada por c/Estación)
47350 Quintanilla De Onesimo - (Valladolid)
☎: +34 677 570 779 - Fax: +34 983 361 005
vegaclara@vegaclara.com
www.vegaclara.com

MARIO VC 2009 T
tempranillo, cabernet sauvignon

90 Colour: cherry, garnet rim. Nose: spicy, creamy oak, toasty, ripe fruit. Palate: powerful, flavourful, toasty, round tannins.

VINNICO EXPORT

Muela, 16
3730 Jávea - (Alicante)
☎: +34 965 791 967 - Fax: +34 966 461 471
info@vinnico.com
www.vinnico.com

AVENTINO 200 BARRELS 2009 T
100% tinta del país

91 Colour: cherry, garnet rim. Nose: spicy, creamy oak, toasty, ripe fruit. Palate: powerful, flavourful, toasty, round tannins.

VINOS HERCAL

Santo Domingo, 2
9300 Roa - (Burgos)
☎: +34 947 541 281
ventas@somanilla.es
www.somanilla.es

BOCCA 2009 T ROBLE
tempranillo

90 Colour: cherry, garnet rim. Nose: spicy, creamy oak, toasty, ripe fruit. Palate: powerful, flavourful, toasty, round tannins.

SOMANILLA 2008 TC
tinto fino

90 Colour: bright cherry. Nose: ripe fruit, sweet spices, creamy oak. Palate: flavourful, fruity, toasty, round tannins.

VIÑA ARNAIZ

Ctra. N-122, km. 281
9463 Haza - (Burgos)
☎: +34 947 536 227 - Fax: +34 947 536 216
www.vinosdefamilia.com

VIÑA ARNÁIZ 2007 TR
85% tempranillo, 10% cabernet sauvignon, 5% merlot

90 Colour: bright cherry. Nose: ripe fruit, sweet spices, creamy oak, expressive, red berry notes. Palate: flavourful, fruity, toasty, round tannins.

VIÑA MAMBRILLA

Ctra. Pedrosa s/n
9317 Mambrilla de Castrejón - (Burgos)
☎: +34 947 540 234 - Fax: +34 947 540 234
bodega@mambrilla.com
www.mambrilla.com

ALIDIS EXPRESIÓN 2009 T
100% tempranillo

93 Colour: cherry, garnet rim. Nose: red berry notes, mineral, expressive, sweet spices, creamy oak. Palate: powerful, flavourful, balanced, long, elegant.

ALIDIS GRAN RESERVA 2006 TGR
100% tempranillo

92 Colour: pale ruby, brick rim edge. Nose: spicy, fine reductive notes, dark chocolate, ripe fruit. Palate: spicy, elegant, long, balanced.

ALIDIS RESERVA 2008 TR
100% tempranillo

90 Color cherry, garnet rim. Aroma ripe fruit, spicy, creamy oak, toasty, complex. Taste powerful, flavourful, toasty, round tannins.

VIÑA SOLORCA

Ctra. Circunvalación, s/n
9300 Roa - (Burgos)
☎: +34 947 541 823 - Fax: +34 947 540 035
info@bodegassolorca.com
www.bodegassolorca.com

GRAN SOLORCA 2006 TR
100% tempranillo

91 Color cherry, garnet rim. Aroma ripe fruit, spicy, creamy oak, toasty, complex. Taste powerful, flavourful, toasty, round tannins.

VIÑA VALDEMAZÓN

Pza. Sur, 3
47359 Olivares de Duero - (Valladolid)
☎: +34 983 680 220
info@valdemazon.com
www.valdemazon.com

VIÑA VALDEMAZÓN VENDIMIA SELECCIONADA 2009 T
100% tempranillo

90 Color cherry, garnet rim. Aroma ripe fruit, spicy, creamy oak, toasty, complex. Taste powerful, flavourful, toasty, round tannins.

VIÑEDOS ALONSO DEL YERRO

Finca Santa Marta - Ctra. Roa-Anguix, Km. 1,8
9300 Roa - (Burgos)
☎: +34 913 160 121 - Fax: +34 913 160 121
mariadelyerro@vay.es
www.alonsodelyerro.com

"MARÍA" ALONSO DEL YERRO 2009 T
100% tempranillo

95 Colour: cherry, garnet rim. Nose: spicy, creamy oak, toasty, complex, mineral, ripe fruit. Palate: powerful, flavourful, toasty, round tannins.

ALONSO DEL YERRO 2009 T
100% tempranillo

94 Colour: cherry, garnet rim. Nose: ripe fruit, spicy, creamy oak, toasty, characterful, expressive. Palate: powerful, flavourful, toasty, round tannins.

VIÑEDOS Y BODEGAS ÁSTER

Ctra. Aranda-Palencia-, Término El Caño
9312 Anguix - (Burgos)
☎: +34 947 522 700 - Fax: +34 947 522 701
aster@riojalta.com
www.riojalta.com

ÁSTER FINCA EL OTERO 2010 T
FERMENTADO EN BARRICA
100% tinta del país

94 Colour: very deep cherry. Nose: mineral, characterful, elegant, floral, fruit expression, creamy oak, sweet spices. Palate: flavourful, complex, good acidity, round.

VIÑEDOS Y BODEGAS GARCÍA FIGUERO

Ctra. La Horra - Roa, Km. 2,2
9311 La Horra - (Burgos)
☎: +34 947 542 127 - Fax: +34 947 542 033
bodega@tintofiguero.com
www.tintofiguero.com

FIGUERO TINUS 2009 T
100% tempranillo

93 Colour: cherry, garnet rim. Nose: ripe fruit, fruit preserve, cocoa bean, dark chocolate, sweet spices, creamy oak. Palate: flavourful, fruity, long, good acidity, fine tannins, elegant.

TINTO FIGUERO 15 MESES BARRICA 2008 TR
100% tempranillo

90 Colour: cherry, garnet rim. Nose: ripe fruit, spicy, aged wood nuances, fine reductive notes, earthy notes. Palate: powerful, flavourful, toasty, round tannins, balanced.

VIÑEDOS Y BODEGAS GORMAZ

Ctra. de Soria, s/n
42330 San Esteban de Gormaz - (Soria)
☎: +34 975 350 404 - Fax: +34 975 351 313
info@hispanobodegas.com
www.hispanobodegas.com

12 LINAJES 2007 TR
tempranillo

90 Colour: bright cherry. Nose: ripe fruit, spicy, creamy oak, toasty, expressive. Palate: powerful, flavourful, toasty, round tannins.

ANIER VENDIMIA SELECCIONADA 2010 T
tempranillo

93 Colour: cherry, garnet rim. Nose: spicy, creamy oak, toasty, complex, fruit expression, red berry notes, mineral, varietal. Palate: powerful, flavourful, toasty, round tannins.

VIÑEDOS Y BODEGAS RIBÓN

Basilón, 15
47350 Quintanilla de Onésimo - (Valladolid)
☎: +34 983 680 015 - Fax: +34 983 680 015
info@bodegasribon.com
www.bodegasribon.com

TINTO RIBÓN 2009 TC
100% tempranillo

90 Colour: cherry, garnet rim. Nose: spicy, creamy oak, toasty, varietal. Palate: powerful, flavourful, toasty, round tannins.

DESCRIPTION

This includes the six wine growing regions of Extremadura. It is among the most extensive vineyards in Spain but also among the most lethargic. All the wines are made with high temperatures despite the differences among sub-regions with up to six wine regions. The region of Tierra de Barros is the epicentre and the most extensive. The character of the local white grapes such as cayetana and pardina should be highlighted as well as the enormous variety of local vines and new foreign vines which are included in this Denomination of Origin.

NUMBER OF HECTARES: 28.312 **ALTITUDES:** 150 m. – 800 m.

PREDOMINANT VARIETIES:

White grapes: alarije, borba, cayetana blanca, pardina, macabeo, chardonnay, chelva, malvar, parellada, pedro ximenez, verdejo, eva, cigüente, perruno, muscatel de Aleandría, small grained muscatel and sauvignon blanc.

Red grapes: garnacha tinta, tempranillo, bobal, cabernet sauvignon, garnacha tintorera, graciano, mazuela, merlot, monastrell, syrah, pinot noir and jaén tinto.

CLIMATOLOGY AND SOILS

The region of Tierra de Barros, where 80% of the vines are concentrated, has a very dry, warm climate. It has flat lands and fertile soils such as those of Matanegra. Those of Cañamero are located on slopes above 800 metres. In Ribera Alta the soils are sandy and in Ribera Baja there are clay soils, both zones have an Atlantic and continental type climatology. Montanchez is composed of hills with very different soils.

BODEGAS TORIBIO VIÑA PUEBLA

Luis Chamizo, 12-21
6310 Puebla de Sancho Pérez - (Badajoz)
☎: +34 924 551 449 - Fax: +34 924 551 449
info@bodegastoribio.com
www.bodegastoribio.com

MADRE DEL AGUA 2009 TC
70% garnacha tintorera, 10% tempranillo, 10% cabernet sauvignon, 10% garnacha

93 Colour: deep cherry, garnet rim. Nose: balanced, complex, expressive, ripe fruit, cocoa bean, scrubland. Palate: fruity, powerful.

VIÑA PUEBLA 2010 BFB
macabeo

90 Colour: bright yellow. Nose: powerfull, ripe fruit, sweet spices, creamy oak, fragrant herbs. Palate: rich, flavourful, good acidity.

VIÑA PUEBLA ESENZIA 2008 TC

90 Color cherry, garnet rim. Aroma ripe fruit, spicy, creamy oak, toasty, complex. Taste powerful, flavourful, toasty, round tannins.

PAGO LOS BALANCINES

Paraje la Agraria, s/n
6475 Oliva de Mérida - (Badajoz)
☎: +34 924 367 399 - Fax: +34 924 367 399
alunado@pagolosbalancines.com
www.pagolosbalancines.com

ALUNADO 2009 BFB
chardonnay

92 Colour: bright yellow. Nose: ripe fruit, sweet spices, fragrant herbs, cocoa bean. Palate: rich, smoky aftertaste, flavourful, fresh, good acidity.

HUNO 2008 T
tempranillo, cabernet sauvignon, merlot, garnacha tintorera

92 Colour: cherry, garnet rim. Nose: balanced, complex, spicy, dark chocolate, ripe fruit. Palate: long, good structure.

LOS BALANCINES FINCA DE MATANEGRA 2009 TC
tempranillo, cabernet sauvignon, garnacha tintorera

96 Colour: cherry, garnet rim. Nose: spicy, dark chocolate, elegant, expressive, balanced, earthy notes, ripe fruit. Palate: flavourful, ripe fruit, spicy, long, fine tannins.

SALITRE 2009 T
100% garnacha tintorera

94 Colour: cherry, garnet rim. Nose: ripe fruit, spicy, creamy oak, toasty, complex, characterful, expressive, varietal. Palate: powerful, flavourful, toasty, round tannins.

VASO DE LUZ 2009 TR
cabernet sauvignon

94 Colour: deep cherry, garnet rim. Nose: red berry notes, ripe fruit, sweet spices, cocoa bean, elegant. Palate: good structure, complex, round tannins, good acidity.

DESCRIPTION

The most recent Denomination of Origin in La Mancha. It is composed almost exclusively of cooperatives which are skilled in the management of foreign sales. On the right bank of the River Júcar, in the lower part, are the most exceptional vineyards, at an altitude of 700 metres and with clay soils covered by pebbles. This is where the tastiest tempranillos can be found.

NUMBER OF HECTARES: 9.200 **ALTITUDES:** 650 m. – 750 m.

PREDOMINANT VARIETIES:

White grapes: muscatel de grano menudo and sauvignon blanc.
Red grapes: cencibel, cabernet sauvignon, merlot, syrah, petit verdot, cabernet franc and bobal.

CLIMATOLOGY AND SOILS

Dry continental, with soils formed by small stones on the surface and clay in the subsoil.

ELVIWINES

Finca "Clos Mesorah" Ctra. T-300 Falset Marça, Km. 1
43775 Marça Priorat - (Tarragona)
☎: +34 935 343 026 - Fax: +34 936 750 316
moises@elviwines.com
www.elviwines.com

NESS KOSHER 2011 RD
100% syrah

90 Color rose, purple rim. Aroma powerfull, ripe fruit, red berry notes, floral, expressive. Taste fleshy, powerful, fruity, fresh.

DESCRIPTION

La Rioja is responsible for 40% of the production of Spanish wine and has approximately 1,200 wineries. Its commercial success is based on the popular Rioja wine with a long period of ageing which is usually produced in the Rioja Alta subzone. This type of Rioja wine was imposed by the Bordeaux wineries and spread throughout the world in the seventies. However, a lot of water has flowed under the bridge since then and the local producer has progressed with a more fruity and complex formula, tied to the character of the soil and the vines, with ageing which is more balanced as regards the needs of each wine and not to the impositions of the regulation times of historical law. The Rioja wine of the year or young wine is produced in the Rioja Alavesa sub-zone, it competes with French Beaujolais and follows the same system of carbonic maceration in which fermentation is begun with complete bunches. The most sun dried and Mediterranean wines are produced in the part nearest to Navarre and the most southerly in the province. Tempranillo, graciano and mazuelo compose the normal combination of traditional Rioja wine although single variety wines now predominate. The white wines with a long period of ageing using long ageing formulas in large clay vessels have been modernized to give rise to complex, creamy, much more harmonized wines.

NUMBER OF HECTARES: 61.960 **ALTITUDES:** 400 m. - 700 m.

SUBZONES:

- **Rioja Alta:** This is the sub-region with the largest production of Rioja wine (36,780 hectares), and concentrates 43% of the wines. This route involves the cultivation of the banks of the River Ebro upstream from Logroño. The wines have body, are aromatic, fruity and with the possibility of long ageing due to their high level of acidity. This zone receives the impact of the Bay of Biscay and is conditioned by the mists of the valley of the River Ebro. The soils where the vines grow are very varied between clay – limestone and clay- ferrous and alluvial.

- **Rioja Alavesa:** This zone is well known for its young wines with carbonic maceration, wines of the year or young wines with lively colours and fruity potential. It is half-way between the Mediterranean and Atlantic climate, the region, whose centre is Laguardia, is protected by the Sierra de Cantabria which defends it from the north winds. The predominant soils are clay – limestone on terraces and in small plots.

- **Rioja Baja:** This is the second region with more volume of wines in La Rioja. The Mediterranean climate provides more full bodied and warmer wines. The vineyards are located on alluvial

AGRÍCOLA LABASTIDA

El Olmo, 8
1330 Labastida - (Álava)
☎: +34 945 331 230 - Fax: +34 945 331 257
info@tierrayvino.com
www.tierrayvino.com

EL BELISARIO 2009 T
100% tempranillo

93 Colour: cherry, garnet rim. Nose: ripe fruit, spicy, creamy oak, toasty, complex, earthy notes, mineral. Palate: powerful, flavourful, toasty, balanced.

EL PRIMAVERA 2011 T
100% tempranillo

90 Colour: cherry, purple rim. Nose: expressive, fresh fruit, red berry notes, floral, spicy. Palate: flavourful, fruity, good acidity, round tannins.

TIERRA 2009 TC
100% tempranillo

90 Colour: cherry, garnet rim. Nose: balanced, ripe fruit, sweet spices. Palate: flavourful, fruity, round tannins.

ALTOS DE RIOJA VITICULTORES Y BODEGUEROS

Ctra. Logroño, s/n
1300 Laguardia - (Alava)
☎: +34 945 600 693 - Fax: +34 945 600 692
altosderioja@altosderioja.com
www.altosderioja.com

ALTOS R 2006 TR
100% tempranillo

90 Colour: cherry, garnet rim. Nose: balanced, ripe fruit, spicy. Palate: fruity, balanced, fine bitter notes, fine tannins.

ALTOS R 2011 B
60% viura, 40% malvasía

90 Colour: bright straw. Nose: fresh fruit, fragrant herbs, citrus fruit. Palate: fruity, flavourful, good acidity.

ALTOS R PIGEAGE 2009 T
90% tempranillo, 10% graciano

93 Colour: deep cherry, garnet rim. Nose: balanced, ripe fruit, sweet spices, creamy oak. Palate: good structure, flavourful, ripe fruit, good acidity.

ALTÚN

Las Piscinas, 30
1307 Baños de Ebro - (Álava)
☎: +34 945 609 317 - Fax: +34 945 609 309
altun@bodegasaltun.com
www.bodegasaltun.com

ALBIKER 2011 T MACERACIÓN CARBÓNICA
95% tempranillo, 5% viura

90 Colour: deep cherry. Nose: powerfull, expressive, varietal, candied fruit, fruit liqueur notes. Palate: spirituous, sweetness, flavourful, powerful, fruity, complex.

ALTÚN 2007 TR
100% tempranillo

90 Colour: bright cherry. Nose: ripe fruit, new oak, toasty. Palate: flavourful, fruity, toasty, round tannins.

ALTÚN 2009 TC
100% tempranillo

90 Colour: cherry, garnet rim. Nose: red berry notes, ripe fruit, sweet spices, creamy oak. Palate: flavourful, spicy, long, correct.

EVEREST 2010 T
100% tempranillo

94 Colour: cherry, garnet rim. Nose: red berry notes, ripe fruit, expressive, mineral, balsamic herbs, spicy, toasty. Palate: powerful, flavourful, complex, balanced, long, toasty.

SECRETO DE ALTÚN 2010 T
100% tempranillo

92 Colour: cherry, garnet rim. Nose: mineral, ripe fruit, red berry notes. Palate: powerful, flavourful, fine bitter notes, round tannins.

ALVAREZ ALFARO

C/ San Bartolome 57
26559 Aldeanueva de Ebro - (La Rioja)
☎: +34 941 144 210 - Fax: +34 941 144 210
info@bodegasalvarezalfaro.com
www.bodegasalvarezalfaro.com

ALVAREZ ALFARO SELECCIÓN FAMILIAR 2009 T
100% tempranillo

90 Color cherry, garnet rim. Aroma ripe fruit, spicy, creamy oak, toasty, complex. Taste powerful, flavourful, toasty, round tannins.

AMADOR GARCÍA CHAVARRI

Avda. Río Ebro, 68 - 70
1307 Baños de Ebro - (Álava)
☎: +34 945 290 385 - Fax: +34 975 290 373
bodegasamadorgarcia@gmail.com
www.bodegasamadorgarcia.com

AMADOR GARCÍA 2008 TC

90 Colour: cherry, garnet rim. Nose: ripe fruit, spicy, creamy oak, toasty. Palate: powerful, flavourful, round tannins, balanced, long.

ARRIAGA Y MIMÉNDEZ COMPAÑÍA DE VINOS

Capitán Cortés, 6. Piso 4º Puerta 3
26003 Logroño - (La Rioja)
☎: +34 687 421 306 - Fax: +34 941 287 072
administracion@arriagaymimendez.com
www.arriagaymimendez.com

LA INVIERNA CORTE UNO 2007 T
100% tempranillo

91 Colour: cherry, garnet rim. Nose: spicy, ripe fruit, tobacco. Palate: good structure, good acidity, fine bitter notes, full.

ARTUKE BODEGAS Y VIÑEDOS

La Serna, 24
1307 Baños de Ebro - (Álava)
☎: +34 945 623 323 - Fax: +34 945 623 323
artuke@artuke.com
www.artuke.com

ARTUKE 2011 T MACERACIÓN CARBÓNICA
95% tempranillo, 5% viura

91 Colour: cherry, purple rim. Nose: lactic notes, raspberry, red berry notes, balanced, expressive. Palate: fresh, fruity, light-bodied, good acidity, flavourful, balanced.

ARTUKE FINCA DE LOS LOCOS 2010 T
80% tempranillo, 20% graciano

95 Colour: bright cherry. Nose: expressive, cocoa bean, toasty, ripe fruit, dark chocolate. Palate: flavourful, fruity, toasty, round tannins.

ARTUKE K4 2010 T
75% tempranillo, 25% graciano

96 Colour: cherry, garnet rim. Nose: spicy, creamy oak, toasty, mineral, characterful, ripe fruit, red berry notes. Palate: powerful, flavourful, toasty, round tannins.

ARTUKE PIES NEGROS 2010 TC
90% tempranillo, 10% graciano

93 Colour: cherry, garnet rim. Nose: ripe fruit, spicy, creamy oak, toasty, complex, mineral. Palate: powerful, flavourful, toasty, round tannins.

BAIGORRI

Ctra. Vitoria-Logroño, Km. 53
1307 Samaniego - (Álava)
☎: +34 945 609 420 - Fax: +34 945 609 407
mail@bodegasbaigorri.com
www.bodegasbaigorri.com

BAIGORRI 2010 BFB
90% viura, 10% malvasía

91 Colour: bright yellow. Nose: powerfull, ripe fruit, sweet spices, dried herbs. Palate: rich, smoky aftertaste, flavourful, fresh, good acidity.

BAIGORRI 2006 TR
100% tempranillo

91 Colour: deep cherry. Nose: powerfull, macerated fruit, expressive, spicy, roasted coffee. Palate: powerful, flavourful, good structure, creamy, spicy.

BAIGORRI 2008 TC
90% tempranillo, 10% otras

91 Colour: deep cherry. Nose: ripe fruit, spicy, creamy oak, toasty, complex, dark chocolate. Palate: powerful, flavourful, toasty, round tannins.

BAIGORRI BELUS 2008 T
70% tempranillo, 20% mazuelo, 10% garnacha

90 Colour: cherry, garnet rim. Nose: ripe fruit, spicy, toasty, complex. Palate: powerful, flavourful, toasty, round.

BAIGORRI DE GARAGE 2007 T
100% tempranillo

93 Colour: cherry, garnet rim. Nose: complex, balanced, expressive, aromatic coffee, ripe fruit, mineral. Palate: good structure, flavourful, good acidity, balanced.

BAIGORRI GARNACHA 2009 T
100% garnacha

93 Colour: very deep cherry, garnet rim. Nose: powerfull, balanced, creamy oak, ripe fruit. Palate: good structure, flavourful.

BARÓN DE LEY

Ctra. Mendavia - Lodosa, Km. 5,5
31587 Mendavia - (Navarra)
☎: +34 948 694 303 - Fax: +34 948 694 304
info@barondeley.com
www.barondeley.com

BARÓN DE LEY 2011 B
85% viura, 15% malvasía

90 Colour: bright straw. Nose: white flowers, fruit expression, fresh, neat, varietal. Palate: powerful, flavourful, fruity, complex.

BARÓN DE LEY FINCA MONASTERIO 2008 T
90% tempranillo, 10% otras

91 Colour: cherry, garnet rim. Nose: spicy, tobacco, ripe fruit, balanced. Palate: balanced, good acidity, fruity.

BARÓN DE LEY VARIETALES TEMPRANILLO 2010 T
100% tempranillo

91 Color cherry, garnet rim. Aroma ripe fruit, spicy, creamy oak, toasty, complex. Taste powerful, flavourful, toasty, round tannins.

BODEGA CONTADOR

Ctra. Baños de Ebro, Km. 1
26338 San Vicente de la Sonsierra - (La Rioja)
☎: +34 941 334 228 - Fax: +34 941 334 537
info@bodegacontador.com
www.bodegacontador.com

CONTADOR 2010 T
99% tempranillo, 1% garnacha

97 Colour: cherry, purple rim. Nose: new oak, toasty, sweet spices, dark chocolate, earthy notes, mineral, fruit expression, ripe fruit. Palate: long, ripe fruit, spicy, balsamic, round tannins, round.

LA CUEVA DEL CONTADOR 2010 T
100% tempranillo

95 Colour: cherry, purple rim. Nose: powerfull, characterful, complex, ripe fruit, creamy oak, cocoa bean. Palate: flavourful, fine bitter notes, good acidity, round tannins.

LA VIÑA DE ANDRÉS ROMEO 2010 T
100% tempranillo

96 Colour: cherry, purple rim. Nose: ripe fruit, fruit expression, fresh, complex, new oak, toasty, scrubland. Palate: fine bitter notes, round, long, ripe fruit, harsh oak tannins.

PREDICADOR 2010 T

93 Colour: cherry, purple rim. Nose: red berry notes, fruit expression, creamy oak, sweet spices. Palate: round tannins, ripe fruit, spicy.

BODEGA DEL MONGE-GARBATI

Ctra. Rivas de Tereso, s/n
26338 San Vicente de la Sonsierra - (La Rioja)
☎: +34 659 167 653 - Fax: +34 941 311 870
bodegamg@yahoo.es
www.vinaane.com

EL LABERINTO DE VIÑA ANE 2009 T
100% tempranillo

90 Colour: deep cherry, garnet rim. Nose: red berry notes, ripe fruit, sweet spices, violets. Palate: powerful, flavourful, good structure.

BODEGA I. PETRALANDA

Avda. La Estación, 44
26360 Fuenmayor - (La Rioja)
☎: +34 941 450 462 - Fax: +34 941 450 620
nonno@vinoart.es
www.zearra.com

NONNO 2007 T
tempranillo, mazuelo

91 Colour: cherry, garnet rim. Nose: complex, medium intensity, balanced, tobacco, ripe fruit, spicy. Palate: flavourful, good structure, good acidity.

BODEGA MONTEALTO

Las Piscinas, s/n
1307 Baños del Ebro - (Alava)
☎: +34 918 427 013 - Fax: +34 918 427 013
contacta@meddissl.com
www.meddissl.com

ROBATIE 2011 T
95% tempranillo, 5% viura

90 Color cherry, purple rim. Aroma expressive, fresh fruit, red berry notes, floral. Taste flavourful, fruity, good acidity, round tannins.

ROBATIE VENDIMIA SELECCIONADA 2009 T
100% tempranillo

92 Colour: cherry, garnet rim. Nose: ripe fruit, spicy, creamy oak, toasty, characterful. Palate: powerful, flavourful, toasty, round tannins.

BODEGA SAN MARTÍN DE ABALOS

Camino del Prado s/n
26211 Fonzaleche - (La Rioja)
☎: +34 941 300 423 - Fax: +34 941 300 423
comercial@bodegasanmartindeabalos.com
www.sanmartindeabalos.com

PORTALON DE SAN MARTÍN 2008 T
15% viura, 5% garnacha, 80% tempranillo

90 Colour: cherry, garnet rim. Nose: ripe fruit, cocoa bean, sweet spices. Palate: good structure, flavourful, spicy.

BODEGA VIÑA EGUILUZ

Camino de San Bartolomé, 10
26339 Abalos - (La Rioja)
☎: +34 941 334 064 - Fax: +34 941 583 022
info@bodegaseguiluz.es
www.bodegaseguiluz.es

EGUILUZ 2006 TR
100% tempranillo

90 Colour: cherry, garnet rim. Nose: ripe fruit, spicy, old leather. Palate: flavourful, toasty, round tannins, balanced.

BODEGA Y VIÑEDOS SOLABAL

Camino San Bartolomé, 6
26339 Abalos - (La Rioja)
☎: +34 941 334 492 - Fax: +34 941 308 164
solabal@solabal.com
www.solabal.es

MUÑARRATE 2011 B
viura, malvasía

90 Colour: bright straw. Nose: fragrant herbs, fresh fruit, floral. Palate: fruity, fresh, complex, flavourful, powerful.

SOLABAL 2007 TR
tempranillo

90 Colour: cherry, garnet rim. Nose: spicy, creamy oak, toasty, characterful. Palate: powerful, flavourful, toasty, round tannins.

VALA DE SOLABAL 2008 T
tempranillo

90 Colour: cherry, garnet rim. Nose: ripe fruit, spicy, creamy oak, toasty, characterful. Palate: powerful, flavourful, toasty, round tannins.

BODEGAS ABEL MENDOZA MONGE

Ctra. Peñacerrada, 7
26338 San Vicente de la Sonsierra - (La Rioja)
☎: +34 941 308 010 - Fax: +34 941 308 010
jarrarte.abelmendoza@gmail.com

ABEL MENDOZA MALVASÍA 2011 BFB
malvasía

90 Colour: bright yellow. Nose: medium intensity, balanced, fresh fruit, citrus fruit, fragrant herbs. Palate: fruity, rich, good acidity, spicy.

ABEL MENDOZA SELECCIÓN PERSONAL 2009 T
tempranillo

93 Colour: dark-red cherry, garnet rim. Nose: cocoa bean, fruit expression, complex, varietal, elegant. Palate: full, rich, flavourful, powerful, spicy, creamy, smoky aftertaste.

ABEL MENDOZA TEMPRANILLO
GRANO A GRANO 2009 T
tempranillo

93 Colour: very deep cherry. Nose: medium intensity, closed, fruit expression, dark chocolate, creamy oak. Palate: powerful, flavourful, complex, balsamic, smoky aftertaste.

BODEGAS ALTANZA

Ctra. Nacional 232, Km. 419
26360 Fuenmayor - (Rioja)
☎: +34 941 450 860 - Fax: +34 941 450 804
altanza@bodegasaltanza.com
www.bodegasaltanza.com

ALTANZA RESERVA ESPECIAL 2004 TR
tempranillo

90 Colour: deep cherry, garnet rim. Nose: spicy, fruit preserve, tobacco, toasty. Palate: balanced, good acidity, fine bitter notes.

LEALTANZA 2007 TR
tempranillo

90 Color cherry, garnet rim. Aroma ripe fruit, spicy, creamy oak, toasty, complex. Taste powerful, flavourful, toasty, round tannins.

LEALTANZA 2004 TGR
tempranillo

90 Colour: pale ruby, brick rim edge. Nose: spicy, fine reductive notes, wet leather, aged wood nuances, fruit liqueur notes, fragrant herbs. Palate: spicy, fine tannins, elegant, long.

LEALTANZA 2011 B
viura, sauvignon blanc

90 Colour: bright straw. Nose: ripe fruit, citrus fruit, scrubland. Palate: flavourful, fruity, fresh.

LEALTANZA AUTOR 2008 T
tempranillo

90 Colour: cherry, garnet rim. Nose: ripe fruit, spicy, creamy oak, toasty, balanced. Palate: powerful, flavourful, toasty, round tannins.

BODEGAS AMAREN

Ctra. Baños de Ebro, s/n,
1307 Villabuena - (Álava)
☎: +34 945 175 240 - Fax: +34 945 174 566
bodegas@bodegasamaren.com
www.bodegasamaren.com

AMAREN 2010 BFB
85% viura, 15% malvasía

91 Colour: bright yellow. Nose: complex, fresh, powerfull, fragrant herbs, candied fruit. Palate: good acidity, elegant, fresh, fruity, full.

AMAREN TEMPRANILLO 2006 TR
100% tempranillo

91 Colour: cherry, garnet rim. Nose: spicy, creamy oak, toasty, fruit liqueur notes, wet leather. Palate: powerful, flavourful, toasty, round tannins.

ÁNGELES DE AMAREN 2008 T
85% tempranillo, 15% graciano

92 Colour: cherry, garnet rim. Nose: ripe fruit, spicy, creamy oak, complex. Palate: powerful, flavourful, toasty, round tannins.

BODEGAS ANTONIO ALCARAZ

Ctra. Vitoria-Logroño, Km. 57
1300 Laguardia - (Álava)
☎: +34 658 959 745 - Fax: +34 965 888 359
rioja@antonio-alcaraz.es
www.antonio-alcaraz.es

ANTONIO ALCARAZ 2007 TR
90% tempranillo, 10% graciano, mazuelo

91 Colour: cherry, garnet rim. Nose: ripe fruit, spicy, toasty, complex. Palate: powerful, flavourful, toasty, round tannins.

ANTONIO ALCARAZ 2009 TC
90% tempranillo, 10% mazuelo

91 Colour: bright cherry, garnet rim. Nose: spicy, ripe fruit. Palate: fruity, flavourful, round tannins.

GLORIA ANTONIO ALCARAZ 2009 TC
100% tempranillo

90 Colour: deep cherry. Nose: expressive, ripe fruit, creamy oak, sweet spices. Palate: balanced, ripe fruit, round tannins.

BODEGAS BASAGOITI

Mas Parxet, s/n
8391 Tiana - (Barcelona)
☎: +34 933 950 811 - Fax: +34 933 955 500
info@parxet.es
www.parxet.es

BASAGOITI 2009 TC
75% tempranillo, 25% garnacha

90 Colour: cherry, garnet rim. Nose: ripe fruit, scrubland, spicy. Palate: powerful, flavourful, long, spicy.

NABARI 2011 T
70% tempranillo, 30% garnacha

90 Colour: cherry, purple rim. Nose: ripe fruit, balsamic herbs. Palate: flavourful, fine bitter notes, good acidity.

BODEGAS BENJAMÍN DE ROTHSCHILD & VEGA SICILIA S.A.

Ctra. Logroño - Vitoria, km. 61
1309 Leza - (Alava)
☎: +34 983 680 147 - Fax: +34 983 680 263
irodriguez@vega-sicilia.com
www.vegasicilia.com

MACÁN 2009 T
100% tempranillo

93 Colour: cherry, garnet rim. Nose: cocoa bean, spicy, ripe fruit, complex, closed. Palate: flavourful, full, balanced, good acidity, fine tannins.

MACÁN CLÁSICO 2009 T
100% tempranillo

95 Colour: cherry, purple rim. Nose: expressive, balanced, elegant, red berry notes, ripe fruit. Palate: flavourful, good acidity, fine tannins, long.

BODEGAS BERCEO

Cuevas, 32-34-36
26200 Haro - (La Rioja)
☎: +34 941 310 744 - Fax: +34 948 670 259
bodegas@gurpegui.es
www.gurpegui.es

BERCEO "NUEVA GENERACIÓN" 2008 TC
tempranillo, graciano, mazuelo

91 Colour: cherry, garnet rim. Nose: ripe fruit, spicy, creamy oak, toasty, complex. Palate: powerful, flavourful, toasty, round tannins, balanced.

LOS DOMINIOS DE BERCEO "RESERVA 36" 2006 TR
tempranillo

90 Colour: deep cherry. Nose: sweet spices, creamy oak, toasty, ripe fruit. Palate: spirituous, good structure, flavourful, powerful, spicy.

LOS DOMINIOS DE BERCEO 2010 TC
tempranillo

92 Colour: cherry, garnet rim. Nose: ripe fruit, spicy, creamy oak, toasty. Palate: powerful, flavourful, toasty, round tannins.

VIÑA BERCEO 2008 TC
tempranillo, garnacha, graciano

91 Colour: deep cherry. Nose: ripe fruit, sweet spices, scrubland. Palate: spicy, fine bitter notes.

BODEGAS BERONIA

Ctra. Ollauri - Nájera, Km. 1,8
26220 Ollauri - (La Rioja)
☎: +34 941 338 000 - Fax: +34 941 338 266
beronia@beronia.es
www.beronia.es

BERONIA 2005 TGR
90% tempranillo, 8% mazuelo, 2% graciano

91 Colour: deep cherry, garnet rim. Nose: caramel, spicy, elegant, ripe fruit. Palate: spicy, classic aged character, powerful, good structure.

BERONIA 2007 TR
90% tempranillo, 5% graciano, 5% mazuelo

90 Colour: dark-red cherry, orangey edge. Nose: cocoa bean, spicy, elegant. Palate: creamy, ripe fruit, powerful, flavourful.

BERONIA SELECCIÓN 198 BARRICAS 2005 TR
90% tempranillo, 7% mazuelo, graciano

92 Colour: dark-red cherry. Nose: ripe fruit, powerfull, damp earth, truffle notes. Palate: elegant, round, full, rich, soft tannins.

BERONIA TEMPRANILLO ELABORACIÓN ESPECIAL 2009 T
100% tempranillo

91 Colour: cherry, garnet rim. Nose: spicy, creamy oak, red berry notes, roasted coffee. Palate: powerful, flavourful, toasty, round tannins.

III A.C., BERONIA 2008 T
92% tempranillo, 4% graciano, 4% mazuelo

92 Colour: dark-red cherry. Nose: ripe fruit, fruit expression, powerfull, characterful, expressive, toasty, creamy oak. Palate: powerful, flavourful, complex, creamy, toasty.

BODEGAS BILBAÍNAS

Estación, 3
26200 Haro - (La Rioja)
☎: +34 941 310 147 - Fax: +34 935 051 567
m.oyono@bodegasbilbainas.com
www.bodegasbilbainas.com

BODEGAS BILBAINAS GARNACHA 2010 T
100% garnacha

92 Colour: cherry, purple rim. Nose: floral, ripe fruit, fresh, balanced, balsamic herbs. Palate: flavourful, fruity, fresh, easy to drink.

BODEGAS BILBAINAS GRACIANO 2007 T
100% graciano

92 Colour: cherry, garnet rim. Nose: ripe fruit, spicy, creamy oak. Palate: powerful, flavourful, toasty, round tannins.

LA VICALANDA 2005 TGR
100% tempranillo

94 Colour: cherry, garnet rim. Nose: spicy, toasty, complex, aromatic coffee, dark chocolate, ripe fruit. Palate: powerful, flavourful, toasty, round tannins.

LA VICALANDA 2007 TR
100% tempranillo

93 Colour: cherry, garnet rim. Nose: elegant, complex, spicy, ripe fruit. Palate: good structure, flavourful, balanced, good acidity, full.

VIÑA POMAL "ALTO DE LA CASETA" 2008 T
100% tempranillo

91 Colour: cherry, garnet rim. Nose: ripe fruit, wild herbs, spicy, creamy oak, fine reductive notes. Palate: balanced, flavourful.

VIÑA POMAL 2007 TR
100% tempranillo

91 Colour: cherry, garnet rim. Nose: spicy, creamy oak, toasty, characterful, candied fruit. Palate: powerful, flavourful, toasty, round tannins.

VIÑA ZACO 2009 T
100% tempranillo

90 Colour: cherry, garnet rim. Nose: balanced, ripe fruit, sweet spices, complex. Palate: good structure, flavourful.

VIÑA ZACO 2010 T
100% tempranillo

90 Colour: bright cherry, garnet rim. Nose: balanced, complex, ripe fruit, cocoa bean. Palate: balanced, ripe fruit, long.

BODEGAS BRETÓN CRIADORES

Ctra. de Fuenmayor, Km. 1,5
26370 Navarrete - (La Rioja)
☎: +34 941 440 840 - Fax: +34 941 440 812
info@bodegasbreton.com
www.bodegasbreton.com

ALBA DE BRETÓN 2005 TR
85% tempranillo, 15% graciano

91 Colour: deep cherry. Nose: undergrowth, damp earth, candied fruit, creamy oak, toasty. Palate: round, powerful, flavourful, spicy, toasty.

DOMINIO DE CONTE 2005 TR
90% tempranillo, 10% graciano

91 Colour: dark-red cherry. Nose: earthy notes, damp earth, fine reductive notes, dark chocolate, sweet spices, cedar wood. Palate: flavourful, rich, complex, spicy, reductive nuances.

L 5 LORIÑÓN 2008 TC
85% tempranillo, 15% graciano

90 Colour: cherry, garnet rim. Nose: ripe fruit, spicy, creamy oak, toasty, characterful. Palate: powerful, flavourful, toasty, round tannins.

BODEGAS CAMPILLO

Ctra. de Logroño, s/n
1300 Laguardia - (Álava)
☎: +34 945 600 826 - Fax: +34 945 600 837
info@bodegascampillo.es
www.bodegascampillo.es

CAMPILLO 2001 TGR
95% tempranillo, 5% graciano

90 Colour: dark-red cherry. Nose: fruit preserve, old leather, damp earth. Palate: powerful, flavourful, toasty, roasted-coffee aftertaste, ripe fruit.

CAMPILLO 2011 BFB
85% viura, 10% malvasía, 5% chardonnay

91 Colour: bright yellow. Nose: ripe fruit, sweet spices, creamy oak, fragrant herbs. Palate: rich, flavourful, fresh, good acidity.

CAMPILLO FINCA CUESTA CLARA 2005 TR
100% tempranillo

93 Colour: cherry, garnet rim. Nose: ripe fruit, spicy, creamy oak, toasty, dark chocolate. Palate: powerful, flavourful, toasty, round tannins.

CAMPILLO RESERVA ESPECIAL 2005 TR
85% tempranillo, 10% graciano, 5% cabernet sauvignon

91 Colour: cherry, garnet rim. Nose: ripe fruit, scrubland, sweet spices, creamy oak. Palate: correct, ripe fruit, round tannins.

CAMPILLO RESERVA SELECTA 2005 TR
100% tempranillo

93 Colour: cherry, garnet rim. Nose: ripe fruit, spicy, creamy oak, toasty, red berry notes, mineral. Palate: powerful, flavourful, toasty, round tannins.

BODEGAS CAMPO VIEJO

Camino de la Puebla, 50
26006 Logroño - (La Rioja)
☎: +34 941 279 900 - Fax: +34 941 279 901
campoviejo@domecqbodegas.com
www.domecqbodegas.com

ALCORTA & CARMEN RUSCADELLA 2008 T
tempranillo

90 Colour: cherry, garnet rim. Nose: ripe fruit, spicy, creamy oak, toasty. Palate: powerful, flavourful, toasty, round tannins.

AZPILICUETA 2007 TR
tempranillo, graciano, mazuelo

91 Colour: cherry, garnet rim. Nose: balanced, expressive, elegant, ripe fruit, spicy. Palate: fruity, round tannins, good acidity.

AZPILICUETA 2009 TC
tempranillo, graciano, mazuelo

91 Colour: cherry, garnet rim. Nose: spicy, creamy oak, toasty, complex, ripe fruit. Palate: powerful, flavourful, toasty, round tannins.

CAMPO VIEJO 2004 TGR
tempranillo, graciano, mazuelo

90 Colour: pale ruby, brick rim edge. Nose: ripe fruit, tobacco, old leather. Palate: spicy, powerful, flavourful, round.

FÉLIX AZPILICUETA COLECCIÓN PRIVADA 2008 T
tempranillo, graciano, mazuelo

93 Colour: cherry, garnet rim. Nose: ripe fruit, spicy, creamy oak, toasty, complex, characterful. Palate: powerful, flavourful, toasty, round tannins.

FÉLIX AZPILICUETA COLECCIÓN PRIVADA 2011 BFB
viura

90 Color bright yellow. Aroma powerfull, ripe fruit, sweet spices, creamy oak, fragrant herbs. Taste rich, smoky aftertaste, flavourful, fresh, good acidity.

BODEGAS CASA PRIMICIA

Camino de la Hoya, 1
1300 Laguardia - (Álava)
☎: +34 945 600 296 - Fax: +34 945 621 252
info@bodegascasaprimicia.com
www.casaprimicia.com

COFRADÍA 2005 TR
100% tempranillo

93 Colour: dark-red cherry, orangey edge. Nose: earthy notes, scrubland, spicy, smoky, cigar, sweet spices. Palate: balanced, flavourful, long, spicy, round tannins.

BODEGAS CASTILLO DE SAJAZARRA

Del Río, s/n
26212 Sajazarra - (La Rioja)
☎: +34 941 320 066 - Fax: +34 941 320 251
bodega@castillodesajazarra.com
www.castillodesajazarra.com

CASTILLO DE SAJAZARRA 2006 TR
100% tempranillo

90 Colour: cherry, garnet rim. Nose: spicy, creamy oak, toasty. Palate: powerful, flavourful, toasty, round tannins.

DIGMA AUTOR 2006 TR
100% tempranillo

94 Colour: deep cherry, garnet rim. Nose: balanced, complex, elegant, ripe fruit, creamy oak. Palate: flavourful, balanced, mineral.

SOLAR DE LÍBANO 2008 TC
97% tempranillo, 3% graciano, garnacha

90 Colour: cherry, garnet rim. Nose: ripe fruit, spicy, creamy oak, toasty, earthy notes. Palate: powerful, flavourful, toasty, round tannins.

SOLAR DE LÍBANO 2008 TR
97% tempranillo, 3% graciano, garnacha

91 Colour: cherry, garnet rim. Nose: ripe fruit, spicy, creamy oak, toasty. Palate: powerful, flavourful, toasty, round tannins.

BODEGAS CONSEJO DE LA ALTA

Avda. de Fuenmayor, s/n
26350 Cenicero - (La Rioja)
☎: +34 941 455 005 - Fax: +34 941 455 010
comercial@consejodelaalta.com
www.consejodelaalta.com

CONSEJO DE LA ALTA 2006 TR
tempranillo

90 Colour: dark-red cherry, orangey edge. Nose: ripe fruit, spicy, creamy oak, fine reductive notes. Palate: good acidity, round, flavourful, spicy.

BODEGAS CORRAL

Ctra. de Logroño, Km. 10
26370 Navarrete - (La Rioja)
☎: +34 941 440 193 - Fax: +34 941 440 195
info@donjacobo.es
www.vinotecadonjacobo.es

ALTOS DE CORRAL 2008 T FERMENTADO EN BARRICA
100% tempranillo

91 Colour: deep cherry. Nose: ripe fruit, sweet spices, dark chocolate. Palate: flavourful, spicy, ripe fruit.

BODEGAS COVILA

Camino del Soto, 26
1306 La Puebla de Labarca - (Álava)
☎: +34 945 627 232 - Fax: +34 945 627 295
comercial@covila.es
www.covila.es

PAGOS DE LABARCA AEX 2009 T
100% tempranillo

91 Colour: cherry, garnet rim. Nose: spicy, creamy oak, toasty, characterful, ripe fruit, mineral. Palate: powerful, flavourful, toasty, round tannins.

BODEGAS DARIEN

Ctra. Logroño-Zaragoza, Km. 7
26006 Logroño - (La Rioja)
☎: +34 941 258 130 - Fax: +34 941 265 285
info@darien.es
www.darien.es

DARIEN 2007 TR
87% tempranillo, 13% graciano

90 Colour: cherry, garnet rim. Nose: spicy, creamy oak, toasty, characterful. Palate: powerful, flavourful, toasty, round tannins.

DELIUS 2004 TR
80% tempranillo, 20% graciano

90 Colour: cherry, garnet rim. Nose: spicy, creamy oak, toasty, characterful. Palate: powerful, flavourful, toasty, round tannins.

BODEGAS DE LOS HEREDEROS DEL MARQUÉS DE RISCAL S.L.

Bodegas de los Herederos del Marqués de Riscal
1340 Elciego - (Álava)
☎: +34 945 606 000 - Fax: +34 945 606 023
marquesderiscal@marquesderiscal.com
www.marquesderiscal.com

BARÓN DE CHIREL 2006 TR
80% tempranillo, 20% otras

92 Colour: bright cherry, orangey edge. Nose: balanced, expressive, ripe fruit, spicy, tobacco. Palate: good structure, flavourful, spicy, long.

FINCA TORREA 2007 TR
tempranillo, graciano

94 Colour: dark-red cherry, orangey edge. Nose: aromatic coffee, creamy oak, toasty, fruit expression, damp earth. Palate: round, powerful, spirituous, balsamic, spicy, ripe fruit.

MARQUÉS DE RISCAL 150 ANIVERSARIO 2004 TGR
tempranillo, graciano, otras

92 Colour: deep cherry. Nose: ripe fruit, aromatic coffee, spicy, wet leather. Palate: flavourful, fine bitter notes, good acidity, fine tannins.

BODEGAS DEL MEDIEVO

Circunvalación San Roque, s/n
26559 Aldeanueva de Ebro - (La Rioja)
☎: +34 941 163 141 - Fax: +34 941 144 204
info@bodegasdelmedievo.com
www.bodegasdelmedievo.com

TUERCE BOTAS 2009 TC
100% graciano

90 Colour: deep cherry. Nose: fruit expression, ripe fruit, fruit liqueur notes, cocoa bean. Palate: fruity, powerful, flavourful, ripe fruit, balsamic.

BODEGAS DINASTÍA VIVANCO

Ctra. Nacional 232, s/n
26330 Briones - (La Rioja)
☎: +34 941 322 013 - Fax: +34 941 322 316
infobodega@dinastiavivanco.es
www.dinastiavivanco.es

COLECCIÓN VIVANCO 4 VARIETALES 2009 TC
70% tempranillo, 15% graciano, 10% garnacha, 5% mazuelo

91 Colour: very deep cherry, garnet rim. Nose: cocoa bean, creamy oak, balanced, ripe fruit. Palate: long, ripe fruit, spicy, balanced, good acidity.

COLECCIÓN VIVANCO DULCE DE INVIERNO 2009 T
50% tempranillo, 20% graciano, 20% garnacha, 10% mazuelo

94 Colour: coppery red. Nose: balanced, expressive, complex, dried fruit, floral. Palate: rich, flavourful, long, balanced, elegant.

COLECCIÓN VIVANCO PARCELAS
DE GARNACHA 2008 T
100% garnacha

93 Colour: cherry, garnet rim. Nose: red berry notes, ripe fruit, earthy notes, sweet spices, toasty. Palate: powerful, flavourful, long, balanced.

COLECCIÓN VIVANCO PARCELAS
DE GRACIANO 2007 T
100% graciano

90 Colour: cherry, garnet rim. Nose: earthy notes, ripe fruit, spicy, creamy oak. Palate: powerful, flavourful, spicy, long, balanced.

COLECCIÓN VIVANCO PARCELAS
DE MATURANA 2009 T
100% maturana

92 Colour: black cherry. Nose: scrubland, grassy, powerfull, expressive. Palate: correct, good acidity, round tannins, fine bitter notes.

VIVANCO TEMPRANILLO GARNACHA 2011 RD
80% tempranillo, 20% garnacha

90 Color rose, purple rim. Aroma powerfull, ripe fruit, red berry notes, floral, expressive. Taste fleshy, powerful, fruity, fresh.

BODEGAS DON SANCHO DE LONDOÑO

Ctra. Ollauri - Nájera s/n
26323 Hormilla - (La Rioja)
☎: +34 941 058 976 - Fax: +34 941 058 976
info@dslbodegas.es
www.dslbodegas.es

LONDOÑO 2009 TC
100% tempranillo

90 Colour: cherry, garnet rim. Nose: ripe fruit, spicy, creamy oak, toasty, complex. Palate: powerful, flavourful, toasty, balanced.

LONDOÑO VENDIMIA SELECCIONADA 2010 BFB
viura, malvasía, garnacha blanca

92 Colour: bright yellow. Nose: ripe fruit, sweet spices, creamy oak, fragrant herbs. Palate: rich, flavourful, fresh, good acidity, elegant.

BODEGAS EXOPTO

Ctra. de Elvillar, 26
1300 Laguardia - (Álava)
☎: +34 650 213 993
info@exopto.net
www.exopto.net

HORIZONTE DE EXOPTO 2009 T
80% tempranillo, 10% garnacha, 10% graciano

91 Colour: cherry, garnet rim. Nose: spicy, ripe fruit. Palate: flavourful, good acidity, round tannins, light-bodied.

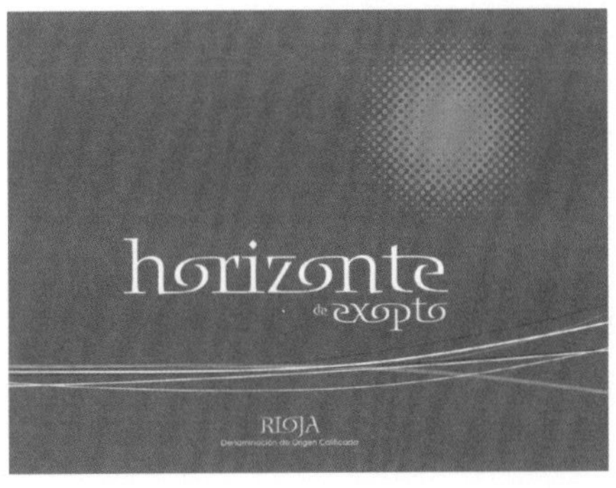

EXOPTO CUVÉE LUCA 2009 T
60% graciano, 30% tempranillo, 10% garnacha,

92 Colour: cherry, garnet rim. Nose: ripe fruit, spicy, creamy oak, toasty. Palate: powerful, flavourful, toasty, round tannins.

HORIZONTE DE EXOPTO 2010 B
80% viura, 10% malvasía, 10% garnacha blanca

90 Colour: bright yellow. Nose: balanced, complex, elegant, ripe fruit, floral. Palate: rich, spicy, fine bitter notes.

BODEGAS FAUSTINO

Ctra. de Logroño, s/n
1320 Oyón - (Álava)
☎: +34 945 622 500 - Fax: +34 945 622 511
info@bodegasfaustino.es
www.bodegasfaustino.es

FAUSTINO DE AUTOR RESERVA ESPECIAL 2006 TR
86% tempranillo, 14% graciano

91 Colour: deep cherry, orangey edge. Nose: spicy, creamy oak, balsamic herbs, fine reductive notes. Palate: flavourful, long, correct, round.

FAUSTINO EDICIÓN ESPECIAL 2001 T
100% tempranillo

93 Color pale ruby, brick rim edge. Aroma elegant, spicy, fine reductive notes, wet leather, aged wood nuances, fruit liqueur notes. Taste spicy, fine tannins, elegant, long.

FAUSTINO I 75 ANIVERSARIO 2004 TGR
92% tempranillo, 8% graciano

92 Colour: pale ruby, brick rim edge. Nose: spicy, wet leather, aged wood nuances, fruit liqueur notes, balanced. Palate: spicy, fine tannins, elegant, long.

BODEGAS FLORENTINO MARTÍNEZ

Ermita, 33
26311 Cordovín - (La Rioja)
☎: +34 941 418 614 - Fax: +34 941 418 614
bodegas@florentinomartinez.com
www.florentinomartinez.com

FLORENTIUS 2011 B
viura, malvasía

90 Colour: bright straw. Nose: fruit expression, complex, varietal, fragrant herbs. Palate: light-bodied, full, flavourful, powerful, fresh, fruity.

TANKA 2005 T
tempranillo

91 Colour: cherry, garnet rim. Nose: ripe fruit, spicy, creamy oak, toasty, characterful. Palate: powerful, flavourful, toasty, round tannins.

BODEGAS FOS

Término de Vialba, s/n
1340 Elciego - (Álava)
☎: +34 945 606 681 - Fax: +34 945 606 608
fos@bodegasfos.com
www.bodegasfos.com

FOS BARANDA 2008 T
100% tempranillo

91 Colour: deep cherry, garnet rim. Nose: balanced, expressive, ripe fruit, dark chocolate, creamy oak. Palate: good structure, complex, flavourful.

BODEGAS FRANCISCO GARCÍA RAMÍREZ E HIJOS

Ctra. Ventas, s/n
26143 Murillo del Río Leza - (La Rioja)
☎: +34 941 432 372 - Fax: +34 941 432 156
info@bodegasgarciaramirez.com

HEREDAD GARBLO 2008 T
85% tempranillo, 5% graciano, 5% mazuelo, 5% garnacha

90 Colour: cherry, garnet rim. Nose: spicy, creamy oak, toasty, ripe fruit. Palate: powerful, flavourful, toasty, round tannins.

BODEGAS FRANCO ESPAÑOLAS

Cabo Noval, 2
26009 Logroño - (La Rioja)
☎: +34 941 251 300 - Fax: +34 941 262 948
francoespanolas@francoespanolas.com
www.francoespanolas.com

BARBARO 2007 T
garnacha, tempranillo, mazuelo

91 Colour: cherry, garnet rim. Nose: ripe fruit, spicy, creamy oak, toasty, fine reductive notes. Palate: powerful, flavourful, toasty, fine tannins.

BARON D'ANGLADE 2005 TR
tempranillo, mazuelo, graciano

92 Colour: dark-red cherry, garnet rim. Nose: fine reductive notes, animal reductive notes, tobacco, ripe fruit, cocoa bean, spicy. Palate: round, rich, powerful, toasty, soft tannins.

BODEGAS GARCÍA DE OLANO

Ctra. Vitoria, s/n
1309 Paganos - La Guardia - (Álava)
☎: +34 945 621 146 - Fax: +34 945 621 146
garciadeolano@telefonica.net
www.bodegasgarciadeolano.com

3 DE OLANO 2009 T
100% tempranillo

90 Colour: cherry, garnet rim. Nose: ripe fruit, creamy oak, toasty, cocoa bean. Palate: powerful, flavourful, toasty, balanced.

BODEGAS GÓMEZ CRUZADO

Avda. Vizcaya, 6
26200 Haro - (La Rioja)
☎: +34 941 312 502 - Fax: +34 941 303 567
bodega@gomezcruzado.com
www.gomezcruzado.com

GÓMEZ CRUZADO "GC" 2009 TC
80% tempranillo, 20% garnacha

92 Color bright cherry. Aroma ripe fruit, sweet spices, creamy oak, expressive. Taste flavourful, fruity, toasty, round tannins.

HONORABLE GÓMEZ CRUZADO 2010 T
90% tempranillo, 10% garnacha

91 Colour: bright cherry. Nose: ripe fruit, sweet spices, creamy oak. Palate: flavourful, fruity, toasty, round tannins.

BODEGAS HERMANOS PECIÑA

Ctra. de Vitoria, Km. 47
26338 San Vicente de la Sonsierra - (La Rioja)
☎: +34 941 334 366 - Fax: +34 941 334 180
info@bodegashermanospecina.com
www.bodegashermanospecina.com

CHOBEO DE PECIÑA 2008 T
100% tempranillo

90 Color cherry, garnet rim. Aroma ripe fruit, spicy, creamy oak, toasty, complex. Taste powerful, flavourful, toasty, round tannins.

GRAN CHOBEO DE PECIÑA 2008 T
100% tempranillo

90 Colour: deep cherry. Nose: characterful, fruit preserve, spicy. Palate: fine bitter notes, spicy, ripe fruit.

SEÑORÍO DE P. PECIÑA 2001 TGR
95% tempranillo, 3% garnacha, 2% graciano

90 Color pale ruby, brick rim edge. Aroma elegant, spicy, fine reductive notes, wet leather, aged wood nuances, fruit liqueur notes. Taste spicy, fine tannins, elegant, long.

BODEGAS IZADI

Herrería Travesía II, 5
1307 Villabuena de Álava - (Álava)
☎: +34 945 609 086 - Fax: +34 945 609 261
club@grupoartevino.com
www.grupoartevino.com

IZADI 2008 TC
100% tempranillo

90 Colour: very deep cherry. Nose: ripe fruit, fruit expression, creamy oak, cocoa bean. Palate: flavourful, fruity, fresh, spicy, round tannins.

IZADI EL REGALO 2006 TR
90% tempranillo, 10% graciano, mazuelo, garnacha

91 Colour: cherry, garnet rim. Nose: creamy oak, dark chocolate, candied fruit, ripe fruit. Palate: spicy, ripe fruit, fine bitter notes.

BODEGAS LA EMPERATRIZ

Ctra. Santo Domingo - Haro, Km. 31,5
26241 Baños de Rioja - (La Rioja)
☎: +34 941 300 105 - Fax: +34 941 300 231
correo@bodegaslaemperatriz.com
www.bodegaslaemperatriz.com

FINCA LA EMPERATRIZ 2007 TR
90% tempranillo, 10% graciano, mazuelo, garnacha

91 Colour: deep cherry. Nose: creamy oak, spicy, cocoa bean, fruit expression. Palate: full, powerful, flavourful, complex.

FINCA LA EMPERATRIZ 2009 TC
95% tempranillo, 3% garnacha, 2% viura

94 Colour: dark-red cherry. Nose: complex, elegant, expressive, fruit expression, sweet spices, cocoa bean. Palate: powerful, flavourful, round, rich, full, toasty, fruity aftestaste.

FINCA LA EMPERATRIZ GARNACHA CEPAS VIEJAS 2010 T
garnacha

93 Colour: cherry, garnet rim. Nose: balanced, expressive, varietal, balsamic herbs, ripe fruit. Palate: good structure, full, round tannins.

FINCA LA EMPERATRIZ PARCELA Nº 1 2010 T
tempranillo

94 Colour: deep cherry. Nose: fruit expression, violet drops, fresh fruit, powerfull, varietal, complex. Palate: creamy, balsamic, complex, fruity.

FINCA LA EMPERATRIZ TERRUÑO 2009 T
tempranillo

94 Colour: cherry, garnet rim. Nose: red berry notes, ripe fruit, sweet spices, creamy oak, toasty. Palate: powerful, flavourful, balanced, toasty.

FINCA LA EMPERATRIZ VIURA 2011 B
viura

90 Colour: bright straw. Nose: fresh, fresh fruit, white flowers. Palate: flavourful, fruity, good acidity, balanced.

FINCA LA EMPERATRIZ VIURA CEPAS VIEJAS 2010 B
viura

92 Colour: bright yellow. Nose: varietal, powerfull, complex, smoky, scrubland. Palate: elegant, spirituous, sweetness, fresh, fruity.

BODEGAS LACUS

Cervantes, 18
26559 Aldeanueva de Ebro - (La Rioja)
☎: +34 649 331 799 - Fax: +34 941 144 128
inedito@bodegaslacus.com
www.bodegaslacus.com

INÉDITO 3/3 2010 T
50% tempranillo, 30% garnacha, 20% graciano

91 Colour: bright cherry. Nose: ripe fruit, sweet spices, creamy oak, fragrant herbs. Palate: flavourful, fruity, toasty, round tannins.

INÉDITO H12 2008 T
75% graciano, 25% garnacha

91 Colour: cherry, garnet rim. Nose: creamy oak, toasty, fruit expression. Palate: powerful, flavourful, toasty, round tannins.

INÉDITO S 2008 T
50% graciano, 40% tempranillo, 10% garnacha

90 Colour: cherry, garnet rim. Nose: spicy, creamy oak, toasty, characterful, ripe fruit. Palate: powerful, flavourful, toasty, round tannins.

BODEGAS LAGUNILLA

Ctra. de Elciego, s/n
26350 Cenicero - (La Rioja)
☎: +34 914 365 924 - Fax: +34 941 453 114
gromero@arcoinvest-group.com
www.berberana.com

LAGUNILLA OPTIMUS (MARQUÉS DE LA CONCORDIA FAMILY OF WINES) 2008 T
100% tempranillo

91 Colour: garnet rim. Nose: ripe fruit, balsamic herbs, aromatic coffee, creamy oak, toasty. Palate: spicy, powerful, flavourful, balanced, round tannins.

BODEGAS LANDALUCE

Ctra. Los Molinos, s/n
1300 Laguardia - (Álava)
☎: +34 620 824 314
asier@bodegaslandaluce.es
www.bodegaslandaluce.es

ELLE DE LANDALUCE 2011 B
60% viura, 40% malvasía

90 Colour: bright straw. Nose: floral, fragrant herbs, balanced, expressive, powerfull. Palate: rich, powerful, flavourful, sweetness, fresh, fruity.

FINCAS DE LANDALUCE 2008 TC
100% tempranillo

91 Colour: cherry, garnet rim. Nose: spicy, creamy oak, toasty, complex, balsamic herbs. Palate: powerful, flavourful, toasty, round tannins.

BODEGAS LAR DE PAULA

Coscojal, s/n
1309 Elvillar - (Álava)
☎: +34 945 604 068 - Fax: +34 945 604 105
info@lardepaula.com
www.lardepaula.com

4 BESOS TEMPRANILLO 2008 T
100% tempranillo

90 Colour: cherry, garnet rim. Nose: ripe fruit, spicy, creamy oak, toasty, red berry notes. Palate: powerful, flavourful, toasty, round tannins.

MERUS.4 2007 T
100% tempranillo

91 Colour: dark-red cherry, orangey edge. Nose: ripe fruit, spicy, creamy oak, fine reductive notes, balsamic herbs. Palate: long, powerful, flavourful.

BODEGAS LARRAZ

Paraje Ribarrey. Pol. 12- Parcela 50
26350 Cenicero - (La Rioja)
☎: +34 639 728 581
info@bodegaslarraz.com
www.bodegaslarraz.com

CAUDUM BODEGAS LARRAZ SELECCIÓN ESPECIAL 2009 T
tempranillo

91 Colour: cherry, garnet rim. Nose: spicy, creamy oak, toasty, expressive, ripe fruit. Palate: powerful, flavourful, toasty, round tannins.

BODEGAS LEZA GARCÍA

San Ignacio, 26
26313 Uruñuela - (La Rioja)
☎: +34 941 371 142 - Fax: +34 941 371 035
bodegasleza@bodegasleza.com
www.bodegasleza.com

LG DE LEZA GARCÍA 2009 T
100% tempranillo

91 Colour: cherry, garnet rim. Nose: ripe fruit, sweet spices, dark chocolate, balsamic herbs. Palate: good structure, flavourful, round tannins.

BODEGAS LOA

Camino de la Hoya, s/n
1300 Laguardia - (Alava)
☎: +34 954 975 375
casalbor@casalbor.es

LOA 2007 T
tempranillo

93 Colour: cherry, garnet rim. Nose: spicy, creamy oak, toasty, ripe fruit, mineral. Palate: powerful, flavourful, toasty, round tannins.

BODEGAS LOLI CASADO

Avda. La Poveda, 46
1306 Lapuebla de Labarca - (Álava)
☎: +34 945 607 096 - Fax: +34 945 607 412
loli@bodegaslolicasado.com
www.bodegaslolicasado.com

POLUS VIURA VENDIMIA TARDÍA 2011 B
100% viura

91 Colour: bright yellow. Nose: ripe fruit, wild herbs, candied fruit. Palate: sweet, fruity, powerful, flavourful, complex.

BODEGAS LUIS ALEGRE

Ctra. Navaridas, s/n
1300 Laguardia - (Álava)
☎: +34 945 600 089 - Fax: +34 945 600 729
luisalegre@bodegasluisalegre.com
www.luisalegre.com

FINCA LA REÑANA 2010 BFB
90% viura, 10% malvasía

90 Colour: bright yellow. Nose: powerfull, ripe fruit, sweet spices, creamy oak. Palate: rich, flavourful, fresh, good acidity.

GRAN VINO PONTAC 2008 T
95% tempranillo, 5% graciano

92 Colour: cherry, garnet rim. Nose: ripe fruit, spicy, creamy oak, cocoa bean, dark chocolate. Palate: powerful, flavourful, toasty, balanced.

KODEN DE LUIS ALEGRE 2010 T
100% tempranillo

91 Colour: cherry, garnet rim. Nose: spicy, creamy oak, toasty, ripe fruit. Palate: powerful, flavourful, toasty, round tannins.

LUIS ALEGRE PARCELA Nº 5 2008 TR
100% tempranillo

90 Colour: black cherry, garnet rim. Nose: creamy oak, dark chocolate, sweet spices, ripe fruit. Palate: flavourful, long, round tannins.

LUIS ALEGRE SELECCIÓN ESPECIAL 2008 TR
95% tempranillo, 5% graciano, mazuelo

90 Colour: dark-red cherry, garnet rim. Nose: ripe fruit, spicy, creamy oak, toasty, complex. Palate: powerful, flavourful, toasty, round tannins.

PONTAC DE PORTILES 2009 T
90% tempranillo, 10% garnacha

92 Colour: bright cherry, garnet rim. Nose: ripe fruit, sweet spices, creamy oak, expressive, earthy notes. Palate: flavourful, fruity, toasty, round tannins, balanced.

BODEGAS LUIS CAÑAS

Ctra. Samaniego, 10
1307 Villabuena - (Álava)
☎: +34 945 623 373 - Fax: +34 945 609 289
bodegas@luiscanas.com
www.luiscanas.com

HIRU 3 RACIMOS 2006 T
100% tempranillo

94 Colour: cherry, garnet rim. Nose: spicy, creamy oak, toasty, complex, earthy notes. Palate: powerful, flavourful, toasty, round tannins.

LUIS CAÑAS 2004 TGR
95% tempranillo, 5% graciano

93 Colour: bright cherry, garnet rim. Nose: spicy, expressive, fine reductive notes, fruit preserve. Palate: balanced, spicy, full.

LUIS CAÑAS 2005 TR
95% tempranillo, 5% graciano

90 Colour: bright cherry, garnet rim. Nose: complex, balanced, elegant, spicy. Palate: balanced, ripe fruit, spicy.

LUIS CAÑAS SELECCIÓN DE FAMILIA 2005 TR
85% tempranillo, 15% otras

91 Colour: cherry, garnet rim. Nose: spicy, creamy oak, toasty, characterful, fruit liqueur notes. Palate: powerful, flavourful, toasty, round tannins.

BODEGAS MARQUÉS DE VITORIA

Camino de Santa Lucía, s/n
1320 Oyón - (Álava)
☎: +34 945 622 134 - Fax: +34 945 601 496
info@bodegasmarquesdevitoria.es
www.marquesdevitoria.com

MARQUÉS DE VITORIA 2004 TGR
100% tempranillo

90 Colour: cherry, garnet rim. Nose: medium intensity, balanced, spicy, neat. Palate: fruity, spicy, good acidity, fine bitter notes.

MARQUÉS DE VITORIA 2005 TR
100% tempranillo

91 Colour: dark-red cherry. Nose: aromatic coffee, spicy, ripe fruit, fruit expression. Palate: full, powerful, flavourful, round, spicy, toasty.

MARQUÉS DE VITORIA 2009 TC
100% tempranillo

90 Colour: cherry, garnet rim. Nose: ripe fruit, balanced, dry stone, spicy, toasty. Palate: fruity, flavourful, creamy, balsamic.

BODEGAS MARTÍNEZ ALESANCO

José García, 20
26310 Badarán - (La Rioja)
☎: +34 941 367 075 - Fax: +34 941 367 075
info@bodegasmartinezalesanco.com
www.bodegasmartinezalesanco.com

NADA QUE VER 2008 TC
100% maturana

90 Colour: cherry, garnet rim. Nose: ripe fruit, scrubland, sweet spices. Palate: powerful, flavourful, balanced, long.

PEDRO MARTÍNEZ ALESANCO 2007 TR
90% tempranillo, 10% garnacha

90 Colour: deep cherry, garnet rim. Nose: balanced, fine reductive notes, ripe fruit, spicy. Palate: good structure, flavourful, long.

BODEGAS MARTÍNEZ CORTA

Ctra. Cenicero, s/n
20313 Uruñuela - (La Rioja)
☎: +34 670 937 520 - Fax: +34 941 374 368
enologia@bodegasmartinezcorta.com
www.bodegasmartinezcorta.com

SOROS 2007 T
100% tempranillo

90 Colour: cherry, garnet rim. Nose: ripe fruit, spicy, cocoa bean, creamy oak. Palate: powerful, flavourful, long, spicy.

BODEGAS MEDRANO IRAZU S.L.

San Pedro, 14
1309 Elvillar - (Álava)
☎: +34 945 604 066 - Fax: +34 945 604 126
amador@bodegasmedranoirazu.com
www.bodegasmedranoirazu.com

LUIS MEDRANO 2009 T
tempranillo

92 Colour: bright cherry, garnet rim. Nose: closed, ripe fruit, spicy. Palate: flavourful, good structure, ripe fruit, good acidity.

MAS DE MEDRANO 2009 T
tempranillo

90 Colour: cherry, garnet rim. Nose: ripe fruit, spicy, toasty, complex, mineral. Palate: powerful, flavourful, toasty, round tannins.

MEDRANO IRAZU RESERVA DE FAMILIA 2006 TR
tempranillo

90 Colour: cherry, garnet rim. Nose: ripe fruit, spicy, creamy oak, toasty, complex. Palate: powerful, flavourful, toasty, round tannins, balanced.

BODEGAS MENTOR

San Antón, 4-Entpta. dcha.
26002 Logroño - (La Rioja)
☎: +34 941 270 795 - Fax: +34 941 244 577
info@puertagotica.es
www.puertagotica.es

MENTOR 2005 TR
100% tempranillo

92 Colour: dark-red cherry, orangey edge. Nose: ripe fruit, wild herbs, spicy, fine reductive notes. Palate: powerful, flavourful, spicy, round tannins.

MENTOR 2007 TC

90 Colour: cherry, garnet rim. Nose: ripe fruit, spicy, creamy oak. Palate: powerful, flavourful, toasty, round tannins.

BODEGAS MITARTE

Avda. San Ginés, 15
1330 Labastida - (Álava)
☎: +34 945 331 069 - Fax: +34 945 331 069
bodegas@mitarte.com
www.mitarte.com

DE FAULA 2006 TR
100% tempranillo

90 Colour: cherry, garnet rim. Nose: ripe fruit, creamy oak, toasty, complex. Palate: powerful, flavourful, toasty, round tannins.

BODEGAS MUGA

Barrio de la Estación, s/n
26200 Haro - (La Rioja)
☎: +34 941 311 825 - Fax: +34 941 312 867
info@bodegasmuga.com
www.bodegasmuga.com

ARO 2006 T
70% tempranillo, 30% graciano

93 Colour: bright cherry. Nose: mineral, powerfull, varietal, characterful, ripe fruit, toasty. Palate: powerful, flavourful, spicy, ripe fruit.

MUGA 2008 TC
70% tempranillo, 20% garnacha, 10% mazuelo, graciano

92 Colour: cherry, garnet rim. Nose: spicy, balanced, medium intensity, ripe fruit. Palate: balanced, fine bitter notes, good acidity.

MUGA 2011 BFB
90% viura, 10% malvasía

91 Colour: bright yellow. Nose: balanced, expressive, ripe fruit, sweet spices. Palate: flavourful, rich, fruity, spicy, good acidity.

MUGA SELECCIÓN ESPECIAL 2006 TR
70% tempranillo, 20% garnacha, 10% mazuelo, graciano

91 Colour: deep cherry. Nose: roasted coffee, spicy, dark chocolate, ripe fruit, complex. Palate: sweetness, spirituous, powerful, flavourful, spicy.

PRADO ENEA 2005 TGR
80% tempranillo, 20% garnacha, mazuelo, graciano

94 Colour: cherry, garnet rim. Nose: complex, elegant, fine reductive notes, waxy notes, spicy. Palate: balanced, fine bitter notes, spicy, long.

TORRE MUGA 2006 T
75% tempranillo, 15% mazuelo, 10% graciano

93 Colour: deep cherry. Nose: cocoa bean, spicy, toasty, fruit expression, elegant, expressive, complex. Palate: long, spicy, round, elegant.

BODEGAS MURÚA

Ctra. Laguardia
1340 Elciego - (Álava)
☎: +34 945 606 260
info@bodegasmurua.com
www.bodegasmurua.com

MURÚA 2004 TR
90% tempranillo, 8% graciano, 2% mazuelo

90 Colour: bright cherry, orangey edge. Nose: balanced, neat, medium intensity, fine reductive notes. Palate: balanced, fine bitter notes, good acidity.

BODEGAS MUSEO ONTAÑÓN

Avda. de Aragón, 3
26006 Logroño - (La Rioja)
☎: +34 941 234 200 - Fax: +34 941 270 482
enoturismo@ontanon.es
www.ontanon.es

ARTESO 2008 TC
75% tempranillo, 15% graciano, 10% garnacha

92 Colour: cherry, garnet rim. Nose: red berry notes, ripe fruit, balsamic herbs, spicy, creamy oak. Palate: balanced, round, powerful, flavourful, round tannins.

COLECCIÓN MITOLÓGICA ONTAÑÓN 2004 TGR
95% tempranillo, 5% graciano

91 Colour: dark-red cherry, orangey edge. Nose: spicy, creamy oak, fruit liqueur notes, balsamic herbs, fine reductive notes. Palate: correct, balanced, flavourful, long.

ONTAÑÓN 2004 TGR
tempranillo, graciano

90 Colour: deep cherry, orangey edge. Nose: fruit preserve, creamy oak, sweet spices. Palate: flavourful, ripe fruit.

ONTAÑÓN 2005 TR
tempranillo, graciano

90 Color cherry, garnet rim. Aroma ripe fruit, spicy, creamy oak, toasty, complex. Taste powerful, flavourful, toasty, round tannins.

VETIVER 2010 B
100% viura

90 Colour: bright yellow. Nose: ripe fruit, fragrant herbs, white flowers, fine lees. Palate: powerful, rich, flavourful.

BODEGAS NAVAJAS

Camino Balgarauz, 2
26370 Navarrete - (La Rioja)
☎: +34 941 440 140 - Fax: +34 941 440 657
info@bodegasnavajas.com
www.bodegasnavajas.com

NAVAJAS 2004 TGR
85% tempranillo, 10% graciano, 5% mazuelo

91 Colour: dark-red cherry, orangey edge. Nose: fine reductive notes, tobacco, expressive, elegant, cocoa bean. Palate: round, full, rich, flavourful, toasty, soft tannins.

BODEGAS OBALO

Ctra. 232 A, Km. 26
26339 Abalos - (Rioja)
☎: +34 941 744 056
www.bodegaobalo.com

ALTINO 2009 TC
100% tempranillo

92 Colour: cherry, garnet rim. Nose: spicy, creamy oak, toasty, characterful. Palate: powerful, flavourful, toasty, round tannins.

OBALO 2007 TR
100% tempranillo

90 Colour: cherry, garnet rim. Nose: ripe fruit, spicy, toasty, complex. Palate: flavourful, toasty, round tannins, good structure.

OBALO 2009 TC
100% tempranillo

93 Colour: cherry, garnet rim. Nose: spicy, creamy oak, toasty, characterful, roasted coffee. Palate: powerful, flavourful, toasty, round tannins.

OBALO 2011 T
100% tempranillo

91 Colour: cherry, purple rim. Nose: expressive, red berry notes, floral, balsamic herbs, mineral, spicy. Palate: flavourful, fruity, good acidity, round tannins.

BODEGAS OLARRA

Avda. de Mendavia, 30
26009 Logroño - (La Rioja)
☎: +34 941 235 299 - Fax: +34 941 253 703
bodegasolarra@bodegasolarra.es
www.bodegasolarra.es

CERRO AÑÓN 2005 TR
80% tempranillo, mazuelo, graciano, garnacha

91 Colour: deep cherry. Nose: ripe fruit, undergrowth, spicy, creamy oak, toasty. Palate: round, powerful, flavourful, good structure, spicy, balsamic, ripe fruit, round tannins.

SUMMA 2006 TR
85% tempranillo, 10% graciano, 5% mazuelo

91 Colour: dark-red cherry. Nose: creamy oak, toasty, sweet spices, aromatic coffee, ripe fruit, elegant. Palate: balanced, round, powerful, flavourful.

BODEGAS ONDALÁN

Ctra. de Logroño, 22
1320 Oyón - Oion - (Álava)
☎: +34 945 622 537 - Fax: +34 945 622 538
ondalan@ondalan.es
www.ondalan.es

ONDALÁN TEMPRANILLO SELECCIÓN 2009 T
100% tempranillo

90 Color cherry, garnet rim. Aroma ripe fruit, spicy, creamy oak, toasty, complex. Taste powerful, flavourful, toasty, round tannins.

BODEGAS ONDARRE

Ctra. de Aras, s/n
31230 Viana - (Navarra)
☎: +34 948 645 300 - Fax: +34 948 646 002
bodegasondarre@bodegasondarre.es
www.bodegasondarre.es

MAYOR DE ONDARRE 2006 TR
88% tempranillo, 12% mazuelo

90 Colour: cherry, garnet rim. Nose: ripe fruit, spicy, creamy oak, toasty. Palate: powerful, flavourful, toasty, round tannins.

ONDARRE 2006 TR
85% tempranillo, 10% garnacha, 5% mazuelo

90 Colour: dark-red cherry. Nose: spicy, creamy oak, toasty, ripe fruit. Palate: soft tannins, elegant, round, flavourful, spicy, creamy.

BODEGAS ORBEN

Ctra. Laguardia, Km. 60
1300 Laguardia - (Álava)
☎: +34 945 609 086 - Fax: +34 945 609 261
club@grupoartevino.com
www.grupoartevino.com

MALPUESTO 2010 T
100% tempranillo

96 Colour: deep cherry, garnet rim. Nose: fruit preserve, creamy oak, sweet spices, new oak. Palate: flavourful, powerful, fine bitter notes, good acidity, ripe fruit, round tannins.

ORBEN 2007 T
97% tempranillo, 3% graciano

92 Colour: dark-red cherry. Nose: complex, elegant, toasty, creamy oak. Palate: spicy, creamy, toasty, ripe fruit.

BODEGAS OSTATU

Ctra. Vitoria, 1
1307 Samaniego - (Álava)
☎: +34 945 609 133 - Fax: +34 945 623 338
ostatu@ostatu.com
www.ostatu.com

GLORIA DE OSTATU 2006 T
100% tempranillo

94 Colour: very deep cherry, garnet rim. Nose: undergrowth, damp earth, fruit expression, cocoa bean, roasted coffee. Palate: complex, powerful, flavourful, round, reductive nuances.

OSTATU 2007 TR
tempranillo

93 Colour: cherry, garnet rim. Nose: ripe fruit, spicy, toasty, complex, earthy notes, new oak, aromatic coffee. Palate: powerful, flavourful, toasty, round tannins.

OSTATU 2009 TC
tempranillo, graciano, mazuelo, garnacha

91 Colour: cherry, purple rim. Nose: ripe fruit, balanced, sweet spices, fragrant herbs. Palate: good structure, flavourful, good acidity.

OSTATU 2011 B
viura, malvasía

90 Colour: bright straw, greenish rim. Nose: balanced, expressive, fresh fruit, citrus fruit. Palate: fruity, flavourful, good acidity.

OSTATU LADERAS DEL PORTILLO 2008 T
tempranillo, viura

90 Colour: cherry, garnet rim. Nose: ripe fruit, aromatic coffee, sweet spices, creamy oak, expressive. Palate: powerful, flavourful, toasty, balanced.

OSTATU SELECCIÓN 2008 T
tempranillo

91 Colour: cherry, garnet rim. Nose: ripe fruit, spicy, toasty, complex, earthy notes, new oak. Palate: powerful, flavourful, toasty, round tannins.

BODEGAS PACO GARCÍA

Crta. Ventas s/n
26143 Murillo de Rio Leza - (La Rioja)
☎: +34 941 432 372 - Fax: +34 941 432 156
info@bodegaspacogarcia.com
www.bodegaspacogarcia.com

BEAUTIFUL THINGS DE PACO GARCÍA 2008 T
90% tempranillo, 10% graciano

90 Colour: dark-red cherry. Nose: characterful, expressive, ripe fruit, sweet spices. Palate: powerful, flavourful, rich, fruity, complex.

PACO GARCÍA 2008 TC
90% tempranillo, 10% garnacha

91 Colour: cherry, garnet rim. Nose: spicy, creamy oak, toasty, ripe fruit. Palate: powerful, flavourful, toasty, round tannins.

PACO GARCÍA SEIS 2010 T
100% tempranillo

92 Colour: dark-red cherry. Nose: ripe fruit, expressive, powerfull, varietal, aromatic coffee. Palate: powerful, flavourful, fruity, sweetness, creamy.

BODEGAS PALACIO

San Lázaro, 1
1300 Laguardia - (Álava)
☎: +34 945 600 057 - Fax: +34 945 600 297
rrpp@bodegaspalacio.es
www.bodegaspalacio.es

COSME PALACIO 2007 TR
100% tempranillo

90 Colour: cherry, garnet rim. Nose: ripe fruit, earthy notes, balsamic herbs, fine reductive notes, sweet spices. Palate: powerful, flavourful, spicy, long.

GLORIOSO 2005 TGR
100% tempranillo

90 Colour: pale ruby, brick rim edge. Nose: spicy, fine reductive notes, wet leather, aged wood nuances, fruit liqueur notes. Palate: spicy, fine tannins, elegant, long.

GLORIOSO 2007 TR
100% tempranillo

91 Colour: dark-red cherry, orangey edge. Nose: aromatic coffee, cocoa bean, ripe fruit, fruit expression. Palate: round, elegant, balanced, powerful, flavourful, rich, creamy.

BODEGAS PALACIOS REMONDO

Avda. Zaragoza, 8
26540 Alfaro - (La Rioja)
☎: +34 941 180 207 - Fax: +34 941 181 628
info@palaciosremondo.com

LA MONTESA 2010 TC

92 Colour: cherry, garnet rim. Nose: spicy, creamy oak, toasty, characterful. Palate: powerful, flavourful, toasty, round tannins.

PLÁCET VALTOMELLOSO 2009 B

93 Colour: bright yellow. Nose: elegant, ripe fruit, wild herbs, dried flowers. Palate: flavourful, rich, fruity, good acidity.

PROPIEDAD VIÑAS TRADICIONALES 2010 T

93 Colour: cherry, garnet rim. Nose: spicy, creamy oak, toasty, complex, fruit preserve, violet drops. Palate: powerful, flavourful, toasty, round tannins.

BODEGAS PATERNINA

Avda. Santo Domingo, 11
26200 Haro - (La Rioja)
☎: +34 941 310 550 - Fax: +34 941 312 778
paternina@paternina.com
www.paternina.com

CONDES DE LOS ANDES 2007 TR
tempranillo, mazuelo, garnacha

90 Colour: cherry, garnet rim. Nose: ripe fruit, creamy oak, toasty, wet leather. Palate: powerful, flavourful, toasty, round tannins.

FEDERICO PATERNINA SELECCIÓN ESPECIAL 2009 T
tempranillo

90 Colour: light cherry. Nose: roasted coffee, spicy, characterful. Palate: fruity, powerful, harsh oak tannins, creamy, spicy.

BODEGAS PATROCINIO

Ctra. Cenicero
26313 Uruñuela - (La Rioja)
☎: +34 941 371 319 - Fax: +34 941 371 435
info@bodegaspatrocinio.com

LÁGRIMAS DE MARÍA 2009 TC
85% tempranillo, 15% graciano

90 Colour: cherry, garnet rim. Nose: ripe fruit, scrubland, aromatic coffee, spicy. Palate: correct, powerful, flavourful.

ZINIO 2011 B
100% viura

90 Colour: bright straw. Nose: balanced, medium intensity, floral, fragrant herbs. Palate: balanced, fine bitter notes, fruity.

ZINIO VENDIMIA SELECCIONADA 2009 TC
100% tempranillo

90 Colour: cherry, garnet rim. Nose: ripe fruit, toasty, spicy. Palate: spicy, ripe fruit, round tannins.

BODEGAS PERICA

Avda. de la Rioja, 59
26340 San Asensio - (La Rioja)
☎: +34 941 457 152 - Fax: +34 941 457 240
info@bodegasperica.com
www.bodegasperica.com

6 CEPAS 6 2011 T
100% tempranillo

90 Colour: cherry, purple rim. Nose: earthy notes, red berry notes, ripe fruit, balsamic herbs, spicy. Palate: powerful, flavourful, long, balanced.

OLAGOSA 2004 TGR
90% tempranillo, 5% garnacha, 5% mazuelo

90 Colour: deep cherry. Nose: aromatic coffee, characterful. Palate: flavourful, spirituous, long.

PERICA ORO RESERVA ESPECIAL 2006 TR
95% tempranillo, 5% graciano

90 Colour: deep cherry. Nose: powerfull, spicy, toasty, creamy oak. Palate: fine bitter notes, good acidity, toasty.

BODEGAS RAMÓN BILBAO

Avda. Santo Domingo, 34
26200 Haro - (La Rioja)
☎: +34 941 310 295 - Fax: +34 941 310 832
info@bodegasramonbilbao.es
www.bodegasramonbilbao.es

MIRTO DE RAMÓN BILBAO 2008 T
100% tempranillo

93 Colour: cherry, garnet rim. Nose: spicy, creamy oak, toasty, complex, earthy notes, mineral, ripe fruit. Palate: powerful, flavourful, toasty, round tannins.

RAMÓN BILBAO 2004 TGR
90% tempranillo, 5% mazuelo, 5% graciano

90 Colour: cherry, garnet rim. Nose: spicy, creamy oak, toasty, complex, wet leather. Palate: powerful, flavourful, toasty, round tannins.

RAMÓN BILBAO 2008 TR
90% tempranillo, 5% mazuelo, 5% graciano

90 Colour: bright cherry. Nose: ripe fruit, sweet spices, creamy oak, spicy. Palate: flavourful, fruity, toasty, round tannins.

RAMÓN BILBAO 2010 TC
100% tempranillo

90 Colour: cherry, garnet rim. Nose: spicy, creamy oak, toasty, characterful, ripe fruit. Palate: powerful, flavourful, toasty, round tannins.

RAMÓN BILBAO TEMPRANILLO EDICIÓN LIMITADA 2010 TC
100% tempranillo

92 Colour: cherry, garnet rim. Nose: spicy, creamy oak, toasty, ripe fruit, characterful, earthy notes. Palate: powerful, flavourful, toasty, round tannins.

RAMÓN BILBAO VIÑEDOS DE ALTURA 2010 TC
50% tempranillo, 50% garnacha

90 Colour: bright cherry. Nose: sweet spices, creamy oak, red berry notes. Palate: flavourful, fruity, toasty, round tannins.

BODEGAS REAL DIVISA

Divisa Real, s/n
26339 Abalos - (La Rioja)
☎: +34 941 258 133 - Fax: +34 941 258 155
realdivisa@fer.es
www.realdivisa.com

MARQUÉS DE LEGARDA 2001 TGR
91% tempranillo, 7% graciano, 2% mazuelo

90 Colour: pale ruby, brick rim edge. Nose: elegant, spicy, fine reductive notes, wet leather, aged wood nuances, fruit liqueur notes. Palate: spicy, fine tannins, elegant, long.

BODEGAS REGALÍA DE OLLAURI

Ctra. de Nájera, Km. 1
26220 Ollauri - (La Rioja)
☎: +34 941 338 373 - Fax: +34 941 338 374
info@bodegasregalia.es
www.bodegasregalia.es

MARQUÉS DE TERÁN SELECCIÓN ESPECIAL 2009 T
tempranillo

91 Color bright cherry. Aroma ripe fruit, sweet spices, creamy oak, expressive. Taste flavourful, fruity, toasty, round tannins.

OLLAMENDI 2007 T
tempranillo

91 Colour: cherry, garnet rim. Nose: ripe fruit, spicy, creamy oak, toasty, mineral. Palate: powerful, flavourful, toasty, round tannins.

BODEGAS REMÍREZ DE GANUZA

Constitución, 1
1307 Samaniego - (Álava)
☎: +34 945 609 022 - Fax: +34 945 623 335
cristina@remirezdeganuza.com
www.remirezdeganuza.com

ERRE PUNTO 2011 T MACERACIÓN CARBÓNICA
90% tempranillo, 5% graciano, 5% viura, malvasía

91 Colour: cherry, purple rim. Nose: floral, red berry notes, lactic notes, fresh, expressive. Palate: powerful, flavourful, fresh, fruity, good acidity, balanced.

FINCAS DE GANUZA 2005 TR
90% tempranillo, 10% graciano

92 Colour: cherry, garnet rim. Nose: spicy, creamy oak, fine reductive notes, balsamic herbs, sweet spices. Palate: powerful, flavourful, toasty, round tannins.

REMÍREZ DE GANUZA 2006 TR
90% tempranillo, 5% graciano, 5% viura, malvasía

95 Colour: dark-red cherry. Nose: undergrowth, damp earth, toasty, complex, balanced. Palate: mineral, creamy, spicy, powerful, flavourful.

TRASNOCHO 2007 T
tempranillo, 10% graciano

94 Colour: dark-red cherry. Nose: ripe fruit, fruit expression, expressive, powerfull, undergrowth, damp earth. Palate: powerful, flavourful, good structure.

VIÑA COQUETA 2007 TR
90% tempranillo, 5% graciano, 5% viura, malvasía

93 Colour: cherry, garnet rim. Nose: ripe fruit, spicy, creamy oak, fine reductive notes, sweet spices. Palate: powerful, flavourful, long, toasty.

BODEGAS RIOJANAS

Estación, 1 - 21
26350 Cenicero - (La Rioja)
☎: +34 941 454 050 - Fax: +34 941 454 529
bodega@bodegasriojanas.com
www.bodegasriojanas.com

GRAN ALBINA 2006 TR
34% tempranillo, 33% mazuelo, 33% graciano

90 Colour: cherry, garnet rim. Nose: spicy, creamy oak, toasty. Palate: powerful, flavourful, toasty, round tannins.

GRAN ALBINA VENDIMIA 2007 T
34% tempranillo, 33% mazuelo, 33% graciano

90 Colour: light cherry. Nose: fine reductive notes, expressive, creamy oak, toasty, ripe fruit. Palate: creamy, ripe fruit, flavourful, powerful, fruity.

MONTE REAL RESERVA DE FAMILIA 2006 TR
100% tempranillo

90 Colour: dark-red cherry, orangey edge. Nose: spicy, aged wood nuances, fruit preserve, dry nuts. Palate: round, powerful, flavourful, spirituous, spicy, smoky aftertaste, ripe fruit.

VIÑA ALBINA SELECCIÓN 2006 TR
80% tempranillo, 15% mazuelo, 5% graciano

90 Colour: cherry, garnet rim. Nose: creamy oak, toasty, spicy. Palate: powerful, flavourful, toasty, round tannins.

VIÑA ALBINA SEMIDULCE 2001 B RESERVA
90% viura, 10% malvasía

92 Colour: bright golden. Nose: candied fruit, creamy oak, toasty, sweet spices. Palate: flavourful, long, ripe fruit.

BODEGAS RODA

Avda. de Vizcaya, 5
26200 Haro - (La Rioja)
☎: +34 941 303 001 - Fax: +34 941 312 703
rodarioja@roda.es
www.roda.es

CIRSION 2009 T
tempranillo

96 Colour: cherry, garnet rim. Nose: ripe fruit, spicy, creamy oak, toasty, complex, earthy notes. Palate: powerful, flavourful, toasty, round tannins.

CIRSION 2010 T
tempranillo

95 Colour: cherry, purple rim. Nose: sweet spices, creamy oak, ripe fruit, red berry notes, mineral. Palate: flavourful, powerful, concentrated, spicy.

RODA 2007 TR
89% tempranillo, 8% garnacha, 3% graciano

93 Colour: dark-red cherry. Nose: complex, elegant, expressive, fruit expression. Palate: flavourful, powerful, spirituous, complex, roasted-coffee aftertaste, spicy.

RODA 2008 TR
90% tempranillo, 6% graciano, 4% garnacha

91 Colour: cherry, garnet rim. Nose: elegant, dark chocolate, sweet spices, ripe fruit. Palate: good structure, flavourful, round tannins.

RODA I 2007 TR
100% tempranillo

94 Colour: deep cherry. Nose: undergrowth, elegant, complex, fruit expression, toasty, aromatic coffee. Palate: round, elegant, flavourful, powerful, full, roasted-coffee aftertaste.

BODEGAS SANTALBA

Avda. de la Rioja, s/n
26221 Gimileo - (La Rioja)
☎: +34 941 304 231 - Fax: +34 941 304 326
santalba@santalba.com
www.santalba.com

ERMITA DE SAN FELICES 2007 TR
100% tempranillo

90 Colour: bright cherry. Nose: ripe fruit, sweet spices, creamy oak, dry stone. Palate: flavourful, fruity, round tannins.

SANTALBA ECOLÓGICO 2010 T
100% tempranillo

91 Colour: cherry, garnet rim. Nose: balanced, ripe fruit, sweet spices, varietal. Palate: good structure, flavourful, fresh.

SANTALBA SINGLE VINEYARD 2005 T
100% tempranillo

92 Colour: deep cherry, orangey edge. Nose: spicy, cocoa bean, mineral, scrubland. Palate: flavourful, long, round tannins.

BODEGAS SOLAR DE SAMANIEGO

Ctra. De Elciego s/n
1300 Laguardia - (Álava)
☎: +34 902 227 700 - Fax: +34 902 227 701
bodega@cofradiasamaniego.com
www.solardesamaniego.com

LA OLVIDADA 2009 T
100% tempranillo

93 Colour: cherry, garnet rim. Nose: ripe fruit, creamy oak, sweet spices, mineral, complex. Palate: powerful, flavourful, toasty, round tannins, balanced.

VALCAVADA 2006 TR
80% tempranillo, 20% graciano

90 Colour: cherry, garnet rim. Nose: spicy, dried herbs, tobacco. Palate: flavourful, good acidity, fine bitter notes.

BODEGAS SONSIERRA, S. COOP.

El Remedio, s/n
26338 San Vicente de la Sonsierra - (La Rioja)
☎: +34 941 334 031 - Fax: +34 941 334 245
sonsierra@sonsierra.com
www.sonsierra.com

PAGOS DE LA SONSIERRA 2008 TR
100% tempranillo

90 Colour: black cherry, garnet rim. Nose: ripe fruit, aromatic coffee, sweet spices, toasty. Palate: spicy, long, toasty, flavourful.

PERFUME DE SONSIERRA DAVID DELFÍN 2009 T
100% tempranillo

92 Colour: bright cherry. Nose: ripe fruit, creamy oak, toasty, complex, sweet spices. Palate: powerful, flavourful, round tannins.

SONSIERRA VENDIMIA SELECCIONADA 2009 TC
100% tempranillo

90 Colour: cherry, garnet rim. Nose: spicy, creamy oak, toasty, characterful. Palate: powerful, flavourful, toasty, round tannins.

BODEGAS TARÓN

Ctra. de Miranda, s/n
26211 Tirgo - (La Rioja)
☎: +34 941 301 650 - Fax: +34 941 301 817
info@bodegastaron.com
www.bodegastaron.com

TARÓN 2005 TR
85% tempranillo, 10% mazuelo, 5% graciano

90 Color cherry, garnet rim. Aroma ripe fruit, spicy, creamy oak, toasty, complex. Taste powerful, flavourful, toasty, round tannins.

TARÓN 4MB 2009 T
100% tempranillo

91 Colour: cherry, garnet rim. Nose: ripe fruit, sweet spices, violets, balanced. Palate: good structure, flavourful.

TARÓN VIÑAS VIEJAS 2010 TR
100% tempranillo

92 Colour: cherry, garnet rim. Nose: ripe fruit, spicy, creamy oak, toasty, complex, mineral. Palate: powerful, flavourful, toasty, round tannins.

BODEGAS TOBÍA

Paraje Senda Rutia, s/n
26214 Cuzcurrita de Río Tirón - (La Rioja)
☎: +34 941 301 789 - Fax: +34 941 328 045
tobia@bodegastobia.com
www.bodegastobia.com

DAIMON 2010 T
56% tempranillo, 22% graciano, 16% garnacha, 6% merlot

90 Colour: cherry, garnet rim. Nose: balanced, complex, ripe fruit, creamy oak, cocoa bean. Palate: flavourful, full, round tannins.

TOBÍA SELECCIÓN 2008 TC
80% tempranillo, 10% graciano, 10% garnacha

90 Colour: bright cherry. Nose: ripe fruit, spicy, creamy oak, cocoa bean. Palate: powerful, flavourful, toasty, round tannins.

BODEGAS VALDELACIERVA

Ctra. Burgos, Km. 13
26370 Navarrete - (La Rioja)
☎: +34 941 440 620 - Fax: +34 941 440 787
info@hispanobodegas.com
www.hispanobodegas.com

IMPAR VENDIMIA SELECCIONADA 2010 T
tempranillo

90 Colour: cherry, garnet rim. Nose: fruit expression, complex, elegant, varietal, cocoa bean. Palate: complex, fruity, powerful, flavourful, balsamic.

BODEGAS VALDELANA

Puente Barricuelo, 67-69
1340 Elciego - (Álava)
☎: +34 945 606 055 - Fax: +34 945 606 587
info@bodegasvaldelana.com
www.bodegasvaldelana.com

DUQUESA DE LA VICTORIA 2006 TR
95% tempranillo, 5% graciano

91 Colour: deep cherry, garnet rim. Nose: cocoa bean, sweet spices, ripe fruit. Palate: balanced, fine bitter notes, round tannins.

DUQUESA DE LA VICTORIA 2011 T
95% tempranillo, 5% viura

91 Colour: cherry, purple rim. Nose: red berry notes, balanced, expressive. Palate: fruity, flavourful, long.

LADRÓN DE GUEVARA DE AUTOR 2009 TC
95% tempranillo, 5% graciano

92 Colour: cherry, garnet rim. Nose: spicy, creamy oak, toasty. Palate: powerful, flavourful, toasty, round tannins.

VALDELANA 2006 TR
95% tempranillo, 5% graciano

90 Colour: deep cherry, garnet rim. Nose: creamy oak, toasty, ripe fruit. Palate: balanced, fine bitter notes, round tannins.

BODEGAS VALDEMAR

Camino Viejo, s/n
1320 Oyón - (Álava)
☎: +34 945 622 188 - Fax: +34 945 622 111
info@valdemar.es
www.valdemar.es

INSPIRACIÓN VALDEMAR EDICIÓN LIMITADA 2008 T
70% tempranillo, 20% experimental, 10% graciano

92 Colour: cherry, garnet rim. Nose: ripe fruit, spicy, creamy oak, toasty, mineral, characterful. Palate: powerful, flavourful, toasty, round tannins.

INSPIRACIÓN VALDEMAR GRACIANO 2005 T
100% graciano

90 Colour: cherry, garnet rim. Nose: scrubland, spicy, wet leather, cigar, earthy notes. Palate: flavourful, long, balanced, spicy.

INSPIRACIÓN VALDEMAR MATURANA 2008 T
92% maturana, 8% tempranillo

92 Colour: cherry, garnet rim. Nose: ripe fruit, spicy, creamy oak, toasty, characterful. Palate: powerful, flavourful, toasty, round tannins.

VALDEMAR TEMPRANILLO 2011 T
100% tempranillo

90 Color cherry, purple rim. Aroma expressive, fresh fruit, red berry notes, floral. Taste flavourful, fruity, good acidity, round tannins.

BODEGAS VINÍCOLA REAL

Ctra. Nalda, km. 9
26120 Albelda de Iregua - (La Rioja)
☎: +34 941 444 233 - Fax: +34 941 444 427
info@vinicolareal.com
www.vinicolareal.com

200 MONGES 2001 TGR
85% tempranillo, 10% graciano, 5% mazuelo

91 Colour: pale ruby, brick rim edge. Nose: elegant, spicy, fine reductive notes, wet leather, aged wood nuances. Palate: spicy, fine tannins, elegant, long.

200 MONGES SELECCIÓN ESPECIAL 2005 TR
100% tempranillo

92 Colour: dark-red cherry, orangey edge. Nose: ripe fruit, earthy notes, balsamic herbs, spicy, fine reductive notes. Palate: flavourful, long, spicy, round tannins.

BODEGAS VIÑA HERMINIA

Camino de los Agudos, 1
26559 Aldeanueva de Ebro - (La Rioja)
☎: +34 941 142 305 - Fax: +34 941 142 303
marketing@caballero.es
www.viñaherminia.es

VIÑA HERMINIA EXCELSUS 2010 T
50% garnacha, 50% tempranillo

91 Colour: cherry, garnet rim. Nose: ripe fruit, spicy, creamy oak, toasty. Palate: powerful, flavourful, toasty, round tannins.

BODEGAS Y VIÑAS SENDA GALIANA

Barrio Bodegas, s/n
26142 Villamediana - (La Rioja)
☎: +34 941 435 375 - Fax: +34 941 436 072
info@sendagaliana.com

SENDA GALIANA 2004 TGR
80% tempranillo, 10% graciano, 10% mazuelo

92 Color pale ruby, brick rim edge. Aroma elegant, spicy, fine reductive notes, wet leather, aged wood nuances, fruit liqueur notes. Taste spicy, fine tannins, elegant, long.

BODEGAS Y VIÑEDOS ALUÉN

Robledal, 18
26320 Baños de Río Tobia - (La Rioja)
☎: +34 607 166 152 - Fax: +34 941 374 851
info@bodegasaluen.com
www.bodegasaluen.com

ALUÉN + 2008 T
100% tempranillo

90 Colour: cherry, garnet rim. Nose: ripe fruit, creamy oak, fine reductive notes, scrubland. Palate: powerful, flavourful, toasty, balanced.

BODEGAS Y VIÑEDOS ALVAR

Camino de Ventosa, s/n
26371 Ventosa - (La Rioja)
☎: +34 941 441 905 - Fax: +34 941 441 917
alvar@bodegasalvar.com
www.bodegasalvar.com

LIVIUS GRACIANO 2007 T
100% graciano

91 Colour: bright cherry, garnet rim. Nose: sweet spices, creamy oak, ripe fruit, balsamic herbs. Palate: balanced; ripe fruit, long.

BODEGAS Y VIÑEDOS ARRANZ-ARGOTE

Mayor Alta, 43
26370 Navarrete - (La Rioja)
☎: +34 699 046 043
bodega@vinoarar.com
www.vinoarar.com

ARAR 2004 T
tempranillo, graciano, garnacha, mazuelo, maturana

90 Colour: cherry, garnet rim. Nose: ripe fruit, spicy, creamy oak, toasty, dark chocolate. Palate: powerful, flavourful, toasty, round tannins.

BODEGAS Y VIÑEDOS ARTADI

Ctra. de Logroño, s/n
1300 Laguardia - (Álava)
☎: +34 945 600 119 - Fax: +34 945 600 850
info@artadi.com
www.artadi.com

ARTADI EL CARRETIL 2010 T
100% tempranillo

98 Colour: cherry, purple rim. Nose: fruit expression, red berry notes, dry stone, creamy oak, sweet spices. Palate: flavourful, powerful, complex, spicy.

ARTADI LA POZA DE BALLESTEROS 2010 T
tempranillo

96 Colour: cherry, garnet rim. Nose: creamy oak, ripe fruit, fruit expression, red berry notes. Palate: flavourful, powerful, good acidity, fine bitter notes, round.

ARTADI PAGOS VIEJOS 2010 T
100% tempranillo

95 Colour: cherry, garnet rim. Nose: ripe fruit, powerfull, characterful, creamy oak. Palate: flavourful, powerful, fine bitter notes, good acidity, round tannins.

ARTADI VALDEGINÉS 2010 T
tempranillo

95 Colour: bright cherry. Nose: sweet spices, creamy oak, mineral, fruit expression, elegant. Palate: flavourful, fruity, toasty, fine tannins.

ARTADI VIÑAS DE GAIN 2010 T
100% tempranillo

92 Colour: bright cherry. Nose: sweet spices, creamy oak, red berry notes, ripe fruit. Palate: flavourful, fruity, toasty, round tannins.

VIÑA EL PISÓN 2010 T
100% tempranillo

96 Colour: cherry, purple rim. Nose: varietal, characterful, complex, ripe fruit, red berry notes, creamy oak. Palate: flavourful, fruity, good acidity, fine bitter notes.

BODEGAS Y VIÑEDOS PUENTE DEL EA

Camino Aguachal, s/n
26212 Sajazarra - (La Rioja)
☎: +34 941 320 405 - Fax: +34 941 320 406
puentedelea@gmail.com
www.puentedelea.com

ERIDANO CRIANZA PLATA 2008 TC
100% tempranillo

90 Colour: deep cherry. Nose: complex, expressive, ripe fruit, fruit expression, spicy, creamy oak. Palate: powerful, flavourful, complex.

ERIDANO SELECCIÓN 2009 T
90% tempranillo, 10% garnacha

90 Colour: cherry, garnet rim. Nose: smoky, aromatic coffee, elegant, fresh, complex, dry stone. Palate: round tannins, fruity, flavourful, powerful, balsamic.

PUENTE DEL EA 2011 BFB
90% viura, 10% chardonnay

90 Color bright yellow. Aroma powerfull, ripe fruit, sweet spices, creamy oak, fragrant herbs. Taste rich, smoky aftertaste, flavourful, fresh, good acidity.

PUENTE DEL EA AUTOR 2009 T
100% tempranillo

90 Color cherry, garnet rim. Aroma ripe fruit, spicy, creamy oak, toasty, complex. Taste powerful, flavourful, toasty, round tannins.

PUENTE DEL EA GARNACHA 2010 T
100% garnacha

91 Colour: cherry, garnet rim. Nose: ripe fruit, spicy, creamy oak, toasty, sweet spices. Palate: powerful, flavourful, toasty, round tannins.

PUENTE DEL EA GRACIANO 2010 T
100% graciano

92 Colour: cherry, garnet rim. Nose: complex, elegant, powerfull, varietal, ripe fruit, fruit expression. Palate: elegant, round, powerful, flavourful, spicy.

BODEGAS Y VIÑEDOS PUJANZA

Ctra. del Villar, s/n
1300 Laguardia - (Álava)
☎: +34 945 600 548 - Fax: +34 945 600 522
gerencia@bodegaspujanza.com
www.bodegaspujanza.com

PUJANZA 2009 T
100% tempranillo

93 Colour: cherry, garnet rim. Nose: mineral, ripe fruit, sweet spices. Palate: flavourful, fine bitter notes, good acidity, round tannins.

PUJANZA AÑADAS FRÍAS 2010 B
100% viura

92 Colour: bright straw. Nose: fresh fruit, citrus fruit, white flowers, mineral. Palate: flavourful, fruity, fresh, good acidity.

PUJANZA CISMA 2009 T
tempranillo

94 Colour: very deep cherry. Nose: red berry notes, fruit expression, scrubland, sweet spices, elegant. Palate: fine bitter notes, good acidity, ripe fruit.

PUJANZA HADO 2010 T
tempranillo

92 Colour: bright cherry. Nose: ripe fruit, sweet spices, creamy oak, expressive, mineral. Palate: flavourful, fruity, toasty, round tannins.

PUJANZA NORTE 2009 T
tempranillo

96 Colour: cherry, garnet rim. Nose: ripe fruit, spicy, creamy oak, toasty, powerfull. Palate: powerful, flavourful, toasty, round tannins.

BODEGAS Y VIÑEDOS VARAL

San Vicente, 40
1307 Baños de Ebro - (Álava)
☎: +34 945 623 321 - Fax: +34 945 623 321
bodegasvaral@bodegasvaral.com
www.bodegasvaral.com

CRIANZA DE VARAL 2008 T
100% tempranillo

90 Colour: deep cherry, garnet rim. Nose: sweet spices, red berry notes, ripe fruit. Palate: fruity, good acidity, flavourful.

ESENCIAS DE VARAL 2007 T
100% tempranillo

91 Colour: cherry, garnet rim. Nose: ripe fruit, spicy, creamy oak, toasty, complex. Palate: powerful, flavourful, toasty, round tannins, balanced.

VARAL VENDIMIA SELECCIONADA 2008 T
100% tempranillo

92 Colour: cherry, garnet rim. Nose: ripe fruit, sweet spices, aromatic coffee, earthy notes. Palate: powerful, flavourful, long, toasty, balanced.

BODEGAS Y VIÑEDOS ZUAZO GASTÓN

Las Norias, 2
1320 Oyón - (Álava)
☎: +34 945 601 526 - Fax: +34 945 622 917
zuazogaston@zuazogaston.com
www.zuazogaston.com

ZUAZO GASTÓN 2007 TR
100% tempranillo

90 Colour: light cherry, orangey edge. Nose: aromatic coffee, creamy oak, fruit expression, fresh fruit. Palate: powerful, flavourful, sweetness, spicy, creamy.

BODEGAS YSIOS

Camino de la Hoya, s/n
1300 Laguardia - (Álava)
☎: +34 945 600 640 - Fax: +34 945 600 520
ysios@pernod-ricard.com
www.ysios.com

YSIOS 2007 TR
100% tempranillo

92 Color cherry, garnet rim. Aroma ripe fruit, spicy, creamy oak, toasty, complex. Taste powerful, flavourful, toasty, round tannins.

YSIOS EDICIÓN LIMITADA 2007 TR
100% tempranillo

94 Colour: bright cherry, garnet rim. Nose: ripe fruit, mineral, spicy, cocoa bean, creamy oak. Palate: powerful, flavourful, long, balanced, elegant.

BODEGAS ZUGOBER

Tejerías, 13-15
1306 Lapuebla de Labarca - (Álava)
☎: +34 945 627 228 - Fax: +34 945 627 281
contacto@belezos.com
www.zugober.com

BELEZOS ECOLÓGICO 2010 T ROBLE
85% tempranillo, 15% graciano

90 Colour: cherry, garnet rim. Nose: balanced, powerfull, complex, cocoa bean. Palate: good structure, ripe fruit, spicy.

BELEZOS VENDIMIA SELECCIONADA 2008 T
90% tempranillo, 5% graciano

90 Colour: cherry, garnet rim. Nose: spicy, creamy oak, toasty, ripe fruit. Palate: powerful, flavourful, toasty, round tannins.

CARLOS SAN PEDRO PÉREZ DE VIÑASPRE

Páganos, 44- Bajo
1300 Laguardia - (Álava)
☎: +34 945 600 146 - Fax: +34 945 600 146
info@bodegascarlossampedro.com
www.bodegascarlossampedro.com

CARLOS SAN PEDRO 2009 T
tempranillo

90 Colour: cherry, garnet rim. Nose: ripe fruit, spicy, toasty, complex, fine reductive notes. Palate: powerful, flavourful, toasty, harsh oak tannins.

CASTILLO DE CUZCURRITA

San Sebastián, 1
26214 Cuzcurrita del Río Tirón - (La Rioja)
☎: +34 941 328 022 - Fax: +34 941 301 620
info@castillodecuzcurrita.com
www.castillodecuzcurrita.com

SEÑORÍO DE CUZCURRITA 2007 T
100% tempranillo

92 Colour: dark-red cherry. Nose: closed, spicy, aged wood nuances, fruit expression. Palate: creamy, mineral, flavourful, powerful.

COMPAÑÍA DE VINOS TELMO RODRÍGUEZ

El Monte
1308 Lanciego - (Álava)
☎: +34 945 628 315 - Fax: +34 945 628 314
contact@telmorodriguez.com
www.telmorodriguez.com

ALTOS DE LANZAGA 2008 T
tempranillo, garnacha, graciano

93 Colour: cherry, garnet rim. Nose: toasty, aromatic coffee, fruit liqueur notes, earthy notes. Palate: flavourful, fine bitter notes, good acidity, round tannins.

LANZAGA 2008 T
tempranillo, graciano, garnacha

90 Colour: cherry, garnet rim. Nose: spicy, aromatic coffee, toasty, ripe fruit. Palate: fine bitter notes, good acidity, round.

LZ 2011 T
tempranillo, garnacha, graciano

93 Colour: cherry, garnet rim. Nose: red berry notes, balsamic herbs, scrubland, spicy. Palate: flavourful, good acidity, fine bitter notes, fine tannins.

CREACIONES EXEO

Costanilla del Hospital s/n
1330 Labastida - (Álava)
☎: +34 649 940 040
carlos@bodegasexeo.com
www.bodegasexeo.com

CIFRAS 2010 B
100% garnacha blanca

91 Colour: bright straw, greenish rim. Nose: fresh fruit, citrus fruit, balanced, fine lees, wild herbs. Palate: rich, fruity, spicy, long.

CIFRAS 2010 T
100% garnacha

92 Colour: cherry, purple rim. Nose: red berry notes, raspberry, ripe fruit, powerfull, expressive, floral. Palate: powerful, flavourful, fruity, complex, long.

LETRAS 2008 T
100% tempranillo

94 Colour: cherry, garnet rim. Nose: red berry notes, ripe fruit, spicy, dark chocolate, cocoa bean, toasty, expressive, mineral. Palate: powerful, flavourful, toasty, balanced.

LETRAS MINÚSCULAS 2010 T
70% tempranillo, 30% garnacha

93 Colour: cherry, garnet rim. Nose: spicy, creamy oak, toasty, fruit expression, red berry notes. Palate: powerful, flavourful, toasty, round tannins.

CVNE - COMPAÑÍA VINÍCOLA DEL NORTE DE ESPAÑA

Barrio de la Estación, s/n
26200 Haro - (La Rioja)
☎: +34 941 304 800 - Fax: +34 941 304 815
marketing@cvne.com
www.cvne.com

CORONA SEMIDULCE 2010 B
85% viura, 15% garnacha blanca, malvasía

92 Colour: pale. Nose: floral, fresh fruit, fragrant herbs. Palate: sweet, good acidity, powerful, flavourful, fruity, fresh.

CUNE 2006 TGR
85% tempranillo, 10% graciano, 5% mazuelo

90 Colour: pale ruby, brick rim edge. Nose: spicy, wet leather, aged wood nuances, elegant. Palate: spicy, fine tannins, elegant, long.

CUNE 2008 TR
85% tempranillo, 15% mazuelo, graciano, garnacha

90 Colour: light cherry, orangey edge. Nose: ripe fruit, spicy, cedar wood, creamy oak. Palate: round, rich, flavourful, powerful.

CUNE WHITE 2011 B
100% viura

90 Colour: bright straw. Nose: fruit expression, fragrant herbs, smoky. Palate: sweetness, fruity, rich, flavourful.

IMPERIAL 2001 TGR
85% tempranillo, 10% graciano, 5% mazuelo

93 Colour: dark-red cherry. Nose: dark chocolate, old leather, waxy notes, tobacco. Palate: round, powerful, flavourful, spicy, reductive nuances.

IMPERIAL 2007 TR
85% tempranillo, 10% graciano, 5% mazuelo

93 Colour: dark-red cherry. Nose: damp earth, complex, expressive, cocoa bean, creamy oak, toasty. Palate: spicy, creamy, roasted-coffee aftertaste, ripe fruit.

REAL DE ASÚA 2005 T
100% tempranillo

93 Colour: very deep cherry. Nose: fine reductive notes, damp earth, undergrowth. Palate: round, complex, powerful, full, flavourful, sweet tannins.

DIEZ-CABALLERO

Barrihuelo, 53
1340 Elciego - (Álava)
☎: +34 944 807 295 - Fax: +34 944 630 938
diez-caballero@diez-caballero.es
www.diez-caballero.es

DÍEZ-CABALLERO VENDIMIA SELECCIONADA 2005 TR
100% tempranillo

90 Colour: cherry, garnet rim. Nose: spicy, creamy oak, toasty, characterful, fruit liqueur notes. Palate: powerful, flavourful, toasty, round tannins.

DÍEZ-CABALLERO VICTORIA 2010 T
100% tempranillo

92 Colour: cherry, garnet rim. Nose: spicy, creamy oak, toasty. Palate: powerful, flavourful, toasty, round tannins.

DIOS ARES

Ctra. de Navaridas s/n
1300 Laguardia - (Alava)
☎: +34 945 600 678 - Fax: +34 945 600 619
export@bodegasdiosares.com

ARES 2008 TR
tempranillo

90 Colour: very deep cherry. Nose: sweet spices, dark chocolate, aromatic coffee. Palate: flavourful, powerful, fine bitter notes.

ARES 2009 TC
tempranillo

92 Color bright cherry. Aroma ripe fruit, sweet spices, creamy oak, expressive. Taste flavourful, fruity, toasty, round tannins.

DOMINIO DE BERZAL

Término Río Salado, s/n
1307 Baños de Ebro - (Álava)
☎: +34 945 623 368 - Fax: +34 945 623 368
info@dominioberzal.com
www.dominioberzal.com

DOMINIO DE BERZAL SELECCIÓN PRIVADA 2009 T
tempranillo

90 Colour: cherry, garnet rim. Nose: spicy, creamy oak, toasty, ripe fruit. Palate: powerful, flavourful, toasty, round tannins.

DSG VINEYARDS

Ctra. Assa
1309 Elvillar - (Alava)
☎: +34 619 600 425
www.dsgvineyards.es

PHINCA ABEJERA 2008 T
tempranillo, graciano, garnacha, viura

94 Colour: light cherry, garnet rim. Nose: red berry notes, ripe fruit, balsamic herbs, sweet spices, creamy oak, expressive, mineral. Palate: flavourful, fresh, fruity, spicy, long, balanced.

PHINCAS 2008 T
tempranillo, mazuelo, garnacha, viura, graciano

90 Colour: cherry, garnet rim. Nose: ripe fruit, spicy, creamy oak, toasty. Palate: powerful, flavourful, toasty, long.

TERCAS 2009 BFB
viura, garnacha blanca, malvasía

90 Colour: bright yellow. Nose: powerfull, ripe fruit, sweet spices, creamy oak, fragrant herbs, roasted coffee. Palate: rich, flavourful, fresh, good acidity.

VUELTA DE TERCAS 2009 T
tempranillo, graciano, garnacha

91 Colour: cherry, garnet rim. Nose: red berry notes, ripe fruit, expressive, mineral, creamy oak, sweet spices, cocoa bean, dark chocolate. Palate: flavourful, fruity, good acidity, balanced, round tannins.

EL COTO DE RIOJA

Camino Viejo de Logroño, 26
1320 Oyón - (Álava)
☎: +34 945 622 216 - Fax: +34 945 622 315
cotorioja@elcoto.com
www.elcoto.com

COTO DE IMAZ 2001 TGR
100% tempranillo

90 Colour: dark-red cherry, brick rim edge. Nose: elegant, complex, fine reductive notes, spicy. Palate: soft tannins, round, full, good structure, flavourful, creamy, toasty.

COTO DE IMAZ 2005 TR
100% tempranillo

91 Colour: cherry, garnet rim. Nose: ripe fruit, spicy, creamy oak, toasty, wet leather. Palate: powerful, flavourful, toasty, round tannins.

COTO DE IMAZ SELECCIÓN ANIVERSARIO 2005 TR
100% tempranillo

90 Colour: dark-red cherry, orangey edge. Nose: spicy, creamy oak, toasty, balsamic herbs. Palate: good structure, flavourful, long.

COTO MAYOR 2008 TC
90% tempranillo, 10% graciano

90 Colour: cherry, garnet rim. Nose: ripe fruit, spicy, balanced. Palate: flavourful, fruity, easy to drink, spicy.

COTO REAL 2005 TR
80% tempranillo, 10% garnacha, 10% graciano

91 Colour: cherry, garnet rim. Nose: spicy, creamy oak, toasty, complex, fruit liqueur notes, balsamic herbs. Palate: powerful, flavourful, toasty, round tannins.

ELVIWINES

Finca "Clos Mesorah" Ctra. T-300 Falset Marça, Km. 1
43775 Marça Priorat - (Tarragona)
☎: +34 935 343 026 - Fax: +34 936 750 316
moises@elviwines.com
www.elviwines.com

HERENZA KOSHER ELVIWINES 2009 TC
100% tempranillo

92 Colour: bright cherry. Nose: sweet spices, creamy oak, red berry notes, fruit expression. Palate: flavourful, fruity, toasty, round tannins.

MATI KOSHER ELVIWINES 2010 T
100% tempranillo

90 Colour: cherry, garnet rim. Nose: floral, scrubland, grassy, lactic notes, complex, elegant, cocoa bean, spicy. Palate: creamy, fruity, full, light-bodied, flavourful, complex.

FINCA ALLENDE

Pza. Ibarra, 1
26330 Briones - (La Rioja)
☎: +34 941 322 301 - Fax: +34 941 322 302
info@finca-allende.com
www.finca-allende.com

ALLENDE 2008 T
100% tempranillo

92 Colour: dark-red cherry. Nose: cocoa bean, creamy oak, toasty, ripe fruit. Palate: round, elegant, full, flavourful, fine tannins.

ALLENDE 2009 B
90% viura, 10% malvasía

92 Colour: bright yellow. Nose: fresh fruit, fragrant herbs, dry stone, smoky. Palate: good acidity, fresh, fruity, sweetness, smoky aftertaste.

ALLENDE 2009 T
100% tempranillo

91 Colour: dark-red cherry. Nose: damp earth, complex, elegant, spicy, cocoa bean. Palate: creamy, powerful, flavourful, fruity, elegant.

ALLENDE 2010 B
90% viura, 10% malvasía

93 Colour: straw. Nose: faded flowers, wild herbs, powerfull, expressive, complex, fresh. Palate: flavourful, powerful, rich, fruity, complex, smoky aftertaste, sweetness, spirituous.

ALLENDE 2010 T
100% tempranillo

92 Colour: cherry, garnet rim. Nose: ripe fruit, spicy, creamy oak, toasty, varietal. Palate: powerful, flavourful, toasty, round tannins.

AVRVS 2008
85% tempranillo, 15% graciano

94 Colour: dark-red cherry. Nose: fruit preserve, fruit liqueur notes, powerfull, complex, spicy, sweet spices, creamy oak. Palate: spirituous, powerful, flavourful, round tannins.

AVRVS 2009 T
85% tempranillo, 15% graciano

96 Colour: deep cherry. Nose: damp earth, mineral, expressive, complex, closed, creamy oak, toasty. Palate: round, elegant, warm, spirituous, ripe fruit, round tannins.

CALVARIO 2008 T
90% tempranillo, 8% garnacha, 2% graciano

92 Colour: cherry, garnet rim. Nose: spicy, creamy oak, toasty, ripe fruit, earthy notes. Palate: powerful, flavourful, toasty, round tannins.

CALVARIO 2009 T
90% tempranillo, 8% garnacha, 2% graciano

94 Colour: cherry, garnet rim. Nose: ripe fruit, mineral, spicy, creamy oak, balsamic herbs, expressive. Palate: flavourful, long, round, spicy, balanced.

MÁRTIRES 2010 B
100% viura

97 Colour: bright yellow. Nose: complex, neat, expressive, ripe fruit, citrus fruit, white flowers, sweet spices. Palate: rich, flavourful, good structure, ripe fruit, good acidity.

MÁRTIRES 2011 B
100% viura

94 Colour: bright yellow. Nose: powerfull, ripe fruit, sweet spices, creamy oak. Palate: rich, smoky aftertaste, flavourful, fresh, good acidity.

FINCA DE LA RICA

Las Cocinillas, s/n
1330 Labastida - (Rioja)
☎: +34 941 509 406
info@fincadelarica.com
www.fincadelarica.com

EL NÓMADA 2009 T
tempranillo, graciano

90 Colour: cherry, garnet rim. Nose: ripe fruit, spicy, creamy oak, toasty, characterful, varietal, expressive. Palate: powerful, flavourful, toasty, round tannins.

FINCA DE LOS ARANDINOS

Ctra. LP 137, km. 4,6
26375 Entrena - (La Rioja)
☎: +34 941 446 065 - Fax: +34 941 446 256
bodega@fincadelosarandinos.com
www.fincadelosarandinos.com

FINCA DE LOS ARANDINOS 2009 TC
75% tempranillo, 20% garnacha, 5% mazuelo

91 Colour: bright cherry. Nose: ripe fruit, sweet spices, creamy oak. Palate: flavourful, fruity, toasty, round tannins.

VIERO SOBRE LÍAS 2010 BFB
100% viura

91 Colour: bright straw. Nose: expressive, complex, fresh fruit, fragrant herbs. Palate: fresh, fruity, light-bodied, powerful, flavourful, spirituous.

FINCA EGOMEI

Ctra. Corella, s/n
26240 Alfaro - (La Rioja)
☎: +34 948 780 006 - Fax: +34 948 780 515
info@egomei.es
www.bodegasab.com

EGOMEI ALMA 2007 T
75% tempranillo, 25% graciano

93 Colour: very deep cherry, garnet rim. Nose: elegant, wild herbs, ripe fruit, mineral. Palate: flavourful, good structure, round tannins.

FINCA NUEVA

Las Eras, 16
26330 Briones - (La Rioja)
☎: +34 941 322 301 - Fax: +34 941 322 302
info@fincanueva.com
www.fincanueva.com

FINCA NUEVA 2005 TR
100% tempranillo

90 Colour: cherry, garnet rim. Nose: ripe fruit, spicy, toasty, complex. Palate: powerful, flavourful, toasty, round tannins.

FINCA NUEVA 2007 TC
100% tempranillo

90 Color cherry, garnet rim. Aroma ripe fruit, spicy, creamy oak, toasty, complex. Taste powerful, flavourful, toasty, round tannins.

FINCA NUEVA 2007 TR
100% tempranillo

90 Colour: cherry, garnet rim. Nose: spicy, ripe fruit, balsamic herbs, old leather. Palate: flavourful, spicy, good acidity.

FINCA NUEVA 2010 BFB
100% viura

91 Colour: bright yellow. Nose: expressive, elegant, fruit expression, fragrant herbs. Palate: creamy, rich, fresh, fruity, powerful, full.

FINCA NUEVA TEMPRANILLO 2011 T
100% tempranillo

90 Colour: dark-red cherry. Nose: sweet spices, creamy oak, ripe fruit. Palate: fruity, powerful, flavourful, fresh.

FINCA VALPIEDRA

Término El Montecillo, s/n
26360 Fuenmayor - (La Rioja)
☎: +34 941 450 876 - Fax: +34 941 450 875
info@bujanda.com
www.familiamartinezbujanda.com

CANTOS DE VALPIEDRA 2009 T
100% tempranillo

92 Colour: cherry, garnet rim. Nose: mineral, fruit expression, elegant, sweet spices, creamy oak. Palate: balanced, fruity, easy to drink.

FINCA VALPIEDRA 2007 TR
92% tempranillo, 6% graciano, 2% maturana

91 Colour: pale ruby, brick rim edge. Nose: ripe fruit, spicy, toasty, complex, wet leather, cigar, dry stone. Palate: powerful, flavourful, toasty, round tannins.

GÓMEZ DE SEGURA

Barrio El Campillar
1300 Laguardia - (Álava)
☎: +34 615 929 828 - Fax: +34 945 600 227
info@gomezdesegura.com
www.gomezdesegura.com

GÓMEZ DE SEGURA VENDIMIA SELECCIONADA 2010 T
100% tempranillo

90 Colour: cherry, garnet rim. Nose: red berry notes, ripe fruit, toasty, sweet spices. Palate: flavourful, fruity, good acidity.

GRANJA NUESTRA SEÑORA DE REMELLURI

Ctra. Rivas de Tereso, s/n
1330 Labastida - (Álava)
☎: +34 945 331 801 - Fax: +34 945 331 802
info@remelluri.com
www.remelluri.com

LA GRANJA REMELLURI 2005 TGR
tempranillo, garnacha, graciano

93 Colour: cherry, garnet rim. Nose: spicy, creamy oak, toasty, overripe fruit, wet leather. Palate: powerful, flavourful, toasty, round tannins.

LINDES DE REMELLURI 2009 T
tempranillo, garnacha, graciano

94 Colour: cherry, garnet rim. Nose: fruit expression, ripe fruit, varietal, expressive, cocoa bean. Palate: powerful, flavourful, complex, balsamic, creamy.

REMELLURI 2007 TR
tempranillo, garnacha, graciano

93 Colour: cherry, garnet rim. Nose: ripe fruit, spicy, creamy oak, toasty. Palate: powerful, flavourful, toasty, round tannins.

GRUPO VINÍCOLA MARQUÉS DE VARGAS

Ctra. Zaragoza, Km. 6
26006 Logroño - (La Rioja)
☎: +34 941 261 401 - Fax: +34 941 238 696
bodega@marquesdevargas.com
www.marquesdevargas.com

MARQUÉS DE VARGAS 2007 TR
75% tempranillo, 10% mazuelo, 5% garnacha, 10% otras

91 Colour: deep cherry. Nose: spicy, aged wood nuances, fruit expression, damp earth, undergrowth. Palate: powerful tannins, flavourful, fruity, powerful, complex, toasty.

MARQUÉS DE VARGAS HACIENDA PRADOLAGAR 2005 TR
40% tempranillo, 10% mazuelo, 10% garnacha, 40% otras

94 Colour: deep cherry. Nose: cocoa bean, spicy, fruit expression, complex, fine reductive notes, damp earth. Palate: flavourful, powerful, round, toasty, roasted-coffee aftertaste, fine tannins.

MARQUÉS DE VARGAS RESERVA PRIVADA 2005 TR
60% tempranillo, 10% mazuelo, 10% garnacha, 20% otras

93 Colour: cherry, garnet rim. Nose: spicy, creamy oak, toasty, ripe fruit. Palate: powerful, flavourful, toasty, round tannins.

HACIENDA GRIMÓN

Gallera, 6
26131 Ventas Blancas - (La Rioja)
☎: +34 941 482 184 - Fax: +34 941 482 184
info@haciendagrimon.com
www.haciendagrimon.com

FINCA LA ORACIÓN 2010 T
100% tempranillo

92 Colour: cherry, garnet rim. Nose: ripe fruit, spicy, creamy oak, complex, earthy notes. Palate: powerful, flavourful, toasty, round tannins, long, balanced.

LABARONA 2007 TR
85% tempranillo, 15% graciano

90 Colour: cherry, garnet rim. Nose: spicy, creamy oak, toasty, dark chocolate. Palate: powerful, flavourful, toasty, round tannins.

HACIENDAS DE ESPAÑA

Ctra. El Ciego, s/n
26350 Cenicero - (La Rioja)
☎: +34 914 365 924
gromero@arcoinvest-group.com
www.haciendas-espana.com

HACIENDA SUSAR (MARQUÉS DE LA CONCORDIA FAMILY OF WINES) 2007 T
100% tempranillo

90 Colour: bright cherry. Nose: ripe fruit, sweet spices, creamy oak, expressive. Palate: flavourful, fruity, toasty, powerful.

HEREDAD UGARTE

Ctra. A-124, Km. 61
1309 Laguardia - (Álava)
☎: +34 945 282 844 - Fax: +34 945 271 319
info@heredadugarte.com
www.egurenugarte.com

ANASTASIO 2007 T
100% tempranillo

91 Colour: bright cherry. Nose: ripe fruit, sweet spices, creamy oak, expressive, cocoa bean, dark chocolate. Palate: flavourful, fruity, toasty, round tannins, round.

CEDULA REAL 2004 TGR
90% tempranillo, 10% mazuelo

90 Colour: pale ruby, brick rim edge. Nose: spicy, fine reductive notes, wet leather, aged wood nuances, fruit liqueur notes. Palate: spicy, fine tannins, long.

MARTÍN CENDOYA 2008 TR
80% tempranillo, 15% graciano, 5% mazuelo

90 Colour: deep cherry. Nose: ripe fruit, spicy, aromatic coffee, toasty. Palate: flavourful, powerful, fine bitter notes.

HERMANOS FRÍAS DEL VAL

Herrerías, 13
1307 Villabuena - (Álava)
☎: +34 945 609 172 - Fax: +34 945 609 172
info@friasdelval.com
www.friasdelval.com

DON PEDUZ 2011 T

90 Colour: cherry, purple rim. Nose: fresh fruit, red berry notes, floral. Palate: flavourful, fruity, good acidity, round tannins.

HERMANOS FRÍAS DEL VAL 2011
T MACERACIÓN CARBÓNICA

90 Colour: cherry, purple rim. Nose: balanced, fruit expression, violets, expressive. Palate: fruity, flavourful, good acidity.

JOSÉ BASOCO BASOCO

Ctra. de Samaniego, s/n
1307 Villabuena - (Álava)
☎: +34 945 331 619 - Fax: +34 945 331 619
info@fincabarronte.com

FINCA BARRONTE 2009 TC
85% tempranillo, 15% graciano

90 Colour: cherry, garnet rim. Nose: medium intensity, ripe fruit, powerfull, dark chocolate. Palate: flavourful, good structure, round tannins.

JUAN CARLOS SANCHA

C° de Las Barreras, s/n - Finca Fuentelacazuela
26320 Baños de Río Tobía - (La Rioja)
☎: +34 941 232 160 - Fax: +34 941 232 160
juancarlossancha@yahoo.es
www.juancarlossancha.com

AD LIBITUM MATURANA TINTA 2010 T
100% maturana

92 Colour: deep cherry. Nose: dark chocolate, spicy, toasty, macerated fruit, fruit expression. Palate: powerful, flavourful, varietal, good structure, powerful tannins.

PEÑA EL GATO GARNACHA 2010 T
100% garnacha

91 Colour: bright cherry. Nose: ripe fruit, sweet spices, creamy oak. Palate: flavourful, fruity, toasty, round tannins.

LA RIOJA ALTA

Avda. de Vizcaya, 8
26200 Haro - (La Rioja)
☎: +34 941 310 346 - Fax: +34 941 312 854
riojalta@riojalta.com
www.riojalta.com

GRAN RESERVA 904 RIOJA ALTA 2000 TGR
90% tempranillo, 10% graciano

93 Colour: pale ruby, brick rim edge. Nose: elegant, spicy, wet leather, aged wood nuances, fruit liqueur notes, cigar. Palate: spicy, fine tannins, elegant, long.

LA RIOJA ALTA GRAN RESERVA 890 1998 TGR
95% tempranillo, 3% graciano, 2% mazuelo

90 Colour: dark-red cherry, orangey edge. Nose: old leather, fruit preserve, spicy, reduction notes. Palate: spicy, good structure, classic aged character.

VIÑA ARANA 2005 TR
95% tempranillo, 5% mazuelo

92 Colour: bright cherry, orangey edge. Nose: elegant, ripe fruit, sweet spices, waxy notes. Palate: balanced, fine bitter notes, fine tannins.

VIÑA ARDANZA 2004 TR
80% tempranillo, 20% garnacha

93 Colour: deep cherry, orangey edge. Nose: fruit liqueur notes, spicy, cigar, old leather, balsamic herbs. Palate: balanced, fine tannins, long, spicy.

LAN

Paraje del Buicio, s/n
26360 Fuenmayor - (La Rioja)
☎: +34 941 450 950 - Fax: +34 941 450 567
info@bodegaslan.com
www.bodegaslan.com

CULMEN 2007 TR
tempranillo, graciano

93 Colour: deep cherry, garnet rim. Nose: balanced, spicy, fine reductive notes. Palate: flavourful, fruity, round tannins, balanced, good acidity.

LAN 2007 TR
90% tempranillo, 5% mazuelo, 5% graciano

90 Colour: cherry, garnet rim. Nose: spicy, creamy oak, toasty, candied fruit. Palate: powerful, flavourful, toasty, round tannins.

LAN A MANO 2008 T
tempranillo, graciano, mazuelo

93 Colour: deep cherry, garnet rim. Nose: complex, ripe fruit, spicy. Palate: good structure, flavourful, balanced, spicy, ripe fruit, round tannins, good acidity.

LAN D-12 2009 T
tempranillo

91 Colour: cherry, garnet rim. Nose: ripe fruit, spicy, creamy oak, toasty, complex. Palate: powerful, flavourful, toasty, round tannins, balanced.

LAUNA

Ctra. Vitoria-Logroño, Km. 57
1300 Laguardia - (Alava)
☎: +34 946 824 108 - Fax: +34 956 824 108
info@bodegaslauna.com
www.bodegaslauna.com

TEO'S 2008 T
100% tempranillo

90 Colour: cherry, garnet rim. Nose: medium intensity, ripe fruit, warm, balanced, sweet spices. Palate: good structure, flavourful, long.

TEO'S 2009 T
100% tempranillo

91 Colour: bright cherry. Nose: ripe fruit, sweet spices, creamy oak, dark chocolate, expressive, balanced. Palate: flavourful, fruity, toasty, round tannins, balanced.

LUBERRI MONJE AMESTOY

Camino de Rehoyos, s/n
1340 Elciego - (Álava)
☎: +34 945 606 010 - Fax: +34 945 606 482
luberri@luberri.com
www.luberri.com

BIGA DE LUBERRI 2005 TC
100% tempranillo

90 Color cherry, garnet rim. Aroma ripe fruit, spicy, creamy oak, toasty, complex. Taste powerful, flavourful, toasty, round tannins.

LUBERRI 2011 T MACERACIÓN CARBÓNICA
95% tempranillo, 5% viura

90 Colour: cherry, purple rim. Nose: neat, fruit expression, violets, expressive. Palate: fruity, easy to drink, balanced.

LUBERRI CEPAS VIEJAS 2006 TC
100% tempranillo

91 Colour: cherry, garnet rim. Nose: cigar, fruit liqueur notes, spicy, toasty, expressive. Palate: balanced, flavourful, spicy, long, elegant.

SEIS DE LUBERRI 2009 T
100% tempranillo

92 Colour: cherry, garnet rim. Nose: spicy, creamy oak, toasty, complex, citrus fruit, red berry notes. Palate: powerful, flavourful, toasty, round tannins.

MARQUÉS DE CÁCERES

Ctra. Logroño, s/n
26350 Cenicero - (La Rioja)
☎: +34 941 454 026 - Fax: +34 941 454 400
export@marquesdecaceres.com
www.marquesdecaceres.com

GAUDIUM GRAN VINO 2005 TR
95% tempranillo, 5% graciano

93 Colour: cherry, garnet rim. Nose: spicy, creamy oak, toasty, complex, earthy notes, ripe fruit. Palate: powerful, flavourful, toasty, round tannins.

MARQUÉS DE CÁCERES 2005 TGR
85% tempranillo, 15% garnacha, graciano

92 Colour: deep cherry. Nose: macerated fruit, fruit expression, powerfull, elegant, cocoa bean, spicy, toasty. Palate: round, full, flavourful, powerful, good structure, spicy, toasty.

MARQUÉS DE CÁCERES 2008 TR
85% tempranillo, 15% garnacha, graciano

92 Colour: cherry, garnet rim. Nose: medium intensity, balanced, neat, sweet spices, mineral. Palate: correct, elegant, balanced.

MARQUÉS DE CÁCERES 2009 TC
85% tempranillo, 15% garnacha, graciano

90 Colour: cherry, garnet rim. Nose: red berry notes, ripe fruit, balsamic herbs, spicy, toasty. Palate: powerful, flavourful, long, toasty.

MARQUÉS DE CÁCERES RESERVA ESPECIAL 2006 TR
85% tempranillo, 15% garnacha, graciano

91 Colour: cherry, garnet rim. Nose: ripe fruit, spicy, creamy oak, toasty, complex. Palate: powerful, flavourful, round tannins.

MC MARQUÉS DE CÁCERES 2010 T
100% tempranillo

93 Colour: cherry, garnet rim. Nose: ripe fruit, mineral, creamy oak, aromatic coffee, roasted coffee. Palate: elegant, powerful, flavourful, toasty.

MARQUÉS DE MURRIETA

Finca Ygay- Ctra. N-232 Logroño-Zaragoza, PK 403
26006 Logroño - (La Rioja)
☎: +34 941 271 374 - Fax: +34 941 251 606
rrpp@marquesdemurrieta.com
www.marquesdemurrieta.com

CAPELLANIA 2007 B
100% viura

91 Colour: bright yellow. Nose: sweet spices, cocoa bean, candied fruit, citrus fruit, fruit liqueur notes. Palate: sweetness, toasty, fine bitter notes, round.

CASTILLO YGAY 2001 TGR
93% tempranillo, 7% mazuelo

97 Color pale ruby, brick rim edge. Aroma elegant, spicy, fine reductive notes, wet leather, aged wood nuances, fruit liqueur notes. Taste spicy, fine tannins, elegant, long.

CASTILLO YGAY 2004 TGR
93% tempranillo, 7% mazuelo

95 Colour: cherry, garnet rim. Nose: toasty, spicy, candied fruit, wet leather. Palate: flavourful, spicy, ripe fruit, good acidity, fine tannins.

DALMAU 2007 TR
85% tempranillo, 8% cabernet sauvignon, 7% graciano

97 Colour: cherry, garnet rim. Nose: ripe fruit, spicy, creamy oak, toasty, characterful, earthy notes. Palate: powerful, flavourful, toasty, round tannins.

DALMAU 2009 TR
73% tempranillo, 13% cabernet sauvignon, 11% graciano

96 Colour: cherry, garnet rim. Nose: spicy, complex, toasty, ripe fruit, fruit expression. Palate: powerful, flavourful, toasty, round tannins.

MARQUÉS DE MURRIETA 2006 TR
88% tempranillo, 7% mazuelo, 3% garnacha, 2% graciano

91 Colour: cherry, garnet rim. Nose: candied fruit, medium intensity, aromatic coffee. Palate: flavourful, powerful, good acidity, fine bitter notes.

MARQUÉS DE MURRIETA 2007 TR
85% tempranillo, 8% garnacha, 6% mazuelo, 1% graciano

92 Colour: cherry, garnet rim. Nose: complex, powerfull, ripe fruit, creamy oak, sweet spices. Palate: flavourful, fine bitter notes, round, spicy, ripe fruit.

MARQUÉS DE ULÍA

Paraje del Buicio, s/n
26360 Fuenmayor - (La Rioja)
☎: +34 941 450 950 - Fax: +34 941 450 567
info@marquesdeulia.com
www.marquesdeulia.com

MARQUÉS DE ULÍA 2005 TR

91 Color cherry, garnet rim. Aroma ripe fruit, spicy, creamy oak, toasty, complex. Taste powerful, flavourful, toasty, round tannins.

MARQUÉS DE ULÍA 2008 TC
tempranillo

90 Colour: cherry, garnet rim. Nose: ripe fruit, spicy, tobacco. Palate: powerful, flavourful, toasty, round tannins, good acidity.

MARQUÉS DEL PUERTO

Ctra. de Logroño, s/n
26360 Fuenmayor - (La Rioja)
☎: +34 941 450 001 - Fax: +34 941 450 051
bmp@mbrizard.com
www.bodegamarquesdelpuerto.com

ROMÁN PALADINO 1995 TGR
88% tempranillo, 7% mazuelo, 5% graciano

90 Color pale ruby, brick rim edge. Aroma elegant, spicy, fine reductive notes, wet leather, aged wood nuances, fruit liqueur notes. Taste spicy, fine tannins, elegant, long.

MARTÍNEZ LACUESTA

Paraje de Ubieta, s/n
26200 Haro - (La Rioja)
☎: +34 941 310 050 - Fax: +34 941 303 748
bodega@martinezlacuesta.com
www.martinezlacuesta.com

MARTÍNEZ LACUESTA 2006 TR
85% tempranillo, 10% graciano, 5% mazuelo

90 Colour: deep cherry, orangey edge. Nose: ripe fruit, sweet spices, creamy oak, fine reductive notes. Palate: flavourful, balanced, long.

MIGUEL ÁNGEL MURO

Avda. Gasteiz, 29
1306 Lapuebla de Labarca - (Álava)
☎: +34 945 607 081 - Fax: +34 945 607 081
info@bodegasmiguelangelmuro.com
www.bodegasmuro.com

AMENITAL 2005 T
80% tempranillo, 20% graciano

90 Colour: cherry, garnet rim. Nose: ripe fruit, spicy, toasty. Palate: flavourful, toasty, spicy, good acidity.

AMENITAL 2009 TC

91 Colour: cherry, garnet rim. Nose: ripe fruit, creamy oak, toasty, mineral, sweet spices. Palate: powerful, flavourful, toasty, balanced.

MURO BUJANDA 2008 TC
100% tempranillo

90 Colour: cherry, garnet rim. Nose: ripe fruit, spicy, creamy oak, complex. Palate: powerful, flavourful, round tannins.

MIRAVINOS

Plaza de Matute 12, - 3º
28012 - (Madrid)
☎: +34 609 119 248
info@miravinos.es
www.miravinos.es

CATAURO 2009 T
tempranillo

90 Colour: very deep cherry. Nose: powerfull, ripe fruit, toasty, dark chocolate, earthy notes. Palate: flavourful, powerful, fine bitter notes, round tannins.

MONTECILLO

Ctra. Navarrete-Fuenmayor, Km. 2
26360 Fuenmayor - (La Rioja)
☎: +34 925 860 990 - Fax: +34 925 860 905
carolina.cerrato@osborne.es
www.osborne.es

CUMBRE MONTECILLO 2006 TR
85% tempranillo, 15% graciano

91 Colour: cherry, garnet rim. Nose: ripe fruit, spicy, creamy oak, toasty. Palate: powerful, flavourful, toasty, round tannins.

MONTECILLO 2005 TGR
100% tempranillo

90 Colour: dark-red cherry, brick rim edge. Nose: sweet spices, toasty, ripe fruit, old leather, fine reductive notes. Palate: powerful, flavourful, spicy, classic aged character.

VIÑA MONTY 2006 TR
100% tempranillo

91 Colour: dark-red cherry, orangey edge. Nose: fine reductive notes, ripe fruit, undergrowth, sweet spices. Palate: round, flavourful, powerful, spicy, toasty, ripe fruit.

VIÑA MONTY 2009 TC
100% tempranillo

90 Colour: dark-red cherry, orangey edge. Nose: spicy, cedar wood, fruit expression. Palate: balsamic, ripe fruit, flavourful, powerful.

OLIVIER RIVIÈRE VINOS

Pepe Blanco, 6 1C
26140 Lardero - (La Rioja)
☎: +34 690 733 541 - Fax: +34 941 452 476
olive_riviere@yahoo.fr

ALTO REDONDO 2010 T
garnacha

95 Colour: cherry, garnet rim. Nose: ripe fruit, fruit expression, grassy, sweet spices, balsamic herbs. Palate: flavourful, fruity, fresh, fine tannins, long.

BASQUEVANAS 2010 B BARRICA
100% albillo

92 Colour: bright golden. Nose: spicy, candied fruit, citrus fruit. Palate: flavourful, fine bitter notes, good acidity, round.

EL QUEMADO 2009 T

92 Colour: cherry, garnet rim. Nose: ripe fruit, spicy, creamy oak, toasty, complex. Palate: powerful, flavourful, toasty, grainy tannins.

GABACHO 2010 T
graciano

90 Colour: very deep cherry. Nose: creamy oak, overripe fruit, balsamic herbs. Palate: flavourful, fruity, good acidity.

GANKO 2009 T
tempranillo, garnacha, mazuelo, graciano

94 Colour: cherry, garnet rim. Nose: characterful, elegant, red berry notes, balsamic herbs, grassy, sweet spices, mineral. Palate: flavourful, fruity, fresh, spicy, fine bitter notes.

GANKO 2010 T
100% garnacha

94 Colour: deep cherry. Nose: red berry notes, fruit expression, grassy. Palate: flavourful, good acidity, fine bitter notes, fine tannins.

JEQUITIBÁ 2010 B
viura, malvasía, garnacha blanca

91 Colour: bright straw. Nose: fresh, fresh fruit, white flowers. Palate: flavourful, fruity, good acidity, balanced.

RAYOS UVA 2011 T
50% tempranillo, 50% graciano

90 Colour: cherry, purple rim. Nose: fresh fruit, red berry notes, floral, earthy notes, scrubland. Palate: flavourful, fruity, good acidity, round tannins.

VIÑAS DEL CADASTRO 2009 T

90 Colour: bright cherry. Nose: sweet spices, creamy oak, fruit expression. Palate: flavourful, fruity, toasty, round tannins.

PAGO DE LARREA

Ctra. Elciego-Cenicero, Km. 1,2
1340 Elciego - (Álava)
☎: +34 945 606 063 - Fax: +34 945 606 697
bodega@pagodelarrea.com
www.pagodelarrea.com

8 DE CAECUS 2008 T
100% tempranillo

90 Colour: cherry, garnet rim. Nose: spicy, creamy oak, toasty, fruit expression. Palate: powerful, flavourful, toasty, round tannins.

PAGOS DE LEZA

Ctra. A-124 Logroño Vitoria
1309 Leza - (Álava)
☎: +34 945 621 212 - Fax: +34 945 621 222
pagosdeleza@pagosdeleza.com
www.pagosdeleza.com

ANGEL SANTAMARÍA VENDIMIA SELECCIONADA 2005 TR

90 Colour: pale ruby, brick rim edge. Nose: elegant, spicy, fine reductive notes, aged wood nuances, toasty. Palate: spicy, elegant, long, flavourful, good structure.

PAISAJES Y VIÑEDOS

Pza. Ibarra, 1
26330 Briones - (La Rioja)
☎: +34 941 322 301 - Fax: +34 941 322 302
comunicacio@vilaviniteca.es

PAISAJES CECIAS 2009 T
garnacha

90 Colour: very deep cherry. Nose: sweet spices, fruit preserve, scrubland. Palate: flavourful, ripe fruit, fine bitter notes, good acidity.

PAISAJES VALSALADO 2009 T
tempranillo, garnacha, graciano, mazuelo

92 Colour: bright cherry. Nose: ripe fruit, sweet spices, creamy oak, balsamic herbs, scrubland. Palate: flavourful, fruity, toasty, round tannins.

PAISAJES VIII LA PASADA 2009 T
tempranillo

92 Colour: cherry, garnet rim. Nose: spicy, creamy oak, toasty, characterful, scrubland. Palate: powerful, flavourful, toasty, round tannins.

QUIROGA DE PABLO

Antonio Pérez, 24
26323 Azofra - (La Rioja)
☎: +34 606 042 478 - Fax: +34 941 379 334
info@bodegasquiroga.es
www.bodegasquiroga.es

HEREDAD DE JUDIMA 2007 TR
100% tempranillo

90 Colour: cherry, garnet rim. Nose: ripe fruit, spicy, toasty, balsamic herbs. Palate: powerful, flavourful, toasty, round tannins.

HEREDAD DE JUDIMA 2009 TC
tempranillo

90 Colour: cherry, garnet rim. Nose: powerfull, creamy oak, new oak, ripe fruit. Palate: long, spicy, powerful, flavourful.

R. LÓPEZ DE HEREDIA VIÑA TONDONIA

Avda. Vizcaya, 3
26200 Haro - (La Rioja)
☎: +34 941 310 244 - Fax: +34 941 310 788
bodega@lopezdeheredia.com
www.tondonia.com

VIÑA TONDONIA 1993 B RESERVA

92 Colour: bright golden. Nose: ripe fruit, dry nuts, powerfull, toasty, aged wood nuances, sweet spices, expressive. Palate: flavourful, fruity, spicy, toasty, long, elegant.

VIÑA TONDONIA 2001 TR

90 Colour: pale ruby, brick rim edge. Nose: spicy, fine reductive notes, aged wood nuances, fruit liqueur notes, varnish. Palate: spicy, fine tannins, elegant, long.

RIOJA VEGA

Ctra. Logroño-Mendavia, Km. 92
31230 Viana - (Navarra)
☎: +34 948 646 263 - Fax: +34 948 645 612
info@riojavega.com
www.riojavega.com

RIOJA VEGA 130 ANIVERSARIO 2006 TR
75% tempranillo, 20% graciano, 5% mazuelo

90 Colour: cherry, garnet rim. Nose: spicy, smoky, old leather, cigar, balsamic herbs. Palate: flavourful, long, correct.

RIOJA VEGA EDICIÓN LIMITADA 2009 TC
90% tempranillo, 10% graciano

90 Colour: cherry, garnet rim. Nose: balanced, complex, expressive, ripe fruit. Palate: fruity, easy to drink, good acidity.

RODRÍGUEZ SANZO

Manuel Azaña, 9
47014 - (Valladolid)
☎: +34 983 150 150 - Fax: +34 983 150 151
comunicacion@valsanzo.com
www.rodriguezsanzo.com

LA SENOBA 2008 T
tempranillo

92 Colour: cherry, garnet rim. Nose: ripe fruit, spicy, creamy oak, toasty, fruit expression, characterful. Palate: powerful, flavourful, toasty, round tannins.

LACRIMUS 2009 TC
85% tempranillo, 15% graciano

90 Colour: deep cherry. Nose: sweet spices, ripe fruit, earthy notes, spicy. Palate: fine bitter notes, long, sweet tannins, balanced.

SEÑORÍO DE SAN VICENTE

Los Remedios, 27
26338 San Vicente de la Sonsierra - (La Rioja)
☎: +34 941 334 080 - Fax: +34 941 334 371
info@eguren.com
www.eguren.com

SAN VICENTE 2008 T
100% tempranillo

96 Colour: cherry, garnet rim. Nose: ripe fruit, spicy, creamy oak, toasty, characterful. Palate: powerful, flavourful, toasty, round tannins, good acidity, round.

SAN VICENTE 2009 T
100% tempranillo

95 Colour: very deep cherry. Nose: ripe fruit, dry nuts, red berry notes, toasty, sweet spices. Palate: spicy, ripe fruit, good acidity, fine bitter notes, round tannins.

SIERRA CANTABRIA

Amorebieta, 3
26338 San Vicente de la Sonsierra - (La Rioja)
☎: +34 941 334 080 - Fax: +34 941 334 371
info@eguren.com
www.eguren.com

AMANCIO 2008 T
100% tempranillo

96 Colour: cherry, garnet rim. Nose: spicy, characterful, fruit expression, red berry notes, new oak. Palate: powerful, flavourful, toasty, round tannins.

AMANCIO 2009 T
100% tempranillo

94 Colour: cherry, garnet rim. Nose: ripe fruit, spicy, creamy oak, dark chocolate. Palate: powerful, flavourful, toasty, round tannins, good acidity.

FINCA EL BOSQUE 2009 T
100% tempranillo

95 Colour: cherry, garnet rim. Nose: spicy, creamy oak, toasty, complex, earthy notes, ripe fruit, raspberry. Palate: powerful, flavourful, toasty, round tannins.

FINCA EL BOSQUE 2010 T
100% tempranillo

96 Colour: very deep cherry. Nose: fruit expression, raspberry, ripe fruit, toasty, creamy oak, sweet spices, mineral. Palate: flavourful, powerful, fine bitter notes, round tannins, good acidity.

SIERRA CANTABRIA 2004 TGR
100% tempranillo

94 Colour: deep cherry. Nose: elegant, spicy, toasty, ripe fruit. Palate: flavourful, spicy, fine bitter notes.

SIERRA CANTABRIA 2008 TC
tempranillo

91 Colour: cherry, garnet rim. Nose: creamy oak, toasty, characterful, fruit expression. Palate: powerful, flavourful, toasty, long.

SIERRA CANTABRIA 2011 RD
tempranillo, garnacha, viura

90 Colour: brilliant rose. Nose: white flowers, red berry notes, citrus fruit. Palate: flavourful, fruity, fresh, good acidity.

SIERRA CANTABRIA COLECCIÓN PRIVADA 2009 T
100% tempranillo

95 Colour: cherry, garnet rim. Nose: ripe fruit, spicy, creamy oak, toasty, complex, characterful, mineral. Palate: powerful, flavourful, toasty, round tannins.

SIERRA CANTABRIA COLECCIÓN PRIVADA 2010 T
100% tempranillo

96 Colour: bright cherry. Nose: sweet spices, creamy oak, expressive, red berry notes. Palate: flavourful, fruity, toasty, round tannins.

SIERRA CANTABRIA CUVÈE ESPECIAL 2008 T
100% tempranillo

92 Colour: deep cherry. Nose: ripe fruit, fruit expression, creamy oak. Palate: flavourful, powerful, spicy, ripe fruit, roasted-coffee aftertaste.

SIERRA CANTABRIA ORGANZA 2010 B
viura, malvasía, garnacha blanca

93 Colour: bright yellow. Nose: powerfull, sweet spices, creamy oak, fragrant herbs, mineral, fruit expression. Palate: rich, flavourful, fresh, good acidity.

SIERRA CANTABRIA ORGANZA 2011 B
viura, malvasía, garnacha blanca

92 Colour: bright straw. Nose: scrubland, lactic notes, ripe fruit, citrus fruit. Palate: round, good acidity, fine bitter notes.

TIERRA ANTIGUA

Urb. Monje Vigilia, 7
26120 Albelda de Iregua - (La Rioja)
☎: +34 941 444 223 - Fax: +34 941 444 427
info@tierrantigua.com
www.tierrantigua.com

TIERRA ANTIGUA 2005 TR
85% tempranillo, 15% graciano, garnacha

92 Colour: cherry, garnet rim. Nose: ripe fruit, spicy, creamy oak, toasty, complex, mineral. Palate: powerful, flavourful, toasty, round tannins, balanced.

TOBELOS BODEGAS Y VIÑEDOS

Ctra. N 124, Km. 45
26290 Briñas - (La Rioja)
☎: +34 941 305 630 - Fax: +34 941 313 028
tobelos@tobelos.com
www.tobelos.com

TAHÓN DE TOBELOS 2008 TR
100% tempranillo

91 Colour: cherry, garnet rim. Nose: ripe fruit, spicy, creamy oak, toasty, characterful. Palate: powerful, flavourful, toasty, round tannins.

TOBELOS TEMPRANILLO 2008 T
100% tempranillo

90 Color cherry, garnet rim. Aroma ripe fruit, spicy, creamy oak, toasty, complex. Taste powerful, flavourful, toasty, round tannins.

TORRE DE OÑA

Finca San Martín
1309 Páganos - (Álava)
☎: +34 945 621 154 - Fax: +34 945 621 154
info@torredeona.com
www.torredeona.com

FINCA SAN MARTÍN 2009 T
90% tempranillo, 10% graciano

90 Colour: cherry, garnet rim. Nose: sweet spices, creamy oak, ripe fruit. Palate: flavourful, powerful, fine bitter notes, good acidity.

TORRE DE OÑA 2008 TR
97% tempranillo, 3% graciano

92 Colour: bright cherry, garnet rim. Nose: ripe fruit, cocoa bean, creamy oak. Palate: good structure, flavourful, round tannins, good acidity.

VIÑA IJALBA

Ctra. Pamplona, Km. 1
26006 Logroño - (La Rioja)
☎: +34 941 261 100 - Fax: +34 941 261 128
vinaijalba@ijalba.com
www.ijalba.com

DIONISIO RUIZ IJALBA 2010 T
maturana

90 Colour: cherry, garnet rim. Nose: red berry notes, ripe fruit, citrus fruit, fragrant herbs, spicy. Palate: powerful, flavourful, spicy.

IJALBA MATURANA 2011 B
100% maturana blanca

91 Colour: bright yellow. Nose: floral, fresh fruit, fragrant herbs. Palate: powerful, flavourful, fruity, fresh, sweetness, full.

IJALBA SELECCIÓN ESPECIAL 2005 TR
50% graciano, 50% tempranillo

91 Colour: cherry, garnet rim. Nose: spicy, ripe fruit, candied fruit, tobacco. Palate: balanced, correct, fine bitter notes.

VIÑA REAL

Ctra. Logroño - Laguardia, Km. 4,8
1300 Laguardia - (Álava)
☎: +34 945 625 255 - Fax: +34 945 625 211
marketing@cvne.com
www.cvne.com

VIÑA REAL 2005 TGR
95% tempranillo, 5% graciano

92 Colour: dark-red cherry. Nose: spicy, creamy oak, fine reductive notes, damp earth, undergrowth. Palate: fine tannins, powerful, flavourful, round, full, rich, elegant.

VIÑA REAL 2006 TR
90% tempranillo, 10% graciano, garnacha, mazuelo

92 Colour: deep cherry. Nose: cocoa bean, spicy, fruit expression, expressive, old leather, tobacco. Palate: round, balanced, flavourful, good structure, spicy, creamy, long.

VIÑA REAL 2010 TC
90% tempranillo, 10% garnacha, mazuelo, graciano

92 Colour: bright cherry, garnet rim. Nose: balanced, expressive, medium intensity, ripe fruit. Palate: flavourful, round tannins.

VIÑA SALCEDA

Ctra. Cenicero, Km. 3
1340 Elciego - (Álava)
☎: +34 945 606 125
info@vinasalceda.com
www.vinasalceda.com

CONDE DE LA SALCEDA 2007 TR
tempranillo

93 Colour: cherry, garnet rim. Nose: ripe fruit, spicy, creamy oak, characterful. Palate: powerful, flavourful, toasty, powerful tannins, mineral, long.

PUENTE DE SALCEDA 2009 T
tempranillo

91 Colour: cherry, garnet rim. Nose: spicy, creamy oak, toasty, red berry notes, ripe fruit. Palate: powerful, flavourful, toasty, round tannins.

VIÑASPRAL

Camino Del Soto s/n
1309 Elvillar - (Álava)
☎: - Fax: +34 628 132 151
info@maisulan.com
www.maisulan.com

HONORATUS AURUM 2008 B
100% viura

91 Colour: bright golden. Nose: ripe fruit, powerfull, toasty, aged wood nuances, sweet spices. Palate: flavourful, fruity, spicy, toasty, long.

HONORATUS FRUCTUS VENDIMIA SELECCIONADA 2009 T
85% tempranillo, 10% graciano, 5% garnacha

92 Colour: cherry, garnet rim. Nose: red berry notes, ripe fruit, balsamic herbs, creamy oak, toasty. Palate: powerful, flavourful, correct, elegant.

MAISULAN SELECCIÓN 2010 T
100% tempranillo

91 Colour: cherry, garnet rim. Nose: spicy, creamy oak, toasty, characterful. Palate: powerful, flavourful, toasty, round tannins.

VIÑEDOS DE ALDEANUEVA S. COOP.

Avda. Juan Carlos I, 100
26559 Aldeanueva de Ebro - (La Rioja)
☎: +34 941 163 039 - Fax: +34 941 163 585
va@aldeanueva.com
www.aldeanueva.com

CULTO 2007 T
60% graciano, 40% tempranillo

90 Colour: cherry, garnet rim. Nose: ripe fruit, spicy, creamy oak, toasty, characterful. Palate: powerful, flavourful, toasty, round tannins.

VIÑEDOS DE ALFARO

Camino de los Agudos s/n
26559 Aldeanueva de Ebro - (La Rioja)
☎: +34 941 142 389 - Fax: +34 941 142 386
info@vinedosdealfaro.com
www.vinedosdealfaro.com

RODILES VENDIMIA SELECCIONADA 2005 T
100% graciano

92 Colour: very deep cherry, garnet rim. Nose: dark chocolate, tobacco, fruit preserve, balsamic herbs. Palate: balanced, fine bitter notes, spicy, good acidity.

VIÑEDOS DE PÁGANOS

Ctra. Navaridas, s/n
1309 Páganos - (Álava)
☎: +34 945 600 590 - Fax: +34 945 600 885
info@eguren.com
www.eguren.com

EL PUNTIDO 2008 T
100% tempranillo

94 Colour: cherry, garnet rim. Nose: ripe fruit, spicy, creamy oak, mineral, toasty. Palate: powerful, flavourful, toasty, round tannins, good acidity, fine bitter notes.

EL PUNTIDO 2009 T
100% tempranillo

95 Colour: cherry, garnet rim. Nose: ripe fruit, spicy, creamy oak, characterful. Palate: powerful, flavourful, toasty, powerful tannins, mineral.

LA NIETA 2009 T
100% tempranillo

95 Colour: bright cherry. Nose: ripe fruit, creamy oak, expressive, mineral, toasty, cocoa bean. Palate: flavourful, fruity, toasty, round tannins, round, spicy.

LA NIETA 2010 T
100% tempranillo

96 Colour: cherry, garnet rim. Nose: spicy, complex, red berry notes, fruit expression, new oak, sweet spices, dry stone. Palate: powerful, flavourful, toasty, round tannins, good acidity.

VIÑEDOS DEL CONTINO

Finca San Rafael, s/n
1321 Laserna - (Álava)
☎: +34 945 600 201 - Fax: +34 945 621 114
laserna@contino.es
www.cvne.com

CONTINO 2005 TGR
70% tempranillo, 15% garnacha, 15% graciano

93 Colour: cherry, garnet rim. Nose: ripe fruit, spicy, creamy oak, toasty, complex, wet leather. Palate: powerful, flavourful, toasty, round tannins.

CONTINO 2007 TR
85% tempranillo, 10% graciano, 5% mazuelo, garnacha

92 Colour: dark-red cherry. Nose: powerfull, expressive, complex, spicy, fruit expression. Palate: powerful, flavourful, complex, spicy, balsamic, toasty.

CONTINO 2008 TR
85% tempranillo, 10% graciano, mazuelo, garnacha

90 Colour: cherry, garnet rim. Nose: elegant, ripe fruit, dark chocolate, spicy. Palate: flavourful, good acidity, balanced.

CONTINO 2010 B
70% viura, 20% garnacha blanca, 10% malvasía

91 Colour: bright straw. Nose: white flowers, fragrant herbs, fine lees, fresh, expressive. Palate: fruity, fresh, complex, elegant.

CONTINO GARNACHA 2009 T
100% garnacha

92 Colour: cherry, garnet rim. Nose: ripe fruit, spicy, creamy oak, toasty, scrubland. Palate: powerful, flavourful, toasty, round tannins.

CONTINO GRACIANO 2007 T
100% graciano

93 Colour: cherry, garnet rim. Nose: ripe fruit, spicy, toasty, complex, earthy notes, scrubland. Palate: powerful, flavourful, toasty, round tannins, balsamic.

CONTINO GRACIANO 2009 T
100% graciano

91 Colour: cherry, garnet rim. Nose: spicy, creamy oak, toasty, complex, ripe fruit, red berry notes. Palate: powerful, flavourful, toasty, round tannins.

CONTINO VIÑA DEL OLIVO 2008 T
88% tempranillo, 12% graciano

93 Colour: deep cherry, garnet rim. Nose: sweet spices, cocoa bean, creamy oak, ripe fruit, complex. Palate: good structure, flavourful, round tannins, good acidity.

CONTINO VIÑA DEL OLIVO 2009 T
90% tempranillo, 10% graciano

93 Colour: cherry, garnet rim. Nose: ripe fruit, spicy, toasty, complex, fruit expression. Palate: powerful, flavourful, toasty, round tannins.

VIÑEDOS DEL TERNERO

Finca El Ternero
9200 Miranda de Ebro - (Burgos)
☎: +34 941 320 021 - Fax: +34 941 302 719
ana@vinedosdelternero.com
www.vinedosdelternero.com

HACIENDA TERNERO 2011 BFB
100% viura

90 Colour: bright yellow. Nose: powerfull, ripe fruit, sweet spices, creamy oak, fragrant herbs. Palate: rich, flavourful, fresh, good acidity.

MIRANDA 2007 TC
95% tempranillo, 5% mazuelo

90 Colour: cherry, garnet rim. Nose: ripe fruit, spicy, creamy oak, toasty, complex. Palate: powerful, flavourful, toasty, round tannins, balanced.

PICEA 650 2008 T
95% tempranillo, 5% mazuelo

93 Colour: bright cherry. Nose: ripe fruit, sweet spices, creamy oak, expressive, mineral, toasty. Palate: flavourful, fruity, toasty, round tannins, balanced, elegant.

VIÑEDOS Y BODEGAS DE LA MARQUESA - VALSERRANO

Herrería, 76
1307 Villabuena - (Álava)
☎: +34 945 609 085 - Fax: +34 945 623 304
info@valserrano.com
www.valserrano.com

FINCA MONTEVIEJO 2007 T
95% tempranillo, garnacha, 5% graciano

92 Colour: cherry, garnet rim. Nose: balanced, ripe fruit, sweet spices, earthy notes. Palate: good structure, flavourful, full, long, fine bitter notes, good acidity.

VALSERRANO 2000 B GRAN RESERVA
95% viura, 5% malvasía

93 Color bright golden. Aroma ripe fruit, dry nuts, powerfull, toasty, aged wood nuances. Taste flavourful, fruity, spicy, toasty, long.

VALSERRANO 2007 TR
90% tempranillo, 10% graciano

90 Colour: cherry, garnet rim. Nose: sweet spices, creamy oak, cocoa bean, ripe fruit. Palate: good structure, flavourful, ripe fruit, long.

VALSERRANO GARNACHA 2009 T
100% garnacha

91 Colour: cherry, garnet rim. Nose: spicy, toasty, ripe fruit, sweet spices. Palate: powerful, flavourful, toasty, round tannins.

VALSERRANO MAZUELO 2008 T
100% mazuelo

90 Colour: cherry, garnet rim. Nose: ripe fruit, spicy, balsamic herbs, tobacco, fine reductive notes. Palate: long, powerful, flavourful, balanced.

WINNER WINES

Avda. del Mediterráneo, 38
28007 Madrid - (Madrid)
☎: +34 915 019 042 - Fax: +34 915 017 794
winnerwines@ibernoble.com
www.ibernoble.com

VIÑA SASETA 2005 TR
90% tempranillo, 5% graciano, 5% mazuelo

90 Colour: cherry, garnet rim. Nose: spicy, ripe fruit, balanced. Palate: balanced, good acidity, round tannins.

DESCRIPTION

This is situated in the provinces of Valladolid, Segovia and Ávila. The character of Rueda is defined by three components: the verdejo grape, which is native to the area, the continental climate and the gravelly soils. The white wines of this variety evoke fennel, are fruity and with a high level of acidity. It is one of the more commercially attractive wines in the world and in Spain.

NUMBER OF HECTARES: 11.739 **ALTITUDES:** 600 m. – 700 m.

PREDOMINANT VARIETIES:

White grapes: verdejo, viura, sauvignon blanc and palomino fino.
Red grapes: tempranillo, cabernet sauvignon, merlot and garnacha.

CLIMATOLOGY AND SOILS

The climatology is continental, the soils are normally stony on the surface, well aired and drained. Loam predominates in the texture of the soils.

AGRÍCOLA CASTELLANA. BODEGA CUATRO RAYAS

Ctra. Rodilana, s/n
47491 La Seca - (Valladolid)
☎: +34 983 816 320 - Fax: +34 983 816 562
info@cuatrorayas.org
www.cuatrorayas.org

CUATRO RAYAS VERDEJO 2011 B
100% verdejo

90 Colour: bright straw. Nose: fresh, fresh fruit, white flowers. Palate: flavourful, fruity, good acidity, balanced.

CUATRO RAYAS VIÑEDOS CENTENARIOS 2011 B
100% verdejo

92 Colour: bright straw. Nose: fresh, white flowers, expressive, mineral, grassy. Palate: flavourful, fruity, good acidity, balanced.

AGRÍCOLA SANZ, S.L.

Ctra. Madrid - Coruña, km. 170
47490 Rueda - (Valladolid)
☎: +34 983 804 132

ANTONIO SANZ 2011 B
100% verdejo

92 Colour: bright straw. Nose: fresh, fresh fruit, white flowers, mineral. Palate: flavourful, fruity, good acidity, balanced.

ÁNGEL RODRÍGUEZ VIDAL

Torcido, 1
47491 La Seca - (Valladolid)
☎: +34 983 816 302 - Fax: +34 983 816 302
martinsancho@martinsancho.com

MARTÍNSANCHO VERDEJO 2011 B
100% verdejo

90 Color bright straw. Aroma fresh, fresh fruit, white flowers, expressive. Taste flavourful, fruity, good acidity, balanced.

AURA (DOMECQ BODEGAS)

Autovía del Noroeste, Km. 175
47490 Rueda - (Valladolid)
☎: +34 983 868 286 - Fax: +34 983 868 168
mcarreir@domecqbodegas.com
www.domecqbodegas.com

AURA SAUVIGNON BLANC 2011 B
100% sauvignon blanc

90 Colour: bright straw. Nose: fresh, fresh fruit, white flowers, grassy. Palate: flavourful, fruity, good acidity, balanced.

AVELINO VEGAS

Real del Pino, 36
40460 Santiuste - (Segovia)
☎: +34 921 596 002 - Fax: +34 921 596 035
ana@avelinovegas.com
www.avelinovegas.com

CIRCE 2011 B
verdejo

90 Colour: bright straw. Nose: fresh, fresh fruit, white flowers, expressive. Palate: flavourful, fruity, good acidity, sweetness.

MONTESPINA SAUVIGNON 2011 B JOVEN
sauvignon blanc

90 Colour: bright straw. Nose: fresh, white flowers, balanced, citrus fruit. Palate: flavourful, fruity, good acidity, balanced.

MONTESPINA VERDEJO 2011 B JOVEN
verdejo

90 Colour: bright straw. Nose: fresh, fresh fruit, white flowers, expressive, fine lees. Palate: flavourful, fruity, good acidity, balanced.

BELLORIVINOS

Cobalto, 37
47012 - (Valladolid)
☎: +34 619 708 546
juan.ortega@syngenta.com

BELLORI 2010 BFB
100% verdejo

94 Colour: bright yellow. Nose: powerfull, ripe fruit, creamy oak, fragrant herbs, dried flowers. Palate: rich, flavourful, fresh, good acidity, balanced.

BELLORI 2011 B
100% verdejo

90 Colour: bright straw. Nose: white flowers, fragrant herbs, ripe fruit, expressive, varietal. Palate: powerful, flavourful, long, balanced.

BELONDRADE

Quinta San Diego - Camino del Puerto, s/n
47491 La Seca - (Valladolid)
☎: +34 983 481 001 - Fax: +34 600 590 024
info@belondrade.com
www.belondrade.com

BELONDRADE Y LURTON 2010 BFB
verdejo

95 Colour: bright yellow. Nose: powerfull, ripe fruit, sweet spices, creamy oak, fragrant herbs. Palate: rich, flavourful, fresh, good acidity.

BODEGA EL ALBAR LURTON

Camino Magarin, s/n
47529 Villafranca del Duero - (Valladolid)
☎: +34 983 034 030 - Fax: +34 983 034 040
bodega@francoislurton.es
www.francoislurton.es

HERMANOS LURTON CUESTA DE ORO 2009 BFB
100% verdejo

93 Colour: bright yellow. Nose: powerfull, ripe fruit, sweet spices, creamy oak, fragrant herbs, expressive. Palate: rich, flavourful, fresh, good acidity, balanced.

HERMANOS LURTON SAUVIGNON BLANC 2011 B
100% sauvignon blanc

90 Colour: bright straw. Nose: white flowers, fresh fruit, herbaceous, fragrant herbs, elegant. Palate: fresh, fruity, flavourful, balanced.

BODEGA EMINA MEDINA DEL CAMPO

Ctra. Medina del Campo - Olmedo, Km. 1,5
47400 Medina del Campo - (Valladolid)
☎: +34 983 800 001 - Fax: +34 902 430 189
eminarueda@emina.es
www.eminarueda.es

EMINA PRESTIGIO VERDEJO 2011 B
100% verdejo

91 Colour: bright straw. Nose: fresh, fresh fruit, white flowers, expressive, varietal, grassy. Palate: flavourful, fruity, good acidity, balanced.

SELECCIÓN PERSONAL CARLOS MORO
EMINA VERDEJO 2009 B
100% verdejo

93 Colour: bright yellow. Nose: powerfull, ripe fruit, fragrant herbs, pattiserie, toasty. Palate: rich, smoky aftertaste, flavourful, fresh, good acidity.

BODEGA GÓTICA

Ctra. Rueda - La Seca, Km. 1,2
47490 Rueda - (Valladolid)
☎: +34 629 458 235 - Fax: +34 983 868 387
mjhmonsalve@ya.com
www.bodegagotica.com

MONSALVE VERDEJO 2011 B
100% verdejo

91 Colour: bright straw. Nose: fresh, white flowers, expressive, ripe fruit, citrus fruit. Palate: flavourful, fruity, good acidity, fine bitter notes.

TRASCAMPANAS VERDEJO 2011 B
100% verdejo

90 Colour: bright straw. Nose: white flowers, expressive, varietal, fresh fruit, wild herbs. Palate: flavourful, fruity, good acidity, balanced.

BODEGA HERMANOS DEL VILLAR

Zarcillo, s/n
47490 Rueda - (Valladolid)
☎: +34 983 868 904 - Fax: +34 983 868 905
info@orodecastilla.com
www.orodecastilla.com

ORO DE CASTILLA VERDEJO 2011 B
100% verdejo

90 Colour: bright straw. Nose: fresh, white flowers, ripe fruit. Palate: flavourful, fruity, good acidity, balanced.

BODEGA LA SOTERRAÑA

Ctra. Valladolid - Madrid N-601, Km. 151
47410 Olmedo - (Valladolid)
☎: +34 983 601 026 - Fax: +34 983 601 026
info@bodegaslasoterrana.com
www.bodegaslasoterrana.com

ERESMA 2009 BFB
100% verdejo

90 Colour: bright straw. Nose: faded flowers, ripe fruit, fragrant herbs, sweet spices, creamy oak. Palate: flavourful, spicy, long.

ERESMA VERDEJO 2011 B
100% verdejo

90 Colour: bright straw. Nose: fresh, white flowers, ripe fruit, grassy. Palate: flavourful, fruity, good acidity, balanced.

BODEGA MONTE BLANCO

Avda. Colón, 146
30205 Cartagena - (murcia)
☎: +34 941 310 295 - Fax: +34 941 310 832
info@bodegas-monteblanco.es
www.bodegas-monteblanco.es

MONTE BLANCO DE RAMÓN
BILBAO VERDEJO 2011 B
100% verdejo

91 Colour: bright straw. Nose: fresh, fresh fruit, white flowers, tropical fruit. Palate: flavourful, fruity, good acidity, balanced.

BODEGA PALACIO DE BORNOS

Ctra. Madrid - Coruña, km. 170,6
47490 Rueda - (Valladolid)
☎: +34 983 868 116 - Fax: +34 983 868 432
info@taninia.com
www.palaciodeborno.com

PALACIO DE BORNOS VERDEJO VENDIMIA SELECCIONADA 2010 BFB
verdejo

92 Colour: bright yellow. Nose: powerfull, ripe fruit, sweet spices, creamy oak. Palate: rich, smoky aftertaste, flavourful, fresh, good acidity.

PALACIOS DE BORNOS LA CAPRICHOSA 2010 B
verdejo

90 Colour: bright straw. Nose: fresh, white flowers, expressive, varietal, mineral. Palate: flavourful, fruity, good acidity, balanced.

PALACIOS DE BORNOS VERDEJO 2010 BFB
verdejo

90 Colour: bright yellow. Nose: powerfull, ripe fruit, sweet spices, creamy oak. Palate: rich, smoky aftertaste, flavourful, fresh, good acidity.

PALACIOS DE BORNOS VERDEJO 2011 B
verdejo

90 Colour: bright straw. Nose: ripe fruit, fresh fruit, fruit expression, grassy. Palate: flavourful, fruity, good acidity.

BODEGA REINA DE CASTILLA

Camino de La Moya, s/n Ctra. La Seca - Serrada
47491 La Seca - (Valladolid)
☎: +34 983 816 667 - Fax: +34 983 816 663
bodega@reinadecastilla.es
www.reinadecastilla.es

EL BUFÓN VERDEJO 2011 B
100% verdejo

91 Colour: bright straw. Nose: fresh, fresh fruit, white flowers, mineral. Palate: flavourful, fruity, good acidity, balanced.

REINA DE CASTILLA SAUVIGNON BLANC 2011 B
sauvignon blanc

91 Colour: bright straw. Nose: fresh, fresh fruit, white flowers, mineral, varietal. Palate: flavourful, fruity, good acidity, balanced.

REINA DE CASTILLA VERDEJO 2011 B
100% verdejo

90 Colour: bright straw. Nose: fresh, white flowers, citrus fruit, fruit expression. Palate: flavourful, fruity, good acidity, balanced.

BODEGA VALDEHERMOSO

Pasión, 13
47001 - (Valladolid)
☎: +34 651 993 680
valdehermoso@valdehermoso.com
www.valdehermoso.com

VIÑA PEREZ 2011 B
100% verdejo

90 Colour: bright straw. Nose: white flowers, expressive, ripe fruit, varietal, balanced. Palate: flavourful, fruity, good acidity, balanced.

BODEGAS BALUARTE

Calle de la Ribera 32
31592 Cintruénigo - (Navarra)
☎: +34 948 811 000
info@bodegaschivite.com

BALUARTE 2011 B
verdejo

90 Colour: bright straw. Nose: fresh, white flowers, tropical fruit. Palate: flavourful, fruity, good acidity, balanced.

BODEGAS CASTELO DE MEDINA

Ctra. CL-602, Km. 48
47465 Villaverde de Medina - (Valladolid)
☎: +34 983 831 932 - Fax: +34 983 831 857
jcortega@castelodemedina.es
www.castelodemedina.es

CASTELO DE LA DEHESA 2011 B
50% verdejo, 30% viura, 20% sauvignon blanc

90 Colour: bright straw. Nose: fresh, fresh fruit, white flowers, expressive. Palate: flavourful, fruity, good acidity, balanced, easy to drink.

CASTELO DE MEDINA SAUVIGNON BLANC 2011 B
100% sauvignon blanc

91 Colour: bright straw. Nose: fresh, fresh fruit, white flowers, expressive, fragrant herbs. Palate: flavourful, fruity, good acidity, balanced.

CASTELO DE MEDINA VERDEJO 2011 B
100% verdejo

91 Colour: bright yellow. Nose: citrus fruit, fresh fruit, fragrant herbs, floral. Palate: flavourful, fresh, fruity, elegant.

CASTELO DE MEDINA VERDEJO VENDIMIA SELECCIONADA 2011 B
100% verdejo

92 Colour: bright straw, greenish rim. Nose: floral, fragrant herbs, citrus fruit, ripe fruit. Palate: powerful, flavourful, fine bitter notes, balsamic.

BODEGAS DE LOS HEREDEROS DEL MARQUÉS DE RISCAL

Ctra. N-VI, km. 172,6
47490 Rueda - (Valladolid)
☎: +34 983 868 029 - Fax: +34 983 868 563
marquesderiscal@marquesderiscal.com
www.marquesderiscal.com

FINCA MONTICO 2011 B
100% verdejo

93 Colour: bright yellow. Nose: dried flowers, fine lees, ripe fruit, citrus fruit, dried herbs, earthy notes. Palate: flavourful, powerful, good acidity, round.

MARQUÉS DE RISCAL LIMOUSIN 2011 B
100% verdejo

93 Colour: bright straw. Nose: powerfull, ripe fruit, sweet spices, creamy oak. Palate: rich, smoky aftertaste, flavourful, fresh, good acidity.

MARQUÉS DE RISCAL RUEDA VERDEJO 2011 B
100% verdejo

92 Colour: bright straw. Nose: fresh, fresh fruit, white flowers, expressive, fragrant herbs, mineral. Palate: flavourful, fruity, good acidity, balanced.

BODEGAS FÉLIX LORENZO CACHAZO S.L.

Ctra. Medina del Campo, Km. 9
47220 Pozáldez - (Valladolid)
☎: +34 983 822 008 - Fax: +34 983 822 008
bodega@cachazo.com
www.cachazo.com

CARRASVIÑAS VERDEJO 2011 B
100% verdejo

90 Colour: bright straw. Nose: floral, tropical fruit, fragrant herbs, medium intensity. Palate: fresh, flavourful, fruity.

MANIA RUEDA VERDEJO 2011 B
100% verdejo

91 Colour: bright straw. Nose: fresh fruit, white flowers, varietal, citrus fruit. Palate: flavourful, fruity, good acidity, balanced.

BODEGAS GARCÍAREVALO

Pza. San Juan, 4
47230 Matapozuelos - (Valladolid)
☎: +34 983 832 914 - Fax: +34 983 832 986
enologo@garciarevalo.com
www.garciarevalo.com

TRES OLMOS LÍAS 2011 B
100% verdejo

90 Colour: straw. Nose: white flowers, ripe fruit, grassy, mineral. Palate: flavourful, good acidity.

BODEGAS GARCIGRANDE

Aradillas s/n
57490 Rueda - (Valladolid)
☎: +34 983 868 561 - Fax: +34 983 868 449
info@hispanobodegas.com
www.hispanobodegas.com

12 LINAJES VERDEJO 2011 B
100% verdejo

90 Colour: bright straw. Nose: fresh, fresh fruit, white flowers, expressive, tropical fruit, grassy. Palate: flavourful, fruity, good acidity, balanced.

ANIER VENDIMIA SELECCIONADA 2011 B
100% verdejo

92 Colour: bright straw. Nose: ripe fruit, fresh fruit, citrus fruit, grassy, mineral. Palate: flavourful, fruity, fresh.

SEÑORÍO DE GARCI GRANDE VERDEJO 2011 B
100% verdejo

91 Colour: bright straw. Nose: fresh, fresh fruit, white flowers, expressive, grassy. Palate: flavourful, fruity, good acidity, balanced.

BODEGAS IMPERIALES

Ctra. Madrid - Irun, Km. 171
9370 Gumiel de Izán - (Burgos)
☎: +34 947 544 070 - Fax: +34 947 525 759
direccion@bodegasimperiales.com
www.bodegasimperiales.com

ABADÍA DE SAN QUIRCE VERDEJO 2011 B
100% verdejo

90 Colour: bright straw. Nose: fresh, white flowers, varietal, ripe fruit. Palate: flavourful, fruity, good acidity, balanced.

BODEGAS JOSÉ PARIENTE

Ctra. Rueda - La Seca, km. 2.5
47491 La Seca - (Valladolid)
☎: +34 983 816 600 - Fax: +34 983 816 620
info@josepariente.com
www.josepariente.com

APASIONADO DE JOSE PARIENTE 2011 B
100% sauvignon blanc

90 Colour: bright straw. Nose: white flowers, candied fruit. Palate: flavourful, fine bitter notes, sweetness.

JOSÉ PARIENTE 2010 BFB
100% verdejo

91 Color bright yellow. Aroma powerfull, ripe fruit, sweet spices, creamy oak, fragrant herbs. Taste rich, smoky aftertaste, flavourful, fresh, good acidity.

JOSÉ PARIENTE SAUVIGNON BLANC 2011 B
100% sauvignon blanc

92 Colour: bright straw. Nose: fresh, white flowers, expressive, varietal, ripe fruit. Palate: flavourful, fruity, good acidity, balanced.

JOSÉ PARIENTE VERDEJO 2011 B
100% verdejo

91 Colour: bright straw. Nose: fresh, white flowers, ripe fruit, citrus fruit, varietal. Palate: flavourful, fruity, good acidity, balanced.

BODEGAS MENADE

Cuatro Calles, s/n
47491 La Seca - (Valladolid)
☎: +34 983 103 223 - Fax: +34 983 816 561
info@sitiosdebodega.com

MENADE SAUVIGNON BLANC DULCE 2011 B
100% sauvignon blanc

90 Colour: bright straw. Nose: fresh, fresh fruit, white flowers, expressive. Palate: flavourful, fruity, good acidity, sweetness.

MENADE VERDEJO 2011 B
100% verdejo

90 Colour: bright straw. Nose: fresh, fresh fruit, white flowers, varietal. Palate: flavourful, fruity, good acidity, balanced.

BODEGAS MOCEN

Arribas, 7-9
47490 Rueda - (Valladolid)
☎: +34 983 868 533 - Fax: +34 983 868 514
info@bodegasmocen.com
www.bodegasantano.com

ALTA PLATA VERDEJO 2011 B
100% verdejo

90 Colour: bright straw. Nose: fresh fruit, white flowers, varietal. Palate: flavourful, fruity, good acidity, balanced.

LEGUILLÓN VERDEJO 2011 B
100% verdejo

90 Colour: straw. Nose: ripe fruit, citrus fruit, dried herbs. Palate: powerful, good acidity, fine bitter notes.

BODEGAS NAIA

Camino San Martín, s/n
47491 La Seca - (Valladolid)
☎: +34 628 434 933
info@bodegasnaia.com
www.bodegasnaia.com

K-NAIA 2011 B
100% verdejo

90 Colour: bright straw. Nose: dried flowers, citrus fruit, fruit expression, fragrant herbs. Palate: fresh, fruity, light-bodied, easy to drink.

NAIA 2011 B
100% verdejo

93 Colour: bright straw. Nose: fresh, white flowers, varietal, ripe fruit, mineral. Palate: flavourful, fruity, good acidity, balanced.

NAIADES 2009 BFB
100% verdejo

94 Colour: bright straw. Nose: powerfull, varietal, ripe fruit, sweet spices, cocoa bean. Palate: flavourful, ripe fruit, spicy.

BODEGAS NIDIA

Ctra. La Seca 17
47400 Medina del Campo - (Valladolid)
☎: +34 983 812 581
danieltorio@laborquo.es

NIDIA 2008 BFB
100% verdejo

90 Colour: bright yellow. Nose: ripe fruit, sweet spices, creamy oak, fragrant herbs. Palate: rich, flavourful, fresh, good acidity, balanced.

BODEGAS NILO

Federico García Lorca, 7
47490 Rueda - (Valladolid)
☎: +34 690 068 682 - Fax: +34 983 868 366
info@bodegasnilo.com
www.bodegasnilo.com

BIANCA 2011 B
verdejo

90 Colour: bright straw. Nose: white flowers, fruit expression, fragrant herbs, expressive. Palate: flavourful, fruity, balanced, long.

BODEGAS ORDÓÑEZ

Bartolomé Esteban Murillo, 11
29700 Vélez- Málaga - (Málaga)
☎: +34 952 504 706 - Fax: +34 951 284 796
office@jorge-ordonez.es
www.grupojorgeordonez.com

NISIA 2011 B
100% verdejo

95 Colour: bright straw. Nose: fresh, fresh fruit, white flowers, expressive, varietal, sweet spices. Palate: flavourful, fruity, good acidity, balanced.

BODEGAS PEÑAFIEL

Ctra. N-122, Km. 311
47300 Peñafiel - (Valladolid)
☎: +34 983 881 622 - Fax: +34 983 881 944
bodegaspenafiel@bodegaspenafiel.com
www.bodegaspenafiel.com

ALBA MIROS 2011 B
100% verdejo

90 Colour: bright straw. Nose: fresh, fresh fruit, white flowers. Palate: flavourful, fruity, good acidity, balanced.

BODEGAS PRADOREY

Ctra. Nacional VI, Km. 172,5
47490 Rueda - (Valladolid)
☎: +34 983 444 048 - Fax: +34 983 868 564
bodega@pradorey.com
www.pradorey.com

PR 3 BARRICAS 2009 BFB
100% verdejo

93 Colour: bright straw. Nose: fresh, white flowers, expressive, ripe fruit, sweet spices, creamy oak. Palate: flavourful, fruity, good acidity, balanced.

PRADOREY SAUVIGNON BLANC 2011 B
100% sauvignon blanc

91 Colour: bright straw. Nose: white flowers, fragrant herbs, fine lees, mineral. Palate: powerful, flavourful, complex, fruity.

PRADOREY VERDEJO 2011 B
100% verdejo

91 Colour: bright straw. Nose: expressive, citrus fruit, fresh fruit, fragrant herbs, mineral. Palate: good acidity, flavourful, fruity, balanced.

BODEGAS PROTOS

Ctra. CL 610, Medina - La Seca Km. 32,5
47491 La Seca - (Valladolid)
☎: +34 983 816 608
bodega@bodegasprotos.com
www.bodegasprotos.com

PROTOS 2010 B BARRICA
100% verdejo

92 Colour: bright golden. Nose: ripe fruit, dry nuts, powerfull, toasty, aged wood nuances, fragrant herbs. Palate: flavourful, fruity, spicy, toasty, long.

PROTOS VERDEJO 2011 B
100% verdejo

91 Colour: bright straw. Nose: fresh fruit, white flowers, fine lees, powerfull. Palate: flavourful, fruity, good acidity, balanced.

BODEGAS RUEDA PÉREZ

Boyón
47220 Pozáldez - (Valladolid)
☎: +34 650 454 657 - Fax: +34 983 822 049
satruedaperez@terra.es
www.bodegasruedaperez.es

VIÑA BURÓN VERDEJO 2011 B
100% verdejo

91 Colour: bright straw. Nose: fresh fruit, white flowers, expressive, mineral. Palate: flavourful, fruity, good acidity, balanced.

BODEGAS VAL DE VID

Ctra. Valladolid - Medina, Km. 23,6
47231 Serrada - (Valladolid)
☎: +34 983 559 914 - Fax: +34 983 559 914
esther.vega@avintec.es

CONDESA EYLO 2011 B
100% verdejo

90 Colour: bright straw. Nose: white flowers, citrus fruit, fruit expression, balsamic herbs, mineral. Palate: powerful, flavourful, fresh, fruity.

VAL DE VID 2011 B
70% verdejo, 30% viura

90 Colour: bright yellow. Nose: white flowers, fragrant herbs, fresh fruit. Palate: powerful, flavourful, long, good acidity, balanced.

VAL DE VID VERDEJO 2011 B
100% verdejo

91 Colour: bright straw. Nose: fresh, fresh fruit, white flowers, expressive, varietal, grassy. Palate: flavourful, fruity, good acidity, balanced.

BODEGAS VERACRUZ S.L.

Juan A. Carmona, 1
47500 Nava del Rey - (Valladolid)
☎: +34 670 581 157
j.benito@bodegasveracruz.com
www.bodegasveracruz.com

ERMITA VERACRUZ VERDEJO 2011 B
verdejo

92 Colour: bright straw. Nose: fresh, fresh fruit, white flowers, varietal, mineral, dried herbs. Palate: flavourful, fruity, good acidity, balanced.

BODEGAS VERDEAL

Nueva, 8
40200 Cuéllar - (Segovia)
☎: +34 921 140 125 - Fax: +34 921 142 421
info@bodegasverdeal.com
www.bodegasverdeal.com

VERDEAL 2011 B
100% verdejo

90 Colour: bright straw. Nose: dried herbs, ripe fruit, citrus fruit. Palate: flavourful, fruity, fresh, easy to drink, varietal.

BODEGAS VICENTE GANDÍA

Ctra. Cheste a Godelleta, s/n
46370 Chiva - (Valencia)
☎: +34 962 524 242 - Fax: +34 962 524 243
vuboldi@vicentegandia.com
www.vicentegandia.es

NEBLA VERDEJO 2011 B
100% verdejo

90 Colour: bright straw. Nose: fresh, fresh fruit, white flowers, varietal. Palate: flavourful, fruity, good acidity, balanced.

BODEGAS VIORE

Camino de la Moy, s/n
47491 La Seca - (Valladolid)
☎: +34 941 454 050 - Fax: +34 941 454 529
bodega@bodegasriojanas.com
www.bodegasriojanas.com

VIORE VERDEJO 2011 B
100% verdejo

90 Colour: bright straw. Nose: fresh fruit, white flowers, neat, powerfull, varietal. Palate: flavourful, fruity, balanced, fine bitter notes, correct.

BODEGAS Y VIÑEDOS ÁNGEL LORENZO CACHAZO

Estación, 53
47220 Pozaldez - (Valladolid)
☎: +34 983 822 481 - Fax: +34 983 822 012
bodegamartivilli@jet.es
www.martivilli.com

MARTIVILLÍ VERDEJO 2011 B

91 Colour: bright straw. Nose: complex, scrubland, white flowers, ripe fruit. Palate: flavourful, fruity, fresh, fine bitter notes.

BODEGAS Y VIÑEDOS NEO

Ctra. N-122, Km. 274,5
9391 Castrillo de la Vega - (Burgos)
☎: +34 947 514 393 - Fax: +34 947 515 445
info@bodegasconde.com
www.bodegasneo.com

PRIMER MOTIVO VERDEJO 2011 B
100% verdejo

90 Colour: bright straw. Nose: fragrant herbs, dried flowers, fruit expression, varietal. Palate: fine bitter notes, powerful, flavourful, fruity.

BODEGAS Y VIÑEDOS SHAYA

Ctra. Aldeanueva del Codonal s/n
40642 Aldeanueva del Codonal - (Segovia)
☎: +34 968 435 022
info@orowines.com
www.orowines.com

SHAYA 2011 B
100% verdejo

92 Colour: bright straw. Nose: fresh, fresh fruit, white flowers, varietal, ripe fruit, mineral. Palate: flavourful, fruity, good acidity, balanced.

SHAYA HABIS 2010 BFB
100% verdejo

94 Colour: bright yellow. Nose: powerfull, ripe fruit, sweet spices, creamy oak, fragrant herbs. Palate: rich, smoky aftertaste, flavourful, fresh.

CAMPOS DE SUEÑOS

Avda. Diagonal, 590, 5º 1ª
8021 - (Barcelona)
☎: +34 660 445 464
info@vinergia.com
www.vinergia.com

CAMPOS DE SUEÑOS 2011 B
100% verdejo

90 Colour: bright straw. Nose: fresh fruit, white flowers, neat, varietal, complex, grassy. Palate: flavourful, fruity, good acidity, balanced.

COMENGE BODEGAS Y VIÑEDOS

Camino del Castillo, s/n
47316 Curiel de Duero - (Valladolid)
☎: +34 983 880 363 - Fax: +34 983 880 717
admin@comenge.com
www.comenge.com

COMENGE 2011 B
100% verdejo

90 Colour: bright straw. Nose: fresh, fresh fruit, white flowers. Palate: flavourful, fruity, good acidity, balanced.

COMERCIAL GRUPO FREIXENET S.A.

Joan Sala, 2
8770 Sant Sadurní D'Anoia - (Barcelona)
☎: +34 938 917 000 - Fax: +34 938 183 095
freixenet@freixenet.es
www.freixenet.es

VALDUBON VERDEJO 2011 BFB
100% verdejo

90 Colour: bright yellow. Nose: powerfull, ripe fruit, sweet spices, creamy oak, fragrant herbs. Palate: rich, flavourful, fresh, fruity, spicy.

COMPAÑÍA DE VINOS TELMO RODRÍGUEZ

El Monte
1308 Lanciego - (Álava)
☎: +34 945 628 315 - Fax: +34 945 628 314
contact@telmorodriguez.com
www.telmorodriguez.com

EL TRANSISTOR 2010 B
100% verdejo

94 Colour: bright straw. Nose: ripe fruit, grassy, expressive, mineral. Palate: flavourful, powerful, fruity, fine bitter notes, good acidity, round.

DE ALBERTO

Ctra. de Valdestillas, 2
47239 Serrada - (Valladolid)
☎: +34 983 559 107 - Fax: +34 983 559 084
info@dealberto.com
www.dealberto.com

DE ALBERTO VERDEJO 2011 B
verdejo

91 Color bright straw. Aroma fresh, fresh fruit, white flowers, expressive. Taste flavourful, fruity, good acidity, balanced.

GUTI 2011 B
verdejo

90 Colour: bright straw. Nose: fresh fruit, white flowers, varietal. Palate: flavourful, fruity, good acidity, balanced.

DIEZ SIGLOS DE VERDEJO

Ctra. Valladolid Km. 24,5
47231 Serrada - (Valladolid)
☎: +34 983 559 910 - Fax: +34 983 559 020
comercial1@diezsiglos.es
www.diezsiglos.es

DIEZ SIGLOS 2011 B
100% verdejo

90 Color bright straw. Aroma fresh, fresh fruit, white flowers, expressive. Taste flavourful, fruity, good acidity, balanced.

ESTANCIA PIEDRA S.L.

Ctra. Toro a Salamanca, km. 5
49800 Toro - (Zamora)
☎: +34 980 693 900 - Fax: +34 980 693 901
info@estanciapiedra.com
www.estanciapiedra.com

PIEDRA VERDEJO 2011 B
100% verdejo

90 Colour: bright yellow. Nose: fragrant herbs, citrus fruit, ripe fruit, dried flowers, grassy. Palate: powerful, flavourful, fresh, fruity, balanced.

FINCA CASERÍO DE DUEÑAS

Ctra. Cl. 602, km. 50,2
47465 Villaverde de Medina - (Valladolid)
☎: +34 915 006 000 - Fax: +34 915 006 006
pzumft@habarcelo.es
www.habarcelo.es

VIÑA MAYOR 2010 BFB
100% verdejo

90 Colour: bright straw. Nose: fresh, fresh fruit, white flowers, lactic notes, sweet spices. Palate: flavourful, fruity, good acidity, balanced.

FINCA LAS CARABALLAS

Camino Velascálvaro, 2
47400 Medina del Campo - (Valladolid)
info@lascaraballas.com
www.lascaraballas.com

FINCA LAS CARABALLAS 2011 B
100% verdejo

91 Colour: bright straw. Nose: fresh fruit, white flowers, fragrant herbs, mineral. Palate: flavourful, fruity, good acidity, rich.

FINCA LAS CARABALLAS SEMIDULCE 2011 B
50% verdejo, 50% sauvignon blanc

90 Colour: golden. Nose: powerfull, floral, candied fruit, fragrant herbs. Palate: flavourful, sweet, fresh, fruity, good acidity.

FINCA MONTEPEDROSO

DIPUTACIO, S/N
1320 Oyon - (Alava)
☎: +34 983 868 977 - Fax: +34 983 868 055
info@bujanda.com
www.familiamartinezbujanda.com

FINCA MONTEPEDROSO VERDEJO 2011 B
verdejo

91 Colour: bright straw. Nose: fresh, fresh fruit, white flowers, varietal, tropical fruit. Palate: flavourful, fruity, good acidity, balanced.

FRANCISCO JAVIER SANZ CANTALAPIEDRA

San Judas, 2
47491 La Seca - (Valladolid)
☎: +34 983 816 669 - Fax: +34 983 816 639
nacional@ordentercera.com
www.ordentercera.com

ORDEN TERCERA VERDEJO 2011 B JOVEN
100% verdejo

90 Color bright straw. Aroma fresh, fresh fruit, white flowers, expressive. Taste flavourful, fruity, good acidity, balanced.

GRUPO YLLERA

Autovía A-6, Km. 173, 5
47490 Rueda - (Valladolid)
☎: +34 983 868 097 - Fax: +34 983 868 177
grupoyllera@grupoyllera.com
www.grupoyllera.com

VIÑA CANTOSÁN VARIETAL VERDEJO 2011 B
100% verdejo

91 Colour: bright straw. Nose: varietal, floral, fragrant herbs, citrus fruit, fresh fruit, expressive. Palate: rich, flavourful, balsamic, long, balanced.

YLLERA VERDEJO VENDIMIA NOCTURNA 2011 B
verdejo

90 Colour: bright straw. Nose: dried flowers, varietal, wild herbs, earthy notes, expressive. Palate: balsamic, correct, flavourful, light-bodied, fruity.

HACIENDAS DE ESPAÑA*

Avenida Nava del Rey, 8
47490 Rueda - (Valladolid)
☎: +34 914 365 924
comunicacion@arcoinvest-group.com
www.haciendas-espana.com

HACIENDA ZORITA VEGA DE LA REINA VERDEJO (MARQUÉS DE LA CONCORDIA FAMILY OF WINES) 2011 B
100% verdejo

91 Colour: bright straw. Nose: dried flowers, wild herbs, citrus fruit, fruit expression. Palate: powerful, flavourful, complex, long, balanced.

JAVIER SANZ VITICULTOR

San Judas, 2
47491 La Seca - (Valladolid)
☎: +34 983 816 669 - Fax: +34 983 816 639
nacional@jsviticultor.com
www.jsviticultor.com

VILLA NARCISA RUEDA VERDEJO 2011 B
verdejo

90 Colour: bright straw. Nose: fresh, fresh fruit, white flowers, expressive, fragrant herbs. Palate: flavourful, fruity, good acidity, balanced.

LIBERALIA ENOLÓGICA

Camino del Palo, s/n
49800 Toro - (Zamora)
☎: +34 980 692 571 - Fax: +34 980 692 571
liberalia@liberalia.es
www.liberalia.es

ENEBRAL 2011 B
100% verdejo

91 Colour: bright straw. Nose: faded flowers, fragrant herbs, citrus fruit, expressive. Palate: powerful, flavourful, good acidity, correct.

LOESS

C/ Burgohondo, 4
28023 - (Madrid)
☎: +34 983 664 898 - Fax: +34 983 406 579
loess@loess.es
www.loess.es

LOESS COLLECTION 2010 BFB
100% verdejo

91 Colour: bright straw. Nose: fresh, white flowers, ripe fruit, sweet spices. Palate: flavourful, fruity, good acidity, balanced.

MIRAVINOS

Plaza de Matute 12, - 3º
28012 - (Madrid)
☎: +34 609 119 248
info@miravinos.es
www.miravinos.es

NAIPES 2011 B
verdejo

92 Colour: bright straw. Nose: fresh fruit, expressive, floral, varietal, mineral. Palate: flavourful, fruity, good acidity, balanced.

MONTEBACO

Finca Montealto
47359 Valbuena de Duero - (Valladolid)
☎: +34 983 485 128 - Fax: +34 983 485 033
montebaco@bodegasmontebaco.com
www.bodegasmontebaco.com

MONTEBACO VERDEJO SOBRE LÍAS 2011 B
verdejo

90 Colour: bright straw. Nose: fresh fruit, white flowers, expressive, mineral, grassy, varietal. Palate: flavourful, fruity, balanced, fine bitter notes.

OLID INTERNACIONAL

Juan García Hortelano, 21-7ºC
47014 - (Valladolid)
☎: +34 983 132 690
olidinternacional@gmail.com
www.olidinternacional.com

983 2011 B
100% verdejo

90 Colour: bright straw. Nose: fresh fruit, white flowers, citrus fruit, dried herbs. Palate: flavourful, fruity, good acidity, balanced.

PAGO TRASLAGARES

Autovía Noroeste km 166,4 Apdo. 507
47490 Rueda - (Valladolid)
☎: +34 983 667 023
export@traslagares.com
www.traslagares.com

TRASLAGARES VERDEJO 2011 B
100% verdejo

90 Colour: bright straw. Nose: fresh fruit, white flowers, ripe fruit. Palate: flavourful, fruity, good acidity, balanced.

PAGOS DEL REY RUEDA

Avda. Morejona, 6
47490 Rueda - (Valladolid)
☎: +34 983 868 182 - Fax: +34 983 868 182
rueda@pagosdelrey.com
www.pagosdelrey.com

ANALIVIA SAUVIGNON BLANC 2011 B
100% sauvignon blanc

91 Colour: bright straw. Nose: fresh, fresh fruit, white flowers, herbaceous. Palate: flavourful, fruity, balanced, good acidity.

PREDIO DE VASCARLÓN

Ctra. Rueda, s/n
47491 La Seca - (Valladolid)
☎: +34 983 816 325 - Fax: +34 983 816 326
vascarlon@prediodevascarlon.com
www.prediodevascarlon.com

ATELIER VERDEJO 2011 B
100% verdejo

90 Colour: bright straw. Nose: fresh, white flowers, varietal, ripe fruit. Palate: flavourful, fruity, good acidity, balanced, fine bitter notes.

RODRÍGUEZ SANZO

Manuel Azaña, 9
47014 - (Valladolid)
☎: +34 983 150 150 - Fax: +34 983 150 151
comunicacion@valsanzo.com
www.rodriguezsanzo.com

VIÑA SANZO SOBRE LÍAS 2010 B
100% verdejo

93 Colour: bright yellow. Nose: powerfull, sweet spices, fragrant herbs, ripe fruit, citrus fruit. Palate: rich, smoky aftertaste, flavourful, fresh, good acidity.

VIÑA SANZO VERDEJO 2011 B
100% verdejo

91 Colour: bright straw. Nose: fresh fruit, white flowers, expressive. Palate: flavourful, fruity, good acidity, balanced.

TERNA BODEGAS

Cuatro Calles, s/n
47491 La Seca - (Valladolid)
☎: +34 983 103 223 - Fax: +34 983 816 561
info@sitiosdebodega.com
www.sitiosdebodega.com

V3 VIÑAS VIEJAS VERDEJO 2010 BFB
100% verdejo

94 Colour: bright straw. Nose: mineral, ripe fruit, candied fruit, sweet spices. Palate: flavourful, powerful, spicy, ripe fruit.

TERROIR 34

Castellote 26
Aranda de Duero - (Burgos)
☎: +34 606 941 434
info@terroir34.com
www.terroir34.com

TERROIR 34 "SEDUCTION FROM COOL STONES" 2011 B
100% verdejo

91 Colour: bright straw. Nose: fresh, fresh fruit, white flowers, varietal, mineral. Palate: flavourful, fruity, good acidity, balanced.

TOMÁS POSTIGO

Estación, 12
47300 Peñafiel - (Valladolid)
☎: +34 983 873 019 - Fax: +34 983 880 258
administracion@tomaspostigo.es

TOMÁS POSTIGO 2010 BFB
verdejo

91 Colour: bright yellow. Nose: powerfull, ripe fruit, fragrant herbs, spicy, cocoa bean. Palate: rich, smoky aftertaste, flavourful, fresh, good acidity.

UNZU PROPIEDAD

Avda. de la Poveda, 16
1306 Lapuebla - (Álava)
☎: +34 948 812 297
info@unzupropiedad.com
www.unzupropiedad.com

LABORES DE UNZU VERDEJO 2011 B
100% verdejo

91 Colour: bright straw. Nose: fresh, fresh fruit, expressive, varietal. Palate: flavourful, fruity, good acidity, balanced.

VALTRAVIESO

Finca La Revilla, s/n
47316 Piñel de Arriba - (Valladolid)
☎: +34 983 484 030 - Fax: +34 983 484 037
valtravieso@valtravieso.com
www.valtravieso.com

DOMINIO D NOGARA 2011 B
100% verdejo

90 Colour: bright yellow. Nose: white flowers, fruit expression, wild herbs, fragrant herbs. Palate: rich, powerful, flavourful.

VINOS JOC - JORDI OLIVER CONTI

Mas Marti
17467 Sant Mori - (Girona)
☎: +34 607 222 002
info@vinojoc.com
www.vinojoc.com

JOC RUEDA 2011 B
100% verdejo

91 Colour: bright straw. Nose: floral, fragrant herbs, fruit expression, expressive, varietal. Palate: powerful, flavourful, fruity, balanced.

VINOS SANZ

Ctra. Madrid - La Coruña, Km. 170,5
47490 Rueda - (Valladolid)
☎: +34 983 868 100 - Fax: +34 983 868 117
vinossanz@vinossanz.com
www.vinossanz.com

FINCA LA COLINA SAUVIGNON BLANC 2011 B
100% sauvignon blanc

93 Colour: bright straw. Nose: ripe fruit, citrus fruit, white flowers, grassy. Palate: flavourful, good acidity, fine bitter notes.

FINCA LA COLINA VERDEJO CIEN X CIEN 2011 B
100% verdejo

93 Colour: bright straw. Nose: fresh fruit, white flowers, mineral, grassy. Palate: flavourful, fruity, good acidity, balanced.

SANZ CLÁSICO 2011 B
70% verdejo, 30% viura

90 Colour: bright straw. Nose: expressive, varietal, ripe fruit, dried herbs. Palate: flavourful, fruity, fresh.

SANZ SAUVIGNON BLANC 2011 B
100% sauvignon blanc

90 Colour: bright straw. Nose: fresh, white flowers, varietal, ripe fruit, grassy. Palate: flavourful, fruity, good acidity.

SANZ VERDEJO 2011 B
100% verdejo

91 Colour: bright straw. Nose: fresh, fresh fruit, white flowers, dried herbs, fine lees. Palate: flavourful, fruity, good acidity, balanced.

VIÑEDOS DE NIEVA

Camino Real, s/n
40447 Nieva - (Segovia)
☎: +34 921 594 628 - Fax: +34 921 595 409
info@vinedosdenieva.com
www.vinedosdenieva.com

BLANCO NIEVA 2011 B
100% verdejo

91 Colour: bright straw. Nose: fresh, fresh fruit, white flowers, expressive, mineral. Palate: flavourful, fruity, good acidity, balanced.

BLANCO NIEVA PIE FRANCO 2011 B
100% verdejo

93 Colour: bright straw. Nose: white flowers, citrus fruit, fruit expression, fragrant herbs, mineral. Palate: powerful, flavourful, long, balanced.

BLANCO NIEVA SAUVIGNON 2011 B
100% sauvignon blanc

90 Colour: bright straw. Nose: mineral, fresh fruit, citrus fruit, grassy. Palate: flavourful, fruity, fresh, spicy.

LOS NAVALES VERDEJO 2011 B
100% verdejo

90 Colour: bright straw. Nose: fresh, fresh fruit, white flowers, expressive, tropical fruit. Palate: flavourful, fruity, good acidity, balanced.

DESCRIPTION

This is located in Huesca, the northern province of Aragón, the Somontano Denomination of Origin is one of the producer zones which has grown most rapidly in quality and in number of wineries over just 25 years. From three wineries it has passed to 35, all of which have an exemplary vocation to promote wine tourism. Wines are produced with local and international grapes with a certain Atlantic aura.

NUMBER OF HECTARES: 4.887

ALTITUDES: 500 m.

PREDOMINANT VARIETIES:

White grapes: macabeo, garnacha blanca, alcañón, chardonnay, gewürztraminer, riesling and sauvignon blanc.

Red grapes: tempranillo, garnacha tinta, cabernet sauvignon, merlot, moristel, parraleta, pinot noir and syrah.

CLIMATOLOGY AND SOILS

The climate is continental, the vineyards are located mainly in brown – limestone soils on soft materials.

ALDAHARA BODEGA

Ctra. Barbastro, 10
22423 Estadilla - (Huesca)
☎: +34 974 305 236 - Fax: +34 974 305 236
bodega@aldahara.es
www.aldahara.es

VAL D'ALFERCHE 2009 T
100% syrah

90 Colour: cherry, garnet rim. Nose: sweet spices, floral, expressive. Palate: balanced, fruity aftestaste, round tannins, long.

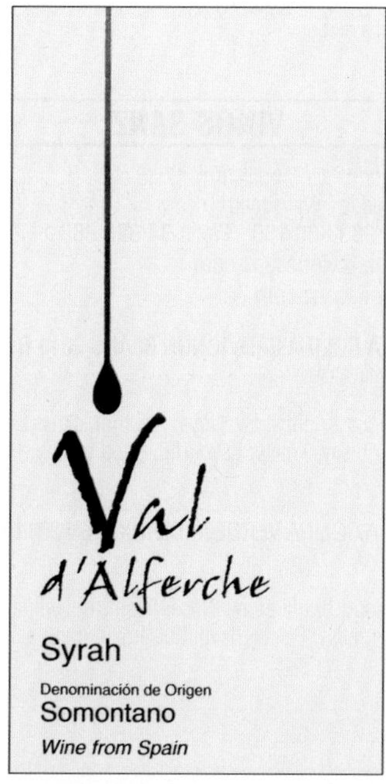

BAL D'ISABENA BODEGAS

Ctra. A-1605, Km. 11,2
22587 Laguarres - (Huesca)
☎: +34 605 785 178 - Fax: +34 974 310 151
info@baldisabena.com
www.baldisabena.com

COJÓN DE GATO 2010 T ROBLE
syrah, merlot

91 Colour: cherry, purple rim. Nose: dark chocolate, sweet spices, expressive, complex, ripe fruit. Palate: fruity, flavourful, full.

COJÓN DE GATO 2011 B
gewürztraminer, chardonnay

90 Colour: bright yellow. Nose: medium intensity, balanced, white flowers. Palate: balanced, flavourful, full, good acidity.

BLECUA

Ctra. Naval, Km. 3,7
22300 Barbastro - (Huesca)
☎: +34 974 302 216 - Fax: +34 974 302 098
marketing@vinasdelvero.es
www.bodegablecua.com

BLECUA 2005 T
garnacha, tempranillo, merlot, cabernet sauvignon

93 Colour: cherry, garnet rim. Nose: ripe fruit, spicy, creamy oak, complex, mineral. Palate: powerful, flavourful, toasty, round tannins.

BLECUA 2007 TR
garnacha, tempranillo, cabernet sauvignon

95 Colour: deep cherry, garnet rim. Nose: complex, elegant, expressive, balsamic herbs, cocoa bean, spicy. Palate: balanced, full, flavourful.

BODEGA PIRINEOS

Ctra. Barbastro - Naval, Km. 3,5
22300 Barbastro - (Huesca)
☎: +34 974 311 289 - Fax: +34 974 306 688
info@bodegapirineos.com
www.bodegapirineos.com

PIRINEOS 2011 RD
merlot, cabernet sauvignon

90 Colour: rose, purple rim. Nose: powerfull, red berry notes, floral, expressive. Palate: , powerful, fruity, fresh, easy to drink.

PIRINEOS SELECCIÓN GEWÜRZTRAMINER 2011 B
gewürztraminer

90 Colour: bright straw. Nose: fresh, white flowers, expressive. Palate: flavourful, fruity, good acidity, balanced, full.

PIRINEOS SELECCIÓN MARBORÉ 2005 T
tempranillo, merlot, cabernet sauvignon, moristel, parraleta

90 Colour: deep cherry, garnet rim. Nose: complex, ripe fruit, sweet spices. Palate: good structure, powerful, flavourful.

PIRINEOS SELECCIÓN MARBORÉ 2010 B

91 Colour: bright straw. Nose: fresh, fresh fruit, white flowers, expressive, sweet spices. Palate: flavourful, fruity, good acidity, balanced.

BODEGAS ALODIA

Ctra. de Colungo, s/n
22147 Adahuesca - (Huesca)
☎: +34 974 318 265
info@alodia.es
www.alodia.es

ALODIA PARRALETA 2009 T
100% parraleta

90 Colour: cherry, garnet rim. Nose: ripe fruit, spicy, creamy oak, earthy notes. Palate: powerful, flavourful, toasty.

BODEGAS BALLABRIGA

Ctra. de Cregenzán, Km. 3
22300 Barbastro - (Huesca)
☎: +34 974 310 216 - Fax: +34 974 306 163
info@bodegasballabriga.com
www.bodegasballabriga.com

NUNC 2007 T
merlot, syrah, garnacha, otras

93 Colour: bright cherry, garnet rim. Nose: elegant, ripe fruit, scrubland, spicy. Palate: long, ripe fruit, complex, round tannins.

PARRALETA EMOCIÓN 2007 T
parraleta

91 Colour: cherry, garnet rim. Nose: expressive, balanced, scrubland, cocoa bean. Palate: fruity, flavourful, good acidity.

PARRALETA EMOTION 2010 T
100% parraleta

90 Colour: cherry, garnet rim. Nose: ripe fruit, earthy notes, scrubland, spicy. Palate: ripe fruit, powerful, flavourful.

PETRET 2008 TC
50% cabernet sauvignon, 50% merlot

91 Colour: pale ruby, brick rim edge. Nose: ripe fruit, scrubland, fine reductive notes, spicy, complex. Palate: balanced, flavourful, long, spicy.

BODEGAS ESTADA

Ctra. A-1232, Km. 6,4
22313 Castillazuelo - (Huesca)
☎: +34 687 891 701
info@bodegasestada.com
www.bodegasestada.com

ESTATA 2020 VICIOUS 2011 BFB
chardonnay

90 Colour: bright yellow. Nose: balanced, powerfull, ripe fruit, jasmine, sweet spices. Palate: flavourful, full, fruity, spicy.

BODEGAS IRIUS

Ctra. N-240, Km. 154,5
22300 Barbastro - (Huesca)
☎: +34 974 269 900
visitairius@bodegairius.com
www.bodegairius.com

ABSUM COLECCIÓN GEWÜRZTRAMINER 2010 B ROBLE
100% gewürztraminer

90 Colour: bright yellow. Nose: complex, expressive, white flowers, elegant, sweet spices. Palate: rich, flavourful, good acidity, balanced.

ABSUM COLECCIÓN MERLOT 2009 T
100% merlot

91 Colour: deep cherry, purple rim. Nose: complex, expressive, creamy oak, cocoa bean, ripe fruit. Palate: good structure, round tannins.

ABSUM COLECCIÓN SYRAH 2009 T
100% syrah

94 Colour: bright cherry. Nose: sweet spices, creamy oak, expressive, red berry notes, ripe fruit. Palate: flavourful, fruity, toasty, round tannins.

ABSUM VARIETALES 2010 T
50% tempranillo, 35% merlot, 10% cabernet sauvignon, 5% syrah

92 Colour: bright cherry, garnet rim. Nose: balanced, expressive, ripe fruit, sweet spices, cocoa bean, creamy oak. Palate: good structure, long, spicy.

ALBAT ELIT 2007 TR
75% tempranillo, 15% cabernet sauvignon, 10% merlot

91 Colour: cherry, garnet rim. Nose: ripe fruit, sweet spices, dark chocolate, cocoa bean, creamy oak. Palate: powerful, flavourful, long, toasty.

IRIUS PREMIUM 2008 T
40% tempranillo, 20% cabernet sauvignon, 20% merlot, 20% syrah

96 Colour: bright cherry, purple rim. Nose: complex, ripe fruit, sweet spices, elegant. Palate: spicy, long, balanced, fine bitter notes, round tannins.

IRIUS SELECCIÓN 2008 T
30% tempranillo, 30% merlot, 25% cabernet sauvignon, 15% syrah

92 Colour: very deep cherry, garnet rim. Nose: powerfull, expressive, dark chocolate, creamy oak, sweet spices, candied fruit. Palate: full, flavourful, good structure, rich.

BODEGAS LAUS

Ctra. N-240, km 154,8
22300 Barbastro - (Huesca)
☎: +34 974 269 708 - Fax: +34 974 269 715
info@bodegaslaus.com
www.bodegaslaus.com

LAUS FLOR DE GEWÜRZTRAMINER 2011 B
100% gewürztraminer

91 Colour: bright straw. Nose: white flowers, fresh fruit, fragrant herbs, expressive. Palate: fresh, fruity, flavourful, varietal, balanced.

BODEGAS MELER

Pico Perdiguero, 13
22300 Barbastro - (Huesca)
☎: +34 974 269 907 - Fax: +34 974 269 907
info@bodegasmeler.com
www.bodegasmeler.com

ANDRES MELER 2006 T
100% cabernet sauvignon

92 Colour: cherry, garnet rim. Nose: spicy, creamy oak, toasty, complex, fragrant herbs. Palate: powerful, flavourful, toasty, round tannins.

MELER 2006 TC
merlot, cabernet sauvignon

90 Colour: cherry, garnet rim. Nose: spicy, fine reductive notes, wet leather, aged wood nuances, fruit liqueur notes. Palate: spicy, fine tannins, elegant, long.

MELER 95 SOBRE ALJEZ CHARDONNAY 2008 B
100% chardonnay

91 Colour: bright yellow. Nose: powerfull, ripe fruit, sweet spices, creamy oak, fragrant herbs. Palate: rich, smoky aftertaste, flavourful, fresh.

BODEGAS OBERGO

Ctra. La Puebla, Km. 0,6
22439 Ubiergo - (Huesca)
☎: +34 669 357 866
bodegasobergo@obergo.es
www.obergo.es

OBERGO "FINCA LA MATA" 2009 T
40% merlot, 40% cabernet sauvignon, 20% garnacha

90 Colour: cherry, garnet rim. Nose: ripe fruit, spicy, toasty, fine reductive notes. Palate: powerful, flavourful, toasty, round tannins.

OBERGO SYRAH 2009 T
100% syrah

92 Colour: cherry, purple rim. Nose: red berry notes, ripe fruit, sweet spices, creamy oak. Palate: powerful, flavourful, balanced.

OBERGO VARIETALES 2009 T
100% cabernet sauvignon

90 Colour: cherry, garnet rim. Nose: ripe fruit, spicy, creamy oak, toasty. Palate: powerful, flavourful, toasty, round tannins.

BODEGAS OLVENA

Paraje El Ariño, s/n
Ctra. Nacional 123, Km. 5
22300 Barbastro - (Huesca)
☎: +34 974 308 481 - Fax: +34 974 308 482
info@bodegasolvena.com
www.bodegasolvena.com

OLVENA CUATRO O EL PAGO DE LA LIBÉLULA 2008 T
tempranillo, merlot, cabernet sauvignon, syrah

90 Colour: cherry, garnet rim. Nose: red berry notes, ripe fruit, fragrant herbs, floral, sweet spices. Palate: round tannins, fresh, fruity, spicy, long.

BODEGAS SERS

Pza. Mayor, 7
22417 Cofita - (Huesca)
☎: +34 652 979 718
info@bodegassers.es
www.bodegassers.es

SÈRS 2008 TR
60% cabernet sauvignon, 30% merlot, 10% syrah

90 Colour: bright cherry, garnet rim. Nose: complex, candied fruit, dark chocolate, creamy oak, aromatic coffee. Palate: flavourful, balanced, long.

SÈRS BLANQUÉ 2011 BFB
100% chardonnay

90 Colour: bright yellow. Nose: balanced, expressive, scrubland, floral, sweet spices. Palate: balanced, spicy.

SÈRS SINGULAR 2010 T
100% parraleta

91 Colour: bright cherry. Nose: ripe fruit, sweet spices, creamy oak, expressive, complex. Palate: flavourful, fruity, toasty, round tannins.

SÈRS TEMPLE 2009 TC
40% merlot, 60% cabernet sauvignon

90 Color bright cherry. Aroma ripe fruit, sweet spices, creamy oak, expressive. Taste flavourful, fruity, toasty, round tannins.

BODEGAS SIERRA DE GUARA

Ctra. A-1 1229, Km. 0,2
22124 Las Cellas - (Huesca)
☎: +34 974 340 671 - Fax: +34 974 319 363
idrias@bodegassierradeguara.es
www.bodegassierradeguara.es

IDRIAS ABIEGO 2009 T
50% merlot, 50% cabernet sauvignon

90 Colour: bright cherry. Nose: ripe fruit, sweet spices, creamy oak, balsamic herbs. Palate: flavourful, fruity, toasty, round tannins.

IDRIAS CHARDONNAY 2007 BFB
100% chardonnay

90 Colour: bright yellow. Nose: ripe fruit, sweet spices, creamy oak, fragrant herbs. Palate: rich, smoky aftertaste, flavourful, fresh, good acidity.

CHESA

Autovía A-22, km. 57
22300 Barbastro - (Huesca)
☎: +34 649 870 637 - Fax: +34 974 313 552
bodegaschesa@hotmail.com
www.bodegaschesa.com

CHESA 2009 T ROBLE
65% merlot, 35% cabernet sauvignon

90 Color bright cherry. Aroma ripe fruit, sweet spices, creamy oak, expressive. Taste flavourful, fruity, toasty, round tannins.

DALCAMP

Constitución, 4
22415 Monesma de San Juan - (Huesca)
☎: +34 973 760 018 - Fax: +34 973 760 523
rdalfo@mixmail.com
www.castillodemonesma.com

CASTILLO DE MONESMA 2007 TR
90% cabernet sauvignon, 10% merlot

90 Color cherry, garnet rim. Aroma ripe fruit, spicy, creamy oak, toasty, complex. Taste powerful, flavourful, toasty, round tannins.

DE BEROZ

Pol. Valle del Cinca - Calle B- 26-24
22300 Barbastro - (Huesca)
☎: +34 974 269 921 - Fax: +34 974 269 921
bodega@deberoz.com
www.deberoz.com

DE BEROZ CRIANZA ESPECIAL 2007 T
cabernet sauvignon, merlot, syrah

90 Colour: bright cherry, garnet rim. Nose: complex, cocoa bean, toasty, wild herbs, ripe fruit. Palate: flavourful, fruity.

DE BEROZ ESENCIA DE BLANCOS 2011 B
90% chardonnay, 10% gewürztraminer

90 Colour: bright straw. Nose: fruit expression, ripe fruit, white flowers, balsamic herbs. Palate: powerful, flavourful, balanced.

DE BEROZ RESERVA FAMILIA 2006 T
cabernet sauvignon, merlot, syrah, tempranillo

91 Colour: bright cherry, garnet rim. Nose: spicy, ripe fruit, balanced, powerfull. Palate: flavourful, good acidity, balanced.

LAR DE BEROZ 2006 T
cabernet sauvignon, syrah, garnacha, parraleta

91 Colour: deep cherry, garnet rim. Nose: toasty, sweet spices, warm, ripe fruit. Palate: good structure, round tannins.

ENATE

Avda. de las Artes, 1
22314 Salas Bajas - (Huesca)
☎: +34 974 302 580 - Fax: +34 974 300 046
bodega@enate.es
www.enate.es

ENATE 2005 TR
100% cabernet sauvignon

92 Colour: cherry, garnet rim. Nose: balanced, powerfull, ripe fruit, spicy, warm, mineral. Palate: flavourful, balanced, fine bitter notes.

ENATE CHARDONNAY 20 ANIVERSARIO 2009 BFB
100% chardonnay

93 Colour: bright yellow. Nose: ripe fruit, honeyed notes, sweet spices, creamy oak. Palate: spicy, powerful, toasty, long, flavourful, roasted-coffee aftertaste.

ENATE CHARDONNAY 2009 BFB
100% chardonnay

92 Colour: bright yellow. Nose: powerfull, ripe fruit, sweet spices, creamy oak, fragrant herbs. Palate: rich, flavourful, roasted-coffee aftertaste.

ENATE CHARDONNAY-234 2011 B
100% chardonnay

90 Colour: bright straw. Nose: fresh, white flowers, expressive, balanced. Palate: flavourful, fruity, good acidity, balanced.

ENATE MERLOT-MERLOT 2008 T
100% merlot

92 Colour: cherry, garnet rim. Nose: spicy, creamy oak, toasty, complex, candied fruit. Palate: powerful, flavourful, toasty, round tannins.

ENATE RESERVA ESPECIAL 2006 TR
65% cabernet sauvignon, 35% merlot

94 Colour: cherry, garnet rim. Nose: ripe fruit, cocoa bean, spicy, dark chocolate, toasty, elegant. Palate: powerful, flavourful, spicy, balanced.

ENATE SYRAH-SHIRAZ 2007 T
100% syrah

92 Colour: bright cherry, garnet rim. Nose: expressive, creamy oak, dark chocolate, ripe fruit. Palate: flavourful, full.

ENATE UNO 2005 T
60% cabernet sauvignon, 20% merlot, 20% syrah

93 Colour: deep cherry, garnet rim. Nose: expressive, cocoa bean, ripe fruit, powerfull, scrubland. Palate: full, complex, good structure, round tannins.

ENATE VARIETALES 2006 T
40% merlot, 40% cabernet sauvignon, 20% syrah

91 Colour: cherry, garnet rim. Nose: balanced, scrubland, ripe fruit, dark chocolate. Palate: flavourful, powerful, long, full.

VINSOM

Ctra. Berbegal, Km. 2,5
22300 Barbastro - (Huesca)
☎: +34 974 269 188 - Fax: +34 974 269 188
info@lafirmadevinos.com
www.docelunas.es

12 LUNAS 2008 T
55% tempranillo, 20% syrah, 20% cabernet sauvignon, 5% garnacha

91 Colour: cherry, garnet rim. Nose: ripe fruit, sweet spices, creamy oak, toasty. Palate: powerful, flavourful, balanced, complex.

12 LUNAS 2011 B
90% chardonnay, 10% gewürztraminer

90 Colour: bright straw. Nose: white flowers, fruit expression, ripe fruit, expressive. Palate: powerful, flavourful, full, long, balanced.

VIÑAS DEL VERO

Ctra. Naval, Km. 3,7
22300 Barbastro - (Huesca)
☎: +34 974 302 216 - Fax: +34 974 302 098
marketing@vinasdelvero.es
www.vinasdelvero.es

VIÑAS DEL VERO CHARDONNAY COLECCIÓN 2011 B
100% chardonnay

92 Colour: bright yellow, greenish rim. Nose: elegant, balanced, medium intensity, floral. Palate: fruity, full, fine bitter notes.

VIÑAS DEL VERO CLARIÓN 2010 B

91 Colour: bright yellow. Nose: medium intensity, fresh fruit, wild herbs, faded flowers. Palate: flavourful, fruity, fine bitter notes.

VIÑAS DEL VERO CLARIÓN MAGNUM 2008 B

92 Colour: bright yellow, greenish rim. Nose: elegant, ripe fruit, floral, sweet spices, fragrant herbs. Palate: flavourful, fine bitter notes, balanced.

VIÑAS DEL VERO GEWÜRZTRAMINER COLECCIÓN 2011 B
100% gewürztraminer

90 Colour: bright straw. Nose: fresh, fresh fruit, white flowers, expressive, varietal. Palate: flavourful, fruity, good acidity, balanced, easy to drink.

VIÑAS DEL VERO GRAN VOS 2005 TR

90 Colour: cherry, garnet rim. Nose: complex, spicy, fine reductive notes. Palate: flavourful, full, ripe fruit, long, spicy.

VIÑAS DEL VERO LA MIRANDA DE SECASTILLA 2009 T
garnacha, parraleta, syrah

90 Colour: bright cherry, purple rim. Nose: elegant, medium intensity, red berry notes, ripe fruit, scrubland. Palate: ripe fruit, powerful.

VIÑAS DEL VERO MERLOT COLECCIÓN 2007 T
100% merlot

91 Colour: bright cherry, garnet rim. Nose: medium intensity, ripe fruit, balanced, complex. Palate: flavourful, ripe fruit, good acidity.

VIÑAS DEL VERO SECASTILLA 2008 T
garnacha

92 Colour: bright cherry, garnet rim. Nose: elegant, cocoa bean, creamy oak, aromatic coffee, ripe fruit. Palate: flavourful, balanced.

DESCRIPTION

This lies on the northern side of Tenerife, where 35% of Canary Island wines are produced. Here there is a particular phenomenon involving the formation of clouds due to the trade winds striking the warm soil. This gives rise to Atlantic type wines, which are fresh and fruity with an earthy taste, a result of the volcanic soils.

NUMBER OF HECTARES: 1.174

ALTITUDES: 0 m. – 1.000 m.

PREDOMINANT VARIETIES:

White grapes: güal, listán blanco, malvasía, muscatel, verdello, vijariego, pedro ximénez, forastera blanca, albillo, sabro, breval, bastardo blanco, burrablanca and torrontés.

Red grapes: bastardo negro, cabernet sauvignon, castellana negra, listán negro, listán prieto, malvasía rosada, muscatel negro, negramoll, pinot noir, rubí cabernet, syrah, tempranillo, tintilla and vijariego negro.

CLIMATOLOGY AND SOILS

This is typically Atlantic, the temperatures are mild thanks to the influence of the trade winds which provide a high level of humidity. The soils are volcanic, with a red colour, composed of organic material and trace elements.

BODEGA DOMÍNGUEZ CUARTA GENERACIÓN

Calvario, 79
38350 Tacoronte - (Santa CruzTenerife)
☎: +34 922 572 435 - Fax: +34 922 572 435
administracion@bodegadominguez.es
www.bodegadominguez.com

DOMÍNGUEZ MALVASÍA CLÁSICO 2010 B
malvasía

91 Colour: old gold. Nose: complex, elegant, candied fruit, faded flowers, sweet spices. Palate: rich, flavourful, balanced.

BODEGAS CRATER

San Nicolás, 122
38360 El Sauzal - (Santa Cruz de Tenerife)
☎: +34 922 573 272 - Fax: +34 922 573 272
crater@bodegasbutens.com
www.craterbodegas.com

CRÁTER 2008 TC
70% listán negro, 30% negramoll

92 Colour: deep cherry, garnet rim. Nose: complex, balanced, ripe fruit, creamy oak, sweet spices, fragrant herbs. Palate: full, flavourful, good structure, round tannins.

MAGMA DE CRÁTER 2008 TC
80% negramoll, 20% syrah

93 Colour: cherry, garnet rim. Nose: mineral, complex, expressive, ripe fruit, neat, powerfull, elegant. Palate: good structure, spicy, long.

BODEGAS INSULARES TENERIFE

Vereda del Medio, 48
38350 Tacoronte - (Santa Cruz de Tenerife)
☎: +34 922 570 617 - Fax: +34 922 570 043
bitsa@bodegasinsularestenerife.es
www.bodegasinsularestenerife.es

HUMBOLDT 1997 BLANCO DULCE
100% listán blanco

95 Colour: light mahogany. Nose: petrol notes, candied fruit, balanced, elegant, honeyed notes. Palate: rich, powerful, flavourful, full, long.

HUMBOLDT 2001 TINTO DULCE
100% listán negro

95 Colour: deep cherry, garnet rim. Nose: complex, balanced, expressive, spicy, aromatic coffee, fruit liqueur notes. Palate: balanced, rich, good structure, sweet tannins, full.

HUMBOLDT MALVASÍA 2008 B
100% malvasía

94 Colour: bright yellow. Nose: expressive, complex, candied fruit, floral, honeyed notes, sweet spices, pattiserie. Palate: good structure, flavourful, good acidity, rich.

HUMBOLDT VENDIMIA TARDÍA 2005 B
100% listán blanco

92 Colour: old gold, amber rim. Nose: complex, expressive, acetaldehyde, candied fruit. Palate: creamy, balanced, long.

HUMBOLDT VERDELLO 2005 BLANCO DULCE
100% verdello

94 Colour: bright yellow. Nose: candied fruit, faded flowers, caramel, sweet spices, petrol notes. Palate: rich, flavourful, good acidity.

DESCRIPTION

This is the doyen of the Catalonian Denominations of Origin. The zone takes in all the province of Tarragona, but has been supplanted by lighter Denominations of Origin such as Priorat and Montsant. Most of the wineries survive as suppliers of cava or maintain the tradition of liqueur wines which are classified as such varied wines as mistelas, garnachas, local sweet wines and muscatels. In recent years, pleasant, fruity wines made from local grapes such as sumoll have appeared.

NUMBER OF HECTARES: 6.600

ALTITUDES: 160 m.

PREDOMINANT VARIETIES:

White grapes: chardonnay, macabeo, xarel.lo, garnacha blanca, parellada, muscat of Alexandria, muscatel de Frontignan, sauvignon blanc and malvasía.

Red grapes: samsó, garnacha, ull de llebre, cabernet sauvignon, merlot, monastrell, pinot noir, syrah, sumoll and carigane.

CLIMATOLOGY AND SOILS

Mediterranean in its more northerly part (El Camp) and somewhat more extreme in the zone of Ribera, with warm winters and summers. The soils are light and of a limestone type.

AGRÍCOLA I S.C. MONTBRIÓ DEL CAMP

Avda. Sant Jordi, 19-21
43340 Montbrió del Camp - (Tarragona)
☎: +34 977 826 039 - Fax: +34 977 826 576
montebrione@retemail.es
www.montebrione.com

MOSCATELL MONTEBRIONE BLANCO DULCE

90 Colour: bright yellow. Nose: balanced, expressive, candied fruit, pattiserie, white flowers. Palate: flavourful, fruity.

AGRÍCOLA Y SECCIÓ DE CRÉDIT DE RODONYA

St. Sebastia, 3
43812 Rodonya - (Tarragona)
crodonya@telefonica.net

SUMOI CAPVESPRE S/C T

90 Colour: light cherry. Nose: overripe fruit, powerfull, expressive, sweet spices, caramel. Palate: good structure, flavourful, long.

BODEGAS J. M. BACH I FILLS

Camí Vell de Cambrils 180
43480 Vilaseca - (Tarragona)
☎: +34 977 353 099 - Fax: +34 977 353 154
closbarenys@closbarenys.com
www.closbarenys.com

CLOS BARENYS MARIANA RESERVA ESPECIAL DE FAMILIA MAGNUM 2007 T
100% cabernet sauvignon

90 Colour: cherry, garnet rim. Nose: balanced, expressive, sweet spices, scrubland. Palate: good structure, flavourful, balsamic, ripe fruit, long.

DE MULLER

Camí Pedra Estela, 34
43205 Reus - (Tarragona)
☎: +34 977 757 473 - Fax: +34 977 771 129
lab@demuller.es
www.demuller.es

DE MULLER AVREO SECO AÑEJO
70% garnacha, 30% garnacha blanca

91 Colour: mahogany. Nose: roasted almonds, balanced, acetaldehyde. Palate: good structure, flavourful, fine bitter notes.

DE MULLER AVREO SEMIDULCE AÑEJO
garnacha, garnacha blanca

91 Colour: light mahogany. Nose: spicy, fruit liqueur notes, fruit liqueur notes, toasty, aromatic coffee. Palate: powerful, sweet.

DE MULLER CHARDONNAY 2011 BFB
100% chardonnay

91 Colour: bright golden. Nose: balanced, expressive, faded flowers, citrus fruit, honeyed notes. Palate: fine bitter notes, balanced, good acidity, ripe fruit.

DE MULLER GARNACHA SOLERA 1926 SOLERA
100% garnacha

94 Color iodine, amber rim. Aroma powerfull, complex, elegant, dry nuts, toasty. Taste rich, fine bitter notes, fine solera notes, long, spicy.

DE MULLER MOSCATEL AÑEJO VINO DE LICOR
moscatel de alejandría

90 Colour: light mahogany. Nose: powerfull, varietal, fruit liqueur notes, honeyed notes. Palate: fine bitter notes, good acidity, spirituous.

DE MULLER RANCIO SECO VINO DE LICOR
garnacha, cariñena

91 Colour: light mahogany. Nose: balanced, expressive, roasted almonds, sweet spices, acetaldehyde. Palate: good structure, flavourful, complex.

PAJARETE SOLERA 1851 RANCIO
moscatel de alejandría, garnacha, garnacha blanca

93 Color iodine, amber rim. Aroma powerfull, complex, elegant, dry nuts, toasty. Taste rich, fine bitter notes, fine solera notes, long, spicy.

VINO DE MISA DULCE SUPERIOR
60% garnacha blanca, 40% macabeo

90 Colour: old gold. Nose: fruit liqueur notes, honeyed notes, sweet spices, aged wood nuances, spicy. Palate: long, rich, powerful, flavourful, balanced.

VINOS PADRÓ

Avda. Catalunya, 64-70
43812 Brafim - (Tarragona)
☎: +34 977 620 012 - Fax: +34 977 620 486
info@vinspadro.com
www.vinspadro.com

IPSIS 2009 TC
tempranillo, merlot

90 Colour: bright cherry, purple rim. Nose: sweet spices, toasty, ripe fruit. Palate: ripe fruit, long, round tannins.

VINYES DEL TERRER

Camí del Terrer, s/n
43480 Vila-Seca - (Tarragona)
☎: +34 977 269 229 - Fax: +34 977 269 229
info@terrer.net
www.terrer.net

NUS DEL TERRER 2009 T
55% cabernet sauvignon, 45% garnacha

93 Colour: cherry, garnet rim. Nose: ripe fruit, spicy, creamy oak, toasty, complex, cigar. Palate: powerful, flavourful, toasty, round tannins.

NUS DEL TERRER 2010 T
65% cabernet sauvignon, 35% garnacha

93 Colour: cherry, garnet rim. Nose: ripe fruit, spicy, creamy oak, toasty, complex, fruit expression, red berry notes. Palate: powerful, flavourful, toasty, round tannins, round.

TERRER D'AUBERT 2010 T
95% cabernet sauvignon, 5% garnacha

92 Colour: cherry, garnet rim. Nose: spicy, creamy oak, toasty, characterful. Palate: powerful, flavourful, toasty, round tannins.

DESCRIPTION

The wines of this zone, a past exporter, received the name from its centre of operations: Gandesa, to the east of the city of Tarragona. Its most attractive product is the white wine with a high level of alcohol. This is a Mediterranean type wine, favoured by the garnacha blanca variety of grape, with an aromatic, herbaceous style. In order to highlight these wines, the special seal "100 x 100 garnacha blanca" has been created.

NUMBER OF HECTARES: 5.755 **ALTITUDES:** 350 m. – 500 m.

PREDOMINANT VARIETIES:

White grapes: chardonnay, garnacha blanca, parellada, macabeo, muscat of Alexandria, muscatel de grano pequeño, sauvignon blanc, chenin, pedro ximénez and viognier.

Red grapes: cabernet sauvignon, cariñena, garnacha tinta, garnacha peluda, merlot, samsó, syrah, tempranillo, petit verdot, marselane and caladoc.

CLIMATOLOGY AND SOILS

Mediterranean but with continental influences and the presence of the Cierzo and the Garbi (southwest) winds. The soils are of a limestone type and the texture is mainly clay, poor in organic material and with an abundance of pebbles.

AGRÍCOLA SANT JOSEP

Estació, 2
43785 Bot - (Tarragona)
☎: +34 977 428 035 - Fax: +34 977 428 192
info@coopbot.com
www.coopbot.com

LLÀGRIMES DE TARDOR 2010 BFB
100% garnacha blanca

92 Color bright yellow. Aroma powerfull, ripe fruit, sweet spices, creamy oak, fragrant herbs. Taste rich, smoky aftertaste, flavourful, fresh, good acidity.

LLÀGRIMES DE TARDOR MISTELA NEGRA 2011 VINO DE LICOR
100% garnacha

90 Colour: cherry, garnet rim. Nose: fruit liqueur notes, sweet spices, creamy oak, dark chocolate. Palate: rich, powerful, flavourful, balanced.

LLÀGRIMES DE TARDOR SELECCIÓ 2006 TC
30% cariñena, 23% cabernet sauvignon, 23% syrah, 14% merlot, 10% garnacha

91 Colour: cherry, garnet rim. Nose: ripe fruit, spicy, creamy oak, toasty. Palate: powerful, flavourful, toasty, round tannins.

CELLER BÁRBARA FORÉS

Santa Anna, 28
43780 Gandesa - (Tarragona)
☎: +34 977 420 160 - Fax: +34 977 421 399
info@cellerbarbarafores.com
www.cellerbarbarafores.com

COMA D'EN POU BÀRBARA FORÉS 2008 T
45% garnacha, 30% syrah, 25% cabernet sauvignon

91 Colour: cherry, garnet rim. Nose: ripe fruit, spicy, creamy oak, complex, wild herbs. Palate: powerful, flavourful, round tannins.

EL TEMPLARI BÁRBARA FORÉS 2010 T
55% garnacha, 45% morenillo

92 Colour: deep cherry. Nose: ripe fruit, red berry notes, earthy notes. Palate: ripe fruit, good acidity, balanced.

VI DOLÇ NATURAL BÁRBARA FORÉS 2009 B
garnacha blanca

93 Colour: bright golden. Nose: candied fruit, acetaldehyde, expressive, balanced. Palate: flavourful, rich, balanced.

CELLER BATEA

Moli, 30
43786 Batea - (Tarragona)
☎: +34 977 430 056 - Fax: +34 977 430 589
cellerbatea@cellerbatea.com
www.cellerbatea.com

EQUINOX B

91 Color golden. Aroma powerfull, floral, honeyed notes, candied fruit, fragrant herbs. Taste flavourful, sweet, fresh, fruity, good acidity, long.

EQUINOX S/C MISTELA
garnacha

90 Colour: black cherry. Nose: toasty, fruit preserve. Palate: flavourful, long, concentrated, powerful, sweet, fruity.

CELLER COOPERATIU GANDESA

Avda. Catalunya, 28
43780 Gandesa - (Tarragona)
☎: +34 977 420 017 - Fax: +34 977 420 403
perefiguereo@coopgandesa.com
www.coopgandesa.com

GANDESA VI RANCI RANCIO
100% garnacha blanca

90 Color iodine, amber rim. Aroma powerfull, complex, elegant, dry nuts, toasty. Taste rich, fine bitter notes, fine solera notes, long, spicy.

CELLER JORDI MIRÓ

Sant Marc, 96
43784 Corbera d'Ebre - (Tarragona)
☎: +34 650 010 639
jordi@ennak.com
www.jordimirodiego.blogsopt.com

ENNAK 2010 TC
garnacha, tempranillo, merlot, cabernet sauvignon

91 Colour: cherry, garnet rim. Nose: ripe fruit, spicy, creamy oak, toasty, complex, earthy notes. Palate: powerful, flavourful, toasty, round tannins.

CELLER PIÑOL

Avda. Aragón, 9
43786 Batea - (Tarragona)
☎: +34 977 430 505 - Fax: +34 977 430 498
info@cellerpinol.com
www.vinospinol.com

FINCA MORENILLO 2010 T
100% morenillo

90 Colour: bright cherry. Nose: expressive, overripe fruit, spicy. Palate: fine bitter notes, good acidity, long.

JOSEFINA PIÑOL VENDIMIA TARDÍA 2010 TINTO DULCE
100% garnacha

91 Colour: cherry, garnet rim. Nose: red berry notes, fruit liqueur notes, spicy, dark chocolate, creamy oak. Palate: powerful, flavourful, spirituous, long.

L'AVI ARRUFÍ 2008 T
60% cariñena, 30% garnacha, 10% syrah

92 Colour: bright cherry. Nose: ripe fruit, sweet spices, creamy oak, toasty. Palate: flavourful, fruity, toasty, round tannins.

L'AVI ARRUFÍ 2010 BFB
garnacha blanca

92 Colour: bright yellow. Nose: powerfull, ripe fruit, sweet spices, creamy oak. Palate: rich, smoky aftertaste, flavourful, fresh, good acidity.

MATHER TERESINA SELECCIÓN DE VIÑAS VIEJAS 2008 T
50% garnacha, 30% cariñena, 20% morenillo

91 Colour: cherry, garnet rim. Nose: spicy, creamy oak, toasty, complex. Palate: powerful, flavourful, toasty, round tannins.

PORTAL N. SRA. PORTAL 2010 T ROBLE
50% garnacha, 20% cariñena, 15% merlot, 15% syrah

90 Color cherry, garnet rim. Aroma ripe fruit, spicy, creamy oak, toasty, complex. Taste powerful, flavourful, toasty, round tannins.

PORTAL N. SRA. PORTAL 2011 B
80% garnacha blanca, 10% sauvignon blanc, 10% viognier

91 Colour: bright straw. Nose: fresh, fresh fruit, white flowers. Palate: flavourful, fruity, good acidity, balanced.

CELLER TERN

Ctra. Vilalba, s/n
43786 Batea - (Tarragona)
☎: - Fax: +34 977 430 433
ternobradordevi@gmail.com
www.ternobradordevi.com

TERN 2011 B
garnacha blanca

90 Colour: bright yellow. Nose: powerfull, ripe fruit, sweet spices, fragrant herbs. Palate: rich, smoky aftertaste, flavourful, fresh, good acidity.

CELLERS TARRONÉ

Calvari, 22
43786 Batea - (Tarragona)
☎: +34 977 430 109 - Fax: +34 977 430 183
inma@cellerstarrone.com
www.cellerstarrone.com

MERIAN DULCE NATURAL 2011 T
100% garnacha

90 Colour: cherry, garnet rim. Nose: fruit preserve, fruit liqueur notes, sweet spices. Palate: powerful, flavourful, sweet.

EDETÀRIA

Finca El Mas
43780 Gandesa - (Tarragona)
☎: +34 977 421 534 - Fax: +34 977 421 534
info@edetaria.com
www.edetaria.com

EDETANA MAGNUM 2010 B
70% garnacha blanca, 30% viognier

91 Colour: bright straw. Nose: white flowers, fresh fruit, fragrant herbs, sweet spices, creamy oak. Palate: powerful, flavourful, fresh, fruity, spicy, balanced.

EDETÀRIA 2008 B
85% garnacha blanca, 15% macabeo

94 Colour: bright yellow. Nose: smoky, dry nuts, fragrant herbs, dry stone, sweet spices, creamy oak. Palate: round, rich, flavourful, long, spicy, balanced.

EDETÀRIA 2008 T
60% garnacha peluda, 30% syrah, 5% cariñena, cabernet sauvignon

91 Colour: cherry, garnet rim. Nose: ripe fruit, spicy, toasty, aromatic coffee, earthy notes. Palate: powerful, flavourful, toasty, long, balanced.

EDETÀRIA 2010 B
85% garnacha blanca, 15% macabeo

92 Colour: bright yellow. Nose: citrus fruit, candied fruit, balsamic herbs, mineral, dark chocolate, cocoa bean, sweet spices, toasty. Palate: rich, flavourful, fruity, fresh, good acidity, balanced.

EDETÀRIA DOLÇ 2007 T
70% garnacha, 30% cabernet sauvignon

91 Colour: cherry, garnet rim. Nose: ripe fruit, spicy, toasty, balsamic herbs, earthy notes. Palate: powerful, flavourful, toasty, round tannins, balanced.

EDETÀRIA DOLÇ 2009 T
70% garnacha, 30% cariñena

90 Colour: bright cherry. Nose: ripe fruit, sweet spices, creamy oak, dark chocolate, cocoa bean. Palate: flavourful, fruity, toasty, round tannins.

VÍA TERRA 2011 B
100% garnacha blanca

90 Colour: bright straw. Nose: fresh, fresh fruit, white flowers, complex, characterful. Palate: flavourful, fruity, good acidity, balanced.

LAFOU CELLER

Can Figueras, Plaza Catalunya, 34
43786 Batea - (Tarragona)
☎: +34 938 743 511 - Fax: +34 938 737 204
info@lafou.net
www.lafou.net

LAFOU 2008 T
75% garnacha, 15% syrah, 10% cabernet sauvignon

91 Colour: cherry, garnet rim. Nose: spicy, creamy oak, toasty, characterful, overripe fruit. Palate: powerful, flavourful, toasty, round tannins.

SOMDINOU

Avda. Catalunya, 28
43780 Gandesa - (Tarragona)
☎: +34 977 420 017 - Fax: +34 977 420 403
joanmariariera@hotmail.com
www.somdinou.cat

PURESA 2007 T
100% cariñena

91 Colour: cherry, garnet rim. Nose: spicy, creamy oak, toasty. Palate: powerful, flavourful, toasty, round tannins.

VINS SAT LA BOTERA

Sant Roc, 26
43786 Batea - (Tarragona)
☎: +34 977 430 009 - Fax: +34 977 430 801
labotera@labotera.com
www.labotera.com

BRUNA DOLÇ 2010 T
garnacha, syrah

91 Colour: deep cherry. Nose: fruit preserve, fruit liqueur notes, powerfull. Palate: long, creamy, pruney.

DESCRIPTION

This is located to the south of the province of León, but also includes towns of Valladolid, a zone which is distinguished by more extreme temperatures than those of Bierzo. Its recognition was due to the character of the prieto picudo grape, a variety with compact bunches pointed grapes which give wines with an intense colour and aromas similar to mencía grapes, it is very tasty. This vine is also the raw material for the sparkling rosé wines produced with a very old technique called "madreo" which consists of adding complete bunches during fermentation. With this process the wine maintains remains of carbonic gas.

NUMBER OF HECTARES: 1.321

ALTITUDES: 750 m.

PREDOMINANT VARIETIES:

White grapes: albarín, verdejo, godello, palomino and malvasía
Red grapes: prieto picudo, mencía, garnacha and tempranillo.

CLIMATOLOGY AND SOILS

Continental type with Atlantic influences. Both the brown and the limestone soils are alluvial.

BODEGAS MARGÓN

Avda de Valencia de Don Juan, s/n
24209 Pajares de los Oteros - (León)
☎: +34 987 750 800 - Fax: +34 987 750 481
comercial@bodegasmargon.com
www.bodegasmargon.com

PRICUM 2011 RD
prieto picudo

90 Colour: onion pink. Nose: elegant, candied fruit, dried flowers, red berry notes. Palate: light-bodied, flavourful, good acidity, long, spicy.

PRICUM ALBARÍN 2010 B BARRICA
albarín

90 Colour: bright yellow. Nose: powerfull, sweet spices, creamy oak, ripe fruit, citrus fruit. Palate: rich, smoky aftertaste, flavourful, fresh, good acidity.

PRICUM ALDEBARÁN VENDIMIA TARDÍA 2008 B
100% verdejo

95 Colour: bright yellow. Nose: ripe fruit, citrus fruit, dried flowers, fragrant herbs, expressive, complex. Palate: elegant, unctuous, fresh, fruity, flavourful, balanced.

PRICUM PARAJE DEL SANTO 2008 T
prieto picudo

92 Color cherry, garnet rim. Aroma ripe fruit, spicy, creamy oak, toasty, complex. Taste powerful, flavourful, toasty, round tannins.

PRICUM PARAJE DEL SANTO 2009 T
100% prieto picudo

91 Color cherry, garnet rim. Aroma ripe fruit, spicy, creamy oak, toasty, complex. Taste powerful, flavourful, toasty, round tannins.

PRICUM PRIETO PICUDO 2008 T
prieto picudo

91 Colour: cherry, garnet rim. Nose: sweet spices, creamy oak, candied fruit, balsamic herbs, scrubland. Palate: flavourful, fruity, spicy, ripe fruit.

PRICUM PRIETO PICUDO 2009 T
100% prieto picudo

90 Colour: cherry, garnet rim. Nose: ripe fruit, red berry notes, creamy oak, spicy. Palate: flavourful, powerful, spicy, ripe fruit.

PRICUM PRIMEUR 2010 T
prieto picudo

94 Colour: cherry, garnet rim. Nose: powerfull, varietal, fresh, mineral. Palate: fruity, flavourful, mineral.

PRICUM VALDEMUZ 2008 T
prieto picudo

91 Colour: cherry, garnet rim. Nose: ripe fruit, spicy, creamy oak, toasty, mineral. Palate: powerful, flavourful, toasty, round tannins.

VALDEMUZ 2009 T
100% prieto picudo

90 Colour: bright cherry. Nose: ripe fruit, sweet spices, creamy oak. Palate: flavourful, fruity, toasty, round tannins.

LEYENDA DEL PÁRAMO

Ctra. de León s/n, Paraje El Cueto
24230 Valdevimbre - (León)
☎: +34 626 194 347
info@leyendadelparamo.com
www.leyendadelparamo.com

EL MÉDICO 2010 T ROBLE
100% prieto picudo

94 Colour: cherry, garnet rim. Nose: red berry notes, ripe fruit, mineral, sweet spices, cocoa bean, dark chocolate, balsamic herbs, scrubland. Palate: powerful, flavourful, complex, long, toasty. Personality.

EL MÚSICO 2009 T
100% prieto picudo

91 Colour: cherry, garnet rim. Nose: powerfull, ripe fruit, red berry notes, toasty, new oak. Palate: flavourful, powerful, spicy, ripe fruit.

MITTEL 2011 B
100% albarín

90 Colour: straw. Nose: fruit expression, fresh, varietal, expressive, balanced. Palate: fruity, varietal, good acidity, sweetness, balanced.

TAMPESTA

La Socollada, s/n
24230 Valdevimbre - (León)
☎: +34 987 351 025 - Fax: +34 987 351 025
bodegas@tampesta.com
www.tampesta.com

TAMPESTA 2011 RD
prieto picudo

90 Colour: onion pink. Nose: elegant, candied fruit, dried flowers, red berry notes. Palate: light-bodied, flavourful, good acidity, long, spicy.

TAMPESTA GOLÁN 2009 T
prieto picudo

90 Colour: dark-red cherry. Nose: fruit expression, creamy oak, varietal. Palate: flavourful, creamy, toasty, harsh oak tannins.

VIÑEDOS Y BODEGA PARDEVALLES

Ctra. de León, s/n
24230 Valdevimbre - (León)
☎: +34 987 304 222 - Fax: +34 987 304 222
info@pardevalles.es
www.pardevalles.com

PARDEVALLES CARROLEÓN 2008 T
100% prieto picudo

91 Colour: bright cherry. Nose: sweet spices, creamy oak, ripe fruit. Palate: flavourful, fruity, toasty, round tannins.

PARDEVALLES GAMONAL 2009 T
100% prieto picudo

91 Colour: cherry, garnet rim. Nose: powerfull, expressive, sweet spices, dark chocolate, mineral. Palate: flavourful, powerful, fine bitter notes, good acidity.

DESCRIPTION

The vineyards of this zone are located to southeast of the province of Zamora, a region which, until now, was relegated to being the poor relative of Toro. The very dry climate and very old vines at a higher altitude than in Toro provide the context for producing wines from very concentrated tempranillo grapes, which are quite fresh. Its wines made from verdejo and malvasía grapes are a hidden treasure.

NUMBER OF HECTARES: 707 **ALTITUDES:** 700 m.

PREDOMINANT VARIETIES:

White grapes: malvasía, small grained muscatel, verdejo, albillo, palomino and godello.
Red grapes: tempranillo, cabernet sauvigon and garnacha.

CLIMATOLOGY AND SOILS

The temperatures are extreme as corresponds to a dry continental climate. The predominant soils are alluvial owing to the presence of the River Duero.

VIÑAS DEL CÉNIT

Ctra. de Circunvalación, s/n
49708 Villanueva de Campeán - (Zamora)
☎: +34 980 569 346 - Fax: +34 980 569 328
info@bodegascenit.com
www.bodegascenit.com

CENIT 2008 T
100% tempranillo

95 Colour: cherry, garnet rim. Nose: powerfull, varietal, ripe fruit, fruit expression, creamy oak, toasty. Palate: flavourful, powerful, good acidity, round tannins.

VIA CENIT 2010 T
100% tempranillo

94 Colour: cherry, garnet rim. Nose: spicy, creamy oak, toasty, complex, mineral, fruit expression, red berry notes. Palate: powerful, flavourful, toasty, round tannins.

DESCRIPTION

Toro is situated in the province of Zamora, in the far west of the region of Castile and León. The key wine in this region is the Toro red grape, a clone of tempranillo which, in this terrain, is cultivated in warmer conditions and in soils with older vines. In recent years, there have appeared a multiplicity of equally potent red wines but with more elegant tannins thanks to ageing in the Bordeaux style.

NUMBER OF HECTARES: 5.783 **ALTITUDES:** 620 m. – 750 m.

PREDOMINANT VARIETIES:

White grapes: malvasía and verdejo.
Red grapes: tinta de toro and garnacha.

CLIMATOLOGY AND SOILS

Continental with Atlantic influences and quite arid. The soils are fundamentally brown – limestone.

BODEGA BURDIGALA (F. LURTON & M. ROLLAND)

Camino Magarín, s/n
47529 Villafranca del Duero - (Valladolid)
☎: +34 983 034 030 - Fax: +34 983 034 040
bodega@burdigala.es
www.francoislurton.com

CAMPESINO 2009 T
100% tinta de Toro

92 Colour: cherry, garnet rim. Nose: spicy, creamy oak, toasty. Palate: powerful, flavourful, toasty, round tannins.

CAMPO ALEGRE 2009 T
100% tinta de Toro

91 Colour: cherry, garnet rim. Nose: balanced, complex, ripe fruit, sweet spices, creamy oak. Palate: good structure, powerful, full.

CAMPO ELISEO 2006 T
100% tinta de Toro

92 Colour: cherry, garnet rim. Nose: spicy, creamy oak, toasty, complex, overripe fruit. Palate: powerful, flavourful, toasty, round tannins.

BODEGA ELÍAS MORA

Juan Mora, s/n
47530 San Román de Hornija - (Valladolid)
☎: +34 983 784 029 - Fax: +34 983 784 190
info@bodegaseliasmora.com
www.bodegaseliasmora.com

2V PREMIUM 2008 T
tinta de Toro

91 Colour: cherry, garnet rim. Nose: spicy, creamy oak, toasty, complex, ripe fruit. Palate: powerful, flavourful, toasty, round tannins.

ELÍAS MORA 2009 TC
100% tinta de Toro

91 Colour: cherry, garnet rim. Nose: ripe fruit, cocoa bean, creamy oak, complex. Palate: balanced, round tannins, long.

VIÑAS ELÍAS MORA 2010 T ROBLE
tinta de Toro

90 Colour: cherry, garnet rim. Nose: ripe fruit, spicy, creamy oak, toasty, earthy notes. Palate: powerful, flavourful, toasty.

BODEGA NUMANTHIA

Real, s/n
49882 Valdefinjas - (Zamora)
☎: +34 980 699 147 - Fax: +34 980 699 164
www.numanthia.com

NUMANTHIA 2010 T
tinta de Toro

96 Colour: very deep cherry. Nose: ripe fruit, red berry notes, fruit expression, sweet spices, dark chocolate. Palate: flavourful, concentrated, powerful, fine bitter notes, good acidity, round, mineral.

TERMANTHIA 2010 T
100% tinta de Toro

97 Colour: bright cherry. Nose: ripe fruit, sweet spices, creamy oak, expressive, fruit expression, red berry notes, mineral. Palate: flavourful, fruity, toasty, round tannins, long, mineral.

TERMES 2010 T
tinta de Toro

94 Colour: cherry, purple rim. Nose: fresh fruit, red berry notes, floral, lactic notes. Palate: flavourful, fruity, good acidity, round tannins.

BODEGA PAGO DE CUBAS

Ctra. Toro Valdefinjas, Km. 6,9
49882 Valdefinjas - (Zamora)
☎: +34 626 410 524 - Fax: +34 980 059 965

INCRÉDULO 2009 T
100% tinta de Toro

90 Color cherry, garnet rim. Aroma ripe fruit, spicy, creamy oak, toasty, complex. Taste powerful, flavourful, toasty, round tannins.

BODEGAS ABANICO

Pol. Ind Ca l'Avellanet - Susany, 6
8553 Seva - (Barcelona)
☎: +34 938 125 676 - Fax: +34 938 123 213
info@exportiberia.com
www.bodegasabanico.com

ETERNUM VITI 2009 T
100% tinta de Toro

91 Colour: cherry, garnet rim. Nose: ripe fruit, spicy, creamy oak, toasty, earthy notes. Palate: powerful, flavourful, toasty, balanced.

LOS COLMILLOS 2009 T
100% tinta de Toro

90 Colour: bright cherry. Nose: ripe fruit, sweet spices, creamy oak, balsamic herbs, earthy notes. Palate: flavourful, fruity, toasty, round tannins.

BODEGAS CARMEN RODRÍGUEZ

Ctra. Salamanca, ZA 605, Km. 1,6
49800 Toro - (Zamora)
☎: +34 980 568 005
info@carodorum.com
www.carodorum.com

CARODORUM SELECCIÓN 2009 TC
tinta de Toro

92 Colour: black cherry, garnet rim. Nose: ripe fruit, scrubland, earthy notes, sweet spices. Palate: flavourful, long, round, balanced.

BODEGAS FARIÑA

Camino del Palo, s/n
49800 Toro - (Zamora)
☎: +34 980 577 673 - Fax: +34 980 577 720
comercial@bodegasfarina.com
www.bodegasfarina.com

COLEGIATA 2011 RD
100% tinta de Toro

90 Colour: rose, purple rim. Nose: powerfull, ripe fruit, red berry notes, floral. Palate: , powerful, fruity, fresh.

COLEGIATA 2011 T
100% tinta de Toro

90 Colour: cherry, purple rim. Nose: fresh fruit, red berry notes, floral. Palate: flavourful, fruity, good acidity, round tannins.

GRAN COLEGIATA CAMPUS 2008 TC
100% tinta de Toro

93 Colour: cherry, garnet rim. Nose: ripe fruit, spicy, creamy oak, toasty, complex, balanced. Palate: powerful, flavourful, toasty, round tannins, round.

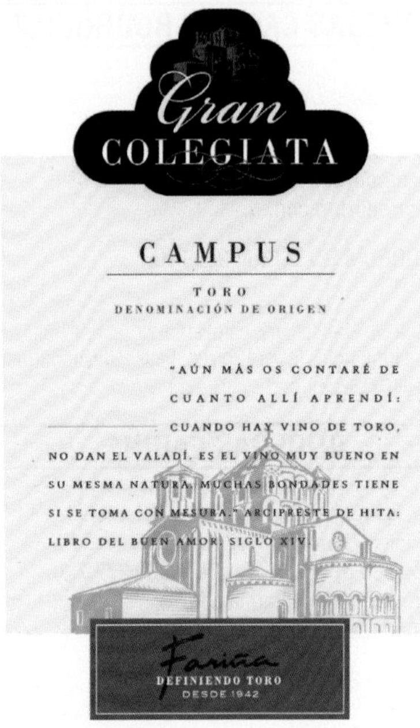

GRAN COLEGIATA ROBLE FRANCÉS 2008 TC
100% tinta de Toro

90 Colour: cherry, garnet rim. Nose: balanced, expressive, spicy, powerfull, ripe fruit. Palate: good structure, fruity.

BODEGAS FRONTAURA

Santiago, 17 - 4º
47001 - (Valladolid)
☎: +34 983 360 284 - Fax: +34 983 345 546
info@bodegasfrontaura.es
www.bodegasfrontaura.es

APONTE 2006 T
100% tinta de Toro

93 Colour: cherry, garnet rim. Nose: complex, ripe fruit, sweet spices, expressive. Palate: good structure, flavourful, round tannins, long.

DOMINIO DE VALDELACASA 2009 T
100% tinta de Toro

90 Colour: cherry, garnet rim. Nose: red berry notes, ripe fruit, mineral, sweet spices, creamy oak. Palate: powerful, flavourful, toasty.

FRONTAURA 2005 TR
100% tinta de Toro

92 Colour: cherry, garnet rim. Nose: balanced, complex, sweet spices, ripe fruit. Palate: good structure, flavourful, complex.

FRONTAURA 2006 TC
100% tinta de Toro

90 Colour: cherry, garnet rim. Nose: earthy notes, spicy, creamy oak, ripe fruit, fine reductive notes. Palate: flavourful, long, round tannins.

BODEGAS GIL LUNA

Ctra. Toro - Salamanca, Km. 2
49800 Toro - (Zamora)
☎: +34 980 698 509 - Fax: +34 980 698 294
pbgiluna@giluna.com
www.giluna.com

TRES LUNAS 2008 T
95% tinta de Toro, 5% garnacha

91 Color cherry, garnet rim. Aroma ripe fruit, spicy, creamy oak, toasty, complex. Taste powerful, flavourful, toasty, round tannins.

TRES LUNAS VERDEJO 2011 B
100% verdejo

91 Colour: bright straw. Nose: fresh, fresh fruit, white flowers, expressive, tropical fruit. Palate: flavourful, fruity, good acidity, balanced.

BODEGAS ITURRIA

Avda. Torrecilla De La Abadesa 2.2e
47100 Tordesillas - (Valladolid)
☎: +34 600 523 070
contact@bodegas-iturria.com

TINTO ITURRIA 2009 T
90% tinta de Toro, 10% garnacha

91 Colour: cherry, garnet rim. Nose: spicy, creamy oak, toasty, complex, fragrant herbs. Palate: powerful, flavourful, toasty, round tannins.

BODEGAS LIBA Y DELEITE

Paseo De Zorrilla, 77 – 3º Dcha.
47007 - (Valladolid)
☎: +34 983 355 543 - Fax: +34 983 340 824
acontia@acontia.es
www.acontia.es

ACONTIA '12 ROBLE ESPAÑOL 2009 T
85% tinta de Toro, 15% garnacha

90 Colour: cherry, garnet rim. Nose: ripe fruit, spicy, toasty, scrubland. Palate: flavourful, spicy, balanced.

BODEGAS MATARREDONDA

Ctra. Toro - Valdefinjas, km. 2,5
49800 Toro - (Zamora)
☎: +34 687 965 280 - Fax: +34 980 059 981
libranza@vinolibranza.com
www.vinolibranza.com

JUAN ROJO 2006 T
100% tinta de Toro

90 Colour: cherry, garnet rim. Nose: ripe fruit, macerated fruit, dark chocolate, sweet spices. Palate: full, powerful, round tannins.

BODEGAS MONTE LA REINA

Ctra. Toro - Zamora, Km. 436,7
49881 Toro - (Zamora)
☎: +34 980 082 011 - Fax: +34 980 082 012
bodega@montelareina.es
www.montelareina.es

CASTILLO DE MONTE LA REINA
VENDIMIA SELECCIONADA 2005 T
100% tempranillo

90 Colour: cherry, garnet rim. Nose: spicy, creamy oak, toasty. Palate: powerful, flavourful, toasty, round tannins.

INARAJA 2006 T
100% tempranillo

91 Colour: dark-red cherry, garnet rim. Nose: ripe fruit, creamy oak, sweet spices, earthy notes. Palate: concentrated, powerful, flavourful, balanced.

BODEGAS REJADORADA S.L.

Rejadorada, 11
49800 Toro - (Zamora)
☎: +34 980 693 089 - Fax: +34 980 693 089
rejadorada@rejadorada.com
www.rejadorada.com

BRAVO DE REJADORADA 2009 T
100% tinta de Toro

90 Colour: bright cherry. Nose: ripe fruit, sweet spices, creamy oak, toasty. Palate: flavourful, fruity, toasty, round tannins.

NOVELLUM REJADORADA 2008 TC
100% tinta de Toro

90 Colour: cherry, garnet rim. Nose: ripe fruit, spicy, creamy oak, toasty. Palate: powerful, flavourful, toasty, round tannins.

BODEGAS TORREDUERO

Pol. Ind. Norte - Parcela 5
49800 Toro - (Zamora)
☎: +34 941 454 050 - Fax: +34 941 454 529
bodega@bodegasriojanas.com
www.bodegasriojanas.com

MARQUÉS DE PEÑAMONTE COLECCIÓN PRIVADA 2009 T
100% tinta de Toro

90 Colour: cherry, garnet rim. Nose: ripe fruit, spicy, creamy oak, toasty, complex. Palate: powerful, flavourful, toasty, balanced.

BODEGAS VEGA SAUCO

Avda. Comuneros, 108
49810 Morales de Toro - (Zamora)
☎: +34 980 698 294 - Fax: +34 980 698 294
vegasauco@vegasauco.com
www.vegasauco.com

ADOREMUS 2005 TR
100% tinta de Toro

91 Colour: cherry, garnet rim. Nose: dark chocolate, tobacco, ripe fruit. Palate: good structure, flavourful, spicy, round tannins, long.

ADOREMUS 1998 TGR
100% tinta de Toro

91 Colour: pale ruby, brick rim edge. Nose: elegant, fine reductive notes, wet leather, aged wood nuances, fruit liqueur notes. Palate: spicy, fine tannins, elegant, long.

ADOREMUS 2004 TR
100% tinta de Toro

90 Colour: cherry, garnet rim. Nose: fruit preserve, cigar, old leather, aged wood nuances. Palate: spicy, flavourful, spirituous, long.

BODEGAS Y VIÑEDOS ANZIL

Ctra. Camino El Pego s/n, Ctra. Toro a Villabuena del Puente, km. 9,400
49800 Toro - (Zamora)
☎: +34 915 006 000 - Fax: +34 915 006 006
www.bodegasanzil.es

VIÑA MAYOR TORO 2010 T
100% tempranillo

90 Colour: cherry, garnet rim. Nose: spicy, creamy oak, toasty. Palate: powerful, flavourful, toasty, round tannins.

BODEGAS Y VIÑEDOS MAURODOS

Ctra. N-122, Km. 412 - Villaester
47112 Pedrosa del Rey - (Valladolid)
☎: +34 983 784 118 - Fax: +34 983 784 018
comunicacion@bodegasmauro.com
www.bodegasanroman.com

SAN ROMÁN 2009 T
100% tinta de Toro

94 Colour: cherry, garnet rim. Nose: spicy, creamy oak, toasty, complex, red berry notes, dark chocolate. Palate: powerful, flavourful, toasty, round tannins.

BODEGAS Y VIÑEDOS PINTIA

Ctra. de Morales, s/n
47530 San Román de Hornija - (Valladolid)
☎: +34 983 680 147 - Fax: +34 983 680 263
rhernan-perez@vega-sicilia.com
www.bodegaspintia.com

PINTIA 2009 T
100% tinta de Toro

95 Colour: cherry, garnet rim. Nose: powerfull, ripe fruit, cocoa bean, expressive. Palate: good structure, full, fine tannins, spicy.

BODEGUEROS QUINTA ESENCIA

Eras, 37
47520 Castronuño - (Valladolid)
☎: +34 605 887 100 - Fax: +34 983 866 391
ferrin@bodeguerosquintaesencia.com
www.bodeguerosquintaesencia.com

SOFROS 2010 T
100% tinta de Toro

91 Colour: cherry, garnet rim. Nose: spicy, creamy oak, toasty, mineral, ripe fruit. Palate: powerful, flavourful, toasty, round tannins.

COMPAÑÍA DE VINOS TELMO RODRÍGUEZ

El Monte
1308 Lanciego - (Álava)
☎: +34 945 628 315 - Fax: +34 945 628 314
contact@telmorodriguez.com
www.telmorodriguez.com

PAGO LA JARA 2008 T
100% tinta de Toro

93 Colour: very deep cherry. Nose: powerfull, varietal, characterful, ripe fruit, toasty, earthy notes. Palate: good acidity, fine bitter notes, round, powerful, round tannins.

CORAL DUERO

Ascensión, s/n
49154 El Pego - (Zamora)
☎: +34 980 606 333 - Fax: +34 980 606 333
rompesedas@rompesedas.com
www.rompesedas.com

ROMPESEDAS 2006 T
100% tinta de Toro

90 Colour: bright cherry. Nose: ripe fruit, sweet spices, creamy oak. Palate: flavourful, fruity, toasty, round tannins.

ROMPESEDAS FINCA LAS PARVAS 2006 T
100% tinta de Toro

93 Colour: cherry, garnet rim. Nose: ripe fruit, spicy, creamy oak, complex. Palate: powerful, flavourful, round tannins, full.

DOMAINES MAGREZ ESPAGNE

Pza. de la Trinidad, 5
49800 Toro - (Zamora)
☎: +34 980 698 172 - Fax: +34 980 698 172
ventas@vocarraje.es
www.bernard-magrez.com

PACIENCIA 2008 T
100% tinta de Toro

93 Colour: cherry, garnet rim. Nose: spicy, creamy oak, toasty, complex, fragrant herbs, mineral. Palate: powerful, flavourful, toasty, round tannins.

DOMINIO DEL BENDITO

Pza. Santo Domingo, 8
49800 Toro - (Zamora)
☎: +34 980 693 306 - Fax: +34 980 694 991
info@bodegadominiodelbendito.es

DOMINIO DEL BENDITO EL PRIMER PASO 2010 T ROBLE

90 Colour: bright cherry. Nose: sweet spices, creamy oak, ripe fruit. Palate: flavourful, fruity, toasty, round tannins.

DOMINIO DEL BENDITO LAS SABIAS 16 MESES 2008 T

92 Colour: cherry, garnet rim. Nose: spicy, creamy oak, toasty, characterful, ripe fruit. Palate: powerful, flavourful, toasty, round tannins.

EL TITÁN DEL BENDITO 2009 T

94 Colour: bright cherry. Nose: ripe fruit, sweet spices, creamy oak, expressive, toasty, mineral. Palate: flavourful, fruity, toasty, balanced.

ESTANCIA PIEDRA S.L.

Ctra. Toro a Salamanca, km. 5
49800 Toro - (Zamora)
☎: +34 980 693 900 - Fax: +34 980 693 901
info@estanciapiedra.com
www.estanciapiedra.com

PIEDRA AZUL 2011 T
100% tinta de Toro

90 Colour: cherry, purple rim. Nose: expressive, fresh fruit, red berry notes, floral, lactic notes, mineral. Palate: flavourful, fruity, good acidity, balanced.

PIEDRA PAREDINAS 2007 T
100% tinta de Toro

93 Colour: dark-red cherry, garnet rim. Nose: ripe fruit, earthy notes, spicy, creamy oak, toasty. Palate: long, powerful, flavourful, spicy.

PIEDRA PLATINO SELECCIÓN 2006 TR
100% tinta de Toro

92 Colour: pale ruby, brick rim edge. Nose: elegant, spicy, fine reductive notes, aged wood nuances, ripe fruit. Palate: spicy, fine tannins, elegant, long, balanced.

PIEDRA ROJA 2009 TC
100% tinta de Toro

92 Colour: cherry, garnet rim. Nose: ripe fruit, creamy oak, toasty, sweet spices, earthy notes. Palate: powerful, flavourful, toasty, long.

FRUTOS VILLAR (TORO)

Eras de Santa Catalina, s/n
49800 Toro - (Zamora)
☎: +34 983 586 868 - Fax: +34 983 580 180
bodegasfrutosvillar@bodegasfrutosvillar.com
www.bodegasfrutosvillar.com

MURUVE 2008 TR
tinta de Toro

90 Colour: cherry, garnet rim. Nose: balanced, powerfull, ripe fruit, dark chocolate, sweet spices. Palate: balanced, fine bitter notes.

HACIENDA TERRA DURO

Campanas, 4, 1º A
47001 - (Valladolid)
☎: +34 983 362 591 - Fax: +34 983 357 663
manueldenicolas@gmail.com
www.terraduro.com

TERRA D'URO FINCA LA RANA 2010 T
tinta de Toro

90 Colour: bright cherry. Nose: ripe fruit, sweet spices, creamy oak, fragrant herbs. Palate: flavourful, fruity, toasty, round tannins.

TERRA D'URO SELECCIÓN 2008 T
tinta de Toro

92 Colour: cherry, garnet rim. Nose: ripe fruit, earthy notes, spicy, creamy oak. Palate: flavourful, powerful, spicy, long, balanced.

TERRA D'URO SELECCIÓN 2009 T
tinta de Toro

90 Colour: cherry, garnet rim. Nose: earthy notes, fruit preserve, spicy, toasty. Palate: powerful, flavourful, long, spicy.

URO 2008 T
tinta de Toro

91 Color cherry, garnet rim. Aroma ripe fruit, spicy, creamy oak, toasty, complex. Taste powerful, flavourful, toasty, round tannins.

URO 2009 T
tinta de Toro

91 Colour: deep cherry. Nose: earthy notes, overripe fruit, toasty, dark chocolate. Palate: powerful, fine bitter notes, spicy.

LIBERALIA ENOLÓGICA

Camino del Palo, s/n
49800 Toro - (Zamora)
☎: +34 980 692 571 - Fax: +34 980 692 571
liberalia@liberalia.es
www.liberalia.es

LIBER 2005 TGR
100% tinta de Toro

91 Colour: cherry, garnet rim. Nose: spicy, creamy oak, toasty, ripe fruit. Palate: powerful, toasty, round tannins.

LIBERALIA CABEZA DE CUBA 2007 TC
100% tinta de Toro

90 Colour: cherry, garnet rim. Nose: ripe fruit, spicy, creamy oak, cocoa bean, fine reductive notes. Palate: powerful, flavourful, long, toasty.

LIBERALIA CINCO 2006 TR
100% tinta de Toro

92 Colour: deep cherry. Nose: characterful, dark chocolate, spicy. Palate: spicy, ripe fruit, round tannins.

LIBERALIA CUATRO 2008 TC
100% tinta de Toro

91 Colour: cherry, garnet rim. Nose: ripe fruit, spicy, creamy oak, toasty, characterful, varietal. Palate: powerful, flavourful, toasty, round tannins.

MARQUÉS DE OLIVARA

Eras de Santa Catalina, s/n
49800 Toro - (Zamora)
☎: +34 980 693 425 - Fax: +34 980 693 409
marquesdeolivara@marquesdeolivara.com
www.marquesdeolivara.com

MARQUÉS DE OLIVARA VENDIMIA SELECCIONADA 2009 T
100% tinta de Toro

90 Colour: cherry, garnet rim. Nose: complex, balanced, ripe fruit, creamy oak. Palate: full, flavourful, long.

PAGOS DEL REY D.O. TORO

Avda. de los Comuneros, 90
49810 Morales de Toro - (Zamora)
☎: +34 980 698 023 - Fax: +34 980 698 020
toro@pagosdelrey.com
www.pagosdelrey.com

FINCA LA MEDA 2010 TC
100% tinta de Toro

90 Colour: cherry, purple rim. Nose: ripe fruit, medium intensity, sweet spices. Palate: flavourful, fruity, good finish.

FINCA LA MEDA ALTA EXPRESIÓN 2011 T
100% tinta de Toro

90 Colour: deep cherry, purple rim. Nose: powerfull, candied fruit, creamy oak, sweet spices, macerated fruit. Palate: long, spicy.

GRAN BAJOZ DE AUTOR 2011 T
100% tinta de Toro

91 Colour: cherry, purple rim. Nose: red berry notes, ripe fruit, spicy, creamy oak, dark chocolate, cocoa bean.

QUINOLA SUÁREZ

Paseo de Zorrilla, 11- 4 izq.
47007 Valladolid - (Valladolid)
☎: +34 625 227 321
garagewine@quinola.es
www.quinola.es

QUINOLA GARAGE WINE 2009 T ROBLE
100% tinta de Toro

93 Colour: cherry, garnet rim. Nose: ripe fruit, spicy, creamy oak, toasty, complex, mineral, powerfull. Palate: powerful, flavourful, toasty, round tannins.

QUINTA DE LA QUIETUD

Camino de Bardales, s/n
49800 Toro - (Zamora)
☎: +34 980 568 019
info@quintaquietud.com
www.quintaquietud.com

QUINTA QUIETUD 2007 T
100% tinta de Toro

94 Colour: cherry, garnet rim. Nose: ripe fruit, spicy, creamy oak, toasty, complex, earthy notes, varietal. Palate: powerful, flavourful, toasty, round tannins.

RODRÍGUEZ SANZO

Manuel Azaña, 9
47014 - (Valladolid)
☎: +34 983 150 150 - Fax: +34 983 150 151
comunicacion@valsanzo.com
www.rodriguezsanzo.com

DAMALISCO 2009 TC
tinta de Toro

92 Colour: cherry, garnet rim. Nose: ripe fruit, spicy, creamy oak, toasty, complex, earthy notes. Palate: powerful, flavourful, toasty, round tannins.

TERRAS DE JAVIER RODRÍGUEZ 2009 T
100% tinta de Toro

93 Colour: bright cherry. Nose: ripe fruit, sweet spices, creamy oak, dark chocolate. Palate: flavourful, fruity, toasty, round tannins.

TESO LA MONJA

Paraje Valdebuey- Ctra. ZA-611, Km. 6,3
49882 Valdefinjas - (Zamora)
☎: +34 980 568 143 - Fax: +34 980 508 144
info@eguren.com
www.eguren.com

ALABASTER 2009 T
100% tinta de Toro

95 Colour: cherry, garnet rim. Nose: ripe fruit, spicy, creamy oak, toasty, complex, aromatic coffee, dark chocolate. Palate: powerful, flavourful, toasty, round tannins, round.

ALABASTER 2010 T
100% tinta de Toro

96 Colour: cherry, garnet rim. Nose: ripe fruit, spicy, creamy oak, toasty, complex, earthy notes. Palate: powerful, flavourful, toasty, round tannins, round, fine bitter notes, good acidity.

ALMIREZ 2010 T
100% tinta de Toro

94 Colour: bright cherry. Nose: ripe fruit, sweet spices, creamy oak, red berry notes. Palate: flavourful, fruity, toasty, round tannins.

ROMANICO 2010 T
100% tinta de Toro

91 Colour: cherry, purple rim. Nose: fruit expression, ripe fruit, spicy. Palate: flavourful, good acidity, ripe fruit.

TESO LA MONJA 2008 T
tinta de Toro

97 Colour: cherry, garnet rim. Nose: ripe fruit, toasty, expressive, characterful, sweet spices, cocoa bean, earthy notes. Palate: powerful, toasty, round, long, fine tannins, elegant.

VICTORINO 2009 T
100% tinta de Toro

97 Colour: cherry, garnet rim. Nose: spicy, creamy oak, toasty, characterful, varietal, powerfull. Palate: powerful, flavourful, toasty, round tannins, good acidity, round.

VICTORINO 2010 T
100% tinta de Toro

96 Colour: cherry, garnet rim. Nose: ripe fruit, spicy, creamy oak, toasty, complex, fruit expression, red berry notes, earthy notes. Palate: powerful, flavourful, toasty, round tannins.

VALBUSENDA

Ctra. Toro - Peleagonzalo s/n
49800 Toro - (Zamora)
☎: +34 980 699 560 - Fax: +34 980 699 566
bodega@valbusenda.com
www.valbusenda.com

VALBUSENDA CEPAS VIEJAS 2008 T
100% tinta de Toro

90 Colour: cherry, garnet rim. Nose: spicy, creamy oak, toasty, fruit expression. Palate: powerful, flavourful, toasty, round tannins.

VETUS

Ctra. Toro a Salamanca, Km. 9,5
49800 Toro - (Zamora)
☎: +34 945 609 086 - Fax: +34 980 056 012
vetus@bodegasvetus.com
www.bodegasvetus.com

CELSUS 2010 T
100% tinta de Toro

94 Colour: very deep cherry. Nose: ripe fruit, fruit expression, creamy oak, sweet spices, cocoa bean. Palate: round, powerful, good acidity, fine bitter notes, round tannins.

FLOR DE VETUS 2010 T
100% tinta de Toro

91 Colour: bright cherry. Nose: sweet spices, creamy oak, red berry notes. Palate: flavourful, fruity, toasty, round tannins.

VINOS Y VIÑEDOS DE LA CASA MAGUILA

Ctra. El Piñero, s/n - Pol. Ind. 1 - parc. 715
49153 Venialbo - (Zamora)
☎: +34 616 262 549
administracion@casamaguila.com
www.casamaguila.com

CACHITO MÍO 2011 T
100% tinta de Toro

91 Colour: bright cherry. Nose: ripe fruit, sweet spices, creamy oak, balsamic herbs. Palate: flavourful, fruity, toasty, round tannins.

VIÑAGUAREÑA

Ctra. Toro a Salamanca, Km. 12,5
49800 Toro - (Zamora)
☎: +34 980 568 013 - Fax: +34 980 568 134
info@vinotoro.com
www.vinotoro.com

MUNIA 2009 TC
100% tinta de Toro

90 Colour: cherry, garnet rim. Nose: spicy, creamy oak, toasty, complex, ripe fruit. Palate: powerful, flavourful, toasty, round tannins.

MUNIA ESPECIAL 2008 T ROBLE
100% tinta de Toro

90 Colour: bright cherry. Nose: sweet spices, creamy oak. Palate: flavourful, fruity, toasty, round tannins.

PICTOR 2008 T ROBLE
100% tinta de Toro

91 Colour: bright cherry. Nose: sweet spices, creamy oak, expressive, ripe fruit, red berry notes, fragrant herbs. Palate: flavourful, fruity, toasty, round tannins.

VIÑEDOS ALONSO DEL YERRO

Finca Santa Marta - Ctra. Roa-Anguix, Km. 1,8
9300 Roa - (Burgos)
☎: +34 913 160 121 - Fax: +34 913 160 121
mariadelyerro@vay.es
www.alonsodelyerro.com

PAYDOS 2009 T
100% tinta de Toro

90 Colour: cherry, garnet rim. Nose: ripe fruit, earthy notes, fruit preserve, spicy, toasty. Palate: powerful, flavourful, complex, toasty.

VIÑEDOS DE VILLAESTER

49800 Toro - (Zamora)
☎: +34 948 645 008 - Fax: +34 948 645 166
info@familiabelasco.com
www.familiabelasco.com

VILLAESTER 2004 T
100% tinta de Toro

91 Colour: pale ruby, brick rim edge. Nose: elegant, spicy, fine reductive notes, wet leather, aged wood nuances, fruit liqueur notes. Palate: spicy, fine tannins, elegant, long, balanced.

VOCARRAJE

Ctra. San Román, s/n
49810 Moral de Toro - (Zamora)
☎: +34 630 084 080 - Fax: +34 980 698 172
info@vocarraje.es
www.vocarraje.es

ABDÓN SEGOVIA 2009 TC
100% tinta de Toro

91 Colour: cherry, garnet rim. Nose: spicy, creamy oak, toasty, varietal. Palate: powerful, flavourful, toasty, round tannins.

DESCRIPTION

This Denomination of Origin is in Castile - La Mancha and its vineyards lie in two provinces: Toledo and Cuenca. The latter has the largest proportion of vineyards. Most of the vineyards are concentrated in the area of Tarancón.

NUMBER OF HECTARES: 1.700 **ALTITUDES:** 500 m. – 1.200 m.

PREDOMINANT VARIETIES:

White grapes: verdejo, small grained muscatel, chardonnay, sauvignon blanc and viura.
Red grapes: tempranillo, merlot, cabernet sauvignon, garnacha and syrah.

CLIMATOLOGY AND SOILS

Despite taking in two provinces with different types of soils, there is a common type of soils in most of the vineyards. The soils are deep, not very fertile, with sandy and sandy-loam textures, with an abundance of clay as we approach the banks of the River Riansares and the River Bendija. The mountain range of Altamira forms gently sloping undulations which rise from 600 to 1,200 metres, generating alterations in the continental climate which is less extreme here, milder with a Mediterranean component. This is why there is little rainfall, more typical of a semiarid climate.

FONTANA

Extramuros, s/n
16411 Fuente de Pedro Naharro - (Cuenca)
☎: +34 969 125 433 - Fax: +34 969 125 387
gemag@bodegasfontana.com
www.bodegasfontana.com

ESENCIA DE FONTANA 2010 TC
90% tempranillo, 10% merlot

91 Colour: bright cherry, garnet rim. Nose: medium intensity, ripe fruit, balsamic herbs, creamy oak. Palate: good structure, full, long, round tannins.

DESCRIPTION

The Denomination of Origin extends through the plateau of Utiel-Requena, and a continuation in the province of Valencia. This region supplies bulk bobal grape wines to other Spanish zones due to the intense colour of its wines. By their work the new generations of oenologists have discovered a new facet of this vine with less rusticity and more freshness. Utiel, which lies between the Mediterranean and Castile, with a good altitude, has fertile soil for the perfect maturing of vines of any origin.

NUMBER OF HECTARES: 36.633 **ALTITUDES:** 600 m. – 900 m.

PREDOMINANT VARIETIES:

White grapes: tardana, macabeo, merseguera, chardonnay and sauvignon blanc.
Red grapes: bobal, tempranillo, garnacha, cabernet sauvignon, merlot, syrah and pinot noir.

CLIMATOLOGY AND SOILS

The climate is continental with Mediterranean influences. The soils are brown almost reddish with a limestone composition, poor in organic material and with good permeability.

BODEGA Y VIÑEDOS CARRES

Francho, 1
46352 Casas de Eufema - (Valencia)
☎: +34 675 515 729
torrescarpiojl@gmail.com
www.bodegacarres.com

EL OLIVASTRO 2009 T
100% bobal

90 Colour: cherry, garnet rim. Nose: ripe fruit, scrubland, earthy notes, spicy, toasty. Palate: powerful, flavourful, long, toasty.

BODEGAS ARANLEÓN

Ctra. Caudete, 3, Los Marcos
46310 Venta del Moro - (Valencia)
☎: +34 963 631 640 - Fax: +34 962 185 150
vinos@aranleon.com
www.aranleon.com

ARANLEÓN HELIX 2007 T ROBLE
tempranillo

90 Colour: bright cherry. Nose: creamy oak, ripe fruit, cocoa bean. Palate: flavourful, fruity, toasty, round tannins.

ARANLEÓN SÓLO 2011 B
60% chardonnay, 40% sauvignon blanc

90 Color bright straw. Aroma fresh, fresh fruit, white flowers, expressive. Taste flavourful, fruity, good acidity, balanced.

BODEGAS COVIÑAS

Avda. Rafael Duyos, s/n
46340 Requena - (Valencia)
☎: +34 962 300 680 - Fax: +34 962 302 651
covinas@covinas.com
www.covinas.com

AL VENT SAUVIGNON BLANC 2011 B
100% sauvignon blanc

90 Color bright straw. Aroma fresh, fresh fruit, white flowers, expressive. Taste flavourful, fruity, good acidity, balanced.

AULA MERLOT 2008 TC
100% merlot

90 Colour: cherry, garnet rim. Nose: sweet spices, dark chocolate, ripe fruit. Palate: flavourful, spicy.

BODEGAS HISPANO SUIZAS

Ctra. N-322, Km. 451,7 El Pontón
46357 Requena - (Valencia)
☎: +34 661 894 200
info@bodegashispanosuizas.com
www.bodegashispanosuizas.com

BASSUS PINOT NOIR 2010 T
pinot noir

92 Colour: cherry, garnet rim. Nose: ripe fruit, sweet spices, aromatic coffee, tobacco. Palate: powerful, flavourful, spicy, toasty.

BASSUS PREMIUM 2009 T
bobal, cabernet sauvignon, merlot, syrah

92 Colour: deep cherry, garnet rim. Nose: fruit liqueur notes, spicy, aromatic coffee, dark chocolate. Palate: fine bitter notes, good acidity, spirituous.

IMPROMPTU 2011 B
sauvignon blanc

93 Colour: bright straw. Nose: fresh, fresh fruit, white flowers, varietal. Palate: flavourful, fruity, good acidity, balanced.

QUOD SUPERIUS 2008 T
bobal, cabernet sauvignon, merlot, syrah

93 Colour: cherry, garnet rim. Nose: ripe fruit, spicy, creamy oak, toasty, complex, mineral. Palate: powerful, flavourful, toasty, round tannins.

BODEGAS MURVIEDRO

Ampliación Pol. El Romeral, s/n
46340 Requena - (Valencia)
☎: +34 962 329 003 - Fax: +34 962 329 002
murviedro@murviedro.es
www.murviedro.es

CUEVA DE LA CULPA 2009 T
60% bobal, 40% merlot

91 Colour: cherry, garnet rim. Nose: ripe fruit, sweet spices, creamy oak. Palate: flavourful, powerful, good acidity, round tannins.

CUEVA DE LA ESPERA 2011 B
80% chardonnay, 20% pinot noir

90 Colour: bright straw. Nose: fresh, fresh fruit, white flowers, characterful. Palate: flavourful, fruity, good acidity, balanced.

BODEGAS PALMERA

Corral Charco de Agut, 19, 23
46300 Utiel - (Valencia)
☎: +34 626 706 394
klauslauerbach@hotmail.com
www.bodegas-palmera.com

L'ANGELET 2008 TC
55% tempranillo, 27% cabernet sauvignon, 18% merlot

90 Colour: pale ruby, brick rim edge. Nose: earthy notes, balsamic herbs, ripe fruit, fine reductive notes, spicy. Palate: balanced, powerful, flavourful.

BODEGAS SIERRA NORTE

Pol. Ind. El Romeral. Transporte- Parc. C2
46340 Requena - (Valencia)
☎: +34 962 323 099 - Fax: +34 962 323 048
info@bodegasierranorte.com
www.bodegasierranorte.com

CERRO BERCIAL 2004 TR
tempranillo, bobal, cabernet sauvignon

90 Color cherry, garnet rim. Aroma ripe fruit, spicy, creamy oak, toasty, complex. Taste powerful, flavourful, toasty, round tannins.

CERRO BERCIAL 2009 T BARRICA
tempranillo, bobal

91 Colour: bright cherry. Nose: ripe fruit, sweet spices, cocoa bean. Palate: flavourful, powerful, ripe fruit, fine bitter notes.

CERRO BERCIAL 2010 B
chardonnay, sauvignon blanc, macabeo

90 Colour: bright straw. Nose: creamy oak, spicy, ripe fruit. Palate: ripe fruit, spicy, creamy.

CERRO BERCIAL PARCELA "LADERA LOS CANTOS" 2006 T
bobal, cabernet sauvignon

91 Colour: cherry, garnet rim. Nose: dry stone, ripe fruit, fine reductive notes, spicy. Palate: good acidity, powerful, flavourful, spicy.

PASION DE BOBAL 2010 T
bobal

91 Colour: cherry, garnet rim. Nose: red berry notes, ripe fruit, balsamic herbs, sweet spices, creamy oak. Palate: powerful, flavourful, fruity, spicy.

PASION DE BOBAL 2011 RD
bobal

90 Colour: rose, purple rim. Nose: powerfull, ripe fruit, red berry notes, floral, expressive, elegant. Palate: , powerful, fruity, fresh, balanced.

TEMPERAMENTO DE BOBAL 2010 T
bobal

90 Colour: cherry, garnet rim. Nose: red berry notes, ripe fruit, spicy, toasty. Palate: powerful, flavourful, harsh oak tannins.

BODEGAS UTIELANAS

San Fernando, 18
46300 Utiel - (Valencia)
☎: +34 962 171 157 - Fax: +34 962 170 801
info@bodegasutielanas.com
www.bodegasutielanas.com

VEGA INFANTE MADURADO EN BARRICA 2011 T
bobal, tempranillo

91 Colour: cherry, purple rim. Nose: red berry notes, fragrant herbs, sweet spices, creamy oak. Palate: powerful, flavourful, spicy.

BODEGAS VICENTE GANDÍA

Ctra. Cheste a Godelleta, s/n
46370 Chiva - (Valencia)
☎: +34 962 524 242 - Fax: +34 962 524 243
vuboldi@vicentegandia.com
www.vicentegandia.es

GENERACIÓN 1 2006 T
70% bobal, 15% cabernet sauvignon, 15% syrah

90 Colour: cherry, garnet rim. Nose: ripe fruit, fruit liqueur notes, balsamic herbs, old leather, tobacco, spicy. Palate: powerful, flavourful, long, spicy.

CERROGALLINA

Travesía Industria, 5
46352 Campo Arcis - (Valencia)
☎: +34 676 897 251 - Fax: +34 962 338 135
info@cerrogallina.com
www.cerrogallina.com

CERROGALLINA 2009 T
100% bobal

93 Colour: cherry, garnet rim. Nose: mineral, red berry notes, ripe fruit, cocoa bean, sweet spices, creamy oak. Palate: powerful, flavourful, complex, balanced.

CHOZAS CARRASCAL

Vereda San Antonio Pol. Ind. Catastral, 16 Parcelas 136-138
46340 San Antonio de Requena - (Valencia)
☎: +34 963 410 395 - Fax: +34 963 168 067
chozas@chozascarrascal.es
www.chozascarrascal.es

EL CF DE CHOZAS CARRASCAL 2010 T
cabernet franc

94 Colour: cherry, garnet rim. Nose: mineral, earthy notes, balsamic herbs, toasty. Palate: flavourful, complex, fine tannins. Personality.

JUANPEDRÓS 2009 T

90 Colour: deep cherry. Nose: candied fruit, spicy, toasty. Palate: ripe fruit, spicy, fine bitter notes, round tannins.

LAS DOSCES 2011 B
80% macabeo, 20% sauvignon blanc

90 Color bright straw. Aroma fresh, fresh fruit, white flowers, expressive. Taste flavourful, fruity, good acidity, balanced.

LAS DOSCES 2011 T
bobal, tempranillo, syrah

90 Colour: cherry, purple rim. Nose: expressive, fresh fruit, red berry notes, floral, creamy oak, sweet spices. Palate: flavourful, fruity, good acidity, round tannins.

LAS OCHO 2008 T
bobal, monastrell, garnacha, tempranillo, cabernet franc, syrah, merlot

92 Colour: cherry, garnet rim. Nose: ripe fruit, spicy, creamy oak, toasty, earthy notes. Palate: powerful, flavourful, toasty, round tannins.

DOMINIO DE LA VEGA

Ctra. Madrid - Valencia, Km. 270,6
46390 San Antonio. - (Valencia)
☎: +34 962 320 570 - Fax: +34 962 320 330
info@dominiodelavega.com
www.dominiodelavega.com

ARTE MAYOR III 2005/2006/2007 T
bobal

91 Colour: cherry, garnet rim. Nose: spicy, creamy oak, candied fruit. Palate: powerful, flavourful, toasty, round tannins.

PRIMUM BOBAL

Constitución, 50 pta. 6
46340 Requena - (Valencia)
☎: +34 625 464 377
vinos@primumbobal.com
www.primumbobal.com

PRIMUM BOBAL 2011 T
100% bobal

90 Color cherry, purple rim. Aroma expressive, fresh fruit, red berry notes, floral. Taste flavourful, fruity, good acidity, round tannins.

TORRE ORIA

Ctra. Pontón - Utiel, Km. 3
46390 Derramador - Requena - (Valencia)
☎: +34 962 320 289 - Fax: +34 962 320 311
info.torreoria@torreoria.es
www.torreoria.com

MARQUÉS DE REQUENA 2006 TR
tempranillo

90 Colour: cherry, garnet rim. Nose: ripe fruit, spicy, creamy oak, toasty. Palate: powerful, flavourful, toasty, round tannins.

UNIÓN VINÍCOLA DEL ESTE

Pl. Ind. El Romeral- Construcción, 74
46340 Requena - (Valencia)
☎: +34 962 323 343 - Fax: +34 962 349 413
cava@uveste.es
www.uveste.es

BESO DE RECHENNA 2009 T

90 Colour: cherry, garnet rim. Nose: ripe fruit, spicy, creamy oak, toasty, wild herbs. Palate: powerful, flavourful, toasty, round tannins.

VERA DE ESTENAS

Junto N-III, km. 266 - Paraje La Cabeuzela
46300 Utiel - (Valencia)
☎: +34 962 171 141 - Fax: +34 962 174 352
estenas@estenas.es
www.estenas.es

CASA DON ÁNGEL BOBAL 2007 T
100% bobal

93 Colour: cherry, garnet rim. Nose: ripe fruit, fragrant herbs, sweet spices, toasty, earthy notes. Palate: long, balanced, powerful, flavourful, spicy.

VERA DE ESTENAS 2009 TC
60% bobal, 25% cabernet sauvignon, 15% tempranillo, 15% merlot

90 Colour: cherry, garnet rim. Nose: ripe fruit, toasty, spicy. Palate: powerful, flavourful, toasty, round tannins.

VIÑA LIDÓN 2011 BFB
100% chardonnay

91 Colour: bright yellow. Nose: powerfull, ripe fruit, sweet spices, creamy oak, fragrant herbs. Palate: rich, flavourful, fresh, good acidity.

VINOS PASIEGO

Avda. Virgen de Tejeda, 28
46320 Sinarcas - (Valencia)
☎: - Fax: +34 962 306 175
bodega@vinospasiego.com
www.vinospasiego.com

PASIEGO DE AUTOR 2005 TC
47% cabernet sauvignon, 33% bobal, 20% tempranillo

91 Colour: cherry, garnet rim. Nose: spicy, creamy oak, toasty, dark chocolate, ripe fruit. Palate: powerful, flavourful, toasty, round tannins.

PASIEGO LAS SUERTES 2010 B
60% chardonnay, 40% sauvignon blanc

90 Colour: bright straw. Nose: fresh, fresh fruit, white flowers, expressive, creamy oak, sweet spices. Palate: flavourful, fruity, good acidity, balanced.

VIÑEDOS LA MADROÑERA

Traginers, 9
46014 Valencia - (Valencia)
☎: +34 963 992 400 - Fax: +34 963 992 451
pguzman@grupoguzman.com
www.viñedoslamadronera.com

DULCE DE CONSTANTIA 2009 T
merlot, cabernet sauvignon

90 Colour: cherry, garnet rim. Nose: ripe fruit, fruit liqueur notes, toasty, aromatic coffee, acetaldehyde. Palate: powerful, flavourful, spirituous, toasty.

DESCRIPTION

This is located to the northwest of the province of Ourense, near to the province of León. The godello grape is from Galicia, but in these areas it is almost a prolongation of the berciana grape. The difference is that it gives off floral aromas and has a more oily texture, therefore, it has more capacity for ageing or ageing on lees.

NUMBER OF HECTARES: 2.700 **ALTITUDES:** 350 m. – 700 m.

PREDOMINANT VARIETIES:

White grapes: godello, dona blanca and palomino.
Red grapes: mencía, merenzao, grao negro and garnacha.

CLIMATOLOGY AND SOILS

Continental with Atlantic influences. The soils are quite varied, and the outstanding soils are those on slate, shallow and with an abundance of stones and a silt texture.

A TAPADA S.A.T.

Finca A Tapada
32310 Rubiá - (Ourense)
☎: +34 988 324 197 - Fax: +34 988 324 197

GUITIÁN GODELLO 2010 BFB
godello

94 Colour: bright yellow. Nose: ripe fruit, sweet spices, cocoa bean, creamy oak. Palate: spicy, ripe fruit, long, mineral.

GUITIÁN GODELLO 2011 B

91 Colour: bright straw. Nose: fruit expression, fragrant herbs, ripe fruit. Palate: flavourful, fruity, fresh, fine bitter notes.

GUITIÁN GODELLO SOBRE LÍAS 2011 B
godello

93 Colour: bright straw. Nose: fresh, fresh fruit, white flowers, fine lees, mineral, burnt matches. Palate: flavourful, fruity, good acidity, balanced.

ADEGA A COROA

A Coroa, s/n
32350 A Rúa - (Ourense)
☎: +34 988 310 648 - Fax: +34 988 311 439
acoroa@acoroa.com
www.acoroa.com

A COROA "LÍAS" 2010 B
100% godello

90 Colour: bright straw. Nose: lactic notes, ripe fruit, citrus fruit, scrubland, sweet spices. Palate: flavourful, sweetness, concentrated.

ADEGA DA PINGUELA

Camino del Disco, 17 Petín
32350 A Rúa - (Ourense)
☎: +34 654 704 753
adega@adegadapinguela.com
www.adegadapinguela.com

MEMORIA DE VENTURA GARNACHA 2011 T
100% garnacha tintorera

91 Colour: very deep cherry. Nose: powerfull, ripe fruit, raspberry, spicy, cocoa bean. Palate: powerful, concentrated, complex.

MEMORIA DE VENTURA MENCÍA 2011 T
100% mencía

94 Colour: cherry, purple rim. Nose: expressive, fresh fruit, red berry notes, floral, mineral, balsamic herbs. Palate: flavourful, fruity, good acidity, round tannins.

ADEGA MELILLAS E FILLOS

A Coroa, 22
32350 A Rúa - (Ourense)
☎: +34 988 310 510
info@adegamelillas.com
www.adegamelillas.com

LAGAR DO CIGUR 2011 T
mencía, alicante

90 Colour: cherry, purple rim. Nose: ripe fruit, red berry notes, scrubland. Palate: flavourful, powerful, fine bitter notes, good acidity.

ADEGA O CASAL

Malladín, s/n
32310 Rubiá - (Ourense)
☎: +34 689 675 800
casalnovo@casalnovo.es
www.casalnovo.es

CASAL NOVO MENCÍA 2011 T
100% mencía

90 Colour: cherry, purple rim. Nose: fresh fruit, red berry notes, floral, ripe fruit. Palate: flavourful, fruity, good acidity, round tannins.

ADEGA O CEPADO

O Patal, 11
32310 Rubia de Valdeorras - (Ourense)
☎: +34 666 186 128
info@cepado.com
www.cepado.com

CEPADO GODELLO 2011 B
godello

90 Colour: bright straw. Nose: fresh, fresh fruit, white flowers, dried herbs. Palate: flavourful, fruity, good acidity, balanced.

ADEGA QUINTA DA PEZA

Ctra. Nacional 120, km.467
32350 A Rua de Valdeorras - (Ourense)
☎: +34 988 311 537 - Fax: +34 981 232 642
quintadapeza@gmail.com
www.quintadapeza.es

QUINTA DA PEZA GODELLO 2011 B
godello

90 Colour: bright yellow. Nose: ripe fruit, citrus fruit, white flowers, balsamic herbs, fragrant herbs. Palate: flavourful, rich, fruity.

BODEGA ELADIO SANTALLA PARADELO

Conde Fenosa, 36
32300 O Barco de Valdeorras - (Ourense)
☎: +34 686 240 374
eladio@bodegaseladiosantalla.com
www.bodegaseladiosantalla.com

HACIENDA UCEDIÑOS 2011 B
godello

92 Colour: bright straw. Nose: fresh, white flowers, grassy, ripe fruit. Palate: flavourful, fruity, good acidity, balanced.

BODEGAS ABANICO

Pol. Ind Ca l'Avellanet - Susany, 6
8553 Seva - (Barcelona)
☎: +34 938 125 676 - Fax: +34 938 123 213
info@exportiberia.com
www.bodegasabanico.com

TEMPESTAD 2011 B
100% godello

91 Colour: bright yellow. Nose: citrus fruit, wild herbs, balsamic herbs, ripe fruit, mineral, balanced. Palate: powerful, flavourful, long, good acidity, balanced.

BODEGAS AVANTHIA

Bartolomé Esteban Murillo, 11
29700 Vélez- Málaga - (Málaga)
☎: +34 952 504 706 - Fax: +34 951 284 796
office@jorge-ordonez.es
www.jorge-ordonez.es

AVANTHIA GODELLO 2011 B
100% godello

92 Colour: bright straw. Nose: ripe fruit, floral, dried herbs. Palate: flavourful, fruity, good acidity, balanced.

AVANTHIA MENCÍA 2009 T
100% mencía

91 Colour: bright cherry, garnet rim. Nose: ripe fruit, sweet spices, balsamic herbs, mineral, aromatic coffee. Palate: flavourful, fruity, toasty, round tannins.

BODEGAS GODEVAL

Avda. de Galicia, 20
32300 El Barco de Valdeorras - (Ourense)
☎: +34 988 108 282 - Fax: +34 988 325 309
godeval@godeval.com
www.godeval.com

GODEVAL CEPAS VELLAS 2011 B

92 Colour: bright straw. Nose: fresh, white flowers, expressive, ripe fruit, scrubland. Palate: flavourful, fruity, good acidity, balanced.

BODEGAS RUCHEL

Ctra. de Cernego, s/n
32340 Vilamartín de Valdeorras - (Ourense)
☎: +34 986 253 345 - Fax: +34 986 253 345
info@vinosruchel.com
www.vinosruchel.com

RUCHEL MENCÍA 2011 T
mencía

90 Colour: cherry, purple rim. Nose: expressive, fresh fruit, red berry notes, floral, mineral. Palate: flavourful, fruity, good acidity, balanced.

BODEGAS SAMPAYOLO

Ctra. de Barxela, s/n
32358 Petín de Valdeorras - (Ourense)
☎: +34 679 157 977
info@sampayolo.com
www.sampayolo.com

SAMPAYOLO GODELLO 2010 B BARRICA
100% godello

90 Colour: bright yellow. Nose: powerfull, ripe fruit, sweet spices, creamy oak, fragrant herbs. Palate: rich, flavourful, fresh, good acidity.

BODEGAS VALDESIL

Ctra. a San Vicente OU 807, km. 3
32348 Vilamartín de Valdeorras - (Ourense)
☎: +34 988 337 900 - Fax: +34 988 337 901
valdesil@valdesil.com
www.valdesil.com

PEDROUZOS MAGNUM 2010 B
godello

96 Colour: bright yellow. Nose: balsamic herbs, scrubland, ripe fruit, citrus fruit, fruit expression, mineral. Palate: fine bitter notes, good acidity, fruity, long, mineral.

PEZAS DA PORTELA 2010 BFB
godello

93 Colour: bright straw. Nose: powerfull, characterful, varietal, ripe fruit, fruit expression. Palate: flavourful, good acidity, fine bitter notes, elegant.

VALDERROA 2011 T
mencía

92 Colour: cherry, purple rim. Nose: floral, red berry notes, expressive, scrubland. Palate: flavourful, fruity, good acidity, round tannins.

VALDERROA CARBALLO 2009 T
mencía

92 Colour: bright cherry. Nose: medium intensity, balsamic herbs, scrubland, ripe fruit, earthy notes. Palate: flavourful, fine bitter notes, good acidity, balsamic.

VALDESIL GODELLO SOBRE LÍAS 2011 B
godello

93 Colour: bright yellow. Nose: white flowers, balsamic herbs, fragrant herbs, mineral, expressive. Palate: powerful, flavourful, elegant.

CARBALLAL

Ctra. de Carballal, km 2,2
32356 Petín de Valdeorras - (Ourense)
☎: +34 988 311 281 - Fax: +34 988 311 281
bodegascarballal@hotmail.com

EREBO GODELLO 2011 B
godello

91 Colour: bright yellow. Nose: fresh fruit, white flowers, wild herbs. Palate: rich, flavourful, fruity, balanced.

COMPAÑÍA DE VINOS TELMO RODRÍGUEZ

El Monte
1308 Lanciego - (Álava)
☎: +34 945 628 315 - Fax: +34 945 628 314
contact@telmorodriguez.com
www.telmorodriguez.com

AS CABORCAS 2010 T
mencía, merenzao, garnacha, godello

95 Colour: bright cherry. Nose: fruit expression, red berry notes, scrubland, balsamic herbs. Palate: flavourful, ripe fruit, spicy, long.

GABA DO XIL GODELLO 2011 B
godello

92 Colour: bright straw. Nose: expressive, fresh, ripe fruit, white flowers. Palate: flavourful, fruity, ripe fruit, long.

GABA DO XIL MENCÍA 2010 T
100% mencía

90 Colour: bright cherry. Nose: red berry notes, scrubland, balsamic herbs. Palate: flavourful, fruity, fresh.

GUITIAN Y BLANCO (BODEGAS D'BERNA)

Córgomo
32340 Villamartín de Valdeorras - (Ourense)
☎: +34 988 324 557 - Fax: +34 988 324 557
info@bodegasdberna.com
www.bodegasdberna.com

D'BERNA GODELLO 2011 B
100% godello

91 Colour: bright straw. Nose: fresh fruit, white flowers, expressive, grassy. Palate: flavourful, fruity, good acidity, balanced.

JOAQUÍN REBOLLEDO

San Roque, 11
32350 A Rúa - (Ourense)
☎: +34 988 372 307 - Fax: +34 988 371 427
info@joaquinrebolledo.com
www.joaquinrebolledo.com

JOAQUÍN REBOLLEDO 2010 T BARRICA
mencía, tempranillo, otras

93 Colour: cherry, garnet rim. Nose: red berry notes, dry stone, earthy notes, fragrant herbs, spicy, expressive. Palate: balanced, flavourful, fruity, complex.

JOAQUÍN REBOLLEDO GODELLO 2011 B
godello

92 Colour: bright straw. Nose: white flowers, citrus fruit, fresh fruit, dried herbs, mineral. Palate: powerful, flavourful, good acidity, balanced.

JOAQUÍN REBOLLEDO MENCÍA 2011 T
mencía

94 Colour: cherry, purple rim. Nose: expressive, fresh fruit, red berry notes, floral, balsamic herbs, mineral. Palate: flavourful, fruity, good acidity, round tannins.

MANUEL CORZO RODRÍGUEZ

Chandoiro, s/n
32372 O Bolo - (Ourense)
☎: +34 629 893 649
manuelcorzorodriguez@hotmail.com

VIÑA CORZO GODELLO 2011 B
100% godello

90 Color bright straw. Aroma fresh, fresh fruit, white flowers, expressive. Taste flavourful, fruity, good acidity, balanced.

RAFAEL PALACIOS

Avda. de Somoza, 81
32350 A Rúa de Valdeorras - (Ourense)
☎: +34 988 310 162 - Fax: +34 988 310 643
bodega@rafaelpalacios.com
www.rafaelpalacios.com

AS SORTES 2011 B
100% godello

95 Colour: bright straw. Nose: powerfull, ripe fruit, fragrant herbs, grassy. Palate: rich, flavourful, fresh, good acidity.

LOURO DO BOLO 2011 B
88% godello, 12% treixadura

93 Colour: bright straw. Nose: fresh, white flowers, varietal, ripe fruit. Palate: flavourful, fruity, good acidity, balanced.

SANTA MARTA BODEGAS

Córgomo, s/n
32348 Villamartín de Ourense - (Ourense)
☎: +34 988 324 559 - Fax: +34 988 324 559
info@vinaredo.com
www.vinaredo.com

VIÑAREDO GODELLO 2011 B
100% godello

92 Colour: bright straw. Nose: powerfull, varietal, ripe fruit, citrus fruit. Palate: flavourful, powerful, good acidity, fine bitter notes.

VIÑAREDO SOUSÓN 2009 T BARRICA
100% sausón

90 Colour: cherry, purple rim. Nose: floral, rose petals, violet drops, sweet spices. Palate: flavourful, fruity, good acidity, round tannins.

VIÑA SOMOZA BODEGAS Y VIÑEDOS

Avda. Somoza, s/n
32350 A Rúa - (Ourense)
☎: +34 988 310 918 - Fax: +34 988 310 918
bodega@vinosomoza.com
www.vinosomoza.com

VIÑA SOMOZA GODELLO SELECCIÓN 2010 B ROBLE
100% godello

92 Colour: bright golden. Nose: ripe fruit, powerfull, toasty, aged wood nuances, expressive. Palate: flavourful, fruity, spicy, toasty, long.

VIÑA SOMOZA GODELLO SOBRE LIAS 2011 B
100% godello

91 Colour: bright straw. Nose: fresh, white flowers, expressive, citrus fruit, mineral, grassy. Palate: flavourful, fruity, good acidity, balanced.

VIRXEN DE GALIR

Las Escuelas, s/n Estoma
32336 O Barco de Valdeorras - (Ourense)
☎: +34 988 335 600 - Fax: +34 988 335 592
bodega@virxendegalir.es
www.virxendegalir.es

PAGOS DEL GALIR GODELLO 2011 B
godello

93 Colour: bright yellow. Nose: white flowers, balsamic herbs, fragrant herbs, fresh fruit, expressive. Palate: flavourful, fruity, rich, balanced, complex. Personality.

VÍA NOVA GODELLO 2011 B
godello

90 Colour: bright straw. Nose: fresh, fresh fruit, ripe fruit. Palate: flavourful, fruity, good acidity, balanced.

VÍA NOVA MENCÍA 2011 T
mencía

90 Colour: cherry, purple rim. Nose: fresh fruit, red berry notes, floral, characterful, scrubland. Palate: flavourful, fruity, good acidity, round tannins.

DESCRIPTION

This lies at the southern edge of the southern plateau in the province of Ciudad Real, in the heart of Castile- La Mancha. In the past, Valdepeñas had a prestige which has lost its lustre today. This Denomination of Origin belongs to the correct model of Spanish wine, fundamentally red wine at economical prices.

NUMBER OF HECTARES: 25.430 **ALTITUDES:** 640 m. – 880 m.

PREDOMINANT VARIETIES:

White grapes: airén, macabeo, chardonnay and sauvignon blanc.
Red grapes: cencibel, garnacha, cabernet sauvignon, merlot and syrah.

CLIMATOLOGY AND SOILS

The climate is purely continental with brown - reddish and brown – limestone soils with a high lime content. The level of rainfall is low.

None of the wines tasted achieve the minimum required scoring

DESCRIPTION

In the province of Valencia, one of the most exporting zones in Spain, it has volume wines with new productions which defend a new prestige image for the zone. The best samples of white and red wines come from the subzone of Clariano, to the south of Valencia and are termed Valencia Castellana. Dry and sweet muscatel wines continue to be produced in the centre of the Denomination of Origin.

NUMBER OF HECTARES: 13.079 **ALTITUDES:** 300 m. – 1.000 m.

VARIEDADES PREDOMINANTES:

White grapes: macabeo, malvasía, merseguera, muscat of Alexandria, small grained muscatel, pedro ximénez, plantafina, plantanova, tortosí, verdil, chardonnay, semillon blanc, sauvignon blanc, verdejo, riesling and viognier. Red grapes: garnacha, monastrell, tempranillo, tintorera, forcallat, bobal, cabernet sauvignon, merlot, pinot noir, syrah, graciano, malbec, mandó, marselan, mencía, mazuelo and petit verdot.

CLIMATOLOGY AND SOILS

Mediterranean, marked by strong storms in summer and autumn. Most of the soils are brown, with limestone content and good permeability.

BODEGA J. BELDA

Avda. Conde Salvatierra, 54
46635 Fontanars dels Alforins - (Valencia)
☎: +34 962 222 278 - Fax: +34 962 222 245
info@danielbelda.com
www.danielbelda.com

CA'BELDA 2007 T FERMENTADO EN BARRICA
monastrell, garnacha tintorera

91 Colour: cherry, garnet rim. Nose: toasty, spicy, aromatic coffee, ripe fruit. Palate: powerful, spicy, ripe fruit.

BODEGA LA VIÑA

Portal de Valencia, 52
46630 La Font de la Figuera - (Valencia)
☎: +34 962 290 078 - Fax: +34 962 232 039
info@vinosdelavina.com
www.vinosdelavina.com

ICONO SYRAH 2011 T
syrah

90 Colour: cherry, purple rim. Nose: fresh fruit, red berry notes, ripe fruit, rose petals. Palate: flavourful, fruity, good acidity, round tannins.

JUAN DE JUANES 2009 T
syrah, merlot, cabernet sauvignon, cabernet franc

90 Color cherry, garnet rim. Aroma ripe fruit, spicy, creamy oak, toasty, complex. Taste powerful, flavourful, toasty, round tannins.

VENTA DEL PUERTO 12 2009 T
tempranillo, cabernet sauvignon, merlot, syrah

90 Colour: cherry, garnet rim. Nose: spicy, creamy oak, roasted coffee, overripe fruit. Palate: powerful, flavourful, toasty, round tannins.

BODEGAS ARANLEÓN

Ctra. Caudete, 3, Los Marcos
46310 Venta del Moro - (Valencia)
☎: +34 963 631 640 - Fax: +34 962 185 150
vinos@aranleon.com
www.aranleon.com

EL ÁRBOL DE ARANLEÓN 2008 TC
30% monastrell, 30% tempranillo, 20% cabernet sauvignon, 10% merlot, 10% syrah

92 Colour: cherry, garnet rim. Nose: spicy, creamy oak, toasty, characterful, ripe fruit. Palate: powerful, flavourful, toasty, round tannins.

BODEGAS ARRAEZ

Arcediano Ros, 35
46630 Fuente La Higuera - (Valencia)
☎: +34 962 290 031 - Fax: +34 962 290 339
info@bodegasarraez.com
www.antonioarraez.com

LAGARES 2009 TC
cabernet sauvignon

90 Colour: bright cherry. Nose: ripe fruit, sweet spices, creamy oak, complex, characterful. Palate: flavourful, fruity, toasty, round tannins.

MALA VIDA 2010 T ROBLE
cabernet sauvignon, syrah, tempranillo, monastrell

91 Colour: bright cherry. Nose: ripe fruit, sweet spices, creamy oak, characterful. Palate: flavourful, fruity, toasty, round tannins.

BODEGAS EL ANGOSTO

Ctra. Fontanars CV-660, km. 24
46870 Ontinyent - (Valencia)
☎: +34 962 380 638 - Fax: +34 962 911 349
info@bodegaelangosto.com
www.bodegaelangosto.com

ALMENDROS 2010 T
garnacha tintorera, syrah, marselan

93 Colour: dark-red cherry, bright cherry. Nose: red berry notes, ripe fruit, mineral, creamy oak, expressive. Palate: powerful, flavourful, elegant, long, spicy.

ALMENDROS 2011 B
33% chardonnay, 33% sauvignon blanc, 33% riesling

93 Colour: bright yellow. Nose: powerfull, ripe fruit, sweet spices, creamy oak, fragrant herbs, complex. Palate: rich, smoky aftertaste, flavourful, fresh, good acidity. Personality.

ANGOSTO BLANCO 2011 B
sauvignon blanc, moscatel grano menudo, chardonnay, riesling

91 Colour: bright straw. Nose: fresh fruit, white flowers, fresh, complex, fine lees. Palate: flavourful, fruity, good acidity, balanced.

ANGOSTO TINTO 2010 T
garnacha tintorera, syrah, cabernet franc

92 Colour: bright cherry. Nose: ripe fruit, sweet spices, creamy oak. Palate: flavourful, fruity, toasty, round tannins.

JEFE DE LA TRIBU 2010 T
50% touriga, 50% marselan

90 Colour: bright cherry. Nose: ripe fruit, sweet spices, creamy oak, aromatic coffee, roasted coffee, mineral. Palate: flavourful, toasty, round tannins.

LA TRIBU 2011 T
garnacha tintorera, syrah, monastrell

91 Color cherry, purple rim. Aroma expressive, fresh fruit, red berry notes, floral. Taste flavourful, fruity, good acidity, round tannins.

BODEGAS ENGUERA

Ctra. CV - 590, Km. 51,5
46810 Enguera - (Valencia)
☎: +34 962 224 318 - Fax: +34 961 364 167
oficina@bodegasenguera.com
www.bodegasenguera.com

BLANC D'ENGUERA 2011 B
verdil, sauvignon blanc, chardonnay, viognier

90 Colour: bright yellow. Nose: ripe fruit, sweet spices, creamy oak, fragrant herbs. Palate: rich, smoky aftertaste, flavourful, fresh, good acidity.

MEGALA 2009 T
monastrell, syrah

91 Colour: cherry, garnet rim. Nose: red berry notes, ripe fruit, sweet spices, creamy oak. Palate: flavourful, balanced, toasty, long.

PARADIGMA 2008 T
monastrell

93 Colour: deep cherry. Nose: candied fruit, raspberry, grassy, expressive, scrubland, balsamic herbs, toasty. Palate: spicy, ripe fruit, easy to drink, long.

SUEÑO DE MEGALA 2007 T
monastrell, merlot, tempranillo

91 Colour: cherry, garnet rim. Nose: ripe fruit, toasty, complex, new oak, sweet spices, scrubland. Palate: powerful, flavourful, toasty, round tannins.

BODEGAS LOS FRAILES

Casa Los Frailes, s/n
46635 Fontanaresdels Alforins - (Valencia)
☎: +34 962 222 220 - Fax: +34 963 363 153
info@bodegaslosfrailes.com
www.bodegaslosfrailes.com

BILOGÍA 2008 T
50% monastrell, 50% tempranillo

90 Colour: cherry, garnet rim. Nose: powerfull, warm, fruit preserve, toasty, creamy oak. Palate: powerful, flavourful, sweetness, spicy.

BLANC DE TRILOGÍA 2011 B
70% sauvignon blanc, 10% moscatel, 20% verdil

90 Colour: bright yellow. Nose: sweet spices, creamy oak, fragrant herbs, white flowers. Palate: rich, flavourful, fresh, good acidity, elegant.

LA DANZA DE LA MOMA 2009 T BARRICA
50% monastrell, 50% marselan

92 Colour: cherry, garnet rim. Nose: ripe fruit, spicy, creamy oak, scrubland. Palate: powerful, flavourful, toasty, round tannins.

BODEGAS LOS PINOS

Casa Los Pinos, s/n
46635 Fontanars dels Alforins - (Valencia)
☎: +34 962 222 090 - Fax: +34 600 584 397
bodegaslospinos@bodegaslospinos.com
www.bodegaslospinos.com

DOMINIO LOS PINOS 2010 TC
merlot, monastrell, cabernet sauvignon

91 Colour: cherry, garnet rim. Nose: spicy, creamy oak, toasty, characterful. Palate: powerful, flavourful, toasty, round tannins.

BODEGAS MURVIEDRO

Ampliación Pol. El Romeral, s/n
46340 Requena - (Valencia)
☎: +34 962 329 003 - Fax: +34 962 329 002
murviedro@murviedro.es
www.murviedro.es

ALBA DE MURVIEDRO 2011 B
60% sauvignon blanc, 40% moscatel

90 Colour: bright yellow. Nose: white flowers, tropical fruit, fragrant herbs, expressive. Palate: full, flavourful, easy to drink.

CUEVA DEL PECADO 2008 T
60% tempranillo, 40% cabernet sauvignon

93 Colour: cherry, garnet rim. Nose: ripe fruit, spicy, creamy oak, toasty. Palate: powerful, flavourful, toasty, round tannins.

MURVIEDRO 2009 TC
50% tempranillo, 30% monastrell, 20% syrah

90 Colour: cherry, garnet rim. Nose: ripe fruit, spicy, creamy oak, toasty, balanced. Palate: powerful, flavourful, toasty, round tannins.

MURVIEDRO COLECCIÓN PETIT VERDOT 2011 T
petit verdot

90 Colour: cherry, purple rim. Nose: ripe fruit, balsamic herbs, spicy. Palate: flavourful, good acidity, fine bitter notes.

BODEGAS SIERRA NORTE

Pol. Ind. El Romeral. Transporte- Parc. C2
46340 Requena - (Valencia)
☎: +34 962 323 099 - Fax: +34 962 323 048
info@bodegasierranorte.com
www.bodegasierranorte.com

MARILUNA 2010 T
bobal, tempranillo, monastrell

90 Colour: bright cherry. Nose: expressive, red berry notes, raspberry, sweet spices. Palate: flavourful, fruity, round tannins, balanced.

BODEGAS Y DESTILERÍAS VIDAL

Pol. Ind. El Mijares, c/Valencia, 16
12550 Almazora - (Castellón)
☎: +34 964 503 300 - Fax: +34 964 560 604
jordan@bodegasvidal.com
www.bodegasvidal.com

UVA D'OR MOSCATEL MISTELA
moscatel

90 Colour: golden. Nose: powerfull, floral, honeyed notes, candied fruit, fragrant herbs, citrus fruit. Palate: flavourful, sweet, fresh, fruity, good acidity, long. Personality.

CELLER DEL ROURE

Ctra. de Les Alcusses, Km. 11,1
46640 Moixent - (Valencia)
☎: +34 962 295 020 - Fax: +34 962 295 142
info@cellerdelroure.es

LES ALCUSSES 2008 T
60% monastrell, 10% garnacha tintorera, 10% cabernet sauvignon, 15% merlot, 5% syrah

91 Colour: bright cherry. Nose: ripe fruit, sweet spices, creamy oak. Palate: flavourful, fruity, toasty, round tannins.

MADURESA 2008 T
25% mandó, 25% syrah, 15% petit verdot, 15% garnacha tintorera, 10% monastrell, 10% cabernet sauvignon

93 Colour: cherry, garnet rim. Nose: earthy notes, red berry notes, ripe fruit, creamy oak. Palate: powerful, flavourful, complex, fine tannins.

SETZE GALLETS 16 2011 T
30% garnacha tintorera, 30% monastrell, 15% mandó, 25% merlot

91 Colour: bright cherry. Nose: ripe fruit, sweet spices, creamy oak. Palate: flavourful, fruity, toasty, round tannins.

COOP. V. SAN PEDRO APÓSTOL. MOIXENT

Pza. de la Hispanidad, 4
46640 Moixent - (Valencia)
☎: +34 962 260 020 - Fax: +34 962 260 560
info@closdelavall.com
www.closdelavall.com

CLOS DE LA VALL PX 2010 BFB
pedro ximénez

90 Colour: bright golden. Nose: ripe fruit, dry nuts, powerfull, toasty, sweet spices. Palate: flavourful, fruity, spicy, toasty, long.

HERETAT DE TAVERNERS

Ctra. Fontanars - Moixent, Km. 1,8
46635 Fontanars dels Alforins - (Valencia)
☎: +34 962 132 437 - Fax: +34 962 222 298
info@heretatdetaverners.com
www.heretatdetaverners.com

HERETAT DE TAVERNERS GRACIANO 2008 TR

91 Colour: cherry, garnet rim. Nose: earthy notes, scrubland, toasty, dark chocolate. Palate: powerful, fine bitter notes, good acidity.

HERETAT DE TAVERNERS REIXIU 2011 BC

90 Colour: bright yellow. Nose: powerfull, ripe fruit, sweet spices, creamy oak, white flowers. Palate: rich, flavourful, fresh, good acidity.

PUNT DOLÇ T

91 Colour: cherry, purple rim. Nose: expressive, red berry notes, ripe fruit, spicy, toasty. Palate: flavourful, fruity, good acidity, sweetness, toasty.

PAGO CASA GRAN

Ctra. Mogente Fontanares, km. 9,5
46640 Mogente - (Valencia)
☎: +34 962 261 004 - Fax: +34 962 261 004
comercial@pagocasagran.com
www.pagocasagran.com

CASA BENASAL CRUX 2008 T
garnacha tintorera, monastrell, syrah

90 Colour: cherry, garnet rim. Nose: creamy oak, toasty, dark chocolate, sweet spices, overripe fruit. Palate: powerful, flavourful, toasty, round tannins, balanced.

FALCATA ARENAL 2007 T
garnacha tintorera, monastrell

91 Colour: cherry, garnet rim. Nose: balsamic herbs, mineral, ripe fruit, spicy. Palate: flavourful, spicy, long, good acidity, round tannins.

RAFAEL CAMBRA

Naus Artesanals, 14
46635 Fontanars dels Alforins - (Valencia)
☎: +34 626 309 327 - Fax: +34 962 383 855
rafael@rafaelcambra.es
www.rafaelcambra.es

EL BON HOMME 2011 T
50% cabernet sauvignon, 50% monastrell

91 Colour: cherry, purple rim. Nose: ripe fruit, red berry notes, fragrant herbs. Palate: flavourful, fruity, fine bitter notes, round.

MINIMUM 2009 T

94 Colour: cherry, garnet rim. Nose: spicy, creamy oak, toasty, ripe fruit, characterful. Palate: powerful, flavourful, toasty, round tannins.

RAFAEL CAMBRA DOS 2010 T
cabernet sauvignon, cabernet franc

91 Colour: bright cherry. Nose: sweet spices, creamy oak, ripe fruit. Palate: flavourful, fruity, toasty, round tannins.

RAFAEL CAMBRA UNO 2009 T
monastrell

91 Colour: cherry, garnet rim. Nose: ripe fruit, spicy, creamy oak, toasty, mineral. Palate: powerful, flavourful, toasty, round tannins.

VALSAN 1831

Ctra. Cheste - Godelleta, Km. 1
46370 Chiva - (Valencia)
☎: +34 962 510 861 - Fax: +34 962 511 361
cherubino@cherubino.es
www.valsan1831.com

CUVA VELLA MOSCATEL
moscatel

93 Colour: light mahogany. Nose: powerfull, candied fruit, fruit liqueur notes, dry nuts, honeyed notes, aromatic coffee, dark chocolate. Palate: powerful, sweet, spirituous.

VIÑAS DEL PORTILLO S.L.

P.I. El Llano F2 P4 Apdo. 130
46360 Buñol - (Valencia)
☎: +34 962 504 827 - Fax: +34 962 500 937
vinasdelportillo@vinasdelportillo.es

ALTURIA 2011 B
malvasía, moscatel de alejandría

90 Colour: bright straw. Nose: fresh, fresh fruit, white flowers, fragrant herbs. Palate: flavourful, fruity, good acidity, balanced. Personality.

VIÑEDOS Y BODEGAS VEGALFARO

Ctra. Pontón - Utiel, Km. 3
46430 El Derramador - Requena - (Valencia)
☎: +34 962 320 680 - Fax: +34 962 321 126
info@vegalfaro.com
www.vegalfaro.com

PASAMONTE 2010 T
100% garnacha tintorera

90 Color bright cherry. Aroma ripe fruit, sweet spices, creamy oak, expressive. Taste flavourful, fruity, toasty, round tannins.

DESCRIPTION

This is in the island of Tenerife and is a prolongation of the Valle de la Orotava, to the south of Santa Cruz de Tenerife. The soils are of volcanic origin and the trade winds predominate. These are more marked than in Abona and define the character and personality of the wine. The atomization of the vineyards is the rule and this is shown by the 5,559 wine growers who work on only 572 hectares, where wines of all colours are produced.

NUMBER OF HECTARES: 560 **ALTITUDES:** 70 m. – 1.450 m.

PREDOMINANT VARIETIES:

White grapes: güal, listán blanco, malvasía, muscatel, verdello and vijariego.
Red grapes: bastardo negro, listán negro, malvasía tinta, muscatel negro, negramoll, vijariego negro, cabernet sauvignon, merlot, pinot noir, ruby cabernet, syrah and tempranillo.

CLIMATOLOGY AND SOILS

There is a diversity of microclimates with notable contrasts between daytime and night-time. The soils are volcanic at higher levels.

SAT VIÑA LAS CAÑAS

Barranco Badajoz, s/n
38500 Güimar - (Santa Cruz de Tenerife)
☎: +34 637 592 759 - Fax: +34 922 512 716
vegalascanas@hotmail.com

GRAN VIRTUD 2010 BFB

91 Colour: bright straw. Nose: ripe fruit, sweet spices, creamy oak, jasmine. Palate: fruity, flavourful, good acidity, fine bitter notes.

GRAN VIRTUD 2010 T FERMENTADO EN BARRICA

90 Colour: cherry, purple rim. Nose: ripe fruit, dark chocolate, medium intensity, wild herbs. Palate: rich, fruity, round tannins.

DESCRIPTION

This is located in the Canary Islands, in the northern part of the island of Tenerife. It has a border to the west with the Denomination of Origin Ycoden-Daute-Isora and to the east with the Denomination of Origin Tacoronte-Acentejo. It extends from the sea to the foot of the Teide mountain.

NUMBER OF HECTARES: 519 **ALTITUDES:** 250 m. – 700 m.

PREDOMINANT VARIETIES:

White grapes: güal, malvasía, verdello, vijariego and albillo.
Red grapes: listán negro, tintilla and negramoll.

CLIMATOLOGY AND SOILS

The meteorological conditions are influenced by the trade winds. These are constant winds which blow from the polar areas of the two hemispheres (high pressures) to the equatorial areas (low pressures). There is substantial Atlantic influence, which makes the temperature of the coastal zones milder and provides high levels of humidity.

BODEGA TAJINASTE

El Ratiño, 5
38315 La Orotava - (Santa Cruz de Tenerife)
☎: +34 696 030 347 - Fax: +34 922 308 720
bodega@tajinaste.net
www.tajinaste.net

CAN 2010 T
listán negro, vijariego negro

90 Colour: deep cherry, garnet rim. Nose: balanced, ripe fruit, cocoa bean, creamy oak, sweet spices. Palate: good structure, flavourful, long.

PROPIEDAD VITÍCOLA SUERTES DEL MARQUÉS

Tomás Zerolo, 15
38300 La Orotava - (Santa Cruz de Tenerife)
☎: +34 922 501 300 - Fax: +34 922 503 462
ventas@suertesdelmarques.com
www.suertesdelmarques.com

SUERTES DEL MARQUÉS CANDIO 2010 T
100% listán negro

90 Colour: cherry, garnet rim. Nose: complex, balanced, spicy, balsamic herbs, ripe fruit. Palate: fruity, good structure, long, good acidity.

SUERTES DEL MARQUÉS EL CIRUELO 2011
100% listán negro

90 Colour: light cherry. Nose: floral, fragrant herbs, ripe fruit, varnish, sweet spices, expressive. Palate: fresh, fruity, light-bodied, flavourful, balanced.

DESCRIPTION

The southern zone of the province of Madrid takes in three regions, the most extensive of which is the region of Arganda which uses tempranillo for red wines and malvar for white wines. Despite being city wines, the wines of Madrid have grown in quality and authenticity thanks to the garnacha in granite soils in San Martín de Valdeiglesias and albillo in the zone bordering with Ávila.

NUMBER OF HECTARES: 8.152 **ALTITUDES:** 500 m. – 1.000 m.

PREDOMINANT VARIETIES:

White grapes: malvar, airén, albillo, macabeo, parellada, torrontés and small grained muscatel. Red grapes: tinta fino, garnacha, garnacha tintorera, merlot, cabernet sauvignon y syrah.

CLIMATOLOGY AND SOILS

The climate is extreme continental; the soils are not very fertile and there is granite subsoil in the subzone of San Martín de Valdeiglesias; in Navalcarnero, there are poor, brown soils, with coarse clay sands; the subzone of Arganda is characterized by brown soils, acidic ph and granite subsoil.

BERNABELEVA

Ctra. Avila Toledo (N-403), Km. 81,600
28680 San Martín de Valdeiglesias - (Madrid)
☎: +34 915 091 909
bodega@bernabeleva.com
www.bernabeleva.com

BERNABELEVA "ARROYO DE TÓRTOLAS" 2010 T
100% garnacha

93 Colour: bright cherry. Nose: ripe fruit, scrubland, floral, dry stone, cocoa bean, dark chocolate, spicy, expressive. Palate: long, flavourful, spicy, complex, balanced.

BERNABELEVA "CARRIL DEL REY" 2010 T
100% garnacha

93 Colour: bright cherry. Nose: red berry notes, ripe fruit, scrubland, mineral, spicy, toasty, balanced. Palate: powerful, flavourful, long, good acidity.

BERNABELEVA VIÑA BONITA 2010 T
garnacha

94 Colour: cherry, purple rim. Nose: expressive, red berry notes, floral, sweet spices, creamy oak, mineral, fragrant herbs. Palate: flavourful, fruity, fresh.

CANTOCUERDAS ALBILLO 2010 B
100% albillo

93 Colour: bright yellow. Nose: powerfull, ripe fruit, sweet spices, fragrant herbs, faded flowers, mineral. Palate: rich, smoky aftertaste, flavourful, fresh, balanced, long.

CANTOCUERDAS MOSCATEL DE BERNABELEVA 2010 B
100% moscatel

94 Colour: bright golden. Nose: floral, jasmine, fragrant herbs, citrus fruit, candied fruit. Palate: flavourful, fresh, fruity, complex, good acidity, elegant.

NAVAHERREROS 2010 T
100% garnacha

93 Colour: bright cherry. Nose: sweet spices, creamy oak, red berry notes, ripe fruit, dark chocolate, fragrant herbs. Palate: flavourful, fruity, toasty, round tannins.

NAVAHERREROS BLANCO DE BERNABELEVA 2010 B
60% albillo, 40% macabeo

92 Colour: bright yellow. Nose: citrus fruit, ripe fruit, mineral, dried flowers, wild herbs, expressive. Palate: powerful, flavourful, rich, long, balanced.

BODEGA MARAÑONES

Hilero, 7 - Nave 9
28696 Pelayos de la Presa - (Madrid)
☎: +34 918 647 702
fernandogarcia@bodegamaranones.com
www.bodegamaranones.com

LABROS 2010 T
100% garnacha

91 Colour: bright cherry. Nose: candied fruit, wild herbs, spicy, mineral, earthy notes, expressive. Palate: balanced, flavourful, fresh, fruity, spicy.

MARAÑONES 2010 T
garnacha

93 Colour: light cherry. Nose: red berry notes, ripe fruit, fragrant herbs, floral, violets, sweet spices, creamy oak, expressive. Palate: balanced, elegant, flavourful, fresh, fruity. Personality.

PEÑA CABALLERA 2010 T
garnacha

94 Colour: cherry, garnet rim. Nose: spicy, creamy oak, toasty, fragrant herbs, dry stone, fruit liqueur notes. Palate: powerful, flavourful, toasty, round tannins, elegant.

PICARANA 2011 B
100% albillo

93 Colour: bright yellow. Nose: mineral, earthy notes, citrus fruit, ripe fruit, dried flowers, dry nuts. Palate: powerful, rich, flavourful, spicy, long, balanced, elegant.

PIESDESCALZOS 2011 B
100% albillo

92 Colour: bright yellow. Nose: ripe fruit, sweet spices, fragrant herbs, dried flowers, earthy notes. Palate: rich, flavourful, fresh, good acidity, fine bitter notes.

TREINTA MIL MARAVEDÍES 2010 T
garnacha, syrah

92 Colour: bright cherry. Nose: ripe fruit, sweet spices, creamy oak, cocoa bean, caramel. Palate: flavourful, fruity, toasty, fresh, balanced.

BODEGAS EL REGAJAL

Antigua Ctra. Andalucía, Km. 50,5
28300 Aranjuez - (Madrid)
☎: +34 913 078 903 - Fax: +34 913 576 312
isabel@elregajal.es

EL REGAJAL SELECCIÓN ESPECIAL 2010 T
tempranillo, merlot, syrah, cabernet sauvignon

92 Colour: deep cherry. Nose: fruit expression, overripe fruit, creamy oak, spicy, toasty. Palate: ripe fruit, flavourful, powerful, fine bitter notes, good acidity.

LAS RETAMAS DEL REGAJAL 2010 T
tempranillo, merlot, syrah, cabernet sauvignon

91 Colour: deep cherry. Nose: ripe fruit, scrubland, toasty, spicy. Palate: flavourful, powerful, fine bitter notes, good acidity.

BODEGAS ORUSCO

Alcalá, 54
28511 Valdilecha - (Madrid)
☎: +34 918 738 006 - Fax: +34 918 738 336
esther@bodegasorusco.com
www.bodegasorusco.com

ARMONIUM 2008 T
70% merlot, 30% cabernet sauvignon

90 Colour: bright cherry. Nose: ripe fruit, sweet spices, creamy oak, fragrant herbs. Palate: flavourful, fruity, toasty, round tannins, balanced.

COMANDO G

Villamanin, 27 - 4° E
28011 - (Madrid)
☎: +34 696 366 555
daniel@jimenezlandi.com

LA BRUJA AVERÍA 2011 T
100% garnacha

94 Colour: deep cherry. Nose: fresh fruit, red berry notes, balsamic herbs, scrubland. Palate: good acidity, fine bitter notes, ripe fruit, long.

LAS UMBRÍAS 2010 T
100% garnacha

93 Colour: bright cherry. Nose: medium intensity, elegant, balanced, red berry notes. Palate: flavourful, fine bitter notes, ripe fruit.

LA CASA DE MONROY

José Moya, 12
45940 Valmojado - (Toledo)
☎: +34 918 170 102
info@bodegasmonroy.es
www.bodegasmonroy.es

LA CASA DE MONROY "EL REPISO" 2009 TC
70% tempranillo, 20% cabernet sauvignon, 10% garnacha

90 Colour: cherry, garnet rim. Nose: ripe fruit, spicy, creamy oak, wild herbs, balsamic herbs. Palate: powerful, flavourful, toasty, round tannins.

LA CASA DE MONROY SELECCIÓN VIÑAS VIEJAS 2008 T
90% garnacha, 5% garnacha tintorera, 5% syrah

91 Colour: ruby red, orangey edge. Nose: fruit liqueur notes, scrubland, spicy, earthy notes, balanced. Palate: powerful, flavourful, long, balsamic, spicy.

LA CASA DE MONROY SELECCIÓN VIÑAS VIEJAS 2010 T
95% garnacha, 5% syrah

90 Colour: cherry, garnet rim. Nose: earthy notes, wild herbs, ripe fruit, fruit liqueur notes, spicy, toasty. Palate: powerful, flavourful, spicy, long.

LAS MORADAS DE SAN MARTÍN

Ctra. M-541, Km. 4,7. Pago de Los Castillejos Apdo. Correos 25
28680 San Martín de Valdeiglesias - (Madrid)
☎: +34 691 676 570 - Fax: +34 915 417 590
bodega@lasmoradasdesanmartin.es
www.lasmoradasdesanmartin.es

LAS MORADAS DE SAN MARTÍN LAS LUCES 2007 T
100% garnacha

91 Colour: cherry, garnet rim. Nose: toasty, dark chocolate, fruit liqueur notes, mineral. Palate: fine bitter notes, good acidity, spicy, warm.

PAGOS DE FAMILIA MARQUÉS DE GRIÑÓN

Finca Casa de Vacas - Ctra. CM-4015, Km. 23
45692 Malpica de Tajo - (Toledo)
☎: +34 925 597 222 - Fax: +34 925 789 416
service@hotmail.com
www.pagosdefamilia.com

EL RINCÓN 2007 T
95% syrah, 5% garnacha

90 Color cherry, garnet rim. Aroma ripe fruit, spicy, creamy oak, toasty, complex. Taste powerful, flavourful, toasty, round tannins.

RICARDO BENITO

Las Eras, 5
28600 Navalcarnero - (Madrid)
☎: +34 918 110 097 - Fax: +34 918 112 663
bodega@ricardobenito.com
www.ricardobenito.com

ASIDO 2008 T
tinto fino, merlot, cabernet sauvignon

90 Colour: deep cherry. Nose: ripe fruit, toasty, dark chocolate. Palate: powerful, fine bitter notes, good acidity.

DIVO 2007 T

93 Colour: cherry, garnet rim. Nose: ripe fruit, spicy, creamy oak, toasty, characterful. Palate: powerful, flavourful, toasty, round tannins.

TAGONIUS

Ctra. Ambite, Km. 4,4
28550 Tielmes - (Madrid)
☎: +34 918 737 505 - Fax: +34 918 746 161
director@tagonius.com
www.tagonius.com

TAGONIUS 2004 TR
merlot, tempranillo, syrah, cabernet sauvignon

91 Colour: pale ruby, brick rim edge. Nose: spicy, fine reductive notes, wet leather, aged wood nuances, fruit liqueur notes, toasty. Palate: fine tannins, long, spicy, balsamic.

TAGONIUS MARIAGE 2005 T
tempranillo, merlot

90 Colour: ruby red, orangey edge. Nose: ripe fruit, fruit liqueur notes, scrubland, fine reductive notes. Palate: long, balsamic, spicy, spirituous, round.

TAGONIUS MERLOT 2006 T
merlot

90 Colour: pale ruby, brick rim edge. Nose: fruit liqueur notes, fruit liqueur notes, fragrant herbs, old leather, cigar, tobacco. Palate: spicy, balsamic, powerful, flavourful, long, balanced.

UVAS FELICES

Agullers, 7
8003 Barcelona - (Barcelona)
☎: +34 902 327 777
www.vilaviniteca.es

EL HOMBRE BALA 2010 T
100% garnacha

94 Colour: deep cherry. Nose: spicy, ripe fruit, fruit expression, balsamic herbs, scrubland. Palate: fine bitter notes, round tannins, good acidity.

VINOS JEROMÍN

San José, 8
28590 Villarejo de Salvanés - (Madrid)
☎: +34 918 742 030 - Fax: +34 918 744 139
comercial@vinosjeromin.com
www.vinosjeromin.com

FÉLIX MARTÍNEZ CEPAS VIEJAS 2008 TR
90% tempranillo, 10% otras

90 Colour: bright cherry. Nose: ripe fruit, sweet spices, creamy oak, expressive. Palate: flavourful, fruity, toasty, round tannins, balanced.

GREGO 2009 TC
tempranillo, syrah, garnacha

90 Colour: bright cherry. Nose: sweet spices, creamy oak, ripe fruit. Palate: flavourful, fruity, toasty, round tannins.

MANU VINO DE AUTOR 2007 TC
tempranillo, syrah, garnacha, cabernet sauvignon, merlot

90 Colour: cherry, garnet rim. Nose: spicy, creamy oak, toasty, characterful, ripe fruit. Palate: powerful, flavourful, toasty, round tannins.

PUERTA DE ALCALÁ 2009 TC
tempranillo

90 Colour: cherry, garnet rim. Nose: sweet spices, toasty, ripe fruit, scrubland. Palate: flavourful, powerful, fine bitter notes.

BODEGA OTAZU

Señorío de Otazu, s/n
31174 Etxauri - (Navarra)
☎: +34 948 329 200 - Fax: +34 948 329 353
otazu@otazu.com
www.otazu.com

SEÑORÍO DE OTAZU 2007 T
cabernet sauvignon, tempranillo, merlot

94 Colour: cherry, garnet rim. Nose: ripe fruit, spicy, creamy oak, toasty, complex, characterful, mineral. Palate: powerful, flavourful, toasty, round tannins.

SEÑORÍO DE OTAZU ALTAR 2006 T
90% cabernet sauvignon, 10% tempranillo

95 Colour: cherry, garnet rim. Nose: spicy, creamy oak, toasty, complex, mineral, earthy notes, ripe fruit. Palate: powerful, flavourful, toasty, round tannins.

SEÑORIO DE OTAZU VITRAL 2007 TC
95% cabernet sauvignon, 5% tempranillo

93 Colour: cherry, garnet rim. Nose: spicy, creamy oak, toasty, complex, ripe fruit, overripe fruit, dark chocolate. Palate: powerful, flavourful, toasty, sweet tannins.

BODEGAS MUÑANA

Finca Peñas Prietas - Ctra. Graena a La Peza
18517 Cortes y Graena - (Granada)
☎: +34 958 670 715 - Fax: +34 958 670 715
bodegasmunana@gmail.com
www.bodegasmunana.com

MUÑANA 3 CEPAS 2009 T
syrah, cabernet sauvignon, merlot

90 Colour: cherry, garnet rim. Nose: red berry notes, ripe fruit, mineral, balsamic herbs, spicy. Palate: light-bodied, flavourful, long, round.

DESCRIPTION

The name is taken from the kingdoms of the Guanche, Ycoden and Daute epochs, and the dominions of the princess Isora. It takes in the wide region of the northwest of Tenerife. The wines are cultivated at several altitudes. Outstanding in volume are the expressive white wines made from listán blanca.

NUMBER OF HECTARES: 250 **ALTITUDES:** 50 m. – 1.400 m.

PREDOMINANT VARIETIES:

White grapes: bermejuelo o marmajuelo, gual, malvasía, muscatel, pedro ximénez, verdello, vijariego, albillo, baboso blanco, bastardo blanco, forastera blanca, listán blanca, sabro and torrontés.

Red grapes: tintilla and listán negro.

CLIMATOLOGY AND SOILS

Mediterranean with various micro-climates depending on the altitude and other geographical circumstances. Soils of volcanic rock and ash in the higher areas and clay in the lower areas.

None of the wines tasted achieve the minimum required scoring

DESCRIPTION

This is in the northeast of the province of Murcia. The zone combines several areas at different altitudes for making wines which are more Mediterranean or more continental. Thus, it has become an engine for the export of monastrell with an average price of six euros due to the initiatives of a few wineries with commercial vision.

NUMBER OF HECTARES: 6.150 **ALTITUDES:** 400 m. – 800 m.

PREDOMINANT VARIETIES:

White grapes: merseguera, airén, macabeo, malvasía and chardonnay. Red grapes: monastrell, garnacha tinta, cabernet sauvignon, cencibel, merlot, tintorera and syrah.

CLIMATOLOGY AND SOILS

Continental-Mediterranean. The soils are basically limestone, deep and with good permeability.

BODEGAS CASTAÑO

Ctra. Fuenteálamo, 3 - Apdo. 120
30510 Yecla - (Murcia)
☎: +34 968 791 115 - Fax: +34 968 791 900
info@bodegascastano.com
www.bodegascastano.com

CASA CISCA 2010 T
100% monastrell

96 Colour: cherry, garnet rim. Nose: spicy, creamy oak, toasty, complex, expressive, ripe fruit, lactic notes. Palate: powerful, flavourful, toasty, round tannins.

CASTAÑO COLECCIÓN 2009 T
75% monastrell, 25% cabernet sauvignon

92 Color cherry, garnet rim. Aroma ripe fruit, spicy, creamy oak, toasty, complex. Taste powerful, flavourful, toasty, round tannins.

CASTAÑO MONASTRELL DULCE 2009 T
100% monastrell

90 Colour: cherry, garnet rim. Nose: spicy, toasty, ripe fruit, dried fruit, dark chocolate. Palate: powerful, flavourful, complex.

POZUELO 2008 TR

90 Colour: cherry, garnet rim. Nose: ripe fruit, mineral, balsamic herbs, dark chocolate, cocoa bean, creamy oak. Palate: spicy, long, flavourful, toasty.

VIÑA DETRÁS DE LA CASA CABERNET SAUVIGNON-TINTORERA 2007 TC

93 Colour: cherry, garnet rim. Nose: ripe fruit, expressive, balsamic herbs, earthy notes, creamy oak. Palate: powerful, flavourful, long, toasty.

VIÑA DETRÁS DE LA CASA SYRAH 2007 T
syrah

94 Colour: cherry, garnet rim. Nose: expressive, earthy notes, ripe fruit, spicy. Palate: powerful, flavourful, complex, balanced, long, toasty.

BODEGAS SEÑORÍO DE BARAHONDA

Ctra. de Pinoso, km. 3
30510 Yecla - (Murcia)
☎: +34 968 718 696 - Fax: +34 968 790 928
info@barahonda.com
www.barahonda.com

59H 35' 03" 2010 T

91 Colour: bright cherry. Nose: ripe fruit, sweet spices, creamy oak. Palate: flavourful, fruity, toasty, round tannins.

ZONA ZEPA 2008 T

90 Colour: cherry, garnet rim. Nose: spicy, creamy oak, toasty, ripe fruit. Palate: powerful, flavourful, toasty, round tannins.

TRENZA WINES S.L.

Avda. Matías Saenz Tejada, s/n. Edif. Fuengirola Center - Local 1
29640 Fuengirola - (Málaga)
☎: +34 615 343 320 - Fax: +34 952 588 467
david@vinnico.com
www.trenzawines.com

LA NYMPHINA 2011 T
100% monastrell

90 Colour: bright cherry. Nose: ripe fruit, sweet spices, scrubland. Palate: flavourful, fruity, toasty, round tannins.

TRENZA FAMILY COLLECTION 2009 T
58% monastrell, 24% cabernet sauvignon, 12% syrah, 6% garnacha tintorera

93 Color cherry, garnet rim. Aroma ripe fruit, spicy, creamy oak, toasty, complex. Taste powerful, flavourful, toasty, round tannins.

VINNICO EXPORT

Muela, 16
3730 Jávea - (Alicante)
☎: +34 965 791 967 - Fax: +34 966 461 471
info@vinnico.com
www.vinnico.com

ALMEZ ORGANIC MONASTRELL SHIRAZ 2011 T
85% monastrell, 15% syrah

90 Colour: cherry, purple rim. Nose: red berry notes, floral, ripe fruit. Palate: flavourful, fruity, good acidity, round tannins.

DO PAGO AYLÉS

DESCRIPTION

It is located in the municipal area of Mezalocha, Zaragoza, within the limits of the Cariñena Denomination of Origin. The production zone is in the basin of the River Ebro, in the sub-basin of the River Huerva.

NUMBER OF HECTARES: 75 **ALTITUDES:** 600 m.

PREDOMINANT VARIETIES:
Red grapes: garnacha, merlot, tempranillo and cabernet sauvignon.

CLIMATOLOGY AND SOILS

The climate is temperate continental with low average rainfall (250 and 550 mm. annually). Its soils are composed of limestone, loam and conglomerates.

FINCA AYLÉS

Finca Aylés. Ctra. A-1101, Km. 24
50152 Mezalocha (Zaragoza)
7: +34 976 140 473 - Fax: +34 976 140 268
info@pagoayles.com
www.pagoayles.com

"A" DE AYLÉS 2010 T
tempranillo, merlot, garnacha, cabernet sauvignon

90 Colour: bright cherry. Nose: ripe fruit, sweet spices, creamy oak, cocoa bean, dark chocolate. Palate: flavourful, fruity, toasty, round tannins.

"Y" DE AYLÉS 2010 T
tempranillo, merlot, garnacha, cabernet sauvignon

93 Colour: cherry, garnet rim. Nose: ripe fruit, spicy, creamy oak, complex, scrubland, new oak. Palate: powerful, flavourful, toasty, round tannins.

DO PAGO CALZADILLA

DESCRIPTION

This is located in Cuenca and belongs to the Autonomous Community of Castile La Mancha, in the Alcarria area of Cuenca. Its vineyards have steep slopes with inclinations of more than 40%, which means that cultivation is carried out on slopes and terraces following the bends in the levels.

NUMBER OF HECTARES: 20 **ALTITUDES:** 845-1.005 m.

PREDOMINANT VARIETIES:
Red grapes: tempranillo, cabernet sauvignon, garnacha and syrah.

CLIMATOLOGY AND SOILS

It has a Mediterranean continental climate, with cold temperatures in winter and mild temperatures in summer. It has an important thermal integral, which is especially notable in hottest months. The soils are basically limestone.

PAGO CALZADILLA

Ctra. Huete a Cuenca, Km. 3
16500 Huete - (Cuenca)
☎: +34 969 143 020 - Fax: +34 969 147 047
info@pagodecalzadilla.com
www.pagodecalzadilla.net

CALZADILLA ALLEGRO 2007 T
syrah

90 Colour: cherry, purple rim. Nose: balanced, sweet spices, creamy oak. Palate: ripe fruit, round tannins.

CALZADILLA CLASSIC 2007 T
tempranillo, cabernet sauvignon, garnacha, syrah

90 Colour: cherry, garnet rim. Nose: balanced, ripe fruit, cocoa bean, creamy oak. Palate: good structure, flavourful, good acidity.

GRAN CALZADILLA 2006 T
70% tempranillo, 30% cabernet sauvignon

91 Colour: bright cherry, garnet rim. Nose: complex, sweet spices, creamy oak, cocoa bean. Palate: balanced, fine bitter notes, good acidity.

DO PAGO CAMPO DE LA GUARDIA

DESCRIPTION

This estate belongs to Bodegas Martúe La Guardia. Its vineyards are situated in the municipal area of La Guardia, in the northeast of the province of Toledo (Castile La Mancha).

NUMBER OF HECTARES: 81 **ALTITUDES:** 700 m.

PREDOMINANT VARIETIES:

White grapes: chardonnay.

Red grapes: tempranillo (14 hectares), malbec (3 hectares), cabernet sauvignon (16 hectares), merlot (19 hectares), syrah (19 hectares) and petit verdot (7 hectares).

CLIMATOLOGY AND SOILS

The soils of this estate are deep, composed of silt-limestone and clay-sand. The summers are very warm and the winters cold and dry, a continental type climate. The River Tagus to the north and the Mountains of Toledo to the south mean that there is less rainfall than in neighbouring areas.

None of the wines tasted achieve the minimum required scoring

DO PAGO CASA DEL BLANCO

DESCRIPTION

This belongs to the winery with the same name. this estate is in the centre of the province of Ciudad Real, Castile La Mancha, in the Campo de Calatrava, in the municipal area of Manzanares.

NUMBER OF HECTARES: 92,7 **ALTITUDES:** 617 m.

PREDOMINANT VARIETIES:

White grapes: chardonnay y sauvignon blanc.

Red grapes: tempranillo, merlot, petit verdot, cabernet sauvignon, syrah, malbec and cabernet franc.

CLIMATOLOGY AND SOILS

It has a climate with Mediterranean/continental influences and silt-sandy soils with a high lithium content, probably from the volcanic past of the zone.

None of the wines tasted achieve the minimum required scoring

DO PAGO DEHESA DEL CARRIZAL

DESCRIPTION

This is located in the Mountains of Toledo, in the north of the province of Ciudad Real (Retuerta del Bullaque, and has a border with Toledo, it benefits from privileged continental characteristics in order to produce wines with cabernet sauvignon and other French grapes.

NUMBER OF HECTARES: 22 **ALTITUDES:** 900 m.

PREDOMINANT VARIETIES:

White grapes: chardonnay.
Red grapes: merlot, syrah, cabernet sauvignon and tempranillo.

DEHESA DEL CARRIZAL

Ctra. de Retuerta a Navas de Estena, Km. 5
13194 Retuerta del Bullaque - (Ciudad Real)
☎: +34 925 421 773 - Fax: +34 926 867 093
bodega@dehesadelcarrizal.com
www.dehesadelcarrizal.com

DEHESA DEL CARRIZAL CABERNET SAUVIGNON 2007 T
cabernet sauvignon

91 Colour: cherry, garnet rim. Nose: ripe fruit, scrubland, varietal, sweet spices. Palate: spicy, powerful, flavourful, complex.

DEHESA DEL CARRIZAL COLECCIÓN PRIVADA 2007 T
cabernet sauvignon, syrah, merlot, petit verdot

90 Color cherry, garnet rim. Aroma ripe fruit, spicy, creamy oak, toasty, complex. Taste powerful, flavourful, toasty, round tannins.

DEHESA DEL CARRIZAL SYRAH 2008 T
syrah

92 Colour: cherry, garnet rim. Nose: ripe fruit, balsamic herbs, earthy notes, spicy, creamy oak. Palate: full, flavourful, toasty.

DO PAGO DOMINIO DE VALDEPUSA

DESCRIPTION

Malpica de Tajo (Toledo) was a pioneer in the launch of cabernet sauvignon and chardonnay in Spain by Carlos Falcó.

NUMBER OF HECTARES: 49 **ALTITUDES:** 300 m. – 400 m.

PREDOMINANT VARIETIES:

Red grapes: syrah, cabernet sauvignon, petit verdot, merlot and graciano.

CLIMATOLOGY AND SOILS

The climate is continental with substantial contrasts between daytime and night-time. It has an average temperature of 17°C. The soils are formed by a clay surface on a limestone subsoil.

PAGOS DE FAMILIA MARQUÉS DE GRIÑÓN

Finca Casa de Vacas - Ctra. CM-4015, Km. 23
45692 Malpica de Tajo - (Toledo)
☎: +34 925 597 222 - Fax: +34 925 789 416
service@hotmail.com
www.pagosdefamilia.com

CALIZA 2008 T
70% syrah, 30% petit verdot

90 Colour: deep cherry, garnet rim. Nose: fruit preserve, dark chocolate, fruit liqueur notes, tobacco. Palate: balanced, fine bitter notes, round tannins.

MARQUÉS DE GRIÑÓN CABERNET SAUVIGNON 2007 T
100% cabernet sauvignon

91 Colour: bright cherry, garnet rim. Nose: elegant, ripe fruit, scrubland, varietal. Palate: full, spicy, ripe fruit.

MARQUÉS DE GRIÑÓN EMERITVS 2007 TR
63% cabernet sauvignon, 32% petit verdot, 5% syrah

93 Colour: cherry, garnet rim. Nose: spicy, creamy oak, toasty, characterful, ripe fruit, mineral. Palate: powerful, flavourful, toasty, round tannins.

MARQUÉS DE GRIÑÓN PETIT VERDOT 2007 T
100% petit verdot

91 Colour: bright cherry, garnet rim. Nose: complex, wild herbs, balanced. Palate: flavourful, ripe fruit, round tannins.

SVMMA VARIETALIS 2007 T
45% cabernet sauvignon, 42% syrah, 13% petit verdot

92 Colour: cherry, garnet rim. Nose: expressive, creamy oak, ripe fruit, cocoa bean, wild herbs. Palate: good structure, complex, full.

DO PAGO EL TERRERAZO

DESCRIPTION

This estate belongs to the Bodega Mustiguillo. It is located in the Spanish Levante, between Utiel and Sinarcas, in the Autonomous Community of Valencia.

NUMBER OF HECTARES: 87 **ALTITUDES:** 850 m.

PREDOMINANT VARIETIES:
Red grapes: bobal.

CLIMATOLOGY AND SOILS

This has a Mediterranean – continental climate. Its proximity to the Mediterranean sea, 80 km. distant, means that its vineyards are influenced by the wet winds from the sea. The soils are basically clay and limestone, with pebbles and sand.

MUSTIGUILLO VIÑEDOS Y BODEGA

Ctra. N-330, km 196,5 El Terrerazo
46300 Utiel - (Valencia)
☎: +34 962 168 260 - Fax: +34 962 168 259
info@bodegamustiguillo.com
www.bodegamustiguillo.com

FINCA TERRERAZO 2010 T
100% bobal

95 Colour: bright cherry. Nose: ripe fruit, expressive, mineral, cocoa bean. Palate: flavourful, fruity, toasty, round tannins.

DO PAGO FINCA ÉLEZ

DESCRIPTION

This is the Denomination of Origin corresponding to the Manuel Manzaneque winery, situated in the town of El Bonillo, in the province of Albacete in the mountain range, Sierra de Alcaraz, to the southeast of La Mancha. This estate wine became known due to a chardonnay from barrels which was a pioneer wine in La Mancha.

NUMBER OF HECTARES: 40 **ALTITUDES:** 1.000 m.

PREDOMINANT VARIETIES:

White grapes: chardonnay.

Red grapes: syrah, cabernet sauvignon, tempranillo and merlot.

CLIMATOLOGY AND SOILS

It has a continental climate with silt-clay-sandy soils and silt-clay soils.

VIÑEDOS Y BODEGA MANUEL MANZANEQUE

Ctra. Ossa de Montiel a El Bonillo, Km. 11,500
2610 El Bonillo - (Albacete)
☎: +34 967 585 003 - Fax: +34 967 370 649
info@manuelmanzaneque.com
www.manuelmanzaneque.com

MANUEL MANZANEQUE CHARDONNAY 2008 BFB
chardonnay

90 Colour: bright yellow. Nose: powerfull, ripe fruit, sweet spices, creamy oak, fragrant herbs. Palate: rich, flavourful, fresh, good acidity.

MANUEL MANZANEQUE ESCENA 2007 T
90% tempranillo, 10% cabernet sauvignon

93 Colour: cherry, garnet rim. Nose: ripe fruit, spicy, toasty, fine reductive notes, balsamic herbs. Palate: powerful, flavourful, toasty, round tannins.

MANUEL MANZANEQUE NUESTRA SELECCIÓN 2007 T
70% tempranillo, 20% cabernet sauvignon, 10% merlot

91 Colour: cherry, garnet rim. Nose: ripe fruit, spicy, creamy oak, toasty, complex, balsamic herbs. Palate: powerful, flavourful, toasty, round tannins, elegant.

MANUEL MANZANEQUE SYRAH 2007 T
syrah

90 Colour: cherry, garnet rim. Nose: ripe fruit, violets, earthy notes, spicy, creamy oak. Palate: powerful, flavourful, balanced, round tannins.

DO PAGO FLORENTINO

DESCRIPTION

This is composed of terrain located in the municipal area of Malagón (Ciudad Real), and is protected by natural lakes to the south and by the mountain range, Sierra de Malagón, to the north.

NUMBER OF HECTARES: 58,12 **ALTITUDES:** 630-670 m.

PREDOMINANT VARIETIES:
Red grapes: tempranillo, syrah and petit verdot

CLIMATOLOGY AND SOILS

Sandy soils, with remains of limestone. The subsoil is composed of slate and limestone and the surface also has a portion of small stones (fragments of loose rock). Its climate is characterized as being somewhat more temperate and dry than in the neighbouring towns.

None of the wines tasted achieve the minimum required scoring

DO PAGO GUIJOSO

DESCRIPTION

The wines produced in the Finca El Guijoso, owned by Bodegas Sánchez Muliterno, located in El Bolillo, between Albacete and Ciudad Real (Castile La Mancha) are recognized.

NUMBER OF HECTARES: 58,12 **ALTITUDES:** 630-670 m.

PREDOMINANT VARIETIES:
White grapes: chardonnay and sauvignon blanc.
Red grapes: tempranillo, merlot, cabernet and syrah.

CLIMATOLOGY AND SOILS

It is surrounded by evergreen oak and savin woods, the vineyard has silt-sandy soils, with angular pebbles (limestone and pebbles (silica) with up to 80% of stone. The predominant climate is continental.

BODEGAS Y VIÑEDOS SÁNCHEZ MULITERNO

Tesifonte Gallego, 5
2002 (Albacete)
7: +34 967 193 222 - Fax: +34 967 193 292
bodegas@sanchez-muliterno.com
www.sanchez-muliterno.com

MAGNIFICUS 2006 T
100% syrah

91 Colour: dark-red cherry, orangey edge. Nose: ripe fruit, mineral, cocoa bean, sweet spices, creamy oak, fine reductive notes. Palate: balanced, powerful, flavourful, long, round tannins.

DO PAGO LOS BALAGUESES

DESCRIPTION

The estate Pago los Balagueses is located to the southwest of the region of Utiel, 20 Km. from Requena, in the Autonomous Community of Valencia.

NUMBER OF HECTARES: 18 **ALTITUDES:** 750 m.

PREDOMINANT VARIETIES:

White grapes: sauvignon blanc.

Red grapes: syrah, bobal, garnacha tintorera and merlot.

CLIMATOLOGY AND SOILS

The climate is continental with Mediterranean influences, its vineyards record annual rainfall of 450 millimetres. The vineyards are on a gently sloping hillside surrounded by pine trees, almond trees and olive trees.

VIÑEDOS Y BODEGAS VEGALFARO

Ctra. Pontón - Utiel, Km. 3
46340 Requena (Valencia)
☎: +34 962 320 680 - Fax: +34 962 321 126
rodolfo@vegalfaro.com
www.vegalfaro.com

PAGO DE LOS BALAGUESES SYRAH 2009 TC
syrah

93 Colour: cherry, garnet rim. Nose: spicy, creamy oak, toasty, characterful, earthy notes, ripe fruit. Palate: flavourful, toasty, round tannins.

DO PAGO PRADO DE IRACHE

DESCRIPTION

This is a recent Denomination of Origin granted to Bodegas Irache, a classical Navarre winery in the town of Ayegui owning 150 hectares in the region of Tierra Estella. Its best product is Prado Irache, a blend of tempranillo, cabernet and merlot.

NUMBER OF HECTARES: 17 **ALTITUDES:** 450 m.

PREDOMINANT VARIETIES:
Red grapes: tempranillo, cabernet sauvignon, merlot, mazuelo, graciano and garnacha.

CLIMATOLOGY AND SOILS

A continental and Atlantic type climate. Silt loam soils.

IRACHE

Monasterio de Irache, 1
31240 Ayegui (Navarra)
☎: +34 948 551 932 - Fax: +34 948 554 954
irache@irache.com
www.irache.com

PRADO IRACHE VINO DE PAGO 2006 T
tempranillo, cabernet sauvignon, merlot

90 Colour: bright cherry, orangey edge. Nose: ripe fruit, woody, scrubland, sweet spices, creamy oak, earthy notes. Palate: long, spicy, powerful, flavourful, round tannins.

DO PAGO DE OTAZU

DESCRIPTION

Otazu is located between mountain ranges, Sierra del Perdón and Sierra de Etxauri, and is the most northerly vineyard in the country. It specializes in very fresh Atlantic type red wines, produced from vines in limestone soils with a predominance of pebbles.

NUMBER OF HECTARES: 92 **ALTITUDES:** 380 m.

PREDOMINANT VARIETIES:
White grapes: chardonnay.
Red grapes: tempranillo, merlot and cabernet sauvignon.

CLIMATOLOGY AND SOILS

A fresh wine growing area with an Atlantic tendency with strong continental contrasts between daytime and night-time. Limestone type soils in Pamplona with a predominance of pebbles.

BODEGA OTAZU

Señorío de Otazu, s/n
31174 Etxauri (Navarra)
☎: +34 948 329 200 - Fax: +34 948 329 353
otazu@otazu.com
www.otazu.com

SEÑORÍO DE OTAZU 2007 T
cabernet sauvignon, tempranillo, merlot

95 Colour: cherry, garnet rim. Nose: ripe fruit, spicy, creamy oak, toasty, complex, characterful, mineral. Palate: powerful, flavourful, toasty, round tannins.

SEÑORÍO DE OTAZU ALTAR 2006 T
90% cabernet sauvignon, 10% tempranillo

95 Colour: cherry, garnet rim. Nose: spicy, creamy oak, toasty, complex, mineral, earthy notes, ripe fruit. Palate: powerful, flavourful, toasty, round tannins.

SEÑORIO DE OTAZU VITRAL 2005 TC
95% cabernet sauvignon, 5% tempranillo

94 Colour: cherry, garnet rim. Nose: spicy, creamy oak, toasty, complex, ripe fruit, overripe fruit, dark chocolate. Palate: powerful, flavourful, toasty, sweet tannins.

DO PAGO SEÑORÍO DE ARINZANO

DESCRIPTION

This is located in the northwest of Spain in Estella, Navarre. Its vineyards are located in a valley formed by the foothills of the Pyrenees and are divided by the River Ega which moderates the temperature.

NUMBER OF HECTARES: 128 **ALTITUDES:** 600 m.

PREDOMINANT VARIETIES:

White grapes: chardonnay.
Red grapes: tempranillo, merlot and cabernet sauvignon.

CLIMATOLOGY AND SOILS

Its climate is influenced by the Atlantic, with a substantial thermal differential. The vineyards in this estate are located in a geologically complex area, with variable proportions of silt, loam, clay and the degradation of limestone-calcareous rock.

SEÑORÍO DE ARÍNZANO

Crta. NA-132, km. 3,1
31292 Aberin (Navarra)
7: +34 948 555 258
info@arinzano.com
www.bodegaschivite.com

ARÍNZANO 2004 T

95 Colour: cherry, garnet rim. Nose: ripe fruit, spicy, creamy oak, toasty, complex, elegant, balanced, mineral. Palate: powerful, flavourful, toasty, round tannins, long.

ARÍNZANO LA CASONA 2008 T

95 Colour: bright cherry. Nose: sweet spices, creamy oak, powerfull, red berry notes, fruit expression. Palate: flavourful, fruity, toasty, round tannins, round.

DESCRIPTION

To date in Spain, there are only six zones which have acquired the label "Quality Wine": Cangas, Granada, Lebrija, Sierra de Salamanca, Valles de Benavente and Valtiendas, distinguished as VCPRD (Quality Wines Produced in Specified Regions). This entails training for those zones which aspire to achieve the Denomination of Origin category, but this term continues to be imprecise for the buyer.

CANGAS

BODEGAS OBANCA

Obanca, 12
33800 Cangas del Narcea - (Asturias)
☎: +34 626 956 571 - Fax: +34 985 811 539
informacion@obanca.com
www.obanca.com

CASTRO DE LIMÉS OROCANTABRICO 2011 BFB
albarín

91 Colour: bright yellow. Nose: powerfull, ripe fruit, sweet spices, creamy oak, fragrant herbs. Palate: rich, flavourful, fresh, good acidity.

LLUMES 2010 T
verdejo negro

91 Colour: bright cherry. Nose: creamy oak, spicy, red berry notes, ripe fruit, balsamic herbs, mineral. Palate: flavourful, fruity, toasty, round tannins, elegant.

DOMINIO DEL UROGALLO

Pol. Obanca, C. Empresas, nave 2
33819 Cangas de Narcea - (Asturias)
☎: +34 626 568 238
info@dominiodelurogallo.com
www.dominiodelurogallo.com

PESICO 2010 B
100% albarín

92 Colour: bright straw. Nose: dried flowers, ripe fruit, fragrant herbs, dry stone. Palate: fresh, fruity, light-bodied, good acidity, balanced.

PESICO 2010 T
60% carrasquín, 20% verdejo negro, 10% albarín tinto, 10% mencía

90 Colour: cherry, garnet rim. Nose: ripe fruit, creamy oak, toasty, balsamic herbs, mineral. Palate: powerful, flavourful, toasty, round tannins, balanced.

GRANADA

DOMINIO BUENAVISTA

Ctra. de Almería, s/n
18480 Ugíjar - (Granada)
☎: +34 958 767 254 - Fax: +34 958 990 226
info@dominiobuenavista.com
www.dominiobuenavista.com

VELETA NOLADOS 2009 T
40% cabernet sauvignon, 40% cabernet franc, 20% tempranillo

90 Colour: cherry, garnet rim. Nose: ripe fruit, spicy, creamy oak, toasty, balsamic herbs, earthy notes. Palate: powerful, flavourful, toasty, spicy.

MARQUÉS DE CASA PARDIÑAS C.B.

Finca San Torcuato
18540 Huélago - (Granada)
☎: +34 630 901 094 - Fax: +34 958 252 297
info@spiracp.es
www.marquesdecasapardiñas.com

SPIRA VENDIMIA SELECCIONADA 2010 T
60% tempranillo, 35% cabernet sauvignon, 5% merlot

90 Color bright cherry. Aroma ripe fruit, sweet spices, creamy oak, expressive. Taste flavourful, fruity, toasty, round tannins.

NESTARES RINCÓN VINOS Y BODEGAS

C/ Moret, 1
☎: +34 655 959 500 - Fax: +34 958 272 125
info@alpujarride.com
www.alpujarride.com

NESTARES RINCÓN 1.0 2011 T
tempranillo, syrah, merlot

90 Colour: cherry, garnet rim. Nose: red berry notes, floral, balsamic herbs, earthy notes. Palate: good acidity, powerful, flavourful, long.

SALAMANCA

CÁMBRICO

Paraje El Guijarral
37658 Villanueva del Conde - (Salamanca)
☎: +34 923 281 006 - Fax: +34 923 213 605
alberto@cambrico.com
www.cambrico.com

VIÑAS DEL CÁMBRICO 2010 T
52% tempranillo, 41% rufete, 7% garnacha

91 Colour: cherry, garnet rim. Nose: red berry notes, expressive, mineral, sweet spices, creamy oak.

VINOS LA ZORRA

C/ Sampedro, s/n
37610 Mogarraz - (Salamanca)
☎: +34 923 418 042
estanverdes@vinoslazorra.es
www.vinoslazorra.es

LA VIEJA ZORRA 20 BARRICAS SELECCIÓN ESPECIAL 2010 T
52% rufete, 43% tempranillo, 5% garnacha

93 Colour: bright cherry. Nose: sweet spices, creamy oak, expressive, scrubland, ripe fruit. Palate: flavourful, fruity, toasty, round tannins.

LA ZORRA 2010 T
80% rufete, 20% tempranillo

90 Colour: cherry, purple rim. Nose: fresh fruit, red berry notes, floral, sweet spices. Palate: flavourful, fruity, good acidity, round tannins.

VALTIENDAS

BODEGAS VAGAL

La Fuente, 19
40314 Valtiendas - (Segovia)
☎: +34 921 527 331 - Fax: +34 921 527 332
jose.vagal@gmail.com
www.vagal.com

VAGAL PAGO ARDALEJOS 2009 T
tinta del país

91 Colour: cherry, garnet rim. Nose: red berry notes, ripe fruit, sweet spices, creamy oak. Palate: powerful, flavourful, balanced, long, toasty.

VAGAL SELECCIÓN 2009 T

92 Colour: cherry, garnet rim. Nose: ripe fruit, spicy, toasty, earthy notes, balsamic herbs. Palate: powerful, flavourful, toasty, round tannins.

BODEGAS ZARRAGUILLA

Iglesia, 14
40237 Sacramenia - (Segovia)
☎: +34 678 610 090 - Fax: +34 921 527 270
informacion@bodegaszarraguilla.es
www.bodegaszarraguilla.es

RESERVA DE MARTÍN 2008 T
tempranillo

90 Colour: bright cherry. Nose: ripe fruit, sweet spices, creamy oak, fresh. Palate: flavourful, fruity, toasty, round tannins.

DESCRIPTION

The number of regional wines is becoming more and more important (46) taking into account that the producers are only obliged to specify the geographical name, the grapes or the alcohol level. For some, this is a successful outlet for their most risky projects which are not included under the rules of Denomination of Origin, as occurs especially in the more extensive Autonomous Communities such as La Mancha, Castile and León and Extremadura. For the majority, it is a brand which protects areas of vineyards with quality potential, a portfolio of grapes and notable production, a type of waiting-room for recognition as a Denomination of Origin.

ALTIPLANO DE SIERRANEVADA

BODEGAS MUÑANA

Finca Peñas Prietas - Ctra. Graena a La Peza
18517 Cortes y Graena (Granada)
☎: +34 958 670 715- Fax: +34 958 670 715
bodegasmunana@gmail.com
www.bodegasmunana.com

MUÑANA 3 CEPAS 2009 T
syrah, cabernet sauvignon, merlot

90 Colour: cherry, garnet rim. Nose: red berry notes, ripe fruit, mineral, balsamic herbs, spicy. Palate: light-bodied, flavourful, long, round.

MARQUÉS DE CASA PARDIÑAS C.B.

Finca San Torcuato
18540 Huélago (Granada)
☎: +34 630 901 094- Fax: +34 958 252 297
info@spiracp.es
www.marquesdecasapardiñas.com

SPIRA VENDIMIA SELECCIONADA 2011 T
80% tempranillo, 20% cabernet sauvignon

91 Colour: cherry, garnet rim. Nose: red berry notes, ripe fruit, balsamic herbs, scrubland, roasted coffee. Palate: fine bitter notes, flavourful, long, balsamic, toasty.

BAJO ARAGÓN

AMPRIUS LAGAR

C/ Los Enebros, 74-2º planta
44002 (Teruel)
☎: +34 978 623 077
pedrocasas@ampriuslagar.es
www.ampriuslagar.es

LAGAR D'AMPRIUS CHARDONNAY 2011 B
chardonnay

90 Colour: bright straw. Nose: white flowers, candied fruit, wild herbs. Palate: flavourful, fruity, good acidity.

CELLER D'ALGARS

Cooperativa, 9
44622Arenys De Lledó (Teruel)
☎: +34 978 853 147- Fax: +34 978 853 147
info@cellerdalgars.com
www.enigmma.es

VIRTUTIS CAUSA 2007 T
50% syrah, 35% garnacha, 15% cabernet sauvignon

91 Colour: cherry, garnet rim. Nose: ripe fruit, spicy, creamy oak, toasty, expressive, mineral. Palate: powerful, flavourful, toasty, round tannins.

DOMINIO MAESTRAZGO

Royal III, B12
44550 Alcorisa (Teruel)
☎: +34 978 840 642- Fax: +34 978 840 642
bodega@dominiomaestrazgo.com
www.dominiomaestrazgo.com

DOMINIO MAESTRAZGO 2010 T ROBLE
65% garnacha, 20% tempranillo, 15% syrah

91 Colour: cherry, garnet rim. Nose: red berry notes, ripe fruit, scrubland, spicy, creamy oak. Palate: long, powerful, flavourful, spicy.

REX DEUS 2005 T ROBLE
85% garnacha, 10% syrah, 5% cabernet sauvignon

90 Colour: bright cherry. Nose: ripe fruit, creamy oak, earthy notes, spicy, toasty, dry stone. Palate: flavourful, fruity, toasty, balanced.

EVOHE BODEGAS

Ignacio de Ara, 3
50002 Zaragoza (Zaragoza)
☎: +34 976 461 056- Fax: +34 976 461 558
nosotros@evohegarnacha.com
www.evohegarnacha.com

EVOHÉ GARNACHA 2011 T
100% garnacha

90 Colour: cherry, purple rim. Nose: floral, red berry notes, scrubland, earthy notes. Palate: full, powerful, flavourful, long, balsamic.

VENTA D'AUBERT

Ctra. Valderrobres a Arnes, Km. 28
44623 Cretas (Teruel)
☎: +34 978 769 021- Fax: +34 978 769 031
ventadaubert@gmx.net
www.ventadaubert.com

VENTA D'AUBERT SYRAH 2006 T
syrah

90 Color cherry, garnet rim. Aroma ripe fruit, spicy, creamy oak, toasty, complex. Taste powerful, flavourful, toasty, round tannins.

VENTA D'AUBERT 2011 B
chardonnay, garnacha blanca, viognier

91 Colour: bright golden. Nose: floral, ripe fruit, fragrant herbs, mineral, spicy. Palate: powerful, flavourful, long, spicy, balanced.

VENTA D'AUBERT VIOGNIER 2011 B
viognier

90 Colour: bright straw. Nose: white flowers, fragrant herbs, citrus fruit, fruit expression, mineral. Palate: flavourful, fresh, balanced.

CADIZ

FINCA MONCLOA

Manuel María González, 12
11403 Jerez de la Frontera (Cádiz)
☎: +34 956 357 000- Fax: +34 956 357 043
nacional@gonzalezbyass.com
www.gonzalezbyass.com

FINCA MONCLOA 09 BARRICAS 2009 T
52,2% cabernet sauvignon, 28,3% syrah, 13% petit verdot, 6,5% tintilla de rota

90 Colour: cherry, garnet rim. Nose: red berry notes, scrubland, mineral, toasty. Palate: balanced, flavourful, spicy, toasty.

CASTILLA

BODEGA ABAXTERRA

CMM 3200, Km. 27,500
13343 Villamanrique (Ciudad Real)
☎: +34 635 295 098- Fax: +34 916 925 426
info@bodegas-abaxterra.com
www.bodegas-abaxterra.com

ABAXTERRA 2010 T
70% tempranillo, 30% syrah

90 Colour: cherry, garnet rim. Nose: ripe fruit, sweet spices, creamy oak. Palate: powerful, flavourful, long, toasty.

BODEGA DEHESA DE LUNA

CM-3106, km. 16
2630 La Roda (Albacete)
☎: +34 967 548 508- Fax: +34 967 548 022
contacto@dehesadeluna.com
www.dehesadeluna.com

DEHESA DE LUNA TEMPRANILLO 2010 T
100% tempranillo

90 Colour: deep cherry. Nose: creamy oak, sweet spices, ripe fruit, mineral. Palate: flavourful, powerful, complex, good acidity.

BODEGA GARCÍA DE LA ROSA (AGROCONGOSTO S.L.)

Pol. La Carbonera, Podadores, 12
45350 Noblejas (Toledo)
☎: +34 925 140 605- Fax: +34 925 140 605
carlosgarciarosa@bodegagarciadelarosa.es
www.bodegagarciadelarosa.es

GARCÍA DE LA ROSA 2010 T ROBLE
tempranillo

90 Colour: cherry, purple rim. Nose: lactic notes, ripe fruit, sweet spices, creamy oak. Palate: balanced, powerful, flavourful, toasty.

BODEGA LOS ALJIBES

Finca Los Aljibes
2520 Chinchilla de Montearagón (Albacete)
☎: +34 918 843 472- Fax: +34 918 844 324
info@fincalosaljibes.com
www.fincalosaljibes.com

ALJIBES CABERNET FRANC 2007 T
100% cabernet franc

90 Colour: cherry, garnet rim. Nose: red berry notes, ripe fruit, balsamic herbs, mineral, sweet spices. Palate: balanced, powerful, flavourful, long.

SELECTUS 2007 T
syrah, cabernet franc, merlot, cabernet sauvignon

91 Colour: cherry, garnet rim. Nose: ripe fruit, balsamic herbs, cocoa bean, earthy notes. Palate: powerful, spicy, long, balanced.

BODEGAS BARREDA

Ramalazo, 2
45880 Corral de Almaguer (Toledo)
☎: +34 925 207 223- Fax: +34 925 207 223
nacional@bodegas-barreda.com
www.bodegas-barreda.com

TORRE DE BARREDA PAÑOFINO 2008 T
100% tempranillo

91 Colour: cherry, garnet rim. Nose: red berry notes, ripe fruit, fragrant herbs, mineral, creamy oak, toasty. Palate: balanced.

BODEGAS CASAQUEMADA

Ctra. Ruidera, Km. 5,5
13710 Argamasilla de Alba (Ciudad Real)
☎: +34 628 621 187- Fax: +34 926 511 515
casaquemada@casaquemada.es
www.casaquemada.es

ALBA DE CASA QUEMADA 2008 T
100% syrah

91 Colour: cherry, garnet rim. Nose: fruit liqueur notes, fragrant herbs, violets, earthy notes, spicy, toasty. Palate: powerful, flavourful, spicy, long.

ANEA DE CASAQUEMADA 2005 T
100% syrah

90 Colour: cherry, garnet rim. Nose: ripe fruit, spicy, creamy oak, balsamic herbs. Palate: powerful, flavourful, toasty, balanced.

BODEGAS ERCAVIO

Camino de los Molinos, s/n
45312 Cabañas de Yepes (Toledo)
☎: +34 925 122 281- Fax: +34 925 137 033
masquevinos@fer.es
www.bodegasercavio.com

EL SEÑORITO DE ERCAVIO 2009 T
100% tempranillo

90 Colour: cherry, garnet rim. Nose: powerfull, characterful, ripe fruit, raspberry, spicy, toasty. Palate: flavourful, fine bitter notes, round tannins.

LA BUENA VID 2009 T
80% tempranillo, 20% graciano

91 Colour: bright cherry. Nose: creamy oak, medium intensity, red berry notes, ripe fruit, fresh. Palate: flavourful, fruity, toasty, round tannins.

LA MALVAR DE ERCAVIO 2011 B
100% malvar

90 Colour: bright straw. Nose: fresh, fragrant herbs, balanced, medium intensity, citrus fruit. Palate: good structure, spicy, long.

LA MESETA 2010 T
50% tempranillo, 50% syrah

91 Colour: deep cherry, garnet rim. Nose: balanced, expressive, ripe fruit. Palate: complex, balanced, flavourful, round tannins.

LA PLAZUELA 2007 T

92 Colour: cherry, garnet rim. Nose: ripe fruit, spicy, creamy oak, complex. Palate: powerful, flavourful, toasty, round tannins.

BODEGAS FINCA LA ESTACADA

Ctra. N-400, Km. 103
16400 Tarancón (Cuenca)
☎: +34 969 327 099- Fax: +34 969 327 199
enologia@fincalaestacada.com
www.fincalaestacada.com

SECUA CABERNET-SYRAH 2008 T
cabernet sauvignon, syrah

90 Colour: cherry, garnet rim. Nose: ripe fruit, spicy, creamy oak, toasty, complex, earthy notes. Palate: powerful, flavourful, toasty, round tannins.

SECUA CRIANZA EN LÍAS 2010 B
viognier, sauvignon blanc

92 Colour: bright yellow. Nose: powerfull, ripe fruit, sweet spices, creamy oak, fragrant herbs. Palate: rich, flavourful, good acidity, long. Personality.

BODEGAS MANO A MANO

Ctra. CM-412, Km. 100
13248 Alhambra (Ciudad Real)
☎: +34 619 349 394- Fax: +34 926 691 162
info@bodegamanoamano.com
www.bodegamanoamano.com

VENTA LA OSSA 2010 TC
100% tempranillo

92 Colour: cherry, garnet rim. Nose: ripe fruit, dark chocolate, sweet spices, creamy oak. Palate: powerful, flavourful, complex, long.

VENTA LA OSSA SYRAH 2009 T
100% syrah

94 Colour: cherry, garnet rim. Nose: ripe fruit, floral, sweet spices, creamy oak. Palate: round, flavourful, fruity, full, complex, balanced.

VENTA LA OSSA TNT 2010 T
75% touriga nacional, 25% tempranillo

93 Colour: cherry, garnet rim. Nose: ripe fruit, aromatic coffee, creamy oak, scrubland, balsamic herbs. Palate: flavourful, full, long, toasty.

BODEGAS MONTALVO WILMOT

Ctra. Ruidera, km. 10,2 Finca Los Cerrillos
13710 Argamasilla de Alba (Ciudad Real)
☎: +34 926 699 069- Fax: +34 926 699 069
silvia@montalvowilmot.com
www.montalvowilmot.com

MONTALVO WILMOT SYRAH 2010 T ROBLE
100% syrah

90 Colour: cherry, garnet rim. Nose: ripe fruit, sweet spices, creamy oak, toasty, floral, lactic notes. Palate: powerful, flavourful, toasty.

BODEGAS MUREDA

Ctra. N-IV, Km. 184,1
13300 Valdepeñas (Ciudad Real)
☎: +34 926 318 058- Fax: +34 926 318 058
administracion@mureda.es
www.mureda.es

MUREDA SYRAH 2011 T
syrah

91 Color cherry, purple rim. Aroma expressive, fresh fruit, red berry notes, floral. Taste flavourful, fruity, good acidity, round tannins.

BODEGAS RÍO NEGRO

Ctra. CM 1001, Km. 37,400
19230 Cogolludo (Guadalajara)
☎: +34 639 301 817- Fax: +34 913 026 750
info@fincarionegro.es
www.fincarionegro.com

FINCA RÍO NEGRO 2009 T
80% tempranillo, 20% syrah

92 Colour: cherry, garnet rim. Nose: balsamic herbs, floral, red berry notes, ripe fruit, sweet spices, creamy oak. Palate: powerful, flavourful, fruity, toasty, balanced.

BODEGAS VERUM

Juan Antonio López Ramírez, 4
13700 Tomelloso (Ciudad Real)
☎: +34 926 511 404- Fax: +34 926 515 047
administracion@bodegasverum.com
www.bodegasverum.com

VERUM 2009 T
50% merlot, 40% cabernet sauvignon, 10% tempranillo

90 Colour: cherry, garnet rim. Nose: red berry notes, ripe fruit, sweet spices, toasty, dark chocolate, expressive. Palate: powerful, flavourful, balanced, round tannins.

CASALOBOS

Ctra. Porzuna CM-412, Km. 6,5
13196 Picón (Ciudad Real)
☎: +34 926 600 002
bodega@casalobos.es
www.casalobos.es

CASALOBOS 2007 T
syrah, cabernet sauvignon, petit verdot, tempranillo

90 Colour: cherry, garnet rim. Nose: ripe fruit, scrubland, earthy notes, spicy, creamy oak. Palate: flavourful, long, fine bitter notes, round tannins.

DEHESA DE LOS LLANOS

Ctra. Peñas de San Pedro, Km. 5,5
2006 (Albacete)
☎: +34 967 243 100- Fax: +34 967 243 093
info@dehesadelosllanos.es
www.dehesadelosllanos.com

MAZACRUZ CIMA 2008 T
cabernet sauvignon, syrah, merlot, petit verdot

90 Colour: cherry, garnet rim. Nose: ripe fruit, balsamic herbs, earthy notes, creamy oak. Palate: balanced, powerful, flavourful, complex.

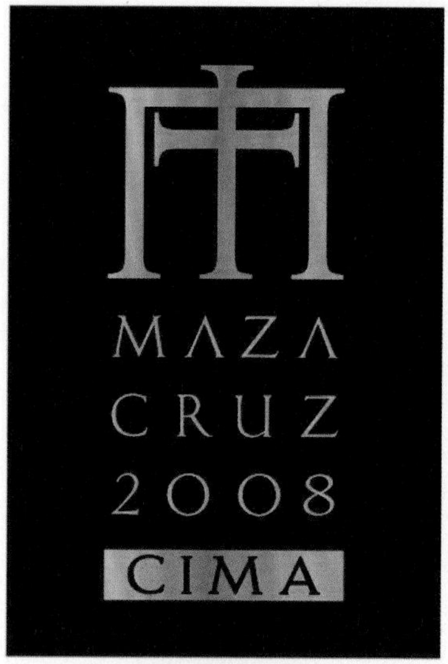

DOMINIO DE EGUREN

Camino de San Pedro, s/n
1309 Páganos (Álava)
☎: +34 945 600 117- Fax: +34 945 600 590
info@eguren.com
www.eguren.com

CÓDICE 2010 T
100% tempranillo

90 Colour: cherry, purple rim. Nose: floral, red berry notes, lactic notes, expressive, roasted coffee. Palate: powerful, flavourful, fresh, fruity.

FINCA CONSTANCIA

Camino del Bravo, s/n
45543 Otero (Toledo)
☎: +34 914 903 700- Fax: +34 916 612 124
lslara@gonzalezbyass.es
www.gonzalezbyass.es

ALTOS DE LA FINCA 2009 T
petit verdot, syrah

90 Colour: black cherry, garnet rim. Nose: overripe fruit, scrubland, fine reductive notes, toasty. Palate: long, flavourful, harsh oak tannins.

FINCA LA VALONA VIÑEDOS Y BODEGAS

D. Victoriano González, 39
16220 Quintanar del Rey (Cuenca)
☎: +34 967 496 600- Fax: +34 967 495 495
info@fincalavalona.com
www.fincalavalona.com

LA VALONA SELECCIÓN 2007 T
100% tempranillo

90 Colour: cherry, garnet rim. Nose: ripe fruit, wild herbs. Palate: flavourful, full, long.

FONTANA

Extramuros, s/n
16411 Fuente de Pedro Naharro (Cuenca)
☎: +34 969 125 433- Fax: +34 969 125 387
gemag@bodegasfontana.com
www.bodegasfontana.com

DUETO DE FONTANA 2004 TC
50% merlot, 50% cabernet sauvignon

90 Colour: cherry, garnet rim. Nose: ripe fruit, tobacco, spicy. Palate: fine bitter notes, good structure, ripe fruit, round tannins.

GRAN FONTAL VENDIMIA SELECCIONADA 2007 TR
100% tempranillo,

90 Colour: cherry, garnet rim. Nose: balanced, expressive, fruit expression, sweet spices. Palate: balanced, fruity, spicy.

QUERCUS 2007 TC
100% tempranillo

91 Colour: bright cherry, garnet rim. Nose: complex, elegant, spicy, ripe fruit, dark chocolate. Palate: fruity, rich, round tannins, long.

PAGO DE VALLEGARCÍA

Claudio Coello, 35 Bajo C
28001 Madrid (Madrid)
☎: +34 925 421 407- Fax: +34 925 421 822
comercial@vallegarcia.com
www.vallegarcia.com

HIPPERIA 2008 T
47% merlot, 46% cabernet sauvignon, 5% petit verdot, 2% cabernet franc

92 Colour: cherry, garnet rim. Nose: ripe fruit, spicy, creamy oak, toasty, complex, mineral. Palate: powerful, flavourful, toasty, round tannins, balanced.

PETIT HIPPERIA 2010 T
38% merlot, 37% cabernet sauvignon, 16% petit verdot, 5% syrah, 4% cabernet franc

91 Colour: cherry, purple rim. Nose: earthy notes, spicy, balsamic herbs, ripe fruit. Palate: elegant, full, flavourful, long.

VALLEGARCÍA SYRAH 2008 T
100% syrah

92 Colour: bright cherry. Nose: ripe fruit, sweet spices, creamy oak. Palate: flavourful, fruity, toasty, round tannins.

VALLEGARCÍA VIOGNIER 2010 BFB
100% viognier

94 Colour: bright yellow. Nose: powerfull, ripe fruit, sweet spices, fragrant herbs, mineral. Palate: rich, smoky aftertaste, flavourful, fresh, good acidity.

VIÑEDOS BALMORAL

Mayor, 32 - 1º
2001 (Albacete)
☎: +34 967 508 382- Fax: +34 967 235 301
info@vinedosbalmoral.com
www.edone.es

MARAVIDES 2010 T

90 Colour: bright cherry. Nose: ripe fruit, sweet spices, creamy oak, roasted coffee. Palate: flavourful, fruity, toasty, round tannins.

VIÑEDOS Y BODEGAS EL CASTILLO

Ctra. Ossa de Montiel, Km. 1,8
2600 Villarrobledo (Albacete)
☎: +34 967 573 230- Fax: +34 967 573 048
info@bodegaselcastillo.com
www.bodegaselcastillo.com

ROBLE PARRA 2008 T
100% tempranillo

90 Colour: deep cherry. Nose: powerfull, expressive, characterful, ripe fruit, toasty, new oak. Palate: flavourful, powerful, concentrated, fine bitter notes.

FINCA MUÑOZ CEPAS VIEJAS 2008 T
100% tempranillo

90 Colour: cherry, garnet rim. Nose: ripe fruit, spicy, toasty, fine reductive notes, acetaldehyde. Palate: powerful, flavourful, toasty, ripe fruit.

CASTILLA Y LEÓN

ABADÍA RETUERTA

Ctra. N-122 Soria, km. 332,5
47340 Sardón de Duero (Valladolid)
☎: +34 983 680 314- Fax: +34 983 680 286
elena.revilla@abadia-retuerta.es
www.abadia-retuerta.com

ABADÍA RETUERTA LE DOMAINE 2010 B
80% sauvignon blanc, 20% verdejo

92 Colour: bright yellow. Nose: ripe fruit, sweet spices, creamy oak, fragrant herbs, expressive. Palate: rich, flavourful, fresh, balanced.

ABADÍA RETUERTA PAGO NEGRALADA 2009 T BARRICA
100% tempranillo

95 Colour: dark-red cherry, garnet rim. Nose: ripe fruit, sweet spices, creamy oak, balanced. Palate: long, spicy, powerful, flavourful, round.

ABADÍA RETUERTA PAGO VALDEBELLÓN 2009 T BARRICA
100% cabernet sauvignon

95 Colour: cherry, garnet rim. Nose: ripe fruit, earthy notes, fragrant herbs, spicy, toasty, balanced. Palate: powerful, flavourful, balsamic, spicy, round tannins. Personality.

ABADÍA RETUERTA SELECCIÓN ESPECIAL 2009 T
75% tempranillo, 15% cabernet sauvignon, 10% syrah

92 Colour: bright cherry. Nose: sweet spices, creamy oak, expressive, red berry notes, ripe fruit, balanced, mineral. Palate: flavourful, fruity, toasty, round tannins, long.

PAGO LA GARDUÑA SYRAH 2009 T
100% syrah

93 Colour: cherry, garnet rim. Nose: ripe fruit, violets, dark chocolate, sweet spices, creamy oak. Palate: powerful, flavourful, long, toasty, round tannins.

ALTOS DE SAN ESTEBAN

Ildefonso Sánchez del Río, 4 - 3ºB
33001 Oviedo (Asturias)
☎: +34 660 145 313
mamarques@telecable.es

ALTOS DE SAN ESTEBAN LA MENDAÑONA 2008 TC
100% mencía

92 Colour: cherry, garnet rim. Nose: red berry notes, ripe fruit, wild herbs, earthy notes, mineral, expressive. Palate: balanced, powerful, flavourful, spicy.

ALTOS DE SAN ESTEBAN VIÑAS DE MONTE 2009 TC
85% mencía, 12% cabernet sauvignon, 3% merlot

90 Colour: cherry, garnet rim. Nose: ripe fruit, spicy, complex, earthy notes, scrubland. Palate: powerful, flavourful, toasty, round tannins.

ARRIAGA Y MIMÉNDEZ COMPAÑÍA DE VINOS

Capitán Cortés, 6. Piso 4º Puerta 3
26003 Logroño (La Rioja)
☎: +34 687 421 306- Fax: +34 941 287 072
administracion@arriagaymimendez.com
www.arriagaymimendez.com

MITERNA CORTE UNO 2006 T BARRICA
100% prieto picudo

91 Colour: cherry, garnet rim. Nose: earthy notes, cigar, old leather, aged wood nuances, ripe fruit, balsamic herbs. Palate: elegant, powerful, flavourful, long, balanced.

BEATRIZ HERRANZ

Cuesta de las descargas, 11 bis
28005 Madrid (Madrid)
☎: +34 655 890 949

BARCO DEL CORNETA 2010 B
100% verdejo

90 Colour: bright straw. Nose: powerfull, ripe fruit, citrus fruit, sweet spices, grassy. Palate: flavourful, good acidity, spicy.

BELONDRADE

Quinta San Diego - Camino del Puerto, s/n
47491 La Seca (Valladolid)
☎: +34 983 481 001- Fax: +34 600 590 024
info@belondrade.com
www.belondrade.com

QUINTA APOLONIA BELONDRADE 2011 B
100% verdejo

91 Colour: bright straw. Nose: fresh, fresh fruit, white flowers, varietal. Palate: flavourful, fruity, good acidity.

BODEGA ALISTE

Pza. de España, 4
49520 Figueruela de Abajo (Zamora)
☎: +34 676 986 570- Fax: +34 944 231 816
javier@hacedordevino.com
www.vinosdealiste.com

MARINA DE ALISTE 2010 T
90% tempranillo, 10% syrah

90 Colour: cherry, garnet rim. Nose: spicy, creamy oak, ripe fruit, earthy notes. Palate: powerful, flavourful, long, spicy.

BODEGA DON JUAN DEL AGUILA

Real de Abajo, 100
5110 El Barraco (Ávila)
☎: +34 920 281 032
bodegadonjuandelaguila@gmail.com
www.donjuandelaguila.es

GAZNATA FINCA MARIANO 2009 T
garnacha

93 Colour: light cherry, garnet rim. Nose: fruit liqueur notes, scrubland, mineral, dry stone, spicy, creamy oak. Palate: balanced, flavourful, complex, spicy, long, round.

BODEGA EL ALBAR LURTON

Camino Magarin, s/n
47529 Villafranca del Duero (Valladolid)
☎: +34 983 034 030- Fax: +34 983 034 040
bodega@francoislurton.es
www.francoislurton.es

EL ALBAR LURTON BARRICAS 2008 T
100% tinta de Toro

90 Colour: cherry, garnet rim. Nose: mineral, ripe fruit, sweet spices, creamy oak. Palate: flavourful, toasty, ripe fruit, long.

EL ALBAR LURTON EXCELENCIA 2008 T
100% tempranillo

92 Colour: cherry, garnet rim. Nose: ripe fruit, expressive, sweet spices, toasty. Palate: spicy, powerful, flavourful.

BODEGA Y VIÑEDOS GARMENDIA

Finca Santa Rosalia, s/n
34260 Vizmalo (Burgos)
☎: +34 947 166 171- Fax: +34 947 166 147
maria@bodegasgarmendia.com
www.bodegasgarmendia.com

GARMENDIA 2011 B
verdejo, viura

90 Colour: bright straw. Nose: fresh, fresh fruit, white flowers, fragrant herbs. Palate: flavourful, fruity, good acidity, balanced.

BODEGAS ALDEASOÑA

Ctra. Peñafiel - San Idelfonso, s/n
40235 Aldeasoña (Segovia)
☎: +34 983 878 052- Fax: +34 983 873 052
bodega@bodegaconvento.com

ALDEASOÑA 2006 T
100% aragones

90 Colour: cherry, garnet rim. Nose: ripe fruit, expressive, sweet spices, dark chocolate, creamy oak. Palate: powerful, flavourful, toasty.

BODEGAS CANOPY

Avda. Barber, 71
45004 (Toledo)
☎: +34 619 244 878- Fax: +34 925 283 681
achacon@bodegascanopy.com

K OS 2008 T
garnacha

93 Colour: very deep cherry. Nose: powerfull, ripe fruit, mineral, earthy notes, toasty, smoky. Palate: mineral, powerful, good acidity, fine bitter notes, round tannins.

BODEGAS CASTELO DE MEDINA

Ctra. CL-602, Km. 48
47465 Villaverde de Medina (Valladolid)
☎: +34 983 831 932- Fax: +34 983 831 857
jcortega@castelodemedina.es
www.castelodemedina.es

SYTÉ 2008 T
60% syrah, 40% tempranillo

91 Colour: cherry, garnet rim. Nose: ripe fruit, spicy, creamy oak, toasty, complex, balanced. Palate: powerful, flavourful, toasty, round tannins, good acidity.

BODEGAS GARCÍA NIÑO

Avda. Julio, s/n
9410 Arandilla (Burgos)
☎: +34 916 192 294- Fax: +34 916 126 072
fernando@bodegasgarcianino.es
www.altorredondo.es

PAGO DE COSTALAO 24 MESES 2009 TC
100% tempranillo

90 Colour: cherry, garnet rim. Nose: ripe fruit, dark chocolate, sweet spices, toasty, mineral. Palate: powerful, flavourful, toasty, balanced.

BODEGAS GODELIA

Antigua Ctra. N-VI, Km. 403,5
24547 Pieros (Cacabelos) (León)
☎: +34 987 546 279- Fax: +34 987 548 026
info@godelia.es
www.godelia.es

LIBAMUS 2010 T
100% mencía

91 Colour: cherry, garnet rim. Nose: red berry notes, ripe fruit, dark chocolate, cocoa bean, sweet spices, creamy oak. Palate: powerful, flavourful, fruity, full.

BODEGAS LEDA

Mayor, 48
47320 Tudela de Duero (Valladolid)
☎: +34 983 520 682- Fax: +34 983 520 682
info@bodegasleda.com
www.bodegasleda.com

MÁS DE LEDA 2009 TC
100% tempranillo

92 Colour: cherry, garnet rim. Nose: ripe fruit, balsamic herbs, spicy, cocoa bean. Palate: powerful, flavourful, balanced, toasty.

BODEGAS MAURO

Cervantes, 12
47320 Tudela de Duero (Valladolid)
☎: +34 983 521 972- Fax: +34 983 521 439
comunicacion@bodegasmauro.com
www.bodegasmauro.com

MAURO 2010 TC
tempranillo, syrah

90 Colour: cherry, purple rim. Nose: ripe fruit, floral, earthy notes, sweet spices, toasty. Palate: powerful, flavourful, complex, balanced, toasty.

MAURO VENDIMIA SELECCIONADA 2007 T
100% tempranillo

91 Colour: cherry, garnet rim. Nose: ripe fruit, spicy, creamy oak, fine reductive notes, mineral. Palate: powerful, flavourful, full, toasty.

TERREUS 2009 TC
100% tempranillo

92 Colour: cherry, garnet rim. Nose: fruit preserve, mineral, spicy, toasty, creamy oak. Palate: powerful, flavourful, full, complex, long, toasty.

BODEGAS TRITÓN

Pol.1 Parc. 146/148 Paraje Cantagrillos
49708 Villanueva de Campeán (Zamora)
☎: +34 968 435 022- Fax: +34 968 716 051
info@orowines.com
www.orowines.com

TRIDENTE ENTRESUELOS 2010 T
100% tempranillo

90 Colour: bright cherry. Nose: ripe fruit, sweet spices, creamy oak, balanced. Palate: flavourful, fruity, toasty, round tannins.

TRIDENTE TEMPRANILLO 2010 T
100% tempranillo

92 Colour: cherry, garnet rim. Nose: ripe fruit, dark chocolate, sweet spices, creamy oak, mineral. Palate: powerful, flavourful, long, balanced, toasty.

BODEGAS Y VIÑEDOS EL CODONAL

Pza. de la Constitución, 3
40462 Aldeanueva del Codonal (Segovia)
☎: +34 921 582 063
pedro.gomez@bodegaselcodonal.com
www.bodegaselcodonal.com

CODONAL VINUM NOBILE 2010 B
verdejo

90 Colour: bright yellow. Nose: powerfull, ripe fruit, sweet spices, fragrant herbs. Palate: rich, flavourful, fresh, good acidity.

BODEGAS Y VIÑEDOS LA MEJORADA

Monasterio de La Mejorada
47410 Olmedo (Valladolid)
☎: +34 606 707 041- Fax: +34 983 483 061
contacto@lamejorada.es
www.lamejorada.es

LA MEJORADA LAS CERCAS 2009 T ROBLE
tempranillo, syrah

92 Colour: bright cherry. Nose: ripe fruit, sweet spices, creamy oak, scrubland. Palate: flavourful, fruity, toasty, round tannins, balanced.

LA MEJORADA LAS NORIAS 2009 T ROBLE
tempranillo

91 Colour: bright cherry. Nose: ripe fruit, sweet spices, creamy oak. Palate: flavourful, fruity, toasty, round tannins, balanced.

BODEGAS Y VIÑEDOS MENTO

Calvario, 13
47320 Tudela de Duero (Valladolid)
☎: +34 983 521 233
info@bodegasmento.com
www.entudeladeduero.com

MENTO VENDIMIA SELECCIONADA 2006 T ROBLE
100% tempranillo

90 Colour: cherry, garnet rim. Nose: ripe fruit, dark chocolate, cocoa bean, creamy oak, tobacco. Palate: powerful, flavourful, spicy, long.

CLUNIA

Camino Torre, 1
9410 Coruña del Conde (Burgos)
☎: +34 607 185 951- Fax: +34 948 818 574
pavez@principedeviana.com

CLUNIA SYRAH 2010 T
100% syrah

92 Colour: cherry, purple rim. Nose: ripe fruit, violets, mineral, complex, expressive. Palate: flavourful, full, spicy, long, balanced.

CLUNIA TEMPRANILLO 2010 T
100% tempranillo

91 Colour: cherry, garnet rim. Nose: complex, expressive, ripe fruit, earthy notes, sweet spices. Palate: powerful, flavourful, spicy, balanced.

COMANDO G

Villamanin, 27 - 4º E
28011 (Madrid)
☎: +34 696 366 555
daniel@jimenezlandi.com

RUMBO AL NORTE 2010 T
100% garnacha

94 Colour: deep cherry. Nose: mineral, candied fruit, red berry notes, floral, scrubland, balsamic herbs, spicy. Palate: flavourful, spicy.

COMPAÑÍA DE VINOS TELMO RODRÍGUEZ

El Monte
1308 Lanciego (Álava)
☎: +34 945 628 315- Fax: +34 945 628 314
contact@telmorodriguez.com
www.telmorodriguez.com

PEGASO "BARRANCOS DE PIZARRA" 2009 T
100% garnacha

93 Colour: deep cherry. Nose: spicy, ripe fruit, fruit expression, earthy notes. Palate: ripe fruit, long, fruity, elegant.

PEGASO "GRANITO" 2009 T
100% garnacha

93 Colour: bright cherry. Nose: mineral, red berry notes, spicy, floral. Palate: flavourful, warm, elegant, fine tannins.

DANIEL EL TRAVIESO S.L.

Cuesta de las Descargas, 11 bis
28005 Madrid (Madrid)
☎: +34 696 366 555
daniel@jimenezlandi.com

EL REVENTÓN 2010 T
100% garnacha

96 Colour: light cherry. Nose: fragrant herbs, floral, earthy notes, mineral, expressive, red berry notes, ripe fruit. Palate: balanced, fresh, fruity, long, elegant. Personality.

LAS UVAS DE LA IRA 2010 B
100% albillo

93 Colour: bright yellow. Nose: powerfull, warm, candied fruit, honeyed notes, fragrant herbs, sweet spices. Palate: flavourful, sweetness, fine bitter notes, good acidity.

ZERBEROS A + P 2009 T ROBLE
garnacha

92 Colour: light cherry, orangey edge. Nose: red berry notes, ripe fruit, balsamic herbs, mineral, dry stone, spicy. Palate: light-bodied, balanced, flavourful, complex.

DANIEL V. RAMOS (ZERBEROS FINCA)

Real de Abajo, 100
5110 El Barraco (Ávila)
☎: +34 687 410 952
dvrcru@gmail.com
winesdanielramosvinos.blogspot.com

ZERBEROS ARENA 2009 T ROBLE
garnacha

93 Colour: cherry, garnet rim. Nose: ripe fruit, balsamic herbs, mineral, sweet spices, creamy oak, expressive. Palate: powerful, flavourful, full, complex, long, spicy, elegant.

ZERBEROS DELTIEMBLO 2010 T
garnacha

93 Colour: light cherry, garnet rim. Nose: red berry notes, fruit liqueur notes, mineral, creamy oak, spicy, fragrant herbs. Palate: flavourful, powerful, balanced, long, balsamic.

DEHESA DE CADOZOS

Pº Pintor Rosales, 72 Bajo
28008 (Madrid)
☎: +34 914 550 252- Fax: +34 915 448 142
nmaranon@cadozos.com
www.cadozos.com

CADOZOS 2007 T
80% tinto fino, 20% pinot noir

90 Colour: cherry, garnet rim. Nose: earthy notes, ripe fruit, scrubland, spicy, creamy oak. Palate: balanced, powerful, flavourful, harsh oak tannins.

DOMINIO DE DOSTARES

P.I. Bierzo Alto, Los Barredos, 4
24318 San Román de Bembibre (León)
☎: +34 987 514 550- Fax: +34 987 514 570
info@dominiodetares.com
www.dominiodostares.com

CUMAL 2010 T
100% prieto picudo

93 Colour: cherry, garnet rim. Nose: ripe fruit, spicy, dark chocolate, creamy oak, mineral. Palate: powerful, flavourful, long, toasty.

LEIONE 2008 T
100% prieto picudo

91 Colour: black cherry, garnet rim. Nose: ripe fruit, cocoa bean, dark chocolate, spicy, creamy oak. Palate: powerful, flavourful, toasty.

ERMITA DEL CONDE

Camino de la Torre, 1
9410 Coruña del Conde (Burgos)
☎: +34 682 207 160- Fax: +34 913 193 279
bodega@ermitadelconde.com
www.ermitadelconde.com

ERMITA DEL CONDE 2009 T
100% tinto fino

91 Colour: cherry, garnet rim. Nose: ripe fruit, mineral, spicy, creamy oak. Palate: powerful, flavourful, spicy, long.

PAGO DEL CONDE 2009 T
tinto fino

93 Colour: cherry, garnet rim. Nose: ripe fruit, cocoa bean, dark chocolate, sweet spices, mineral. Palate: powerful, flavourful, complex, toasty, long.

FINCA CÁRDABA

Coto de Cárdaba, s/n
40314 Valtiendas (Segovia)
☎: +34 921 527 470- Fax: +34 921 527 470
info@fincacardaba.com
www.fincacardaba.com

FINCA CÁRDABA SELECCIÓN 2005 T
100% tempranillo

90 Colour: dark-red cherry, orangey edge. Nose: ripe fruit, balsamic herbs, old leather, tobacco, spicy. Palate: powerful, flavourful, spicy.

FINCA LA RINCONADA

Castronuño
47520 Castronuño (Valladolid)
☎: +34 914 901 871- Fax: +34 916 620 430
info@barcolobo.com
www.fincalarinconada.es

BARCOLOBO 12 MESES BARRICA 2009 T
75% tempranillo, 20% syrah, 5% cabernet sauvignon

90 Colour: cherry, garnet rim. Nose: red berry notes, ripe fruit, floral, sweet spices, creamy oak. Palate: balanced, elegant, powerful, flavourful, toasty.

FINCA TORREMILANOS BODEGAS PEÑALBA LÓPEZ

Finca Torremilanos, s/n
9400 Aranda de Duero (Burgos)
☎: +34 947 510 377- Fax: +34 947 512 856
torremilanos@torremilanos.com
www.torremilanos.com

PEÑALBA-LÓPEZ PINOT NOIR 2009 T
100% pinot noir

90 Colour: cherry, garnet rim. Nose: ripe fruit, spicy, creamy oak, toasty, complex, scrubland. Palate: powerful, flavourful, toasty, round tannins.

GARNACHA ALTO ALBERCHE

Camino del Pimpollar, s/n
5100 Navaluenga (Ávila)
☎: +34 616 416 542
sietenavas@live.com
www.altoalberche.es

7 NAVAS 2011 T
100% garnacha

91 Colour: cherry, purple rim. Nose: expressive, red berry notes, floral, fragrant herbs, mineral. Palate: flavourful, fruity, good acidity, round tannins.

7 NAVAS DULCE NATURAL 2010 T
100% garnacha

92 Colour: cherry, garnet rim. Nose: acetaldehyde, dried fruit, wild herbs, dried flowers, dark chocolate, toasty. Palate: balanced, sweet, powerful, flavourful, spicy.

7 NAVAS FINCA CATALINO 2009 T
100% garnacha

94 Colour: cherry, garnet rim. Nose: ripe fruit, scrubland, earthy notes, spicy, expressive. Palate: fresh, flavourful, complex, spicy, long, balanced.

GARNACHAS ÚNICAS C.B.

Los Pinillas, 1 Bajo B
28032 (Madrid)
☎: +34 615 163 719
carlos@maldivinas.es
www.maldivinas.es

LA MOVIDA 2010 T
100% garnacha

92 Colour: cherry, garnet rim. Nose: floral, fruit preserve, balsamic herbs, sweet spices, creamy oak, mineral. Palate: spirituous, powerful, flavourful, long.

GRUPO YLLERA

Autovía A-6, Km. 173, 5
47490 Rueda (Valladolid)
☎: +34 983 868 097- Fax: +34 983 868 177
grupoyllera@grupoyllera.com
www.grupoyllera.com

YLLERA 25 ANIVERSARIO 2005 T
tempranillo

90 Colour: dark-red cherry, garnet rim. Nose: ripe fruit, wild herbs, toasty, spicy, creamy oak, mineral. Palate: fine tannins, flavourful, spicy.

YLLERA DOMINUS GRAN SELECCIÓN VIÑEDOS VIEJOS 2005 T
100% tempranillo

90 Colour: ruby red, garnet rim. Nose: ripe fruit, balsamic herbs, earthy notes, spicy, creamy oak, fine reductive notes. Palate: long, spicy, flavourful, round tannins.

HACIENDAS DE ESPAÑA***

Hacienda Zorita, Ctra. Ledesma, Km. 12
37115 Valverdón (Salamanca)
☎: +34 914 365 924
comunicacion@arcoinvest-group.com
www.haciendas-espana.com

HACIENDA ZORITA NATURAL RESERVE (MARQUÉS DE LA CONCORDIA FAMILY OF WINES) 2009
100% syrah

90 Colour: cherry, garnet rim. Nose: red berry notes, ripe fruit, violets, sweet spices, creamy oak. Palate: flavourful, fresh, fruity, complex, balanced.

HEREDAD DE URUEÑA

Ctra. Toro a Medina de Rioseco, km 21,300
47862 Urueña (Valladolid)
☎: +34 915 610 920- Fax: +34 915 634 131
direccion@heredaduruena.com
www.heredaduruena.com

FORUM ETIQUETA NEGRA 2010 T
tinta de Toro, tinta del país

92 Colour: cherry, garnet rim. Nose: ripe fruit, earthy notes, creamy oak, dark chocolate, toasty. Palate: powerful, flavourful, long, balanced.

SANTOS MERLOT 2010 T
merlot, cabernet sauvignon

90 Color cherry, garnet rim. Aroma ripe fruit, spicy, creamy oak, toasty, complex. Taste powerful, flavourful, toasty, round tannins.

SANTOS SYRAH 2010 T
syrah

91 Colour: cherry, garnet rim. Nose: floral, ripe fruit, toasty, sweet spices. Palate: balanced, powerful, flavourful, long, toasty.

LEYENDA DEL PÁRAMO

Ctra. de León s/n, Paraje El Cueto
24230 Valdevimbre (León)
☎: +34 626 194 347
info@leyendadelparamo.com
www.leyendadelparamo.com

FLOR DEL PÁRAMO 2011 B
100% albarín

90 Colour: bright straw. Nose: fresh, fresh fruit, white flowers, citrus fruit. Palate: flavourful, fruity, good acidity, balanced, elegant.

OSSIAN VIDES Y VINOS

San Marcos, 5
40447 Nieva (Segovia)
☎: +34 696 159 121- Fax: +34 921 594 207
ossian@ossian.es
www.ossian.es

OSSIAN 2009 BFB
100% verdejo

94 Color bright yellow. Aroma powerfull, ripe fruit, sweet spices, creamy oak, fragrant herbs. Taste rich, smoky aftertaste, flavourful, fresh, good acidity.

PEÑALBA LA VERDE BODEGAS VIZAR

Ctra. N 122, Km. 341
47329 Villabámez (Valladolid)
☎: +34 983 682 690- Fax: +34 983 682 125
info@bodegasvizar.es
www.bodegasvizar.es

VIZAR SELECCIÓN ESPECIAL 2009 T
tempranillo, syrah

92 Colour: deep cherry, purple rim. Nose: elegant, complex, ripe fruit, sweet spices. Palate: fruity, complex, good structure, round tannins.

VIZAR SYRAH 2009 T
100% syrah

92 Colour: bright cherry, purple rim. Nose: complex, elegant, sweet spices, violets. Palate: good structure, fine tannins, fruity.

QUINTA SARDONIA

Casa, s/n - Granja Sardón
47340 Sardón de Duero (Valladolid)
☎: +34 650 498 353- Fax: +34 983 032 884
jbougnaud@quintasardonia.com
www.quintasardonia.es

QUINTA SARDONIA QS 2008 T
57,7% tinto fino, 29,5% cabernet sauvignon, 4,5% syrah, 4% merlot, 4,3% otras

93 Colour: cherry, garnet rim. Nose: ripe fruit, balsamic herbs, earthy notes, spicy, creamy oak. Palate: powerful, flavourful, long, toasty, balanced.

RODRÍGUEZ SANZO

Manuel Azaña, 9
47014 (Valladolid)
☎: +34 983 150 150- Fax: +34 983 150 151
comunicacion@valsanzo.com
www.rodriguezsanzo.com

SANZO VERDEJO FRIZZANTE 2011 B
100% verdejo

90 Colour: bright straw. Nose: fresh fruit, white flowers, expressive, fragrant herbs. Palate: flavourful, fruity, good acidity, fine bead.

RUBEN DIAZ Y JOSE BRAGADO VITICULTORES

Nueva, 26
5260 Cebreros (Ávila)
☎: +34 654 975 456- Fax: +34 918 631 346
ruben.cerberux10@gmail.com

CERRO DE LA ESTRELLA 2009 T
garnacha

94 Colour: light cherry, garnet rim. Nose: ripe fruit, scrubland, mineral, spicy, creamy oak. Palate: powerful, flavourful, long, mineral.

TERNA BODEGAS

Cuatro Calles, s/n
47491 La Seca (Valladolid)
☎: +34 983 103 223- Fax: +34 983 816 561
info@sitiosdebodega.com
www.sitiosdebodega.com

E TERNA PRIETO PICUDO 2009 T
100% prieto picudo

91 Colour: cherry, garnet rim. Nose: red berry notes, ripe fruit, balsamic herbs, spicy, mineral. Palate: powerful, flavourful, complex, long, toasty.

VINOS DE ARGANZA

Río Ancares, 2
24560 Toral de los Vados (León)
☎: +34 987 544 831- Fax: +34 987 563 532
admon@vinosdearganza.com
www.vinosdearganza.com

LAGAR DE ROBLA 2008 T
mencía

90 Colour: cherry, garnet rim. Nose: ripe fruit, spicy, creamy oak, toasty, complex, expressive. Palate: powerful, flavourful, toasty, fine tannins, elegant.

VINOS MALAPARTE

Avda. Camilo José Cela, 2
40200 Cuéllar (Segovia)
☎: +34 921 105 204
info@vinosmalaparte.es
www.vinosmalaparte.es

MALAPARTE 2009 T
tinta del país

91 Color bright cherry. Aroma ripe fruit, sweet spices, creamy oak, expressive. Taste flavourful, fruity, toasty, round tannins.

VIÑAS DEL CÉNIT

Ctra. de Circunvalación, s/n
49708 Villanueva de Campeán (Zamora)
☎: +34 980 569 346- Fax: +34 980 569 328
info@bodegascenit.com
www.bodegascenit.com

ALEO 2010 T ROBLE
100% tempranillo

90 Colour: bright cherry. Nose: ripe fruit, sweet spices, creamy oak, cocoa bean, dark chocolate. Palate: flavourful, fruity, toasty, round tannins.

VENTA MAZARRÓN 2010 T
100% tempranillo

92 Colour: very deep cherry. Nose: powerfull, aromatic coffee, spicy, ripe fruit. Palate: powerful, spicy, ripe fruit, roasted-coffee aftertaste.

CUMBRES DE GUADALFEO

BODEGA GARCÍA DE VERDEVIQUE

Los García de Verdevique
18439 Castaras (Granada)
☎: +34 958 957 025
info@bodegasgarciadeverdevique.com
www.bodegasgarciadeverdevique.com

LOS GARCÍA DE VERDEVIQUE 2007 T BARRICA
tempranillo, cabernet sauvignon, syrah

90 Colour: cherry, garnet rim. Nose: ripe fruit, earthy notes, mineral, balsamic herbs, sweet spices. Palate: correct, powerful, flavourful, spicy.

EIVISSA

CAN RICH DE BUSCATELL

Camí de Sa Vorera, s/n
7820 San Antonio (Illes Balears)
☎: +34 971 803 377- Fax: +34 971 803 377
info@bodegascanrich.com
www.bodegascanrich.com

CAN RICH 2011 B
50% chardonnay, 50% malvasía

90 Colour: bright yellow. Nose: fresh, white flowers, expressive. Palate: flavourful, fruity, good acidity, balanced, fine bitter notes.

LAUSOS CABERNET SAUVIGNON 2007 T
100% cabernet sauvignon

92 Colour: bright cherry. Nose: expressive, balanced, varietal, balsamic herbs, ripe fruit. Palate: full, good structure, spicy.

TOTEM WINES

Post Box 654 San Mateo, s/n (a las afueras)
7830 San José (Illes Balears)
☎: +34 654 507 809
laurentfresard@yahoo.fr
www.totemwines.com

TÓTEM 2008 T
monastrell

90 Colour: bright cherry, garnet rim. Nose: medium intensity, ripe fruit, sweet spices. Palate: good structure, flavourful, spicy.

EXTREMADURA

BODEGA DE MIRABEL

Buenavista, 31
10220 Pago de San Clemente (Cáceres)
☎: +34 927 323 154- Fax: +34 927 323 154
bodegademirabel@hotmail.com

MIRABEL 2009 T
75% tempranillo, 25% cabernet sauvignon

91 Colour: cherry, garnet rim. Nose: ripe fruit, spicy, creamy oak, scrubland. Palate: powerful, flavourful, long, balanced.

BODEGA MARQUÉS DE VALDUEZA

Autovía de Extremadura A-5 Km. 360
6800 Mérida (Badajoz)
☎: +34 913 191 508- Fax: +34 913 088 450
contact@marquesdevaldueza.com
www.marquesdevaldueza.com

MARQUÉS DE VALDUEZA 2007 T
47% syrah, 38% cabernet sauvignon, 21% merlot

93 Colour: cherry, garnet rim. Nose: balanced, medium intensity, spicy, cocoa bean, mineral. Palate: good structure, fruity, flavourful, round tannins.

MARQUÉS DE VALDUEZA 2008 T
cabernet sauvignon, merlot, syrah

94 Colour: cherry, garnet rim. Nose: red berry notes, ripe fruit, wild herbs, spicy. Palate: flavourful, spicy, sweet tannins.

MARQUÉS DE VALDUEZA ETIQUETA ROJA 2009 T
58% cabernet sauvignon, 42% syrah

90 Colour: deep cherry, purple rim. Nose: medium intensity, ripe fruit, sweet spices, wild herbs. Palate: fruity, good structure, ripe fruit.

VALDUEZA 2009 T
53% syrah, 29% cabernet sauvignon, 18% merlot

91 Colour: deep cherry, purple rim. Nose: scrubland, powerfull, ripe fruit. Palate: fruity, long, spicy, round tannins.

BODEGAS DE OCCIDENTE

Granados, 1
6200 Almendralejo (Badajoz)
☎: +34 662 952 801
info@bodegasdeoccidente.es
www.bodegasdeoccidente.es

GRAN BUCHE 2009 T
tempranillo

90 Colour: cherry, garnet rim. Nose: ripe fruit, spicy, creamy oak, complex. Palate: powerful, flavourful, round tannins, spicy.

PAGO DE LAS ENCOMIENDAS, VIÑEDOS Y BODEGA

Carmen, 37
☎: +34 924 118 280
pagodelasencomiendas@pagodelasencomiendas.es
www.pagodelasencomiendas.es

XENTIA 2009 T
30% petit verdot, 40% tempranillo, 20% syrah, 10% graciano

90 Colour: bright cherry, purple rim. Nose: powerfull, characterful, ripe fruit, creamy oak, sweet spices, complex. Palate: good structure, full, long, spicy.

FORMENTERA

CAP DE BARBARIA S.L.

Elisenda de Pinos, 1 Casa A
8034 (Barcelona)
☎: +34 609 855 556
info@capdebarbaria.com
www.capdebarbaria.com

CAP DE BARBARIA 2009 T
35% cabernet sauvignon, 35% merlot, 25% monastrell, 5% fogoneu

93 Colour: cherry, garnet rim. Nose: complex, expressive, spicy, scrubland, mineral. Palate: good structure, long, round tannins, ripe fruit.

TERRAMOLL

Ctra. de La Mola, Km. 15,5
7872 El Pilar de la Mola (Illes Balears)
☎: +34 971 327 257- Fax: +34 971 327 293
info@terramoll.es
www.terramoll.es

TERRAMOLL ES MONESTIR 2009 TC
100% monastrell

91 Colour: bright cherry. Nose: elegant, complex, balanced, ripe fruit, sweet spices. Palate: flavourful, good structure, round tannins.

TERRAMOLL PRIMUS 2006 TC
merlot, monastrell

90 Colour: bright cherry, garnet rim. Nose: balanced, ripe fruit, sweet spices. Palate: fruity, flavourful, good acidity.

ILLA DE MENORCA

HORT

Cami de Sant Patrici, s/n
7750 Ferreries (Illes Balears)
☎: +34 971 373 702- Fax: +34 971 155 193
info@santpatrici.com
www.santpatrici.com

HORT MERLOT 2009 T
merlot

90 Color bright cherry. Aroma ripe fruit, sweet spices, creamy oak, expressive. Taste flavourful, fruity, toasty, round tannins.

LAUJAR ALPUJARRA

BODEGA ECOLÓGICA EL CORTIJO DE LA VIEJA

Paraje de la Vieja, s/n Ctra. A-348 Km. 75
4480 Alcolea (Almería)
☎: +34 950 343 919- Fax: +34 950 343 919
comercial@iniza.net
www.iniza.net

INIZA 2011 T MACERACIÓN CARBÓNICA
garnacha, tempranillo

90 Colour: cherry, purple rim. Nose: expressive, fresh fruit, red berry notes, floral, lactic notes. Palate: flavourful, fruity, good acidity, round tannins.

LIÉBANA

BODEGA RÍO SANTO

Cillorigo de Liébana
39584 Esanos (Cantabria)
☎: +34 652 286 474
info@riosanto.es
www.riosanto.es

LUSIA 2010 T ROBLE
85% mencía, 15% tempranillo

91 Colour: cherry, purple rim. Nose: mineral, red berry notes, ripe fruit, floral, sweet spices, creamy oak. Palate: powerful, flavourful, long, toasty.

MALLORCA

4 KILOS VINÍCOLA

1ª Volta, 168 Puigverd
7200 Felanitx (Illes Balears)
☎: +34 660 226 641- Fax: +34 971 580 523
fgrimalt@4kilos.com
www.4kilos.com

12 VOLTS 2010 T
syrah, merlot, cabernet sauvignon, callet, fogoneu

93 Colour: bright cherry. Nose: expressive, dark chocolate, ripe fruit. Palate: flavourful, fruity, toasty, round tannins.

4 KILOS 2010 T
callet, cabernet sauvignon, merlot

94 Colour: cherry, garnet rim. Nose: spicy, creamy oak, toasty, mineral, earthy notes, characterful, fruit expression. Palate: powerful, flavourful, toasty, round tannins.

GRIMALT CABALLERO 2010 T
100% callet

94 Colour: bright cherry. Nose: fruit expression, balsamic herbs, scrubland, earthy notes. Palate: flavourful, good acidity, long, mineral.

ÁN NEGRA VITICULTORS S.L.

3ª Volta, 18 - Apdo. 130
7200 Faianitx (Illes Ballears)
☎: +34 971 584 481- Fax: +34 971 584 482
info@annegra.com
www.animanegra.com

ÀN 2010 T
95% callet, 5% manto negro, fogoneu

93 Colour: cherry, garnet rim. Nose: elegant, ripe fruit, sweet spices. Palate: good structure, fine tannins, complex, fruity.

BINIGRAU

Fiol, 33
7143 Biniali (Illes Balears)
☎: +34 971 512 023- Fax: +34 971 886 495
info@binigrau.es
www.binigrau.es

BINIGRAU SELECCIÓ 2008 T
manto negro, callet, merlot

94 Colour: bright cherry. Nose: complex, elegant, expressive, creamy oak, ripe fruit. Palate: flavourful, good structure, balanced, good acidity.

E NEGRE DE BINIGRAU 2010 T
manto negro, merlot

92 Colour: cherry, purple rim. Nose: elegant, complex, warm, ripe fruit, sweet spices. Palate: fruity, full, balanced, good acidity.

NOU NAT 2011 B
prensal, chardonnay

92 Colour: bright yellow. Nose: white flowers, fresh fruit, expressive, sweet spices. Palate: ripe fruit, fruity, flavourful, fine bitter notes, good acidity.

OBAC DE BINIGRAU 2009 TC
manto negro, callet, merlot, cabernet sauvignon, syrah

90 Colour: bright cherry. Nose: fresh, balsamic herbs, scrubland, dark chocolate, spicy. Palate: ripe fruit, round tannins, balanced.

OBAC DE BINIGRAU 2010 TC

91 Colour: cherry, garnet rim. Nose: expressive, ripe fruit, sweet spices, new oak, toasty. Palate: mineral, long, spicy, ripe fruit.

BODEGAS ÁNGEL

Ctra. Sta María - Sencelles, km. 4,8
7320 Santa María del Camí (Illes Balears)
☎: +34 971 621 638- Fax: +34 971 621 638
info@bodegasangel.com
www.bodegasangel.com

ÁNGEL GRAN SELECCIÓ 2009 T ROBLE
cabernet sauvignon, merlot, callet, manto negro

91 Colour: cherry, garnet rim. Nose: ripe fruit, spicy, creamy oak, toasty, complex, mineral. Palate: powerful, flavourful, toasty, round tannins, elegant.

ÁNGEL NEGRE 2010 T ROBLE
manto negro, merlot, cabernet sauvignon, callet, syrah

92 Colour: light cherry, garnet rim. Nose: ripe fruit, balsamic herbs, mineral, spicy, creamy oak. Palate: powerful, flavourful, round, balanced.

BODEGAS CA'N VIDALET

Ctra. Alcudia - Pollença Ma 2201, Km. 4,85
7460 Pollença (Illes Balears)
☎: +34 971 531 719- Fax: +34 971 535 395
info@canvidalet.com
www.canvidalet.com

CA'N VIDALET SO DEL XIPRER-GRAN SELECCIÓN 2008 T
20% merlot, 80% cabernet sauvignon

92 Colour: bright cherry, garnet rim. Nose: cocoa bean, creamy oak, red berry notes, ripe fruit, mineral. Palate: full, fruity, elegant.

CA'N VIDALET TERRA FUSCA 2009 T
100% syrah

91 Colour: bright cherry. Nose: ripe fruit, sweet spices, creamy oak, expressive, medium intensity, floral. Palate: flavourful, fruity, toasty, round tannins.

BODEGAS RIBAS

Muntanya, 2
7330 Consell (Illes Balears)
☎: +34 971 622 673- Fax: +34 971 622 746
info@bodegaribas.com
www.bodegaribas.com

RIBAS DE CABRERA 2010 T
50% manto negro, 35% syrah, 10% merlot, 5% cabernet sauvignon

91 Colour: bright cherry, garnet rim. Nose: toasty, sweet spices, creamy oak, candied fruit, violets. Palate: complex, good structure, round tannins.

SIÓ 2010 T
40% manto negro, 25% cabernet sauvignon, 15% syrah, 20% merlot

91 Colour: bright cherry, purple rim. Nose: ripe fruit, sweet spices, creamy oak, complex. Palate: flavourful, fruity, easy to drink.

COMERCIAL GRUPO FREIXENET S.A.

Joan Sala, 2
8770 Sant Sadurní D'Anoia (Barcelona)
☎: +34 938 917 000- Fax: +34 938 183 095
freixenet@freixenet.es
www.freixenet.es

SUSANA SEMPRE MAIOR NEGRE 2009 T
cabernet sauvignon, merlot, manto negro

90 Colour: bright cherry. Nose: ripe fruit, creamy oak, expressive, balsamic herbs. Palate: flavourful, fruity, toasty, round tannins.

FINCA SON BORDILS

Ctra. Inca - Sineu, Km. 4,1
7300Inca (Illes Balears)
☎: +34 971 182 200- Fax: +34 971 182 202
info@sonbordils.es
www.sonbordils.es

FINCA SON BORDILS CHARDONNAY 2011 BFB
100% chardonnay

91 Colour: bright yellow. Nose: powerfull, ripe fruit, creamy oak, fragrant herbs. Palate: rich, flavourful, fresh, good acidity.

FINCA SON BORDILS MERLOT 2006 T
93,1% merlot, 3,7% manto negro, 2,4% cabernet sauvignon, callet, monastrell

90 Colour: cherry, garnet rim. Nose: ripe fruit, spicy, creamy oak, fragrant herbs. Palate: powerful, flavourful, toasty, round tannins.

SON BORDILS BLANC DE RAÏM BLANC 2011 B
90,7% prensal, 9,3% chardonnay

90 Colour: bright straw. Nose: fresh fruit, white flowers, dried herbs, balanced. Palate: flavourful, fruity, balanced.

SON BORDILS BLANC DOLC 2011 B
70% pansa blanca, 30% moscatel grano menudo

90 Colour: bright yellow. Nose: floral, citrus fruit, ripe fruit, fragrant herbs, fresh. Palate: fine bitter notes, good acidity, powerful, flavourful, sweet.

SON BORDILS ROSAT DE MONASTRELL 2011 RD
100% monastrell

90 Colour: rose, purple rim. Nose: powerfull, ripe fruit, red berry notes, floral, expressive. Palate: , powerful, fruity, fresh, easy to drink, balanced.

SON CAMPANER

Pou Bauza 19ª, Pol Ind. Binissalem
7350 Binissalem (Mallorca)
☎: +34 971 870 004
info@soncampaner.es
www.soncampaner.es

SON CAMPANER MERLOT 2010 T
merlot

90 Colour: cherry, garnet rim. Nose: ripe fruit, sweet spices, earthy notes, fragrant herbs. Palate: spicy, flavourful, long, toasty.

SON PRIM PETIT

Ctra. Inca - Sencelles, Km. 4,9
7140 Sencelles (Mallorca)
☎: +34 971 872 758
correo@sonprim.com
www.sonprim.com

SON PRIM CABERNET 2009 T
cabernet sauvignon

92 Colour: cherry, garnet rim. Nose: earthy notes, dry stone, ripe fruit, balsamic herbs, spicy, creamy oak. Palate: long, flavourful, elegant, round tannins.

SON PRIM CUP 2009 T BARRICA
manto negro, cabernet sauvignon, merlot

92 Colour: bright cherry. Nose: sweet spices, mineral, red berry notes, ripe fruit. Palate: flavourful, fruity, toasty, round tannins, balanced.

SON PRIM MERLOT 2009 T
merlot

90 Colour: cherry, garnet rim. Nose: ripe fruit, spicy, toasty, fragrant herbs. Palate: powerful, flavourful, toasty, balanced.

SON PRIM SYRAH 2009 T
syrah

91 Colour: bright cherry. Nose: ripe fruit, sweet spices, creamy oak, balsamic herbs, violets. Palate: flavourful, fruity, toasty, round tannins.

SON VIVES

Font de la Vila, 2
7191 Banyalbufar (Illes Ballears)
☎: +34 609 601 904- Fax: +34 971 718 065
toni@darder.com
www.sonvives.com

N SELECCIO 2007

90 Colour: bright cherry, orangey edge. Nose: spicy, toasty, ripe fruit, complex. Palate: powerful, correct, balanced.

VINYES MORTITX

Ctra. Pollensa Lluc, Km. 10,9
7315 Escorca (Illes Balears)
☎: +34 971 182 339- Fax: +34 971 182 340
info@vinyesmortitx.com
www.vinyesmortitx.com

L'U DE MORTITX 2007 TC
64% syrah, 24% merlot, 12% cabernet sauvignon

91 Colour: cherry, purple rim. Nose: medium intensity, creamy oak, cocoa bean, ripe fruit. Palate: fruity, flavourful, good acidity.

RIBERA DEL ANDARAX

FINCA ÁNFORA

Paraje Barranco del Obispo, s/n.
4729 Enix (Almería)
☎: +34 950 520 336- Fax: +34 950 341 614
info@vegaenix.com
www.vegaenix.com

VEGA ENIX DAMARIS 2006 T
100% syrah

90 Colour: cherry, garnet rim. Nose: ripe fruit, creamy oak, sweet spices, balsamic herbs. Palate: powerful, flavourful, toasty, round tannins.

VEGA ENIX LAURENTI 2006 T
100% cabernet sauvignon

90 Colour: pale ruby, brick rim edge. Nose: ripe fruit, aged wood nuances, spicy, creamy oak, earthy notes. Palate: powerful, flavourful, long, spicy.

VEGA ENIX XOLAIR 2006 T
100% merlot

91 Colour: pale ruby, brick rim edge. Nose: ripe fruit, scrubland, spicy, creamy oak, fine reductive notes. Palate: flavourful, long, spicy, balanced.

PAGOS DE INDALIA

Paseo de los Baños, 2
4458 Padules (Almería)
☎: +34 950 510 728
juanma@pagosdeindalia.com
www.pagosdeindalia.com

INDALIA 2010 T
tempranillo, cabernet franc, cabernet sauvignon

91 Colour: cherry, garnet rim. Nose: earthy notes, balsamic herbs, floral, red berry notes, ripe fruit, spicy, creamy oak. Palate: powerful, flavourful, balanced, round tannins.

RIBERA DEL GÁLLEGO

BODEGA PEGALAZ

Ctra. A-1202, Km. 7 Desvío Ermita Santa Quiteria
22806 Santa Eulalia de Gállego (Zaragoza)
☎: +34 625 643 440
bodegaspegalaz@gmail.com
www.pegalaz.com

FIRÉ 2007 T
cabernet sauvignon, merlot, tempranillo

93 Colour: cherry, garnet rim. Nose: spicy, creamy oak, complex, fresh, red berry notes, ripe fruit. Palate: powerful, flavourful, toasty, round tannins.

FIRÉ 2009 B

92 Color bright yellow. Aroma powerfull, ripe fruit, sweet spices, creamy oak, fragrant herbs. Taste rich, smoky aftertaste, flavourful, fresh, good acidity.

RIBERA DEL JILOCA

VINAE MURERI

Ctra. Murero-Atea - Finca La Moratilla
50366 Murero (Zaragoza)
☎: +34 976 808 033
info@vinaemureri.com
www.vinaemureri.com

MURERO ÉLITE 2005 T
100% garnacha

92 Colour: cherry, garnet rim. Nose: mineral, ripe fruit, sweet spices, cocoa bean, toasty. Palate: spicy, powerful, flavourful, toasty, balanced.

DESCRIPTION

Beyond the environment of the wines classified as quality wines, table wines are those wines which are not produced following the precepts of any of the above categories nor the wines of the land which are also classified as table wines according to the Law on Wine. The Guide contains 41 table wines graded as excellent, which indicates that it is necessary to eliminate old beliefs that these wines are simply volume wines.

BODEGA KIENINGER

Los Frontones, 67
29400 Ronda - (Málaga)
☎: +34 952 879 554
martin@bodegakieninger.com
www.bodegakieninger.com

7 VIN 2010 T
50% blaufraenkisch, 50% zweigelt

91 Colour: cherry, garnet rim. Nose: balanced, expressive, ripe fruit, spicy, complex. Palate: long, spicy, fruity, good acidity.

BODEGA MAS L'ALTET

Mas L'Altet Partida de la Creu, s/n
3838 Alfafara - (Alicante)
☎: +34 609 759 708
nina@bodegamaslaltet.com
www.bodegamaslaltet.com

AVI DE MAS L'ALTET 2009 T
65% syrah, 26% cabernet sauvignon, 5% merlot, 4% garnacha

91 Colour: cherry, garnet rim. Nose: balanced, ripe fruit, cocoa bean, spicy, wild herbs. Palate: ripe fruit, long, round tannins.

AVI DE MAS L'ALTET 2010 T
58% syrah, 25% cabernet sauvignon, 13% garnacha, 4% merlot

90 Colour: deep cherry, purple rim. Nose: powerfull, ripe fruit, fruit preserve, scrubland, spicy. Palate: concentrated, fruity.

LUKA 2008 T
65% syrah, 26% cabernet sauvignon, 5% merlot, 4% garnacha

91 Colour: cherry, garnet rim. Nose: spicy, creamy oak, toasty, characterful, mineral. Palate: powerful, flavourful, toasty, round tannins.

BODEGAS DEL NÉVALO

Tomás Carretero, 42
14300 Villaviciosa de Córdoba - (Córdoba)
☎: +34 957 050 387
info@bodegasdelnevalo.com
www.bodegasdelnevalo.com

BLANCO NÉVALO B
airén, pedro ximénez, palomino

90 Color iodine, amber rim. Aroma powerfull, complex, elegant, dry nuts, toasty. Taste rich, fine bitter notes, fine solera notes, long, spicy.

BODEGAS OBANCA

Obanca, 12
33800 Cangas del Narcea - (Asturias)
☎: +34 626 956 571 - Fax: +34 985 811 539
informacion@obanca.com
www.obanca.com

CASTRO DE LIMÉS 2009 T
100% carrasquín

93 Colour: cherry, garnet rim. Nose: ripe fruit, mineral, dark chocolate, creamy oak, toasty, balsamic herbs. Palate: powerful, flavourful, long, balanced, good acidity.

DESCARGA 2011 T
verdejo negro, carrasquín, mencía, albarín tinto

90 Colour: cherry, garnet rim. Nose: red berry notes, ripe fruit, sweet spices, fragrant herbs, creamy oak. Palate: long, flavourful, fresh, fruity, spicy.

LA DESCARGA 2009 T
albarín tinto, verdejo negro, carrasquín, mencía

90 Colour: cherry, garnet rim. Nose: ripe fruit, creamy oak, toasty, sweet spices, scrubland. Palate: powerful, flavourful, round tannins, spicy.

LA DESCARGA 2011 B
albarín, albillo

90 Colour: bright straw. Nose: white flowers, fragrant herbs, mineral, fresh fruit, elegant. Palate: rich, fruity, flavourful, long.

BRUNO MURCIANO & DAVID SAMPEDRO GIL

8 Avenida Banda De Musica El Angel
46315 Caudete de las Fuentes - (Valencia)
☎: +34 962 319 096
bru.murciano@yahoo.es

LA MALKERIDA 100% BOBAL 2011 T
100% bobal

90 Colour: cherry, purple rim. Nose: expressive, red berry notes, floral, balsamic herbs, mineral. Palate: flavourful, fruity, good acidity, round tannins.

CARRIEL DELS VILARS

Mas Can Carriel Els Vilars
17753 Espolla - (Girona)
☎: +34 972 563 335
carrieldelsvilars@hotmail.com

CARRIEL DELS VILARS 2011 T
50% garnacha, 30% syrah, 15% cabernet sauvignon, 5% samsó

90 Colour: cherry, garnet rim. Nose: fruit preserve, scrubland, damp earth, mineral, petrol notes, wet leather. Palate: fresh, fruity, flavourful, round tannins.

ESCUMÒS D'ANYADA 2009 ESP
macabeo, xarel.lo, parellada, garnacha blanca

90 Colour: bright golden. Nose: dry nuts, fragrant herbs, lees reduction notes, pattiserie, citrus fruit. Palate: powerful, flavourful, good acidity, fine bitter notes.

ESCUMÒS RESERVA ANYADA 2001 ESP
macabeo, xarel.lo, parellada, garnacha blanca

93 Colour: bright golden. Nose: dry nuts, complex, lees reduction notes, aged wood nuances, faded flowers, toasty. Palate: powerful, flavourful, good acidity, fine bead, fine bitter notes. Personality.

CELLER LA MUNTANYA

Compositor Paco Esteve, 13
3830 Muro de l'Alcoi - (Alicante)
☎: +34 607 902 235 - Fax: +34 965 531 248
info@cellerlamuntanya.com
www.cellerlamuntanya.com

ALMOROIG 2007 T
69% monastrell, 16% giró, 15% garnacha tintorera

91 Colour: deep cherry, garnet rim. Nose: scrubland, balanced, complex, expressive. Palate: good structure, flavourful, balanced, fine bitter notes.

CELLER LA MUNTANYA DOLÇ NATURAL 2009 B
100% malvasía

92 Colour: golden. Nose: powerfull, honeyed notes, candied fruit, fragrant herbs, citrus fruit. Palate: flavourful, sweet, fresh, fruity, good acidity, long.

CELLER LA MUNTANYA NEGRE 2009 T
65% monastrell, 10% giró, 10% garnacha tintorera, 8% bobal, 7% bonicaire

92 Colour: bright cherry, garnet rim. Nose: elegant, balanced, scrubland, spicy, mineral, dark chocolate. Palate: good structure, flavourful, round tannins.

LLIURE ALBIR 2010 B
50% malvasía, 35% garnacha blanca, 15% verdil

92 Colour: bright yellow. Nose: powerfull, ripe fruit, sweet spices, creamy oak, fragrant herbs, dry nuts. Palate: rich, smoky aftertaste, flavourful, fresh, good acidity, long.

COTO DE GOMARIZ

Barrio de Gomariz
32429 Leiro - (Ourense)
☎: +34 671 641 982 - Fax: +34 988 488 174
gomariz@cotodegomariz.com
www.cotodegomariz.com

VX CUVÉE PRIMO 2007 T
sousón, caiño longo, caiño da Terra, carabuñeira, mencía

93 Colour: very deep cherry. Nose: mineral, earthy notes, red berry notes, fruit expression, creamy oak, sweet spices. Palate: flavourful, powerful, ripe fruit, long, mineral.

DANIEL V. RAMOS (ZERBEROS FINCA)

Real de Abajo, 100
5110 El Barraco - (Ávila)
☎: +34 687 410 952
dvrcru@gmail.com
winesdanielramosvinos.blogspot.com

ZERBEROS VIENTO ZEPHYROS 2009 B ROBLE
albillo, sauvignon blanc

91 Colour: bright yellow. Nose: ripe fruit, dried herbs, spicy, creamy oak, mineral. Palate: spicy, long, good acidity, elegant.

ZERBEROS VINO PRECIOSO 2010 B
albillo

90 Colour: bright golden. Nose: faded flowers, dry stone, earthy notes, ripe fruit. Palate: flavourful, spicy, long, balanced.

ECCOCIWINE

GIV 6701, km. 4
17462 San Martí Vell - (Girona)
☎: +34 616 863 209
info@eccociwine.com
www.eccociwine.com

ECCOCI TINTO PREMIUM 2009 T
merlot, cabernet franc, marselan

90 Colour: cherry, garnet rim. Nose: ripe fruit, scrubland, earthy notes, fine reductive notes, spicy. Palate: flavourful, balsamic, balanced.

ECCOMI TINTO SUPER PREMIUM 2009 TC
merlot, cabernet franc, marselan

92 Colour: cherry, garnet rim. Nose: red berry notes, ripe fruit, balsamic herbs, mineral, creamy oak. Palate: long, rich, flavourful, toasty, elegant.

ENVINATE

Gran Vía, 2 1ºC
27600 Sarría - (Lugo)
☎: +34 682 207 160
asesoria.envinate@gmail.com

DAS LOUSAS MENCÍA 2010 T
mencía

91 Colour: cherry, purple rim. Nose: red berry notes, medium intensity, dry stone, spicy. Palate: fruity, flavourful, complex, long, spicy.

PUZZLE 2010 T
tempranillo, garnacha, listán negro, touriga

93 Colour: dark-red cherry, garnet rim. Nose: fruit preserve, sweet spices, balsamic herbs, dark chocolate. Palate: rich, round tannins, long, toasty.

TINTA AMARELA 2011 T
100% Trincadeira preta

93 Colour: bright cherry, purple rim. Nose: red berry notes, ripe fruit, expressive, balsamic herbs, toasty. Palate: full, flavourful, round tannins, balanced.

EQUIPO NAVAZOS

Cartuja, 1 - módulo 6
11401 Jerez de la Frontera - (Cádiz)
equipo@navazos.com
www.equiponavazos.com

NAVAZOS NIEPOORT 2011 B
100% palomino

93 Colour: bright yellow. Nose: elegant, faded flowers, flor yeasts, fine lees. Palate: balanced, fine bitter notes, complex. Personality.

JUAN JESÚS PÉREZ Y ADRIÁN

Bajada al Puerto de Santo Domingo
38787 Garafia - (Santa Cruz de Tenerife)
☎: +34 618 309 374
tagalguen@hotmail.com

PRAXIS VINO DE PASAS B
malvasía, listán blanco, gual, marmajuelo

90 Colour: light mahogany. Nose: powerfull, floral, honeyed notes, candied fruit, fragrant herbs. Palate: flavourful, sweet, fresh, fruity, good acidity, long, roasted-coffee aftertaste.

KAIROS

Dels Nostris, 26-A
8185 Lliça de Vall - (Barcelona)
☎: +34 938 436 061 - Fax: +34 938 439 671
kairos@vinodegaraje.com
www.kairosvino.com

KAIROS 2011 T
100% tempranillo

90 Colour: cherry, garnet rim. Nose: earthy notes, mineral, floral, ripe fruit, spicy. Palate: powerful, flavourful, balanced, long.

LA CALANDRIA. PURA GARNACHA

Camino de Aspra, s/n
31521 Murchante - (Navarra)
☎: +34 630 904 327
luis@lacalandria.org
www.lacalandria.org

TIERGA 2010 T
100% garnacha

92 Colour: cherry, purple rim. Nose: ripe fruit, wild herbs, creamy oak, dry stone. Palate: full, flavourful, fruity aftestaste, long.

MAS COMTAL

Mas Comtal, 1
8793 Avinyonet del Penedès - (Barcelona)
☎: +34 938 970 052 - Fax: +34 938 970 591
mascomtal@mascomtal.com
www.mascomtal.com

GRAN ANGULAR - IN.M 100% 2010 B
Incroccio manzoni

92 Colour: bright straw. Nose: fresh, white flowers, fragrant herbs, mineral. Palate: flavourful, fruity, good acidity, balanced. Personality.

GRAN ANGULAR INCROCIO MANZONI CHARDONNAY 2010 B
80% Incroccio manzoni, 20% chardonnay

90 Colour: bright yellow. Nose: fine lees, citrus fruit, dried herbs, floral, mineral. Palate: good acidity, balanced, flavourful, long, complex.

LYRIC LICOROSO
merlot

92 Colour: light mahogany. Nose: varnish, caramel, spicy, dark chocolate, candied fruit, dry nuts. Palate: powerful, flavourful, long, spicy, balanced.

MAS DE LA REAL DE SELLA

Avda. País Valencia 8, Bajo
3570 Villajoyosa - (Alicante)
☎: +34 699 308 250 - Fax: +34 965 890 819
info@masdelarealdesella.es
www.masdelarealdesella.es

MAS DE SELLA VINO DE AUTOR 2008 T
cabernet sauvignon, cabernet franc, garnacha tintorera, syrah, marselan

90 Colour: cherry, garnet rim. Nose: ripe fruit, spicy, creamy oak, toasty, complex, earthy notes. Palate: powerful, flavourful, toasty, round tannins.

MUSTIGUILLO VIÑEDOS Y BODEGA

Ctra. N-330, km 196,5 El Terrerazo
46300 Utiel - (Valencia)
☎: +34 962 168 260 - Fax: +34 962 168 259
info@bodegamustiguillo.com
www.bodegamustiguillo.com

MESTIZAJE 2010 B
63% merseguera, 30% viognier, 7% malvasía

93 Colour: bright straw. Nose: expressive, characterful, lactic notes, white flowers, ripe fruit. Palate: flavourful, fine bitter notes, long, ripe fruit.

MESTIZAJE 2011 T

91 Colour: cherry, purple rim. Nose: expressive, fresh fruit, red berry notes, floral, mineral, lactic notes. Palate: flavourful, fruity, good acidity, round tannins.

PAGO DEL MARENOSTRUM

Ctra. A-348, Km. 85-86
4460 Fondón - (Almería)
☎: +34 926 666 027 - Fax: +34 670 099 520
info@pagodelvicario.com

1500 H PINOT NOIR 2007 T
100% pinot noir

90 Colour: deep cherry, garnet rim. Nose: balanced, elegant, spicy, tobacco. Palate: powerful, good structure, fine bitter notes.

PEDRO MANUEL RODRÍGUEZ PÉREZ

Sanmil, 43 - Santa Cruz de Brosmos
27425 Sober - (Lugo)
☎: +34 982 152 508 - Fax: +34 982 402 000
adegasguimaro@gmail.com

GBG 2011 B
80% godello, 15% treixadura, 5% dona blanca

91 Colour: bright yellow. Nose: ripe fruit, faded flowers, sweet spices, dried herbs, earthy notes. Palate: rich, powerful, flavourful, long.

PRÍNCIPE ALFONSO DE HOHENLOHE

Estación de Parchite, 104
29400 Ronda - (Málaga)
☎: +34 914 365 900
gromero@arcoinvest-group.com
www.haciendas-espana.com

ÁNDALUS PETIT VERDOT (MARQUÉS DE LA CONCORDIA FAMILY OF WINES) 2006 T
petit verdot

90 Colour: cherry, garnet rim. Nose: ripe fruit, spicy, toasty, scrubland, aged wood nuances. Palate: powerful, flavourful, toasty, fine bitter notes.

SEDELLA VINOS

Término Las Viñuelas, s/n
29715 Sedella - (Málaga)
☎: +34 687 463 082 - Fax: +34 967 140 723
info@sedellavinos.com
www.sedellavinos.com

SEDELLA 2009 T
romé, garnacha

91 Colour: cherry, garnet rim. Nose: ripe fruit, scrubland, earthy notes, spicy, creamy oak. Palate: powerful, flavourful, long, round tannins.

VALQUEJIGOSO

Ctra, Villamanta - Méntrida, s/n
28610 Villamanta - (Madrid)
☎: +34 650 492 390
aureliogarcia@valquejigoso.com
www.valquejigoso.com

VALQUEJIGOSO V2 2007 T
cabernet sauvignon, syrah, petit verdot, cabernet franc, merlot, negral

94 Colour: very deep cherry. Nose: powerfull, ripe fruit, toasty, dark chocolate, mineral, earthy notes. Palate: flavourful, powerful, fine bitter notes, good acidity, round tannins.

VERA DE ESTENAS

Junto N-III, km. 266 - Paraje La Cabeuzela
46300 Utiel - (Valencia)
☎: +34 962 171 141 - Fax: +34 962 174 352
estenas@estenas.es
www.estenas.es

CASA DON ÁNGEL MALBEC 7-8 T
malbec

92 Colour: cherry, garnet rim. Nose: spicy, creamy oak, ripe fruit. Palate: powerful, flavourful, toasty, round tannins.

VINS DE TALLER

Nou, 5
17469 Siurana d'Empordà - (Girona)
☎: +34 972 525 578 - Fax: +34 934 816 434
info@vinsdetaller.com
www.vinsdetaller.com

VINS DE TALLER MM 2009 TC
merlot, marcelan

90 Colour: cherry, garnet rim. Nose: fruit preserve, dry stone, earthy notes, spicy, cocoa bean, expressive. Palate: powerful, flavourful, complex, long.

VINS DE TALLER VRM 2010 BFB
viognier, roussanne, marsanne, cortese

90 Colour: bright yellow. Nose: ripe fruit, fine lees, earthy notes, fragrant herbs, sweet spices. Palate: rich, flavourful, long, toasty.

VINS TONI GELABERT

Camí dels Horts de Llodrá Km. 1,3
7500 Manacor - (Illes Balears)
☎: +34 610 789 531
info@vinstonigelabert.com
www.vinstonigelabert.com

TORRE DES CANONGE BLANC 2010 B
giró

90 Colour: bright yellow. Nose: balanced, expressive, candied fruit, dried herbs, sweet spices. Palate: fruity, rich, toasty.

VIÑEDO Y BODEGA HERETAT DE CESILIA

Paraje Alcaydias, 4
3660 Novelda - (Alicante)
☎: +34 965 605 385 - Fax: +34 965 604 763
administracion@heretatdecesilia.com
www.heretatdecesilia.com

AD GAUDE 2006 T
70% monastrell, 15% syrah, 15% petit verdot

91 Colour: very deep cherry. Nose: spicy, ripe fruit, aromatic coffee. Palate: flavourful, powerful, fine bitter notes, good acidity.

CARDENAL ÁLVAREZ 2007 TINTO
60% monastrell, 20% cabernet sauvignon, 20% petit verdot

92 Colour: dark mahogany. Nose: dry nuts, acetaldehyde, dark chocolate, sweet spices, roasted coffee, dried fruit. Palate: powerful, flavourful, complex, long, toasty, sweet.

VIÑEDOS CULTURALES

Plaza Constitución, 8 - 1º
3380 Bigastro - (Alicante)
☎: +34 966 770 353 - Fax: +34 966 770 353
vinedosculturales@gmail.com
vinedosculturales.blogspot.com.es

PARQUE NATURAL "EL CARRO" 2011 B
100% moscatel de alejandría

93 Color bright straw. Aroma fresh, fresh fruit, white flowers, expressive. Taste flavourful, fruity, good acidity, balanced.

PARQUE NATURAL "LA VIÑA DE SIMÓN" 2011 B
100% merseguera

92 Colour: bright straw. Nose: spicy, candied fruit, ripe fruit, citrus fruit, violet drops, faded flowers. Palate: flavourful, sweetness, fine bitter notes.

VIÑEDOS Y BODEGAS VEGALFARO

Ctra. Pontón - Utiel, Km. 3
46430 El Derramador - Requena - (Valencia)
☎: +34 962 320 680 - Fax: +34 962 321 126
info@vegalfaro.com
www.vegalfaro.com

PAGO DE LOS BALAGUESES SYRAH 2009 TC
syrah

93 Colour: cherry, garnet rim. Nose: spicy, creamy oak, toasty, characterful, earthy notes, ripe fruit. Palate: flavourful, toasty, round tannins.

PEÑÍN GUIDE
TOP WINES FROM

MÉXICO

DATA ON MEXICO:

POPULATION: 112.322.757 habitantes
SURFACE AREA: : 1.972.550 km^2
SURFACE AREA OF VINEYARDS: 27.872 has.
PREDOMINANT VARIETIES:
RED GRAPES: the varieties of French origin are very extended although the most important in alphabetical order are the following: *barbera, cabernet franc, cabernet sauvignon, claret, garnacha, merlot, misión, nebbiolo, syrah and tempranillo.*
White grapes: chardonnay, chenin blanc, colombard, fumé blanc, sauvignon blanc and semillón.
WHITE GRAPES: *chardonnay, chenin blanc, colombard, fumé blanc, sauvignon blanc and semillón.*
HARVEST DATES: the harvest dates begin at the end of July and end in the first week of November as in Spain.
CLIMATE: there are three very differentiated climatic zones: the arid zone, the temperate zone and the tropical zone. This means that the temperatures are generally high although there are substantial oscillations in the interior and with low rainfall. In the more desert regions, it was necessary to adapt the soil to the crops and, above all, channel water which was often difficult to find. The temperate zones have the best conditions for cultivating vines owing to the milder temperatures and somewhat more abundant rainfall. These climatic conditions become milder especially in the region of Sonora although alternative irrigation systems are also required there.
PRODUCTION 2012: 38.000 grape tonnes
ALTITUDE: average altitude 300 m. and maximum altitude 800 m.

INTRODUCTION

Today Mexico is a country where there is a nervous feeling of uncertainty as the country undergoes a fully fledged process of creation. This country is now fully involved in the launch of the wine industry at international level and the creation of rules which foster quality wines and eliminate fraud.

Despite the fact that there are historical wineries, fundamentally in the most developed wine growing region, Lower California. It is now that all the agents involved are positioning themselves in order to lay the foundations for the development of all this region's industries in the near future.

The current situation entails two opposing states of mind. On the one hand there are the winery owners and the oenologists who are aware of the importance of the times they are living in and are immensely happy with the grand achievements their wines can attain and the long creative road which lies ahead. On the other hand, there is the uncertainty and the dizzy feeling caused by the need to achieve sufficient unity in order to give greater force to their requirements. Undoubtedly the steps taken now will condition future development.

The first big challenge to Mexican wine is the creation of sound legislative foundations which regulate and limit the production as well as regulating the quality of wine. The Guía Peñín is aware that the first approaches are being made by associations of producers. However, it is true that, at the present time, the sector does not have full governmental backing. Wine is very highly taxed, 42% of its value, which contradicts the official message that the institutions openly support the sector.

Lower California has the responsibility to be the engine of Mexican wine as it produces almost 85% of all the wine made in Mexico. As can be expected, Lower California is the standard bearer as regards the most modern production methods in the country, and the most visionary and curious oenologists have gone there thus boosting its recognition and international dissemination.

The coexistence of wine and gastronomy in a clearer and more direct fashion is another matter to be dealt with. The key to this will lie in knowing how to link the wines with the most delicate gastronomic aspect. In this area, much progress has ben made with initiatives such as the wine route set up by the Government of Lower California (www.descubrebajacalifornia.com).

Creating the culture medium for the proper development of the industry must be a priority for the competent authorities and together with the accumulated experience of other producer countries which will undoubtedly help to avoid committing errors of the past.

MAP OF THE WINE GROWING ZONES

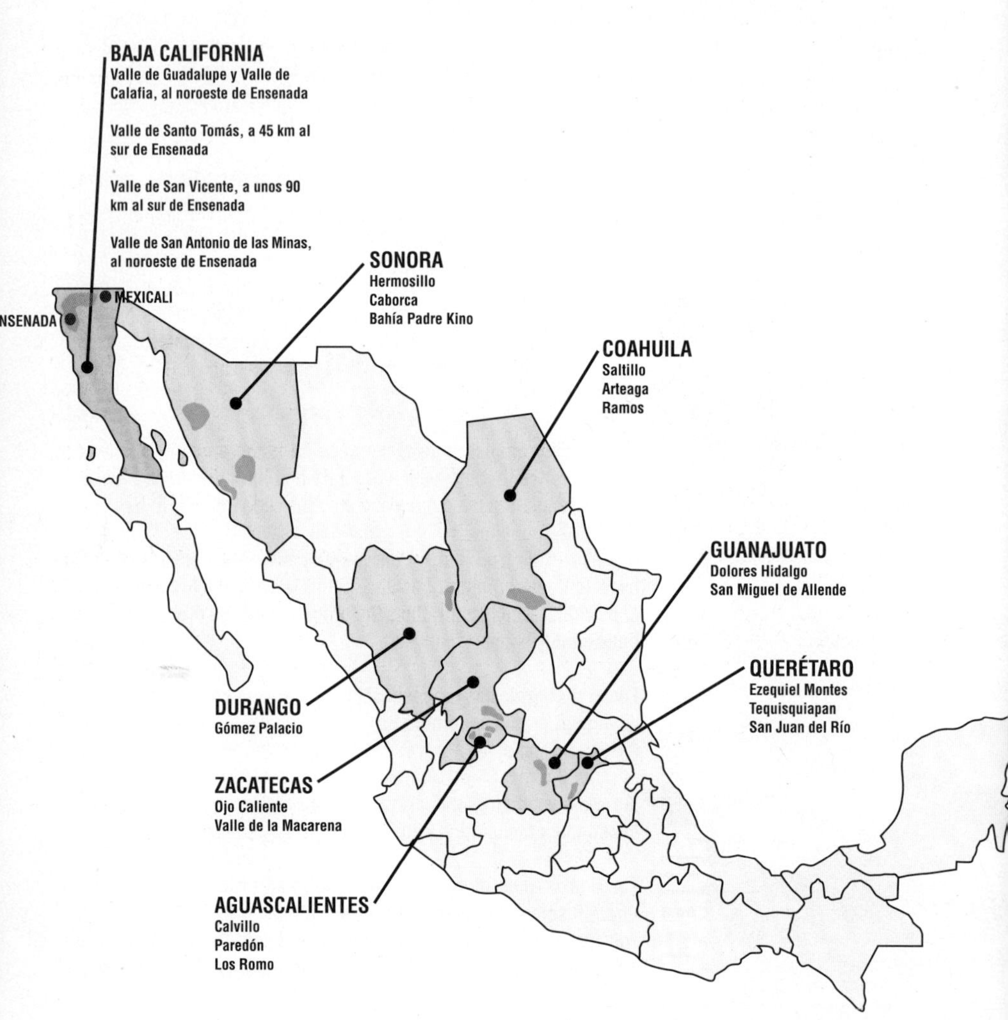
BAJA CALIFORNIA
Valle de Guadalupe y Valle de Calafia, al noroeste de Ensenada
Valle de Santo Tomás, a 45 km al sur de Ensenada
Valle de San Vicente, a unos 90 km al sur de Ensenada
Valle de San Antonio de las Minas, al noroeste de Ensenada
MEXICALI
ENSENADA
SONORA
Hermosillo
Caborca
Bahía Padre Kino
COAHUILA
Saltillo
Arteaga
Ramos
GUANAJUATO
Dolores Hidalgo
San Miguel de Allende
QUERÉTARO
Ezequiel Montes
Tequisquiapan
San Juan del Río
DURANGO
Gómez Palacio
ZACATECAS
Ojo Caliente
Valle de la Macarena
AGUASCALIENTES
Calvillo
Paredón
Los Romo

THE KEYS TO THE YEAR

Talking about Mexican wine is inevitably to talk about Lower California, where there is the greatest concentration of vineyards and brands in the country and where there is the greatest oenological awareness. Today Lower California is the production zone which is the standard bearer of change and internationalization of Mexican wine, most Mexican wines, 90 points, is mainly from lower California, which the reader will verify in this Guide.

Lower California has a number of valleys which make it a very diverse area. The valleys have a warm Mediterranean climate, with more or less influence from the Pacific depending on the proximity to this ocean. The greatest concentration of vineyards, almost 80% of the production of Lower California, is in this valley, very near to the city of Ensenada, followed by other equally interesting valleys such as Santo Tomás, San Antonio de las Minas, San Vicente, Ojos Negros and Las Grullas (Ejido-Uruapán). The crucible of varieties which coexist in these valleys show that there is still indefiniteness as regards varieties in the zone. Definiteness remains to be created. Red varieties such as nebbiolo, garnacha, barbera, cabernet sauvignon, petit syrah, merlot, misión and white varieties such as chardonnay, chenin blanc, savignon blanc and viognier coexist in greater or lesser competition in valleys dominated by sandy soils and, to a lesser extent, clay.

In Lower California water is the major player and directly defines the quality of harvests. This is due to the low rainfall, which is approximately 250 mm. annually (Napa Valley: 400 mm. Rioja about 600 mm. Burdeos 600 mm). Although it may not seem so, wines are achieved here by drip irrigation (obviously) and a wine is produced with good balance, fruitiness and even singularity (the irrigation water normally has a greater amount of salt than in other zones, which gives the wines a certain amount of salinity). This capacity to create wines of a similar level shows that the power to develop grand wines is in the hands of the producers and the greater or lesser skill of the Mexican wine growers and oenologists will be decisive when it comes to making this happen.

Until a short time ago, Mexican idiosyncrasy restrained the capacity of the wine to reach its best level. However, fundamental players such as the oenologist Hugo D'Acosta (involved in several oenological projects), Laura Zamora

(Bodegas Santo Tomás), José Luis Durand (Bodegas Sinergy), Camilo P. Magoni (Bodegas L.A. Cetto) and the Austrian Thomas Egli (Casa de Piedra) have made it possible to steer the wine of Lower California on the right course. All these oenologists, each of whom is immersed in projects with differing philosophies, represent the diversity and capacity of the wine in the zone, therefore, they must be considered as references for other producers to be able to discern their capacity to become grand players with Mexican wines. Currently Lower California has very important responsibility for Mexican wine. Its proper development will undoubtedly condition growth in other producer zones such as Guanajuato, Queretaro, etc.

With regard to tasting, the red wines with the highest scores are those which have been created as blends which endeavour to balance maturity, the fruit and the acidity with the right contribution of wood. Fauno 2009 (nebbiolo, cabernet sauvignon and zinfandel), Vino de Piedra 2009 (tempranillo and Cabernet Sauvignon) and Liceaga Etiqueta L 2008 (syrah, merlot) are three of the highest scoring creations in this new edition. At individual level we find that nebbiolo is the variety with the best capacity of expression, which is demonstrated by Nebbiolo Bella Terra 2010 and Nebbiolo Las Nubes 2009.

Despite being the red grape varieties being the most represented on the Mexican wines podium, it is white wine which has the responsibility to lead the decision that Lower California must make in order to create its wine-gastronomy offer, especially as regards one of its star gastronomic products, seafood. This is how future developments can benefit all the producers. The typology now seems to be well defined to that extent that the wines are white, mature, fatty and full-bodied.

The four wines mentioned here are from Lower California. All of them were produced in the most productive and popular valley in the State, the Valle de Guadalupe, located 25 kilometres from the Pacific. Sauvignon blanc and chardonnay are present in the blends of wines with the highest scores. All of them have been in wood, so their nuances will appear to a greater or lesser extent under the influence of well blended oak. The warm climate, which is similar to the Mediterranean climate, together with sandy-loam and silt-loam soils, condition the work in the vineyards which is of the utmost importance in this area of Mexico. Among the most relevant of the year are Llave Blanca 2006 (sauvignon blanc, chenin blanc), Nuva 2010 (chardonnay, sauvignon blanc and moscato canelli), Kuiiy 2011 (sauvignon blanc, chardonnay) the highest scoring young wine and L.A. Cetto Chardonnay Reserva Privada 2009.

GENERAL CHARACTERISTICS OF THE WINES

Mexico produces very full bodied wines with mature preserve tastes although they maintain their fruity expression, with notable mature tannins and a sweet, long and balanced final. The selected varieties are those which define and contribute the finest and most personal nuances to each wine. The best white wines evoke mature fruit and are tasty and consistent although there are also wines which, owing to the greater or lesser influence of the ocean, are fresh with a fruity expression and hints of flowers.

HISTORY

The history of Mexico started, as happened in Argentina and Chile, as result of the work of the first colonists after the discovery of America. Mexico is the country where vines were first cultivated on the continent. There is even talk of a wine growing history before the arrival of the Spaniards by the natives who used wild vines to produce their own drinks, adding other fruits. The entry of the wine growing culture to the country is said to start in the XV century. Catholicism and the customs of the colonists enabled the development of the wine culture in the country as it formed part of the diet of the colonists and served as a component of the religious rituals. This is how the cultivation of vines began to extend thanks to the first evangelizing missions, which were responsible for the first modern wine making in the country.

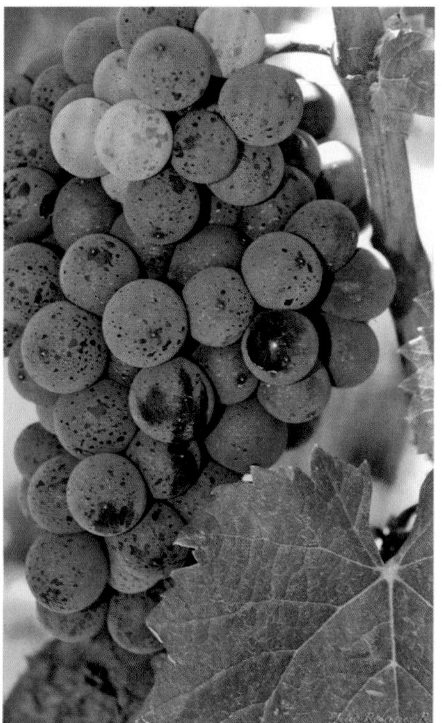

Mexico City, the ancient capital of the Spanish Viceroyalty, is considered to be the epicentre of the oenological movement. The cultivation of vines began to extend from this city towards the more southerly regions such as Querétaro, Guanajuato and San Luís de Potosí, then, there was movement towards Lower California, Sónora, Coahuila and Valle de Parras, due, among other things, to the incentive of the colonists to cultivate vines. However, a brake was put on the situation by the Spanish colonists, who soon saw that the cultivation of vines in Mexico was a drisk to their own wine making trade. This led to the imposition of prohibitions on the cultivation of vines, which, fortunately, was impossible to ensure owing to the vast extension of the country.
Despite the course of history, the decisive century for Mexico as a wine producing country was the XIX century. Again immigration was responsible for the point of inflexion. The travellers who arrived in the Gulf of Mexico brought oenological knowledge from Europe. However, the feared phylloxera (a vine parasite which directly attacks the roots and disable the plant for ever) also arrived, while the country was having political and social problems which would reach their climax in the Mexican Revolution of 1910. The phylloxera almost totally destroyed the Mexican vines.

Despite this, the plague was also a chance to remodel the Mexican vineyards. New varieties of grapes were planted brought fundamentally from France and little by little new technologies of oenology and wine growing brought from Europe were applied.

The XX century was not as beneficial for Mexico as it was in other countries with wine growing traditions. The historical non- involvement of the governments of the country gave an advantage to countries such as Chile and Argentina in the development of this industry. As from the eighties, Mexico underwent a change in its mentality and decided to focus its efforts on boosting its wine growing industry with common action oriented towards creating a Mexican brand. Today this policy continues its process of growth.

WINE GROWING AREAS

Mexico does not have legislation which regulates the areas of production in the country, nor does it have labelling. Despite this legal vacuum, the producers have grouped together in the zones where there is a greater concentration of vines. There are seven more relevant producer areas in the county: Lower California, Sonora, Coahuila, Durango, Aguascalientes, Zacatecas and Queretaro.

Lower California is the producer and exporter engine for Mexican wines, nearly 84% of the wine produced in the country belongs to this characteristic zone.

EXPORTATION

As can be supposed, the exportation figures for Mexico do not achieve the wine growing levels of Argentina and Chile. The latest data we have been able to collect for the Guide are those related to 2010, which are a little out of date, and which show that there is a lack of interest as regards the registering and control of their wine trade. Despite all this, the number of labels in Mexico is growing year by year, which leads us to believe that this data will slowly achieve market quotas over the years.

During 2010, Mexico obtained a total of 2.96 million dollars from exports, a figure lower than that of 2009, with graph peaks which show the lack of stability of a young oenological country. These almost three million dollars of exportation contrast with the 1,500 million dollars of the Chilean export balance, which shows that it is more an importer than an exporter country at the present time. Wine is consumed, but this is imported. The main purchases come fundamentally from Spain (37%) and Chile (25%). Most Mexican exports are concentrated in the United States and Canada, followed by Belgium and the United Kingdom.

The internal consumption figures are also low, which is much lower than the first wine producing countries in the world. This entails 0.16 litres per person per year as opposed to 16 litres for Chile, which places Mexico in position 65 as regards per capita consumption at global level. This low consumption is explained by two factors: the climate of the country, which is more inclined to the consumption of refreshing drinks, while the high duty on wine increases the final price so that it becomes a luxury product.

DESCRIPTION

It is known as the wine strip as it is responsible for nearly 85% of the production of wine in Mexico. It is located in the far northwest of Mexico, between California and the Tropic of Cancer.

ALTITUDES: between 200 metres and 900 metres in Valle de Ojos Negros.

NUMBER OF HECTARES: 2.551

PREDOMINANT VARIETIES:

Red wines: *cabernet sauvignon, merlot, syrah, nebbiolo* and *barbera.*
White wines: *chardonnay, sauvignon blanc* and *chenin blanc.*

CLIMATOLOGY AND SOILS

The climate is Mediterranean with wet winters, hot summers moderated by the fresh winds from the northwest Pacific and a scarcity of rainfall, and in some cases this means there is a need to irrigate vineyards. In the vineyards of Lower California, as a consequence of the influence of the ocean, there are substantial differences between the daytime and the night-time temperatures, which is beneficial for the correct grape maturing process.

The proximity of the vineyards to the Pacific Ocean provides the wines with a very peculiar hint of salinity as a result of the movements of the sea winds which mitigate the temperatures, transforming a warm climate to a temperate one. Although there are a variety of soils in Lower California, the most common are those of a sandy-clay nature.

PRODUCER ZONES

The vineyards of Lower California are concentrated within a radius of 90 kilometres from the city of Ensenada. The most important producer valleys are Valle de Guadalupe, Valle de Calafia, Valle de Santo Tomás, Valle de San Vicente and Valle de San Antonio de las Minas.

Valle de San Vicente: this is located 90 kilometres south of Ensenada, with altitudes from 350 metres to 420 metres above sea level. This is the valley which is nearest to the coast. The ocean is only 11 kilometres away, therefore, the sea influence is stronger than in the other valleys in Lower California. It has the advantage that there is a small mountain range located between the ocean and the vineyards of the valley, which prevents the massive entry of humidity. The wines of this valley have mineral nuances thanks to the clay-ferrous soils.

Valle de Ojos Negros: this is located towards the interior of the Peñínsula, at approximately 30 Km. from Ensenada. This valley lies at an altitude of 800 metres above sea level and its soils are clay-sandy. At the present time, there is only one producer in the zone, Bodega San Rafael. The average temperatures in the middle of the maturing process go from 15º to 35ºC.

Valle de Santo Tomás: this lies 45 kilometres south of Ensenada. This valley has very deep clay soils. Its climate is very hot in summer, with maximum temperatures of approximately 40ºC, which leads to full bodied wines, dominated by very mature fruit and may even be candied.

Valle de San Antonio de las Minas: this is located to the northwest of Ensenada and continues to extend to the start of the Valle de Guadalupe. Its vineyards are located fundamentally at the foot of a mountain with soil which is rich in granite. Its climate is very similar to the famous Valle de Guadalupe except that its proximity to the sea mitigates its daytime and night-time temperatures.

Valle de Guadalupe: this is the most well known of all and lies 25 kilometres from the Pacific Ocean, which notably affects the vines and the wine. It has a wide diversity of soils depending on the location and altitude, although the dominant edaphology is clay on the slopes with a granite composition which shape the valleys and very sandy in the centre, where the river beds run. This valley has a peculiarity which makes it different from the rest, and this is the salinity of the water which is used to irrigate the fields. In rainy years, this water will be less concentrated and will provide the wine with mineral sensations and saline hints in the mouth. However, in very dry years, the salt concentrates in the water hindering the maturing of the grape and providing excessively notable hints of salt. The Valle is characterized by very warm summers, with temperatures of approximately 35-40º in the daytime and 15-20º at night-time. Some summers there occurs the climatic phenomenon called the Santana effect which is the entry of a very warm, dry wind from the interior desert (in the area of Sonora), similar to the Saharan calimas. In these years, the grapes receive a heat wave which blocks and paralyzes them, therefore, care must be taken with the irrigation as the grapes can quickly lose their concentration of water and become overripe.

Valle de la Grulla: this is situated on the slopes of the Sierra de San Pedro Martir, at only 30 kilometres to the south of Ensenada. The vineyard lies on very sandy soils on the surface and clay in the intermediate layers. A crack or ravine in the mountain range makes it possible for the fresh, wet winds to come in from the ocean which makes this valley the freshest in Lower California. The excellent climatic and geographic qualities of the valley mean that it is a producer zone with substantial potential. The need for water for its vineyards is supplied due to its proximity to the mountain range, which provides water to the vineyards naturally.

ALXIMIA

Camino Vecinal al Tigre, Valle de Guadalupe
22800 Ensenada (Lower California)
☎: +52 646 947 5256
vino@alximia.com
www.alximia.com

GAIA 2011 T
cabernet sauvignon, tempranillo, syrah — Valle de Guadalupe

92 Colour: cherry, garnet rim. Nose: expressive, balsamic herbs, ripe fruit. Palate: flavourful, fruity, spicy, long, soft tannins.

HELIOS 2012 B
grenache — Valle de Guadalupe

90 Colour: onion pink. Nose: floral, wild herbs, saline, candied fruit. Palate: powerful, flavourful, fresh.

BELLA TERRA

Rancho Franchi s/n,
22750 Valle de Guadalupe (Lower California)
☎: +52 646 183 9013
josefranciscoperezk@gmail.com

BELLA TERRA MERLOT 2011 T
merlot — Valle de Guadalupe

91 Colour: bright cherry. Nose: ripe fruit, sweet spices, creamy oak, balsamic herbs. Palate: flavourful, fruity, toasty, round tannins.

NEBBIOLO BELLA TERRA 2010 T
nebbiolo — Ensenada

92 Colour: cherry, garnet rim. Nose: spicy, creamy oak, toasty, characterful, varietal, ripe fruit. Palate: powerful, flavourful, toasty, round tannins.

NEBBIOLO BELLA TERRA 2011 T
Ensenada

90 Colour: bright cherry. Nose: sweet spices, creamy oak, fruit preserve. Palate: flavourful, fruity, toasty, balanced.

PETIT SYRAH BELLA TERRA 2010 T
petite syrah — Valle de Guadalupe

90 Colour: deep cherry, purple rim. Nose: medium intensity, red berry notes, ripe fruit. Palate: balanced, round tannins, fine bitter notes.

BODEGA ABORIGEN

Ctra. Tecate - Ensenada, Km. 93.5, San Antonio de las Minas
22766 Ensenada (Lower California)
☎: +52 646 156 5312 - Fax: +52 646 156 5267
gloriaelenaramos@hotmail.com

CLANDESTINO T
garnacha, syrah — Valle de Guadalupe

90 Colour: bright cherry. Nose: spicy, ripe fruit, scrubland. Palate: flavourful, spicy, ripe fruit.

FECHA "1 DE OCTUBRE" 2009 T
cariñena — Valle de Guadalupe

91 Colour: cherry, garnet rim. Nose: complex, sweet spices, red berry notes, ripe fruit. Palate: good structure, good acidity, fine bitter notes.

BODEGA Y VIÑEDOS ERNESTO CAMOU Y CAMOU

22750 Valle de Guadalupe (Lower California)
☎: +52 646 156 8014 - Fax: +52 646 156 8014
ernestocamou2@yahoo.com

CABERNET SAUVIGNON A LA USANZA DE MEDOC 2010 T
cabernet sauvignon — Valle de Guadalupe

90 Colour: bright cherry. Nose: ripe fruit, sweet spices, creamy oak, wild herbs. Palate: flavourful, fruity, toasty, round tannins.

CENTENARIO 9 CHARDONNAY 2010 B
chardonnay — Valle de Guadalupe

90 Colour: bright yellow. Nose: powerfull, ripe fruit, sweet spices, creamy oak. Palate: rich, smoky aftertaste, flavourful, fresh, good acidity.

TEMPRANILLO A LA USANZA DE RIBERA DEL DUERO 2010 T
tempranillo — Valle de Guadalupe

90 Color cherry, garnet rim. Aroma ripe fruit, spicy, creamy oak, toasty, complex. Taste powerful, flavourful, toasty, round tannins.

BODEGAS SAN RAFAEL, S.P.R. DE R.L.

Parcela 73, Z1 P1 s/n, Ejido Real del Castillo
22770 Ensenada (Lower California)
☎: +52 646 178 3664 - Fax: +52 646 178 3664
contacto@bodegassanrafael.com
www.vinospassion.com

PASSIÓN 2008 T
cabernet sauvignon, cabernet franc, merlot, petit verdot, malbec
Valle de Ojos Negros

91 Colour: cherry, garnet rim. Nose: ripe fruit, spicy, creamy oak, toasty, complex. Palate: powerful, flavourful, toasty, round tannins.

BODEGAS SANTO TOMAS

Miramar, 666 Zona Centro
22800 Ensenada (Lower California)
☎: +52 646 178 8464
israelcontreras@grupopando.com
www.santo-tomas.com

SANTO TOMÁS BARBERA 2008 T
Barbera Valle de Santo Tomás

90 Colour: cherry, garnet rim. Nose: spicy, toasty, complex, ripe fruit, fruit expression, scrubland. Palate: powerful, flavourful, toasty, round tannins.

SANTO TOMÁS CABERNET SAUVIGNON 2009 T
Valle de Santo Tomás

90 Colour: cherry, garnet rim. Nose: red berry notes, ripe fruit, wild herbs, sweet spices, creamy oak. Palate: powerful, flavourful, good structure, toasty.

SANTO TOMÁS CHARDONNAY 2009 B
Valle de Santo Tomás

91 Color bright yellow. Aroma powerfull, ripe fruit, sweet spices, creamy oak, fragrant herbs. Taste rich, smoky aftertaste, flavourful, fresh, good acidity.

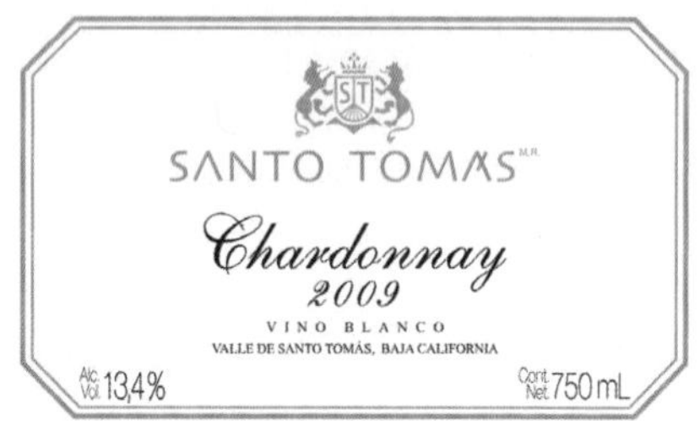

SANTO TOMÁS MERLOT 2011 T
merlot Valle de Santo Tomás

91 Colour: bright cherry. Nose: ripe fruit, sweet spices, creamy oak, expressive. Palate: flavourful, fruity, toasty, balanced.

SANTO TOMÁS TEMPRANILLO CABERNET 2011 T
Valle de Santo Tomás

90 Colour: cherry, garnet rim. Nose: wild herbs, ripe fruit, spicy, creamy oak. Palate: powerful, flavourful, fleshy, balsamic.

SANTO TOMÁS VIOGNIER 2011 B
viognier — Valle de Santo Tomás

90 Colour: bright straw. Nose: balanced, white flowers, jasmine, neat, saline. Palate: flavourful, full, ripe fruit.

SIROCCO 2006 T
syrah — Valle de Santo Tomás

91 Colour: cherry, garnet rim. Nose: ripe fruit, creamy oak, toasty, dark chocolate, complex. Palate: powerful, flavourful, toasty, round tannins.

TARDO MERLOT 2007 T
merlot — Valle de Santo Tomás

90 Colour: bright cherry. Nose: fruit preserve, sweet spices, aromatic coffee, cocoa bean. Palate: balanced, correct, good finish.

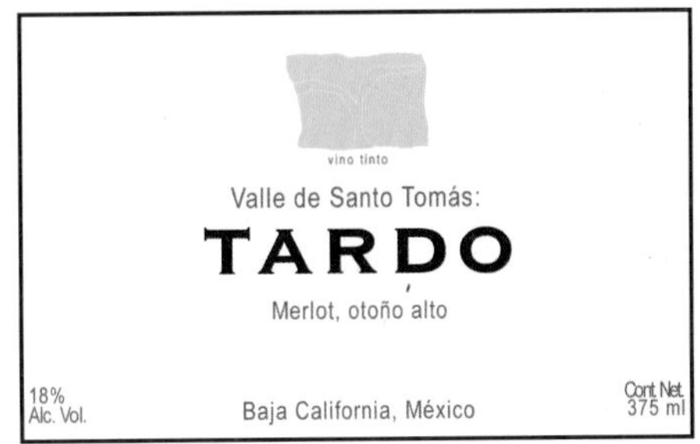

UNICO 2006 T
65% cabernet sauvignon, 35% merlot — Valle de Santo Tomás

90 Colour: cherry, garnet rim. Nose: elegant, spicy, aged wood nuances, fruit liqueur notes, expressive. Palate: spicy, long, elegant, fine tannins.

UNICO 2007 T

Valle de Santo Tomás

93 Colour: pale ruby, brick rim edge. Nose: elegant, spicy, fine reductive notes, wet leather, aged wood nuances. Palate: spicy, fine tannins, elegant, long.

VULTUS 2006 T

syrah, tempranillo, cabernet sauvignon

Valle de San Antonio de las Minas

91 Colour: cherry, garnet rim. Nose: creamy oak, toasty, complex, fruit preserve, overripe fruit, spicy. Palate: powerful, flavourful, toasty, round tannins.

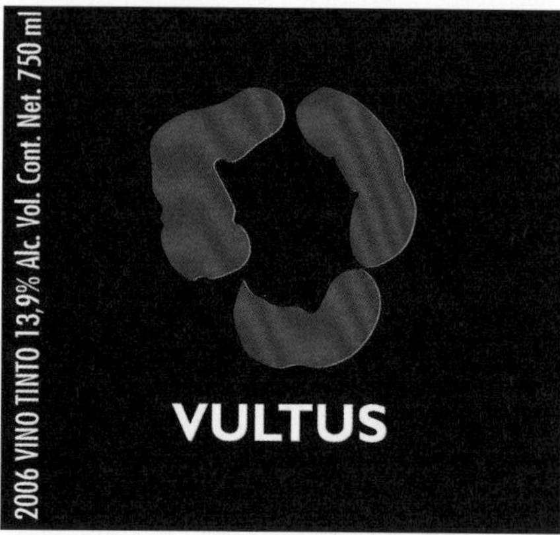

VULTUS 2008 T

Valle de San Antonio de las Minas

92 Colour: bright cherry. Nose: ripe fruit, sweet spices, creamy oak, expressive, balsamic herbs, mineral. Palate: flavourful, fruity, toasty, round tannins, balanced.

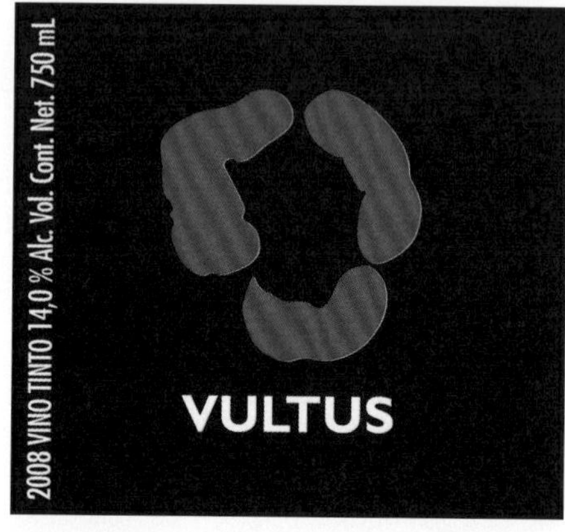

XALOC 2005 T

Valle de Santo Tomás

91 Colour: pale ruby, brick rim edge. Nose: elegant, aged wood nuances, fruit liqueur notes, toasty. Palate: spicy, fine tannins, long, elegant.

XALOC 2008 T

Valle de Santo Tomás

91 Colour: cherry, garnet rim. Nose: ripe fruit, spicy, creamy oak, toasty, complex, mineral, elegant. Palate: powerful, flavourful, toasty, round tannins, balanced.

YAGO 2008 T
cariñena, syrah, cabernet sauvignon

Valle de San Antonio de las Minas

90 Colour: cherry, garnet rim. Nose: spicy, creamy oak, toasty, complex, overripe fruit. Palate: powerful, flavourful, toasty, round tannins.

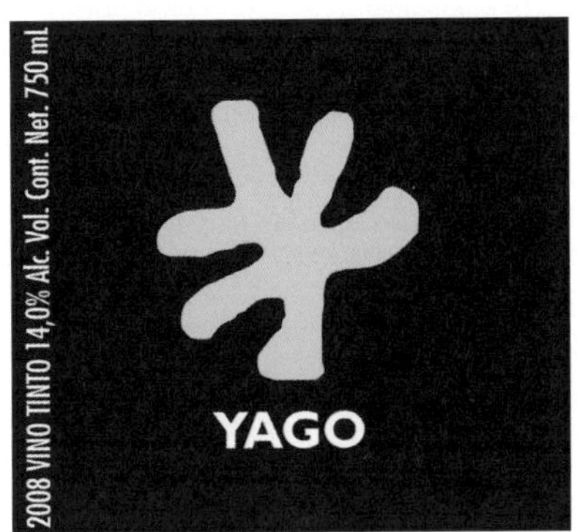

CASA DE PIEDRA

Ctra. Tecate-Ensenada, km 93,5 San Antonio de las Minas
22766 Ensenada (Lower California)
☎: +52 646 156 5267 - Fax: +52 646 156 5267
acpiedra@prodigy.net.mx
www.vinoscasadepiedra.com

CONTRASTE 2009 T
tempranillo, cabernet sauvignon, cariñena, garnacha, syrah

Valle de Guadalupe

91 Colour: cherry, garnet rim. Nose: spicy, creamy oak, toasty. Palate: powerful, flavourful, toasty, round tannins.

ENSAMBLE COLINA 2008 T
cabernet sauvignon, merlot, petite syrah, zinfandel, barbera

Valle de Guadalupe

91 Colour: bright cherry. Nose: ripe fruit, sweet spices, creamy oak, mineral, scrubland. Palate: flavourful, fruity, toasty, round tannins.

VINO DE PIEDRA 2009 T
50% tempranillo, 50% cabernet sauvignon Valle de Guadalupe

92 Colour: cherry, garnet rim. Nose: ripe fruit, balsamic herbs, balanced, expressive. Palate: good structure, flavourful, complex, good acidity, fine bitter notes, round tannins.

VINO DE PIEDRA 2010 T

Valle de Guadalupe

92 Colour: cherry, garnet rim. Nose: ripe fruit, balsamic herbs, mineral, earthy notes, saline, creamy oak, expressive. Palate: powerful, flavourful, complex, fleshy, spicy, balsamic, elegant.

CASA PEDRO DOMECQ PERNOD RICARD

Paseo de Tamarindos, 100
05120 Bosques de las Lomas (D.F.)
☎: +52 551 105 9537 - Fax: +52 551 105 9538
ines.delabarra@pernod-ricard.com
www.pernod-ricard.com

RESERVA MAGNA DOMECQ 2007 T
40% nebbiolo, 20% syrah, 20% cabernet sauvignon, 20% merlot

Valle de Guadalupe

90 Colour: cherry, garnet rim. Nose: ripe fruit, spicy, creamy oak, toasty, characterful. Palate: powerful, flavourful, toasty, round tannins.

CASTA VITIVINÍCOLA

Paseo de los Héroes, 9415 Local 27, Zona Río
Tijuana (Lower California)
☎: +52 664 648 3161
castadevinos.mx@gmail.com
www.castadevinos.com

CARDÓN 2011 T
60% syrah, 30% cabernet sauvignon, 10% mouvedre
Valle de Guadalupe

91 Colour: cherry, garnet rim. Nose: balanced, powerfull, balsamic herbs, spicy. Palate: balanced, spicy, long, round tannins.

CAVAS DEL MOGOR

Ctra. Ensenada –Tecate Km 85.5, San Antonio de las Minas
Ensenada (Lower California)
☎: +52 646 156 8156
natalia_badan@hotmail.com

CHASSELAS DEL MOGOR 2010 B
chasselas Valle de San Antonio de las Minas

90 Colour: bright straw. Nose: grassy, ripe fruit, citrus fruit. Palate: flavourful, spicy, long.

CUATRO CUATROS

Carretera Tijuana – Ensenada km 89 s/n
22760 Ensenada B.C. (El Tigre)
☎: +52 646 174 6595
luise.esquivel@hotmail.com
www.cuatrocuatros.mx

CUATRO CUATROS 2009 T
cabernet sauvignon, merlot, tempranillo Ensenada

90 Colour: bright cherry. Nose: ripe fruit, sweet spices, creamy oak. Palate: flavourful, fruity, toasty, round tannins.

CUATRO CUATROS 2010 B
sauvignon blanc Ensenada

90 Colour: yellow, greenish rim. Nose: complex, expressive, scrubland. Palate: flavourful, balanced, good acidity, fine bitter notes.

ESTACION DE OFICIOS / ESCUELITA

Avda. Emiliano Zapata, s/n Manzana 9, El Porvenir
22755 Ensenada (Lower California)
☎: +52 646 156 5267 - Fax: +52 646 156 5267
info@estacionporvenir.org
www.estacionporvenir.org

ESTACION PORVENIR 2009 T
petite syrah, cabernet sauvignon, zinfandel, barbera
Valle de Guadalupe

92 Colour: cherry, garnet rim. Nose: ripe fruit, spicy, creamy oak, toasty. Palate: powerful, flavourful, toasty, round tannins.

TXTURA 1 2008 T
tempranillo, zinfandel, garnacha Valle de Guadalupe

91 Colour: cherry, garnet rim. Nose: sweet spices, ripe fruit, toasty, mineral. Palate: flavourful, spicy, ripe fruit.

TXTURA 2 2008 T
cabernet sauvignon, merlot, petite syrah Valle de Guadalupe

91 Colour: cherry, garnet rim. Nose: expressive, complex, spicy, ripe fruit, elegant. Palate: balanced, fruity, good structure.

TXTURA 3 2009 T
cariñena Valle de Guadalupe

90 Colour: cherry, garnet rim. Nose: elegant, ripe fruit, spicy, complex. Palate: fruity, full, good acidity.

FIRMAMENTO

Parcela Escolar No. 85 Z-1 P1 4, El Porvenir
22755 Ensenada (Lower California)
☎: +52 646 156 5267 - Fax: +52 646 156 5267
gloriaelenaramos@hotmail.com

5 ESTRELLAS 2009 T
cabernet sauvignon, merlot, tempranillo, cinsault, garnacha
Valle de Guadalupe

91 Colour: cherry, garnet rim. Nose: ripe fruit, spicy, creamy oak, toasty, characterful, powerfull. Palate: powerful, flavourful, toasty, round tannins.

GRUPO PRODUCTOR CENTINELA

Dr. Flores Troncoso 63
21350 Mexicali (Lower California)
☎: +52 686 554 8926 - Fax: +52 686 554 8926
gpcvinos@yahoo.com.mx

RAÍCES COLONIALES DE BAJA CALIFORNIA 2011 T
nebbiolo — Valle de Guadalupe

90 Colour: cherry, garnet rim. Nose: balanced, powerfull, ripe fruit, dried herbs. Palate: fruity, good acidity, long.

RAÍCES COLONIALES DE BAJA CALIFORNIA 2011 T
merlot — Valle de Guadalupe

90 Colour: bright cherry, garnet rim. Nose: ripe fruit, fruit preserve, sweet spices. Palate: spicy, toasty, balanced.

RAÍCES DE BAJA CALIFORNIA 2009 T
100% merlot — Valle de Guadalupe

91 Colour: cherry, garnet rim. Nose: ripe fruit, spicy, creamy oak, toasty. Palate: powerful, flavourful, toasty, round tannins.

L.A. CETTO

Avda. Cañón Johnson, 2108 Col. Hidalgo
22465 Tijuana (Lower California)
☎: +52 664 685 3031 - Fax: +52 664 685 4450
valle@gpocetto.com
www.cettowines.com

ANGELO CETTO 2004 T
cabernet sauvignon, nebbiolo, montepulciano — Valle de Guadalupe

91 Colour: pale ruby, brick rim edge. Nose: elegant, spicy, fine reductive notes, wet leather, aged wood nuances, fruit liqueur notes. Palate: spicy, fine tannins, elegant, long.

CABERNET SAUVIGNON L.A. CETTO 2009 T
cabernet sauvignon — Valle de Guadalupe

90 Colour: cherry, garnet rim. Nose: ripe fruit, spicy, creamy oak, toasty. Palate: powerful, flavourful, toasty, round tannins.

CHARDONNAY L.A. CETTO 2011 B
chardonnay — Valle de Guadalupe

90 Colour: bright straw. Nose: fresh, fresh fruit, white flowers. Palate: flavourful, fruity, good acidity, balanced.

L.A. CETTO CHARDONNAY RESERVA PRIVADA 2009 B
chardonnay — Valle de Guadalupe

91 Colour: bright straw. Nose: powerfull, ripe fruit, citrus fruit, sweet spices, creamy oak. Palate: powerful, sweetness, fruity.

L.A. CETTO CHENIN BLANC 2011 B
chenin blanc — Valle de Guadalupe

90 Colour: bright straw. Nose: fresh, fresh fruit, white flowers. Palate: flavourful, fruity, good acidity, balanced.

L.A. CETTO FUMÉ BLANC 2001 B
sauvignon blanc — Valle de Guadalupe

90 Colour: bright straw. Nose: fresh, fresh fruit, white flowers, expressive, varietal. Palate: flavourful, fruity, good acidity, balanced.

MALBEC BOUTIQUE 2007 T
100% malbec — Valle de Guadalupe

90 Colour: cherry, garnet rim. Nose: powerfull, fruit liqueur notes, toasty, sweet spices. Palate: powerful, spicy, ripe fruit.

NEBBIOLO R.P. 2007 T
nebbiolo Valle de Guadalupe

91 Colour: cherry, purple rim. Nose: spicy, scrubland, balanced, ripe fruit. Palate: fruity, good acidity, round tannins.

PETITE SIRAH L.A. CETTO 2009 T
petite syrah Valle de Guadalupe

91 Colour: deep cherry. Nose: powerfull, complex, characterful, ripe fruit, sweet spices, toasty. Palate: powerful, flavourful, spicy, ripe fruit.

SANGIOVESE BOUTIQUE 2007 T
100% sangiovese Valle de Guadalupe

90 Colour: cherry, garnet rim. Nose: ripe fruit, spicy, creamy oak, toasty, mineral. Palate: powerful, flavourful, toasty, round tannins.

LAS NUBES BODEGAS Y VIÑEDOS

Callejón Emiliano Zapata, Ejido El Porvenir
22755 Ensenada (Lower California)
☎: +52 646 176 8120 - Fax: +52 646 176 9766
vicsegura@prodigy.net.mx
www.vinoslasnubesbc.com

CUMULUS 2009 T
garnacha, cariñena, tempranillo Valle de Guadalupe

90 Colour: bright cherry. Nose: sweet spices, creamy oak, ripe fruit, smoky. Palate: flavourful, fruity, toasty, round tannins.

KUIIY 2011 B
sauvignon blanc, chardonnay Valle de Guadalupe

91 Color bright straw. Aroma fresh, fresh fruit, white flowers, expressive. Taste flavourful, fruity, good acidity, balanced.

NEBBIOLO LAS NUBES 2009 T
nebbiolo Valle de Guadalupe

92 Colour: cherry, garnet rim. Nose: ripe fruit, spicy, creamy oak, toasty, characterful. Palate: powerful, flavourful, toasty, round tannins.

NIMBUS 2009 T
merlot, cabernet sauvignon, tempranillo Valle de Guadalupe

91 Colour: deep cherry. Nose: powerfull, expressive, ripe fruit, spicy. Palate: flavourful, ripe fruit, fine bitter notes.

MONTAÑO BENSON VINICULTORES

Ave Lopez Mateos 925-11b
22800 Ensenada (Lower California)
☎: +52 646 175 7865
montanobenson@yahoo.com

ESTELA 2010 T
95% zinfandel, 5% petit syrah Valle de Guadalupe

90 Colour: cherry, garnet rim. Nose: ripe fruit, spicy, creamy oak, toasty, complex. Palate: powerful, flavourful, toasty, round tannins, balanced.

MURMULLO 2009 T
barbera Valle de Guadalupe

91 Colour: cherry, garnet rim. Nose: candied fruit, sweet spices, mineral, dark chocolate. Palate: good structure, flavourful, long.

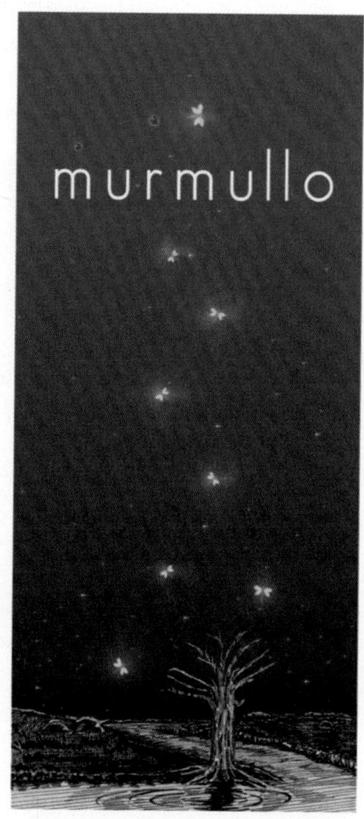

MONTE XANIC

Calle Principal a Ejido Francisco Zarco Rancho Monte Xanic s/n,
22750 Valle de Guadalupe - Ensenada (Lower California)
☎: +52 646 174 6155 - Fax: +52 555 545 1113
ventas@montexanic.com.mx
www.montexanic.com.mx

CALIXA CABERNET SAUVIGNON SYRAH 2010 T
60% cabernet sauvignon, 40% syrah — Valle de Guadalupe

91 Colour: bright cherry. Nose: ripe fruit, sweet spices, creamy oak, mineral. Palate: flavourful, fruity, toasty, round tannins.

MONTE XANIC CABERNET FRANC EDICIÓN LIMITADA 2011 T
cabernet franc — Valle de Guadalupe

90 Colour: cherry, garnet rim. Nose: medium intensity, spicy, balsamic herbs, mineral. Palate: balanced, fine tannins, long.

MONTE XANIC CHARDONNAY 2011 B
Valle de Guadalupe

90 Colour: bright yellow. Nose: powerfull, ripe fruit, sweet spices, creamy oak. Palate: rich, flavourful, fresh, good acidity.

MONTE XANIC GRAN RICARDO 2009 T
72% cabernet sauvignon, 18% merlot, 10% petit verdot
Valle de Guadalupe

90 Colour: cherry, garnet rim. Nose: ripe fruit, spicy, creamy oak, toasty, powerfull. Palate: powerful, flavourful, toasty, round tannins.

MONTE XANIC GRAN RICARDO 2011 T
Valle de Guadalupe

93 Colour: cherry, garnet rim. Nose: red berry notes, ripe fruit, sweet spices, creamy oak, mineral, expressive. Palate: powerful, flavourful, correct, long, toasty, balanced.

MONTE XANIC MERLOT 2011 T
merlot — Valle de Guadalupe

90 Colour: cherry, garnet rim. Nose: balanced, ripe fruit, scrubland. Palate: flavourful, spicy, round tannins.

MONTE XANIC SAUVIGNON BLANC 2011 B
100% sauvignon blanc — Valle de Guadalupe

90 Colour: bright straw. Nose: white flowers, citrus fruit, ripe fruit. Palate: flavourful, correct, fine bitter notes.

MONTE XANIC SAUVIGNON BLANC 2012 B
sauvignon blanc — Valle de Guadalupe

91 Colour: bright straw. Nose: fresh, fresh fruit, white flowers, tropical fruit. Palate: flavourful, fruity, good acidity, balanced.

NATIVO VINÍCOLA

San Antonio de las MInas
Ensenada (Lower California)
☎: +52 664 130 1306
nahara@nativovinicola.com
www.nativovinicola.com

PAI PAI NATIVO CABERNET SAUVIGNON 2010 T
cabernet sauvignon, carignan — Valle de San Antonio de las Minas

90 Colour: cherry, garnet rim. Nose: ripe fruit, spicy, creamy oak, complex. Palate: powerful, flavourful, toasty, round tannins.

SINERGI VITICULTURA

Granada, 2100 A Fracc. Granados
22480 Ensenada (Lower California)
☎: +52 646 176 5852
joseluisdurand@gmail.com
www.sinergi-vt.com

ICARO 2009 T
nebbiolo, cabernet sauvignon, petite syrah, petit verdot, merlot
Ensenada

90 Colour: black cherry, purple rim. Nose: red berry notes, balanced, sweet spices, fruit preserve. Palate: flavourful, rich.

TRES VALLES

Ignacio Comonfort, San Antonio de las Minas
22760 Ensenada (Lower California)
☎: +52 646 178 8052 - Fax: +52 646 178 2255
tres-valles@prodigy.net.mx
www.vinostresvalles.com

KOJÁA 2009 T
petit sirah — Valle de Guadalupe

90 Colour: cherry, garnet rim. Nose: powerfull, ripe fruit, fruit preserve, dark chocolate. Palate: good structure, sweet tannins.

KUWAL 2010 T
tempranillo, Grenache Noir, Ruby Cabernet Valle de Guadalupe

90 Colour: cherry, garnet rim. Nose: red berry notes, ripe fruit, saline, spicy, creamy oak. Palate: powerful, flavourful, balsamic, balanced.

VENA CAVA

Hotel La Villa del Valle - Rancho San Marcos - Toros Pintos, s/n Valle de Guadalupe
22750 Ensenada (Lower California)
☎: +52 646 156 8007 - Fax: +52 646 156 8007
info@lavilladelvalle.com
www.venacavawine.com

VENA CAVA 2010 T
Valle de Guadalupe

90 Colour: cherry, garnet rim. Nose: ripe fruit, creamy oak, toasty, spicy, balsamic herbs. Palate: powerful, flavourful, toasty, round tannins.

VENA CAVA BIG BLEND 2009 T
45% petit syrah, 32% zinfandel, 16% cabernet sauvignon, 7% garnacha Valle de Guadalupe

90 Colour: bright cherry. Nose: ripe fruit, sweet spices, creamy oak, expressive, mineral. Palate: flavourful, fruity, toasty, round tannins.

VINÍCOLA ADOBE GUADALUPE S. DE R.L. DE C.V.

Parcela A-1, s/n Col. Rusa de Guadalupe
22750 Ensenada (Lower California)
☎: +52 646 155 2094 - Fax: +52 646 155 2093
info@adobeguadalupe.com
www.adobeguadalupe.com

GABRIEL 2010 T
38% merlot, 30% cabernet sauvignon, 9% cabernet franc
Valle de Guadalupe

91 Colour: deep cherry, garnet rim. Nose: complex, expressive, ripe fruit, balsamic herbs, spicy. Palate: balanced, flavourful, good structure, round tannins.

KERUBIEL 2010 T
44% syrah, 22% cinsault, 17% garnacha, 17% mourvedre
Valle de Guadalupe

92 Colour: cherry, garnet rim. Nose: complex, balanced, expressive, ripe fruit. Palate: spicy, long, good acidity.

RAFAEL 2010 T
cabernet sauvignon, nebbiolo Valle de Guadalupe

90 Colour: cherry, garnet rim. Nose: red berry notes, ripe fruit, balsamic herbs, sweet spices. Palate: powerful, flavourful, long, toasty.

VINÍCOLA FRATERNIDAD

Adolfo López Mateos, 2025 Col. Obrera
22830 Ensenada (Lower California)
☎: +52 646 176 1959 - Fax: +52 646 176 1959
www.vinicolafraternidad.com.mx

BOCETO 2009 T
tempranillo, cabernet sauvignon, nebbiolo Valle de Guadalupe

90 Colour: bright cherry. Nose: ripe fruit, sweet spices, creamy oak, expressive. Palate: flavourful, fruity, toasty, round tannins.

NUVA 2010 B
chardonnay, sauvignon blanc, moscato canelli Valle de Guadalupe

91 Color bright yellow. Aroma powerfull, ripe fruit, sweet spices, creamy oak, fragrant herbs. Taste rich, smoky aftertaste, flavourful, fresh, good acidity.

TRAZO 2009 T
tempranillo, cabernet sauvignon, merlot, petit verdot
Valle de Guadalupe

90 Colour: cherry, garnet rim. Nose: balanced, cocoa bean, creamy oak, ripe fruit, mineral. Palate: good structure, fruity, round tannins.

VINÍCOLA LA TRINIDAD

Paseo de las Rosas, 213, Fracc. Villa Las Rosas
22760 Ensenada (Lower California)
☎: +52 646 947 6161
patricia@latrinidadvinos.com
www.latrinidadvinos.com

FAUNO 2009 T
nebbiolo, cabernet sauvignon, zinfandel Valle de Guadalupe

93 Colour: cherry, garnet rim. Nose: ripe fruit, spicy, toasty, complex. Palate: powerful, flavourful, toasty, round tannins.

FAUNO 2011 T
nebbiolo, cabernet sauvignon, zindandel Valle de Guadalupe

91 Colour: deep cherry, garnet rim. Nose: wild herbs, red berry notes, ripe fruit, dry stone. Palate: flavourful, powerful, long, round tannins.

MINOTAURO 2011 T
cabernet sauvignon, zifandel Valle de Guadalupe

90 Colour: cherry, garnet rim. Nose: balanced, expressive, ripe fruit, spicy. Palate: balanced, long, good acidity.

VINÍCOLA NORTE 32

Fondo Calle Diez , s/n Francisco Zarco, Valle de Guadalupe
2275 Ensenada (Lower California)
☎: +52 646 947 8052
tintosdelnorte32@yahoo.com.mx
www.norte32.com

NORTE 32 ETIQUETA BLANCA 2009 T
cabernet sauvignon Valle de Guadalupe

91 Colour: cherry, garnet rim. Nose: ripe fruit, spicy, expressive. Palate: powerful, flavourful, toasty, round tannins.

NORTE 32 ETIQUETA BLANCA 2011 T
cabernet sauvignon Valle de Guadalupe

91 Colour: cherry, garnet rim. Nose: complex, balsamic herbs, spicy. Palate: balanced, good acidity, round tannins.

NORTE 32 ETIQUETA NEGRO 2010 T
tempranillo, syrah Valle de Guadalupe

91 Colour: cherry, garnet rim. Nose: powerfull, ripe fruit, fruit expression, warm, dark chocolate, toasty. Palate: powerful, flavourful, fleshy, spicy.

NORTE 32 ETIQUETA NEGRO 2011 T
Valle de Guadalupe

91 Colour: deep cherry, garnet rim. Nose: toasty, spicy, ripe fruit. Palate: good structure, flavourful, round tannins.

TEZIANO 2009 T
cabernet sauvignon Valle de Guadalupe

90 Colour: cherry, garnet rim. Nose: ripe fruit, mineral, elegant. Palate: good acidity, flavourful, powerful, balanced.

VINÍCOLA RINCÓN DE GUADALUPE

Calle Seginda entre Guadalupe e Hidalgo, Local 11
22800 Ensenada (Lower California)
☎: +52 646 177 0577 - Fax: +52 646 177 0577
vinicola@rincondeguadalupe.com
www.rincondeguadalupe.com

BRISA DE SUR 2008 T
cabernet sauvignon, merlot Valle de San Vicente

90 Colour: cherry, garnet rim. Nose: candied fruit, powerfull, warm, sweet spices. Palate: ripe fruit, long, round tannins.

VINÍCOLA TORRES ALEGRE Y FAMILIA

Valle de Guadalupe
22840 Ensenada (Lower California)
☎: +52 646 176 3345
contacto@torresalegre.com
www.vinicolatorresalegreyfamilia.com

LA LLAVE BLANCA 2006 B
sauvignon blanc, chenin blanc Valle de Guadalupe

91 Colour: bright yellow. Nose: candied fruit, sweet spices, balanced, expressive. Palate: balanced, good acidity, fine bitter notes, ripe fruit.

NEBBIOLO CRU GARAGE 2006 T
nebbiolo Valle de Guadalupe

90 Colour: cherry, garnet rim. Nose: dark chocolate, ripe fruit, sweet spices. Palate: ripe fruit, long, correct, round tannins.

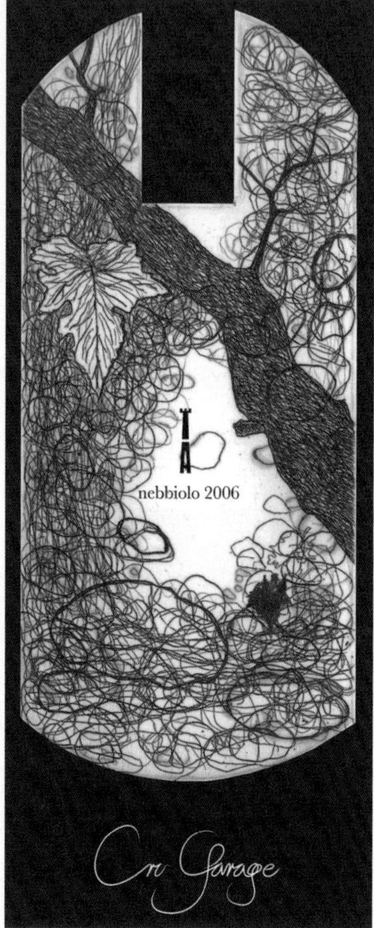

VINÍCOLA VI

Privada Sauce, 3288 Terrazas El Gallo
22850 Ensenada (Lower California)
☎: +52 646 171 6914 - Fax: +52 646 174 5189
mmorales@uabc.edu.mx

VI 2008 T
cabernet sauvignon Valle de Guadalupe

90 Colour: cherry, garnet rim. Nose: ripe fruit, spicy, creamy oak, toasty, complex. Palate: powerful, flavourful, toasty, round tannins.

VINISTERRA

San Antonio de las Minas
22800 Ensenada (Lower California)
☎: +52 646 178 3350
contacto@vinisterra.com
www.vinisterra.com

MACOUZET TEMPRANILLO 2007 T
tempranillo Valle de Guadalupe

91 Colour: deep cherry, garnet rim. Nose: expressive, balanced, ripe fruit, sweet spices. Palate: good structure, flavourful, ripe fruit, long.

PIES DE TIERRA 2009 T
Valle de Guadalupe

93 Colour: cherry, garnet rim. Nose: ripe fruit, spicy, creamy oak, toasty, complex, earthy notes. Palate: powerful, flavourful, toasty, round tannins, balanced.

VINOS EL CIELO

Parcela No. 118 km. 7,5 Ctra. Guadalupe - El Tigre Ejido
El Porvenir, Ensenada (Lower California)
contacto@vinoselcielo.com
www.vinoselcielo.com

CASSIOPEA 2012 B
sauvignon blanc Lower California

90 Colour: bright straw. Nose: citrus fruit, wild herbs, floral, expressive. Palate: correct, fleshy, fresh, fruity, flavourful, balanced.

EL CIELO CAPRICORNIUS 2011 B
chardonnay Lower California

91 Color bright yellow. Aroma powerfull, ripe fruit, sweet spices, creamy oak, fragrant herbs. Taste rich, smoky aftertaste, flavourful, fresh, good acidity.

VINOS XECUE

Km. 89,1 Ctra. Ensenada - Tecate Camino Vecinal
Rancho El Chivatillo, San Antonio de las Minas
22750 Ensenada (Lower California)
☎: +52 646 175 3830 - Fax: +52 646 175 3830
aceja37@yahoo.com.mx
www.xecue.com

RELATO MEXICANO 2010 T
cabernet sauvignon, merlot, zinfandel, malbec Valle de Guadalupe

91 Colour: bright cherry. Nose: ripe fruit, sweet spices, creamy oak, expressive, mineral. Palate: flavourful, fruity, toasty, round tannins, good acidity.

XECUE CABERNET SAUVIGNON 2010 T
cabernet sauvignon Valle de San Antonio de las Minas

90 Colour: cherry, garnet rim. Nose: ripe fruit, spicy, creamy oak, toasty, fruit preserve. Palate: powerful, flavourful, toasty, round tannins.

VIÑA DE LICEAGA

Ctra. Tecate-Ensenada, Km. 93, San Antonio De Las Minas
22766 Ensenada (Lower California)
☎: +52 646 156 5313 - Fax: +52 646 178 2922
info@vinosliceaga.com
www.vinosliceaga.com

LICEAGA ETIQUETA L 2008 T
80% syrah, 20% merlot Valle de San Antonio de las Minas

92 Color cherry, garnet rim. Aroma ripe fruit, spicy, creamy oak, toasty, complex. Taste powerful, flavourful, toasty, round tannins.

LICEAGA MERLOT 2007 TGR
95% merlot, 5% cabernet sauvignon
Valle de San Antonio de las Minas

90 Colour: pale ruby, brick rim edge. Nose: expressive, spicy, cocoa bean, ripe fruit. Palate: flavourful, powerful, spicy.

VIÑAS DE GARZA

Rancho Mogorcito, Ctra. Tecate-Ensenada, Km. 87
Valle de Guadalupe
Ensenada (Lower California)
☎: +52 646 175 8883
informacion@vinosdegarza.com
www.vinosdegarza.com

AMADO IV 2007 T
Valle de Guadalupe

91 Colour: cherry, garnet rim. Nose: ripe fruit, spicy, creamy oak, toasty, characterful. Palate: powerful, flavourful, toasty, round tannins.

COLINA NORTE 2008 T
Valle de Guadalupe

90 Colour: cherry, garnet rim. Nose: ripe fruit, spicy, creamy oak. Palate: powerful, flavourful, toasty, round tannins.

VIÑAS PIJOAN

Km. 12 + 800 Ctra. El Tigre a Valle de Guadalupe
22750 Ensenada (Lower California)
☎: +52 646 178 3482
info@vinospijoan.com
www.vinospijoan.com

CARMEN MARÍA 2008 T
petite syrah, cabernet sauvignon Valle de Guadalupe

90 Colour: cherry, garnet rim. Nose: spicy, creamy oak, sweet spices, dark chocolate, overripe fruit. Palate: powerful, flavourful, toasty, round tannins.

LEONORA 2009 T
cabernet sauvignon, merlot Valle de Guadalupe

90 Colour: cherry, garnet rim. Nose: powerfull, ripe fruit, sweet spices, toasty. Palate: flavourful, spicy, ripe fruit, long.

VIÑAS TIERRA SANTA

Camino a Tierra Santa, parcela 196
Ejido El Porvenir, Valle de Guadalupe (Lower California)
☎: +52 646 178 2071 - Fax: +52 646 178 2071
nomuraens@hotmail.com

MISION LORETO CABERNET SAUVIGNON 2008 T
cabernet sauvignon Valle de Guadalupe

91 Colour: cherry, garnet rim. Nose: spicy, creamy oak, toasty, characterful. Palate: powerful, flavourful, toasty, round tannins.

MISION LORETO SYRAH 2008 T
syrah Valle de Guadalupe

90 Colour: bright cherry. Nose: ripe fruit, sweet spices, creamy oak, expressive. Palate: flavourful, fruity, toasty, long, round tannins.

VIÑEDOS ALDO CÉSAR PALAFOX

Km. 42,5 Ctra. TransPeñínsular Ensenada La Paz
22800 Ensenada (Lower California)
☎: +52 646 174 6145 - Fax: +52 646 174 6145
correo@aldopalafox.com
www.aldopalafox.com

TRIBUTO 2010 T
cabernet sauvignon, merlot Valle de Santo Tomás

91 Colour: deep cherry, garnet rim. Nose: scrubland, complex, ripe fruit. Palate: good structure, good acidity, round tannins.

VIÑEDOS MALAGÓN

Calle Sexta, 75
Francisco Zarco (Ensenada)
☎: +52 646 155 2102
info@vinedosmalagon.com
www.vinedosmalagon.com

MALAGON EL GRENACHE 2009 T
garnacha Valle de Guadalupe

90 Colour: pale ruby, brick rim edge. Nose: candied fruit, fruit liqueur notes, toasty, spicy. Palate: powerful, flavourful, spicy.

MALAGON RESERVA DE LA FAMILIA 2009 T
grenache, petite syrah, cabernet sauvignon, merlot
Valle de Guadalupe

90 Colour: bright cherry. Nose: medium intensity, ripe fruit, fruit liqueur notes, spicy, aromatic coffee. Palate: flavourful, powerful, spicy.

VIÑEDOS TIERRA DE GRACIA

Lázaro Cárdenas, 1601 4ª Col. La Bodega
21377 Mexicali (Lower California)
☎: +52 686 577 5410 - Fax: +52 686 577 5410
info@tierradegracia.com.mx
www.tierradegracia.com.mx

AMARO 2009 T
barbera, zinfandel, merlot, petite syrah Valle de Guadalupe

91 Colour: cherry, garnet rim. Nose: powerfull, ripe fruit, sweet spices. Palate: flavourful, powerful, good acidity.

CASTA VITIVINÍCOLA

Paseo de los Héroes, 9415 Local 27, Zona Río
Tijuana (Lower California)
☎: +52 664 648 3161
castadevinos.mx@gmail.com
www.castadevinos.com

CASTA TINTA 2011 T
syrah Valle de Guadalupe

90 Colour: cherry, garnet rim. Nose: ripe fruit, violet drops, spicy, balsamic herbs. Palate: balanced, powerful, flavourful, fleshy, long, toasty.

CIRIO 7 BARRICAS 2011 T
50% mourvèdre, 50% cabernet sauvignon Valle de Guadalupe

90 Colour: cherry, garnet rim. Nose: scrubland, spicy, ripe fruit. Palate: flavourful, good structure, ripe fruit, fine tannins.

DESCRIPTION

This is located in the northeast of the country; it has borders with the States of Chihuahua and Durango, in the south with another producer zone of Mexico, Zacatecas, in the east with Nuevo León and in the north with the United States.

ALTITUDES: The vineyards lie at an average altitude of 1,000 metres above sea level.

PREDOMINANT VARIETIES:
Red wines: *cabernet sauvignon, merlot, syrah, tempranillo, lenoir y rosa del Perú.*
White wines: *chardonnay, chenin blanc, semillón y colombard.*

CLIMATOLOGY AND SOILS

In this area, due to its extension, there are several different types of climates although the most common is the arid climate. Despite this, most of the vineyards are concentrated in the south of the State owing fundamentally to the continental-Mediterranean temperate climate with fresh winters and warm summers.

Coahuila is dominated by the presence of Sierra Madre Oriental, a mountain range which crosses the State from north to south. It is over 1,300 kilometres long and has altitudes reaching 3,000 metres above sea level. As well as this characteristic mountainous location, there are also wide desert and semi-desert zones.

PRODUCER ZONES

Most of the vineyards of the zone are concentrated in the southernmost part of the State, in the towns of Parras de la Fuente, Arteaga and Saltillo.

None of the wines tasted achieve the minimum required scoring

DESCRIPTION

This is located in the centre of Mexico, between the end of the Sierra Madre Occidental and the Sierra Madre Oriental. The State of Guanajuato to the north with San Luís de Potosí, to the south with Michoacán, to the east with Querétaro and to the west with Jalisco. This is the State where the movement for independence arose which would end the Spanish domination of Mexico more than 200 years ago. This marked the beginning of a new horizon for the formation of the country.

ALTITUDES: average altitude 1,900 metres above sea level.

PREDOMINANT VARIETIES:

Red wines: *cabernet sauvignon, merlot, syrah, cabernet franc, tempranillo and malbec.*
White wines: *semillón.*

CLIMATOLOGY AND SOILS

The climatic conditions of Guanajuato involve several factors. The greater or lesser proximity to the sea, the influence of the polar winds and the influence of the mountain range of Sierra Madre, factors which define the climate of each zone. Thus, although there are three types of climates in the State depending on the proximity to the mountains, the production area of the grapes has a temperate climate, with temperatures of approximately 18ºC and with rainfall generally in the summer months. The vineyards of Guanajuato have sandy-loam soils.

PRODUCER ZONES

The towns of Dolores Hidalgo and San Miguel de Allende are responsible for the production of wine in the zone, with approximately 20 hectares of cultivated vineyards.

BODEGAS VEGA MANCHON

Ctra. Dolores Hidalgo a San Luis de la Paz
37800 El Rosillo (Guanajuato)
☎: +52 415 152 8205
cynthia@cunadetierra.com.mx
www.cunadetierra.com.mx

CLOS LA MAR 2010 T
nebbiolo, merlot, syrah — Guanajuato

90 Colour: bright cherry. Nose: ripe fruit, sweet spices, creamy oak, dried herbs. Palate: flavourful, fruity, toasty, round tannins.

DESCRIPTION

Located in the centre of the country it has a border to the north with San Luis Potosí, to the west with Guanajuato, to the east with Hidalgo and to the southwest with Michoacán.

ALTITUDES: the region has altitudes which go from 760 metres to 3,300 metres in the northernmost part.

PREDOMINANT VARIETIES:

Red wines: *cabernet sauvignon, merlot, pinot noir, gamay, pinot gris and malbec.*
White wines: *saint emilion, chenin, sauvignon blanc and macabeo.*

CLIMATOLOGY AND SOILS

There are a number of climates due fundamentally to the Sierra Madre Oriental in the north of the State. The climate is predominantly dry with the exception of the northern region, where there are moderate temperatures and more abundant rainfall than in the south.

Located in the heart of Mexico, the region has the Sierra Madre Oriental which gives its northern zone a climate different from the rest of the State. The vineyards are located far from this mountain range, in a zone dominated by the valleys and by lower altitudes than in the northern region. The absence of rainfall obliges the producers to make use of springs near the vineyards so as to benefit their vineyards. There are up to nine water bearing channels in Querétaro used to supply the State with water.

PRODUCER ZONES

The main wine production zones of Querétaro are located in the centre-south of the State in the towns of San Juan del Río and Ezequiel Montes, where the dominant climate is temperate semi-dry.

None of the wines tasted achieve the minimum required scoring

GLOSSARY AND INDEXES

TERMINOLOGY RELATED TO COLOUR

AMBER. The first step in the oxidative ageing of sherry generoso wines, brandies, whiskies and rum, somewhere between yellow and coppery red.

BEADS. The slow rising string of bubbles in a sparkling wine.

BRICK RED. An orangey hue, similar to that of a brick, used to describe reds aged in bottle for more than 10 years or inbarrel for longer than six.

BRILLIANT. Related to a young and neat wine.

CANDY CHERRY. This is used to define a colour lighter than a red but darker than a rosé.

CLEAN. Utterly clean, immaculate.

CLOUDY. Lacking clarity.

COPPERY. A reddish nuance that can be appreciated in whites aged in wood for a long period, generally amontillados and some palo cortados.

CHERRY. Commonly used to express red colour. It can take all sort of degrees from 'light' all the way to 'very dark' or almost 'black cherry'.

DARK. This often refers to a tone slightly lighter than 'deep' and synonymous to "medium-intensity".

DEEP. A red with a very dark colour, which hardly lets us see the bottom of the glass.

DULL. A wine lacking in liveliness, usually with an ochre hue.

GARNET RED. A common nuance in medium to light reds. If the wine is an intense cherry red it could have a garnet rim only if it comes from cooler regions; if it is more luminous and open than the violet rim of a dark wine, it generally would be a young wine.

GOLDEN. Gold in colour with yellow –predominantly– to reddish tones.

GLIMMER. A vague brilliance.

IODINE. A tone similar to iodine tincture stains (old gold and brownish) displayed by rancio and generoso wines have after their long oxidative ageing.

LIVELY. A reflection of the youth of a wine through bright, brilliant colours.

MAHOGANY. Describes the second stage of ageing in brandies, rum and generoso sherry (fortified) wines. A hue between brown and yellow displayed by wines when long aged.

OCHRE. Yellow-orangey hue, the last colour phase of a table wine, generally found in wines with a long oxidative ageing; it is a sign of their decline.

OILY. A wine that appears dense to the eye, usually sweet and with high alcohol content.

OLD GOLD. Gold colour with the brownish tones found in amontillados and a bit lighter than the mahogany nuance predominant in oloroso sherry.

ONION SKIN. A touch lighter than salmon colour.

OPAQUE. A wine with such depth of colour we cannot see the bottom of the glass. Generally found in very old pedro ximénez and therefore akin to caramelised notes.

OPEN. Very pale, not at all intense.

ORANGEY EDGE. Intermediate phase between a deep red and brick red found towards the rim in red wines of a medium age. It generally appears sooner in wines with higher alcohol content and it is also typical of wines made from pinot noir.

RASPBERRY. Sort of pinkish colour with a bluish rim, it is the optimal colour for rosé wines since it denotes freshness, youth and a good acidity.

RIM. Also known as 'edge', it refers to the lighter colour the wine displays at the edge of the oval when we hold the glass at 45º, as opposed to the 'core' or main body of colour right in the centre. If it is a young red, it will show normally violet or raspberry nuances; when slightly older, it will be a deeper red or garnet, and if has been in the bottle for more than five years it might be anything from ruby to tawny through brick red and orangey.

RUBY. Slightly orangey hue with a yellow nuance found in old wines that have lost part of their original cherry colour.

SALMON. A tone slightly redder than pink found in rosé wines with less acidity and more alcohol.

STEELY. Pale colour with metallic reflections (reminiscent of those from steel) found in some whites.

STRAW-COLOURED. This term should be understood asstraw yellow, the colour found in the majority of young white wines, halfway between yellow and green. It can also be described as "lemony".

TERMINOLOGY RELATED TO AROMA

ACETONE. Very close notes to those of nail varnish, typical of very old eau de vie.

ALCOHOL. It is not a pejorative term for an excess of alcohol –in which case we would refer to it as burning–, but just a predominant, non-aggressive note.

ALDEHYDE. A sensory note of oxidized, slightly rancid alcohol, typical of old wines with high alcohol content that have undergone oxidative ageing.

ANIMAL. Not a positive note, generally the result of long storage in bottle, also referred to as 'wet dog' or 'wet hide' and normally associated with a lack of hygiene. If it is found in younger vintages, then it could be a symptom of "brett" (see brett).

ATTIC. An aroma associated with that of old dry wood and dust typical of attics, mainly found in fortified wines aged in wood and in very old wines aged for a long period in old barrels which happen to have also been bottled for more than ten years.

BALSAMIC. A trait usually associated to wood-aged wines in hot regions, where high temperatures accelerate their evolution. It also refers to the aroma of dry herbs such as eucalyptus and bay leaf, as well as incense and tar.

BLACK FRUIT. It refers to the sort of toasted aromas of very ripe grapes, those almost 'burnt skin' notes found in reds that have undergone a long vatting period in contact with the skins.

"BRETT". This is the abbreviation for a new term (brettanomyces) to describe an old problem: the aroma of stables, henhouse, and wet new leather generally found along with reductive off-odours in wines that have been in the bottle for more than ten years. These aromas were considered part of the sensory complexity of old wines and therefore tolerated. Nowadays, due to better olfactory research and more hygienic working conditions in the wineries, they are easily detected and considered more a defect. In addition, today brett is often found in younger wines as this particular bacteria or yeast usually develops better in wines with higher ph levels.
The increase in the ph of wines is quite common these days due to global warming, riper grapes and the use of fertilizers over the past thirty-five years.

BROOM. An aroma reminiscent of Mediterranean shrubs, only a bit dryer.

CANDIED FRUIT. This is a sweet nuance, somewhere between toasted and jammy, which is found in whites with a long oxidative ageing and in some sweet white wines.

CAROB. Anybody who has chewed or smelt one of those beans cannot would easily recall its typical blend of sweetness and toasted notes, as well as the slightly rustic nuance. It is usually found in old brandy aged in soleras of pedro ximénez and in deep, concentrated wines made from very ripe grapes.

CEDAR. The somewhat perfumed aroma of cedar, a soft wood commonly found in Morocco.

CITRUS. An aroma reminiscent of lemon, orange and grapefruit.

CLASSIC RIOJA. A note named after the more traditional and popular style of Rioja, with predominantly woody notes (normally from very old wood) along with a typical character of sweet spices and occasionally candle wax nuances instead of fruit, given the oxidative character provided by long ageing periods.

CLEAR. A wine with no defects, neither in the nose nor in the palate.

CLOSED. A term to describe a faint or not properly developed nose. Almost always found in concentrated wines from a good vintage, which evolve very slowly in the bottle, but it can also be found in wines recently bottled.

COCOA. Delicate, slightly toasted aroma found in wines aged in wood for a moderately long time that have evolved very well in the bottle.

COMPLEX. A wine abundant in aromas and flavours related either to grape variety, soil or ageing, although none of those features is particularly prominent.

CREAMY. Aroma of finely toasted oak (usually French) with notes of caramelised vanilla.

DATES. A sweet aroma with hints of dates and a raisiny nuance.

EARTHY. An aroma somewhere between clay and dust typical of red wines made from ripe grapes and with high alcohol content. It can also refer in some wines to a mineral nuance.

ELEGANT. A harmonious combination of fine, somewhat restrained aromatic notes related to perfumed wood, and a light, pleasantly balanced richness or complexity (see complex).

ETHEREAL. This is used to describe spirits, fortified wines and wines with a certain intensity of alcohol in their oxidative evolution; the strength of the alcohol reveals the rancid-type aromas. It has a lot to do with age.

WITHERED FLOWERS. This is a sort of 'toasty' nuance typical of good champagnes made with a high percentage of pinot noir and some cavas which have aged perfectly in the bottle and on their lees for a long time.

FINE. A synonym for elegant.

FINE LEES. This is an aroma between herbaceous and slightly toasty that is produced by the contact of the wine with the lees (dead yeasts cells) after the fermentation has taken place, a process called autolysis that helps to make the wine more complex and to give it a richer aroma.

FLOR. This is a pungent, saline aroma typically found in sherry wines, particularly fino, manzanilla and, to a lesser degree, amontillado. It is caused by a film-forming yeast known as 'flor' in Spanish (literally flower), which transfers to the wine its singular smell and flavour.

FLORAL. Reminiscent of the petals of certain flowers –such as roses and jasmine–noticeable in certain northern withes or in quality reds after a bottle-ageing spell that also delivers some spicy notes.

FRAGRANT HERBS. An aroma similar to soaps and perfumes made from lavender, rosemary, lemon, orange blossom or jasmine. It is found in white wines that undergo pre-fermentative cold skin maceration.

FRESH. A wine with lively aroma and hardly any alcohol expression.

FRESH FRUIT. These are fruity notes produced by a slow grape-ripening cycle typical of mild climates.

FRUIT EXPRESSION. Related to different flavours and aromas reminiscent of various fruits and fine herbs.

FRUITY. Fruit notes with a fine herbal character and even hints of green grass.

HERBACEOUS. A vague note of vine shoots, scrub and geranium leaf caused by an incomplete maturation of the grape skin.

INTENSE. A powerful aroma that can be immediately referred to as such when first nosing the wine.

IODINE. This refers to iodine tincture, a combination of the sweetish smell of alcohol, toasted notes, liniment and varnish or lacquer.

JAM. Typical notes of very ripe black fruit slightly caramelised by a slow oxidative ageing in oak barrels. Very similar to forest fruit jam (prunes, blackberries, blueberries, redcurrants, cherries…). Found in red wines –generally from southern regions– with a high concentration of fruit notes giving that they are made resorting to long vatting periods, which provide longer contact with the skins.

MACERATION. These are aromas similar to those produced during fermentation and that –logically– found in young wines.

MEDITERRANEAN. An aroma where various prominent notes (sweetness, alcohol, burning and raisiny notes, caramel…) produced by grapes grown in hot regions blend in to characterize the wines.

MINERAL NOTES. Used to describe wines that have a subtle nose with plenty of notes reminiscent of flint, slate, hot stones or dry sand.

MUSK. A term to describe the sweet and grapey notes typical of highly aromatic varieties such as moscatel, riesling and gewürztraminer.

ROASTED COFFEE. (See terms of taste).

SUBDUED FRUIT. It generally refers to aromas produced by a fast ripening of the grapes typical of warm climates.

EVOLUTION NOTES. Generally used to describe wines aged prematurely by either oxygen or heat, e.g., a wine that has been left in a glass for several hours.

NUTS. Notes generally found in white wines with oxidative ageing; the oxygen in the air gives rise to aromas and flavours reminiscent of nuts (bitter almond, hazelnut, walnut…). When ageing spells are longer and –most importantly– take place in older casks, there will appear notes that are closer to fruits like figs, dates and raisins.

ORANGE PEEL. Typical fruity aroma found in certain white wines with, above all, a vibrant spicy character.

ORGANIC NOTES. A way to define the fermentative aromas –essentially related to yeast– and typical of young white wines and also fortified generoso wines from the sherry region.

OVERRIPE FRUIT. An aroma typical of young wines that are already slightly oxidized and reminiscent of grape bunches with some signs of rot –noble or not–, or simply bruised or recently pressed grapes.

OXIDATIVE EVOLUTION. Notes related to the tendency of a wine to age by the action of oxygen that passes through the pores of the cask or barrel (micro-oxidation), or during racking.

PATISSERIE. An aroma between sweet and toasted with hints of caramelised sugar and vanilla typical of freshly baked cakes. It is found in wines –generally sweet– that have been aged in oak for a long time and it is caused by both oxidative evolution and the aromatic elements (mainly vanillin) found in oak.

PEAT. A slightly burnt aroma that occurs when the notes of ripe grapes blend in with the toasted aromas of new oak in wines with a high alcohol content.

PHENOLIC. A short and derivative way to describe polyphenols (a combination of the tannins and anthocyanins, vegetal elements of the grape), it describes aromas of grape skins macerated for a long time that yield notes somewhere between ink and a pressed bunch of grapes.

TAR. The pitchy, petrolly aromas of very toasted wood, associated with concentrated red wines with lots of colour, structure and alcohol.

PORT. This is the sweet aroma of wine made from somewhat raisiny or overripe grapes and reminiscent of the vintage Ports made with a short oxidative ageing.

PUNGENT. A prominent aromatic note produced by the combination of alcohol, wood and flor notes and typical of –particularly– fino sherry wines.

RANCIO. This is not a defect but a note better known as "sherryfied" and brought about by oxidative ageing.

RED FRUIT. An aromatic note that refers to forest red fruits (blackberries, redcurrants, mulberries) as well as slightly unripe cherries and plums.

REDUCTION. A wine aroma caused by the lack of oxygen during long bottle ageing, which gives rise to notes like tobacco, old leather, vanilla, cinnamon, cocoa, attic, dust, etc.

REDUCTION OFF-ODOURS. This is a negative set of aromas, halfway between boiled cabbage and boiled eggs, produced by the lees in wines that have not been properly aerated or racked.

REDUCTIVE TANK OFF-ODOURS. A smell between metal and boiled fruit typical of wines stored in large vats at high temperatures. The sulphur added –probably in excess– combines with the wine and reduces its freshness and the expression of fruit notes. This phenomenon is largely found in the production of bulk wines.

RIPE GRAPE SKIN. The aroma that a very ripe grape gives off when squeezed, similar to that of ink or of ripe grape bunches just pressed.

SALINE. This is the note acquired by a fino that has aged in soleras under flor yeast.

SEASONED WOOD. It refers to notes that may appear in wines aged in barrel for a long period –more than four or five years– which have lost the fine toasted aromas and flavours of new oak.

SHRUB. An aroma typically herbal found in Mediterranean regions, a mixture of rosemary, thyme and other typically semi-arid herbs. It refers to the dry, herbaceous note found generally in white and red wines from warmer regions.

SOLERA. An aroma close to the damp, seasoned, aged aroma of an old bodega for oloroso wines.

SPICY. It refers to the most common household spices (pepper, cloves, cinnamon) that appear in wines that undergo long and slow oxidative ageing in oak casks or barrels.

SPIRITUOUS. Both a flavour and an olfactory feature related to high alcohol content but without burning sensations. It is an almost 'intellectual' term to define alcohol, since that product is nothing else but the "spirit of wine".

STEWED FRUIT. Notes of stewed or 'cooked' fruit appear in wines made from well-ripened –not overripe– grapes and are similar to those of jam.

TERROIR. An aromatic note determined by the soil and climate and therefore with various nuances: mountain herbs, minerals, stones, etc.

TOASTED SUGAR. Sweet caramelised aromas.

TOFFEE. A note typical of the milk coffee creams (lactic and toasted nuances mixed together) and present in some crianza red wines.

TROPICAL NOTES. The sweet white fruit aromas present in white wines made from grapes that have ripened very quickly and lack acidity.

TRUFFLE. Similar note to that of a mixture of damp earth and mushrooms.

UNDERGROWTH. This is the aromatic nuance between damp earth, grass and fallen leaves found in well-assembled, wood-aged reds that have a certain fruity expression and good phenolic concentration.

VANILLA. A typical trait of wines –also fortified– aged in oak, thanks to the vanillin, an element contained in that type of wood.

VARIETAL EXPRESSION. This is the taste and aroma of the variety or varieties used to make the wine.

VARNISH. A typical smell found in very old or fortified wines due to the oxidation of the alcohol after a long wood-ageing period. The varnished-wood note is similar to the aroma of eau de vie or spirits aged in wood.

VISCOUS. The sweet taste and aromatic expression of wines with high alcohol content.

VOLATILE. A note characteristic of wines with high volatile acidity, i.e., just the first sign of them turning into vinegar. It is typical of poorly stabilized young wines or aged wines either with a high alcohol content or that have taken on this note during the slow oxidative wood-ageing phase, although we should remember it is a positive trait in the case of generoso wines.

WINE PRESS. The aroma of the vegetal parts of the grape after fermentation, vaguely reminiscent of pomace brandy, grapeskins and ink.

CHARACTERFUL. Used to express the singularity of a wine above the rest. It may refer to winemaking, terroir or the peculiarities of its ageing.

WOODY. It describes an excess of notes of wood in a wine. The reason could be either a too long ageing period or the wine's lack of structure.

VARNISHED WOOD. A sharp note typical of wines aged in wood for a long period, during which the alcohol oxidises and gives off an aroma of acetone, wood or nail varnish.

YEASTY. The dry aroma of bread yeast that can be perceived in young cavas or champagnes, or wines that have just been bottled.

TERMINOLOGY RELATED TO THE PALATE

ALCOHOL. A gentle, even sweet note of fine spirits; it is not a defect.

ALCOHOLIC EDGES. A slight excess of alcohol perceived on the tongue, but which does not affect the overall appreciation of the wine.

BITTER. A slight, non-aggressive note of bitterness, often found in some sherry wines (finos, amontillados) and the white wines from Rueda; it should not be regarded as a negative feature, quite on the contrary, it helps to counterbalance soft or slightly sweet notes.

CARAMELISED. A very sweet and toasted note typical of some unctuous wines aged in oloroso or pedro ximénez casks.

DENSE. This is related to the body of the wine, a thick sensation on the palate.

FATNESS. "Gordo" (fat) is the adjective used in Jerez to describe a wine with good body; it is the antonym of "fino" (light).

FLABBY. Used to describe a wine low in acidity that lacks freshness.

FLAVOURFUL. A pronounced and pleasant sensation on the palate produced by the combination of various sweet nuances.

FULL. A term used to describe volume, richness, some sweetness and round tannins; that is, a wine with a fleshy character and an almost fat palate.

AMPLE. A term used to describe richness. It is a sensation generally experienced on the attack.

LIGHT. The opposite of meaty, dense or concentrated; i.e., a wine with little body.

LONG. This refers to the persistence of the flavour after the wine has been swallowed.

MEATY. A wine that has body, structure and which can almost literally be "chewed".

NOTES OF WOOD. Well-defined notes somewhere between woody and resin generally found in wines matured in younger casks.

OILY. This is the supple, pleasantly fat sensation produced by glycerine. It is more prominent in older wines –thanks to the decrease in acidity– or in certain varieties such as riesling, gewürztraminer, chardonnay, albariño and godello.

OXIDATIVE AGEING. It refers to the influence of the air in the evolution of wine. Depending on the level of oxygen in the air, oxidation will take place in wine to a greater or lesser extent. Oxidative ageing happens when the air comes in contact with the wine either during racking –which ages the wine faster– or through the pores of the wood.

PASTY. This is not a pejorative term, simply a very sweet and dense taste.

ROASTED COFFEE. The sweet and toasted note of caramelised sugar typically found in wines aged in oak barrels –generally burnt inside–, or else the taste of very ripe (sometimes even overripe) grapes.

ROUGH TANNINS. Just unripe tannins either from the wood or the grape skins.

ROUND. This is an expression commonly used to describe a wine without edges, supple, with volume and body.

SWEETENED. Related to sweetness, only with an artificial nuance.

SWEETNESS. A slightly sweet note that stands out in a wine with an overall dry or tannic character.

SOFT TANNINS. Both alcohol and adequately ripened grapes help to balance out the natural bitter character of the tannins. They are also referred to as fat or oily tannins.

TANNIC. This is term derived from tannin, a substance generally found in the skin of the grape and in the wood that yields a somewhat harsh, vegetal note. In wines, it displays a slightly harsh, sometimes even grainy texture.

UNCTUOUS. This refers to the fat, pleasant note found in sweet wines along with their somewhat sticky sweetness.

VELVETY. A smooth, pleasant note on the palate typical of great wines where the tannins and the alcohol have softened down during ageing.

VIGOROUS. A wine with high alcohol content.

WARM. The term speaks of alcohol in a more positive way.

WELL-BALANCED. A term that helps to define a good wine: none of the elements that are part of it (alcohol, acidity, dry extract, oak) is more prominent than the other, just pure balance.

ARGENTINA

CHILE

SPAIN

MEXICO

ARGENTINA

CHILE

SPAIN

MEXICO